Los Angeles
An Architectural Guide

*Dedicated to the memory of
Esther McCoy*

Los Angeles
An Architectural Guide

David Gebhard and Robert Winter
Julius Shulman, *Photographic Consultant*

SALT LAKE CITY

This is a Peregrine Smith Book, published by
Gibbs Smith, Publisher
P.O. Box 667
Layton, UT 84041

Designed and produced by J. Scott Knudsen, Park City, Utah
Printed and bound in Salt Lake City, Utah

Library of Congress Cataloging-in-Publication Data
Gebhard, David.
Los Angeles : an architectural guide / David Gebhard and Robert Winter.
p.   cm.
Includes bibliographical references and index.
ISBN 0-87905-627-4
1. Architecture—California—Los Angeles—Guidebooks.
2. Los Angeles (Calif.)—Buildings, structures, etc.—Guidebooks.
I. Winter, Robert. II. Title.
NA735.L55G44 1994
720'.9794'93—dc20
                           93-42654
                           CIP

CONTENTS

Preface vii
Acknowledgements ix
Photo Credits x
Guide to this Guide xi
Introduction xiii
Historic Preservation in Los Angeles xxvii
The Los Angeles Freeway System xxix
Area Reference Map xxx
Public Transportation in Los Angeles xxxii
The Los Angeles Public Murals xxxiv
1. Malibu 1
2. Pacific Palisades, North 8
3. Pacific Palisades, South 12
4. Santa Monica, North 20
5. Santa Monica, South; Ocean Park 31
6. Venice; Marina Del Rey 36
7. Los Angeles International Airport 45
8. South Beach Area 50
9. Palos Verdes, North 53
10. Palos Verdes, South 57
11. Santa Catalina Island 58
12. San Pedro 61
13. Wilmington 64
14. Torrance 66
15. Long Beach, Downtown and West 69
16. Long Beach, East; Naples;
    and Seal Beach 75
17. Long Beach, North 78
18. Inglewood; Hawthorne 80
19. Gardena 84
20. Baldwin Hills; Culver City 84
21. Brentwood 94

22. Bel Air 101
23. Westwood, West 105
24. Westwood, South and East 110
25. UCLA 114
26. Beverly Hills, North 121
27. Beverly Hills, South 127
28. Century City 133
29. Carthay Circle 134
30. South Carthay 135
31. West Hollywood 135
32. Central Hollywood 147
33. Hollywood Hills 163
34. East Hollywood; Los Feliz;
    Griffith Park 166
35. Silver Lake 177
36. Angelino Heights; Echo Park;
    Elysian Park 183
37. Wilshire Boulevard District;
    Hancock Park 186
38. MacArthur Park, West 198
39. MacArthur Park, North 206
40. MacArthur Park, East 208
41. Downtown 216
42. Downtown, Civic Center 241
43. Downtown, Plaza and Northeast 249
44. Downtown, South 254
45. Boyle Heights 257
46. Exposition Park, West; Leimert Park ... 263
47. Exposition Park, East 267
48. University of Southern California 273
49. Vernon; Commerce; Huntington Park;
    South Gate; Bell; Maywood 278

50. Highland Park 285	87. La Cañada-Flintridge 361
51. Mount Washington 291	88. Route 66—San Gabriel Valley 364
52. Eagle Rock 293	89. Pasadena 364
53. Lincoln Heights 297	90. Upper Arroyo Seco 367
54. Alhambra 300	91. Lower Arroyo Seco, North 374
55. Montebello; Pico Rivera 304	92. Lower Arroyo Seco, South 384
56. Whittier 306	93. Oak Knoll 388
57. Santa Fe Springs 310	94. Pasadena, Central Business District 392
58. Downey 311	95. East Pasadena 402
59. Norwalk 312	96. North Pasadena 406
60. Artesia 312	97. Altadena 408
61. Bellflower 313	98. South Pasadena, Central Section 412
62. San Fernando Valley 314	99. San Marino 415
63. Glendale 315	100. San Gabriel Valley 422
64. Burbank 321	101. Sierra Madre 424
65. Universal City 324	102. Arcadia 427
66. North Hollywood 326	103. Monrovia 429
67. Toluca Lake 327	104. Duarte 432
68. Studio City 328	105. Bradbury 432
69. Pacoima 333	106. Azusa 432
70. Sherman Oaks 333	107. Glendora 433
71. Encino 336	108. San Dimas 433
72. Tarzana; Woodland Hills 338	109. La Verne 434
73. Calabasas 340	110. Temple City; El Monte 434
74. Highway 101 West 341	111. Covina; West Covina; El Monte;
75. Canoga Park 344	Irwindale; Glendora 435
76. Chatsworth 347	112. Industry; La Puente 436
77. Northridge 348	113. Pomona 438
78. Granada Hills; Mission Hills 349	114. Diamond Bar 441
79. Van Nuys; Panorama City; Sepulveda .. 349	115. Claremont 441
80. Mission San Fernando Rey de España .. 351	Readings 447
81. San Fernando 352	Index 461
82. Newhall; Saugus; Valencia 354	
83. Palmdale; Lancaster 356	
84. La Crescenta Valley 356	
85. Tujunga 358	
86. La Crescenta 360	

PREFACE

This is the fourth guide the authors have written on the architecture of Los Angeles, the first having been published in 1965. Our earlier two guides (1965 and 1977) presented the architecture of Los Angeles as well as that of the whole of Southern California. The 1977 guide indicated that this approach—in the number of entries and the physical size of the book itself—was simply getting out of hand. Therefore, this volume like the earlier 1985 edition, is devoted only to Los Angeles and Los Angeles County. It is our goal to produce a second volume which will present the rest of Southern California. It could well be that with the tremendous growth experienced over the past quarter of a century, especially in Orange and San Diego counties, that three volumes will eventually be needed.

Our first guide in 1965 arose from special circumstances. Although we recognized a general need for a survey of architecture in Southern California, we were especially interested at the time in providing a guide for Easterners and Midwesterners who would be coming to the joint meeting of the College Art Association and the Society of Architectural Historians taking place in Los Angeles in winter of 1964. We knew that without some sort of help, these outlanders would find it difficult to cope with the vast distances of Los Angeles and would, therefore, miss outstanding examples of architecture.

Circumstances beyond our control put off publication until 1965, but this special intention of the guide was to give it some quirks. We figured that the visitors would not be much interested in nineteenth-century Victorian architecture since they had so much around them at home. Nor (considering the high fashion for Modernism at the time) did we feel that

they would have an interest in Los Angeles's great surge of traditional imagery of the years 1900 through 1941. Less understandably, we all but neglected the Craftsman movement. We consciously weighted our selections toward twentieth-century High Art Modernist buildings, particularly those designed after 1920. The result was to underrate the nineteenth century and early twentieth century.

Something else has happened since 1964. We ourselves have become older, even mature. Our taste has broadened, perhaps even become a bit perverse (or perhaps, as some of our friends have said, we no longer have any taste). It is amusing to look back at our pride in our catholic taste. We are still rather proud of some of the things we included that went against the high-art Modernist taste of the time. Art Deco and Streamline Moderne, and Hansel and Gretel, and the Period Revival styles of the 1920s, were given some prominence, though not as much as they should have had. We left a back door open when we noted that the book might become "a period piece," but we did not realize how right we were.

Since 1964, moreover, long friendship and the consequent appreciation of each other's attitudes has brought us to the point of almost invariable agreement on what should be included and why it is important. The elder of us was brought up and thoroughly conscious in the 1930s. He was told that the Streamline Moderne (then called "Modernistic") architecture was petit-bourgeois. When he went to college he learned to despise "eclectic" architecture and learned the terms *dishonest, meaningless ornament,* etc. He has, under the influence of his somewhat younger colleague, discovered that ornament, wherever it occurs, usually has great meaning and that dishonesty in art is sometimes just as well-intentioned and aesthetically successful as honesty.

A concern for the difference between the East and West still preoccupies us, both Midwesterners by birth and rearing. In choosing buildings to list, we have had to make our single most important criterion the necessity of emphasizing the areas where Southern California and Los Angeles are strongest—often stronger than other parts of the country, even Northern California.

There is no question that we have widened our list of buildings, both in our 1977 and 1985 editions of the guide, and once again in this new book. Nevertheless, it is by no means a complete listing of works by major architects. We have in almost all cases tried to limit the list to buildings that can be seen from the street, but this high motive has been difficult to enforce. So many of the buildings that were easily seen in 1964, 1977, and 1985, are today immersed in foliage, thanks to plentiful water and fertilizer and notwithstanding our recent drought. Some of these are so important in the history of architecture, or in an important architect's aesthetic development, that we had to list them in the hope that you might have a chance to see them someday. We do try to let you know about the problems of viewing particular monuments.

It should be noted, though, that a number of major buildings (particularly houses) have not been included, either because they cannot be seen from a public road, or because the owner or architect has requested us not to provide an address.

Very early in our studies we found it impossible to map everything in a totally logical fashion, not surprising in an area whose cities' boundaries often defy logic. Enclaves of outstanding buildings, such as in Pasadena, West Los Angeles, and Pacific Palisades, occur rarely in the greater Los Angeles area, and even in these places the idea of walking from one major building to another is usually ridiculous. In general we have tried to use freeways to separate regions, but every student of the area knows freeways, particularly when they are depressed below the land or raised above it, do not set limits except on maps. The problem remains that you may visit one building only to find later that there was another that you wanted to see just a few blocks away, but it was on another map. We suggest planning.

Another insoluble problem has been our inability to develop maps to please everyone. Difficulties occasionally arise from our very efforts to make it easy for you to go from one place to another. We have, for instance, usually left out minor streets where nothing that we have recommended exists. The maps vary in scale depending on the number of outstanding buildings in an area and their proximity to each other. Orientation is the same in all cases, with north being at the top of the map. In many areas you may want a more detailed map. We suggest buying at least *The Thomas Guide,* Los Angeles County edition, which is updated annually and available at major bookstores.

A final plea: the inclusion of buildings in this guide does not mean that the owners have given permission to enter the grounds or the building. Privacy and security are especially sacred today. Some people love to show you through their houses, honored that you would think enough of their taste to notice them. But this attitude is becoming increasingly rare, especially among owners who have houses by well-known architects. Some people don't even want their homes photographed from the street. We counsel diplomacy in the form of a telephone call to the architect, who may arrange a visit for you. Where that is impossible, a note to the occupant may have good results. A few rebuffs are par for the course. But please do respect the privacy of the occupants of these buildings.

We hope that in publishing this guide to architecture in Los Angeles we have not omitted anything that is really important. We know, however, that because we have not been able to cover every road and every street, we may have left out some good things. We invite your comments and criticisms. Everyone will be the wiser for them when we publish the next edition.

ACKNOWLEDGEMENTS

Although in a book of this sort the authors must take full responsibility for its errors as well as its strong points, the final result must be a compilation of the work and knowledge of many people, most of whom will have to go unsung except as they may recognize themselves in this enterprise. We are grateful for the many leads that we have received in telephone calls, in comments after lectures, or in casual conversation. To the literally hundreds of people who have contributed to this volume, we acknowledge our enormous debt.

All cannot be relegated to anonymity. The late Esther McCoy recognized the architectural richness of the Los Angeles area long before we arrived on the scene and was a constant source of information as well as a close friend. Julius Shulman and Marvin Rand have been generous with their photographs and their knowledge. John Chase and the late John Beach, both enthusiasts for the city, have donated ideas and given inspiration to us. Ray Girvigian, the late Carleton M. Winslow, Jr., and Jay Frierman opened their files to us, as did Ileana Welch, formerly the coordinator of the Cultural Heritage Program in the Cultural Affairs Department at City Hall.

John Miller and Richard Mouck have continued to prowl the area looking for things we missed in our earlier books and have turned up some wonders. The Los Angeles Conservancy, with Ruth Ann Lehrer, Paul Gleye, and Linda Dishman in the lead, has called our attention to other important architecture that needs preservation or that is simply outstanding. Tom Owen, the encyclopedic mind at the Los Angeles Public Library, continues to mete out delicious morsels, as have other librarians around the city and county. Surely the Pasadena City Urban Conservation Program, formerly under the direction of Jane Ellison and Paul Gleye, and now of Mary Jo Winder, remains one of the best such organizations in the state. Its survey, formerly spearheaded by Leslie Heumann, Ann Scheid, Denver Miller, and now by Stephanie DeWolfe, has archives that have enabled us to identify the architects and dates of buildings that would otherwise be poorly documented.

Besides the extensive photographic collections of Marvin Rand and Julius Shulman, we have used those of the History Center of the Los Angeles Branch of the California Historical Society, the History Section of the Los Angeles County Museum of Natural History supervised by William Mason, the Huntington Library and Art Gallery, the Los Angeles Public Library, the Special Collections of the UCLA Research Library, and the Architectural Drawing Collection of the University Art Museum, University of California, Santa Barbara. As has always been the case, Patricia Gebhard has, as an editor, helped to hold everything together.

For frequent contributions to our knowledge of Los Angeles architecture, we would also like to thank the following (several of whom are now deceased):

Gregory Ain
Robert Alexander
Timothy Andersen
Margaret Bach
Mary and Reyner Banham
Mary Ann Beach
Harriette von Breton
Lauren Weiss Bricker
David Bricker
Douglas Byles
Regula Campbell
David Cameron
Richard Carrott

Alson Clark
Norman Cohen
Richard Crissman
Jane Ellison
Frank O. Gehry
Joseph Giovannini
Paul Gleye
Calvin Gogerty
Barbara Goldstein
Tim Gregory
Marlene Grossman
Harwell H. Harris
Leslie Heumann
Allen Hess
T. M. Hotchkiss
Thomas Hines
Shelley Kappe
Paul Laszlo
Eugene and Sally Lesner
James and Janeen Marrin
Cliff May
Margaret Meriwether
John Merritt
Kennon Miedema
Denver Miller
Charles W. Moore
Dion Neutra
Dione Neutra
Helen Park
John Pastier
Jean Bruce Poole
James Pulliam
John August Reed
John Ripley
Ann Scheid
Pauline Schindler
Kathryn Smith
David A. Stupplebech
Msgr. Francis J. Weber
Betty Lou Young
Marilyn Zubler

M ost of the photographs were taken by the authors. Exceptions are as follows:

Julius Shulman: pp. 20; 36(#6); 44; 48; 80; 104; 112; 113(#12); 120; 121(#35); 124; 125(#25); 141; 154(#19); 164; 171(#74); 174; 181(#35); 184; 186(#21); 188(#4); 194(#1); 207(#38); 268; 278; 322(right); 447(top); 452(bottom); 453; 455(bottom); 456(bottom)

Marvin Rand: pp. 19; 36(#7); 72(#12); 75(#12); 87; 170(#65); 364; 376(#11); 426; 429(bottom); 451(bottom)

C. Winslow: p. 16

Miles Berné: p. 58

Jack Laxer: pp. 100; 488

Luckhaus Studio: p. 128; 443(bottom)

Graphic Studio: p. 142(#21)

Maynard L. Parker: pp. 145(#6); 192; 448(bottom)

D. C. Lang: p. 145(#3)

Ralph Samuels: p. 185(#14)

W. P. Woodcock: pp. 143(#17); 198; 483

W. M. Clarke: pp. 277; 389; 438(top)

Robert C. Cleveland: p. 309(#5, 10)

Vanguard Photography: pp. 326; 333; 419(bottom)

Hiller Studios: p. 336
Padilla Studios: pp. 390(#27); 485

Frederick W. Martin: p. 416

Norbert Lopez: p. 450(top)

Tom Vinetz: p. 464(top)

GUIDE TO THIS GUIDE

This is a guide to the man-made structures, gardens, parks, and other features that make up the physical environment of Los Angeles County. The time span covered began with the Missions of Spanish California and ends with projects to be completed in 1994.

We suggest that a good way to begin exploring Los Angeles is to start wandering down the beach, and then proceed slowly inland. So we start off with Malibu, proceed all the way around Palos Verdes Peninsula to Long Beach, then go back up north. Eventually we reach the San Fernando, San Gabriel, and Pomona valleys.

The entries section comprises the bulk of the guide. Each entry lists the building, design date, name of architect or designer (if available), address, and brief comments. In our citation of buildings we generally move from west to east.

Federal, state, county, and city public buildings are generally open between the hours of 10 A.M. and 5 P.M. on weekdays. We have included a number of historic buildings open to the public. Information about these buildings is included either in the introduction to the section or in the individual entry, although it should be noted that these hours often are subject to change. Museums are generally closed on Mondays; check with each institution for their specific hours.

INTRODUCTION

The Pueblo of Los Angeles was founded on the banks of the Los Angeles River in 1771 by the Spanish governor of California, Felipe de Neve (Crouch, Garr and Mundigo, 1982). The future city followed the codes laid down for planning in Spain's "Laws of the Indies," though, as Daniel Garr has pointed out, one element of these laws was ignored, namely that the siting of a new town should be situated away from existing settlements. In this instance, the Spanish placed their new Pueblo adjacent to the Native American Gabrielino village of Yangna (Yabit).

The placing of the Pueblo of Los Angeles upon the upper river plain was a logical one, for water was available all year and the distance from the sea made the site less accessible to attack. Probably the presence of the Gabrielino Indians was looked upon as providing cheap labor. In the fashion of Spanish city planning, the early buildings of the new Pueblo were arranged around a plaza, with the planned expansion developed as a rectangular grid in all directions. Because of flooding, the plaza and its buildings were moved on two and possibly three occasions (Frierman and Greenwood, 1992; also Robinson, 1981), so the present Plaza area is a final, not a beginning, step as far as Hispanic Los Angeles is concerned

From early descriptions and drawings, the Pueblo had taken shape by the early 1840s, boasting a number of two-story adobes in the style that we now call Monterey. One of these, the Vicente Sanchez adobe, may, as a matter of fact, have antedated both the Larkin Adobe in Monterey and the Thompson Adobe in Santa Barbara.

At the time of the Anglo-American conquest of California grid blocks, subdivided into lots, had been laid out east and west of the plaza. In the 1840s, under Mexican rule, Los Angeles was California's largest settlement, and it turned out to be the de facto seat of civilian government (with the military governor being located in Monterey). Hispanic Los Angeles, even in the 1820s and on through the 1850s, was a mixed affair of Hispanics and Anglos (mostly Americans from the east). This was reflected in the architecture, with the increased use of imported milled wood (usually from northern California and Oregon), prebuilt doors and windows, and even wood-shingle roofs. By the 1860s, both Hispanics (Latinos) and Anglos had discarded the adobe with its aura of provincialism and turned to masonry and wood construction and to architectural styles derived mostly from the eastern United States. This is well evidenced in Pio Pico's Pico House Hotel of 1869–70, which is a sophisticated version of the Italianate (with some Romanesque overtones).

From the 1870s on, downtown Los Angeles crept around the two large hills to the south—Bunker Hill and Fort Moore Hill. For all practical purposes the old Plaza area had little to do with the new nineteenth-century urban core of the city. The Plaza was rescued as a symbol with the advent of regionalism expressed in the Mission Revival and the later Spanish Colonial Revival. The history of the Plaza area, including its function as a late-nineteenth- and early-twentieth-century "Chinatown," illustrates how layers of cultural and architectural values were superimposed upon one another.

This brings us to the broader issue of how people have responded to the place, Los Angeles. The views and reactions which Los Angeles has evoked have been highly varied and usually ardent. Every American city, large or small, has always had its boosters, and most have attracted at least a smattering of critics.

Los Angeles's distinction has always been the intensity of these reactions ranging from vehement hatred to gushing enthusiasm. In a way, many Angelinos have always enjoyed this, for, as Jack Smith, the columnist for the *Los Angeles Times,* has sagely observed, almost everything people say about Los Angeles has some truth in it.

Los Angeles, like all of Southern California, sometimes seems to be as much a mirage as a reality. Walter Lindley and J. P. Widney were at pains to create this image when they wrote their extremely popular *California of the South,* first published in 1888. "The healthseeker who, after suffering in both mind and body, after vainly trying the cold climate of Minnesota and the warm climates of Florida, after visiting Mentone, Cannes, and Nice, after traveling to Cuba and Algiers, and noticing that he is losing ounce upon ounce of flesh, that his cheeks grow more sunken, his appetite more capricious, his breath more hurried, that his temperature is no longer normal. . . , turns with a gleam of hope toward the Occident [i.e. to California]." Many followed that gleam and found that it was something more than hope.

The Southland (always, it should be noted, capitalized) provided a place that, given water, fertilizer, toil, and imagination, could be transformed into almost anything that the human mind could conceive. A Midwestern farm, a Southern plantation or, best of all, a South American jungle—or perhaps something that had never before been seen. And the environment could be changed in a hurry so that the settler could enjoy the fruits of his or her labor in but a few months or a few years at the most. Foreigners and Americans had, of course, been busy transforming the continent since the seventeenth century, but in Southern California instant paradise was possible.

A place which lends itself so readily to transformation is by its very nature a fragile environment. Casual Southern California living hinges at best on a harmonious interplay of cool ocean breezes and warm desert air. A protracted period of Santa Ana winds, when air is drawn down and baked on the mountain slopes then suffused over the lower lands, can be dis-

astrous, as can an overly wet rainy season. Rain usually appears in good amounts (often causing landslides) in the winter months, but when it does not (and it often does not), water must be hoarded in almost every area except Los Angeles, which in the early part of this century literally bought the Owens River Valley to the north and dried it up in order to get a constant water supply from the High Sierra.

The Big Orange, as Jack Smith has called L.A., also lives on Colorado River water, and more recently on Feather River water, both of which it pipes hundreds of miles. All this costs millions, but it has worked up to the moment. Nevertheless, and because of the danger that all this might be cut off, Los Angeles with its teeming millions is the most tenuous civilization in Southern California, utterly at the mercy of human caprice or error—not to mention divine intervention. Nietzsche told us to live dangerously. In Los Angeles there is no other choice.

If the supreme existential predicament exists in this area, its residents are all but oblivious to it. They are intent upon an individualistic hedonism rarely experienced on such a wide scale since Sodom and Gomorrah. On the surface it would seem that people who, like the Athenians, live out of doors and who are constantly swarming at shopping centers, beaches, Disneyland would have developed public virtues to their highest point. Not so. Southern Californians are among the most privacy-conscious people on earth. Outdoor living means backyard swimming pool areas, not the Agora. Historians have recently noted that the settlement of America was achieved not by Daniel Boone looking for Lebensraum, but by groups of people moving together to establish communities. But once the communities were settled, the myth of the self-made man (and woman) has predominated over the concept of community.

Southern California is the most complete realization of the myth of the self-made, self-reliant, self-oriented individual that the world has ever seen. Its denizens live by one of the most ingenious and complex commercial, industrial, and transportational systems ever developed. Yet they accept this marvelous concatenation of forces as given, assuming that its main reason for being is to serve individual needs. The ideal of a democratic society in which public and private enterprises and activities are intended to enhance the pursuit of individual happiness is at the very heart of the Southern California experience.

This attitude has some negative ramifications, the most important naturally being a gross shirking of social responsibility, as the riots of 1965 and 1991 so aptly demonstrated. Signs of this lack of public concern are everywhere apparent, especially in central Los Angeles. The breaking up of communities by freeways and urban renewal (more intense in building high-rise office buildings than housing) and the destruction of the past in the name of progress are only the most glaring signs. When faced with this problem, Southern Californians are in the habit of saying that in a real emergency they will come together, but in the meantime—privacy. Sometimes they are right, but often they sense the emergency too late, and they reap the whirlwind.

On the other hand, positive physical symbols of individualistic hedonism occur— single-family dwellings, shopping centers, and freeways. The latter, besides servicing real-estate promotion in distant places, were built to get the individual into the landscape and as far away from the city as possible. Someone has said American history is mainly the story of the westward movement, and because Americans have always been moving, a proliferation of freeways is the natural reaction of people who, when stopped by the sea, want to keep going. There is poetry in this, but it is more likely that the reason for the freeways is to give the Southern Californians a means by which to roam into places where they can be free. It is true that the freeways have caused a sort of fungus growth that has helped to wipe out the landscape that the Southern Californians were seeking, but it is also true that the multiplication of freeways gives Southern California an identity, for good or bad, different from any other region of the globe. That is one reason, for instance, why it is absurd to compare Los Angeles to any other city on earth, save perhaps London. It simply cannot be measured by conventional standards set by cities which are centripetal. Los Angeles is a pioneer, and, unless you have some tolerance for the mobility provided by freeways, you will misunderstand Los Angeles and other Southland cities. Probably you will hate them.

Freeways, though appearing on the scene rather late, are closely related to the other much older architectural embodiment of the ideal of individual freedom—the single-family dwelling situated in suburbia. It is significant that in America the terms "house" and "home" are used interchangeably, and that when viewing American architectural history, domestic architecture is usually emphasized much more strongly than government, ecclesiastical, or even commercial building. There has been in this country a sentiment for the single-family dwelling from the seventeenth century to the present when the apartment house, even in California, is encroaching on the American dream. Moreover, it has been the house standing on a good-sized lot, providing space for a garden and, in the twentieth century, a swimming pool that has drawn people to California. In fact, it is a part of the "myth of the garden" that the house should be only an element in the richness of nature, closing a vista as a temple or pagoda in an English landscape garden. Needless to say, the ideal has been honored in the breach. Rarely does any section (excepting Bel Air and portions of Palos Verdes, Pasadena, and San Marino) resemble Frank Lloyd Wright's idea of "Broadacre City." But the semblance of an estate surrounds even the humblest bungalow. Even as the apartment house and condominium craze struck the area, it is significant that many of these continue to be called garden apartments, though the garden may simply be a swimming pool with a few potted plants (sometimes artificial) strung around to keep up pretenses.

The history of Los Angeles architecture is essentially an analysis of the process by which Americans adapted European ideas to the special needs of an unusual environment. The missions, all derived from Mexican design, had to be relatively simple in comparison to Mexican churches. The simplicity of life and the paucity of workmen who understood the fine points of Spanish Churrigueresque or Neo-Classical design mitigated against an elaborate civilization. Thus the special excitement of a relatively sophisticated facade such as that on the mission at Santa Barbara. The interiors were also chaste, with some painting, usually done by the Franciscan monks or their Indian converts, decorating the area near the altar and the trim along the lower parts of the walls. Remember that most of the present glittering altars have been added since 1900.

Early domestic architecture was equally simple, the chief material being adobe brick like that used in Mexico. No mansions the size of the Casa Grande at the Vallejo rancho near Petaluma were ever built in the Southland, though it should be noted that the first two-story porched Monterey adobe (the Thompson Adobe in Santa Barbara of 1834–36) was built in the Southland, not as myth would have it in Monterey to the north. For those who enjoy a romance with the early adobes of California it is somewhat disappointing to discover that most of the adobes which are still around were built after the Anglo-American incursion by gringos who made that adaptation of the Classical Revival to adobe architecture that we have come to call the Monterey style. And, as in the case of the mission churches, most of these adobes have been imaginatively restored, particularly in the 1920s, so that only rarely can the observer sense the plainness of their existence before 1850.

After 1850, Southern California architecture reflected the current fashions in New York, Boston, Philadelphia, or later of St. Louis and Chicago. One normally would think that as one went into the provinces that there would be an appreciable time lag. But this was generally not so. The Anglo architects and clients who came to California in the last half of the nineteenth century were generally well aware of the latest architectural fashions, and that is what they wished to create in building in their new homeland. Thus, before the more intense use of land —urban renewal and freeway construction—

wiped most of them out, there were many examples of the late Federal/Greek Revival, the Italianate vogue in its various phases, the Eastlake craze, the Richardsonian Romanesque and the Shingle, Queen Anne, and Colonial Revival styles. As in Northern California, there was a curious mixture of the Queen Anne and Eastlake that would not often be found in the East. Nevertheless, except for palm trees and exotic flowers and shrubs, Los Angeles in 1895 would have greatly resembled most smaller eastern and midwestern cities.

But if the architecture was similar, the role of the architect was somewhat more expansive. The eastern architect, from Charles Bulfinch onward, had often been a speculator in futures as well as a designer of buildings. But the great land boom of the 1880s threw the Southern California architect directly into large speculative enterprises. Architectural firms, such as the famous partnership of Samuel and Joseph Cather Newsom, devoted a considerable amount of their professional energies to designing new towns, housing developments, hotels, and office buildings, and sometimes even invested their own monies in these speculative ventures. This was often done foolishly. The collapse of the boom at the end of the 1880s did in most of these architects. But we see here the beginning of the special Southern California invention of the large architectural firm that was in every way a business enterprise, promoting progress as much as any booster in the Chamber of Commerce. Moreover, we see in the late nineteenth century the full emergence of the architectural office involved as much with planning and financing as with the design of buildings.

It has been noted often that in California, material and spiritual values tend to become confused. Just as the architect was becoming a businessman, the culture spawned the Mission style, a symbolic attack on the materialism which had made California. Again, the intellectual background of this "truly California style" was eastern. There has always been ambivalence in American ideas about progress. Usually the aggressive spirit is credited with having made America great, but always there has been a parallel feeling that its end result may be catastrophe. There are many aspects of this mood in American literature, art, and even politics. The architectural manifestation of it was expressed, as Vincent Scully, Jr. has noted in his volume *The Shingle Style,* in several Colonial revivals toward the end of the nineteenth century. People coming west naturally brought these styles (Colonial Revival, Shingle, and Tudor) with them, and there are still examples of all these styles to be found in Los Angeles and Southern California. But their incongruity amidst palm trees was not missed by some émigrés. What was indigenous and Colonial in the Southland? The most obvious relics were the missions, reminders, like seventeenth- and eighteenth-century eastern architecture, of a better day before the industrial technological revolution swept over "the Virgin Land."

The result was the beginning of the restoration of the missions, almost all of them moldering into ruins since the Mexican secularization of their lands in the 1820s. Self-made scholars such as Charles F. Lummis and his arch-rival George Wharton James propagandized for the missions both at home and nationally as did the architects Arthur B. Benton and Sumner Hunt. In 1894 Lummis and other celebrants of the Spanish-Mexican culture founded the California Landmarks Club, one of the earliest statewide preservation organizations to be established in the United States. The members not only talked about missions, but also involved themselves in the actual stabilization and restoration of several of the mission buildings.

Even more interesting was the wholesale exploitation of mission elements, often with Moorish effects that the Franciscans had not thought of, into a new style—the Mission Revival or simply the Mission Style (circa 1891–1915). The first great ode to the Mission was the California Building at the 1893 World Columbian Exposition at Chicago. The style quickly spread over the whole of California, and A. B. Benton designed what came to be its greatest monument, the Mission Inn at Riverside (1902 and later). But other architects such as Lester S. Moore and Sumner Hunt were just as successful in adapting it to houses, museums, railroad stations, school buildings, city halls, and churches, to the point that— much more than in Northern California—it became an emblem of a region.

Ironically, like Frederick Jackson Turner's winds of democracy, the Mission style blew east, becoming a favored style for amusement parks and recreational buildings and here and there a house (regrettably without palm trees). There was, indeed, a Mission Revival band instrument factory in Elkhart, Indiana, and a 1905 recreation building in Loring Park in Minneapolis. More importantly, the style looked two ways. On one hand it heralded the treasure trove of Iberia and anticipated the San Diego Fair of 1915 where Churrigueresque, Plateresque, and Moorish details were displayed, causing a craze for a Spanish Colonial Revival in the 1920s. On the other hand, the broad white-stucco surfaces and deep recesses indicated the possibilities of a style which would reflect the Spanish-Mexican heritage and the climate of a country where the sun usually shines and, at the same time, an economy of ornament which might lead to a new style. Thus, while buildings in the Mission style are often awkward (even ugly), in the hands of a consummate artist such as Irving J. Gill the style could be beautiful. In fact, Gill's work often resembled the later European International Style Modern. But Gill was far in advance of his European contemporaries in his sensitivity to nature—to the environment in general. Where foreign designs seem to have been intended to contrast with the natural surroundings, Gill took great interest in bringing nature to the house. His favorite device was the indoor/outdoor space of the pergola, but it is also significant that he went so far as to put an almost imperceptible green tint into what otherwise seems to be white paint and used it on exterior and interior walls in order to complement the natural surroundings.

Unfortunately, Gill was almost a prophet without honor in his own country. His essays in abstraction and simplification were rarely imitated, and what has happened to most of his buildings forms a sorry chapter in the history of the destruction of the usable past.

The mention of Gill and his connection with the Mission style should be a reminder that both he and his style were part and parcel of the contemporaneous Arts and Crafts or Craftsman movement. The Craftsman movement is usually associated with the woodsy mountain cabin, and Gill with stucco and concrete. But read Gill's article, "The Home of the Future," in Gustav Stickley's magazine *The Craftsman* (1916) and you will find him very conscious of his fascination with fine craftsmanship, albeit often in a different material.

The epicenter of the American Craftsman movement was not East Aurora, Eastwood, Oak Park, or even Berkeley, but Southern California. It is surprising that a style which used so much wood as a symbol of the love of work that the machine had wiped out should have gained such enormous popularity in an area where there are few forests and where the danger of dry rot and infestation by termites would seem to make it the worst possible material. It has been suggested that the opening of the harbor at San Pedro was accompanied by a promotional campaign which was extremely successful with the lumber barons of the north. This would perhaps explain, in part, the popularity of the wood frame, but it does not explain the use of so much exposed wood on exteriors in the form of shakes or shingles and in interiors in the form of paneling and beamed ceilings. Rather, its use has intellectual, even ideological, sources. It is not surprising in light of the vision which promoted Southern California as a haven from the cruelties of life, and automatically promoted a style which would fit into picturesque surroundings. This explains the popularity of the style in the Arroyo Seco at Pasadena where it was particularly favored by the intellectual and artistic elite who are always conscious of the necessity to wage eternal war on crass materialism even though, more often than not, ending up taking full advantage of it.

It was also in Southern California that the bungalow, the apotheosis of William Morris's notion of a proletarian art that he could never himself attain, found its true home. Here a young family on the make, a sick family on the mend, or an old family on meager savings could build a woodsy place in the sun with palm trees and a rose garden. The California bungalow, whatever its size or quality of workmanship, was the closest thing to a democratic art that Anglo-America has ever produced. Even when it became a high-art product, as in the work of Charles and Henry Greene of Pasadena, it was as much a tribute to the carpenters who lovingly put together the wood details as to the architects who designed them. The high-art Gamble House and the low-art bungalow both convey a message that you can do it yourself if you only have the moral conviction. In the bungalow court—another of Southern California's great inventions—which started around 1910 in Pasadena, the adventageous bungalow was reduced to dollhouse-like dwellings which still managed to convey the sense of the single-family dwelling set in a garden.

A very important concern was the relationship of house to garden. *The Craftsman* magazine became a devoted admirer of Southern California architecture and gardens. *The Ladies Home Journal* and the *Architectural Record* were no less enthusiastic. Old pictures of the Blacker House by the Greenes show its broad-sweeping eaves and horizontal lines blending into magnificently landscaped grounds—the house a kind of continuation of the garden. What is not now noticeable about this house and its surroundings, since the gardens have been subdivided, is that the living room chandeliers, with water lilies designed in Tiffany glass, were intended to echo the aquatic plants that once graced the lily pond near the living room windows. Even more striking is the intent, dimly apparent in many bungalow books but very explicit in Eugene O. Murmann's *California Gardens* (1914), that the person of modest means should live in a house set in a landscaped garden.

Popular and widespread as the Craftsman aesthetic became, it was, nevertheless, the Spanish Colonial Revival (or more broadly the Mediterranean Revival) of the 1920s which captured the imagination of the popular and professional journals and architects and critics in the East as well as the West. Here was a style which reflected the storybook romance associated with Californians—one into which Anglo-Americans, tired of the nastiness of war and modern life, could retreat. The highly successful Los Angeles partnership of Morgan, Walls, and Clements was one of several firms which introduced the elaborate details of Spanish and Mexican Churrigueresque and Plateresque forms.

Though the Southland was eventually to become intensely involved with the myth of her Spanish heritage, classical Beaux Arts forms were popular from 1900 on for the staid conservatism of business establishments and, above all, for financial institutions. Downtown L.A. still possesses an array of ten- to twelve-story office blocks built within the Neo-Classic tradition of McKim, Mead, and White, and Daniel Burnham (Burnham and Company). And most of the towns and cities of the region have one or more exercises in this mode. These Beaux Arts designs, which were produced from 1905 through 1925, are in many cases sophisticatedly designed buildings, and they are little different from what we find elsewhere in the county. Almost all of these designs were produced by one or another of the large architectural firms—Morgan, Walls, and Clements, Albert C. Martin, John Austin, Parkinson and Parkinson, and Walker and Eisen. These firms employed designers such as Stiles Clements who were trained in the East and brought the prestige of their Parisian-derived education to the Southland.

The well-organized Beaux Arts traditions underlay the work of most influential architectural offices and were openly enunciated in the more circumspect and controlled Italian designs of Myron Hunt, Sumner Spaulding, Gordon B. Kaufmann, and Reginald D. Johnson. But the most remarkable evidence of Parisian influence was the "City Beautiful" movement that had touched California city planning as early as 1900 and that had, by the 1920s, been embraced by all the major cities and many small ones in the region. Los Angeles, Long Beach, and Pasadena seized upon planning

during the first decades of the century with the same enthusiasm with which they had accepted the Mission style and the Spanish Colonial Revival. Considering that Los Angeles has the aura of the unplanned city, it is surprising to note that it was the first city in the United States to adopt (1909) a comprehensive zoning ordinance. In 1915 a city planning association was organized. In 1920 an official Planning Commission for the huge Los Angeles area was organized.

Some of the outlying communities such as Palos Verdes went several steps further than Los Angeles. They created architectural and landscape architectural reviewing agencies that extended the force of planning far beyond the conventional American practice in the 1920s and 1930s, which was almost always solely concerned with zoning (land use) and street planning. In a sense, as these review boards directed the transformation of the dry hills and flatlands into a jungle and the domain of the Spanish Colonial Revival, they were reinforcing familiar symbols of a golden past. The results of their efforts at Palos Verdes and in several other Los Angeles enclaves are most impressive.

Planning is traditionally the work of an elite and is often most visible to the layman on maps. The buildings of the 1920s speak more loudly of the Age of Prosperity. From a high-art point of view, the Spanish Colonial Revival was generally at its best when drawing upon the vernacular architecture of Andalusia and rural Mexico. In spite of the occasional flourish of a Churrigueresque doorway, the message of Spain and Mexico was simplicity, even when the house was very expensive and lavish in its spaces and gardens. The major architects of this style—George Washington Smith, Roland E. Coate, Reginald D. Johnson, John Byers, Wallace Neff, Gordon B. Kaufmann, and the firm of Marston, Van Pelt and Maybury—left a legacy of buildings which mark a high point in American domestic architecture.

Unquestionably the most talented of the Spanish Colonial Revivalists was the Montecito architect George Washington Smith. His houses and villas in and around Santa Barbara, up the coast, and in Bel Air and Pasadena still seem remarkable for an informality of plan, studied abstract composition, and in the studied relationship between the building and its landscape. Indeed, at risk of sounding one note, the concern of the architects of the 1920s for the manipulation of outdoor spaces in the planting of flowers and trees and the building of terraces and garden walls has often been lost in our present romance of white-stucco walls and red-tile roofs. The nineteenth-century horticulturists, men like Joseph Sexton and Francesco Franceschi, set the stage for the brilliant landscape architects who began to practice after 1900: Olmsted and Olmsted, Charles Gibbs Adams, Kate Sessions, Mildred Davis, Edward Huntsman-Trout, Katherine Bashford, Paul Thiene, Lloyd Wright, Florence Yoch, Lucile Council, A. E. Hanson, W. D. Cook, Lockwood de Forest, Ralph D. Cornell, and more recent figures like Garrett Eckbo, Emmet Wemple, and Campbell and Campbell.

It is obvious to anyone who has looked at the popular home magazines and the professional architectural journals of the 1920s that the Spanish or Mediterranean revivals were not the only styles that were beautifully designed. All architects were equally proficient in other historic modes (they referred to them as "Types")—the Norman French Provincial, the English Tudor, the Colonial Revival, and later the Monterey Revival and even the Art Deco and Streamline Moderne).

The 1920s dipped into three other historic images that are of great interest. The Egyptian Revival, touched off by the discovery of King Tut's tomb in 1922, and the themes of the ancient Nile presented through the silent Hollywood films and their exotic stage sets are certainly delightful. The apartment houses designed and built by J. M. Close suggest in their decorative detail that the return to Karnak was a gag. But Bertram G. Goodhue's use of Egyptian elements in the Los Angeles Public Library must be taken somewhat more seriously.

The truth is that the spirit of the 1920s recognized that architecture, like the other arts, is an art of effect. If the effect is good, try anything. Perhaps this explains the Pueblo Revival

and the pre-Columbian Revival, both of which also occurred in the 1920s. In these revivals the architect Robert B. Stacy-Judd is a name to reckon with, though it should be noted that an interest in pre-Columbian architecture had been reflected as early as 1912 in the Cordova and Abbey Hotels (Hener and Skilling; now destroyed) in downtown Los Angeles and in the entrance and tunnel to the elevator of the Southwest Museum (Hunt and Burns) built in 1917. By the 1920s free and imaginative design in that idiom was being produced by large and small architectural firms. Probably the maddest of these efforts were the Aztec Hotel (1924–25) in Monrovia by Stacy-Judd and the Mayan Theater (1926) by Morgan, Walls and Clements in downtown Los Angeles. Fortunately both are still standing and must be seen to be believed.

Some have suggested that the popularity of pre-Columbian motifs may have something to do with the adoption of the Native American art of the Southwest by the Santa Fe Railroad, an interesting idea. It is also possible that the special interest of the *National Geographic Magazine* in the Yucatan and Peru during this period may, at least in part, have touched off pre-Columbian notions. But another source is even more likely. Frank Lloyd Wright, well recognized in the early twentieth century, had been deeply influenced by pre-Columbian architecture as early as the second decade of the twentieth century and had given the first dramatic evidence of this influence in his Midway Gardens in Chicago of 1914, followed by his A. D. German Warehouse in Richland Center, Wisconsin, in 1915.

When Wright set up shop in Los Angeles in the late teens (actually his first California dwelling was built in Montecito in 1909) he continued his exploration of Native American forms. The Barnsdall House (1917–22) was a variation on the cruciform plan of his earlier Prairie style to which he applied Mayan and Zapotec massing and detail, adding such standards of Southern California as patios and pergolas. The pre-Columbian motif persisted in his impressive series of precast concrete block houses, ranging from the Millard House ("La Miniatura," 1923) in Pasadena to the Ennis

House (1924) which has the effect of a terraced Mayan temple on a hill.

Wright's oldest son Lloyd supervised a number of these buildings (and did the gardens) and even added elements of his own. Lloyd Wright had come to California in 1911 as a landscape architect with the firm of Olmsted and Olmsted, then developing plans for the Panama California Exposition at Balboa Park in San Diego. Wright then worked for Irving J. Gill, and later came to the Los Angeles area working first with Olmsted and Olmsted on the new city of Torrance, and then to join with the landscape architect Paul G. Thiene. As his practice moved from landscape architecture to buildings in the 1920s, it was not surprising that he continued to see architecture as an environment where human designs and natural features were in harmony. Neither should it be surprising that he picked up on his father's interest in pre-Columbian forms. His Sowden House (1926) in Hollywood and other of his buildings in and outside of the Los Angeles area demonstrate his recognition of Native American influences as well as his knowledge of Art Deco and Expressionism.

As if to prove that from Frank Lloyd Wright all blessings flow, the exciting ideas of the Master also drew two other immigrants to Los Angeles in the 1920s—the Austrians, R. M. Schindler and Richard J. Neutra. Of the two, Schindler was closer to Wright in his romantic personalism in design and in his complex manipulation of spaces. Nevertheless, his knowledge of early modern architecture in his native Vienna prompted him to develop forms which were not in Wright's vocabulary. His own 1922 house on Kings Road in West Hollywood was one of the most radical designs (both socially and aesthetically) in America at the time (and in many ways, still is today). The orientation of his complex spaces to nature indicates how quickly he came to understand what was now a Southern California tradition. In a very different setting his Lovell Beach House (1922–26) at Newport Beach is unquestionably one of the true monuments of twentieth-century modern architecture. And Schindler continued to produce ingenious experiments in form and

space until his death in 1953, all of them characterized by ideas not always fully carried out, but certainly stimulating. In fact, in many instances his great charm is a quality of improvisation not quite complete.

Schindler, like Gill, was until recently admired but not tremendously influential. Richard J. Neutra, however, was without doubt the most influential Los Angeles Modernist architect from the late 1920s until his death in 1970. His steel-frame Lovell House (1929) in the Hollywood Hills is, like Schindler's beach house for the same client, one of the very few buildings in America in the 1920s which deserve to be called monuments in the history of the Modern movement in architecture. But he was not just another talented International Style Modern architect. His sensitivity to the natural environment, existing and potential, caused him to go further than anyone before him to bring house and garden together (literally, in the Perkins House [1955] in Pasadena, bringing the garden into the house). Neutra's example was not lost on his younger contemporaries in the 1930s—Harwell H. Harris, Gregory Ain, and Raphael S. Soriano—who, with a little help from their clients, simply landscaped their brilliant designs out of sight.

The decade of the 1920s represented a period of phenomenal growth throughout Southern California. In Los Angeles, for instance, the population increased from 576,000 in 1920 to 1,238,000 in 1930. In this same period as the city grew 114.7 percent, Los Angeles County advanced by 136.9 percent. One essential ingredient of this dispersal of population was the convenience of an interurban railroad network, the Pacific Electric "Big Red Cars," certainly one of the finest public transportation systems developed in this country until its planned obsolescence. But more and more Southern Californians came to rely on the automobile, a kind of extension of the single-family dwelling.

This turn to the automobile was accompanied by linear (or strip) commercial development, the classic example being Wilshire Boulevard, which as early as the 1920s was beginning to take on its present look of being lined by commercial and multiple housing units from downtown Los Angeles to the palisades of Santa Monica. Also significant, and closely related, was the development beginning in the 1920s of retail shopping centers, large and small, still evidenced rather quaintly in cut-out street corners (the area in front for parking, of course) with Spanish Colonial or Art Deco buildings arranged in an L-form back of the cars. The orientation of stores to parking lots rather than the main street was to become a major break with commercial architecture of the past.

No less innovative was the development of eye-catchers to attract passing motorists— Programmatic buildings such as a real estate office in the shape of a sphinx, an orange juice stand sculpted as a large orange, and restaurants, premonitory of the sculpture of Claes Oldenburg, looking like brown derbies, hotdogs, owls, milk cans, toads, dogs, igloos, shoes, and doughnuts. Most of these delightful structures have vanished, but they looked forward in many ways to the less naturalistic but more dramatic pop-culture city scenery of today.

It was inevitable that an era of growth would also make Southern California rich in the fashionable styles of the times. Certainly, next to New York City, Los Angeles exhibits, even today, more examples of the Art Deco than any other part of the country. Bullock's Wilshire (1928), by Parkinson and Parkinson, is the best remaining example of Art Deco in the area, but there are literally hundreds of examples in Los Angeles, Pasadena, Long Beach, and even San Pedro. Sadly, the greatest of these, the shimmering black-and-gold-sheathed Richfield Building (1928–29; Morgan, Walls, and Clements) is no longer with us.

Southern California was deeply affected by the depression of the 1930s. Ironically, it is for this reason that the area has so many outstanding examples of Streamline and Classical (PWA) Moderne buildings. The depression was generally catastrophic to the building industry in California as well as throughout the country. But one operation that was not curtailed was the building of moving-picture theaters, the cheap movie ticket being one of the few luxuries still available to most Americans during the 1930s. Even more important to architecture was public building, stimulated by the United States Public Works Administration (PWA) and other governmental agencies which helped to finance schools, libraries, and post offices in order in part to give people work. Its companion relief organization was, of course, the Works Progress Administration (WPA) whose Federal Arts Project engaged in the revolutionary act of giving work to artists. The results of the activities of these federal agencies are everywhere, especially in the Classical Moderne (PWA Moderne) mode.

As historians have continually noted, not many millionaires jumped out of skyscrapers or off bridges as a result of the Great Crash in 1929. Generally, after a period of shock, the rich and the well-to-do went on (in generally a more low-keyed fashion) building houses in the period revival styles of the 1920s, giving employment to architects of these period styles. Wallace Neff, Paul R. Williams, Roland E. Coate, John Byers and Edla Muir, and H. Roy Kelley developed free-flowing interior spaces and indoor/outdoor relationships, then clothed them in forms which delicately suggested the past—the Spanish Monterey, the English Halftimber, the Colonial, and the Regency. By the end of the decade, Cliff May and others had fully developed the California Ranch house which was to dominate not only Southern California but the whole of America after World War II.

A casual look through the pages of the national architectural journals, *Pencil Points* (later *Progressive Architecture*), *Architectural Record,* or *Architectural Forum,* readily attests to the recognition which the Southern California proponents of modern architecture received during the 1930s. In addition to the "Old Masters"—R. M. Schindler, Richard J. Neutra, and Lloyd Wright—there were the European expatriates—Kem Weber, J. R. Davidson, and Paul Laszlo. And by the mid-1930s there was an impressive younger generation of modernists including Harwell H. Harris, Gregory Ain, Raphael S. Soriano, Whitney R. Smith, Wayne Williams, A. Quincy Jones,

Richard Lind, and John Lautner.

World War II was a great stimulus to business and often directed architecture into previously untouched areas. There was little work in mansions or public and commercial buildings, but for the first time since the First World War the federal government took an interest in public housing. By the end of 1942, Los Angeles had twelve public housing projects. In general these differed greatly from similar projects in other parts of the United States. The density of all of them was decidedly low, and they were styled in forms ranging from the California Ranch house to the International Style Modern. Unquestionably the most impressive of these projects was Neutra's Channel Heights Project (1941–42) above San Pedro, as always in Neutra's hands, beautifully sited and landscaped. It is a matter of public shame that this project has been allowed to disintegrate and for all practical purposes disappear.

The war years also set the stage for an increased dispersal of population. In 1941 the Los Angeles Regional Planning Commission drew up the basic guidelines for development for the next quarter century. Los Angeles was not to be a classical city with one or two centers but a complex entity with a variety of commercial and industrial centers. The region was to continue to stress the single-family house. To realize this scheme, the private automobile was to be cultivated as the major means of transportation. All this meant a complete devotion to freeways, or as they were more often than not labeled Parkways. The Arroyo Seco Parkway (1934–41, now Pasadena Freeway) had been the first freeway in the West. By 1941 the first sections of the Cahuenga (now Hollywood) Freeway were finished, connecting Los Angeles with the San Fernando Valley. The next two decades saw a freeway mania. By the 1970s, when building tapered off due to the economy and a growing skepticism, almost everyone in Los Angeles was less than four miles from a freeway, the goal of the transportation experts.

In the period after World War II, Southern California experienced a building boom, mostly of tract housing, which demolished the orange groves of the San Fernando Valley and populated almost every square inch of it. The same development spread east almost to San Bernardino and south to the point that, at least along the coast, Southern California had indeed become a megalopolis. Only territories far beyond the reaches of Los Angeles, such as the Owens River Valley, the San Joaquin Valley, and the Mojave Desert, preserved communities that today still reflect some of the old charm of small-town America. Nevertheless, within Los Angeles and other cities of California the chief building type, the Ranch house, continued to exhibit the old values: the two-car garage or carport near the street, the open family room and adjoining patio, the outdoor living space. Again, California pioneered a style of life for America.

In the same period, and especially after 1960, high art came to be high architecture. In an effort, often only cosmetic, at urban renewal, almost all the cities went to medium- or highrise in their downtown areas. These buildings, without exception, were clothed in the machine image International Style Modern garb, many, following Mies, displaying dark and, later, reflective glass walls and creating in most instances an unbearable monotony. Domestic architecture fared better. Whitney Smith and Wayne Williams, Harwell H. Harris, and A. Quincy Jones (Jones and Emmons) maneuvered the International Style Modern in a mellow, woodsy fashion (as was occurring in the Bay Region of northern California). A domestic housing experiment, the Case Study House program (1945–60) of John Entenza and his magazine *Arts and Architecture* was launched with fear and foreboding. No one really thought very many people would be interested in the high-art designs of Richard J. Neutra, Charles and Ray Eames, Raphael S. Soriano, Gregory Ain, J. R. Davidson, Craig Ellwood, Pierre Koenig, and others. However, the first six houses that were opened received 368,554 visitors, though the architects rarely made any attempt to cultivate the popular taste. As Esther McCoy noted (*Perspecta* 15, 1975) the popularity of these avant-garde buildings spread as well to the beautifully designed furniture exhibited in them. A number of retail outlets for the products of such designers as Charles and Ray Eames, Harry Bertoia, Eero Saarinen, and Hendrick Van Keppel were opened, and they were a huge success. Later, the attendance at Eudorah Moore's "California Design" exhibitions in Pasadena was a clear sign that "modern design" had caught on with an influential Anglo minority of Southern Californians.

Naturally, there were counter-tendencies to the Miesian "less is more" machine aesthetic. Throughout the post-war period, John Lautner's highly imaginative designs had a small but intense group of followers, as did the decorative modern Los Angeles buildings of Edward D. Stone and Associates, and others. Through the post-World War II years, and up to the present, there were the Ahmanson and Home Savings banks (almost all of which were designed by Millard Sheets), which in their design and use of sculpture, mosaics, and murals proclaimed that the Classical tradition was not dead and that "more was more." In the domestic architecture of the 1960s and 1970s, the movie set image of the 1930s Hollywood Regency was replaced by the French Empire mode with its applique of mansard roofs, elongated windows, double front doors, and classical urns. Here, as John Chase has indicated in his 1982 book, *Exterior Decoration,* the Hollywood boudoir was indeed turned inside out.

Architecturally and environmentally the early and mid-1970s were a confused period for Los Angeles and Southern California, probably much more so than for the rest of the country. Like a balloon, the ideologies of progress, growth, upward, and onward seemed to have burst, and no one seemed sure of the future any longer. Smog, the congestion of people (and their extension—the automobile), the continual destruction of productive farmland, and potential and real water shortages created doubts of such magnitude that even the usual boosterism of Southern California found it increasingly difficult to reassert the old beliefs. At first the negativism of these reactions produced a number of positive results. A surge of interest in planning occurred, ranging from the initiation of statewide coastal planning to elaborate requirements of environmental review for industrial and other types of projects. Architectural design itself became subject to public scrutiny. It appeared the days of architectural laissez-faire were over.

The desire for continuity with the past also reasserted itself in the 1970s and on into the 1990s—albeit in a far different fashion than in the decades from 1900 through the 1930s. Though interest in historic preservation in Southern California had begun early, this involvement generally restricted itself to the missions and the adobes of the early 1800s. In the late 1960s Angelinos and others began to look at other inheritances from the past: from Victorian architecture of the late nineteenth century to the Streamline Moderne of the 1930s, to, more recently, coffee shops of the 1950s. This involvement became evident in the demand to retain living relics and in the increased usage of historic images derived from California's delightful, but at times mad, past.

The popular California Ranch house, which had slowly assumed Modern elements in the 1950s, began to revert to its Hispanic sources. Acres of tract houses, apartments, and later condominium row houses appeared, some on the remaining open land of the San Fernando Valley, others on leftover bits of land near the Orange County line. Retail establishments and shopping centers exhibited Hispanic themes of stucco, arches, towers, and tile roofs. But all of this, at best, testified to lacking conviction. Still, there was an inkling of the past and, in this case, California's own past.

The Modernist image was, however, in no way abandoned in the 1970s and later. The established L. A. corporate architectural firms such as Albert C. Martin and Associates, Welton Becket and Associates, the Charles Luckman partnership, and William Pereira and Associates stood by the machine image of the Modern. As was the case in Albert C. Martin and Associates' Atlantic Richfield Towers (ARCO Plaza, 1968) they clothed the building in polished stone, but its image remained faithful to the Modern, the Corporate International Style.

Unquestionably, the most impressive of the larger commercial designs came from the offices of Daniel, Mann, Johnson, and Mendenhall and from Gruen Associates. Operating out of these offices, Cesar Pelli and Anthony J. Lumsden took up the fashionable theme of the fragile glass and metal sheathed box, employing it to create impressive pieces of minimalist sculpture. One wonders, however, what these fragile pieces of glass sculpture had to do with Los Angeles's physical environment or its history. Cesar Pelli was perhaps conscious of this when he designed his small Pacific Savings Bank in San Bernardino (1972), with its masonry walls and drive-in facility composed of a regimented forest of palm trees. One of the ironies of the 1970s and 1980s in Los Angeles was that at the same time there was an increased awareness of environment and history, the design and imagery of the city's larger buildings became more arbitrary (more in the nature of art objects rather than architecture), and much of it was certainly anti-regional.

Just as we can, for the convenience of history, present certain individuals and events as touchstones for changes in the past, so we can look to particular personages and events of the 1970s which helped set the stage for Los Angeles of the 1980s. Though Cesar Pelli left the Southland for Yale at the end of the 1970s, he left an inheritance that encouraged a rather specific L.A. brand of High Tech imagery, International Post Modernism, and/or Deconstructionism. On the local scene these versions of High Tech developed along several slightly different paths. One was a direct descendant of the thinly clad metal and glass sheathed box; another approach delighted in playing with building and mechanical technology to create High Art objects and most importantly interior spaces. The first approach can be seen in the multiplicity of low- and high-rise buildings constructed from the palisades of Santa Monica to Lake Avenue in Pasadena. These machine image buildings, such as the 1982–83 Wells Fargo Building (Albert Martin and Associates) in downtown Los Angeles, are, like their predecessors, purposely oblivious to their world,

though it might be noted they are often detailed with sophistication.

The second contingent of High Tech practitioners carries on the Victorian division of architectural practitioners into the separate camps of art-architects and architects. Our present cadre of art-architects looks at technology not through the eyes of the contemporary computer, but through the historic and nostalgic eyes of the early Modernist artists and architects of the 1920s. While some of the younger L.A. practitioners of the 1980s and 1990s have looked back to figures such as Le Corbusier, most have been inspired by the more off-beat modernists of these early years, the European Constructivists, Expressionists, and Surrealists. In addition to looking carefully at the buildings of Schindler (particularly his late work), L.A.'s impressive Modernist contingent of the 1980s and 1990s has been strongly influenced by such figures of the 1920s as the German Surrealist sculptor Kurt Schwitters and others.

Most examples of these late High Tech buildings have been new or remodeled small-scaled buildings, generally designed by younger practitioners. The vigor of many of these buildings is there for anyone to see, though one is often left with the feeling that their cultivation of the irrational, or their play between the popular and the refined would disappear if they were, like Alice, miniaturized and placed in an art gallery. (Often, for example, their work comes through best in elaborate isometric drawings seen best on the walls of a museum.)

Other "events" of the decades of the 1970s through the 1990s have impacted the L.A. scene. Though Charles W. Moore's first Los Angeles building dates from 1968–69, his real influence came through both the Southern California importation of his Sea Ranch image for hundreds if not thousands of town house condominium units and through the direct effect of his work and presence at UCLA. His involvement in history and his fascination with the long tradition of the stucco box in Southern California has inspired many architects practicing in the area.

A second figure of inspiration for the

1980s and 1990s has been Frank O. Gehry. His use and visual "misuse" of commonplace materials and structures, from chain link to exposed wood studs, has indeed created a new chapter for Robert Venturi's *Complexity and Contradiction.* Gehry carries the game a step further by playing off the practical everyday architect against the art-architect (the latter triumphing, of course). In his more recent work, such as the Disney Concert Hall which is now under construction in downtown Los Angeles, Gehry has plunged full force into the Expressionist/Surrealist (plus a pinch of Constructivism) art and architecture world of the 1920s. His Disney Concert Hall will very likely emerge as the great symbol of L.A. at the end of the century.

The lessons provided by Gehry and indirectly by Moore have been energetically taken up by a whole new group of L.A. practitioners, including Eric Owen Moss, Steven Ehrlich, Morphosis (Thom Mayne and Michael Rotundi), Rebecca Bender, Frank D. Israel, Katherine Diamond, and others. While no one would question the demanding presence and even humor of the buildings produced by these avant-gardists, there is on occasion a self-indulgent narcissistic quality that can be disturbing. There can be no question that this new work is vigorous and sometimes highly imaginative. These forms in the landscape, with their cultivated complexities and, above all, contradictions, play on our intellectual, art and architectural sensibilities. Perhaps, one of the most impressive aspects of these more recent buildings, especially apparent in the work of Isreal and Moss, is their almost Expressionist/Surrealist conception of interior space. It is as if we have found ourselves caught up in the Surrealist stage set of that famous film of 1919, *The Cabinet of Doctor Caligari.*

Popular architecture in Southern California never abandoned traditional imagery. Most domestic tract housing of the 1970s through the 1990s retained some links with the past. And, as noted, California's Hispanic/Mediterranean tradition had reasserted itself as early as the 1960s. As in the 1920s and 1930s,

recent versions of the Hispanic/Mediterranean tradition have increasingly shared the limelight with other historic borrowings—the Medieval, whether English Tudor or French Norman, and the American Colonial. These images were and are employed for the complete gamut of building types, from single-family housing to apartments and restaurants. Interestingly, it is in the smaller shopping centers of the 1980s that the concept of California as the New Spain seems to predominate. Regrettably, few of these recent interpretations of historicism give evidence that their architects or landscape architects have any real understanding of the language they are using.

There are, however, notable exceptions. The J. Paul Getty Museum (Langdon and Wilson; Stephen Garrett; Norman Neuerberg) at Malibu, characterized by the period-piece critics of the "old" Modernism as "camp," stands as perhaps the major California monument of the 1970s. And in the 1980s the Getty has been joined by a few other commendable historic image buildings, including the 1982–83 Virginia Steele Scott Gallery of American Art (Warner and Grey) at the Huntington Museum and Library in San Marino. J. Paul Getty looked to Rome and the lava-covered Villa of the Papyri near Herculaneum for his inspiration. At the same time the Huntington's architects had recourse to Rome in the buildings of one of America's great twentieth-century classicists, John Russell Pope. The fine line between illusion and reality embodied in these two buildings, as well as in the designs of the L.A.'s avant-garde architects, is one of the often-repeated themes in the architectural history of Los Angeles and Southern California. The current task in the 1990s and on into the opening years of the next century is how to apply these aesthetic lessons to a wide range of pressing social issues.

HISTORIC PRESERVATION IN LOS ANGELES

Contrary to popular belief, organized preservation efforts have had a long history in Los Angeles. The California Landmarks Club, founded in 1894 under the leadership of Charles F. Lummis and the architects Arthur B. Benton and Sumner Hunt, pioneered conservation of historic architecture, though, to be sure, these efforts were largely limited to a few missions.

In the late 1920s Christine Sterling and many local merchants set out to save and restore notable structures in the Old Plaza area including Olvera Street, a project in which the city, county, and state took an interest in the 1950s and administered jointly for awhile. Saddened by the destruction of Victorian Bunker Hill in the same period, a group of citizens joined to found the Cultural Heritage Foundation (1969) and moved the last two derelicts on the Hill to a newly designated Heritage Square on an unused piece of land next to the Arroyo Seco and the Pasadena Freeway in Highland Park.

In 1978 the private nonprofit Los Angeles Conservancy appeared as a watchdog and galvanizer of preservation energy throughout the city. In fact, the 1970s saw an active development of urban conservation programs, notably in Pasadena, South Pasadena, Santa Monica, Claremont, and more recently Long Beach, and other communities in Los Angeles County.

The Conservancy has entered many frays. It has not always been a winner, but over and over again it has caused governmental bodies to focus on the value of old buildings, or of entire districts. Compromises have, of course, been made, and its activities have not been limited to restraining development as such. In many ways it has encouraged individual property owners to restore and sometimes to recycle old buildings. Through its annual awards it has recognized outstanding examples of restoration and raised the standards for refurbishing the past.

Needless to say the Conservancy has been faced with one problem after another. At the moment (late 1993) Bullocks Wilshire Department Store building, a major national monument of the Art Deco, has been closed due mainly to demographics, but also due to the economic crunch of the last few years. How do you find a new use for such a large building without inviting the destruction of a work of art? And how do you preserve access to it by the general public? The solution to these problems will certainly tax the ingenuity of the Conservancy.

The Cultural Heritage Foundation, whose Heritage Square has been dubbed "an architectural petting zoo" by one critic, has been criticized for its inactivity, limited scope, and tendency to channel its monies into the moving of houses onto a rather undesirable piece of land, charges lacking in appreciation of the fact that the foundation has saved some very distinguished pieces of architecture that would otherwise have been destroyed by the bulldozer or other vandals.

The historic Plaza in downtown Los Angeles is another matter. Until recently the effect of the tripartite administration of the Plaza area has been a disaster for true preservation to the point that, although Olvera Street is a business success, the nearby Pico House, Garnier Block, Masonic Lodge, and Merced Theater are unfinished and, except for the theater, unused. Not all the blame can rest on managerial rivalry. Even ethnic jealousies have entered the fray, and now that the project is under the single administration of the city, it is obvious that the problems, now mainly political, have not ended.

Similarly, the old Landmarks Club's concern for the missions has gone somewhat astray. At San Gabriel and San Fernando, the efforts at preservation, particularly at the latter, have resulted in elaborate misinterpretations of history that would have led even the staunch believer in restoration, Eugene Viollet-le-Duc, to wince, and that sainted preservationist, William Morris, to renew his battle to limit preservation to shoring up old buildings. At the moment (1993) the great preservation battle in regard to the missions has to do with San Gabriel, which was severely damaged in the 1987 earthquake. Those who believe that the approach should be a complete restoration (à la Viollet-le-Duc) are being led by Norman Neuerburg—may they persevere.

All the while, the official city agency responsible for urban conservation has been the Los Angeles Cultural Heritage Board (now Commission). Founded by ordinance in 1962 it is thus one of the oldest such municipal agencies in the country and, among the large cities of the United States, one of the weakest. Ironically, when the ordinance was written, largely by Carl Dentzel (then the director of the Southwest Museum) and William L. Woolett (of the American Institute of Architects), it was one of the strongest. Under its provision that the board can withhold permits for demolition or extensive remodeling for up to one year if progress is shown in efforts to preserve them, many old and treasured buildings are today standing that otherwise would be demolished. But, until recently, the board has felt limited by the ordinance to designating "cultural-historic monuments" and under the ordinance has been specifically barred from owning property or handling money. In 1980 an inventory of the architecture and other resources of the city was inspired by the board but it has been administered by the city's Department of Engineering. It is doing fine work but is discovering that the process of surveying a huge, sprawling city is long and painstaking. Meanwhile, much destruction of important buildings is taking place.

But the Cultural Heritage Commission has moved on from designating individual "cultural-historical monuments" to the much more important task of declaring neighborhoods inviolate. The most visual product of this approach is the Angelino Heights neighborhood, but there are others where an association of city officials and residents rules on restoration and development.

It is a tragedy that the county government's

preservation legislation is almost nonexistent. Furthermore, it must be stated candidly that, in spite of the hopeful signs that we have noted, architectural preservation in the Los Angeles area does not have the community-wide elan that it has in Charleston or even New York. After all, in spite of the victories of the L.A. Cultural Heritage Commission and the Los Angeles Conservancy and similar commissions and preservation organizations in the County of Los Angeles, the retention of old or even middle-aged buildings depends on the will of the owner to save and, if necessary, recycle them. The owner's mind may be swayed by public opinion, but concentrated, well-directed public opinion is still very hard to come by in the City of Los Angeles and in Los Angeles County.

In the period since World War II Los Angeles has been one of the few American cities to expand economically and to flourish even in a period of recession. It is very difficult for the staunchest preservationist to knock destruction in the name of progress. Recently, largely due to the strong and well-deserved publicity given to the restoration work being done by the developers Ratkovitch and Bowers, the idea is getting around that preservation can pay off financially. The success of this observation broadly interpreted, will, we believe, conserve more buildings than municipal ordinances can protect.

A revision of the old Cultural Heritage Ordinance is in the works and, if passed, promises to strengthen the official arm. Already an excellent Historic District Ordinance has been established by the City Council. Historic Preservation Zones can now be set up under the supervision of the Cultural Heritage Commission and the Planning Department. One, the Angelino Heights District has its machinery in order, and two others (South Carthay and the Plaza) have been recommended to the City Council. Again, this work is probably more important than designating individual landmarks, but, in a city where there are few concentrations of distinguished buildings but many isolated landmarks, the Cultural Heritage Commission must keep in the business of individual designation.

THE LOS ANGELES FREEWAY SYSTEM

Planning for what was to become the most famous freeway system in the world started in the early 1930s. By 1940 the Los Angeles Regional Planning Commission had adopted a "Parkway" scheme for the whole of the Los Angeles basin. In the following year the Pasadena Freeway (the Arroyo Seco Parkway) was completed, and the Cahuenga Pass section of the Hollywood Freeway was open to traffic. During the years of the Second World War, two freeways were started—the San Bernardino and the Santa Ana. But it was the fifteen-year period between 1950 and 1965 that most of the freeways of the system were begun. The glory of this freeway renaissance was the wonderful landscaping which occurred in almost every section. These were indeed conceived of as high-speed roadways through urban (visual only) parks.

In the chronological list below we have indicated the date when construction, (not planning) began, and the date they were basically completed. A number of the freeways have not yet been completed, and a number will most likely never be built.

Pasadena Freeway (Arroyo Seco Parkway) 1934–41

Hollywood Freeway 1940–68

San Bernardino Freeway 1943–57

Santa Ana Freeway 1944–64

Harbor Freeway 1952–70

Long Beach Freeway 1951–65 (not completed)

Golden State Freeway 1955–76

Foothill Freeway 1955–76

Artesia Freeway 1956–75

Ventura Freeway 1958–71

San Diego Freeway 1957–64

Corona Freeway 1958 (not completed)

Glendale Freeway 1958 (not completed)

Santa Monica Freeway 1961–66

Santa Paula Freeway 1963 (not completed)

San Gabriel River Freeway 1963–71

Antelope Valley Freeway 1963–73

Garden Grove Freeway 1963 (not completed)

Pomona Freeway 1965-71

San Fernando Valley Freeway 1968–84

Orange Freeway 1969–73

Century Freeway 1970–94

As the list above indicates, there have been very few additions to the Los Angeles freeway system in the last ten years. The one exception is the Century Freeway I-105 (Glen Anderson Freeway). The 17.3-mile Century Freeway, from El Segundo to Norwalk (which includes the Metro Greenline), was opened in the fall of 1993. Certainly, the aesthetic high point of the Century Freeway is its complexed pattern of connector ramps with the Harbor Freeway, and with several of the other freeways it connects with. Since 1965 there has been the continual running battle between the City of South Pasadena and CALTRANS as to whether the Long Beach Freeway will ever be built into Pasadena; one can only hope that this never takes place.

There is also some activity in double-decking existing freeways, but with the high cost of constructing such multilayered solutions, it will probably never be extensive. So far, the proposal has been to double-deck the Harbor Freeway, and a section between Adams Boulevard and Martin Luther King Boulevard has been completed. Perhaps the most apparent change in the freeways over the past few years has been the addition of masonry noise-barrier walls along many sections, and the addition of concrete barriers in the central medians. None of this hardscape is sensitively designed, and one continues to hope that vines and other vegetation will eventually cover over these not-very-handsome walls.

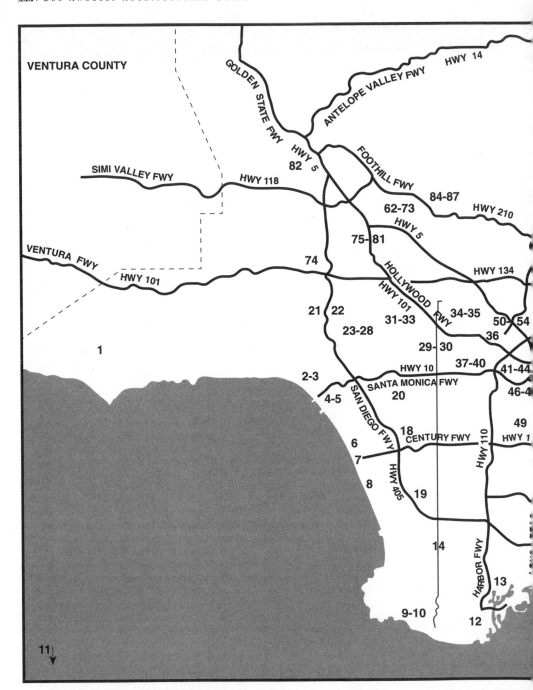

VENTURA COUNTY

GOLDEN STATE FWY

ANTELOPE VALLEY FWY   HWY 14

HWY 5
82

FOOTHILL FWY

SIMI VALLEY FWY   HWY 118

84-87

HWY 210

62-73

HWY 5

75-81

VENTURA FWY

HWY 101   74

HOLLYWOOD FWY

HWY 134

HWY 101   34-35   50-54

21 22   31-33   36

23-28   29- 30   37-40   41-44

1   2-3   HWY 10   46-4

4-5   SAN DIEGO FWY   SANTA MONICA FWY   49

20   HWY 110   HWY 1

18 CENTURY FWY

6

7   HWY 405   19

8

14   HARBOR FWY   13

9-10   12

11

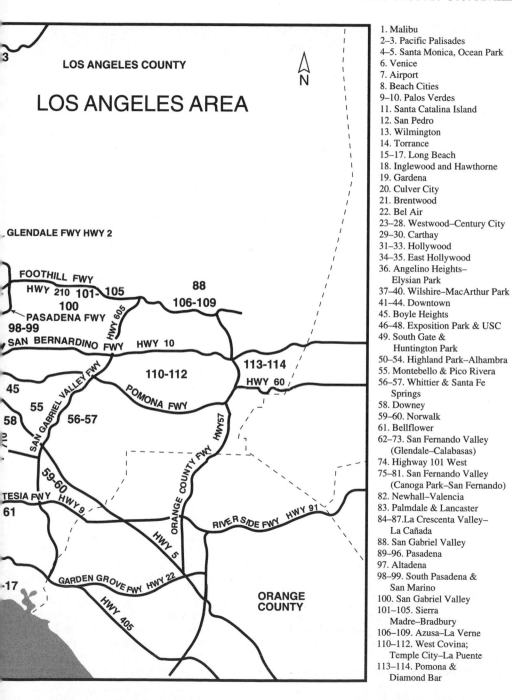

1. Malibu
2–3. Pacific Palisades
4–5. Santa Monica, Ocean Park
6. Venice
7. Airport
8. Beach Cities
9–10. Palos Verdes
11. Santa Catalina Island
12. San Pedro
13. Wilmington
14. Torrance
15–17. Long Beach
18. Inglewood and Hawthorne
19. Gardena
20. Culver City
21. Brentwood
22. Bel Air
23–28. Westwood–Century City
29–30. Carthay
31–33. Hollywood
34–35. East Hollywood
36. Angelino Heights–
    Elysian Park
37–40. Wilshire–MacArthur Park
41–44. Downtown
45. Boyle Heights
46–48. Exposition Park & USC
49. South Gate &
    Huntington Park
50–54. Highland Park–Alhambra
55. Montebello & Pico Rivera
56–57. Whittier & Santa Fe
    Springs
58. Downey
59–60. Norwalk
61. Bellflower
62–73. San Fernando Valley
    (Glendale–Calabasas)
74. Highway 101 West
75–81. San Fernando Valley
    (Canoga Park–San Fernando)
82. Newhall–Valencia
83. Palmdale & Lancaster
84–87. La Crescenta Valley–
    La Cañada
88. San Gabriel Valley
89–96. Pasadena
97. Altadena
98–99. South Pasadena &
    San Marino
100. San Gabriel Valley
101–105. Sierra
    Madre–Bradbury
106–109. Azusa–La Verne
110–112. West Covina;
    Temple City–La Puente
113–114. Pomona &
    Diamond Bar

Public Transportation—The Twentieth Century

The history of public transportation in Los Angeles and the county pretty well mirrored what came about elsewhere in the country. In 1911 the electric railroad system was consolidated by Edward H. Harrington and Henry E. Huntington. This new combined public rail facility was one of the most extensive in the country, and it worked very well. But with the advent of the automobile, the life of this "Red Car" system (again as experienced throughout the country) slowly came to an end. In the 1920s and on, public transit was relegated to buses, and that system continues down to the present moment.

From the early 1920s on, the public commitment for transportation was the street, boulevard, highway, and eventually the freeway. And, as we are all aware, when this system works (i.e. is not overcrowded), it is both in fact and illusion the best mode of transportation. Numerous factors have worked against the freeway and auto in Southern California in recent years, ranging from smog to the overcrowding of the system, and finally to the fact that the pre-World War II planning to effectively create dispersal centers has never really taken place.

With great reluctance, the city and the county have abandoned their futuristic image of such machines as the helicopter-auto and have returned to the past in an effort to solve public transit, i.e., to the building of mixed light and heavy surface rail system, and the beginnings of a subway system. In 1980 a bond measure was passed and plans were laid for a surface rail system 150 miles long. The first phase of this Los Angeles Metro system opened up in July 1990, with the **Blue Line,** the rail system between downtown Los Angeles and downtown Long Beach. Other new increments will be the **Green Line,** which will run down the

I-105 (Glen Anderson Freeway) to Norwalk and to the International Airport (LAX). This is planned to be completed in 1994. Other links in the public transit system are the **Metrolink Trains,** which connect a number of the outlying cities to Los Angeles. It is once again possible to travel easily by rail to San Bernardino to the east, to Moorpark to the northwest, or to San Diego to the south. Several **Metrolink Train Stations** have opened in the past few years. Among these is the **El Monte Station** (1992) designed by Frederick Fisher. An extensive project related to **Metrolink** is the Union Gateway Project. This has been designed by Ehrenkrantz and Eckstut. Construction on this project started in 1991.

The **Blue Line** has now been in use for several years and appears quite successful. The open platform stations were designed by several architectural firms. These include: **Slauson, Imperial, Del Almo and Firestone Stations,** designed by Siegel Diamond; **Pacific Coast Highway/Long Beach Boulevard Station** (plus the other seven Long Beach Stations), designed by La Canada Group, James Goodell and Associates (with Parsons, Brinkerhoff, Quade and Douglas and Miralles and Associates).

In the mid–1920s a plan was drawn up for a combined subway and elevated rail system— not too different from that developed much later as BART in the San Francisco Bay area. The first part of this system, a downtown subway, was actually constructed but was soon abandoned with the advent of the Great Depression of the 1930s.

Construction of the present new subway system (the **Metro Red-Line**), started in the 1980s, and plans are eventually to open a system from downtown Los Angeles to the west, and eventually to develop a system leading to the San Fernando Valley. A small 4.4-mile segment of this system from Union Station to Westlake/MacArthur Park was opened early in 1993. One's general impression so far is that it is well planned and works in a utilitarian sense, but it has none of the elegance of the Washington, D.C., system, nor the general overall design sophistication of BART.

The following Metro Red-Line stations and their accompanying art are either completed, under construction, or planned:

Pershing Square Station
Arthur Erickson Architect
Mural, Jessica Cusick and Roberto Gil

Civic Center Station
Arthur Erickson Architects
Sculpture, Jonathan Borofsky

Union Station
Harry Weese and Associates
Ceramic tile mural, Terry Schoonhoven; sculptural mural, Cynthia Carlson; sculpture, Christopher Sproat

Westlake-MacArthur Park Station
McLarand, Vasquez and Partners; Gensler and Associates
Murals, Francisco Letelier; sculpture, Therman Statom

7th Street/Metro Center Station
Dworsky Associates
Ceramic tile murals, Joyce Kozloff; fiber-optical panels, Tom Eatherton; ceramic tile mural, Roberto Gil de Montes

Other stations in progress (design and/or construction) include:

Hollywood/ Western Station
Master plan by Meyer and Allen

Hollywood/ Vine Station
Master plan by Urban Innovations, Levin and Associates, Gensler and Associates, and Kaku Associates

Vermont/Santa Monica Station
This station, designed by Koning/Eizenberg (with the artist Robert Miller) is projected to open in 1998.

Hollywood/Highland Station
Barton Myers Associates

THE LOS ANGELES PUBLIC MURALS

Los Angeles has always had its share of public murals ranging from the impressive high-art work of Jose Orozco and Howard Warshaw to the populist work of Hugo Ballin and Millard Sheets. In the 1920s, as was true across the country, murals (and sculpture) occur on both private commercial buildings as well as on public structures. During the depression years of the 1930s a number of interior murals were painted as part of the Federal Arts Project in post offices, schools, and other public buildings. During the late 1940s and 1950s large-scale billboards and the exterior murals and mosaics of the Home Savings Association branch offices constituted the major outlet for public art. It was in the 1960s that Los Angeles began to experience a growing rash of external wall murals. The two centers for this art were East Los Angeles and Venice. In the 1970s and 1980s the public mural affair spread all across the city (generally within commercial strips and adjacent to the freeways). To the world of murals, one would have to add the all-encompassing world of the grafitti which plagues almost all of Los Angeles County.

As with other major American cities, the murals of the 1960s and later readily divide themselves into two categories: (1) those which are really folk painted by amateur and self-trained artists (almost always ethnic, and aimed generally at conveying a political or social message); and (2) those which aspire to high art (with their message occasionally social, but usually art for art's sake). In the 1950s the Fine Arts Squad produced a number of epic pieces, a few of which are still around. In 1973 the City of Los Angeles officially started its Inner City Mural Program, and this has continued down to the present day. Starting in 1983 both the city and the state (through the California

Department of Transportation) promoted an array of murals related to the Olympic Games—either as to subject or to help spruce up the city's visual image for the games. While most of these are well executed, they still cannot compete with the giant lighted billboards of Sunset Strip and elsewhere throughout the city and county. Certainly today (1993), the most powerful of the city's murals are those painted by Kent Twitchell—several of which are apparent from the downtown freeways.

It is questionable whether most of these recent public murals (whether by professionals or by amateurs) really contribute much aesthetically to the city, or whether they really acknowledge their sites and its surroundings. They seem to exist in and of themselves, as if they were a large painting which should be in an art gallery, rather than being misplaced on a public street. If one looks back at the murals of Millard Sheets and others, these are (in most instances) very carefully and thoughtfully related to their surroundings. Perhaps, as the years go by, our new group of public muralists will take a moment to learn from the past.

The rapid comings and goings, and the sheer number of public murals in Los Angeles, make it impossible in a Guide such as this to provide a comprehensive and up-to-date list. We have included a select number of public murals, especially when they are related (pro or con) to a building or group of buildings. If you are interested in seeing them, the best solution is to drive the freeways, and then visit Venice and East Los Angeles. If you wish to be more complete in your search, then consult Robin J. Dunitz's excellent book, *Street Gallery: Guide to 1000 Los Angeles Murals* (Los Angeles: RJD Enterprises, P.O. Box 64668, Los Angeles, CA 90064; 1993).

MALIBU

Malibu Beach did not begin its development until 1929, when the Pacific Coast Highway finally was forced through the Rindge Ranch. In 1926, some land at Malibu la Costa had been put up for lease, but the construction of houses at the edge of the beach did not take place until after 1928. It was in the 1930s that the Malibu Colony became a fashionable place to have a beach house. The hilly coastland west of Malibu Colony remained basically rural and untrammeled until the 1960s. Increasingly in recent years, that area between the highway and the beach is being filled with numerous large-scale houses. In the 1960s and early 1970s, most of these houses were loosely Modern in imagery, but in recent years historicism (usually grossly misunderstood) ranging from the Medieval to the Spanish Colonial Revival has prevailed. The land adjacent to the highway is slowly being condominiumized, again with generally disappointing versions of varied architectural images. In the early 1990s, Malibu was incorporated as an independent city, and it will be interesting to see how it develops its own personality in the years to come.

The Malibu Colony continues to acquire houses of distinguished design, but the colony is a private, well-guarded world and is not open to the public. Within it are houses designed by John Lautner, Richard Meier, and others.

1. Sagheb House, 1990
John Lautner
32402 Pacific Coast Highway

Since the 1960s, John Lautner has designed and overseen a number of fascinating houses on the Malibu coast. Most of these are of reinforced concrete devised in a highly organic form. Regrettably, these houses are not easy to see from the roads and highway, but at high tide, an adventuresome person wandering along the beach can catch an occasional glimpse of them. Other Lautner houses in the Malibu area are the **Krause House** (1983) at 24444 Malibu Road, and the **Segel House** (1983) at 22426 Pacific Coast Highway. Lautner's early **Stevens House** (1968) at 78 Malibu Colony Drive is within the private gated colony and cannot be seen.

2. Pierson House, 1961–64
Craig Ellwood
32320 Pacific Coast Highway
Architecture as art. The architect wrote in 1955, "The substance of architecture is *form,* and this alone has a survival value." The Pierson house is a precise, carefully delineated volume, closed off from the road by thin, paperlike walls and an intervening courtyard. It has an urban design on three sides and an open beach pavilion on the west.

3. Berns House, 1951
Gordon Drake
31654 W. Broad Beach Road, Trancas Beach
A screened patio forms the center of this dwelling. The frame is articulated by vertical wood posts having an infill primarily of glass. Rational, but warm. The house in recent years has been remodeled by its current owner, Gerald Frost.

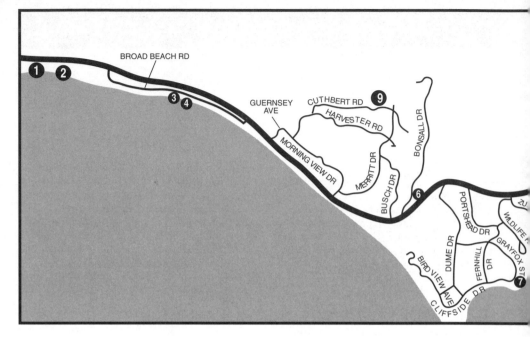

BROAD BEACH RD

① ②

③ ④

GUERNSEY AVE

CUTHBERT RD

⑨

HARVESTER RD

MORNING VIEW DR

MERRITT DR

BUSCH DR

BONSALL DR

⑥

PORTSHEAD DR

WILDLIFE R

ZU

DUME DR

FERNHILL DR

GRAYFOX ST

BIRD VIEW AVE

CLIFFSIDE DR

⑦

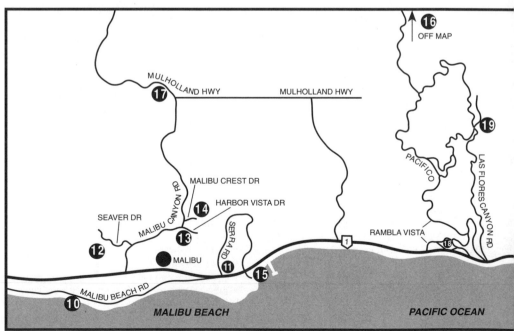

⑯

OFF MAP

MULHOLLAND HWY

MULHOLLAND HWY

⑰

⑲

PACIFICO

LAS FLORES CANYON RD

MALIBU CREST DR

SEAVER DR

MALIBU CANYON RD

HARBOR VISTA DR

⑭

SERRA RD

RAMBLA VISTA

1

⑱

⑬

MALIBU

⑫

⑪

⑮

MALIBU BEACH RD

⑩

MALIBU BEACH

PACIFIC OCEAN

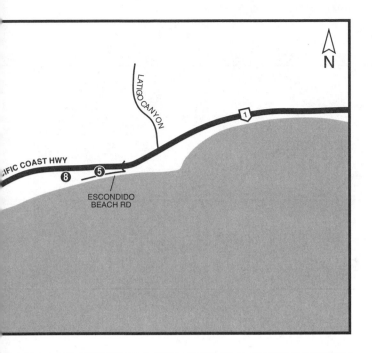

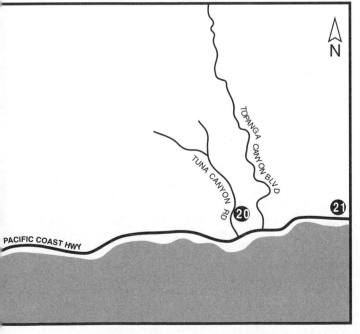

4. Downey House, 1991

4. Downey House, 1991
Melinda Grey
31616 Broad Beach Road, Trancas Beach
The three main sections of this two-story dwelling suggest not a single building but an informal group of buildings. The architect wrote of the house that it was a "playful series of pavilions created by vaults, gables, cylinders, and squares connected by the landscape elements that start out formally and drift into casual directedness." The house is sheathed in natural and pink colored stucco combined with a thin slate base.

5. House, 1962
David Ming-Li Lowe
27320 West Pacific Coast Highway,
Escondido Beach Road
A two-story pavilion suggestive of the faraway Orient; the structure utilizes glued, laminated arch-vaults.

6. LeBrun House, 1963
Thornton M. Abell
6339 Bonsell Drive, Zuma Beach
An entrance gallery, small courtyard, and office connect the living wing to the studio section of the house. Enclosed terraces and gardens effectively carry the interior space outward. Certainly one of Abell's most successful houses.

7. Lyndon House, 1950
Maynard Lyndon
28820 Cliffside Drive, Paradise Cove
A 1950s Modern ranch house expressing the classic post-and-beam tradition of the Case Study Houses.

8. Holiday House Motel, 1950
Richard J. Neutra; 1954, Dion Neutra
27400 Pacific Coast Highway
Two layouts of living/sleeping rooms, each with its own balcony, look out over the ocean. The upper unit has two stories, the lower has one. Balconies are supported by L-shaped outriggers, and the buildings are sheathed in board and batten. The original buildings plus the twelve units added by Dion Neutra in 1954 are effectively worked into the hillside bluff.

9. Davis House, 1972
Frank O. Gehry and Associates
29715 W. Cuthbert Road, Trancas Beach

9. Davis House, 1972

A trapezoidal building covered by a low-pitched shed roof creates a neutral interior space which can be arranged at will. The exterior, including roof, is sheathed in corrugated metal. The shape as you see it from a distance creates some unusual problems of perspective.

10. Hunt House, 1955–57
Craig Ellwood
24514 Malibu Beach Road
The Case Study House image of the 1950s—Miesian, cardboardy, and fragile in a Southern California manner. Facing the road are two boxes, each of which houses a garage; a small entrance court is enclosed between them. A wooden bridge leads down to the house. The plan of the house is the classic Modernist H-scheme. The front leg of the H contains the two bedrooms, both of which look out on their own court. A wood decked terrace extends along the beach side of the house.

11. Office Building, 1987
Goldman/Firth/Associates
LA Group and Isabelle Greene, landscape architects
24955 Pacific Coast Highway

The architects have broken up a 20,000-square-foot building into a series of one-, two-, and three-story volumes, so that it reads as a Modernist village. A rectangular grid framework moves up and down at the base and above are occasional metal and glass penthouses. The project is still on the raw side and needs the softening effect of large-scale plant material.

12. Pepperdine University, 1971–73
William Pereira Associates
Armstrong and Sharfman,
landscape architects
Seaver Drive, west of Malibu Canyon Road
A vast green lawn conveying the feel of a golf course intervenes between the Coast Highway and the university buildings up the hill. These meticulously maintained lawns, plantings, and trees convey a sense of being in Beverly Hills. The buildings employ the '70s composition of cut-into stucco volumes picturesquely set on a hillside location. One of the most recent buildings on the campus is **Odell McConnell Law Center** (1979; Neptune and Thomas), which continues the architectural forms originally established in 1971.

13. Rucker House, 1971
Douglas W. Rucker
Off Malibu Canyon Road at 23704 Harbor
Vista Drive
This well-detailed and theatrically situated hill-side house can be seen as far away as the Pacific Coast Highway. The architect has borrowed the theme of Schindler's hillside houses of the 1930s and maneuvered it into the mid-1980s.

14. Hodges Castle, 1977–79
Thomas Hodges
23800 Malibu Crest Drive
Dr. Hodges's towered and crenelated castle is poised, just as a castle should be, on a high hill overlooking and guarding the inland approaches to Malibu.

15. Adamson House, 1928
Morgan, Walls, and Clements (Stiles Clements)
Pacific Coast Highway at Serra Road
The Adamson House is now included in Malibu Lagoon State Park and can best be viewed from the beach itself. It is one of the few domestic commissions of Stiles Clements, who is best known for his many commercial and institutional designs either within Morgan, Walls, and Clements, or on his own after 1936. The house is a two-story Andalusian farmhouse which exhibits some splendid examples of metalwork and also decorative glazed tile produced by the Malibu Tile Company. Arrangements to see the house and its garden can be made through the Malibu Historical Society.

16. Arch Oboler House, 1940, 1941, 1944, 1946
Frank Lloyd Wright
32436 Mulholland Drive
The grand and spectacular main house "Eagle Feather" was never built. From the road you can see the gate house (1940); below is the small wood and stone "retreat" built in 1941 and added to in 1944 and 1946. The vocabulary that Wright used here is directly related to the 1939 Sturges House in West Los Angeles and the burned 1940 Pauson House in Paradise

Valley north of Phoenix. This house was badly damaged in a November 1977 fire.

17. Mr. Blanding's Dream House, 1947–48
Malibu Creek State Park; 3800 Solstice Canyon Road, Malibu Canyon Road between Mulholland Highway & Cold Canyon Road
America's post-World War II ideal of a dwelling was built for the popular film *Mr. Blanding Builds His Dream House,* produced by RKO and starring Myrna Loy and Cary Grant. It was built as a stage set on the land owned by movie producer George Hunter, who converted it into his own ranch house. As one would expect, the 2,476-square-foot house is pure Anglo Colonial Revival (referred to at the time as "Connecticut Colonial").
According to the publicity release for the film, "identical houses" were built across the country, including one in Los Angeles. The house is now used for the offices of the Santa Monica Mountains Conservancy Foundation.

18. Reed House, 1960
John Reed
21536 W. Rambla Vista, Malibu
Projecting horizontal and vertical volumes in wood create a dramatic hillside composition.

19. Lyman House, circa 1963
Frederick Lyman
3810 Las Flores Canyon Road,
Las Flores Beach
Two rows of heavy posts support a corrugated metal roof. Glass doors open between each pair of vertical posts. As a design it seems simple, yet is highly sophisticated.

20. Walker House, 1992
Melinda Grey
2935 Tuna Canyon Road
The architect described this dwelling as "toys in a playpen connected by an invisible string of timber and glass gridwork." The dwelling with walls of logs appears indeed like a child's delightful village. To the right is a curved roof form which houses the living room (with garage below). A high pyramidal roof covers the central "house," and to the right is a

21. J. Paul Getty Museum, 1972–73

gable-roofed building with a projecting semi-circular bay for sleeping.

21. J. Paul Getty Museum, 1972–73
Langdon and Wilson; Stephen Garrett; Norman Neuerberg, consultant; Emmet L. Wemple and Associates, landscape architects
17985 Pacific Coast Highway

Here is Southern California as it should be—the past as seen through the perceptive eyes of the 1970s, in a landscape which puts the Old World of the Mediterranean to shame. The museum is modeled after an ancient Roman villa, the Villa of the Papyri, which was buried in the famous eruption of Mount Vesuvius in A.D. 79 and excavated in the eighteenth century by tunneling under the hard lava crust. J. Paul Getty, who commissioned the building, wrote: "What could be more logical than to display it [classical art] in a classical building?" You approach the building through a Roman gate along a Roman road to enter the parking garage, which is within the podium. Ascending to the courtyard, you obtain a view of the Pacific Ocean (with no idea that the busy Coast Highway and beach lie below). Turning around, you face the main museum building across the long reflecting pool. Inside the building, a cross axis from the central atrium leads to smaller atriums and walled gardens (one of which contains a restaurant). The classical Greek and Roman sculptures and mosaics all appear at their best in this environment—one created by the building as well as the landscaping. As the architects planned, the building and landscaping have mellowed and improved each year. You must call three or four days in advance for reservations to visit the museum, which is open 10 A.M.–5 P.M. daily, except holidays and Mondays.

PACIFIC PALISADES, NORTH

The area inland from the coast from Malibu to Santa Monica is rich in important High Art architecture, and fortunately much of it is visible from the streets. If Highland Park was the art center of Los Angeles at the turn of the century, Pacific Palisades took the title from the 1920s through the 1940s. Motion picture figures soon discovered that it was only a short distance by Pierce-Arrow from Hollywood to the coast, and settled in. Then writers, artists, and musicians—many of them fleeing Nazi Germany—found it a haven for their creativity. And under the leadership of John Entenza, the

editor and publisher of *Arts and Architecture,* Pacific Palisades and nearby Santa Monica Canyon attracted the most advanced Modernist taste in architecture.

This community began its architectural life in the late 1860s when Los Angelinos came for the summer breezes off the ocean and pitched their tents just north of where Channel Road now cuts off from the Pacific Coast Highway. It remained a summer beach colony until 1921, when a group of Methodists, sensing a perfect place for chautauqua and a resting place for their retired ministers, established a colony on the highlands.

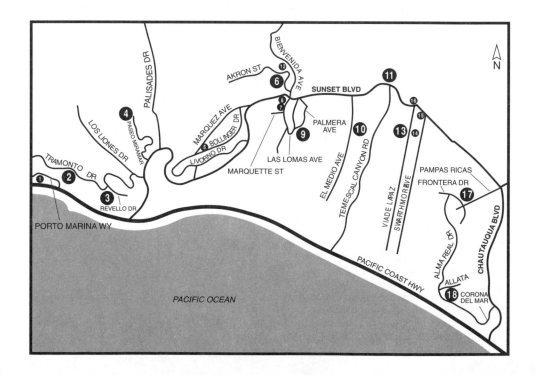

Castellammare, which lies to the north of Pacific Palisades, was developed in the 1920s by Alphonzo Bell, Sr., who had already profited handsomely from the development of Bel Air. Some Mediterranean villas were built on the hills and cliffs overlooking the Pacific, but like the Methodists to the south, Bell never saw his posh Riviera realized.

As you travel up the hill on Sunset Boulevard from the Pacific Coast Highway, take note of the "Lake Shrine" at 17190 Sunset Boulevard. Here, in the middle of what looks like an African jungle, is a spring-fed lake (with houseboat), a "Golden Lotus" archway, and domes of gold. This earthly paradise was built by the Self-Realization Fellowship in 1950, under the direction of Paramahanda Yogananda. The fellowship and its instant Eden are pure Southern California.

1. Villa de Leon, 1927
  Kenneth MacDonald
  17948 Porto Marina Way
A memorable feature of the coast drive as you come down from Santa Barbara is this classical Mediterranean villa perched high on the edge of the cliff overlooking the entrance to the Getty Museum. Much of its splendid landscaping has disappeared in continual landslides, but the house is still sensational, not only from the ocean side but also close-up. Other Spanish and Italian villas of the twenties are situated nearby.

2. House, circa 1935
  Mr. Bird
  17526 Tramonto Drive
The name of the architect is also a description of the house—quaint beyond dreams of sugar plums.

3. Beagles House, 1963
  Pierre Koenig
  17446 Revello Drive
A sophisticated and successful assertion of the '50s and early '60s "less is more" school. Incidentally, unless you follow a recent map you will probably get into trouble, since part of Revello Drive collapsed in a mud slide a few years ago.

4. Times Demonstration House, 1927–28
  Mark Daniels, architect and landscape architect
  520 Paseo Miramar
There were a good number of model and demonstration houses built in the Los Angeles area in the 1920s and 1930s. Mark Daniels was a leading exponent of the Mediterranean/Spanish Colonial Revival in the 1920s, and he designed a number of houses and gardens in the west Los Angeles area. The **Times Demonstration House** is a romantic hillside Spanish house, two stories to the front, three to the rear. As with all of Daniels's work, he both understood the language of historicism and had a wonderful command of forms. As one would expect of an architect/landscape architect, the house is carefully integrated into its site and has a close relationship with its garden.

5. Hill and Dale Nursery and Kindergarten, 1949, 1965
  Lloyd Wright
  16706 Marquez Avenue at Bollinger Drive
A handsome, horizontal redwood structure.

6. House, 1952
  Jones and Emmons
  16310 Akron Street
A single-level post-and-beam spec house for the Southdown development which was never completely realized. The plan is an open one, with the rooms oriented outward towards terraces and garden.

7. House, 1952
  Jones and Emmons
  North of northwest corner of Bienveneda Avenue and Marquette Street
Another variation on the small Southdown development spec housing developed by this firm.

8. Soffer House, 1973
  Eric Wright (remodeling)
  665 Bienveneda Avenue
Austere on the street front and all glass on the garden side, this house has all the good qualities of Wright's grandfather's (Frank Lloyd) Usonian houses and none of the bad ones.

10. 708 House, 1979–82

9. House, circa 1935
  Attributed to John Byers and Edla Muir
  630 Palmera Avenue
A very quaint Anglo-Norman cottage.

10. 708 House, 1979–82
  Eric Owen Moss
  708 El Medio Avenue
A major remodeling has produced one of Moss's characteristic buildings. The architecture here is High Art, but fortunately it's tinged with a sense of delight and humor. Though radical in form and color, it really fits well within a street of typical California spec ranch houses. The original house (1949; James H. Caughey) was a sophisticated Modern version of the California Ranch house.

11. Presbyterian Conference Grounds,
  1922–later
  North end of Temescal Canyon Road
Once this belonged to the Methodists and was the site of the yearly chautauqua performances which were so much a part of the cultural "uplift movement" for the common man at the turn of the century. By the time the small cottages were built to service the huge tent shows, the chautauqua movement was already declining. The Presbyterians took over the grounds and used it as a retreat. Behind it are some beautiful nature trails which may be used by permission of the caretaker at the main gate.

12. St. Matthew's Episcopal Church,
1982–83
Charles W. Moore (Moore, Ruble, Yudell)
Campbell and Campbell (Regula
Campbell), landscape architects
1030 Bienveneda Avenue
The present church is the third structure on the site. The original Carleton M. Winslow church of 1942 was moved to the site in the early 1950s and was then remodeled in 1953 by Jones and Emmons. That building burned in 1978 in a hillside fire. The present church by Moore is close to being domestic in scale. It manages to declare its public nature by the barnlike contours and tall campanile, while at the same time snuggling into its site and the excellent landscape scheme of Campbell and Campbell. Internally, the sanctuary has the quality of an informal meeting hall dominated by a pair of wooden arches and an apse which suggest a traditional cruciform plan. North of the church are remains (including windmill) of the French Norman Barnett Estate designed by John Byers and Edla Muir.

Arrangements for visits can be made by calling the church office.

13. Community United Methodist Church,
1929
801 Via de la Paz
The church was organized in 1922, but this structure was not begun until 1929. Even then the congregation was small, hinting that Methodism would not triumph. The edifice began in the usual Spanish Colonial Revival mode, with the bell tower showing the influence of the Moderne. Much of the original character of the building was covered up by newer (1972) facilities.

14. Palisades Elementary School, 1930
800 Via de la Paz
Spanish Colonial Revival again, this school with Moorish tower was slated for destruction after the 1971 earthquake. Even though it suffered no serious damage, the building's construction did not meet contemporary safety standards. A wise citizenry, proud of the architecture of the old building, engaged an architect who showed that gutting the building, reinforcing the walls, and constructing new interiors would not only satisfy the building inspectors but would cost less than building a new structure. As in the case of the Lapiths and the Centaurs, civilization occasionally wins.

15. Santa Monica Land and Water Company, 1924
Clinton Nourse
Southwest corner of Sunset Boulevard
A fine Spanish Colonial Revival business block. The very name suggests that promoters were early trying to lure buyers to their Riviera.

16. Department of Water and Power Building, 1935
Frederick L. Roehrig
Northeast corner of Sunset Boulevard and Via de la Paz
Did you ever think you would see an example of Regency Moderne? Now you have!

17. House, circa 1929
629 Frontera Drive
This beautifully turned-out Monterey Revival house must be by John Byers. But the real reason we take you into this area is that we want you to experience the town planning of Olmsted and Olmsted, who also laid out Palos Verdes Estates. The houses are all expensive. Some, like this one, are good. Most date after 1929, which says something about the gravity of the Great Depression for the rich.

18. Harrison House, 1950
Paul Sterling Hoag
14926 Altata Drive
At least from the street, this two-story gable-roofed house has the atmosphere of a contemporary version of California's Monterey tradition. It has a two-story porch, board and batten siding, and some walls of adobe brick. The dwelling rests comfortably within a grove of large eucalyptus trees.

Pacific Palisades, South

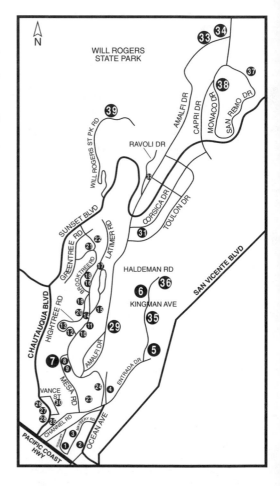

anta Monica Canyon initially contained small, quite modest summer beach houses and year-round cottages. In the later 1930s, it began to acquire serious examples of Modern design by Harwell H. Harris, Richard J. Neutra, and others. After 1945, other prime examples of high art Modernism were built, especially in the area around Chautauqua Boulevard.

The Olmsted brothers, whose father had laid out Central Park in New York City, platted a picturesque maze west of Chautauqua Boulevard, where some of the most pleasant houses in the traditional imagery of the twenties and thirties remain. The old canyons attracted a varied coterie, from the Uplifters on Latimer Road to Will Rogers and Thomas Mann in the highlands.

1. Bradbury House, 1922
  John Byers
  102 Ocean Way
One of the first adobe houses that Byers designed, this was instrumental in establishing his reputation as a Spanish Colonial Revivalist.

2. Sten-Frenke House, 1934
  Richard J. Neutra
  126 Mabery Road, off Ocean Avenue
A classic Neutra with a Streamline Moderne curved-glass bay which overlooks the Pacific. The house, which is nearly impossible to see, lies up the hill behind the street wall and garage. It was sensitively modernized in 1982 by Gwathmey, Siegel and Associates.

3. Guerra House, 1992
  Melinda Grey
  138 Mabery Road
A two-story house composed as a village of

barrel-vaulted and gable-roofed forms, all very delicately handled. The central gable section, which is perpendicular to the street, centers on a partially enclosed circular court.

3. Guerra House, 1992

4. Canyon Elementary School, 1894
 Northeast of intersection of Ocean Avenue
 and Channel Road
A nice Classical Revival one-room schoolhouse
(now a children's library) said to be the second
oldest school building in Los Angeles County.

5. Pumphrey House, 1939
 Harwell H. Harris
 615 Kingman Avenue
This horizontal, wood-battened house is quite
Wrightian and very difficult to see behind
fences and foliage.

6. Delores del Rio House, 1929
 Douglas Honnold and Cedric Gibbons
 757 Kingman Avenue
This impressive example of the early Modern
was designed by the set designer Cedric
Gibbons. It has a formal Art Deco quality on
the street side, but to the rear it is almost pure
doctrinaire International Style Modern in the
two-story facade which overlooks Santa
Monica Canyon. The gardens were renovated
between 1989 and 1993 by the Santa Monica
firm of Campbell and Campbell.

7. Entenza House, 1937
 Harwell H. Harris
 475 Mesa Road
Built for John Entenza, the editor and publisher
of *Arts and Architecture,* as a declaration of his
commitment to modernity. His curved-wall carport, spiral staircase, and metal railing make it
more Streamline Moderne than classical
International style. The Entenza House was
Harris's only realized example of Streamline
Moderne.

8. Abell House, 1937
 Thornton M. Abell
 469 Upper Mesa Road
A gem of the regionalized International Style
Modern, this house depressed on the side of the
hill is barely visible. The house consists of a
series of stucco volumes stepped down a steep
hillside. It is all quite nautical in feeling.

9. Haines House, 1943
 Thornton M. Abell
 477 Upper Mesa Road
An angled, single-floor, Modern image (stucco
volumes) dwelling set far down the hillside.
The garden side of this wood-frame, concrete

block, and fiberglass structure is almost entirely glass, taking advantage of the view. At the base of the hill is a combined studio and garage. This house and Abell's own, just two doors away, are equally difficult to see.

10. Kaplan House, 1973
    Michael Leventhal
    514 Latimer Road
Parts of old wharfs and houses have been used to construct and decorate this highly expressionistic monument of the late Craftsman movement.

11. House, 1976
    Paul Thoryk
    532 Latimer Road
A tribute to the enormous popularity of the Moore and Turnbull ideas of the late 1960s, this house turns out in the end to be another example of the late Craftsman style.

12. House, circa 1925
    Southwest corner of Latimer and
    Hilltree roads
Additions have been made to this house, which was once a tiny Hansel and Gretel delight.

13. Gertler House, 1970
    Raymond Kappe
    14623 Hilltree Road
A handsome wedding of the woodsy Craftsman aesthetic of Frank Lloyd Wright and Charles and Henry Greene to the bold angular forms of the International style. Kappe, whose own house is nearby, has a very personal style well-suited to these ancient groves of eucalyptus and cypress.

14. Uplifters Club, 1923
    William J. Dodd
    Haldeman and Latimer roads
The watered-down Spanish Colonial Revival of the clubhouse is certainly not as interesting as the club itself. In the early teens the members of a splinter group of the Los Angeles Athletic Club devoted themselves to High Jinx. In the early 1920s under the leadership of Harry Marston Haldeman, a local executive of the Crane Plumbing Company, and L. Frank Baum, the author of the Wizard of Oz books, the club

bought property on Latimer Road (named for one of its members) and set out a sort of retreat, not to be confused with the later settlement of high-minded Methodists on the highlands above. Cottages were built (some log cabins) and, later, more elaborate houses. While not really important individually, as a group they compose a fascinating complex, a significant reflection of the change in taste during the late teens and early 1920s. Although we have not thoroughly researched the architects of each of these houses, it would appear from a review of meager records and general observation that the firm most responsible for the whimsical styles found here was that of Arthur S. Heineman, whose brother Alfred was the chief designer.

The log cabins—some of them authentic, some stage sets—are probably of chief interest. The first, at 1 Latimer Road, is the **Kley House** (1923), a log-faced lodge, now almost completely cut off from public view. It is probably by the Heinemans, as are other log-faced cabins at 3 and 18 Latimer Road. Others are on Haldeman Road at 31, 32, and 34. At 36, 37, and 38 are authentically constructed log cabins, of which 38, the **Marco Hellman Cabin,** is the most interesting.

15. Marco Hellman Cabin, 1923–24
    Alfred Heineman
    38 Haldeman Road
Tradition has it that this house, as well as those at 36 and 37 Haldeman Road, was part of a movie set transported to the canyon by Hellman, a very rich banker. Alfred Heineman, who designed the Hellman banks in the Los Angeles area under the firm name of his brother Arthur, was responsible for the rustic decor of the interior of Hellman's own cabin. It is probable that Heineman was also responsible for the interiors of the other cabins as well as the interior and exterior design of Heather Hill (1922–23) at 7 Latimer Road, whose shingled roof in imitation of thatch was a trademark of a number of Heineman houses in Pasadena.

16. Abel House, 1978
    Charles W. Moore, Ron Frank, and Robert
    Yudell (Urban Innovations Group)
    747 Latimer Road

This elongated house picturesquely rambles over its Rustic Canyon site, but, as in many of Moore's designs, a thin central core holds all of the wings and bays together. The entrance and a walled courtyard are in the fashion of the late-seventeenth-century New England Colonial house. A large chimney and stairs dominate the design both externally and internally.

17. Ruben House, 1936
  Richard J. Neutra
  50 Haldeman Road
This is a rare case of a Neutra remodeling. The original shingled ranch-style house was built in 1923–24 by Ralph Hamlin, a bicycle manufacturer who had the dubious distinction of owning the first motorcycle west of the Rockies.

   We have by no means listed all of the interesting architecture in Rustic Canyon; much of it is well hidden from public view. A case in point is the extensive remodeling (1982) of an older California Ranch house by architectural historian Charles Jencks and architect Buzz Yudell. This is a classic example of Post Modernism, but it cannot be seen from the road. The student of lifestyles in the 1920s and 1930s will find many more houses of significance. After all, Aldous Huxley, Emil Ludwig, Johnnie Weissmuller, and other worthies once lived in this area.

18. Emmons House, 1954
  Jones and Emmons
  661 Brooktree Road
A very neat post-and-beam International Style Modern product which has weathered the years extremely well.

19. Anderson House, 1950
  Craig Ellwood
  656 Hightree Road
A thin brick wall and aluminum garage door form the austere street facade of this house by one of Los Angeles's most distinguished followers of Mies van der Rohe.

20. Elton House, 1951
  Craig Ellwood
  635 Hightree Road
If the Anderson House is private, this Miesian house is very open and a strikingly different style from its neighbor.

23. Burns House, 1974

21. Kappe House, 1968
  Raymond Kappe
  715 Brooktree Road
A virtual tree house poised over a steep hillside. Glass has been used almost exclusively as the infill between the vertical and horizontal wood frame of the building. Within, wood bridges and staircases join the principal interior spaces. This house is another example of Kappe's inventive ability to meld the Craftsman aesthetic and the International Style Modern into a very personal style. Other examples of Kappe's work are nearby: the **Pregerson House** (1966) at 680 Brooktree Road, and the **Gates-Dorman House** (1961) at 737 Brooktree Road.

22. Harrison House, 1950
  Paul Sterling Hoag
  728 Brooktree Road
An early 1950s Modernist dwelling rendered in stone and wood, with some exposed structural members. The stone walls are treated as slabs without any penetration of openings. Designs such as this illustrate how the Modernists were able to accommodate "warm" traditional materials into their style.

23. Burns House, 1974
  Charles W. Moore
  230 Amalfi Drive
A 1970s version of the Spanish Colonial Revival of the 1920s. The pink stucco dwelling

21. Kappe House, 1968

boasts an array of shed roofs and skylights, along with the basic necessities of Hispanic Los Angeles—a walled and tiled entrance court and a swimming pool. Within, an organ dominates the two-story living room.

24. Haines House, 1951
Thornton M. Abell
247 Amalfi Drive
A refined pavilion sheathed in horizontal redwood, with a flat roof, brick chimney, and brick terraces.

25. West House, 1948
Rodney A. Walker
199 Chautauqua Boulevard
A romantically sited, single-floor, five-room house sheathed in striated plywood. This was one of the early Case Study House projects.

26. Eames House and Studio, 1947–49
Charles and Ray Eames
203 Chautauqua Boulevard
One of America's great twentieth-century houses, which is as impressive today as when it was built as part of John Entenza's Case Study House program. The two metal-framed boxes, set against a eucalyptus-covered hillside, dramatically illustrate how personal and humane the image of the machine can be in the hands of a gifted designer. The interior furnishings were chosen and arranged by both Ray and Charles Eames as an integral part of the design.

27. Entenza House, 1949
Charles Eames and Eero Saarinen
205 Chautauqua Boulevard
The steel-frame-and-roof design is not as assertive in this Case Study House as in the adjacent Eames House. A single rectangular form contains all of the spaces, including the two-car garage. As with the Eames House, the open interior was most impressive with the furnishings of Saarinen chairs and built-in angular sofa.

28. Bailey House, 1946–48
Richard J. Neutra (with later additions by Neutra)
219 Chautauqua Boulevard

26. Eames House and Studio, 1947–49

Esther McCoy has noted the similarity of this house to Neutra's Nesbitt House of 1942, where he "made a virtue of redwood—even brick." The property is partly enclosed by a serpentine brick wall. A Case Study House.

29. Cernitz House, 1938
Milton J. Black
601 Amalfi Drive
If you look carefully behind the post-World War II remodeling, you will see one of Black's Streamline Moderne delights.

30. Anderson House, 1922
390 Vance Street
Anderson, whose first name seems to have disappeared, was supposed to have been a merchant who brought treasures from all over the world to this tiny house. Most of his travels seem, however, to have been in Mexico. This house, with its magnificent tile, art-glass windows, and mosaic of Mexican dancers in front of a mission arcade, is a real stunner. The house has been extensively rebuilt (from 1986 on) by its present owners, David and Margaret Lederer, who, with the architect Finn Kappe, retained the charm of the original in what amounts to a new house.

30. Anderson House, 1922

31. Kenaston House, 1936–37
 John Byers, Edla Muir; remodeled in 1963
 by Edla Muir
 914 Corsica Drive
The Spanish Colonial Revival made modern.

32. C. S. H. House, 1950
 Raphael S. Soriano
 1080 Ravoli Drive
Almost invisible now, this is the first of the
pure steel-frame Case Study Houses sponsored
by *Arts and Architecture* magazine. It has been
extensively remodeled.

33. Kingsley Houses, 1946
 J. R. Davidson
 1620 and 1630 Amalfi Drive
Absolutely simple builders' houses, distinguished only by the name of their architect.

34. House, circa 1925
 John Byers (with Edla Muir)
 1650 Amalfi Drive
One of the loveliest of Byers's designs. A long,
unfenestrated wall in front opens only at a gate,
which allows you to see into the central patio of
this Spanish Colonial Revival house.

35. Ehrlich House, 1988
 Steven Ehrlich Architects
 624 Kingman Avenue
From the street, the house reads as two separate
structures. The wall surface between is recessed
and dark in color. The imagery of the woven
white surfaces is Modern, via a subtle glance at
the 1930s work of R. M. Schindler. To the rear,
the dwelling opens up to a terraced hillside garden. Views of the ocean are possible from the
upper terraces of the house.

36. Gold-Friedman House, 1991
 Steven Ehrlich Architects
 728 Kingman Avenue
Bold, projecting stucco volumes break up the
front facade of the house. The walkway and
steps wind their way around a rectangular pattern of retaining walls. As with Ehrlich's own
house down the street, this building opens up to
a courtyard and terraced garden to the rear.
Skylights enhance the vertical space of the interior, making the whole light and airy.

37. Mann House, 1941
 J. R. Davidson
 1550 San Remo Drive
It is almost impossible to see this stucco and
glass two-story Modern image house which
was built for the great novelist Thomas Mann.
It is a pity, since the Manns were so deeply
involved with the planning. We list it because
of the thrill of knowing it is there.

38. Barclay House, circa 1927
 John Byers (with Edla Muir)
 1425 Monaco Drive
Monterey Revival.

36. Gold-Friedman House, 1991

39. Will Rogers Ranch, 1921–later
  14243 Sunset Boulevard
This is one of those houses that is more important in evoking the spirit of its owner than for
its architecture, though the house does succeed
very well in conveying the feeling of early
California. It was where Will could occupy
himself "messing around doing this and that
and not much of either. Get on old 'Soapsuds'
and ride off up a little canyon I got here."

When the Rogers's moved to the ranch perma-
nently in 1928, they expanded their simple
vacation cottage. Again in 1933 when his wife
and daughter were in Palestine, Will "raised the
roof" of the living room in order to make room
for him to do his rope tricks comfortably. The
house, full of curios, is open to the public
10 A.M.–5 P.M. daily. See also the barn, whose
two bays are actually the halves of an old barn
Rogers found in west Los Angeles.

SANTA MONICA, NORTH

Dubbed the "Zenith City of the Sunset Sea," Santa Monica was open ranch land until Senator John P. Jones of Nevada went into partnership with Colonel Robert S. Baker, the owner of the ranch, and laid out a town which he believed would become the port of Los Angeles, given railroad connections. A map of the town, with a characteristic grid pattern of streets, was filed with the recorder on July 10, 1875. A few days later, lots went on sale. In nine months, Santa Monica had 1,000 residents and seemed destined, with the railroad and wharf built by Senator Jones, to become one of the great ports of America. Though it gained more residents during the land boom of the late 1880s, the idea of a major metropolis was doomed when San Pedro and Wilmington became the ports of Los Angeles.

Santa Monica was, and still is to a degree, a beach city. Senator Jones and Mrs. Baker, the widow of the ranch owner, gave the land on top of the palisades to the city as a park. Palisades Park is one of the few places in California where a city has maintained the ocean view for the enjoyment of the people, and the people are there, every day of the week in the summer and on good weekends in the winter, playing cards, sunning, jogging, and chatting in a babble of tongues.

Below the Palisades cliff, between the highway and the beach, the sale of lots meant that the beach became accessible in only a few places. Since the 1940s, the state has bought back many of these properties; but a few houses remain, including several new ones. These beach-side locations for dwellings are, needless to say, in great demand.

The town on the highland developed slowly. Third Street (now Santa Monica Mall) became the main commercial street, with residential areas moving northwest, particularly in the 1920s and 1930s. Grand hotels were built. The Arcadia, long gone, was a Queen Anne pile near the pier at Colorado Street. Later, hotels took to the highlands across from Palisades Park. Now, the Miramar (some parts dating from the 1920s) is the only hotel reflecting any part of its former glory, though its gardens have been filled in with a new building. The whole frontage of Ocean Avenue has changed over the past decades, commercial buildings and high-rise apartments taking the place of the old summer homes of wealthy Angelinos. From a distance, the ocean frontage of Santa Monica is beginning to approach the wall-like look we associate with Miami Beach.

Most of Santa Monica's dwellings of the teens, 1920s, and 1930s were modest in size, but in and around San Vicente Boulevard the upper-middle-class quality of neighboring Pacific Palisades and Brentwood prevailed. Santa Monica was the home of the architect John Byers and has many houses designed by him, often in association with Edla Muir. Though Byers was self-trained as an architect, he early developed an interest and sensitivity to the Hispanic architecture tradition. His adobe, Spanish, English, French Norman, and American Colonial designs set an example which others followed to good effect, making northern Santa Monica an architectural monument of traditional images of the twenties and thirties.

Within the past decade, Santa Monica has been transformed bit by bit. The modest single-family houses are being replaced by large houses, or more often by condominium units. The newest of these condominiums spans a wide range of images, from High Tech to Spanish Colonial Revival and Tudor. And in the downtown areas, high-rise office buildings

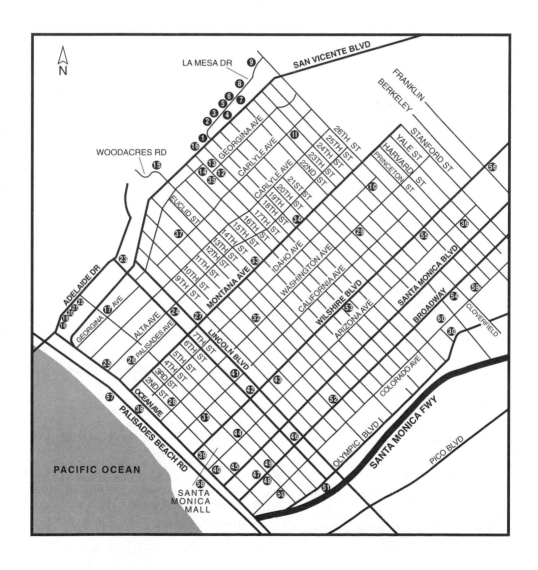

N

LA MESA DR

SAN VICENTE BLVD

FRANKLIN

BERKELEY

WOODACRES RD

PACIFIC OCEAN

SANTA MONICA MALL

SANTA MONICA FWY

PALISADES BEACH RD

OCEAN AVE

ADELAIDE DR

GEORGINA AVE

ALTA AVE

PALISADES AVE

MONTANA AVE

LINCOLN BLVD

EUCLID ST

GEORGINA AVE

CARLYLE AVE

CARLYLE AVE

9TH ST

10TH ST

11TH ST

12TH ST

13TH ST

14TH ST

15TH ST

16TH ST

17TH ST

18TH ST

19TH ST

20TH ST

21ST ST

22ND ST

23RD ST

24TH ST

25TH ST

26TH ST

2ND ST

3RD ST

4TH ST

5TH ST

6TH ST

7TH ST

IDAHO AVE

WASHINGTON AVE

CALIFORNIA AVE

WILSHIRE BLVD

ARIZONA AVE

COLORADO AVE

OLYMPIC BLVD

PICO BLVD

SANTA MONICA BLVD

BROADWAY

PRINCETON ST

HARVARD ST

YALE ST

STANFORD ST

CLOVERFIELD

are beginning to line Wilshire Boulevard and other major streets.

Santa Monica went through the usual affair of finding its downtown retail district deteriorating after World War II. The solution, of course, was to close several blocks of Third Street and create a pedestrian mall. Like almost all other malls of this type, it was economically and aesthetically a failure. From 1988–89, the mall was redesigned with a partial drive-through section and renamed the "Promenade." This seems to be working, due in part to the creation of Santa Monica Place, the introduction of 4,900 movie picture seats, and the construction of adjoining parking structures. As a design, the Promenade is adequate but not earthshaking, and as often occurs in contemporary urban design, hardscape dominates the scene.

1. La Mesa Drive
    Enter opposite 19th Street off San Vicente
    Boulevard
No other street in Los Angeles County (not even Prospect Boulevard in Pasadena) is so beautifully landscaped. In this case, Moreton Bay figs, seemingly planted by the pioneers, line the parkways on both sides of the street. The architecture is worthy of the trees. You will have your own favorites, but we begin with:

2. Crenshaw House, 1925–26
    Gable and Wyant
    1923 Mesa Drive, Santa Monica
The romantic ideal of the Spanish house.

3. Thompson House, 1924–25
    John Byers
    2021 La Mesa Drive
A blend of Spanish, Mexican, and California details.

4. Byers House, 1924
    John Byers
    2034 La Mesa Drive
The architect chose the balconied Monterey style for his second home in Santa Monica. It was within walking distance of his office.

5. Zimmer House, 1924
    John Byers
    2101 La Mesa Drive
A single-floor adobe with a high central portal enclosed by end walls. Uncluttered stucco walls and the low-pitched tile roofs are the dominant theme.

6. Bundy House, 1925
    John Byers
    2153 La Mesa Drive
A good example of Byers's personal version of the Hispanic tradition.

7. Tinglof House, 1925–26
    John Byers
    2210 La Mesa Drive
Hispanic.

8. Nables House, 1949
    Lloyd Wright
    2323 La Mesa Drive
A low-lying yellow brick house, almost impossible to see.

9. Stothart-Phillips House, 1937–38
    J. R. Davidson
    2501 La Mesa Drive
You can catch only a glimpse of this elegant 1930s International Style Modern house. The principal front of this house, with extensive glass doors and windows, overlooks the terrace and has a view to the west. The house has regrettably been changed and remodeled.

10. Koning-Eizenberg House, 1988–89
    Koning/Eizenberg Architecture
    909 25th Street
With the growth of trees, all you can see from the street is the second-floor glass pavilion, which looks very woodsy. The base of the glass box exhibits a diamond pattern in its stucco surface, and the corner is cut out to accommodate a small deck off the living room. The major section of the house extends as a two-story hooped roof rectangle to the rear of the lot.

11. Hromadka House, 1937
    2320 Carlyle Avenue
Southern California's version of what the eighteenth-century Colonial house should have looked like.

12. Fuller House, 1920–22
John Byers
304 18th Street at Georgina Avenue
A typical early Byers design, with living and
sleeping quarters separated by a pergolated
patio. Certainly this is one of his best designs,
only slightly less interesting than his similar
house on Amalfi Drive in Pacific Palisades.

13. Laidlow House, 1924
John Byers
217 17th Street
Byers as a medievalist—in this case French
Norman.

14. Carrillo House, 1925
John Byers
1602 Georgina Avenue at 16th Street
A monumental California adobe. The house
next door at 1638 Georgina Avenue was
designed by G. C. McAlister in 1937.

15. Ullman House, 1955
Thornton M. Abell
800 Woodacres Road (in Pacific Palisades;
extension of 14th Street, Santa Monica)
This concrete block and vertical wood batten
house in a rationalist version of the post-World
War II International Style Modern is just
visible through a magnificent grove of trees.

16. Armstrong-Cobb House, 1926
John Byers
1717 San Vicente Boulevard
A large-scale version of a Spanish farmhouse
(*cortijo*). Especially successful is the varied
layering of the tile roofs, which conveys a
sense that the dwelling has been added to over
the years.

17. MacBennel House, 1921–22
John Byers
404 Georgina Avenue at 4th Street
One of Byers's first real adobes. At this stage in
his career, he was a manufacturer of adobe
bricks, a builder, and an architectural designer.

18. Jones House, 1907
130 Adelaide Drive
A big, wholesome example of the turn-of-the-
century Colonial Revival.

19. Weaver House, 1910–11
Milwaukee Building Company (later Meyer
and Holler)
142 Adelaide Drive
A gorgeous example of Craftsman orientalism,
worthy of Charles and Henry Greene.

20. Milbank House, 1910–11
236 Adelaide Drive
A two-story Craftsman masterpiece, with a
strong surge of oriental details, romantically
situated in a lovely garden.

21. Gorham-Holliday House, 1923–24
John Byers
326 Adelaide Drive
Certainly one of Byers's most impressive
Andalusian houses. A patio occupies the center
of the U, and a projecting Monterey balcony
overlooks the patio and garden.

22. Gorham House, 1910
Robert Farquhar
Southwest corner of Adelaide Drive and 4th
Street
A low stucco house, reminiscent of the
Pasadena Culbertson House by the Greenes.
The entrance, otherwise classical, is capped by
an oriental porch roof.
Across 4th Street (southeast corner) is the
Gillis House (1906), a large T-shaped structure
set out around a patio. It was designed by
Myron Hunt and Elmer Grey during their
woodsy, Arts and Crafts period.

23. Worrel House, 1926
Robert B. Stacy-Judd
710 Adelaide Drive
A Pueblo Revival/Maya fantasy, more fantastic
the longer you look at it. The architect wrote of
this house, "I was at a loss to designate the type
of architecture, but it has come to be known as
the 'Zuni' type." The plan of the house is
highly rational, but needless to say the interior
and exterior imagery is not. This house was
designed shortly after the architect's famous
Aztec Hotel in Monrovia.

24. Byers House, 1917
John Byers
547 7th Street near Alta Avenue

29. Gehry House, 1978

Board and batten and stucco walls hint more at the hills of Berkeley than the highlands of Santa Monica. This was the first house Byers designed for himself. The Craftsman bungalow (**Jones House,** circa 1913) at the northeast corner of Alta Avenue and 7th Street is well worth a look, as is the 1925 **Boswell House** (John Byers) at 624 Alta Avenue.

25. Shorecliff Tower Apartments, 1963
Jones and Emmons
535 Ocean Avenue at Alta Avenue
A quiet, elegant version of the late International Style Modern of the early 1960s.

26. Witbeck House, 1917
Charles and Henry Greene
226 Palisades Avenue
A two-story, faintly Tudor dwelling, sheathed in shingles.

27. Roosevelt School, 1935
Marsh, Smith, and Powell
801 Montana Avenue and Lincoln Boulevard

The PWA Streamline Moderne, leaning towards the International style. Do note the wonderful lettering over the major entrance.

28. Sovereign Hotel and Apartments, 1928–29
Meyer Radon
205 Washington Avenue
There was no reticence here on the part of the architect in showing how many Spanish Colonial Revival forms and details could be used.

29. Gehry House, 1978
Frank O. Gehry and Associates
Southeast corner of Washington Avenue and 22nd Street
A helpless Dutch Colonial has been maneuvered into one of Gehry's perplexing compositions. A new wall separates the house from the street to the north, and to the rear a courtyard has been created. Fragments of the two-by-four-inch studs of the original house have been revealed, new windows have been added here and there, and of course there is the usual swatch of chain-link fence. Inside, not withstanding the asphalt-driveway floor of the kitchen, the atmosphere is Craftsman. Recent additions (1992) of concrete retaining walls, gates, planting (by Nancy Powers), a fountain, and even a lap pool dramatically reduce the sharpness of the original design, making the whole more mellow and suburban in nature.

30. The Peter Boxenbaum Arts Education Center/Crossroads School, 1984–89
Moore, Ruble, Yudell
1714 21st Street
A former concrete warehouse was remodeled to house the school. The principal street facade is horizontally banded, interrupted by a high, deep-set entrance—all beautifully proportioned. Facing the alley/plaza are classrooms, an art gallery, and a grand stairway.

34. Villa de Malaga Townhouse, 1982–83

31. Claremont Apartments, 1929–30
  Max Meltzmann
  330 California Avenue
Spanish Colonial Revival of the late 1920s with
a splash of colored tile in the forecourt.

32. Voss Apartments, 1937–47
  953 11th Street, near Washington Avenue
Exuberant Streamline Moderne. There was a
surge of multiple housing units built in Santa
Monica at the end of the 1930s. The two
favored images were the Streamline Moderne
and the classical-flavored Hollywood Regency.

33. Montana Collection, 1992
  Kanner Architects
  Northwest corner Montana Avenue and
  14th Street
A characteristic approach of the late 1980s and
early 1990s—to divide a project into a series of
separate parts. This design approach has been
very well carried out in this project. There are
three independent units: a tall white volume with
a slanted parapet (which is a stair tower), a
corner pavilion with a round vaulted roof, and
then a long and low white stucco pavilion held
up by tall piers. Parking is on the roof.

34. Villa de Malaga Townhouse, 1982–83
Miguel Angelo Flores and Associates
926–930 20th Street, near Montana Avenue
Two-story townhouses in the Andalusian mood,
organized around a central courtyard. In this
instance, the Hispanic of the early 1980s has
been carried out with both knowledge and reticence. The long central court of the complex
successfully conveys the feeling of a Spanish
village street.

35. Bernini House, 1991
Michael McDonough
242 17th Street
The building's thin slab roof, corner metal windows, and smooth stucco surface suggest that
this might be a modern design of the 1930s. But
a closer look at the stepped curves of the
entrance wall and other details reveal its 1990
origins. Inside, the angled hood of the double-
sided fireplace and the Mayan-like doorways
draw one to the Art Deco and the Mayan
Revival of Robert B. Stacy-Judd.

36. Condominiums, 1980
Urban Forms (Steve Andre and Alan
Tossman)
1319 Harvard Street
Contemporary High Art surface pattern,
accompanied by a sense of mechanical
technology to suggest that it is all rational.

37. Jacobs Studio, 1984
John Chase and Claudia Carol
303 12th Street
An addition to L.A.'s recent spate of small, two-
story, rear-lot studios. This one delightfully suggests a Craftsman image which seems to live a
strange life of its own, separate from the building.

38. Gates to Palisades Park, circa 1912
Sylvanus Marston
Across from entrance to Idaho Avenue
Craftsman orientalized gates with tile by Ernest
Batchelder of Pasadena.

39. Lawrence Welk Plaza, 1973; **General
Telephone Building; Wilshire West
Apartments**
Daniel, Mann, Johnson, and Mendenhall
(Cesar Pelli; P. J. Jacobson, and Dwight
Williams)

Wilshire Professional Building, 1979–80
Gensler and Associates
100 Wilshire Boulevard at Ocean Avenue
Ocean Avenue facing on to Palisades Park is
still a fascinating blend of new, middle-aged,
and old architecture, though the old and
middle-aged buildings of modest size are
continually being replaced by modest high-rise
buildings. The **Lawrence Welk Plaza** should
have been a major focal point not only for
Santa Monica but also for L.A., for here
Wilshire Boulevard reaches its western terminus with only the Pacific beyond. The DMJM
buildings are at best dull; the newer eleven-
story **Wilshire Professional Building,** with its
stepped-back floors and angle to the street, is a
better building; but while it is more satisfactory
as a design, it still does not really establish the
importance of this intersection.

40. Shangri-la Apartments, 1939–40
William E. Foster
Southeast corner of Ocean and Arizona
avenues
An eight-story Streamline Moderne block, with
a suggestion of a curved tower dominating the
street corner of the building. Next door (at least
at the moment) is a charming Eastlake-Queen
Anne dwelling (1890).

41. St. Monica's Roman Catholic Church,
1925
Albert C. Martin
Northwest corner of California Avenue and
7th Street
A stone-sheathed Romanesque church with an
impressive barrel-vaulted interior. The exterior
sculpture is by Joseph Conradi. As intended,
the building presents the case for traditional
imagery realized through the modern technology of reinforced concrete.

**42. Miles Memorial
Playhouse,** 1929
John Byers
In Lincoln Park on Lincoln Boulevard
between Wilshire Boulevard and California
Avenue
A public auditorium theater in the guise of an
Andalusian building.

43. Drive-in Market, 1928
  Paul R. Williams
  Northeast corner of
  Wilshire Boulevard and
  9th Street
Drive-in retail markets
became a popular form in
Southern California in the
late 1920s. By the mid-
1930s, they were replaced
by the larger-scale super-
markets with their accom-
panying parking lots. In this
complex, Paul Williams utilized the Spanish Colonial
Revival image.

**44. Santa Monica Post
Office,** 1937
  Neal A. Melick and
  Robert A. Murray
  1248 5th Street, at
  Arizona Avenue
A single-story PWA
Moderne building with
excellent ornament. The
offset of the interior
horizontal planking evokes
the pioneering nineteenth
century of the West. The Art
Deco (Zigzag) Moderne
decoration, especially that of
the interior chandeliers, hints
more at the Native American art of the
Southwest than of Paris.

48. Ken Edwards Center for Community Services, 1986–89

**45. Bay City Guaranty Building and Loan
  Association Building** (now **Crocker
  Bank**), 1929–30
  Walker and Eisen
  1225 Santa Monica Mall
For a number of decades, this was Santa
Monica's only tall office building. The ground
floor has been altered and signage has hidden
the corner clock tower, but you can still make
out the Art Deco (Zigzag) Moderne ornament.

46. Central Tower Building, 1929
  Eugene Durfee
  1424 7th Street
An eight-story classical Art Deco Moderne

building that seems to have had problems
getting off of the ground.

47. Keller Block, circa 1890
  Northwest corner of Broadway and 3rd
  Street
A rare pre-1900 building which still retains its
cast-iron street front.

**48. Ken Edwards Center for Community
  Services,** 1986–89
  Koning/Eizenberg Architecture
  1527 4th Street
The structure is designed as a broken composition of four structures on the street and a fifth to
the rear. Roof forms vary from flat and hipped to
a hooped-roof building to the right. Though
there is a wide glass entrance, the real way of

getting into the building appears to be the wide driveway situated under the hooped-roof element. On top of the central building is a horizontal louvered screen, which seems reminiscent of the low tower on the nearby City Hall.

49. Santa Monica Place, 1979–81
  Frank O. Gehry and Associates
  315 Broadway
The downtown enclosed shopping mall has enjoyed popularity throughout America since the late 1970s. Though the multi-story mall space is tight, Gehry's design conveys a sense of being rational and delightful. Gehry's chain-link fencing of the exterior surface of the parking garage creates a strange visual illusion, especially with its signage and palm trees on the south and west facades. Within the mall, Frank O. Gehry and Associates (1981) have designed the interior of **Bubar's Jewelers.**

50. Store and Office Building, 1927
  Eugene Durfee
  1501–1515 4th Street
Los Angeles's own improved version of Spanish and Mexican Churrigueresque.

51. Santa Monica Bus (Transportation) Center, 1982–84
  Kappe, Lotery, and Boccato
  Between Olympic Boulevard, 5th and 7th streets, just north of the Santa Monica Freeway
The imagery of the futuristic machine a la Buck Rogers brought up-to-date via science fiction films of the early 1980s.

52. Van Tilburg Office Building, 1979
  Johannes van Tilburg and Partners
  1101 Broadway
A formal composition of a white stucco box, with cut-in patterns accompanied by projecting volumes.

53. Packard Show Rooms, 1928
  Edward James Baume
  Southwest corner of Wilshire Boulevard and 17th Street
Spanish Colonial Revival with wrought-iron grillwork reminiscent of old Spanish choir screens. Since the last edition of this book, this building has been badly damaged in a fire. The rebuilding involved some simplification of detail, but it is well done.

54. Frank O. Gehry Offices, 1988
  Frank O. Gehry Associates
  1520-B Cloverfield Boulevard
On the building's southeast (alley) side, Gehry has provided a new entrance to his own offices and has also created, by steel members, a thick-lined linear composition along the entire back of the building.

55. Home Savings and Loan Association Building, 1969
  Millard Sheets
  Southeast corner of Wilshire Boulevard and 26th Street
Another of Home Savings's attacks on the coldness and dullness of post-World War II Modern. The exterior mosaics are by Nancy Colbath, the stained-glass window by Susan Hertel.

56. The Wave, 1989
  Tony DeLapp
  Wilshire Boulevard, just northeast of Franklin Street
The artist has created a ceremonial arch as the gateway into Santa Monica. The curved form of this metal arch suggests a wave that one might encounter at the Santa Monica beach. The artist is quoted as saying, "I thought it would be nice to do something that integrated with the automobile."

57. Flint Houses, 1928
  John Byers
  701 and 703 Palisades Beach Road
  (Highway 1)
Here Byers utilized the form of a Barcelona urban house, oriented around a high-spaced interior court. There are a few other houses still standing on this strand of Pacific Beach Road. Among them is John Byers's **Netcher House** (1926) at 1020 Pacific Beach Road and Richard J. Neutra's **Lewin House** (1938) at 512 Ocean Front.

58. Israel House,
1990

58. Israel House, 1990
  Steven Ehrlich Architects
  1273 Palisades Beach Road (Highway 1)
A narrow and tall beach house poses as a small
gable-roofed cottage placed on a high base. The
walls of the lower podium read as masonry, the
upper cottage as a stuccoed box.

59. Colorado Place, 1981–84
  Welton Becket Associates
  North side of Colorado Avenue between
  Cloverdale Boulevard and 26th Street.
A mixed-use development consisting of offices,
shops, and eventually a 392-room hotel. The
first phase consisted of low-rise exposed concrete volumes that are insistently Modern in
their horizontal striping of dark window bands
and light-colored spandrels. A small public

60. Sony Music Campus, 1992

park is tucked into one corner, but at this moment the most noticeable elements are the parking garages with their important auto entrances.

60 Sony Music Campus, 1992
 Steven Ehrlich Architects
 2100 Colorado Avenue
The design themes are many and varied in this complex, ranging from the horizontal strip of band windows and pilotis, which is so closely associated with the International style, to the curved forms of the Streamline Moderne, countered by sharp angular volumes. The buildings make a nod to traditionalism in their elegant stone cladding. From the public streets, they are viewed through groves of palm trees. Entrance to the buildings is, of course, via the automobile court, which is equally well-landscaped.

SANTA MONICA, SOUTH; OCEAN PARK

The section of Santa Monica south of the Santa Monica Freeway has always been mixed in its use—small beach cottages west of Ocean Avenue, then a mixture of residential and commercial buildings reaching up and beyond Lincoln Boulevard. This area, like Venice just to the south, is currently experiencing a growth of multiple housing, ranging from high-rise towers to two- and three-story town houses. Santa Monica's wall of high-rises has continued to work its way south, overlooking the beach. Of these, the Sea Colony at 2910 Nielson Way (1980; Landau Partnership) is unquestionably the best, though it could well be argued that none of these complexes (at least in their present size) should have been built.

1a. Santa Monica Pier, 1909–21
City of Santa Monica Engineering Department
West end of Colorado Avenue
The pier was severely damaged in the heavy storms during the winter of 1982–83, but it is now rebuilt. For decades the pier has been one of the joys of Santa Monica, rain or shine. On weekends the railings are lined with people fishing or just walking and looking.

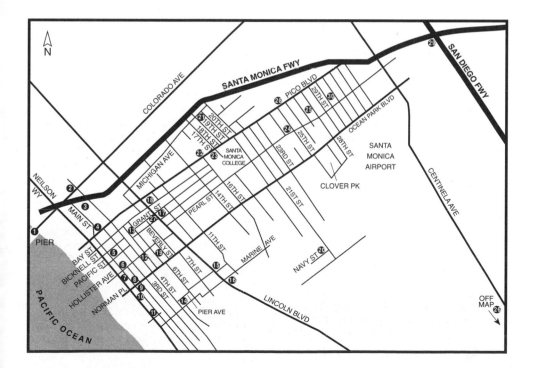

Restaurants, curio shops, and amusement palaces line the south side of the pier. But the hit architecturally (and otherwise as well) is the merry-go-round.

1b. Carousel Park, 1982–86
  Moore Ruble Yudell; Campbell and
  Campbell, landscape architect
The center of the project is an octagonal entry plaza. At the southern edge of the site is a children's park with a playful but menacing dragon which is about to devour a small Viking ship. A fanciful pair of octagonal carousel towers overlook the volleyball courts. These towers are of metal and read as two-dimensional drawings.

2. Sears, Roebuck and Company Store,
  1946–47
  Roland H. Crawford
  Colorado Avenue between 3rd and 4th
  streets
A classic example of a post-World War II Modern retail store building. The design concept is classical Beaux Arts; the fenestration and signage are modern. As with all of the Sears stores, this building was primarily arranged around its parking lot (which was accompanied by its auto service building).

3. Santa Monica City Hall, 1938–39
  Donald B. Parkinson and J. M. Estep
  1685 Main Street
This PWA Moderne building, with its beautiful tile entrance, was to have been the central focus of a formal Beaux Arts grouping of buildings which, as so often happened, never took place. Within the lobby are two Federal Art Project murals by the important West Coast artist Stanton McDonald Wright. These were painted in 1939, and the subject is Colonial Spanish Recreation.

4. Santa Monica Civic Auditorium, 1959
  Welton Becket and Associates
  North corner of Main Street and Pico
  Boulevard
As with so many buildings by this firm, this is a perfect period piece of the late 1950s. Its five 72-foot concrete masts that connect with the entrance canopy match in spirit the tail fins of

automobiles of these years. The masts play against the entire entrance facade, which is composed of a delicate cast-concrete grill.

5. Condominium Town Houses, 1981–82
  Stafford/Bender
  116 Pacific Street
The ultimate in high-tech imagery. Though not specifically derived from classical European Modern of the 1920s, the atmosphere of their constructivist design conveys that feeling. The design of the building, and especially of the facades, is that of pure architectural patterning along the lines of the machine aesthetic.

6. Horatio West Court, 1919–21
  Irving J. Gill
  140 Hollister Avenue
As Esther McCoy has pointed out, this four-unit complex is Gill's closest approximation to the later European International Style Modern of the 1920s. The arched entryways and the small patio courts indicate Gill's attachment to the early Mission Revival of California. The buildings have been restored, and though there have been some changes, they do present an excellent sense of Gill's puritanical and abstract approach to design.

7. Edgemar Development, 1984–88
  Frank O. Gehry and Associates
  2415–2437 Main Street
The name of this project comes from the old Edgemar Farms Dairy which occupied this site. (A fragment of the street wall of the dairy remains at the right side of the project.) Included in the project are commercial spaces, a museum, and a subterranean garage. In certain ways this project may be thought of as a mini-mall; in other regards it harks back to the 1920s in Los Angeles, when a number of theaters were built with forecourts containing retail shops and restaurants. Gehry leads you into the central courtyard through two passages: one defined by the curve of the west building, the other by an angled passageway. Instead of a motion picture theater, the major "theater" is the Santa Monica Museum of Art.
  Aesthetically, the structures are not buildings as we usually think of them, but enlarged

pieces of hard-edged sculpture. The enclosed volumes are clothed in sheet metal and stucco; these are countered by pieces of constructivist sculpture in metal and chain-link fence. The one disappointment is the lack of anything that could be called landscape architecture.

8. Merle Norman Building, 1935–36
George Parr
2525 Main Street
An existing brick building was remodeled and added to, transforming the whole into a Streamline Moderne ship. The south corner of the building suggests an ocean liner with a round tower over an open bridge. The north corner is also streamlined and nautical, hinting in this case at a streamlined warship of the mid-1930s.

9. First Methodist Episcopal Church, 1875–76
2621 2nd Street
As was often the case with nineteenth-century buildings, Santa Monica's first church building has been moved twice: once in 1893, then again in 1900. It is of architectural interest because it could just as well have been built in Iowa City as on the far reaches of the Pacific Coast.

10. Jones House (now Heritage Square Museum), 1894
2620 Main Street
This simply detailed Queen Anne dwelling and its neighbor, the **Trask House** (1903; Hunt and Eggers), were moved to this site in 1977. Both houses, originally from the 1000 block of Ocean Boulevard, have been restored. The Trask House is now the Chronicle Restaurant.

11. Parkhurst Building, 1927
Norman F. Marsh and Company
Northwest corner of Main Street and Pier Avenue
This Spanish Colonial Revival building with its beautiful exposed brickwork might have come out of a Hollywood film on old Seville. It has been restored to its former glory.

12. Two Bungalows, circa 1910
Southeast corner of 4th Street and Hollister Avenue
Almost identical Mission-style bungalows. They were once pink and trimmed in blue.

13. OP12 Dispersed Affordable Housing, 1986–88
Koning/Eisenberg Architecture
2207 6th Street
The three-story block facing onto 6th has the feel of 1920s housing designed by the Dutch architect Gerrit Rietveld. Six units are encompassed in these two buildings, and garden space is provided between. Another affordable Koning and Eizenberg housing project nearby is their **OP12 Dispersed Affordable Housing** at 2400 5th Street. These units, dating from 1986–88, slide over very gently from the world of nondescript builders' products to architecture as art.

Other housing by Koning and Eisenberg in this general area are **St. John's Hospital Housing**, 1314 18th Street (1986–88); **St. Mary's Housing**, 1427 Berkeley Street (1986–88); **St. John's Hospital Housing**, 2121 Arizona Avenue (1987–88), and the **Twenty-two Twenty-Six Town Houses**, 2226 Sixth Street (1990–92). All of these examples of group housing have responded in a highly rational manner to their functional requirements, usually within very modest budgets. And the architects have lifted these buildings out of the commonplace world of the L.A. stucco box to the world of art by twists here and there of form, details, and color.

14. Vawter House, 1900
504 Pier Avenue
A shingled Queen Anne dwelling which, with its extensive porches on two sides, suggests the ideal of the seaside resort that Santa Monica was seeking to create at the turn of the century.

15. Condominium Town House, 1981
Janotta-Breska Associates
1016 Pier Avenue
The high-tech image, perhaps in this instance more romantic than other modernist condominiums of the 1980s and 1990s in Santa Monica and Venice.

16. Condominium Town Houses, 1981
  Janotta-Breska Associates
  1015 Marine Street
A further continuation of the machine image expressed in the condominiums at 1016 Pier Avenue.

17. Condominium Town Houses, 1979
  A Design Group; David Cooper, Michael W. Folonis, George Blain, and Richard Clemenson
  831 Pacific Street
A not-to-be-missed high-tech image that is resplendent with arbitrary high-art forms and surfaces. It gives you the feeling that it belongs in a museum as a model rather than on a city street.

18. Condominium Town Houses, 1981
  A Design Group/Janotta-Breska Associates
  821 Bay Street
This stucco-sheathed unit is a little more believable as High Tech and as a place to live than its neighbor at number 831.

19. Beverly House, 1990
  Michael W. Folonis and Associates
  2522 Beverly Avenue
Though the present building is technically a remodel, it is in fact an entirely new structure. A fascinating play occurs in this design as a strong expression of structure (especially portions of the exposed steel frame) is countered by stucco-sheathed volumes. The architect's intent was to strongly express the layered effect of "three hierarchical forms," and he has certainly carried off this theme.

20. Chambers/Folonis House, 1988
  Michael W. Folonis and Associates
  735 Navy Street
Though this 1,500-square-foot residence occupies much of its 25-foot-wide lot, it fits in well with the older surrounding dwellings. The architect has accomplished this accommodation via the breaking up of his building into what reads as separate volumes. Below, the walls are of concrete block; above is a hooped roof volume clad in sheets of mahogany plywood. On the second floor, an exterior deck separates the parents' space from that of the children.

21. Conference Room, 1982
  Carde/Killefer
  1638 19th Street
A tiny gable-roofed building situated in a garden, it has been treated in part as an abstract exercise of exposed sticks (two-by-four-inch studs, etc.).

22. Woodlawn Cemetery Mausoleum, 1924
  and later
  Pico Boulevard between 7th and 14th streets
The 1924 section of this building (which faces towards the south) can be seen from Pico Boulevard and boasts a handsome Plateresque-inspired facade. Note as well the **BPO Elks Monument** (circa 1910) to the west. It is an open, round, classical temple surrounded by cast-iron elks.

23. Santa Monica City College: Business Education and Vocational Building, 1981
  Daniel, Mann, Johnson, and Mendenhall
  Pico Boulevard at 17th Street
A blend of post-World War II International Style Modern with a suggestion of the Streamline Moderne of the 1930s, and even a slight nod to recent High Tech. Go to the rear (south side) of the building to see this elevation with its exposed metal stairs.

24. Sun-Tech Town Houses, 1981
  Urban Forms; David Van Hoy and Steve Andre
  2433 Pearl Street
An eighteen-unit condominium, the ultimate in Post Modern High Tech imagery. Though the machine is supposedly a rational creature, High Tech imagery such as this is related to Art with a capital *A* more than with pragmatic humane planning. Still, we must admit that it is impressive from the street and from within, especially in the two-story living spaces.

25. Putnam Place Town House, 1983
  2332 28th Street
A perfect model of Post Modernism: classical columns, false walls, and other classical elements.

24. Sun-Tech Town Houses, 1981

26. Condominium Town Houses, 1980
  A Design Group; (Michael Folonis and
  David Cooper)
  Northwest and northeast corners of
  Barrington Avenue and Brookhaven
  Avenue
Yet another example of Post Modern High
Tech. The image in this case is somewhat
stronger in nostalgia for the "Heroic" period of
modern architecture of the 1920s.

27. Condominium Town Houses, 1981
  Tossman/Day
  835 Grant Avenue
A three-story stucco unit whose cut-out forms,
shed roofs, and window pattern directly carry
on Charles W. Moore's late-1970s
vocabulary.

28. Chili Bowls, 1931
  Arthur Whizin
  12244 West Pico Boulevard
By 1933 Arthur Whizen, the "Chili Bowl
King," had established eighteen of these fast-
food stands throughout the L.Λ. area. Only four
remain, in varying states of decay.

**29. Santa Monica Freeway, interchange with
  the San Diego Freeway,** 1961–66
  Lammers, Reed, and Reece; Engineers
The Santa Monica Freeway begins at its western end with a graceful swoop through a curved
tunnel, then it proceeds all the way to West
Covina to the east. The interchange with the
San Diego Freeway is certainly one of the most
spectacular interchanges in the world—Norman
Bel Geddes's *Magic Motorways* of 1940 realized in fact. At the freeway's west end are several murals on concrete retaining walls. While
these are folksy, they hardly add a positive note
to the machine image of the freeway or to its
parklike landscaping.

30. 31st Street House, 1992–93
  Koning/Eizenberg
  1527 31st Street
The projecting facade of a charming small
Spanish Colonial Revival house sits as a
Hollywood stage set in front of a modernist
building. But it should be noted that the rectangular modernist building is anything but pure,
with references to popular modernism of the
1920s and to traditionalism.

VENICE; MARINA DEL REY

In January 1906, the architect Norman F. Marsh wrote of California's new improved version of Venice: "Like the Aladdin's lamp of nursery days, wealth and labor have been the wand that has transformed an uninviting landscape in the southern part of California into scenes that delight the aesthetic." In a period of twelve months, the architectural firm of Marsh and Russell had (according to Marsh's words) designed "a magic city (built for the generations) with its stately arcades, shimmering lagoons, floating pennants, and glistening minarets."

Venice was the brainchild of Abbot Kinney, who came to California in 1880. His dream was to create an exotic city resembling the architecture and waterways of the famous northern Italian city. It would not be an ordinary beach community but one devoted to high culture and equipped with a 3,600 seat auditorium and even a "great university or institute." In 1904 Kinney had engaged Norman F. Marsh and his associates to lay out the site plan and to design the

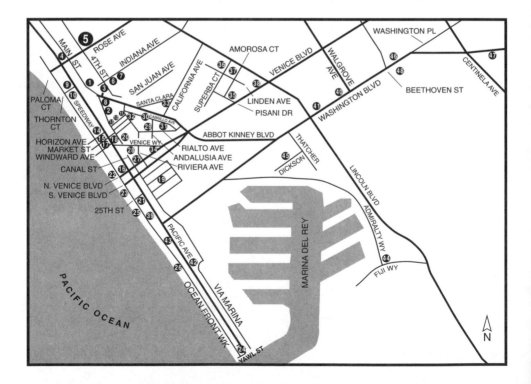

first of the community's buildings. The Italian-born sculptor Luigi Peano was engaged to do the sculpture for the bridges and for a number of the original buildings.

The new city was officially opened by Kinney himself on June 30, 1905. But within a few years, it was evident that the city would only succeed if it oriented itself to amusements and to the beach. In 1907 a casino was constructed, and other entertainment buildings followed, reaching a high point in the 1912 "Race through the Clouds" roller coaster (designed by A. F. Rosenheim).

Nevertheless, while tourists came and went, few palaces were built along Venice's canals. A fair number of dwellings were built, but they were modest in scale and their image was in the lake or seaside manner of the Craftsman mode. Kinney himself died in 1920, and within a few years any thought of Venice as a cultural center was thrown to the winds. The canals began to be filled with silt and junk; many of them were filled in 1930, and the gondoliers went home. Oil wells sprouted along a few of the canals, and the center of Venice in and around Windward and Pacific avenues became increasingly shabby and run down. The final blow came in 1925, when Venice lost its independence and became a part of Los Angeles.

In the 1960s and early 1970s changes began to occur. To the south, Victor Gruen Associates laid out Marina Del Rey (1966–74), a new boat-oriented community checkered by low- and high-rise housing units (located southwest of Lincoln and Washington boulevards). Marina City (Daniel, Mann, Johnson, Mendenhall; Anthony Lumsden, and Richard L. Tipping) was built in 1971 and other additions followed, including Mariner's Village Apartments (1980; Kamnitzer and Marks). In the end, neither the planning nor the buildings in Marina Del Rey are really worth any extended visit, unless you want a lesson on what should not be done.

Over a period of some four and a half years, a proposal has been pursued to develop the former Hughes land, which lies just south of Marina Del Rey. This project, named Playa Vista, was given final approval (for its first phase) in September of 1993. This mixed-use project for the 1,098 acres has preserved appreciable sections of the Balona Wetlands, and it will also include a marina north of Culver Boulevard. Some construction, it is said, will start in 1994. The developers, Maguire Thomas Partners, have indicated that they will be engaging some well-known "name-brand" architects to design this project. We will wait and see what the results will be. We hope that it turns out better than Bunker Hill.

It was in the 1960s and early 1970s that Venice became a Bohemian quarter and began to boast not only artists and their garrets, but also a wide array of public murals. From the late 1970s on, Venice and the southern section of adjoining Santa Monica have emerged as the center for self-conscious, avant-garde, High Art Modern architecture—usually in the form of housing and artists' studios. In Venice itself, and to the north in parts of Santa Monica, one will discover a wide array of multiple- and single-family dwellings as well as smaller commercial projects designed by some of L.A.'s most talented architects of the moment. These include not only such well-published figures as Frank O. Gehry, Eric Owen Moss, Steven Ehrlich and others, but other gifted designers: William Adams, David L. Gray, Tony Greenberg, Miriam Mulder and Richard Katkov, Blake + Au (Perry Austin Blake and Alan Kong Au), David Kellen, and Ron McCoy. A walk and drive through Venice today evoke the feeling of a visit to a stimulating outdoor art gallery of sorts, with many of the new avant-garde buildings posed as enlarged pieces of sculpture. As an appropriate backdrop, the remaining canals and their bridges are being refurbished.

1. Commercial Building, 1987
Sam Davis
916 Main Street
The architect has remodeled an existing building, transforming it into a strong but low-keyed composition. A dark band works itself around the base of the building, and the entrance is marked by a small towerlike form.

2. Chiat/Day/Mojo Advertising Agency Building, 1985–91
Frank O. Gehry Associates; Claes Oldenburg and Coosje van Bruggen
Northeast side of Main Street, between Brooks Avenue and Clubhouse Avenue

To the northwest, the building starts out as an International Style Modern Streamline ocean liner. The liner collides with Claes Oldenburg and Coosje van Bruggen's three-story binoculars, and then to the left, all that remains is a third section of the building, which poses as a rusting steel ruin. In a sense, this adds up to a programmatic building, but as always, Gehry provides us with an impressive art object, plus a gentle but persistent comment on buildings and society.

3. Bright and Associates Building, 1990
Franklin D. Israel Design Associates
901 Abbot Kinney Boulevard (north corner of Abbot Kinney Boulevard and Hampton Drive)

This everyday complex of commercial vernacular buildings had been internally converted in the 1950s, in a very minimal way, into the working studio of Charles and Ray Eames. (They first occupied the building in 1948.) In this, the most recent remodeling of these buildings, Israel has also done very little with their exteriors. The corner gable-roofed building has acquired a metal-sheathed, curved vent above the entrance. The parking lot entrance now is covered by a triangular canopy and an entrance with a panel of glass brick. The real transformation, as one always expects of this architect, are the interiors. The sequence of mysterious space is in part produced via the way that light is introduced and, above all, by color. The varied experiences along the interior "streets" and in the glass-roofed atrium suggest once again (in Israel's designs) an updated and forceful abstraction of the worried Surrealism of the 1920s. In this case, the reference seems to be to the wondrous and weird stage sets by Robert Wiene for the 1919 film *The Cabinet of Dr. Caligari.*

4. Renaissance Building, 1989
Johannes Van Tilburg and Partners
Northwest corner of Main Street and Rose Avenue

4. Renaissance Building, 1989

The inspirations for this three-story, block-long complex were the original Venetian buildings laid out in 1904–6 in central Venice (California, of course). A loggia with elaborate Corinthian columns occurs at the street level. Behind this are retail stores; above the stores are two floors of living units. At the corner of Rose Avenue and Main Street is a giant clown designed by the artist Jonathan Borofsky.

5. Store Building, circa 1937
Mid-block on the north side of Rose Avenue between 4th and 5th streets

A tiny building with an oversized oval window in the Streamline Moderne idiom.

6. Arnoldi Triplex, 1981
Frank O. Gehry and Associates
322 Indiana Avenue

Everything looks ordinary until you consider the boxlike volume at the corner which seems

6. Arnoldi Triplex, 1981

to have been tipped on end. From the side the building gives the appearance of being three separate dwellings.

7. Hopper House, 1989
   Brian Murphy
   326 Indiana Avenue
A Gehry-like design in corrugated metal. It is connected near the rear to the adjoining Gehry Triplex.

8. Duplex, 1978–81
   Frederick Meyer (George Mayers, developer and builder)
   921–923 Abbot Kinney Boulevard
A late 1970s Victorian Revival via details derived, at least in spirit, from an Eastlake pattern book.

9. House, 1986
   Arata Isosaki
   16 Paloma Court
A simple, elongated stucco box is enriched by fasciated corners of glass and metal roofs.

10. Michich-Small House, 1981
   Milica Dedijer-Michich
   120 Thornton Court
Viewed from the walkway, its stuccoed angles and curved columns and balconies come from the Modern of the 1920s and 1930s. On the alley side, an angled greenhouse is almost a rationalist image via James Stirling.

11. Apartment Building, circa 1905
   Attributed to Marsh and Russell
   235 San Juan Avenue

This is one of several of the early designs of Marsh and Russell which reflect the influence of the Midwest work of Louis H. Sullivan and of Frank Lloyd Wright.

12. Caplin House, 1979
   Frederick Fisher and Thane Roberts
   229 San Juan Avenue
A white stucco box with a partial barrel roof, *a la* Adolf Loos and Vienna in the early years of the century. The facades, on the other hand, are self-consciously composed of a pattern of rectangular openings and seem to have more to do with art than architecture.

13. Store Building, circa 1937
   1332–1380 Main Street between San Juan and Horizon avenues
A two-story complex of shops and offices, clothed in the popular Streamline Moderne.

14. Spiller House, 1980
   Frank O. Gehry and Associates
   39 Horizon Avenue
A three-level town house with roof deck. Most of the building is clad in galvanized corrugated metal, while sticks (two-by-fours) and plywood occur in part of the inner court of the living room. Within, the sticklike quality of some exposed posts of the building creates a woodsy Craftsman atmosphere.

15. Gagosian Art Gallery and Apartments,
   1980–81
   Studio Works; Hodgetts and Mangurian;
   with Frank Lupe and Audrey Mitlock
   51 Market Street
The gray stucco street elevation with its upper curved studio facade with glass brick suggests the Streamline Moderne of the 1930s. Inside, a circular court interrupts the basic volume of the buildings.

16. Rebecca's Restaurant, 1982–85
   Frank O. Gehry and Associates
   2025 Pacific Avenue (main entrance on North Venice Boulevard)
Tree trunks help to support the ceiling, and two of Frank Gehry's 18-foot-long crocodiles float from the ceiling and are joined by one of his octopus chandeliers. The tin-collage entrance

doors are by Tony Berlant, the window murals are by Ed Moses, and a painting on black velvet is by Peter Alexander.

17. Venice Center, 1904–5
   Windward Avenue between Pacific Avenue and Speedway
The best remaining group of the original buildings are those on the north side of Windward Avenue. At the northeast corner of Windward and Pacific avenues is the arcaded three-story **Hotel Saint Mark** (Marsh and Graham).

18. Speedway Cafe, 1991
   Franklin D. Israel Design Associates
   Corner of 17th Street and Pacific Avenue
The stuccoed exterior of the cafe plays between plain and ordinary commercial vernacular and sophisticated European. Inside, sheets of plywood, layered on sections of the walls and ceiling, suggest that we have returned to the Surrealist/Constructivist world of Kurt Schwitters in the 1920s.

19. Venice Canals, 1904–5
   Southeast of Pacific Avenue and Venice Boulevard in the Strong and Dickerson Canal Subdivision
Venice's major system of canals and the Venice Lagoon have long since been filled in. To the north, Venice Canal is now San Juan Avenue, and to the south, the Grand Canal is now Grand Boulevard. A few of the canals still exist south of Venice Boulevard, and four of the Venetian bridges still stand. Several of the later canals have been rebuilt, and the ducks and geese that had, over the years, proliferated have been removed. Venice, once the center of the Hippie movement (Alan Ginsberg and all that), has rapidly become arty and yuppie.

20. Windward Circle
   Steven Ehrlich and Associates
   Ace Market (1989), 185 Windward Avenue
   Windward Circle Art Building (1988), 211 Windward Avenue
   Race Through the Clouds (1987), 1600 Main Street
The architect was presented with the unique opportunity of designing three of the buildings

which define the center of Venice. The first of these buildings, Race Through the Clouds (named after the original roller coaster which was located on the site), captures the spirit of the roller coaster via a neon-edged, galvanized metal track which goes in and out around the building. The Windward Circle Art Building abstracts the traditional architecture of Venice through a recessed ground-level loggia, accompanied by the suggestion of three towers. The three-story Ace Market displays vertical projecting arms meant to suggest the steam shovels used to dredge the Venice canals.

21. Norton House, 1982–84
   Frank O. Gehry and Associates
   2509 Ocean Front at the end of 25th Street
This project is supposedly a remodel, but it is really a new house. Steps lead up from the beach in a grand fashion, seemingly all the way to the top of the building. Hovering over the single front section of the house is a viewing study, set as a box on a pole. As with so much of Gehry's work, what appears to be arbitrary and capricious turns out, in plan, to be highly rational.

22. Snipper House, "La Rotonda," 1988
   Miguel Angelo Flores and Associates
   2511 Ocean Front Walk
A modular framed box (on a lavender-colored podium) is placed within a light steel box. To the side one can see portions of the stucco and glass-brick cylinder which forms the core of the house. Contrast it with the Gehry house next door to sense two very different modernist approaches to design and to a beach house with much public exposure.

23. House, 1990
   Steven Ehrlich
   2311 Ocean Front Walk
A raised two-story stucco sheathed volume exhibits a frontispiece of banded concrete block. A high loggia occurs at the first floor; above the center of the upper porch is a glass bay. The architect has designed several other residences in Venice that should be mentioned. These include the **Ed Moses Studio** (1987) at 1233 Palais Boulevard, the **Okulick Studio**

20c. Race Through the Clouds (1987)

(1989) at 604 South Hampton Drive, the **Ripple House** (1989) at 1338 Preston Way, and the **Douroux Canal House** (1991) at 2570 Grand Canal.

24. Doumani House, 1982
Robert Graham
Southwest corner of Ocean Front Walk and Yawl Court

The sculptor as architect. A white stucco U-shaped volume. Its step-pattern windows and the sculptured open-metal grillwork at ground level tilt the design toward the Art Deco Moderne of the 1920s.

25. Douroux House, 1989–90
Antoine Predock
Ocean Front Walk

Facing the ocean and the public walkway is a cast-in-place rectangular armature, open at the top, filled in with glass below. The most eye-catching feature of this facade is the large, overscaled, flipped window. The house extends in a narrow fashion along the public passage-way. The interior ends up being quite open to view from those on the beachside walkway.

26. Stone Condominium, 1973
Kahn, Kappe, and Lotery
3815 Ocean Front Walk

Stucco volumes and walls serve as a foil for the west-facing glass and wood sections of the building. The placement of the wood members separating the glass areas creates a strong but somewhat unusual horizontal scale.

27. Apartment Building, circa 1910
Northeast corner of Venice Boulevard and Canal Street

A three-story delight, designed in a kind of parody of Oriental Craftsman architecture.

28. Ming-Li Lowe Office Building, 1981
David Ming-Li Lowe
308 Venice Way, near Riviera Way

High Art architecture realized by the common-place (materials, structure, methods of assembly, all of steel). You could easily drive by and not notice the building, but once your attention is fixed, the art of design is apparent. There are really two mirrored buildings in this project; a court occurs between these two units.

29. House, circa 1907
   Northwest corner of Andalusia and Rialto
   avenues
Although altered in recent years, this dwelling
still evidences the exotic, faraway qualities of
Islamic India and the Near East.

30. House, circa 1907
   Cabrillo Avenue and Market Street
An arcaded two-story porch with dome sug-
gests Islamic North Africa or perhaps Moorish
Spain.

31. Multi-Family Residence, 1989
   Ted Tokio Tanaka
   1415–1421 Cabrillo Avenue
Behind this dramatic facade of geometric cut-
outs of squares, triangles, and half circles, four
living units are situated. The interior space is
divided into six levels, including the sunken
parking. The assertiveness of this white stucco
building seems to draw more from the traditional architecture of North Africa than from
the usual Southern California Mediterranean
borrowings.

32. University of Arts, 1904–5
   Marsh and Russell
   1304 Riviera Avenue
One of Abbot Kinney's original buildings, this
one intended as part of his cultural institute.
The design, like others at Venice, is both
Sullivanesque and Wrightian.

33. Venice (Electric) Art Block, 1989–91
   Koning/Eisenberg Architecture; Glenn
   Robert Erickson
   499 Santa Clara Avenue
This 360-foot-long block of twenty artists' lofts
is situated on an abandoned electric streetcar
right-of-way. Though connected, the two-story
buildings read as separate structures. The two
corner buildings, facing the streets, pose as
modernist false fronts. The interior buildings
are sheathed in white stucco, while the end
buildings exhibit a thin galvanized sheet metal
(left as is).

34. 411 Venice House, 1991
   Michael W. Folonis and Associates
   411 Venice Boulevard
Several modernist themes occur in this three-
story dwelling. These range from close looks at
early Modern of the 1930s plus a sense of what
R. M. Schindler and other California modernists were about in the years before 1945. A
barrel roof covers part of the house; the walls
are sheathed in smooth plaster and in copper.
Internally, the space is organized around a
three-story atrium. An upper-level bridge
occurs over sections of the atrium.

35. Police and Fire Station of Venice, circa
   1930
   Northeast corner of Venice Boulevard and
   Pisani Drive
A two-story PWA Moderne building in
exposed concrete, with relief sculptures over
the entrance. Next door, to the west, is the former **Venice City Hall,** a slightly garbled version of the Mission Revival.

36. Sedlak House, 1980
   Morphosis (Thom Mayne and Michael
   Rotundi)
   North side of Superba Court, between
   Linden Avenue and Lincoln Boulevard
One of an increasing number of two-story alley
units built as a second dwelling on a city lot.
This gable-roofed unit plays all sorts of aes-
thetic games with common materials and struc-
tures; but all of this formal inventiveness is
used with delight rather than high seriousness.

37. 2-4-6-8 House, 1979
   Morphosis (Thom Mayne and Michael
   Rotundi)
   North side of Amorosa Court, between
   Linden Avenue and Lincoln Boulevard
A four-part window as a playful theme, set in
front of the pieces of asphalt-shingle siding.
Bright colors enhance the dollhouse quality of
the design.
   Another example of the work of Morphosis
is the **House** at 634½ Sixth Street, which dates
from 1986–87.

38. Brenta Apartments, 1990
Rebecca L. Bender
2207 Brenta Place
The form of the building is essential, a single stucco box which has been articulated by slight projections and recessions to read as a random series of volumes. Another unit nearby by Rebecca L. Bender is the **South Venice Apartments** (1991) at 438 South Venice Boulevard.

39. Gardner House, 1992
Rebecca L. Bender
313 28th Avenue
This two-story house, composed of independent volumes, opens sections of its interior spaces to decks and courtyards. The design is dominated by a towerlike volume to the rear of the house.

40. Stein Building, 1984
Bill Stein
13323 Washington Boulevard
The proliferation of towers, gables, and porches do, indeed, command your attention in this 1980s Queen Anne Revival building.

41. Brig Restaurant, 1990–91
Central Office of Architecture (Ron Golan, Eric Kahn, Russell Thomsen)
Northwest of the corner of Washington and Lincoln boulevards
Facing the street is a free-standing billboard screen. The screen is a modernist modular affair behind which one can see through the glass walls of the enclosed restaurant. The screen is lifted from the ground and is supported by large-sized industrial pipes, painted a light green.

42. House, circa 1989
390 Pacific Avenue (Marina Del Rey)
A house that poses as a delightful streamline motor yacht. The bow of the ship, its second-floor bridge, and its slanted mask look out over Pacific Avenue.

43. Stayden Duplex, 1986
Miguel Angelo Flores and Associates
4112 Pacific Avenue
Particularly from the waterside, this dwelling has the feeling of being a grounded houseboat.

39. Gardner House, 1992

42. House, circa 1989

The dark band at the base effectively separates the building from its site, and the sloped skylight roof hints that this is part of the bridge.

44. Marina Fine Arts Gallery, 1991
    John Lautner
    4716 Admiralty Way, Marina Del Rey
Within a conventional retail store space, John Lautner has placed two curved, bent surfaces that almost meet. The space between and behind seems entirely open to the gallery, but angled planes of glass do occur in this space, effectively enclosing the interior. A remarkable and highly inventive solution for a shop front and, in its own way, a strong and wonderful art object in itself and as an introduction to the wares inside.

45. Hampstead House, 1993
    Steven Ehrlich Architects
    835 Dickson Street
From the street, one experiences a composition of cubes which are colored in contrasts of burnt sienna and yellow ocher. The central cube is open and contains within, the segment of a drum (this is also the entrance). In contrast to the precise rectangular geometry of the building, irregular stone paving leads one up to and into the house.

46. Baldwin Motel, circa 1934
    12823 Washington Boulevard, Culver City
A small Streamline Moderne motel with a drive-through gate.

47. Automobile Service Garage, circa 1925
    12129 Washington Boulevard, Los Angeles County
The onion dome atop the small tower, together with the row of ogee arches, establishes the Islamic image of this L-shaped corner garage unit.

48. Mar Vista Houses, 1946–48
    Ain, Johnson and Day (Gregory Ain)
    Beethoven, Moore and Meier streets, south of Marco Place.
One of Ain's prime interests was low-cost housing. After World War II he designed several small-scale developments of which the Mar Vista Houses were one. Fifty-two single-family houses were initially built in this project, with another 52 planned. These houses of 1,050 square feet were planned so that they could take eight different configurations. They were built for the Advanced Development Company. Ain provided internal flexibility, using sliding walls between one of the bedrooms and the living room, and the other two bedrooms could be united or separated by sliding doors. Most of the houses have been remodeled and added to, but one can still get a sense of Ain's view of inexpensive single-family housing.

LOS ANGELES INTERNATIONAL AIRPORT

ince the 1950s the area directly around the Los Angeles International Airport has developed into an aerospace-related industrial zone, supplemented especially on the east and north by a good supply of hotels and office buildings. North of the airport is Westchester, which is almost exclusively residential housing (with the exceptions of Loyola University and Northrup Institute of Technology). To the west is the beach-oriented community of Playa Del Rey, which in the 1960s was substantially reduced in size by the removal of blocks of residences that once existed at the west end of the airport's runways. All that remains now is the picturesque pattern of the streets. The removal of these houses has meant the loss of a number of excellent Spanish Colonial Revival, French Norman, English Tudor, and Streamline Moderne houses of the 1920s and 1930s.

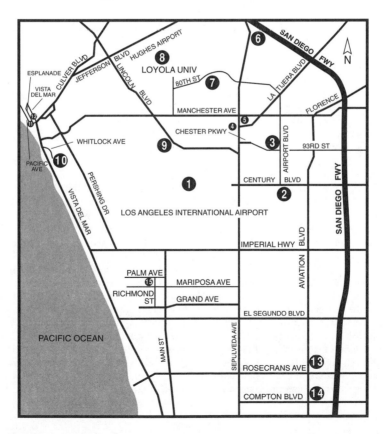

Los Angeles International Airport, Theme Building, 1958

Two major losses were R. M. Schindler's Zaczek Beach House (1936–38), and Thornton M. Abell's Shonerd House (1935). Within the past 20 years, there has been renewed building activity in what remains of Playa Del Rey. The usual pattern of two- and three-story town houses and of attached town houses is occurring, as it is along much of the coast of Southern California.

South of the airport is El Segundo (established in 1917), the name of which was derived from the early (1911) oil fields in the area. The section of El Segundo to the west is composed of single-family spec houses—most of which were built just after World War II—while industrial and commercial activity characterize the eastern and northern portions of the community.

1. Los Angeles International Airport,
1925–present
Enter from the east on Century Boulevard
The site of the airport was at first a general flying field established in 1925. In 1928 it became the municipal airport for the city of Los Angeles. Through much of the 1930s the municipal airport was secondary in public use to other fields located in Burbank, Glendale, and Santa Monica. In 1940–41 Sumner

Spaulding and John Austin were commissioned to design an extensive new passenger terminal and a number of secondary buildings. In 1941 the airport directors appointed a team of architects—Walker and Eisen, McNeal Swasey, Sumner Spaulding, and H. L. Gogerty— to design the new administration building. Because of the Second World War, this expansion of the public aspects of the airport was put aside.

After the war, various studies and some expansion of runways and buildings took place. But the first phase of the airport, as we know it, came about during the years 1957–61. It was in the mid 1950s that William Pereira and Associates, together with Paul R. Williams and Associates, and Welton Becket and Associates, provided a new master plan for the airport, and this was followed later by their designs for a new group of terminals, the administration building, and the central theatrical flying saucer restaurant. Their scheme of a group of terminals built around a central space devoted to parking worked for a time, though the only visual event of great interest for those using the terminals were the Islamic-like domed spaces which hovered over the escalators and staircases. Externally, the character of the place was established by the landscape design, with its reliance on the palm tree. As to buildings, the **Theme Building** by Pereira, Williams, and Becket established the space-age theme of the passenger terminal area. Originally, now regrettably gone, was a second minor theme building, the airport **Standard Service Station**, which was situated east of the theme building. This 1962 station was designed by Charles Luckman, Paul R. Williams, and Welton Becket. Its design repeated the theme of the circle in its wide cantilevered canopy, matched by its small circular drum for an office. This service station won an Architectural Award of Excellence from the national A.I.A. in 1962.

Pereira, Williams, and Becket's scheme for the airport worked well during the 1960s and early 1970s, but eventually the intensity of usage far outstripped what had been planned. Added to this was the traffic congestion on Century Boulevard, the short surface street connecting the airport to the San Diego Freeway. Various proposals were made for the airport, including moving it out onto the northeastern desert at Palmdale, but nothing came of these proposals. Finally, the impetus of the 1984 Olympic Games prompted an extensive rebuilding of the airport, including a new two-layer road system, new and enlarged terminal buildings, and an expanded parking system. This new expansion was designed by William Pereira Associates, Daniel Dworsky and Associates, Bonito A. Sinclair and Associates, and John Williams and Associates. When you fly in and out of the airport, look to the south and you will see a group of Spanish Colonial Revival buildings of the 1920s. The most important of these is **Hangar No. 1,** built in 1929, designed by Gable and Wyant (the hangar is located at 5701 W. Imperial Boulevard). This hangar has recently been restored. The design in the eighties of the multi-layered road system, the addition of new buildings, and the remodeling and expansion of the old have somewhat improved it, but it is hardly a pleasant visual or life experience (either inside or out). One exception, though, would be the remodeled Delta Airline terminal, which provides a pleasant, visually calm space, oriented around a wide-ramped internal space,

lined by palms. This was designed in 1987 by Gensler and Associates, Lawrence Reed Miline Associates, landscape architects.

One of the newest additions to the architecture of the airport is Siegel Diamond's new **Airport Traffic Control Tower and Administrative Base Building** (1993–95). The architects have aptly described their 257-foot-high tower as an "organic imagery of the high tech tree," and as an "adult tree-house." They have taken the paraboloidal arches of the L.A. Airport theme building and used them as their theme. Flattening the arch form, they used it for the lower building and then as the form to cover the traffic control tower. A system of dramatic extended struts are used to support the extended roofs of these two forms. The visual

Airport Control Tower, 1993–95

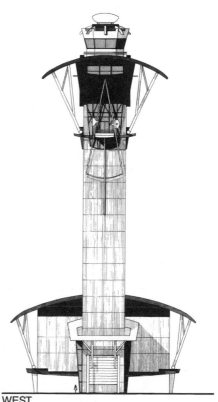

WEST

sense of the new tower is that of an abstracted 1990s version of a World War I airplane with its thin wings and struts.

Entry to the airport will now be via Century Freeway, spoken of as the last of the L.A. freeways. It was completed at the end of 1993. The control tower is located at 245 Worldway North.

2. Worldwide Postal Center, 1967
Daniel, Mann, Johnson, and Mendenhall (DMJM) (Cesar Pelli and Anthony Lumsden)
5800 West Century Boulevard
This building's character is created by the vertical and horizontal units of its two-story frame, left open in parts and filled in others. The exposed concrete frame, thin infills, and rounded corners suggest that the building is some type of fancy machine, housing not postal workers but computers. The siting of the building and its design in no way suggests that it is, in fact, a public building.

3. Hertz Vehicle Maintenance Turnaround Facility, 1982
Daniel, Mann, Johnson, and Mendenhall
9000–9029 Airport Boulevard
A machine object, a two-story curved box with a curved canopy projecting in front of the building.

4. Millron's Department Store Building (now **Broadway**), 1949
Gruen and Krummeck
Northwest corner of Sepulveda Boulevard and Manchester Avenue
The three-block commercial strip on Sepulveda Boulevard (between Manchester Avenue and Lincoln Boulevard), which serves as the center of Westchester, was developed during the years 1948–52. Like the Miracle Mile section of Wilshire Boulevard, the stores on Sepulveda Boulevard face toward the street in a traditional manner, while their parking and major entrances are at the rear. The two-story Millron's Department Store Building not only provides parking at the rear but on its roof as well. Millron's itself and most of the adjoining

stores employ the usual post-World War II motifs—an angular or curved high pylon sign, curved surfaces, and bands of vertical supports.

5. Loyola Theater, 1946
Clarence J. Smale
Southeast corner of Sepulveda Boulevard and Manchester Avenue
Post-World War II Streamline Moderne, partially transformed into Hollywood Regency. The marquee and its curved sign *are* the building. The building has now been remodeled, and it is difficult to really imagine what the original lively facade looked like.

6. Wang Tower, Howard Hughes Center, 1986
Barton Myers Associates
6701 Center Drive West (off of Sepulveda Boulevard and Howard Hughes Parkway)
Barton Myers did a master plan for the site and then designed this 16-story building as the flagship of the project. The stepped facade of granite terminates in a high round tower, all of which is very visible from the San Diego Freeway.

7. Westchester High School (now **Wright Jr. High School**), 1952
Sumner Spaulding and John Rex
Southwest corner of Cowan Avenue and 80th Street
Miesian pavilions arranged around courtyards.

8. Loyola University, 1865–present
80th Street between McConnell Avenue and Fordham Road
Loyola University (at first named Saint Vincent's College) is one of the oldest academic institutions in California. The Westchester site of the university is open and suburban in character. There are several buildings worth visiting. These include:

Sacred Heart Chapel, 1953
M. L. Barker and G. Lawrence
Spanish Colonial Revival carried on successfully into the postwar years. The tower and the street facade work well, especially when seen from a distance.

Loyola University Theater, 1963
Edward D. Stone
A characteristic Stone Palladian Villa, used in this case for an auditorium, all tinselly and lighthearted.

Library, 1977
David C. Martin
A Modern image design with a central sky-lighted atrium.

University Gymnasium, Athletic and Recreational Complex, 1978–80
Kappe, Lotery, Boccato
The graceful, concave shape of the roof is a result of the cable-hung suspension system employed.

9. IBM Aerospace Headquarters, 1963
Eliot Noyes; A. Quincy Jones; and Frederick E. Emmons
9045 Lincoln Boulevard
An exposed concrete grid clothes a late-1950s International Style Modern box.

10. House, circa 1938
5740 Whitlock Avenue
The perfect image for a site overlooking the ocean: a Streamline Moderne design equipped with nautical pipe railing, corner windows, glass brick, flat roofs, and white stucco walls.

11. Esplanade Del Rey Townhouse, 1982
Convoy Street between Esplanade and Culver boulevards
Modern historicism: a block-long row of town houses which seems to hearken back to the 1920s work of J. J. P. Oud in Holland.

12. Duplex, 1977
Eric Owen Moss and James Stafford
6672–6674 Vista Del Mar
Except for its light-yellow color and the exposed metal flues, this Streamline design could have been done in the early 1930s by Norman Bel Geddes.

13. Scientific Data System Building (now Xerox), 1966–68
Craig Ellwood and Associates
555 S. Aviation Boulevard
Once you grant the Miesian design principles

of Ellwood's work, his buildings remain impressive. The symbols of logic and order dominate this three-story post-and-lintel box. The plan is a perfect cruciform with semi-enclosed courtyards at the north and south. The hand of the designer is evident everywhere.

14. Federal Aviation Agency Building, 1973
Daniel, Mann, Johnson, and Mendenhall (Anthony Lumsden, Cesar Pelli, P. J. Jacobson, Dwight Wilson)
15000 S. Aviation Boulevard
An early 1970s image of the machine product, on the fragile and breakable side.

15. El Segundo Elementary School, 1936
Northwest corner of Mariposa Avenue and Richmond Street, El Segundo
PWA Moderne in exposed concrete.

SOUTH BEACH AREA

The South Beach region comprises the communities of Manhattan Beach, Hermosa Beach, and Redondo Beach (also the district called Hollywood Riviera, which is the western part of the City of Torrance).

Manhattan Beach was laid out in 1897 and slowly developed into a quiet bungalow colony. Hermosa Beach to the south was established in 1901, and by the 1920s it was referred to as a "family resort." Both Manhattan Beach and Hermosa Beach received a continual influx of visitors from Los Angeles during the years 1900–1920 via the Pacific Electric Line. The entire beach strand of both communities is public, though you often have to gain access to the beach by what seem to be small, secret spur streets. The beach is mostly well hidden and does not form a strong element in the townscape.

Redondo Beach, the largest of the beach communities, was founded in 1881 with the hope that it would develop as a major port for Los Angeles. At this time a pier, hotel, and narrow-gauge railroad (completed in 1888) to Los Angeles were built. In 1888 the Santa Fe Railroad constructed a line to the town. But the hoped-for commercial harbor never materialized. In 1938 work did begin on a pleasure marina (King Harbor Marina), which was completed after World War II. Redondo Beach, along with the neighboring section of the Hollywood Riviera, possesses an extensive beach park which runs from Vista del Mar to Torrance Boulevard.

Several large-scale town-house condominium projects were built in the beach communities in the 1970s and early 1980s. In other sections of these communities density is being substantially increased. Examples of this can be seen on Blanche Road between 30th and 31st streets in Manhattan Beach, where newer Spanish Colonial Revival town houses (1981

and later) now occupy their entire lots. On Myrtle Street in Hermosa Beach, similar intensification of land use can be experienced, only here the occasional image is "Victorian."

1. Marsh House, 1974
John Blanton
469 28th Street, Manhattan Beach
Located close to the street is this three-story
single dwelling, tied to its site by an extensive
pergola. The slope of the shed roof is interrupted by a slot for a balcony.

2. Provost House, 1975
John Blanton
204 Manhattan Avenue, Manhattan Beach
A tall, thin, vertical shed roof volume with an
assertive composition of windows, the whole
topped by a projecting chimney. Other works of
the 1970s in the area by the same architect are
the McNulty House (1975) at 420 Manhattan
Avenue and the Shelton Apartments (1974) at
480 Rosecrans Avenue.

3. Shelton Apartments #5, 1988
John Blanton
468 Rosecrans Avenue
A stucco box composed in a variation of
Schindler's work of the 1930s.

4. Davidheiser/Kroll House, 1988
John Blanton
120 34th Street
A continuation of the modernist approach of
Neutra and Schindler.

5. Roy Condominiums, 1991
John Blanton
106 Manhattan Avenue, and 109
Bayview Drive
The architect has looked carefully at late 1920s
products of R. M. Schindler, such as his projected Braxton house.

6. House, 1987
Raymond Kappe
1600 The Strand
Mendelsohn-like curved volumes project outward from the concrete frame of the building.
The curved forms are elegantly realized in
wood and metal-framed bands of glass.

7. Tate House, 1989
Melinda Grey
1920 The Strand
A long and narrow residence which makes its
way up the hill. A series of circular or

semicircular spaces establish focal points within
the dwelling. The largest of these spaces is a
"sort of urban Italian courtyard with casement
windows opening out onto the void."

8. House, 1983
Morphosis (Thom Mayne and Michael
Rotundi)
3410 Hermosa Avenue, Hermosa Beach
A borrowing of the Modern image of the thirties with a hint of High Tech, especially in the
walls sheathed with galvanized sheet metal.

9. Garmire/Russell House, 1989
John Blanton
406 North Dianthus Street
A second-floor addition has resulted in the
complete transformation of a small stucco
house. A greenhouse—as half of the gable end
of the building—now projects from the second
floor of the dwelling.

10. Pier Avenue School, 1939
Marsh, Smith, and Powell
Southwest corner of Pier Avenue and
Pacific Coast Highway, Hermosa Beach
Classical PWA Moderne; its conventionalized
ornament suggests Native American art of the
Southwest.

11. Redondo Beach Civic Center, 1962
Victor Gruen and Associates
200 Pacific Coast Highway, Redondo
Beach
A well-sited and handsomely scaled community center, composed of low boxes connected
by free-standing post-and-lintel passages. It is
all early1960s International Style Modern,
designed with delicacy. Regrettably, building
activities in the 1970s and early 1980s have
obscured its civic prominence.

12. Redondo Beach High School, 1931 and later
Allison and Allison
Pacific Coast Highway between Diamond
and Vincent streets, Redondo Beach
PWA Moderne, with the horizontal pattern of
the board forms revealed in the concrete walls.
Note the cast-concrete sculpture on the Manual
Arts Building extolling the virtues of education
and work.

13. Wardrobe Cleaners Building, circa 1950
    120 Catalina Avenue, Redondo Beach
An excellent example of a 1950s commercial
design with angled piers and plate-glass windows, somewhat held in place by a strong horizontal cornice.

14. Eagles Building, 1949
    Northwest corner of Catalina Avenue and
    Garnet Street, Redondo Beach
An almost pure late-1930s Streamline Moderne
building, constructed ten years later. Two
groups of bands run horizontally across the two
facades, connecting all the windows together.
The entrances are emphasized by vertical projections which crawl up and over the parapets.
Recent remodeling has removed the important
horizontal bands.

15. United California Bank Building
    (now **First Interstate Bank**), 1970
    Roland E. Coate, Jr., Stanley Kamebins
    1720 Elena, Redondo Beach
A cutaway passage leads one between two
tightly enclosed volumes. One of the volumes
rises to form a natural pylon for the sign.
Within, warm wood detailing contrasts with the
coldness of concrete surfaces.

16. Riviera Methodist Church, 1957–58
    Neutra and Alexander
    575 Palos Verdes Boulevard, Hollywood
    Riviera, Torrance
A single, long, rectangular block houses the
sanctuary and the Sunday School rooms. An
openwork constructivist post-and-lintel composition of steel and wood emphasizes the
entrance to the sanctuary.

17. Reid House, 1928
    Mark Daniels
    124 Via Monte d'Oro, Hollywood Riviera,
    Torrance
Daniels was one of California's gifted exponents of the Spanish Colonial Revival—in both
architecture and landscape gardening. The Reid
House clearly illustrates his understanding of
Spain's rural Andalusian forms. The house and
its siting also indicate how the original concept
of the Hollywood Riviera was intended to be

composed of large villas, set within ample
grounds—something which did not occur.

18. Von Koerber House, 1931–32
    R. M. Schindler
    408 Via Monte d'Oro, Hollywood Riviera,
    Torrance
Though little known, the Von Koerber House is
one of Schindler's most interesting designs.
The interior is composed of a number of levels
which open outward onto various decks, terraces, and courtyards. Narrow bands of
clerestory windows provide light at the ceiling
levels. Because of design restrictions, Schindler
was required to utilize the Spanish Colonial
Revival image, and he responded with humor
and satire to these requirements. Roof tiles not
only cover the roof but also sections of the
walls, and are even used in an inverted manner
around the fireplace.

18. Von Koerber House, 1931–32

PALOS VERDES, NORTH

In 1913 the New York banker Frank A. Vanderlip acquired 16,000 acres comprising almost all of the Palos Verdes Peninsula. He then engaged Olmsted and Olmsted, Howard Shaw, and Myron Hunt to lay out a "Millionaire's Colony." The entire 16,000-acre tract was planned to include a number of large estates, parks, clubs, an elaborate pattern of roads, and three model villages. The intervention of World War I prevented the project from developing. After the war, a pared-down version of the initial scheme was begun. Between 1922 and 1923 Olmsted and Olmsted, together with Charles H. Cheney, laid

out a master plan for the 3,200 acres which occupied the northwestern portion of the peninsula. They provided for four commercial centers—Lunda Bay, Valmonte, Miraleste, and Malaga Cove. Of these, only Malaga Cove was built (1922–25).

The Spanish (Mediterranean) architectural tradition was established as the official architectural style, and in 1922 an art jury was formed to review all designs. A number of major Spanish Colonial Revival designs were built, including F. L. Olmsted, Jr.'s, house (Myron Hunt and H. C. Chambers, 1924–25), the Buchanan House (Kirkland Cutter, 1927),

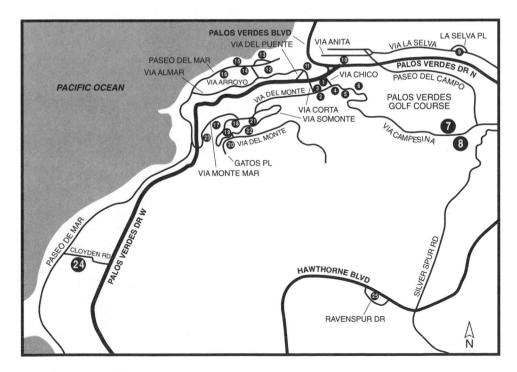

and the Cameron House (Kirkland Cutter, 1926). These and other houses are effectively hidden from view today.

In 1932 the landscape architect A. E. Hanson became the manager of the Palos Verdes Ranch, and it was he who suggested the name Palos Verdes Peninsula to describe the area. The community just kept its head above water during the depression, and finally, with the economic recovery of the late 1930s, A. E. Hanson turned his attention to the northern part of the Ranch and began to develop Rolling Hills, whose theme was "own your own dude ranch." Again, as in Palos Verdes, architecture was to utilize two images—in this case the Anglo-Colonial and the California board-and-batten ranch house. A Western-style gate led into handsome, shake-roofed ranch houses (designed by Lutah Maria Riggs) and to Williamsburg Colonial houses (designed by Paul R. Williams). In 1937 Rolling Hills was incorporated, and it has remained a gate-guarded, upper-middle-class enclave to the present day.

The landscape and architectural beauty of Palos Verdes remains, especially in and around Malaga Cove. Palos Verdes Drive (originally laid out by the Olmsteds) was refurbished and replanted (1983). But one can immediately sense the qualitative difference between planning and design in the 1920s and that of the 1970s by comparing the linear shopping center, which has developed just west of Crenshaw Boulevard on Silver Spur Road, with that of Malaga Cove Plaza. Even tile roofs, stucco walls, and some arches (and a Home Savings Bank with its public art) do not redeem the place.

1. **Malaga Cove Plaza,** 1922 and later
Olmsted and Olmsted; Charles H. Cheney;
Webber, Staunton, and Spaulding
Palos Verdes Drive between Via Corta and
Via Chico
Each of the four community centers planned for Palos Verdes was to be organized around a plaza and lined with two- and three-story arcaded buildings. The Malaga Cove Plaza was the only one built, and it was not fully

completed as planned. The buildings were all designed in 1924 by Webber, Staunton, and Spaulding, while Cheney and the Olmsteds provided the general plan. Both the plan and the architecture are highly successful, including the "Sally Port" over Via Chico. Note the fountain (installed in 1930), which is a two-thirds-reduced reproduction of La Fontana del Nettuno of 1563 in Bologna.

2. **Palos Verdes Public Library,** 1926–30
Myron Hunt and H. C. Chambers
Olmsted and Olmsted, landscape
architects
South of Via Campesina at Via Corta
One of Hunt's most successful designs, fitted with great care into the steep hillside. Stone walls form the base of the building and extend outward to form terrace walls for the garden. The library is on the second level. Below are an exhibition room and public meeting room.

3. **Garden Apartments,** 1937
Attributed to Pierpont Davis
2433 Via Campesina
A 1930s Spanish Colonial Revival complex, including a picturesque minaret.

4. **Apartment Buildings,** 1939
2508, 2510, and 2512 Via Campesina
A reserved but well-organized International Style Modern group of buildings which step up the hillside away from the road.

5. **Stein House,** 1928
Kirkland Cutter
2733 Via Campesina
Spanish Colonial Revival by one of Palos Verdes's major architects of the 1920s. The architect, who had practiced for many years in the state of Washington, transferred his office to the Southland in the 1920s. In addition to designing individual houses, he also designed several of the projected city centers (which were never built). Other designs of his in the Palos Verdes area are the Gilmore House (1927) at 3825 Paseo del Campo, the Paull House (1926) at 3621 Paseo del Campo, the Sisson House (1927) at 1706 Via Montemar, and the Buchanon House (1927) at 700 Via Montemar.

6. Gard House, 1927
   Kirkland Cutter
   2780 Via Campesina
To be read as Spanish, but in truth, many of its
details came from the rural villas of Tuscany.

7. Palos Verdes Golf Course, 1922 and later
   Olmsted and Olmsted; Charles H. Cheney
   3301 Via Campesina
You can obtain a good idea of Olmsted's and
Cheney's approach to designing in California
by driving around the boundaries of the golf
course. Today it all looks natural, but the contours of the land were appreciably modified,
and almost all of the plant material is nonnative. The Spanish Colonial Revival Club
House, designed by C. E. Howard, has been
much altered (and not for the good) over the
years.

8. Bowler House, 1963
   Lloyd Wright
   3456 Via Campesina
The low, hovering roof dramatically extends
the interior outward onto balconies and terraces.

9. Sias House, 1927
   E. Millard
   3405 La Selva Place
An Andalusian farmhouse with a separate
weaving studio.

10. Goodrich House, 1928
   H. Roy Kelley
   2416 Via Anita
This modest dwelling was the 1928 model
home for the Palos Verdes Estates—Spanish
Colonial Revival, of course.

11. Gartz House, 1930
   Wallace Neff
   Northeast corner of Via Almar and Via Del
   Puente
One of Neff's large villas; more Italian than
Spanish.

12. Malaga Cove School, 1926
   Allison and Allison; Olmsted and Olmsted,
   landscape architects
   North of Via Almar at Via Arroyo

Mediterranean, with a tower which seems to be
derived from late-fifteenth- or early-sixteenth-
century Spanish examples.

13. Olmsted House, 1924–25
   Myron Hunt and H. C. Chambers
   Northwest corner of Paseo Del Mar and Via
   Arroyo (on the ocean side)
A rural Spanish farmhouse complex with a
walled garden.

14. Palos Verdes Estates Project House #2,
1925
   W. L. Risley
   408 Paseo Del Mar
A modest Spanish Colonial Revival dwelling,
indicating one of the housing types planned for
Palos Verdes. Other housing types included
connected town houses, garden apartments, and
extensive villas and gardens.

15. Haggerty House (now **Neighborhood
   Church**), 1928
   Armand Monaco; Olmsted and Olmsted,
   landscape architects
   415 Paseo Del Mar
An extensive seaside villa, once again more
Italian than Spanish. The house is impressively
detailed, especially in its ironwork. If Pliny the
Younger could have seen this villa and its gar-
dens, we feel he would have been very happy.

16. Moore House, 1965
   Lloyd Wright
   504 Paseo Del Mar
The extensively cantilevered roof ends in a
sharp, dramatic point, and low horizontal terraces extend the dwelling outward on its site.

17. Stannard House, 1974
   John Blanton
   432 Via Monte Mar
A mid-1970s version of the Hispanic tradition,
with white stucco walls and balconies.

18. Cheney House, 1924
   Charles H. Cheney and C. E. Howard
   657 Via Del Monte
Although not easy to see, this is an important
Spanish Colonial Revival dwelling and garden.
It was designed as his own home by one of

California's foremost city planners, an advocate of community architectural control. While the house is Spanish, the garden tends toward the Italian.

19. La Venta Inn, 1923
Pierpont Davis; Olmsted and Olmsted, landscape architects
736 Via Del Monte

When built, it was one of the landmarks of Palos Verdes. The image was that of a white-washed Mediterranean church set on a steep hillside. Now the planting has grown so high and thick that only the very top of the tower is visible. A pergola encloses one side of the fountained courtyard.

20. Lombardi House, 1965
Lloyd Wright
804 Gatos Place, off Via Del Monte

In this house Lloyd Wright transforms some of the visual excitement of the L.A. commercial strip into domestic architecture.

21. Buchanan House, 1927
Kirkland Cutter
700 Via Somonte

Andalusian Spanish, with an outer and an inner court.

22. Schoolcraft House, 1926
Edgar Cline
749 Via Somonte

A rural Tuscan villa with extensive tile work, ironwork, and windows and doors brought from Italy.

23. Beckstrand House, 1940
Richard J. Neutra
1400 Via Monte Mar

America's own domesticated version of the International Style Modern of the late 1930s. Floor-to-ceiling glass visually connects the interior spaces with the surrounding terraces and gardens.

24. Palos Verdes High School, 1961
Neutra and Alexander
600 Cloyden Road

An effective modernist composition of low-pitched, gabled, tile roofs. The buildings are arranged around courts and connected to one another by low, flat-roofed, open passageways.

25. Ravenspur Condominiums, 1966
Raymond Kappe
5632 Ravenspur Drive, off Hawthorne Boulevard

Constructivism of the 1960s, composed of vertical and horizontal wood members with an infill of wood surfaces and glass.

PALOS VERDES, SOUTH

1. Miller House, 1948
  Thornton M. Abell
  3201 Palos Verdes Drive West
Post-World War II Modern, almost classical in
its clarity and reserve.

2. Wayfarer's Chapel, 1949 and later
  Lloyd Wright
  Portuguese Bend at Abalone Cove, north of
  Palos Verdes Drive South
This chapel is Lloyd Wright's most widely
known and visited building. His concept, as
with so much of his work, was to create a sense
of place via architecture and landscape architecture. His "Natural Church" was a glass structure hidden in a grove of coastal redwoods.
(These did not survive and they were replaced
by other trees.) Today one sees from the road

only the thin, angular, stone-and-concrete tower
rising from the forest. Once inside the building
you will see how successful Lloyd Wright was
in creating a sense of a mysterious, almost
fairy-tale forest.

3. Ekdale House, 1948
  John Rex
  3500 Palos Verdes Drive South
A two-story, glass-walled interior looks out
from a handsome redwood container.

4. Pray House, 1969
  Thornton Abell
  4500 Palos Verdes Drive South
The 1950s Arts and Architecture post-and-lintel
vocabulary successfully carried on a decade or
so later.

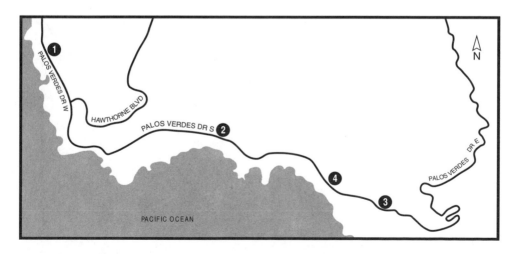

SANTA CATALINA ISLAND

Santa Catalina Island, the largest of the Channel Islands, was first mentioned by the Spanish explorer Cabrillo in 1540. In the 1820s the Island was granted to Pio Pico, who later deeded it to Nicolas Covarrubias. Later in the nineteenth century it was purchased by James Lick, and it was he who introduced sheep and goats to the island. During the American Civil War a barracks was built on the island. But Catalina's architectural history really began when the shipping interests of William Banning established Avalon (1877) as a summer resort with a Hotel Metropole and a tent city. It was G. Shatto who laid the city out into small lots (in 1885). The hotel is long gone, but evidence of this early city remains in the tiny lots now occupied by cottages just behind the commercial strip along the waterfront.

The real development of Avalon came when

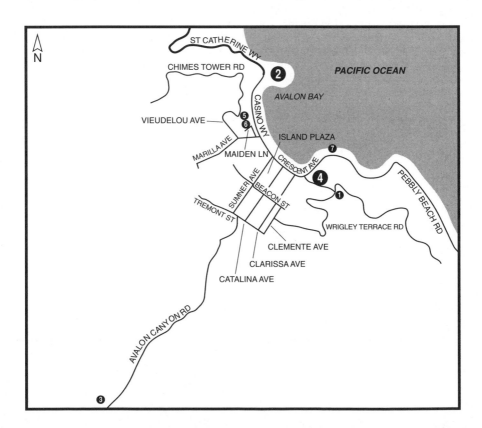

William Wrigley, Jr., bought the island from the Banning interests in 1919. Wrigley, the owner of the Chicago Cubs, wanted a place for his team to do spring training. Also, like so many businessmen of the time, he hankered after the life of a landed aristocrat. The thousand acres of land provided plenty of subsistence for cattle and horses, as well as the buffalo imported and domesticated later for a movie. They can still be seen on the island.

Without attempting to project Catalina as an architectural mecca, we do suggest a number of interesting walks that you can take around the town. There are many old cottages, including a row of Spanish Colonial Revival **workers' cottages** on Fremont Street put up by Wrigley, who further Hispanified the town in 1934–35 by employing commercial artist Otis Shepard to supervise face-lifting the commercial center. It was at this time that controls of signage went into effect, and many of the old wooden fronts were stuccoed and often tiled.

1. Mount Ada, 1921
D. M. Renton; Albert Conrad, landscape architect
Wrigley Terrace Road (From Crescent Avenue take Claressa Avenue to Beacon Street; right one block then right on Clement Avenue. Wrigley Terrace Road begins half a block on the left.)
It would be pleasant to report that Mount Ada, the mansion that Wrigley had built by his Pasadena contractor, David Renton, was an architectural pearl. But like their Pasadena home (now headquarters of the Tournament of Roses), it is more of a curiosity than a work of architecture. It is mildly Anglo-Colonial Revival both inside and out. Its real plus is its wonderful orientation towards magnificent views. One of these, from Wrigley's study, offers an excellent view of the playing field on which the Chicago Cubs worked out. The house is now used by the University of Southern California as a conference center. The grounds, designed by Wrigley's head gardener at his Pasadena home, are well worth a visit, especially the cactus and succulent gardens.

2. Casino, 1928
Webber and Spaulding (Sumner Spaulding)
1 Casino Way (Casino Point, northeast side of Avalon Bay)
Wrigley employed the architect to design a grand casino featuring moving pictures on the first floor and a ballroom on the second floor. Both of these rooms certainly do evoke the spirit of the 1920s, but it is the theater organ, with its bird calls and automobile horn stops, that seems to thrill the tourists most.

The exterior, which looms out of the sea as you approach the island by boat, is a strange mixture of Spanish, Moorish, and Art Deco Moderne styles, along with Art Deco murals on the porch. The ground floor (bay side) houses the headquarters and museum of the Catalina Island Museum Society (open Easter through October, 1–4 P.M. and 7–9 P.M.; weekends and holidays the rest of the year). The wonderful Art Deco nautical murals within the entrance porch are by John Gabriel Beckman.

3. Wrigley Monument, 1924
Bennett, Parsons, and Frost
Top, west end of Avalon Canyon Road 1½ miles from Bay; train service from Island Plaza.
Wrigley's family employed this Chicago planning and landscape firm to design a suitable monument to Wrigley. Its grand staircase, with insets of flamboyant Catalina tile, ends in the austerely Goodhuesque, Spanish with Art Deco enrichment mausoleum, which was apparently never used. The view from the monument is indeed handsome. The memorial is approached through a small but fascinating **botanical garden** (set out by Ralph Roth from 1933 onward). On the way up Avalon Canyon Road you will pass **The Bird Cage**, an aviary now fallen into ruin but still exhibiting some colorful Catalina tile.

4. Gano House, 1889
Attributed to Dr. Gano
718 Crescent Avenue
"Holly Hill," as the Gano House was called, is a large, picturesque Queen Anne cottage recently placed on the National Register of Historic Places. It is occasionally opened under

the supervision of the Catalina Historical
Society, usually for groups by appointment as a
fund-raising project.

5. Wolfe House, 1928
  R. M. Schindler
  124 Chimes Tower Road
The design principles of the Modern expressed
in exposed wood frame and stucco walls. An
exterior ramp leads up to the pergola roof deck.
The house was designed as a double dwelling,
with a shared roof terrace. This monument of
modern architecture in America in the 1920s is
rarely open, but it can easily be seen from the
path below and from the street.

6. Murdock House, 1929
  Elmer Grey
  103 Maiden Lane, on the corner of Crescent
  Avenue
In contrast to Schindler's nearby Wolfe House,
designed about the same time, the image of the
Murdock House is Spanish Colonial Revival,
handled in Grey's usual fashion, so that it ends
up being restrained and classical rather than
picturesque.

7. Cabrillo Mole Terminal Complex,
  1993–94
  Campbell and Campbell
  Pebbly Beach Road, Avalon
For the new terminal for the island ferry, the
architects have designed a small terminal
building, promenade, pergolas, and garden.

SAN PEDRO

The open roadstead east of San Pedro was the harbor for the missions of San Gabriel and San Fernando in the late eighteenth and early nineteenth centuries. Beginning in the 1820s it continued as the principal shipping point for the growing town of Los Angeles and for the surrounding ranches. A revealing portrait of San Pedro in 1834 and its difficult open harbor is contained in Richard Henry Dana, Jr.'s, *Two Years Before the Mast* (1840). In the late 1850s, Wilmington, which was established by Phineas Banning at the entrance to the Los Angeles River (yes, it actually used to have

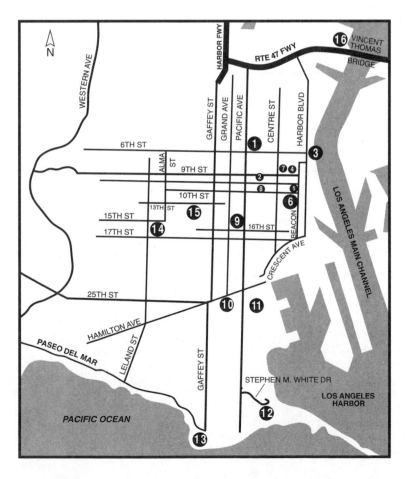

water in it), emerged as the most-used harbor for Los Angeles. The community of San Pedro participated in a marginal way in the various harbor improvements which took place from 1877 on. The most extensive of these improvements began in 1892, and in 1909 both San Pedro and Wilmington were incorporated with Los Angeles.

In 1846 a "five-hundred vara square" had been established by the Mexican government as a governmental reserve. This square, which was located on the low cliff in San Pedro overlooking the harbor, was set aside by the U.S. government in 1888 as a military reservation. In 1914 Fort MacArthur was established, comprising not only the "five-hundred vara square" but extensive acreage in and around Point Fermin. Through the 1950s this installation remained as the principal defense for Los Angeles Harbor.

Just before and during the Second World War, a number of Defense Housing projects were built for ship workers and others. These included Banning Homes (1942), Harbor Hills (1939–41), Rancho San Pedro (1942), and Richard J. Neutra's **Channel Heights Housing Project** (1941–43). Of these the Channel Heights Housing Project was justifiably the most famous, both for its excellent site planning and for the quality of its architecture. Regrettably there is so little left of this project that it is hardly worth a visit.

Though railroads, freeways, and the high **Vincent Thomas Bridge** connect San Pedro and Wilmington to Los Angeles and Long Beach, the feeling of both of these communities is that of a small coastal town, certainly not that of a large seaport.

1. Fox-Warner Brothers Theater, 1931
  B. Marcus Priteca
  478 W. 6th Street
Modest in size, but still a highly effective example of a Moderne Art Deco (Zigzag) theater.

2. YWCA Building, 1918
  Julia Morgan
  437 W. 9th Street
The Bay tradition of San Francisco brought to San Pedro. A board-and-batten building which has been remodeled on several occasions.

3. Municipal Ferry Building (City Hall/Harbor Department Building), 1939–41
  East end of 6th Street at Harbor Boulevard
A PWA Streamline Moderne Building, the Beaux Arts tradition made Moderne. The low, central tower with its clock face and ladder suggest the nautical origin of the Moderne of the 1930s. The building has been recycled by Pullman and Matthews to house a Maritime Museum.

4. U.S. Customs House and Post Office, 1935
  Northwest corner of Beacon and 9th streets
A classic PWA Moderne building. Inside is a forty-foot-long mural by Fletcher Martin.

5. McCafferty Studio House, 1979
  Coy Howard
  1017 Beacon Street
A three-story structure with false gables at each end and a central gabled space which houses the stairway. The highly complex geometry of the street facade does maintain a scale similar to other surrounding structures, but the singular volume does not. This volume, plus its metal industrial sheathing, seems to suggest that it is dockside warehouse rather than a studio dwelling.

6. Seaman's Center Building, 1954 and 1962
  Carleton M. Winslow, Jr., Warren Waltz;
  Andrew Joncich and William Lusby
  Southwest corner of Beacon and 11th streets
The Modern at the end of the 1950s. Here we have one example which has held up well.

7. House, circa 1898
  918–920 Centre Street
A Queen Anne/Colonial Revival dwelling with an expansive, highly detailed corner bay-tower.

8. House, circa 1885
  324 W. 10th Street
An early Queen Anne Revival with some earlier Eastlake details. The house has a two-story spindled porch and a corner bay tower whose third floor is open.

9. Commercial Building, circa 1938
  Northwest corner of Pacific Avenue and 16th
  Street
A Streamline Moderne building with a strong
commitment to the horizontal. If you continue
on down Pacific Avenue you will discover a
good number of fragmented remains of the
1930s Moderne.

10. Old Saint Peter's Episcopal Church,
  1884
  South end of Grand Avenue at 25th Street
A simple, unpretentious carpenter's Gothic in
wood.

11. Fort MacArthur, 1914 and later
  East side of Pacific Avenue between 24th
  and 27th streets
Though the fort is not open to the public (it is
presently being used by the U.S. Air Force),
one can see many of the Mission Revival buildings from Pacific Avenue. These were all constructed between 1916 and 1918. Just barely
visible are some of the double NCO Spanish
Colonial Revival houses which were built in
1933–34. At the east end of the parade grounds
is the site of the **Casa San Pedro** (the Hide
House), which was the first Anglo adobe constructed in Southern California (1823). The former **Trona Corporation Building** at the south
end of the Fort (built in 1917–18) contains a
spectacular timbered interior.
  A second section of **Fort MacArthur, the
Upper Reservation,** is situated on the hillside
off of Gaffey Street and Leavenworth Drive.
These compounds consist of two sets of gun
emplacements. The first of these, the **Osgood-
Farley, Leary-Merrian Emplacements,** are
located off of Leavenworth Drive and Osgood
Farley Road. These emplacements were built in
1916 and consist of four 14-inch disappearing
rifles. A second compound, the **Barlow-Saxton**
(off of Barlow Saxton Road), was also built in
1916 and housed eight 12-inch mortars. As
comments on the machine and earthworks,
these hillside emplacements, with their view
out towards the bay, are very impressive.

12. Cabrillo Maritime Museum, 1981
  Frank O. Gehry and Associates
  3730 Stephen M. White Drive
A pipe framework, open in part and covered in
other areas by chain-link fencing, provides an
introduction to a series of separate enclosed
pavilions. Each pavilion is sheathed in corrugated metal and stucco. The central courtyard,
exhibit spaces, and the auditorium work well.

13. Point Fermin Lighthouse, 1874
  Point Fermin, south end of Gaffey Street
Out of what appears to be a modest Eastlake
dwelling emerges a tapered, four-sided lighthouse tower.

14. San Pedro High School, 1935–37
  Gordon B. Kaufmann
  Leland Street between 15th and 17th streets
The most impressive aspect of this PWA
Moderne building is the curved front auditorium. Its narrow marquee, three louvered
openings above, and the relief sculpture are all
expressive of Beaux Arts design principles of
the 1930s.

15. Dodson House, circa 1887
  859 W. 13th Street
This two-story Eastlake dwelling was first
located at the corner of 7th and Beacon streets.
Much of its former lush ornamentation is now
gone.

16. Vincent Thomas Bridge, 1961–63
  Bridge Division, Division of Highways,
  State of California
  North of the Catalina Terminal; enter from
  the northeast corner of Gaffey and Oliver
  streets
The Thomas Bridge, which connects San Pedro
to Terminal Island and thence to Long Beach,
is California's third-largest suspension bridge.
The bridge is Southern California's one-upmanship to San Francisco's Golden Gate
Bridge and the Bay Bridge. There is something
delightfully stage-set about the Thomas Bridge,
for while it does indeed lead somewhere, one is
not quite sure why it is really there.

WILMINGTON

W ilmington, first named New San Pedro, was founded in 1858 by Phineas Banning. He started the harbor development by constructing a pier and providing warehouses. In 1869 Wilmington was connected to Los Angeles by rail. Though the community was incorporated in 1872, its independence was lost when it was absorbed into Los Angeles in 1909. Banning Park and the Banning House still form, as they did in the last century, the most important place in the community.

1. Los Angeles Department of Social Service Building, circa 1925
Southeast corner of Anaheim Street and Broad Avenue
A two-story Spanish Colonial Revival building.

2. Saint Peter and Saint Paul Roman Catholic Church, 1930
Henry C. Newton and Robert Dennis Murray
515 W. Opp Street
Italian Romanesque, the concrete walls with board pattern of the forms exposed.

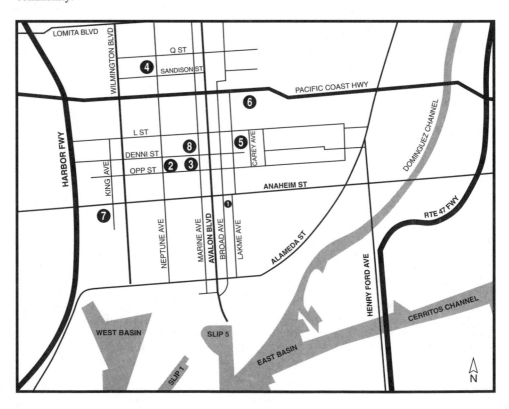

3. Wilmington Branch Public Library, circa 1926
Marston, Van Pelt, and Maybury
309 W. Opp Street
A T-shaped, single-floor Spanish Colonial Revival building. The children's library room leads out onto a pergola and garden.

4. Saint John's Episcopal Church, 1883
1537 Neptune Avenue
A Queen Anne Revival church building, small in size.

5. Drum Barracks, 1859
1053–1055 Cary Avenue
A two-story try at Greek Revival which really ends up more Federal than Greek. The officers' quarters are all that remain of an extensive group of wooden buildings constructed here in the late 1850s and early 1860s.

6. Banning House, 1864
Banning Park at Lakme Avenue and Pacific Coast Highway
A luxurious version (at least for California) of the Greek Revival, resplendent with a two-story balconied porch and elegant entrances on both floors. Glass doors with transoms open out onto the entrance porch and the balcony porch above (the Federal-style front door was added in 1910). The Banning House illustrates how late the Greek Revival as a style continued into the 1860s, not only in California, but also in many areas of the East and Midwest. A central cupola crowns the eighteen-room house. The present park only hints at what the grounds around the house were like in the 1870s. A long avenue of eucalyptus led to the house, and gardens of flowers and shrubs abounded.

6. Banning House, 1864

7. Lucy Banning House, circa 1900
Southwest corner of Anaheim Street and King Avenue
Mission Revival of a sort, with Japanese overtones.

8. Memorial Chapel, Calvary Presbyterian Church, 1870
1160 N. Marine Avenue
A rarity in Southern California—an Italianate church building. The original curved roof of the tower is now missing, and originally there were two entrances, one to each side of the projecting tower.

TORRANCE

The City of Torrance was established in 1911. It was named for its founder, Jared Sidney Torrance, who sought to build an ideal small industrial city. He selected Olmsted and Olmsted to design his new city. They in turn engaged Lloyd Wright to supervise the landscaping and prevailed upon their client to have Irving J. Gill design the first public, commercial, and residential buildings. They organized the city around a two-and-a-half-block park—El Prado. Symbolically the southwest end of the park was terminated by the high

school, while to the northeast the orientation was towards a distant view of Mount San Antonio. A commercial center was placed around the Pacific Electric Station. Beyond this to the north and east the land was laid out for factories and other types of industrial use. The residential areas of the city were placed around El Prado and the high school.

In the mid-1930s a small-scaled civic center was built facing Cravens Street, from El Prado to Post avenues. The 1930s civic center has now been abandoned for a new one located at the northwest corner of Torrance Boulevard

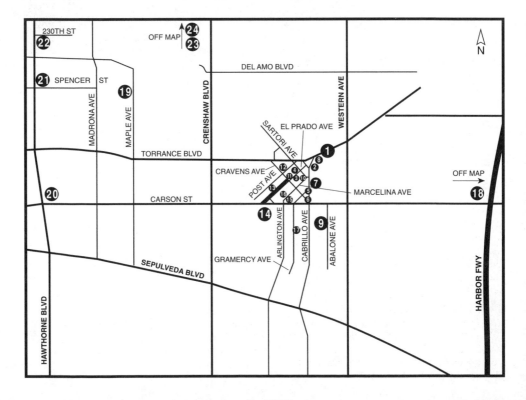

and Maple Avenue. In the 1920s a residential area—the Hollywood Riviera—was developed on the western hills which overlooked the Pacific. In the post-World War II years, there has been a slow infill of the area between the Olmsted center of Torrance and the Hollywood Riviera section. This infill is highly mixed, ranging from office complexes and other commercial uses to single- and multi-family housing.

1. Pacific Electric Railroad Bridge, 1912
Irving J. Gill
Torrance Boulevard between Western and Cabrillo avenues
In effect this reinforced concrete, six-arched bridge serves as a ceremonial entrance into Torrance from the east. This bridge was one of Gill's first projects in Torrance.

2. Pacific Electric Railroad Station, 1912
Irving J. Gill
610 S. Main Street on the west corner of Torrance Boulevard and Cabrillo Avenue
The design of the station originally incorporated a red tile roof and dome, so that it read more effectively as Mission Revival than is currently the case. The two miniature segmented domes on top of the side spur walls illustrate Gill's abstracted use of Mission Revival elements. As with other buildings in Torrance, the structure is of hollow tile and brick, sheathed in stucco.

3. Roi Tan Hotel, 1912
Irving J. Gill
1211 El Prado Avenue
This three-story commercial structure is one of a group of buildings which Gill realized in downtown Torrance. The proportions of the building and of its openings are a hallmark of Gill's approach to design. Architecturally the building sways between the bland and the aesthetically abstract. Though this building was referred to as being of reinforced concrete, it, like his other commercial buildings in Torrance, is of steel, brick, and hollow tile covered with stucco.

4. Murray Hotel, 1912
Irving J. Gill
1210 El Prado Avenue
Similar to the Roi Tan Hotel across the street. The eyebrow of red mission tile at the top has been removed.

5. Colonial Hotel and United Cigar Building, 1912
Irving J. Gill
1601–1605 Cabrillo Avenue on the south corner of Cabrillo and Gramercy avenues
A triangular-shaped building with retail uses on much of the ground level and two floors of hotel rooms above. The narrow brick cornice at the top of the building has been removed.

6. Brighton Hotel, 1912
Irving J. Gill
1639 Cabrillo Avenue, on the north corner of Cabrillo and Cravens avenues
A second triangular building almost identical to the Colonial Hotel, with the usual retail stores on the ground level and hotel rooms and small apartments above.

7. Retail Commercial Building, circa 1928
1420 Cabrillo Avenue
A Spanish Colonial Revival design with a highly dramatic entrance.

8. Fuller Shoe Manufacturing Company Building (Casa Del Amo), 1912
Irving J. Gill
1860 Torrance Boulevard
The single (false) shed roof and the scale of the symmetrical facade convey more of a domestic than a manufacturing quality. The building has been converted into apartments.

9. Salem Manufacturing Company Building, 1913
Irving J. Gill
1805 Abalone Avenue
A single-story box which, though of wood, appears to be of reinforced concrete. Another nearby Gill industrial building is the **Rubbercraft Corporation of California Building** (1913) at 1800 W. 220th Street. This two-story stucco structure has a pair of false-stepped gable ends.

10. Retail Commercial Building, circa 1916
2266 Sartori Avenue
The Mission Revival image is evident here. Buildings such as this had a much wider popular appeal than most of Irving J. Gill's more puritanical buildings.

11. Torrance City Hall and Municipal Auditorium (now **Home Savings Branch Bank**), 1936–37
Walker and Eisen
North corner of Cravens and El Prado avenues
A modest, single-story, PWA-Classicized Moderne Building.

12. Torrance Public Library, 1936
Walker and Eisen
North corner of Cravens and Post avenues
PWA Moderne, one of the group of buildings which composed the original 1930s civic center of Torrance.

13. House, circa 1916
1504 Post Avenue
A two-story bungalow improved by references to the Midwest Prairie style.

14. Torrance High School, 1923; 1929, and circa 1935
Farrell and Miller (original High School Building)
Southwest end of El Prado Avenue at Carson Street
The main building, which was axially oriented to El Prado, utilized a Classical and somewhat Beaux Arts image. The Assembly Hall, with its relief sculpture over its entrance, is an excellent example of the PWA Moderne. Within the foyer of the Assembly Hall is a 1936 Federal Art Project mural by Anna Katharine Skeele. The subject of this mural is Taos Indian Life.

15. Villa Sonora, circa 1922
East corner of Marcelina and Arlington avenues
A Spanish Colonial Revival bungalow court, with single-story units towards the street and a two-story section at the rear of the property.

16. United Methodist Church, circa 1916
Northeast corner of Marcelina and Arlington avenues
Mildly Midwest Prairie in style, the whole terminated by a wonderful octagonal dome.

17. Worker's Single-Family Housing, 1912
Irving J. Gill
Gramercy Avenue contains several of the concrete (actually hollow tile) bungalows designed by Gill. These are located at 1815, 1819, 1903, 1904, 1907, 1916, 1919, and 1920 Gramercy Avenue. These L-shaped single floor dwellings have their entrances to the side within the L. A low-pitched roof projects between the two corner parapets. Gill had planned streets of these and double, connected bungalows for Torrance, but they were not popular with the workers and their families, who much preferred the more romantic and traditional California bungalow.

18. Child/Family Development Center, 1993
Barton Myers Associates
2181 Normandie Avenue
The plan of the low complex is made up of four nurseries which are grouped around a central court. Each of the nurseries is conceived of as a courtyard house with areas for living, sleeping, etc. These nurseries pose as houses overlooking the inner court. The firm of Sussman/Prejza has provided the graphics and the color.

19. South Bay Industrial Park, 1974
Matlin and Dvoretzky
Emmet Wemple and Associates, landscape architects.
300 Maple Avenue
The romantic, picturesque (seemingly natural), landscaped industrial park is what is important here. The unassertive, two-story buildings serve as a backdrop to Wemple's landscape.

20. Ohrbach's Del Amo Fashion Square, 1971
Gruen and Associates (Cesar Pelli)
Northeast corner of Carson Street and Hawthorne Boulevard
A fragile-looking blue container looks out onto acres of parked cars.

21. Bill Hopkins Lincoln-Mercury Agency Building, 1966
Daniel L. Dworsky and Associates
20460 Hawthorne Boulevard (at Spencer Street)
A well-conceived 1960s Modern design of modular brick walls and steel.

22. Tomanjan Professional Building, 1979–80
Neil Stanton Palmer
Northeast corner of Hawthorne Boulevard and 230th Street
A pyramid in brick and stone.

23. "The Courthouse," 1978–79
Northwest corner of Crenshaw Boulevard and 185th Street (just southwest of the San Diego Freeway)
The owner of this building, Dudley Gray, purchased fragments from the 1885 Pottawattamie Courthouse in Council Bluffs, Iowa, and incorporated them into his own version of a classical courthouse. As a design it works best when seen at a distance, from the San Diego Freeway.

24. Castle Park Recreation Center, 1978
2410 Compton Boulevard
In the late 1970s a wonderful group of castle-image recreation centers were built in the Los Angeles area. Within, the castle houses video games of all sorts. Externally, the grounds are a miniature golf course. The castles are large in scale so they can be seen from the freeways—and this one, situated close to the San Diego Freeway, works very well. Within the landscaped grounds are a delightful array of miniature buildings.

LONG BEACH, DOWNTOWN AND WEST

The city was founded in 1880 by the Englishman W. E. Willmore, and it was first named the "American Colony." "The project," it was noted in the local press at the time, "includes an ample town site, college grounds, and all the latest improvements." This plan was especially generous in providing a variety of open public spaces. The entire beach front was to be public, and a number of parks were provided throughout the town site. Shortly after the first sale of land commenced, the city was renamed Willmore City. Though widely advertised, it was not successful. In 1887 it was taken over by the Long Beach Land and Water Company and touted as an ideal seaside resort. A wharf was built and a large wooden resort hotel was constructed on the cliff overlooking the beach. In 1902 the Pacific Electric connected the city with Los Angeles. Four years later, work began on the artificial harbor which eventually would transform Long Beach into a major West Coast port. The culmination of all of these efforts was reached in November 1925, when at long last navigation was open to deep-draft ships.

In the teens and 1920s, efforts were made to incorporate a "City Beautiful" plan for the city. The major axis, Long Beach Boulevard, was to be lined, close to Ocean Beach Boulevard, with classical public buildings. The major result of this scheme was the construction of a Civic Auditorium (1930–32; designed by J. Harold MacDowell of New York, and W. Horace Austin of Long Beach) at the south end of Long Beach Boulevard. In the early1920s a modest City Beautiful City Hall was built on

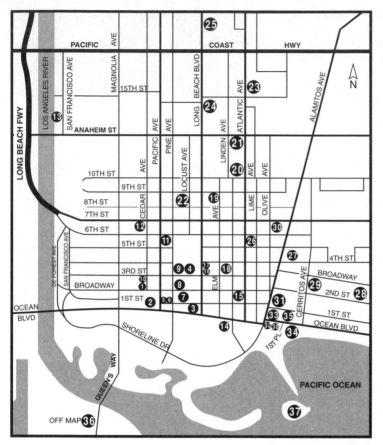

In 1928 the Pacific Southwest Exposition was held in Long Beach. The site for the exposition, at the south end of 7th Street, became an Islamic stage set (it was referred to as "Tunisian"). Regrettably, all of the exposition buildings were temporary (designed by Hugh R. Davies), so that nothing was handed on, not even the site itself.

In 1933 a severe earthquake destroyed or damaged many of the downtown masonry buildings in Long Beach. Many of these buildings were replaced or remodeled into Art Deco Moderne or later into Streamline Moderne buildings.

Like many other

the north side of Lincoln Park (1921; designed by W. Horace Austin). This building was damaged in the March 10, 1933, Long Beach earthquake. The 1921 City Hall was rebuilt, reflecting the latest Art Deco style of the moment (1934; designed by Cecil Shilling and Horace W. Austin). During the 1930s the remodeled City Hall was joined by two other Art Deco (PWA Moderne) public buildings: the Municipal Utilities Building (1932; by Dedrick and Bobbe), and the Veteran's Memorial Building (1936–37; designed by George Kahrs). This wonderful group of Art Deco public buildings was demolished in the 1970s through the usual post-World War II urban renewal.

American cities after the Second World War, Long Beach plunged headlong into urban redevelopment. In this case it happened somewhat later than other cities, in the 1960s and 1970s. In 1981 it was noted, "Major redevelopment surgery has removed six blocks of the city's deteriorated downtown business district to make way for a $100-million mall as part of an investment of more than $1.25 billion in the heart of the city." (*Los Angeles Times,* February 22, 1981, VIII, 1) And as is the continually repeated story of urban redevelopment throughout America, the results are at best mixed. The landscaping of Long Beach Boulevard and parts of Ocean Boulevard is unquestionably a plus. The new plan for the area ignores what little was realized of the earlier Beaux Arts plan. The "surgery" within and without the six-block area destroyed a number of commendable buildings, including the 1930–32 Long Beach Municipal Auditorium with its great colorful mosaic by Henry R. Nord (the mural, *Activities in Long Beach,* has been reinstalled on the south side of the new parking structure), and the group of civic buildings situated facing Lincoln Park—the 1933–34 Long Beach City Hall, the 1932 Long Beach Municipal Utilities Building, and the 1936–37 Long Beach Veteran's Memorial Building. All of these were very good examples of the PWA Moderne.

The inevitable pedestrian mall (**"The Promenade"**) has been built on the east end of Pine Avenue between Ocean Boulevard and 3rd Street. Its only asset is that it does have a symbolic termination at its north end. Here an arched section of the parking structure contains Nord's old Auditorium mosaic, and although the piece was never meant to be seen at eye level and close up, it is still impressive. As with most pedestrian malls, "The Promenade" is not overrun by people.

The high-rise buildings which have been constructed either in or adjacent to the redevelopment area are generally undistinguished. There is more than a hint of overdone theatrics in the twin fourteen-story, semi-cylindrical glass **Arco Center Towers** (at 200–300 Oceangate, 1979–82 Luckman Partnership, Inc.). And nothing very positive can be said for the setting or design of the fasciated, glass-sheathed **Crocker Plaza** office building (at 180 W. Ocean Boulevard, 1980–82; Maxwell Starkman Associates) or the 1974–78 **Long Beach Convention Center** (a sad replacement for the Municipal Auditorium). The 1974–75 **Queen Surf Condominiums**, the 1986–87 **World Trade Center Complex**, and the 1986–87 **Shoreline Square** are at best regrettable. More in keeping with the character of Long Beach is the glass-sheathed six-story **Downtown Plaza** at the corner of Ocean Boulevard and Promenade North (1983; designed by Landau Partnership).

Extensive redevelopment of the beach front took place in the 1980s, but few of the projects

had the effect of retrieving the past glories of Long Beach. At the moment, the one saving element of these newer buildings along Ocean Boulevard and on the beach is the mural painted on the walls of Southern California Edison's Redondo Beach Generating Station. This mural of twelve migrating whales was painted in 1991 by the artist Wyland.

1. California Veteran's Memorial State Office Building, 1981–82
Kenneth S. Wing, Sr., Kenneth S. Wing, Jr.
Northwest corner of Cedar Avenue and Broadway
A four-story constructivist exercise, with much of the exposed metalwork painted blue. As with many Modernist public buildings, there is nothing about this design which suggests the civic and public, nor is it even easy to discover the entrance or to find one's way around.

2. Long Beach City Hall and Public Library, 1973–76
Allied Architects; Hugh Gibbs and Donald Gibbs; Frank Holmelka and Associates; Killingsworth, Brady, and Associates; Kenneth S. Wing, Sr., and Kenneth S. Wing, Jr.
333 W. Ocean Boulevard
The fourteen-story city hall office tower reads as a glass box held in place by projecting concrete piers. The library (if you can find it) is a concrete pillbox hidden in the ground (á la the Oakland Museum). As with the nearby **California Veteran's Building,** there is little of a proud civic sense about the site design or the architecture.

3. Downtown Plaza Building, 1981–82
Gruen Associates
Northeast corner of Ocean Boulevard and Promenade North
A fasciated and stepped glass-sheathed building, more suburban than urban.

4. Parking Structure, 1981–82
Gruen Associates
North end of the Promenade at West 3rd Street
As already mentioned, the arched wall of the parking structure which contains the 1930s

Federal Arts Project mosaic by Henry Nord and others saves not only the parking structure but the mall as well. The adjacent enclosed **Long Beach Plaza** shopping mall was to have many of its ground-floor shops open to the adjacent streets, but this has not really worked.

5. Buffum's Autoport, 1941
J. H. Davis, engineer
North side of 1st Street between Pine and Pacific avenues
A classic example—including its signage—of the Streamline Moderne of the 1930s. Horizontal bands terminate in a vertical plane, from which project three small, curved balconies. The only change is the open concrete grillwork on the street level.

6. First National Bank Building (now **115 Pine Building**), 1900, 1905–6, 1907
Train and Williams
115 Pine Avenue, Northwest corner of Pine Avenue and 1st Street
A rather severe six-story Beaux Arts commercial design. It is saved in every way by the fanciful clock tower added in 1907. The building was restored in 1987 by Lionel Ramirez of Ramirez Design Associates.

7. Security Trust and Savings Building (now **Security Pacific National Bank**), 1923–25
Curlett and Beelman
102 Pine Avenue, northeast corner of Pine Avenue and 1st Street
A fourteen-story Beaux Arts skyscraper. Large two-story windows occur between the fluted pilasters on the ground floor, and elaborate multicolored relief panels are located above the office tower entrances.

8. Rowan Building (Bradley Building), 1930
Northwest corner of Pine Avenue and Broadway
The ground floor of retail shops has been remodeled, but the second floor displays a wonderfully inventive and colorful array of Art Deco motifs in terra cotta. Note also the second floor of the adjoining building to the north—another Art Deco Moderne facade in terra-cotta.

9. Farmers and Merchants Bank Building, 1922
Curlett and Beelman; Horace Austin
Northeast corner of Pine Avenue and 3rd Street
A ten-story, white, terra-cotta-sheathed skyscraper, whose image seems both Beaux Arts and Spanish Renaissance.

10. First Congregational Church, 1914
H. M. Patterson
Southwest corner of Cedar Avenue and 3rd Street
By the mid-teens the northern Italian Romanesque had been found to be highly appropriate for the image of California as the new, improved Mediterranean world.

11. YWCA Building, 1925
Julia Morgan
Southeast corner of Pacific Avenue and 6th Street
A four-story brick Italian Renaissance building. Visit quickly, for it may not be around very long. It has been slated to be replaced by a new structure.

12. Second Church of Christ, Scientist, 1916–25
Elmer Grey
Southwest corner of Cedar Avenue and 7th Street
Pure Beaux Arts, except in this instance there is a hint of the Byzantine rather than the Italian. Most impressive are the four large Corinthian columns, which set off the high entrance porch.

13. Chemical and Physical Testing Laboratories, City of Long Beach, circa 1915
1475 San Francisco Avenue
A single-story Mission Revival building.

14. New Robinson Hotel, 1933, 1934
334 E. Ocean Boulevard
Originally designed as a Gothic revival building, the hotel was remodeled after the 1933 Long Beach earthquake. An Art Deco (Zigzag) Moderne concrete structure set back from the street in a heavily planted garden.

15. Lafayette Hotel Building, 1929
Schilling and Schilling
Southeast corner of Broadway and
Linden avenues
A four-story vertical Art Deco building.
Surveying the scene, perhaps with some reservations, are two large-scaled heads of Native
Americans looking down from the parapet.

16. Post Office and Federal Building,
1931–32
James A. Wetmore; designed by Hugh R.
Davis (Long Beach Architectural Club)
Northeast corner of Long Beach Boulevard
and 3rd Street
PWA Moderne, accomplished with restrained
and sophisticated taste.

**17. Great Western Savings Association
Building,** 1968
Daniel Dworsky and Associates
350 Long Beach Boulevard
A cut-into box with an exposed concrete frame
and an infill of brick. The setback of the building has provided space for planting, brick
walks, and walls.

18. Retail Store Building, 1930
312–16 Elm Avenue
A single-story Art Deco store building with a
pattern of metal grillwork above the store windows.

19. Scottish Rite Cathedral, 1926
Parker O. Wright and Francis H. Gentry
Southwest corner of Elm Avenue and 9th
Street
A classical Italian Romanesque design, covered
with gray mottled terra-cotta which suggests
stone.

20. Saint Mary's Hospital, 1935, 1937
J. E. Loveless
North end of Linden Avenue at 10th Street
A succession of three-story volumes terminated
by a low tower with a hipped roof. It all adds
up to a successful Art Deco composition (with
strong Beaux-Arts overtones).

21. Hancock Motors, 1929
Schilling and Schilling
S.E. corner of Anaheim Street and Linden
Avenue
This single story Art Deco automobile showroom and repair shop is resplendent with cast
relief ornament. Above the corner entrance are
a pair of winged rams' heads.

22. York Rite Masonic Temple Building,
1927
Wright and Gentry
829 Locust Avenue
A severe Beaux-Arts block constructed of a
steel frame and concrete floors.

23. Long Beach Polytechnic High School,
1932–36 and later
Hugh R. Davies
Northeast corner of Atlantic Avenue and
15th Street
The 1934–36 Industrial Arts Building and the
Commercial Arts Building by Davies lean more
towards the International Style Modern of the
1930s than the then-popular Streamline
Moderne. Note the style of lettering for the
buildings. Also, go inside the Industrial Arts
Building to see the Federal Arts Project mural
by Ivan Bartlet and Jean Swiggett.

24. Gasoline Service Station, circa 1925
Southeast corner of Long Beach Boulevard
and 15th Street
An early, prefabricated metal service station
with a single, hipped roof which covers both
the pumps and the office.

25. Pacific Auto Works, 1928–29
Schilling and Schilling
1910 Long Beach Boulevard
Art Deco with both an art and programmatic
intent. The central cartouche suggests a radiator
of an automobile, and the double seashell motif
to each side creates the needed headlights.

26. Robert Louis Stevenson School,
circa 1936
West side of Lime Avenue between 5th and
6th streets
PWA Moderne. The ornament suggests both
the Art Deco and the pre-Columbian.

27. Hot Cha Restaurant, 1936
957 4th Street
A metal coffee pot for a giant sits on top of the clerestory of a small octagonal building.

28. Apartment Building, circa 1928
1436 3rd Street
A two-story Spanish Colonial Revival apartment complex with an open garden court.

29. Ebell Club Building, 1924
Clark Phillip
Southeast corner of Cerritos Avenue and 3rd Street
A great rectangular box of a building with an exuberant Spanish Plateresque facade. The interior was conceived of as a modern version of the Spanish Renaissance.

30. Saint Anthony's Roman Catholic Church, 1952
Barker and Ott
Southeast corner of Olive Avenue and 7th Street
This simple, gable-roofed church was remodeled in 1952. Added to the older building were two fanciful (Gothic?) towers, which now enclose the gable end mosaic depicting Pope Pius XII watching the Virgin's assumption. Below, a three-part entrance is set in a Gothic screen.

31. Apartment Building, circa 1929
917 1st Street
A two-story Streamline Moderne building with all of the needed elements—curved corners, horizontal banded windows, steel railings, and glass bricks.

32. Villa Riviera Apartment Building, 1928
Richard D. King
800 E. Ocean Boulevard
One of the Seashore landmarks of Long Beach. The fourteen-story building contains a one-hundred car garage, plus an "Italian" roof garden. The image—with its dormered, high-pitched, hipped roof and octagonal tower—is French Chateauesque.

33. Pacific Coast Club, 1925–26
Curlett and Beelman
Southwest corner of East Ocean Boulevard and 1st Place.
A romantic French Medieval castle resplendent with towers and all. At the moment it is in need of sympathetic restoration.

34. Tichenor House, 1904
Charles and Henry Greene
852 E. Ocean Boulevard
A much-remodeled, two-story Greene and Greene bungalow. The east facade faces onto 1st Place and contains a remarkable pattern of brick, wood, and glass. Plans have been made to move the house to the campus of California State University, Long Beach.

35. House, circa 1937
936 E. Ocean Boulevard
A Streamline Moderne dwelling, quite nautical in feeling.

36. *The Queen Mary,* 1934
1126 Queen's Way Drive, Pier J, Long Beach Harbor
Another saving element in the harbor area is the great Art Deco/Streamline Moderne 1934 English ocean liner, *The Queen Mary.* Unfortunately, another streamline attraction (in this case of the early 1940s), Howard Hughes's airplane the *Spruce Goose,* has departed for the Pacific Northwest.

37. Oil Drilling Islands, 1967–68
Herb Goldman
Linesch and Reynolds, landscape architects
Long Beach Harbor
A grouping of high, thin, sculptured walls seek to hide the utilitarian equipment of the man-made oil islands from public view on shore. As beautification the results are peculiar, though it is a pure Southern California solution.

LONG BEACH, EAST; NAPLES, AND SEAL BEACH

1. Raymond House, 1918
  Irving J. Gill
  2724 E. Ocean Boulevard
This is one of the few Gill houses in the Los
Angeles area which still remains intact. As with
many of his houses, the Raymond House is a
concrete and hollow tile construction. Its proportions and general detailing are similar to the
destroyed Dodge House in West Hollywood.

2. Bungalow, circa 1915
  2601 1st Street
A single-floor bungalow becomes respectable
with a front porch displaying classical columns.

3. House, circa 1910
  363 Carroll Parkway West
A Mission Revival dwelling.

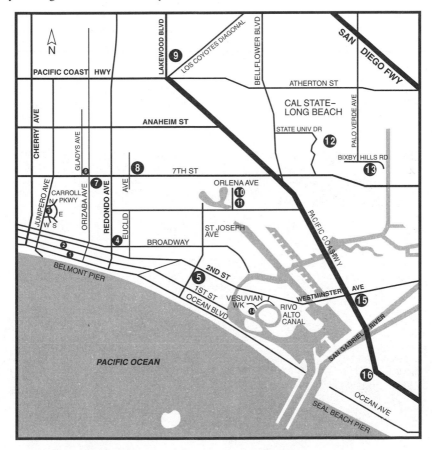

4. Bungalow, circa 1909
    4341 Broadway
An ordinary California bungalow assumes
some importance with the concrete columns of
its front porch cast in the form of rustic tree
trunks.

5. Belmont Theater Building, 1929
    Reginald R. Inwood
    Southeast corner of Saint Joseph Avenue and
    2nd Street
Pre-Columbian architecture "improved"
through the Art Deco. Though it has suffered
the loss of the upper part of its corner tower
with the addition of a new entrance and of a
marquee (in 1948), the building is still exotic.
Recently it has been made "Old West."

6. Newton Rummond House, 1932
    708 Gladys Avenue
Supposedly this is the narrowest dwelling in the
L.A. area—10 feet in width. Its image is that of
a Medieval Hansel and Gretel dwelling, more
French than English.

7. Retail Store and Apartments, circa 1927
    Southeast corner of Orizaba Avenue and 7th
    Street

An imaginative crenelated tower stands guard
over this complex of remodeled structures.
Note the staircase and the entrance into the
tower, and also the pink stucco. Style? Perhaps
we should think of it as Spanish Medieval.

8. Jefferson Junior High School Building,
    1936
    Northeast corner of Euclid Avenue and 7th
    Street
PWA Moderne in exposed concrete. The spiral
motif ornamentation of the piers and spandrels
is impressive.

**9. Duffield Lincoln-Mercury Agency
    Building,** 1963
    Killingsworth, Brady, and Associates
    1940 Lakewood Boulevard
A steel grid frame, which is mostly infilled
with glass, faces onto the street. The late 1950s
Case Study House form enlarged into an elegant auto showroom.

10. House, circa 1936
    376 Orlena Avenue
One of a number of white stucco Streamline
Moderne bungalows to be found in and around
Long Beach.

11. Kimpson-Nixon House, 1939

11. Kimpson-Nixon House, 1939
Raphael S. Soriano
380 Orlena Avenue
Soriano as an advocate of the purist International Style Modern of the 1930s. Boxy volumes are articulated by horizontal bands of windows on both floors.

12. California State University at Long Beach, 1949 and later
State University Drive off Bellflower Boulevard on 7th Street
The architecture of the University, like that of most of the other state universities and colleges, can at best be described as bland "State College Modern." Though architect Edward Killingsworth has for many years been the master-planning architect for the University, the complex still has not developed much above the ordinary. The best element of the campus, and its saving grace, is its landscape architecture. The 1966 **Sculpture Walk** (Killingsworth, Brady, and Associates; Edward Lovell, landscape architect) is a good case in point. Fortunately, the landscape is winning out. A recent addition to the campus collection of art is the log sculpture by Claire Falkenstein (1987).

Also, do visit the **Earl Burns Miller Japanese Garden**. Here on a one-acre site is a traditional Japanese garden with a teahouse, stone lanterns, and other elements. It was designed by the landscape architect Edward R. Lovell, in consultation with Dr. Koichi Kawana of UCLA. The garden is open Tuesday–Thursday, 9:00 A.M.–4:00 P.M., and Sunday, noon–4:00 P.M.

13. La Casa de Rancho Los Alamitos, 1806–later
6400 E. Bixby Hills Road
This single-floor adobe ranch house is, according to tradition, the oldest domestic building still standing in Southern California. Of interest, equal to the adobe house, are the gardens laid out over many years by members of the Bixby family. In the twentieth century many of Southern California's major landscape architects were consulted. These include William Hertrich, Allen Chickering, Ed and Paul J. Howard, Charles Gibbs Adams, and Yoch and Council. Between 1922 and 1936, Yoch and Council laid out the terraces and the geranium, oleander, and jacaranda walks. The ranch house and adjoining grounds are open to the public, Wednesday–Sunday, 1:00–5:00 P.M.

Naples
This waterside community was developed between 1903 and 1905 by Arthur Parson. Like Venice, south of Santa Monica, it was planned around a series of canals. (Needless to say, no

14. Frank House, 1957

one had really looked around the bay of Naples.) The center of the place is an island within Alamitos Bay (itself a fake bay), and it is much more reminiscent of Venice, Italy, than is Santa Monica's Venice. The four romantic concrete bridges over the waterways were designed in 1913 for the Naples Company by Mayberry and Parker.

14. Frank House, 1957
    Killingsworth, Brady, and Smith
    5576 Vesuvian Walk, Naples
Arts and Architecture magazine's Case Study House No. 25. The two-story interior is arranged around a lath-covered interior court. The verticality of space, wall surfaces, and details indicates the course which much of California's Modern was to follow in the later 1960s.

15. The Market Place, 1976–77
    Richard Nagy Martin
    North corner of Pacific Coast Highway and
    Westminster Avenue
Several major shopping centers have been constructed in and around the intersection of Pacific Coast Highway and Westminster Avenue. Of these, The Market Place is, by far, the most pleasant. The high points of the place are the connected lakes, the traditional large-scale Mexican fountain of Guadalajara Canterra stone, and El Torito Restaurant, a wonderful version of California's Mission Revival.

16. Bay City Center, 1979–80
    Irwin and Associates
    Pacific Coast Highway, between 5th and
    Marina streets, Seal Beach (off of map)
The centerpiece of this commercial development is the central thirty-five-foot-high cupola and dome of copper, which, it is said, was modeled after the dome of the 1920s Islamic Bay City Bath House.

LONG BEACH, NORTH

1. Cambridge Investment Inc. Building, 1966
    Killingsworth, Brady, and Associates
    324 E. Bixby Road
An open post and lintel frame building, quite classical in concept.

2. Bixby House, circa 1885–later
    Ernest Coxhead
    11 La Linda Place
We still have no idea how many residences Coxhead designed in Southern California, either during his stay in Los Angeles or after he moved to the Bay Region. This house was designed when he was in San Francisco, and as one would expect, it is similar in certain aspects to his work in the north. In the Bixby House he has blended the Shingle Colonial Revival tradition with the English Arts and Crafts. (Note the house is almost impossible to see from the street.)

3. Reeves House, 1904
   Charles and Henry Greene
   4260 Country Club Drive
A characteristic Greene and Greene two-story bungalow, which was originally built at 306 Cedar Avenue. In 1917 it was moved to 1004 Pine Avenue, and in 1927 it was moved to its present site.

4. Adobe Los Cerritos, 1844
   4600 Virginia Road
This large house was built by Don Juan Temple as the center for his extensive ranch located on the banks of the Los Angeles River. The dwelling is a U-shaped building enclosing a patio which was enclosed by a wall at its open end. The center section of the building is surrounded by a two-story wood porch and gallery. Originally the roof was flat, covered with "brea," but after 1866 a hipped shingle

roof was added. The Adobe Los Cerritos is one of the finest existing Monterey style adobes to be found in Southern California. The romantic gardens around the house were restored by Ralph Cornell.

5. Long Beach Airport Terminal, 1940–41
   Kenneth S. Wing, W. Horace Austin
   West end of Douglas Drive off Lakewood Boulevard
The late 1930s Streamline Moderne moving towards the bland Modern of the post-World War II years. The site planning, with its dominant axial road leading to a park in front of the two-story terminal building, is characteristic of the PWA Moderne. Regrettably the park is now gone as are the Federal Arts Project murals and mosaics by Grace Clements. These murals and mosaics have been covered over and are no longer visible.

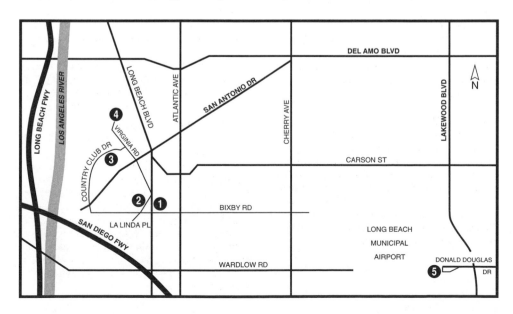

Inglewood, Hawthorne

Inglewood was one of the many boom towns which were established in the late 1880s on the flat plain south of Los Angeles. It was platted in 1887. A large hotel was built, and plans were made for the establishment of the Freeman College of Applied Arts. Then came the bust of 1887–90. The hotel was left standing, but the college never got underway. The town grew very slowly until the late 1930s, when several large tracts of modest spec housing were built, and such streets as Manchester Avenue, Crenshaw Boulevard, and La Cienega Boulevard began to develop as typical, auto-oriented, retail commercial strips. The city's chief fame for years has been the 1937 **Hollywood Turf Club** designed by Stiles Clements. The city today is well supplied with small neighborhood parks and the larger **Centinela Park** (off Florence and Centinela avenues). Much of the city lies right in the center of the east jet pattern for the Los Angeles International Airport, but it has somehow managed to survive remarkably well.

Hawthorne, which lies to the south of Inglewood, was founded in 1906. Its system of grid streets basically continues those of Inglewood.

1. Randy's Donuts, 1954
805 W. Manchester Boulevard

A giant doughnut sits atop a tiny, canted-glass, early 1950s Modern fast-food building. In a Modern fashion, the vertical steel supports for the doughnut plunge right through the building below. A classic example of 1950s programmatic architecture where the sign (the three-dimensional doughnut) is the design, and the building below is merely a base.

2. Centinela Ranch House (Ygnacio Marchado Adobe), after 1844
7636 Midfield Avenue

The Rancho Aguaje de Centinela was granted in 1844, and it is likely that shortly after this date the adobe ranch-house was built. As is generally the case with adobes, the house was added to from time to time, especially in the early 1860s. It is a single-floor adobe with a wood shingle roof, fireplaces, and deep window reveals.

3. Three Speculative Houses, 1940
Edward Lind (office of R. M. Schindler)
423, 429, and 433 Ellis Avenue

Three single-floor spec houses which mirror a number of Schindleresque design motifs. Their garages (at a lower level) face toward the street, and the houses open up to enclosed gardens at the sides and rear.

4. Stanford M. Anderson Water Treatment Plant, 1977
Kappe, Lotery, and Boccato
Southwest corner of Eucalyptus and Beach avenues

A two-story Miesian, steel-and-glass box looks out onto a lively world of brightly painted pipes, tanks, and other machine elements. A colorful diagram on the front wall sign explains it all.

5. Inglewood Civic Center, 1973
Charles Luckman Associates; Robert Herrick Carter, landscape architect
Northwest corner of Manchester Avenue and Hawthorne Boulevard

Within this twenty-nine-acre civic center a nondescript eight-story City Hall has been placed on a two-story base. Set within its own separate garden is the two-story library building. Other buildings located within the Civic Center are a police facility, a fire station, and a public health complex. The vegetation is slowly hiding most of the buildings.

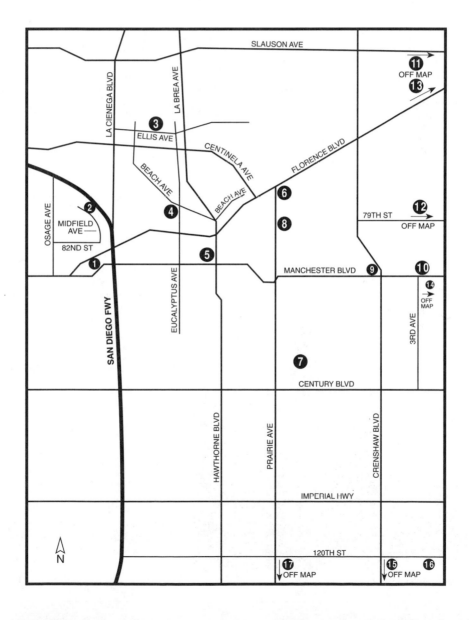

6. Los Angeles Railroad, Inglewood Station, 1928
Southeast corner of Prairie and Florence avenues in Inglewood Park Cemetery
A small Spanish Colonial Revival passenger station which poses as an Andalusian church.

7. Hollywood Turf Club, 1937
Stiles O. Clements, with later additions by Fred Barlow, Jr.; Edward Huntsman-Trout, landscape architect
Northwest corner of Century Boulevard and Prairie Avenue
A Streamline Moderne clubhouse and grandstand, easily visible from Century Boulevard. The master plan, which was laid out by Clements and Huntsman-Trout, can best be seen from the window of your jet as you approach the Los Angeles International Airport.

8. Inglewood Memorial Park, 1905–later

Note that they provided spaces for twenty-two thousand cars (in 1937).

8. Inglewood Memorial Park, 1905–later
Northeast corner of Manchester Avenue and Prairie Avenue
The extensive Inglewood cemetery is situated in low rolling hills, many of which are covered with tall palm trees. The most important monument is the Mausoleum and other buildings at the north side of the park. These reinforced exposed concrete buildings were built between 1933 and 1940, and are Art Deco in style. They were designed by Walter E. Erkes. If you would rather not bother traveling to Santa Barbara to see its famed Mission Church, you can go to the Inglewood Memorial Park Mausoleum and find the "Santa Barbara Mission Window," designed by the Judson Studios.

9. Academy Theater, 1939
S. Charles Lee
3100 Manchester Boulevard
Notwithstanding recent remodelings, this theater marks a high point of the Streamline Moderne in the United States. Stucco-sheathed cylinders play into one another and culminate in a thin, 125-foot-high tower. The spiral fins of this tower and of the parking sign were originally lighted by blue neon tubes.

10. Brownfield Medical Building, 1938
Gregory Ain
Northwest corner of Manchester Boulevard and Third Avenue
A small, tastefully-proportioned "rationalist" design by one of L.A.'s pioneer modernists.

11. Milk Bottle (Knudson's Dairy), circa 1935
1914 W. Slauson Avenue
A good-sized milk bottle sits on top of a dairy building so that we are all aware of what it is about.

12. Pepperdine College,
(old campus) 1937
Thomas Cooper;
Katherine Bashford and
Frederick Barlow, Jr.,
landscape architects
West of 79th Street and
South Vermont Avenue
The college campus con-
tains several excellent
examples of the Streamline
Moderne, and there are sev-
eral buildings which come
close to being 1930s
International Style Modern.
The older **President's
House** at 7851 Budlong
Avenue and the **Pepperdine
Center Building** on the
west side of South Vermont
Avenue at West 78th Street
are Spanish Colonial
Revival.

**13. Mount Carmel High
School Building,** 1934
7011 S. Hoover Avenue
An excellent exercise in the
more abstracted version of
the Spanish Colonial
Revival of the 1930s.

14. The Teapot, circa 1931
607 W. Manchester Avenue
A little programmatic restaurant
in the form of a metal teapot.

**15. One-Hundred Fifty-Third Street School
Building,** 1957
Ain, Johnson, and Day
1605 W. 153rd Street between Harvard
Boulevard and Denker Avenue
A 1950s one-story finger-plan school accom-
plished with Ain's characteristic reticence.

**16. Northrop Electronics Division
Headquarters,** 1982
Daniel L. Dworsky and Associates
2301 W. 120th Street

9. Academy Theater, 1939

International Style Modern made fashionable
through contemporary High Tech imagery.
Many of the glass-walled areas of the building
open onto well-landscaped terraces.

17. Richstone Family Center, 1993–94
Siegel Diamond Architects
13620 Cordary Avenue
The architects have broken the building down
into a series of small readable units. The rectangular block-like volumes are countered by
those with shed roofs and those with barrel-
vaulted roofs.

GARDENA

Gardena, which was located at the junction of the Pacific Electric Railroad lines from San Pedro and Redondo Beach, was founded in 1906. The town center of Gardena (located at Gardena Avenue between Western and Normandie avenues) still conveys a 1920s Spanish Colonial Revival image. Newer buildings of the past three decades have somewhat modified the original unity of the place.

At 2501 W. Rosecrans Avenue is the 1952 Gardena Office of **Great Western Savings and Loan Association,** designed by the San Francisco office of Skidmore, Owings, and Merrill. The building utilizes the then-fashionable Edward Stone Pavilion mode, except that in this case, massive concrete was used. The building has been remodeled, but you can still see the architects' original intent. At 3312 El Segundo Boulevard are the **Goldwater Apartment Buildings** designed by Carl Maston in 1964 with the landscape designed by Emmet L. Wemple and Associates. Each of the fourteen two-story units has its own private court, and in addition there are larger, more public courts. The imagery is early 1960s *Arts and Architecture* post-and-beam Modern with an open courtyard created between the stucco-sheathed boxes and the constructivist pergolas.

Just east of the San Diego Freeway interchange with Redondo Beach Boulevard is **El Camino College** (at 16067 S. Crenshaw Boulevard). The administration building and the library were designed in 1951 by Smith, Powell, and Morgridge. These buildings indicate how well the architects of the immediate post-World War II years could apply both the 1930s lesson of the International Style Modern and the popular Moderne to produce a functional and convincing image.

This section of Los Angeles (county and city) contains the Palms District (laid out in 1886) and Culver City (platted in 1913). Palms, which was established alongside the Santa Monica Railroad, was planned as a grain shipping center, and until the early 1900s, agriculture was the primary use of the land.

Culver City, founded in 1913 by the Nebraska real estate promoter Harry Hazel Culver, has long been famed for the major film studios which began to be located there from the late teens on into the 1920s. Land use in the area now varies considerably. Light industry occurs here and there, extensive commercial strips abound (Venice, Washington, Culver, and Jefferson boulevards). For the vernacular commercial strip fancier, a long, leisurely drive along Rico Boulevard or Washington Boulevard from Santa Monica to downtown Los Angeles is a must. If your interest is in middle-class suburbia and its planning, then visit a development such as **Monte Mar Vista,** a 130-acre development south of Rancho Park (north off the Santa Monica Freeway, east of Overland Avenue, west of Robertson Boulevard). This development was laid out in 1924 by Cook, Hill, and Cornell. In Palms, in and around Overland Avenue between National and Venice boulevards, is **Westside Village,** a spec development of small single-family houses which was built between 1939 and 1941. The small, clapboard houses with their shuttered windows evoke the then-popular Anglo Colonial Revival image. Within the past decade Culver City has emerged as a major center of Post Modern architecture in the Los Angeles area.

BALDWIN HILLS, CULVER CITY

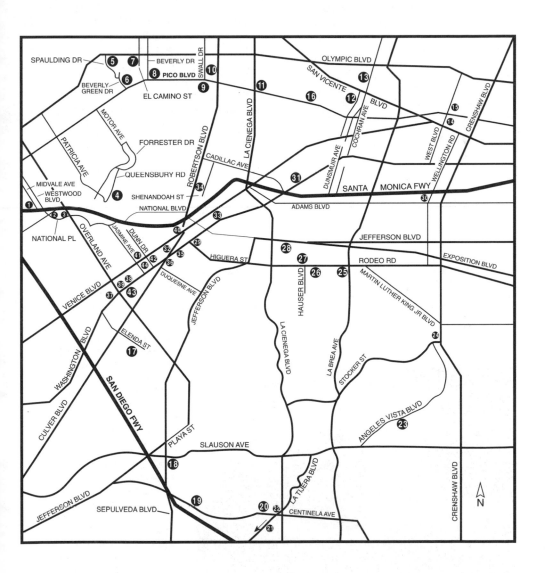

1. Petal House, 1982
  Eric Owen Moss
  2828 Midvale Avenue
This complex of buildings (it is in part a remodeling) displays the architect's inventive ability to carry pedestrian architecture over into the world of high art. The commonest of materials coupled with the most common of architectural forms produces a very uncommon composition. Though the design, including its strong colors, is highly assertive, it fits with ease into a neighborhood of typical, modest, post-World War II spec houses. And, as is true of other designs by Moss, the forms and details of this house convey a sense of charm and delight. See the house close-up from the street, and also observe how it works from the Santa Monica Freeway.

2. Garden Apartment Building, 1955
  Carl L. Maston
  10567 National Boulevard
The building consists of a series of volumes which step down the hillside to the street. The garages are at the street level. Above, each of the units has its own small, enclosed courtyard garden. The building is sheathed in vertical redwood. Glass in horizontal bands occurs between the top of the redwood walls and the thin-fascia flat roofs.

3. National Boulevard Apartment Building, 1954
  Raymond Kappe
  10565 National Boulevard
This building provides a good neighbor for Carl L. Maston's apartments next door. The design concept is similar, except that here Kappe's detailing is more delicate, and in places there is a hint of his later wood constructivism.

4. Strauss-Lewis House, 1940
  Raphael S. Soriano
  3131 Queensbury Road
This single-story dwelling, arranged in a U-shape around a patio (the fourth side to the street is walled in), is far less doctrinaire than most of his other pre-World War II buildings. The house is sheathed in a thin, horizontal pattern of wood.

5. Karaski House, 1960
  Lloyd Wright
  436 Spalding Drive, Beverly Hills
Lloyd Wright at his best; a wonderful essay in stucco, concrete open grillwork, and stone. The grillwork encloses courts and parts of the balconies. The two-story rear of the house has the visual appearance of the bridge of a ship.

6. Colby Apartment Building, 1950
  Raphael S. Soriano
  1312 Beverly Green Drive
Pure post-and-beam design with infill of glass and stucco. Corrugated fiberglass panels are used for the balcony fronts. The whole design is light and airy, characteristic of Soriano's work after 1945 (now demolished).

7. Beverly-Landau Apartment Building, 1949
  Alvin Lustig
  Southwest corner of Olympic Boulevard and El Camino Drive
These two rectangular volumes, set at right angles to each other, have facades which are divided into

4. Strauss-Lewis House, 1940

repeated modules. One
strongly feels here the intent
of a careful designer.

8. Liberty Building, 1966
Kurt Meyer and Associates
1180 S. Beverly Drive
An L.A. version of the 1960s
New Brutalism. Its awk-
wardly proportioned, seven-
story form is a reminder of
how rapidly architectural
fashions come and go.

**9. B'Nai David Synagogue
and School Building,**
circa 1929
South side of Pico
Boulevard at Swall Drive
The pattern of the board forms has been left
exposed in this Art Deco (Zigzag) Moderne
concrete structure. The tower is mildly reminiscent of several of the buildings at the 1925
Paris Exposition of Decorative Arts.

10. Ellwood Office Building, 1965–66
Craig Ellwood Associates
1107–1111 S. Robertson Boulevard
A close to magical transformation of two fifty-
year-old buildings into one of Ellwood's thin,
refined versions of the post-and-beam Miesian
grids.

11. Supermarket Building, circa 1940
Attributed to Stiles Clements
Northeast corner of Pico and La Cienega
boulevards
The Streamline Moderne street facade of this
building culminates in two thin, vertical fin-
signs which turn out to be relief sculpture of a
Hugh Ferriss skyscraper from his 1929
Metropolis of Tomorrow.

12. Dunsmuir Apartment Building, 1937
Gregory Ain
1281 S. Dunsmuir Avenue
A mid-1930s classic of Modernism, often illustrated during those years in magazines and
books on housing. It was this building, presented through the revealing photographs of
Julius Shulman, which established Gregory

12. Dunsmuir Apartment Building, 1937

Ain's national reputation. The building is composed of four two-story units which are stepped
back up the low hillside with a narrow entrance
walkway on one side and a small terrace and
garden for each unit on the other side. Each of
the second-floor bedrooms of the units opens
onto an upper pergola-covered deck.

13. Mackey Apartment Building, 1939
R. M. Schindler
1137–1141 S. Cochran Avenue
Each of the building's elevations is composed
of projecting and cut-into volumes, articulated
by a carefully designed pattern of windows and
doors. Within, some of the spaces are two stories in height.

**14. Sears, Roebuck, and Company Store
Building,** 1939
John Reddon and John G. Raben
Southeast corner of Pico and Westwood
boulevards
This building beautifully presents the ideal of
the pre-World War II suburban department
store. The building itself serves as a quiet
Streamline Moderne backdrop to the automobile, parked either in the large parking lot
to the west or on top of the roof of the store.
The automotive and garden shop buildings are
separate structures within the parking lot.
Originally, small mechanical elevators brought
the merchandise up to the roof parking deck.

15. The Radio Building, circa 1941
4500 block on north side of Pico Boulevard
Pure Streamline Moderne. Also note the 1930s
Art Deco (Zigzag) Moderne building across
Pico Boulevard.

16. Washeteria, circa 1955
5800 Pico Boulevard
A low structure dominated by a giant clothespin.

**17. Robert Lee Frost Auditorium, Culver
City High School and Middle School,** 1964
Flewelling and Moody
South corner of Elenda Street and Franklin
Avenue
The drama of concrete which so excited architects in the 1950s and 1960s is realized in this
structure. A singular curved leg of reinforced
concrete joins onto a curved, partial dome and
folded-roof concrete structure. In the center,
below the concrete forms, is a circular drum
which houses the stage and other rooms. This
firm designed a number of school buildings in
the years after 1945, all of which employed
some version of the Modern.

18. Fox Hills Shopping Mall, 1973-76
Gruen Associates (Cesar Pelli)
Southeast corner of Sepulveda and Slauson
boulevards below the freeway
A form seemingly designed to make an impression from the freeway interchange. The landscaping and buildings do not work as well close up.

*17. Robert Lee Frost Auditorium, Culver City High
School and Middle School, 1964*

19. Hillside Memorial Park
Centinela Avenue, just southeast of Bristol
Parkway
Visible from the San Diego Freeway is the **Al
Jolson Memorial**, designed in 1951 by Paul R.
Williams. The Memorial is an impressive
abstracted version of an open classical temple
which is oriented toward a water cascade.

20. Ladera Center, 1983
Urban Innovations
Corner of La Cienega Boulevard, Centinela
Avenue, and La Tijera Boulevard
A small, older shopping center brought up-to-date by a new stage-set facade, which looks to
the classical tradition (in a strange way). A successful revamping, utilizing the symbols of
Post Modernism.

21. Saint Anselm Church, 1956–57
J. Earl Trudeau
Southwest corner Van Ness Avenue and
70th Street
One of the many Roman Catholic churches
built in Los Angeles that continued the Spanish
image, in this case, based upon Renaissance
examples. The building, its tall tower, and central dome are of reinforced concrete. All of the
exterior and interior ornament, of cast concrete,
are sharp angled and highly simplified.

22. Pann's Restaurant, 1958
Armet and Davis
Northwest corner of La Tijera and La
Cienega boulevards and Centinela Avenue
A classic 1950s L.A. coffee shop designed by
the firm which built so many of L.A.'s restaurants and coffee shops in the post-World War II
years. The restaurant was restored in 1991 and
is now an official Los Angeles landmark.
Towering over the pitched, gable-roofed restaurant is an enormous animated sign. The space
within (with its open kitchen) has been returned
to its original colors, red and white, with
touches of yellow and orange. The low-pitched,
gravel-covered roof is once again lighted, and
the original exotic plant material—phapis
palms, hibiscus, giant birds of paradise—surrounds the restaurant.

22. Pann's Restaurant, 1958

23. California Military Academy (now
   Foundation for the Blind), 1934–36
   Richard J. Neutra
   5300 Angeles Vista Boulevard
A single-floor L-plan building constructed of a
metal frame and sheathing. Each of the classrooms opens to its own outdoor space through
sliding glass walls. Skylights balance the light
in the classrooms and the interior corridors.
(Note that Neutra's buildings lie to the rear of
the site.)

24. Crenshaw Shopping Plaza, 1947–48
   Crenshaw Boulevard between Martin
   Luther King Boulevard and Stocker Road
This was one of the first large suburban shop-
ping malls to be built within Los Angeles after
World War II. It took the lesson learned from
the large department stores along Wilshire
Boulevard and applied it to a suburban situa-
tion. The first increment of the complex was
the **May Company Crenshaw Department
Store**. This three-story department store build-
ing is situated on the northwest corner of
Crenshaw Boulevard and Martin Luther King
Boulevard. This reinforced concrete building
was designed by Albert C. Martin and
Associates and was built in 1946–47. As with
the pre-World War II May Company on
Wilshire, the architects employed a dramatic
curved corner, only in this case, a curved show-

case on the ground level and then three balconies above. Though there were doors to the
street sidewalks, the real entrance was at the
rear where 750 parking spaces were provided.
Albert C. Martin is quoted as saying about this
design that an important "consideration of
design is that of simplicity. Without simplicity
in mass and color treatment, the sole purpose of
designing housing for merchandising is lost."
(*Southwest Builder and Contractor,* Nov. 28,
1947).
   A year later across the street (Martin
Luther King Boulevard), the architect Albert B.
Gardner designed the **Broadway-Crenshaw
Department Store** in 1948. This, too, was
Modern in architectural image and also faced
onto its parking lot to the west. Other stores
were provided with the department store,
including a **Vons Super Market**, designed by
Stiles Clements in 1947–48.

25. Baldwin Hills Shopping Center, 1954
   Robert E. Alexander
   Southwest corner of La Brea Avenue and
   Rodeo Road
A small, neighborhood shopping center
directed primarily to the residences of nearby
Baldwin Hills Village. Changes in shop fronts
and signage have tended to destroy its unity of
design.

26. Baldwin Hills Village, 1940–41
   Reginald D. Johnson, Wilson and Merrill,
   Robert E. Alexander; Clarence S. Stein,
   consultant and site planner; Fred Barlow
   and Fred Edmunson, landscape architects
   5300 Rodeo Road
At the time it was built, and in the years which
have followed, Baldwin Hills Village has continually been mentioned as a successful example
of multiple medium-density housing. The
project was an excellent solution to group
housing. Two-story units are arranged around
open, well-landscaped spaces which lead into
the central tri-part village green. In addition,
each of the units has its own small, walled
courtyard, which helps to separate the buildings
even further from the more public open spaces.
Parking and garage courts were laid out on the
edge of the site, and near the center are the

26. Baldwin Hills Village, 1940–41

clubhouse and the offices. The buildings' low-pitched, hipped roofs are neutral in design, and it is the trees, shrubs, grass, and flowers which dominate. Recently the project has been turned into a condominium, with individual ownership of each unit.

27. University Elementary School, 1948; 1950
    Robert E. Alexander
    Northwest corner of Rodeo Road and
    Hauser Boulevard
Post-and-beam Modern of the 1950s. A good example of the indoor/outdoor classroom building.

28. 8522 National Building, 1986–90
    Eric Owen Moss
    8522 National Boulevard
The architect has remodeled a group of warehouse buildings into an office complex. The complex centers on an interior covered street which meanders through the buildings. The entrance is emphasized by a semicircular open court. Games of high-tech—as structure with materials—occur throughout the project.

29. Paramount Laundry Building, 1987–89
    3960 Ince Boulevard
Lindeblade Tower, 1987–89
    3962 Ince Boulevard
Gary Group Office Building, 1988–90
    9046 Lindblade Street
    Eric Owen Moss
    Southeast corner Ince
    Boulevard and Lindblade
    Street
All three of these adjoining projects utilize portions of older industrial buildings, but they all transform parts of their exteriors and completely revamp the interior space. Serious play is the game in both buildings. Traditionally inspired forms (and references to history) occur in odd and strange places and are countered by fragmented elements of constructivism. The entrance on Lindeblade Street to the Gary Group building conveys the feeling of a high-diving board from which one can plunge to the pavement below. Within the three buildings there are complex arrangements of corridors as streets, interior light courts, and dramatic (via light and forms) endings of passages.

30. Two Retail Commercial Buildings, circa 1934
    4500 block of West Adams Boulevard,
    north of Wellington Road
Two Moderne commercial buildings, more Art Deco (Zigzag) Moderne than Streamline Moderne. Each has a corner tower and splendid cast-concrete (Zigzag) Moderne ornament.

31. Kings Tropical Inn Restaurant Building, 1925
    5879 Washington Boulevard
A domed Islamic building which one supposes was intended to signify the exotic and faraway lands of the tropics.

29. Paramount Laundry Building, 1987–89

29. Gary Group Office Building, 1988–90

32. Tisch/Avnet Building, 1991
    Frank D. Israel design associates
    3815 Hughes Avenue
A new steel-and-glass canopy entrance leads
into the frame of an existing four-
story building. From the entry, one
comes into an interior street
(defined by a long curved wall). At
the center of this street is an oculus.
At right angles to the main street is
a secondary passage which leads
into a three-story conference room.
Certainly one of the most impressive studies in spatial sequences to
be designed in recent years.

33. Helms Bakery Building, 1930
    E. L. Bruner
    8800 Venice Boulevard
The vocabulary of the PWA
Moderne (in this case pre-PWA)
realized in an extensive two-story
building. Now missing is the regimented row of precisely trimmed
shrubs in front of the building and
the central rooftop sign advertising
Helms Olympic Bread.

31. Kings Tropical Inn Restaurant Building, 1925

37. Ship's Culver City Restaurant, 1957

34. La Casa de Rocha, 1865
2400 Shenandoah Street
This story-and-a-half adobe ranch house is surrounded on three sides by a covered corridor. The upper walls of the building are sheathed in shiplap siding.

35. Thomas Ince Studio Building (now
Grayson Potchuck Products), 1915
9336 W. Washington Boulevard
The offices of a motion picture company now poses as its own stage set—in this case a Colonial Revival southern plantation house. The colonnaded two-story porch remains as a free-standing screen in front of a newer building. This was the first major studio building to be constructed in Culver City.

36. Culver Theater, circa 1950
Southeast corner of West Washington
Boulevard and Duquesne Avenue
A post-World War II theater where the facade ends up being all sign. Its design is both Moderne and Baroque (à la Hollywood).

37. Ship's Culver City Restaurant, 1957
Martin Stern, Jr.
Northwest corner of Washington Boulevard and Overland Avenue

Another still-standing Los Angeles coffeehouse of the 1950s. The usual low-pitched, hovering, hipped roof shelters the building below. A composition of wood, stone, and gravel roof. Ship's sign, contained within a circular disk, is accompanied by an angled V, suggesting that a rocket has started its flight.

38. Murphy Buick Showroom and Garage,
circa 1949
A. Quincy Jones
9099 Washington Boulevard
This lively late-1940s Moderne assemblage remains intact, including its wonderful signage. A surprising, but very well carried out, popular image by one of L.A.'s exponents of high art modernism.

**39. Citizen Publishing and Printing
Company Building,** 1929
9355 Washington Boulevard
The pylon-like entrance facade (as an impressive stage set) contains a deep, arched opening, accompanied by classic Art Deco ornamentation.

39. Citizen Publishing and Printing Company Building, 1929

**40. Los Angeles Pacific
Railroad Company,
Ivy Park Substation**
(later **Pacific Electric
Culver Substation**),1907
Northwest corner of
Venice and Culver
boulevards

The Mission Revival image
for a small, single-story
substation. The substation
has now (1992) been
restored, and a small park
has been laid out around it.

40. Los Angeles Pacific Railroad Company, Ivy Park Substation (later Pacific Electric Culver Substation), 1907

**41. Sony Pictures
Entertainment, Child
Care Center,** 1993–94
3845 Clarington Avenue
**Sony Pictures
Entertainment, Digital
Production Building**,
1993–94
10101 Washington Boulevard
Steven Ehrlich Architects; Campbell and
Campbell, landscape architects

For the Child Care Center the architect has
developed a curved masonry wall that supports
the exposed glue lam beams. The undulating
roof establishes the scale and character of the
building. The design is such that, most of the
time, the building can be cooled by natural ventilation. Next door, the Digital Production
Building poses as a miniature castle with corner
towers. It, too, uses curved glue lam beams for
the roof. A large monitor unit on the roof seems
almost to be a distant building. Both the Digital
Production Building and the Child Care Center
are entered through gateways which bring one
into protected inner courts.

42. Garden Apartment Buildings, circa 1925
3819–3825 Dunn Drive

A Medieval fairy-tale world of Hansel and
Gretel cottages in a witch-infested jungle with
pools of water. It is delightfully unbelievable
that it is situated here, only a block from the
center of Culver City.

**43. MGM Studios (Goldwyn Studios)
Building,** 1938–39
Claude Beelman
East corner of Washington Boulevard and
Overland Avenue

The Beaux Arts in the guise of the monumental
PWA Moderne. Rounded corners and decorative panels of concrete make it as official as
any governmental building. The studios were
established at this location in 1923, and there
are both pre- and post-1938 buildings on the
site. The 1923 building is an impressive, classical, columned structure just northeast of the
corner of Washington Boulevard and Overland
Avenue.

44. St. Augustine Roman Catholic Church,
1956–57
J. Earl Trudeau
Northeast corner of Washington Boulevard
and Jasmine Avenue

A Gothic revival church in revealed concrete
with the usual horizontal board patterns as a
surface. All the details are treated in a highly
simplified manner. Within, reinforced-concrete
ribs rise from the floor to support the gabled
roof.

BRENTWOOD

Originally part of the Rancho San Vicente y Santa Monica, modern Brentwood began when the Western Pacific Development Company acquired the land in the early 1900s and named it Brentwood Park. In 1906 the company platted the lots and streets in a manner consciously modeled on the plan of Golden Gate Park in San Francisco. The area, bounded on the east by 26th Street, on the west by Cliffwood Avenue, on the south by San Vicente Boulevard, and on the north by the Santa Monica Mountains was intended, from the first, to be the home of the upper crust of society. It was determinedly residential, with 34 traffic circles interrupting the flow of rapid transit. All but seven of the circles have been eliminated by progress.

Our listing includes the area east to the San Diego Freeway. Originally this was part of the Bel Air District developed in the same period by Alphonzo Bell, Sr. Bell, an early alumnus of Occidental College, for some reason decided to separate his historically coeducational college into men's and women's divisions. The women were to remain in Eagle Rock, and the men moved to Bel Air, not far from where UCLA was soon to settle. The old grads and students were generally disgusted with Bell's idea, and nothing came of it except the name "Tigertail Road" in honor of the Oxy Tigers. His real estate, on both sides of the present freeway, sold well. Like Brentwood Park, it was bought by the upper-middle to upper-upper classes. By and large, the former class hired the better architects.

The new art museum and research center for the **J. Paul Getty Center for the Fine Arts** is now under construction (1992–94) on the high hills just northwest of the junction of Sunset Boulevard and the San Diego Freeway.

Entrance to the museum will be via Getty Center Drive, just off of Sepulveda Boulevard, west of the San Diego Freeway. From a short list composed of Richard Meier, James Stirling, and Fumihiko Maki, the museum selected Meier to design their building. There was some hope that this conservative choice might have led to a sensitively sited complex, and a building which somehow expressed L.A.'s architectural tradition. Such does not seem to have been the case. The buildings in the complex are typical of Meier and would seem to have little to do with Southern California. Even more regrettable has been the insensitive approach to the landscape. In the fashion of an L.A. developer of the 1950s, the hilltops have been leveled off, arroyos filled, and a long, high, insensitively designed wall lines the roadway which scars the hillside as it winds its way up to the complex. This all adds up to the classic environmental arrogance which one associates with so much of the International Style Modern of this century. Those who admire Meier's work will, we assume, applaud this grandiose production; others will obviously have serious design and environmental reservations. By far, the most revealing critical look at the complex is Aaron Betsky's "Shambles Instead of Shangri-La" (*L.A. Architect,* December 1991).

1. Sawtelle Veterans Hospital
Wilshire Boulevard and Sawtelle Avenue
Technically, this is not in Brentwood, but it is so near that it makes a good starting point. It was founded in the 1880s—one of the first veterans' hospitals opened after the Civil War. Regrettably the old buildings, called Domiciliaries, have been destroyed. They were excellent examples of Shingle-style resort architecture. Little remains of the old hospital. The picturesque wooden **Chapel** (1900) is

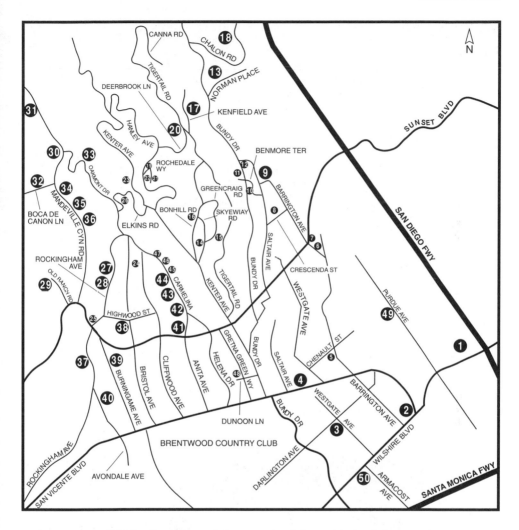

easily seen from Wilshire. Its architect, J. Lee Burton, mixed the Colonial Revival with Gothicism. The same architect designed a tiny Street-car Station (circa 1900) at the corner of Dewey and Pershing, north of the chapel. The station, all arches and posts, is not really Eastlake, but the feeling is.

2. World Savings Center Building, 1982
Maxwell Starkman and Associates
Northwest corner of Wilshire and San Vicente boulevards

A tall, late example of Corporate International Style Modern of no great distinction, but it is so big that you will wonder about it.

3. Four Apartment Units, 1966
J. R. Davidson
955 Westgate Avenue at Darlington Avenue
Naturally stained, diagonal flush boards mark this assemblage.

4. Abell Office Building, 1954
    T. M. Abell
    654 S. Saltair Avenue
This building, though visible, makes its statement from the interior court rather than the street facade. Offices and drafting rooms open into a garden.

5. Shairer House, 1949
    Ain, Johnson, and Day
    11750 Chenault Street
Very Neutraesque, though, as we have noted, the members of the Los Angeles school constantly exchanged ideas, making the subject of influences often beside the point.

6. Shopping Center, circa 1935
    Barrington Avenue and Sunset Boulevard
Mainly Spanish Colonial Revival and dominated by a huge service station with tower. Many a Pierce-Arrow tanked up here on the way to the Hollywood studios.

7. Eastern Star Home, 1931–33
    William Mooser and Company
    11725 Sunset Boulevard
You can see a few pieces here and there of this firm's somewhat earlier Santa Barbara Courthouse, but it lacks the finesse of its northern relative. The huge concrete corbels are grained and painted to resemble wood.

8. Goss House, 1950
    Milton H. Caughey
    11731 Crescenda Street
Understated vertical board and batten with the ends of the roof beams projecting.

9. House, circa 1928
    Northeast corner of Saltair and Barrington avenues
Obviously a work of one of the better architects, this Spanish Revival house dominates its neighborhood.

10. Evans House, 1936
    Lloyd Wright
    12036 Benmore Terrace
Big but less ornamented than most of Wright's work, this house can be seen from 554 N. Bundy Drive below and from its entrance on Benmore.

11. Samuel House, 1934
    Lloyd Wright
    579 N. Bundy Drive
The Bundy facade is saved from austerity by lush foliage. Strangely, the eaves at the side, which are carried into a sort of trellis, do not hold vines.

12. Leslie House, 1950
    Thornton M. Abell
    525 N. Saltair Avenue

As usual, the garage is the street facade, and the International Style Modern house is set below street level.

13. Wyle Guest House, 1983
    Tedesco Architects
    (Lorenzo C. Tedesco)
    1043 Norman Place
A contemporary version of the traditional Japanese farm and tea house, handsomely realized.

7. Eastern Star Home, 1931–33

14. Sturges House, 1939

14. Sturges House, 1939
Frank Lloyd Wright
449 Skyewiay Road
Cantilevered from the hill, this house seems windowless from the street side, although all the major rooms open through glass doors to the balcony deck. It is, of course, one of Wright's monuments. The house is really quite small, some 1,200 square feet, but its open plan and bank of glass doors that lead onto the 21-foot-wide extended deck make it seem large. A roof terrace occurs at the top of the house and, as with most Wright houses of these years, a carport occurs at the rear (which is the entrance to the house).

15. House, 1973–74
Lomax-Mills Associates
548 Greencraig Road
The stucco volume has been dramatically cut into by deep, rectangular openings.

16. Herman House, 1948
Carl Louis Maston
650 Bonhill Road
A good International Style Modern house.

17. Bernheim House, 1961
Raymond Kappe
1000 Kenfield Avenue
A fine essay in fragile wood and glass.

18. Mount St. Mary's College, 1930–
Mark Daniels (1930–31); M. L. Barker and G. Lawrence Ott, 1939–40 and later
12001 Chalon Road
The design theme of these buildings is Hispanic. Bardy Hall, designed during 1930–31 by Mark Daniels, has the feeling of a small Spanish palace; and as with all of this architect's work, it fits itself beautifully into its hillside site. In 1939 Barker and Otto projected a chapel and faculty building which was of "Spanish Gothic Design."

19. Gould House, 1969
Raymond Kappe
12256 Canna Road
Again, glass and wood prevail in this house with stylistic affinities to Schindler's Wolfe House on Santa Catalina Island.

20. Shoor House, 1952
William S. Beckett
12336 Deerbrook Lane
Trim International Style Modern.

21. Mutual Housing Association Community, 1947–50
Whitney Smith, A. Quincy Jones, and Edgardo Contini; James Charlton, Wayne R. Williams and Associates, and Garrett Eckbo, landscape architects.
Hanley Avenue at Rochedale Way
The community comprises a number of houses, some now remodeled. We picked out 717, 727, 738, and 743 Hanley Avenue and 12404, 12408, 12414, and 12428 Rochedale Way as exemplary and visible. There are others on Broom Way and Bramble Way. The community remains a remarkable social, planning, and architectural development by three of Los Angeles's most important architectural figures. The informal siting and the woodsy detail suggest the Bay tradition and Frank Lloyd Wright.

22. Lotery House, 1962
Rex Lotery
1007 Hanley Avenue
This house effectively presents a composition of thin volumes of glass and wood, over which has been delicately placed a thin roof slab, which terminates in an open sunscreen. On the garden side of the house, a broad glass wall opens onto a wood-sheathed balcony.

23. Rodes House, 1978–79
  Moore, Ruble, and Yudell
  1406 N. Kenter Avenue, north end of
  pavement
Moore says that this stucco box was based on
ideas the architects had in their minds of "modernized eighteenth century houses in the south
of France," i.e., Moore's version of the
Hollywood Regency. It has a two-story convex
facade that acts as a stage set for the owner's
amateur theatrical productions.

24. Epstein House, 1949
  Craig Ellwood
  401 N. Cliffwood Avenue
A redwood facade by an architect who was
soon to turn to glass, steel, and brick for
building materials.

25. House, circa 1972
  Northwest corner of Rockingham and
  Burlingame avenues
A house with huge wooden shafts pointing sky-
ward. It must be very dramatic inside.

26. Rich House, 1968
  T. M. Abell
  689 Elkins Road

Unfenestrated stucco walls, broken only by a
simple door. Pure architecture.

27. Avery House, 1934–37
  Lloyd Wright
  365 N. Rockingham Avenue
A pyramid!

28. Temple House, 1935–36
  John Byers (with Edla Muir); Benjamin
  Morton Purdy, landscape architect
  231 N. Rockingham Avenue
This mixture of English and Norman farmhouse
is a real delight. There is a fair view of it from
the entrance gate and a view of an amusing
fragment from Sunset Boulevard below.

29."Mandalay" Cliff May House, 1951–80
  Cliff May
  220 Old Ranch Road
Regrettably, the only element visible from the
public road is the gatehouse. The house itself is
a large-scale ranch house, which was continually being enlarged and remodeled. It began as
a modernist version of a ranch house, and then
in later years, May returned to a more traditional image. As with all of his work, the interior spaces of the house move easily outward

28. Temple House, 1935–36

onto courtyards and terraces. There are a number of Cliff May's smaller ranch houses which can be seen alongside of Old Ranch Road and along the nearby Mandeville Canyon Road. Most of them have been remodeled and enlarged over the years.

30. Rex House #1, 1949
    Edla Muir; Edward Huntsman-Trout, landscape architect
    1888 Mandeville Canyon Road
The feeling is that of an updated Craftsman dwelling, somewhat in the same fashion as one would find in the architecture of San Francisco's Bay tradition during the 1940s and 1950s. The motor court is especially handsome.

31. Rex House #2, 1955
    John Rex
    1900 Mandeville Canyon Road
Orientalism seen through the eye of an International Style Modern architect.

32. Lassoff House, 1989
    Rex Lotery
    13151 Boca de Canon Lane
As in other designs by this architect, the layered effect of roofs is achieved via assertive fascias. In this house he has countered this horizontality by tall V-shaped skylights and by a metal and glass constructivism which faces onto the garden at an upper level. From the street one can see how the architect has made dramatic the series of stepped volumes which work their way up the hillside.

33. Rosen House, 1962
    Craig Ellwood Associates
    910 Oakmont Drive
This was new when our first architecture guide was written. We put a picture of it on the cover. Now the foliage has grown up, mostly obscuring the building. You can still catch a glimpse from the road before you reach the gate.

34. Sperry House, 1953
    Wurster, Bernardi, and Emmons
    2090 Mandeville Canyon Road
A rational, post-and-beam house, rather L.A. in spirit, though by a Bay Area firm.

35. Siple House, 1949–59
    Allen Siple
    2669 Mandeville Canyon Road
This dressed-stone house, obviously a labor of love, was constructed by the architect and his wife, aided by neighbors.

36. Seidel House, 1960
    Pierre Koenig
    2727 Mandeville Canyon Road
Two small Miesian pavilions, delicately articulated, compose this Case Study House.

37. Johnson House, 1919
    Harry Johnson assisted by John Byers;
    Edward Huntsman-Trout,
    landscape architect
    201 S. Rockingham Road
Byers, Harry Johnson's cousin, employed Mexican laborers to make the adobe bricks for the walls of this Spanish Colonial Revival house. It was landscaped with native plants, which have all but obscured the view.

38. Siskin House, 1966
    Thornton M. Abell
    12822 Highwood Street
Set far back from one of the original Brentwood circles, this International Style house contrasts with its wooded environment.

39. Newfield House, 1961
    T. M. Abell
    250 S. Burlingame Avenue
Buff-colored, Roman-laid brick. We thought that the art of the mason was fast disappearing, but here it is in wonderful shape.

40. Nesbitt House, 1942
    Richard J. Neutra
    414 Avondale Avenue
The Nesbitt house marks an early excursion by Neutra into warm, non-machine materials: wood and brick. Unfortunately for the architecture buff, few of its features can be seen from the street.

Carmelina Avenue
There is a series of fascinating houses on Carmelina Avenue just below its intersection with Anita, continuing south to San Vicente Boulevard. The best have been selected for listing here.

42. Hamilton House, 1931–33

41. Boland House, circa 1925
John Byers (with Edla Muir)
12322–12323 Helena Drive
One of Byers's picturesque Spanish Colonial
adventures!

42. Hamilton House, 1931–33
John Byers (with Edla Muir)
193 N. Carmelina Avenue
Monterey Revival.

43. Stedman House, 1935–36
John Byers (with Edla Muir)
363 N. Carmelina Avenue
A path leads from a typical Byers gate through
carefully clipped boxwood hedges to the
Colonial Revival front door.

44. Zimmerman House, 1950
Craig Ellwood
400 N. Carmelina Avenue
An interruption in the Byers boutique. A stark
brick wall faces the street—the beginning of an
L-shaped house which immediately breaks into
glass and steel.

45. Kerr House, 1930
John Byers (with Edla Muir)
428 North Carmelina Avenue
A very different version of the Monterey
Revival when compared with the Hamilton
House.

46. Murray House, circa 1935
John Byers (with Edla Muir)
436 North Carmelina Avenue
Colonial Revival.

47. Schnabel House, 1986-89
Frank O. Gehry and Associates
526 North Carmelina Avenue
Gehry describes this residence as a "Village-
like arrangement of forms." Perhaps it would
be more appropriate to respond to it as a series
of sculptural follies within a Southern
California garden. At the garden side of the
house, these forms sink into what appears to be
a large lake. Regrettably, all that one can see
(but it is still well worth a look) are the metal
sheathed cubes above the entry, dining room,
and library, and then the most dramatic of all,
the Islamic dome over the living room.

48. Drucker Apartments, 1940
J. R. Davidson
Northwest corner of Gretna Green Way and
Dunoon Lane
A curious blending of Schindler and Gill,
though the greatest influence was the
International Style Modern.

49. "Gerb in California" Houses, 1990
David Ming-Li Lowe
1955 Purdue Avenue
Two steel-frame structures are floated on specially designed isolated bases to resist earthquakes. This technology was developed in
Germany and is now being applied to American
buildings by "Gerb in California." The resulting structures are, as you would expect, High
Tech.

50. Armacost Duplex, 1989–90
Rebecca L. Bender
1224 Armacost Avenue
The architect has fitted two 1,500-square-foot
units onto a narrow 25-foot lot. The design
makes it possible for the living areas of the two
units to face onto their own internal patio/deck.
The various volumes of the building assert their
independence via different materials—split
block below, then stucco and fiberboard siding.

BEL AIR

his hilly area above UCLA was developed by Alphonzo Bell in the teens and obviously sold well in the 1920s. It is the last word in respectability, having its own security patrol years before other highbrow enclaves felt the need. It is a gorgeously landscaped area. The entrance to Bel Air is through imposing gates at

Bel Air, Stone Canyon, and Bellagio roads. Much of the planning during the 1920s was by architect Mark Daniels (Elmer Grey Associates), who also designed the **Administration Building** (circa 1928) on Stone Canyon Road just north of the intersection with Bellagio. It is a handsome building of white walls and red tile roofs whose plan focuses on two patios.

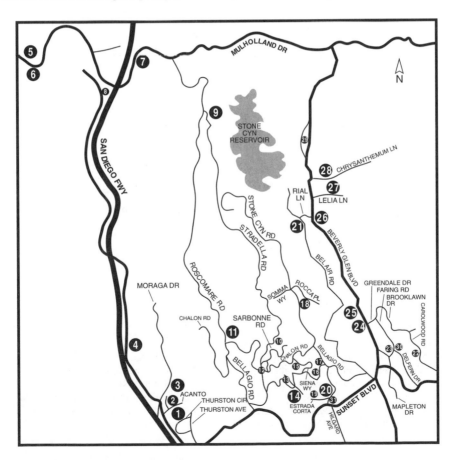

The large and small estates exude wealth, not by the imposing facades (most of which you cannot see), but by beautifully trimmed plantings, literally inundating the sumptuous dwellings. Foliage hides residences by George Washington Smith (his only one in West Los Angeles), Gordon B. Kaufmann, Wallace Neff, Roy Selden Price, Palmer Sabin, Douglas Honnold, George Vernon Russell, Paul R. Williams, and Paul Laszlo. The following list only hints at what is hidden away.

1. Nordlinger House, 1948
A. Quincy Jones
11492 Thurston Circle
Very much under the influence of Frank Lloyd Wright.

2. Winans Apartments (now **Bel Air Gardens**), 1948
A. Quincy Jones
850 Moraga Drive
The jutting roofs are very dramatic.

3. Zeigler House, 1952
Paul Sterling Hoag
1060 Acanto Street
A graceful post-World War II California Ranch house. A low-pitched hipped roof shelters the redwood walls below. Nature, by way of large sycamore trees, dominates the site and house.

4. Leo Baeck Temple, 1962
Victor Gruen Associates
1300 N. Sepulveda Boulevard
A series of apparently thick walls of varying shapes and a great hood of a roof enclose the space of the sanctuary. It all reads well, especially from the San Diego Freeway.

5. Bel Air Presbyterian Church, 1991
Moore, Ruble, and Yudell
16221 Mulholland Drive (west of the San Diego Freeway)
Presbyterians are not supposed to have cathedrals, but this church ranks close to what the Catholics and Episcopalians have produced. Romanesque and Gothic elements have been woven together with some spectacular structural effects as only Charles Moore can manage them.

6. Mirman School, 1972–73
Brent, Goldman, Robbins, and Brown
16180 Mulholland Drive (west of San Diego Freeway, just beyond Mulholland Place)
A good-looking group of stucco buildings obviously influenced by Charles Moore—a good influence.

7. Steven S. Wise Temple, Chapel and School Facilities, 1975
Sidney Eisenstadt
North corner of Mulholland Drive and Casiano Road (east of San Diego Freeway)
Very impressive Expressionism with great, leaning roofs.

8. Singleton House, 1959
Richard J. Neutra
15000 Mulholland Drive, east of Woodcliff Road
Completely private, almost impossible to see that it is there.

9. Rabinowitz House, 1960
J. R. Davidson
2262 Stradella Road
A major design by one of L.A.'s most important modern architects. Most of this architect's houses are either well hidden from public view, or have been remodeled. What a pleasure to actually be able to see an International Style Modern house by this architect.

10. Chappellett House, circa 1925
H. Roy Kelley
848 Stradella Road
A beautiful Monterey Revival dwelling in a style of which Kelley was a master.

11. Beck House, 1955
Thornton M. Abell
952 Roscomare Road
With flush, horizontal wood boards, this house still looks brand new.

12. Brown House, 1955
Richard J. Neutra; Dion Neutra
10801 Chalon Road
A steep hillside house of stucco and redwood, just barely visible from the road.

13. Anderson House, 1951
   Honnold and Rex
   621 Perugia Way
International Style Modern with Las Vegas
stone base.

14. Healy House, 1949-52
   Lloyd Wright
   565 Perugia Way
The Usonian House updated as a California
Ranch house with a little Orientalism added.

15. Norcross House, 1927
   Roland E. Coate
   673 Siena Way
A beautiful Monterey Revival dwelling which
opens onto a high-walled auto court.

16. Japanese Garden, 1961
   Nagao Sakurai, designer, assisted by
   Dudley Fridgett; Kazuo Nakamura, con-
   struction
   Bellagio Road, west of intersection with
   Stone Canyon Road
The original garden was designed and laid out by
A. E. Hanson for Harry Calendar in 1923. At that
time it was picturesque Spanish, not Japanese. It
was transformed into a Japanese garden in 1961.
This beautiful hillside was given to UCLA in
1965. It may be visited 10:00 A.M.–1:00 P.M.,
Tuesday and 12 noon–3:00 P.M., Wednesday, by
calling the UCLA Visitors Center.

17. Miller House, 1932
   Wallace Neff
   10615 Bellagio Road
An enlarged, two-story English cottage with
some inklings of Charles F. A. Voysey's turn-
of-the-century work in England.

18. Nilsson House, 1977
   Eugene Kupper
   10549 Rocca Place (can be seen only from
   end of Somma Way)
An elongated, two-story, skylighted spine
serves as the core of this dwelling. Although
the spaces and their relation to one another are
complex, the general atmosphere of the house
is Classical and Mediterranean. The garden
walls and terraces beautifully integrate the
house to its hillside site.

19. Kranz House, 1989–91
   Barton Phelps and Associates
   245 Estrada Corta
A 1950s California ranch house was removed
and replaced by the present dwelling, which
essentially utilizes the old foundation. A garage
was projected to the street, helping to enclose a
motor court. As in the original house, an angled
living room acts as a hinge between the two
wings of the house. Simple surfaces and geometry dominate the design. A focal point of this
geometry is the tall, canted chimney behind the
glass courtyard entrance.

20. Curtis-Noyes House, 1950
   Raphael S. Soriano
   111 Stone Canyon Road
One of Soriano's largest commissions. About
all that can be seen are the grid-motif garages.

21. Case Study House #16, 1951
   Craig Ellwood
   1811 Bel Air Road
A steel-frame Miesian exercise based upon
eight-foot modules. The infills are of Palos
Verdes stone, wood siding, and glass.

22. Gordon B. Kaufmann House, circa 1929
   Gordon B. Kaufmann; Florence Yoch,
   landscape architect
   245 Carolwood Drive
Mediterranean (Italian) style with Spanish
Colonial aspects, this is much warmer than
most of Kaufmann's houses. The house is close
to the street and beautifully landscaped. Just
below at 230 Carolwood Drive is the **Lohman
House** (1925), also by Kaufmann, in a version
of the Tudor style.

23. Colbert House, 1935
   Lloyd Wright
   615 N. Faring Road
Here Lloyd Wright brings together the
Moderne and the Anglo-Colonial Revival.

24. Broughton House, 1950
Craig Ellwood
909 N. Beverly Glen Boulevard
Modular design, midway between traditional post-and-beam and the insistent Miesian steel beam.

25. Bernatti House, 1947
Rodney Walker
1025 N. Beverly Glen Boulevard
A simple frame structure. You can see the garage best.

26. Lohrie House, 1940
Rodney Walker
1648 Beverly Glen Boulevard
The traditional California Ranch house emerging as a Moderne product with corner windows, sliding glass doors, and extending and overlapping horizontal planes.

27. Phelps-Simonson House, 1981–85
Barton Phelps and Associates
10256 Lelia Lane
One of those creative Los Angeles designs for what would appear to be an impossible site. An arroyo runs through the center of the site, so the house simply bridges over it. The house has a slight feeling of historicism, in this case, what has been labeled Caribbean Colonial. The fenestration is reserved and classical in spirit; the parapeted gable ends and round windows put it into what one could think of as mild-mannered Post Modernism. Internally, the centerpiece is the platformed staircase which takes you to the top of the house.

28. Johnson House, 1949
Harwell H. Harris
10280 Chrysanthemum Lane
Here Harris simplifies and opens up the woodsy style of Charles and Henry Greene to terraces and gardens.

29. Sommer House, 1941
Rodney Walker
2252 Beverly Glen Place
Related to the 1930s San Francisco Bay tradition designs of William W. Wurster, Gardner Dailey, and others.

30. Singleton House, 1973
Wallace Neff
384 Delfern Drive, corner of Faring Road
A French Norman house.

31. House, circa 1926
Northeast corner of Sunset Boulevard and Stone Canyon Road
A splendid Moorish/Spanish house with an abundance of colorful tile work and an impressive, cusped arch loggia looking to the south. The garden, with its terraces, fountains, and water course, is Moorish as well. From time to time in its existence, this house has been highly visible from Sunset Boulevard; on other occasions little could be seen. At the moment, it is as visible as it has ever been.

WESTWOOD, WEST

Westwood was developed by the Janss Investment Company during the early 1920s. The business center of Westwood was designed in 1928 by Leon Deming Tilton, the West Coast representative of the firm of Harland Bartholomew of St. Louis. Janss also prevailed upon the University of California to relocate its "Southern Branch"—UCLA—just north of the business center.

As with many of the new communities established in the 1920s in California, the design of the buildings was reviewed by an art jury. In an article on the village published in the *Architect and Engineer* in 1930, it was noted that "The founders of Westwood Village did not permit, and still do not permit, the erection of any building of any kind whatsoever that does not fit into the picture. The new city is almost entirely constructed of the best type of Mediterranean architecture."

By the end of the decade, the area was composed of upper-middle class, single-family residences, with streets laid out in part to conform to

the irregular pattern of the hilly terrain. In the center was the new UCLA campus, and to the south around Wilshire and Westwood boulevards, was Westwood Village. Many upper-middle class, single-family houses utilized one or another of the historic images—Spanish Colonial Revival, Mediterranean, Monterey

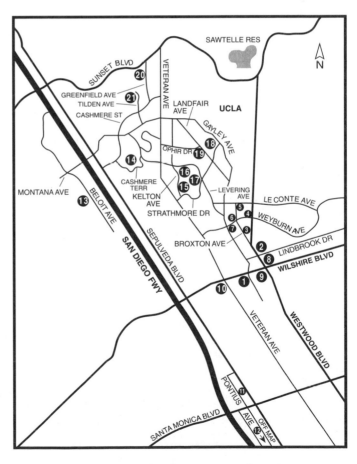

Revival, English and Norman Medieval, the Colonial and Regency. Since the late 1940s, a smattering of Modern housing of one variety or another has been built. Highly respectable, multiple housing developed around the Village, along Wilshire Boulevard and to the east of the UCLA campus (around Landfair Avenue and Strathmore Drive). The quality of these historic-styled houses and apartments is remarkably high, and the buildings, coupled with the quality of the landscaping, make this section one of the most pleasant in L.A.

Before the advent of high-rises around **Westwood Village,** it was one of Southern California's most successful regional suburban shopping centers. The Mediterranean image continued to be used (with some instances of Regency and Streamline Moderne) through the early 1940s. Later remodelings, modernizations, and replacements have somewhat compromised its original character. Probably the greatest losses have been the several Mediterranean-image service stations with their high towers and illuminated signs.

Beginning in the early 1960s, the scale of Westwood Village was challenged (if not to a considerable degree destroyed) by the construction, one after another, of high-rise buildings along Wilshire Boulevard. The earliest of these was designed by such well-known Southern California architects as Claude Beelman, while some of the latest have been projected or built by Eastern name-brand firms.

These include:

1. 10940 Wilshire Tower, 1988
Murphy/Jahn Architects
10940 Wilshire Boulevard
Center West, 1989–90,
Mitchell/Giurgola Architect with
DMJM and Edgardo Cantini
10877 Wilshire Boulevard
Ashton Towers, 1989
Robbins and Brown, Inc., Architects
10930 S. Ashton Avenue
All of these (as well as other buildings) have contributed to the destruction of the scale of the village (and of the residential areas to the northeast), and none have turned out to be

particularly distinguished buildings. There are to be no more high-rises added to this area (the 23-story Center West Building supposedly being the last), which one should be glad for, but still the urban damage has been done.

Since the mid-1980s, when the battle against high-rise was going full steam, there has been a continual urge to somehow revitalize and return Westwood to its original Mediterranean atmosphere. One can only hope that this will come about now in the 1990s, but if it does occur, it will be because social changes have taken place, not primarily because of the acts of planners.

2. Ralph's Grocery Store Building (now a restaurant), 1929
Russell Collins
1150 Westwood Boulevard
Colonnades, extending along the two streets, culminate in a low corner round tower, into which has been placed an impressive, pedimented entrance. The entablature of the tower has a band of corbeled arches, and a small lantern tops the conical roof of the tower. The walls were built in imitation of stone, but they have now been stuccoed over. In style the building is Spanish, both Romanesque and Renaissance.

3. "The Dome" Offices of the Janss Investment Company (now Glendale Federal Savings Association Building), 1929
Allison and Allison
Northwest corner of Westwood Boulevard and Broxton Avenue
This domed, octagonal building still remains as the dominant structure within the village itself. Though the building is on the dry side, the dome with its Islamic (Zigzag) retrieves it all. The new lantern on top of the dome does not help the composition.

4. Holmby Hall, 1929
Gordon B. Kaufmann, John and Donald Parkinson
West side of Westwood Boulevard between Weyburn and LeConte avenues
A Spanish Colonial Revival streetscape of six stores. The corner building at Weyburn Avenue once had a pinnacled tower with four clock faces.

5. Bruin Theater
    S. Charles Lee
    925 Broxton Avenue
A 1930s Moderne theater whose semicircular facade above the marquee housed a lighted sign to advertise the theater.

6. Fox Westwood Village Theater, 1931
    P. O. Lewis
    961 Broxton Avenue
Like "The Dome," the Fox Theater and its tower turn the axis of Broxton Avenue toward the northeast. The theater is essentially Spanish Colonial Revival with a touch of Moderne. The shaft of the tower rises to support projecting single columns and entablatures. On top, a Fox sign is surrounded by Art Deco (Zigzag) Moderne patterns in metal.

7. Weyburn/Gayley Building, 1990–91
    Kanner Associates
    950 Gayley Avenue
A Post Modern design which fits in with the older buildings of the village. A little too classical in its detailing, but the scale works very well.

8. Armand Hammer Museum of Art and Culture, 1989–90
    Edward Larabee Barnes; John M. Y. Lee and Partners with Gruen Associates
    10899 Wilshire Boulevard at Westwood Boulevard
Barnes has produced a handsome but unassertive building. The walls of the building are banded in dark and light Carrara marble which effectively shuts out the busy external world. A segmented arch on the Lindbrook Drive facade of the building emphasizes a second entrance and also provides a view of the upper-level courtyard. As in Barnes' design for the Walker Art Center in Minneapolis, the gallery spaces inside work well for exhibition purposes, being well proportioned and well lighted by natural and artificial light.

6. Fox Westwood Village Theater, 1931

9. Wilshire West Plaza, 1971
    Charles Luckman Associates
    10880 Wilshire Boulevard
Perhaps adequate as an urban high-rise complex, it is devastating in what it and the other high-rises around have done to destroy the scale of Westwood Village.

10. U.S. Federal Office Building, 1970
    Charles Luckman Associates
    11000 Wilshire Boulevard
An immense file cabinet which one can't miss. As depressing a comment on architecture of the 1970s as it is a condemnation of the bureaucracy of our society.

11. Siskin Companies Office Building, 1972
    Thornton M. Abell
    1617 S. Pontius Avenue
A modest, very-well handled, late version of the *Arts and Architecture* aesthetic.

12. Distribution Station #28, Department of Water and Power, 1945–46
    G. E. Benker, Eng.
    Southeast corner Cotner Street and Missouri Avenue

12. Distribution Station #28, Department of Water and Power, 1945–46

One would assume that this water and power station, which is plainly visible from the San Diego Freeway, was built in the 1930s. Its exposed, reinforced-concrete structure is pure PWA Moderne, with strong references to the Classical tradition and the Art Deco. The rows of piers are part of the adjoining wall surfaces, and ornament occurs only around the entrance.

13. Plywood Model Experimental House, 1936
Richard J. Neutra
427 S. Beloit Avenue
This plywood panel house was designed so that it could easily be transported—and so far, it has been moved twice. In the late 1930s, plywood was just coming into its own. The material conveyed modernity and the image of the machine. Neutra's use of it here fulfills these ideals.

14. Buki House, 1941
J. R. Davidson
11149 Cashmere Terrace
Davidson, operating within the stripped-down Regency mode, which was popular in the Los Angeles region before the Second World War.

15. Kelton Apartments, 1942
Richard J. Neutra
646–648 Kelton Avenue
Five apartments are grouped into two buildings. Each apartment is provided with its own outdoor terrace. The fenestration of the building is less insistently International Style Modern than one experiences in Neutra's earlier (1938) nearby Landfair apartments.

16. Elkay Apartments, 1948
Richard J. Neutra
638-642 Kelton Avenue
A post-World War II extension of his earlier Kelton Apartments next door. The Elkay units are more woodsy and less committed to the image of the machine than the 1942 Kelton units.

17. Strathmore Apartments, 1937
Richard J. Neutra
11005 W. Strathmore Drive
In these apartments Neutra updated the Bungalow Court, providing it with a new image (the Modern), more light and air, and more extensive greenery. These four buildings contain eight apartments which, in part, face out onto the central garden and toward UCLA.

18. Sheets (L'Horizon) Apartments, 1949
John Lautner
10901–10919 W. Strathmore Drive
An eight-unit apartment which suggests the futuristic Modern of the twenty-first century. Visually this building is as fresh today as when it was built. Functionally it is a beautiful solution for multiple housing, with each apartment completely separated from the others, and each with its own terraces, decks, and outdoor garden space—all indicative of Lautner's understanding how people will respond to the Modern, as well as the environment of L.A.

19. Landfair Apartments, 1937
Richard J. Neutra
Southwest corner of Landfair Avenue and Ophir Drive
The Landfair Apartments are one of Neutra's most European International Style Modern designs of the decade of the 1930s. This impressive exercise with its roof terrace is

17. Strathmore Apartments, 1937

composed of patterned surfaces of stucco, metal, and glass bands.

20. Tischler House, 1949
R. M. Schindler
175 Greenfield Avenue

Schindler set a 3-D de Stijl composition as a frontispiece for a stucco, gable-roofed volume. The roof of the house was originally made of corrugated fiberglass, which was to have been shaded by parallel rows of eucalyptus planted along each side of the house.

21. Galli Curci House, 1938
Wallace Neff; Florence Yoch and Lucille Council, landscape architects
201 Tilden Avenue

Neff took the theme of the informal rambling Andalusian farmhouse and produced a stunning composition of white stucco volumes terminated by a tile roof. The result, accompanied by one of his tall, picturesque chimneys, illustrates the vigor of the Hispanic tradition in the late 1930s.

21. Galli Curci House, 1938

WESTWOOD, SOUTH AND EAST

1. Kaufmann House, 1937
  Richard J. Neutra
  234 S. Hilgard Avenue
A beautiful example of Neutra's version of the International Style Modern. In this case the building works not only as a symbol of the machine but also as an excellent "machine for

living." The house takes advantage of its site, with the principal public spaces opening toward the garden, away from the street. The bedrooms on the second floor have glass doors leading onto a roof deck. Glass, brick, stainless steel, and interior mirrors add a Moderne note.

2. St. Alban's Episcopal Church, 1940–later
  P. P. Lewis
  Northeast corner of South Hilgard and Westholme avenues
This early 1940s chapel illustrates how strong and vigorous traditional imagery was in this decade—in this case Romanesque (both Italian and French) in brick, rough mortar, and stone trim. The post-1945 parts of the building do not convey any of the strength of the original. The narthex window was produced by the Judson Studios.

3. Doheny Memorial Dormitory for Girls (now YWCA), 1931
  Stanton, Reed, and Hibbard
  794 Hilgard Avenue
If only the smaller buildings on the UCLA campus could have followed the Monterey tradition expressed in this building, well sited on its hillside lot; the landscaping works with the irregular form of the building to create its own world away from the very busy street.

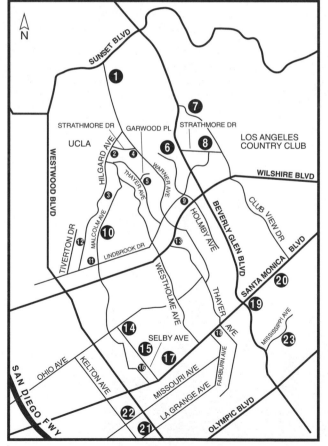

4. Van Cleff House, 1942
    Richard J. Neutra
    651 Warner Avenue
All of the hallmarks of Neutra's Modern image are present in this single-story dwelling, though the roof form and the wood detailing help it to fit in with its neighbors.

5. Greenberg House, 1949
    Richard J. Neutra
    10525 Garwood Place
During the late 1940s Neutra designed several houses with low-pitched shed roofs and walls of stucco and redwood. The Greenberg House exhibits these elements on its hillside site.

6. Dean McHenry House, 1940
    Harwell H. Harris
    624 Holmby Avenue
A two-story stucco dwelling hidden behind a walled enclosure which provides privacy from the street and creates small enclosed garden spaces within. As with many of Harris's dwellings where the garden and the house are really one, we are asked visually to read the dwelling as a series of separate fragments (as with a traditional Japanese house).

7. Mudd House, 1969
    Roland E. Coate, Jr.
    420 Club View Drive
A formal (almost public in scale), wood-sheathed group of pavilions set within a concrete wall and base—a base which has Le Corbusian overtones. The interior spaces and the way in which they extend themselves to the out-of-doors is decidedly axial and Beaux Arts.

8. Maslon House, 1970
    Thornton M. Abell
    10345 Strathmore Drive
A U-shaped stucco volume faces toward the street. To the rear and sides, the interior opens out through glass walls and doors to various terraces and gardens. The atmosphere, though Modern in image, is in fact quite classical.

9. Westwood-Ambassador Apartments, 1940
    Milton J. Black
    10427 Wilshire Boulevard
A textbook image of the Streamline Moderne before the Second World War, this two- and three-story, U-shaped stucco apartment building has horizontal groupings of windows going around the corners, along with curved bays and terraced walls. This architect designed many of Los Angeles's Streamline Moderne apartment buildings of the 1930s.

10. House, circa 1929
    862 Malcolm Avenue
The avenues (not, it should be noted, streets) of Westwood curve in and out of the low hills both east and west of the UCLA campus. They are filled with excellent, well-designed, historic imagery houses of the 1920s and 1930s, all beautifully taken care of, including their grounds. In the 1920s the preference was for Spanish/Mediterranean, English Tudor, and French Norman; in the 1930s it was the Monterey and then the Anglo-Colonial Revival. All of these are present within the eastern section of the Westwood district. These houses illustrate how well the architects of that time could work with traditional images (in this case English Tudor) and at the same time produce a functional house for an upper-middle-class family.

11. Garden Apartment Building, circa 1936
    1001–1009 Malcolm Avenue
Streamline Moderne in a mild manner.

12. Monterey Garden Apartment Building,
    circa 1930
    James N. Conway
    10840 Hilgard Avenue
A two-story garden apartment in the Monterey Style, built around a central court. Another **garden apartment building** is located at 10830 Hilgard Avenue. This one is mildly Spanish Colonial Revival (also circa 1930). South of Wilshire Boulevard at the northeast corner of Westwood Boulevard and Wilkins Avenue is a combined **garden apartment and retail shop,** designed in the Colonial Revival style (circa 1931; J. E. Dolena).

13. Ten-Five-Sixty Wilshire Boulevard, 1980–82
Maxwell Starkman and Associates
10560 Wilshire Boulevard

Wilshire Boulevard between the Los Angeles Country Club to the east and the San Diego Freeway to the west has, since the early 1960s, developed as a high-rise, double-wall corridor of expensive condominium apartment buildings and office towers. It looks great from the air, but its effect on the nearby single-family houses and on Westwood Village itself is devastating. None of the tall apartment buildings or the office towers are outstanding in design, but several of them are so visually aggressive that it is difficult to ignore them. A case in point is this 108-unit, 22-story apartment building. The eight-cornered tower with its crowd of curved balconies does succeed in conveying a sense of transient luxury.

14. Church of St. Paul the Apostle, 1930–31
Newton and Murray
Southeast corner of Ohio and
Selby avenues

A classically reserved design, which the architects say they based on late eighteenth-century Spanish architecture. As with so many of Los Angeles's churches of the late 1920s and early 1930s, it is constructed of reinforced concrete with the exposed surfaces (inside and out) revealing the wood pattern of the forms.

16. Moore/Rogger/Hofflander Condominium Building, 1969–75

15. Ralph Waldo Emerson Junior High School Building, 1937
Richard J. Neutra
1650 Selby Avenue

This is a project which you should walk around and through in order to get an idea of what was going on in the 1930s in school design in California, and how Neutra responded to the California tradition of the open-air school. Though Neutra's image is out-and-out International Style Modern, the plan of the building and of the site is really quite traditional (especially for California). Behind the two-story section of the complex are classrooms which open out to their own individual out-of-doors gardens through sliding glass doors.

16. Moore/Rogger/Hofflander Condominium Building, 1969–75
Charles W. Moore and Richard Chylinski
1725 Selby Avenue

A version of a Spanish Colonial Revival auto court. A ground-level fountain provides the entry theme of this remarkable building. From the street one sees a cascading roof to the north interrupted by stepped dormers. To the south one can see a curved grouping of windows (forming a pattern like spokes of a wheel) that ends in another roof dormer. It is close to impossible to know what is going on inside, which is part of the romance of this design. In fact, it is difficult to know that there are three units in this building. Each of the units faces out to the west, away from the street, and each has walled terraces and balconies.

17. The Los Angeles Temple of The Church of Jesus Christ of Latter-day Saints (Mormon), 1955
Edward O. Anderson
10741 Santa Monica Boulevard

Described by one high-art observer as "Cocktail Lounge Moderne," but it is on a scale which would put any Sunset

Boulevard lounge to shame. The design, in fact, could best be described as modernized Classical. A gold-leaf statue of the angel Moroni graces the summit of the building. As is traditional in the best of L.A.'s public and semi-public buildings, the hilltop site of the Mormon Temple is beautifully landscaped with a precisely manicured lawn and low shrubs. The building and its site form a completely unified composition. The Temple is best seen from the San Diego Freeway.

18. Psychoanalytic Building, 1968–69
  Charles W. Moore and William Turnbull
  1800 Fairburn Avenue
Driving along Little Santa Monica Boulevard, one can easily miss this gem, for its stucco volumes set behind the trees appear right at home in Los Angeles. A complex stage-set gateway composed of a single plane of stucco wall leads into an interior courtyard. Double walls make one wonder what is building and what is screen.

19. "The Grove," Bungalow Court, 1932, 1940
  Allen Siple, Edla Muir
  10500 Santa Monica Boulevard
The front group of bungalows were designed by Allen Siple, while the rear two bungalows were designed in 1940 by Edla Muir. A romantic group of English cottages, actually situated in a thick grove of trees—easily missed if you sail by at thirty-five miles an hour.

20. The Barn, 1965
  A. Quincy Jones
  10300 Santa Monica Boulevard
Quincy Jones's two-and-a-half-story "Barn" served as a place of work, of entertaining, and of living. It is a remodeled structure, though you would not know it once you were inside and able to experience the wonderful central space of the building. As with the best of Quincy Jones's work, it is not openly assertive. But its sense of proportions and detailing make it wear very well.

21. Westwood Hills Congregational Church, 1928
  Northwest corner of Westwood Boulevard and LaGrange Avenue

18. Psychoanalytic Building, 1968–69

A small Spanish Colonial Revival church coupled with some suggestions in detailing of the Art Deco (Zigzag) Moderne.

22. Kelton-Missouri Townhouses, 1980
  Mutlow-Dimster Partnership
  10925 Missouri Avenue
The basic forms of this building look back to the Dutch and German International Style Modern housing of the 1920s. But there are other features, such as the stepped window patterns and the greenhouse elements, which are pure late 1970s and early 1980s.

23. Feitler House, 1993–94
  Siegal Diamond Architects
  10346 Mississippi Avenue
From the street, the visual impact of this dwelling is that of a late 1920s International Style box which has been split open in the middle by a heavy angled solid (very solid) wall and an attached segment of a glass bowl with canted sides. The stucco wall to the left of the entrance exhibits a vertical irregular cut to emphasize even more the split nature of the design. The angled space created by this central wall is a living hall which projects through the whole house and terminates in a private rear terrace.

UCLA

The University of California Los Angeles was established as a State Normal School in 1881 on a five-acre site in downtown L.A., where the Central Los Angeles Public Library is now situated. In 1919 it became a two-year southern campus of UC, and in 1924 it became a four-year school and was named UCLA. The institution's second location, a site at Vermont and Heliotrope avenues, was felt to be far too small for the projected major institution. In 1925 the site in Westwood was selected, and the cities of Los Angeles, Beverly Hills, Santa Monica, and Venice voted bonds to purchase the land. The new campus then became an element within the Janss Corporation development of Westwood. It was to be surrounded by single-family residences (with some multiple housing) on the east, north, and west sides and was to adjoin the commercial district of Westwood Village to the south.

The San Francisco architect George W. Kelham was engaged in 1925 to prepare a master plan for the campus. Two years later Kelham succeeded John Galen Howard as the supervising architect for the University of California, Berkeley campus, and in turn he became the architect for the projected Los Angeles campus. For this hilly site, Kelham developed a dramatic classic cross-axial Beaux Arts scheme. The main axis ran east/west from Hilgard to Westwood

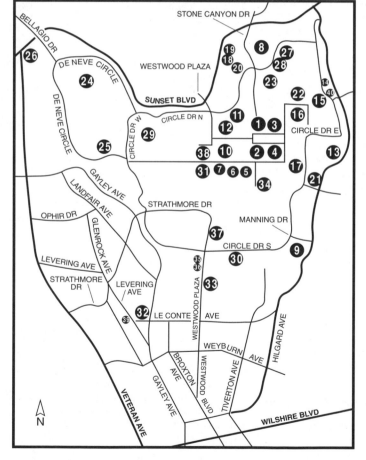

Boulevard. The hilly, irregular site provided the drama of terraces and steps leading down the west side of the hill to Westwood Boulevard. To the east a small arroyo created a contrasting English Romantic garden element, and over this, Kelham placed a bridge (this bridge was the first structure erected on the UCLA Campus; it now lies buried between the north and south sections of the filled-in Dickinson Plaza). A circle on Westwood Boulevard created the major north/south axis.

The architect's initial plan called for forty buildings, and he and the Regents "chose red brick Romanesque architecture of Milan and Genoa because Westwood's rolling hills and gentle climate were reminiscent of northern Italy." The selection of Northern Italian Romanesque for the Westwood campus was not, as the quote would seem to imply, based upon a careful look into appropriate styles. Italian Romanesque in brick was a fashionable style for educational buildings in California during the teens and 1920s. Also, it was the style which had been used in the teens by Allison and Allison for the Vermont Avenue campus of the University ("executed in a style of architecture inspired from the Lombard Romanesque of northern Italy"). By 1932 ten buildings (in addition to the bridge) had been completed at the Westwood campus.

To help create the Italian image, John W. Greg, a well-known Bay area landscape architect and professor of landscape architecture at Berkeley, was engaged to work with Kelham. He presented his plan in 1928, and this was followed through the mid-1930s.

During the depression years of the 1930s, only a few buildings were built. Kelham remained as supervising architect until his death in 1935 when he was replaced by Allison and Allison (David C. Allison). After World War II, David C. Allison and landscape architect Ralph D. Cornell prepared a revision of the Kelham plan. Retaining the essential ingredients of his plan, they still argued for low-rise buildings. They did, though, suggest the filling-in of the arroyo in 1947, which in part now includes Dickson court and plaza, so as to obtain additional building sites. Their most far-

reaching recommendation was to locate the Health Science (Medical School) on the Westwood campus, rather than to separate it as UC Berkeley had done by putting it in San Francisco. This decision and the ideal of having a 25,000-plus student campus eventually led to immense buildings and the commitment to moderate high-rise.

In 1948 the firm of Wurdeman and Becket was appointed as supervising architects (the title was changed to consulting architects). After the death of William Wurdeman, Welton Becket and Associates continued as consulting architects through 1968.

It was during the immediate post-World War II years that the decision was made to abandon the commitment to the historicism of the Northern Italian Romanesque and to embrace the "Modern." At first the Modern was approached in a general but skillful fashion through the style we associated with the designs of Eliel Saarinen. This approach can be seen in such buildings as the first Dickson Art Building (now the School of Architecture and Urban Planning, 1952; Paul Robinson Hunter). Later, variations of the 1950s Corporate International Style Modern were utilized. Today it is very difficult to discover anything positive to say about most of the late modern buildings on the UCLA campus. The pileup of buildings comprising the Court of Sciences and the Medical Center is as depressing a grouping as you can find (and it becomes more so with age). To the west on the hillside above the athletic field is a group of four high-rise dormitories (1959–64; Welton Becket and Associates), which mar this side of the campus and adjacent residential district north of Sunset Boulevard.

The principal saving grace of the campus is the landscaping, which is really outstanding. In 1937 the landscape architect Ralph D. Cornell was appointed. He and his firm continued to develop the wonderful imported vegetation of the place until his death in 1972. Cornell's firm, Cornell, Bridgers, Troller, and Hazlett has continued to work on campus landscaping since 1972 with Jere H. Hazlett as the official landscape architect. While all the landscaping efforts have not been able to hide the tragedies of unfortunate planning and buildings, they have been able to create, throughout the campus, pockets of space which are pleasant, highly visible, and in many instances, simply beautiful.

Since the mid-1970s, there has been a new group of good buildings, including Frank O. Gehry and Associates' Student Placement and Career Planning Center (1976–77), Daniel L. Dworsky and Associates' UCLA Parking Structure (1979–80), Venturi, Scott Brown and Associates' (with Payette Associates') Gordon and Virginia MacDonald Medical Research Laboratories (1990–91), and others. Beginning in the 1980s, a number of the older buildings on the campus have been subjected to seismic retrofitting. These include Royce Hall, the Powell Library, Moore Hall, Haines Hall, Kerckoff Hall, and others.

With the grouping of newer buildings toward the southwest section of the campus and the closing of Westwood Boulevard, it was evident that a new entrance should be provided. The firm of Hodgetts + Fung Design Associates did a master plan for the new **UCLA Gateway** and then instituted its first phase. This consisted of entrance kiosks and pavilion, a pool, plus soft and hard landscaping. This new entrance leads off of Westwood Boulevard and Le Conte Avenue.

To a large degree the present renaissance of architecture at UCLA is due to the campus architect, Charles Warner Oakley. Through his efforts the current architectural scene at UCLA is encouraging, both in the general overall quality of the new buildings and exterior spaces and the sensitivity to the difficult task of retrofitting and revamping the older buildings. Currently (as of mid-1992), there are a number of projects on the boards and under construction. These include:

Microbiology Research Facility, Unit III
by Moore Ruble Yudell
Ackerman Union Addition
by Rebecca Bender
Biochemistry Building
by Anshen and Allen

Chiller Plant and Co-Generation Facility
by Holt, Hinshaw, Pfau and Jones
Anderson School of Management
by Pie, Cobb, Freed and Associates
Tiverton House (Patient Family Guest House)
by Barton Phelps and Associates
It is recommended that the visitor to these buildings obtain a map of the campus from one of the entrance kiosks.

1. Royce Hall, 1928–29
Allison and Allison (David Allison)
Royce Hall set the stage for the adaptation of the Lombardian Romanesque style for the campus. The design of this building was inspired by the Church of St. Ambrosio in Milan, with side glances at other north Italian churches: details gathered from the Cathedral of SS Pietro e Paolo, the Church of Il Santissimo Crocifisso, the Church of St. Sepolcro, and others. It was noted in 1930 that Royce Hall "shows an almost complete symposium of the Romanesque-Italian school of architecture."

The open loggias to each side were originally intended to connect with adjoining buildings. The siting of this building by Kelham and Allison and Allison illustrated how these architects were seeking to convey the image of UCLA as a Lombardian hilltop town. The court between Royce Hall and the Library Building to the south, along with the terraces and stairs leading down to Westwood Boulevard (now closed off) illustrate how they combined the picturesqueness of an Italian city with Beaux Arts axial planning. In 1983–84 Royce Hall was successfully restored and seismically refitted by John Carl Warnecke and Associates (under the direction of Charles Warner Oakley, who later became the campus architect).

2. The Powell Undergraduate Library, 1927–29
George W. Kelham
Italian Romanesque realized in reinforced concrete and steel with a skin of brick and terracotta (manufactured by Gladding McBean and Company). As with Royce Hall, specific northern Italian Romanesque buildings inspired portions of the design: the central dome was

derived from San Ambrosio, while the Church of St. Sepolcro was a source for parts of the interior. The library contains one of the best interiors in the style. Much of the interior was decorated by Julian Ellsworth Garnsey. Especially impressive is the interior of the dome of the Main Reading room.

In 1947 Earl T. Heitschmidt and Charles O. Matcham added a three-story wing at the southeast corner of the building. Though somewhat simplified, this new wing essentially carried on the style of the existing building. Eleven years later, in 1958, Modernism triumphed over traditionalism in an infill stucco box which was inserted between the two south wings by Albert C. Martin and Associates.

Presently the Library is undergoing seismic retrofitting and restoration by Moore, Ruble, and Yudell. Among the changes to the building will be the removal of the 1958 Modernist stack block and the creation of a new historicist facade between the two south wings.

3. Haines Hall, 1928
George W. Kelham
A continuation of the Italian Romanesque image. Particularly fine are the east entrance and the auditorium to the west. Currently being seismically retrofitted, and restored to its original appearance.

4. Physics-Biology Building, 1928–29
Allison and Allison
A version of modernized Romanesque, more picturesque than Kelham's usual approach to this style.

5. Moore Hall of Education, 1930
George W. Kelham
Italian Romanesque with major emphasis placed on the east and south doorways. One of what were a pair of auditoriums on the south side of the building (room 100) has been restored as part of the seismic retrofitting. You can now experience its wood-paneled walls and its stenciled, beamed, and gabled ceiling. The firm of Brenda Levin was the historic architectural consultant for the restoration.

6. Kerckoff Hall, 1930
Allison and Allison (Austin Whittlesey)
A lone Gothic building designed in this style, partly because of the donor's insistence, partly because Berkeley's Student Union (1923, John Galen Howard) was Gothic in style.

7. Ackerman Union Building, 1959–60
Welton Becket and Associates
A late 1950s modular Modernist box, equipped with sun grills. In case you may have missed the thoughtful contextual relationship between the old and the new, the building was (according to an article of the time) "carefully related to its predecessor [Kerckoff Hall] through the use of related materials." Presently, Rebecca Bender is designing an addition, which will not only add space to the existing building but will more sensitively reorganize its presence on Westwood Plaza.

8. University Residence (Chancellor's House), 1930
Reginald D. Johnson
A northern Italian villa, exhibiting Johnson's customary sophistication and reserve.

9. Mira Hershey Residence Hall, 1930
Douglas McLelland
Spanish Colonial Revival rather than the usual brick Italian Romanesque. This complex, with its courtyards, low scale, and planting, is one of the most successful buildings on the campus.

10. Men's Gymnasium, 1932
George W. Kelham
This building and the Women's Gymnasium to the south form the lower terrace grouping for Kelham's main axis.

11. Women's Gymnasium, 1932
Allison and Allison
Lukewarm, brick Italian Romanesque.

12. Temporary Undergraduate Library, 1992–93
Hodgetts + Fung Design Associates
At the base of UCLA's famed staircase and between the two gymnasium buildings is a startling new "found" object. Like many of L.A.'s Post Modernist exercises, this is a sophisticated piece of constructivist garden

sculpture raised, of course, to a grand scale. It is purposely non-contextual, egocentrically asserting its preeminent presence over the landscape and surrounding buildings. The aesthetic theme of the curve and the drum sort of hold it together; its overall composition is openly disjoined.

13. Administration Building, 1937
Allison and Allison
More mild Italian Romanesque.

14. University Guesthouse, 1952
Burnett C. Turner
A two-story, wood-sheathed dwelling, combining the image of the Modern and the California Ranch. This building is scheduled to be removed for additional housing.

15. Business Administration and Economics Building, 1948
John C. Austin
One of the last efforts in the use of the Italian Romanesque style on the campus. As with the earlier buildings, it is sheathed in patterns of brick with limestone trim. The corner tower was designed to contain the mechanical and boiler facilities of the building. Recently, in 1992, a new addition to this building has been completed, returning in this instance to the imagery of the Italian Romanesque style.

16. Dickson Art Building (now **School of Architecture and Urban Planning Building**), 1952
Paul Robinson Hunter
This building attempts to play the game of being twentieth-century Modern and Classical at the same time. It works reasonably well to the south, but the rest tends to be bland, especially the original interiors.

17. Schoenberg Hall, 1955
Welton Becket and Associates
Schoenberg Hall is one of the campus's more successful designs which mirrors the influence of Eliel Saarinen. Above the exterior foyer of the building is a 164-foot mosaic mural by Richard Haines. In sixteen panels he depicts the history of music through the ages.

18. Corinne A. Seeds University Elementary School, 1950, 1957–58
Neutra and Alexander

19. University Nursery-Kindergarten School, 1957–59
Neutra and Alexander
Set in a wooded site near Sunset Boulevard, these single-story buildings illustrate Neutra and Alexander's excellent approach to siting and to the indoor/outdoor planning of educational buildings. In 1990 a proposal was put forward to build the new **John E. Anderson Graduate School of Management** (Pei, Cobb, Freed & Partners; designed by Henry Cobb) on this site. The building is to be completed late in 1994.

20. East Building: Corinne A. Seeds University Elementary School, 1990–93
Barton Phelps and Associates
Neutra and Alexander's 1957–59 building has been replaced by this new complex. It is situated behind and up the hillside next to one of Ralph Cornell's gardens (1954). The two-story building is slightly curved and is broken in the center by a wide passageway and waiting area. The building is dug into the hill so that the upper level is on ground level. The buildings are of concrete block, steel, and glass, designed so as to maintain a sense of intimacy for the users and for the site.

21. Faculty Center, 1959
Hutchinson and Hutchinson
A woodsy California Ranch house. The interiors are pleasant, as are the gardens around the building, but it has none of the vigor of a Cliff May design.

22. Bunche Hall, 1964
Maynard Lyndon
The one and only distinguished high-rise on campus, even though the size of the structure and walk-through scale is poorly related to the adjacent older buildings. The reason for the tower's success has to do with the proportioning of the skin and its components, the relationship of the enclosed box to its base, and the manner in which it projects out of the heavy planting which surrounds the structure. Both in

fact and symbolically, the design of the building consciously separates the students and the faculty by putting lecture and discussion facilities in a separate structure. When the faculty members get on the elevators to go to their offices, they divorce themselves from their teaching function.

23. University Research Library, 1964 and 1967
Jones and Emmons

A modest, non-assertive Modernist building which is very pleasant to work in.

24. Sunset Canyon Recreation Facility, 1964
Smith and Williams

This building climbs up its steep hillside site to create an impression of an elaborate, child's tree house.

25. Northwest Campus Housing and Commons, 1992
Barton Myers Associates; Antoine Predock Architects; Esherick, Homsey, Dodge and Davis; Gensler Associates

The Commons Building and the adjacent housing unit were designed by the Myers firm; Predock's housing units, organized around a triangular courtyard are to the west; and the Esherick, Homsey, Dodge and Davis section lies to the north. The Commons Building makes very direct references to the Classical tradition; the housing is all mildly modernist but very reserved. The Esherick units are the most domestic in their scale and detailing. The site design of the complex responds well to the terrain and to the scale needed in student housing.

26. UCLA Childcare Center, 1987
Charles and Elizabeth Lee
Southeast corner Sunset Boulevard and Veteran Avenue

Though these low, one-story structures were prefabricated off-site, they illustrate how such buildings, with a great care in design, can turn out very well. Within the modular post-and-beam system, the architects have placed window units, doors, and solid panels.

27. Dickson Art Center, 1965
William Pereira and Associates

The only elements of character in this Modern design are the raised terraces and the steps leading up to them.

28. Murphy Sculpture Court, 1969
Cornell, Bridgers, and Troller, landscape architect

Perhaps the landscaping will eventually block out the adjacent buildings so that this space will really have the sense of a court in which are placed free-standing sculptures. Major pieces are by Henry Moore, Jacques Lipschitz, Louis H. Sullivan, and many other important sculptors.

29. Track and Field Stadium, 1969
Daniel Dworsky Associates

This structure might have worked on a site three or four times this size, but what was needed here was an underground non-building.

30. Untitled Mural, 1970
Howard Warshaw

The one and only reason to visit the **Reed Neurological Research Center** is to see the Warshaw mural. In comparison to so much of the well-publicized public mural art of the late 1960s and 1970s, Warshaw's mural illustrates the real understanding needed to accommodate high art to architecture. And in this instance the art easily triumphs over the building.

31. James E. West Alumni Development Center, 1974–76
Caudill Rowlett

Formal, undistinguished Modernism, which is being hidden by trees and shrubs.

32. UCLA Extension Building, 1976
H. Jones

A highly intellectual, rather than spatial, design of hooked-together boxes.

33. Jerry Lewis Neuromuscular Research Center, 1976–79
Daniel Dworsky Associates

A two-story concrete-and-steel structure with a shed roof greenhouse and a terraced patio roof.

34. Student Placement and Career Planning Center, 1976–77
Frank O. Gehry and Associates
This small-scaled, long, low box is loosely post-International Style Modern. Gehry's delight in exposing the equipment and structure hearkens back on the one hand to the Smithsons and the English New Brutalists of the mid-1950s. The suggestion of a building as a machine also ties the design into Los Angeles's own version of the High Tech image of the late 1970s and early 1980s. All of this has been accomplished with a characteristic Gehry high-art image. At the same time, the building is well snuggled into its landscaped site, and the interior spaces have a comfortable, easy-going scale.

35. UCLA Hospital Parking Structure, 1979–80
Daniel Dworsky and Associates
Certain parts of this reinforced concrete parking structure are pure Brutalism—quite impressive as sculpture, especially the top roof deck's layer effect. Other sections of the structure are, as John Dreyfuss of the *Los Angeles Times* noted, "tediously fortresslike."

36. University of California Parking Services and Ridesharing, 1991
Siegel Diamond Architects
The new offices were built within an existing parking structure, and a new inviting entrance was added.

37. Gordon and Virginia MacDonald Medical Research Laboratories, 1991–92
Venturi, Scott Brown and Associates; Payette Associates
Venturi described this six-story structure as a loft space "wrapped with a brick skin." It is similar in design approach to the firm's earlier Lewis Thomas Laboratories at Princeton University: the box and its equipment tower are indeed wrapped in an elegant pattern of multicolor brick and on the lower level by a thin limestone skin. On the northwest side, a primitive Doric column holds the figure of a cutout bear. Behind this column, stairs and a ramp for the handicapped ascend to the building's

forecourt. The south side of the forecourt is contained by a pergola, reminiscent in many ways of the design of Joseph Hoffman at the turn of the century in Vienna. The Venturi firm has provided sketches for an additional building which will occupy the west side of the forecourt. This building is, in the judgment of the authors of this Guide, the most handsome building erected in Los Angeles in recent years.

38. John Wooden Center, 1983
Parkin Architects
A sports center which looks on the exterior like a Southern California supermarket or department store.

39. Le Conte-Levering Faculty Housing, 1982–83
Samuel Wacht Associates
Located off-campus at 827 Levering Avenue
Considering the many examples of distinguished multiple housing around the UCLA campus, ranging from Spanish Colonial Revival bungalow garden courts to the later work of Neutra and Lautner, it strikes us as unfortunate that these new units could not have carried on that tradition. Instead, they have the appearance of inexpensive spec housing.

40. UCLA Guest House, 1982–83
Field and Silverman
A row of shed-roofed stucco boxes not much different from similar attached spec units which one finds all over the Southland.

BEVERLY HILLS, NORTH

Beverly Hills, entirely surrounded by the city and county of Los Angeles, lies on the land known in the early nineteenth century as the Rancho Rodeo de las Aguas, the "gathering of waters" from present-day Benedict, Coldwater, and other canyons near the site of what is now the Beverly Hills Hotel. In the 1850s and 1860s, the Yankees, with Benjamin Wilson, Henry Hancock, William Workman,

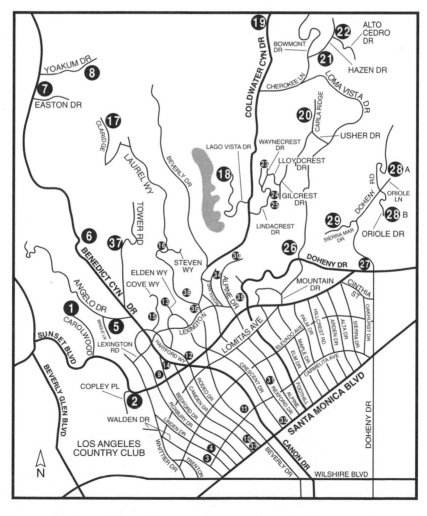

James Whitworth, and Edson A. Benedict in the lead, took over land development and speculation. Several attempts to found a city were made. A German colony was planned in the 1860s, the only remnant of which is Los Angeles Avenue, now Wilshire Boulevard. Until the 1880s the area's chief contribution to civilization was lima beans.

In the 1887 land boom, the town of Morocco was platted, but with the economic collapse the next year the real estate promoters' dream fizzled. The founding finally occurred in 1906 when the Rodeo Land and Water Company, under the leadership of Burton E. Green, conceived of a city for the swells, very much the way Beverly Hills has developed. The landscape architect and planner, Wilbur Cook (assisted by the architect Myron Hunt), planned the present business area with a grid running at forty-five degree angles north from Wilshire Boulevard. He laid out the gently curving streets between Santa Monica Boulevard and the hills to the north. In the hills north of Sunset Boulevard, the landscape architects were the Olmsted Brothers, and they set out streets that undulated picturesquely off into the hills with equally undulating streets crossing them. The result of this plan is that driving, especially at the six-way intersection of Canon Drive, Beverly Drive, and Lomitas Avenue, can be very interesting. In 1912 the extremely fashionable **Beverly Hills Hotel** was built on Sunset Boulevard just above this intersection, and fine houses, most of them on surprisingly small lots, were soon appearing all around. It is usually assumed that these houses were built by the motion-picture crowd, since so many stars live in them now. Actually, the first owners were usually lawyers, doctors, oil men, or wealthy retired people from the frigid zones.

It is remarkable how few of these houses, most of them in the varied styles of the 1920s, have strong architectural or landscape distinction. They are pleasant and highly visible, but not outstanding. It is only when you get into the radically-winding streets in the hills that you will discover distinguished buildings and gardens—some the Modernist work of Neutra, Schindler, Ain, and Harris, and an array of

talented architects who employed period revival images.

The commercial section in the city below Santa Monica Boulevard was originally the strong mixture of Spanish Colonial Revival and Art Deco Moderne that you would expect. Some dazzlers still remain. But the business section has, since the mid-1960s, literally been transformed by high-rise. Some of it, particularly the most recent, has real artistic merit.

As with other upper-middle-class enclaves in Southern California, it is the landscape architecture which makes the place. The impressive rows of palms and other trees along the wide curved streets are mainly due to the efforts of the landscape architect, Raymond E. Page, who was involved in planting them from 1919 through the early 1950s.

1. "Art Pavilion," 1991
   Franklin D. Israel Design Associates
   275 North Carolwood Drive
A classic (in proportions and scale) almost Japanese-like pavilion sits atop a masonry wall and is surrounded by terraces on three sides. There are episodes, such as the large corner windows, that are related to the work of Frank Lloyd Wright and R. M. Schindler in Los Angeles in the 1920s. The main floor of the building is a single gallery space, 28-feet high, with the wood timber trusses of the roof left exposed. A fanciful boatlike balcony projects off the garden side of the building.

2. Helms House, 1933
   Gordon B. Kaufmann
   135 Copley Place
A beautifully and carefully proportioned Spanish dwelling, accompanied by terraces, pools, and a summer house.

3. Spadena House, 1921
   Henry Oliver
   Southeast corner of Carmelita Avenue and
   Walden Drive
Originally designed in Culver City as a movie set and office for Irvin V. Willst Productions, this masterpiece of the Hansel and Gretel mode was moved to a respectable neighborhood and set in an unconventional garden that matches it

beautifully. Apparently it has always been occupied by people who understand and respect its complete madness.

4. Menzies House, 1926
 William Cameron
 604 N. Linden Drive
Tudor with flamboyant stucco enrichment in the gable.

5. Gate House ("Doll's House"), circa 1925
 1808 Angelo Drive
A medieval cottage too sweet for words.

6. Heidemann House, 1972
 Pulliam, Matthews, and Associates
 1236 Benedict Canyon Drive
An award-winning example of the cut-into box. Almost monumental.

7. Vorkapich Garden House, 1938
 Gregory Ain
 2100 Benedict Canyon Drive, just north of Easton Drive
A small, modular plywood house. Here Ain was exploring the idea of prefabricated structure, though it should be noted that the statement of the house as prefabricated architecture is more symbolic than real.

8. Hale House, 1949
 Craig Ellwood Associates
 9618 Yoakum Drive
A single-story Miesian box on stilts.

9. Brown House, 1949
 Craig Ellwood Associates
 902 N. Roxbury Drive
Another box on stilts, this time with balancing, one-story wings. We must say that this house on Roxbury Drive, which Gore Vidal once described as "not so much a drive as a state of mind," remains as an elegant and delicate expression of post-World War II modernism. It is now shrouded in trees as respectable as its Spanish and Tudor neighbors.

10. O'Neill House and Pavilion, 1978–84
 Santa Monica Architectural Group (Tom Oswald)
 507 North Rodeo Drive
The most dramatic structure of this complex is the pavilion which can be seen from the alley

behind 507 N. Rodeo Drive. Eighty years too late, but here is Los Angeles's first real Art Nouveau building—Gaudiesque in the extreme.

11. Forrest House, 1930–31
 Roland E. Coate
 612 N. Beverly Drive
The columned porch suggests both the nineteenth century one-story Monterey house and the later California Ranch house. As befitting its location in Beverly Hills, the Forrest House signals respectability.

12. Beverly Hills Hotel, 1911–12
 Elmer Grey
 9600 Sunset Boulevard
Old photographs reveal a rambling version of the then-popular version of the Mission style. Aesthetically, a great deal has been lost in remodelings and additions, but the building and its lovely garden setting still evoke genteel hospitality. The first extensive additions to the hotel were designed in 1946–47 by Leonard Scultze and Associates of New York and Earl T. Heitschmidt and Charles O. Matcham of Los Angeles. In 1959, Paul R. William and Associates remodeled portions of the building, adding a new elegance to it.

13. Robinson House and Garden, 1911, 1924
 Nathaniel Dryden; Charles Gibbs Adams, landscape architect
 1008 Elden Way
While the Beaux Arts Classical house is impressive, the 1924 Pavilion is the most elegant building on the site. The real glory of the place are the gardens laid out by the Pasadena landscape architect Charles Gibbs Adams, who provided an axis which aligned the house, lawn, pool, and pavilion. The rest of the six-acre estate is arranged in a more informal fashion. The estate was willed by Virgina Robinson to Los Angeles County as a botanical garden. It is open by appointment only.

14. Anthony House, 1909
 Charles and Henry Greene
 910 Bedford Drive at Benedict Canyon Drive
It is significant that Earle C. Anthony, who monopolized the Packard agencies in

California, would employ Bernard Maybeck to do his showrooms in San Francisco and Oakland and get the Greenes to design the interiors of his showroom (demolished) in Los Angeles and his first house, which once stood at the corner of Wilshire and Berendo. When relationships changed (Charles Greene sold his Packard and bought a Hudson), Anthony got Maybeck to design a castle for him near Griffith Park and a large addition to his showroom (also demolished). The Greene and Greene 1909 house has been conscientiously restored by the owners, and is worthy of comparison with its contemporaries, the Gamble and Blacker-Hill houses in Pasadena. The Kerrys, who moved the house to its present site, got Henry Greene to design walls and garden appointments in 1925. A real surprise in an area mainly developed in the revivals of the 1920s.

15. Familian House, 1971
John Lautner
1011 Cove Way

A huge house of stone cairns and wood, just as startling (in a different way) as the Greenes' Anthony House, not far away.

16. Quen House, 1959
Ladd and Kelsey
1211 Laurel Way

Except for the fact that it is all white, this house would pass for the Craftsman style.

17. Epstein House, 1988–89
Barton Phelps and Associates
1462 Claridge Drive

The architect wrote of this house that it "takes a middle route between sculptural fragmentation and the traditional unified exterior envelope." There is a suggestion of Schindler and of Soriano in this design. The entrance is under the house (by the garage) into an entrance garden. Grand steps lead up to the main floor of the house; above are bedrooms and study.

18. English House, 1950
Harwell H. Harris
1261 Lago Vista Drive

A large house whose architect was inspired by Frank Lloyd Wright—in this case almost as if

the Hollyhock house had been divested of ornament. The effect is stunning.

19. Three Houses, 1976
Tom Roberts
2433, 2439, and 2445 Coldwater Canyon Drive

A 1970s version of High Tech. All were once painted a pristine white. Walls and fences have been added.

20. Model House for the Trousdale Development Company, 1965
Rex Lotery
1875 Carla Ridge

A glass, horizontal wood and stucco dwelling built as a model house for this section of Beverly Hills. The high volume of the major living space is countered at right angles by the much lower service wing and accompanying carports. In the instance of this house, the modern image takes on an elegance of materials and detailing one associates with Beverly Hills.

21. Rourke House, 1949
Richard J. Neutra
9228 Hazen Drive (off Coldwater Canyon Drive onto Cherokee Lane, then Bowmont Drive, then Hazen Drive)

Post and beam, stucco with wood trim. Neutra's famous spider-legs (bents) arch the entrance corridor.

22. Rodakiewicz House, 1937
R. M. Schindler
9121 Alto Cedro Drive, beyond Rourke House, right on Alto Cedro Drive—view obtained above on Alto Cedro Drive if you go beyond house, now obscured by tennis court.

Here, with plenty of money to spend, Schindler unleashed all the powers of his romantic vision of de Stijl. This is a classic. It was once set in a tropical rain forest, but the present tennis court pretty much wiped that out.

23. Grossman House, 1949
Greta Magnusson Grossman
1659 Waynecrest Drive

A simple, Modern, brown box sheathed in vertical board and batten.

24. Schulitz House, 1977
 Helmut Schulitz (Urban Innovations
 Group)
 9356 Lloydcrest Drive near southwest cor-
ner of Gilcrest Drive
Another spin-off from Charles Eames's Case
Study House in Santa Monica Canyon. The aes-
thetic of scarcity can go no further.

25. Miller House, 1948
 Ain, Johnson, and Day
 1634 Gilcrest Drive
Very expressionistic for Ain, the roof angles
just every which way. A really handsome
house, easy to see.

26. Doheny House ("Greystone"), 1925–28
 Gordon B. Kaufmann; Paul Thiene, landscape architect
 905 Loma Vista Drive, Greystone Park
Tudor and Jacobean on the grandest possible
scale. The house is no longer open except on
rare occasions, but the glorious gardens are
open every day, 10:00 A.M.–5:00 P.M.
Farther up Loma Vista Drive is the housing
development, much of it on formerly Doheny
land, called **Trousdale Estates.** It is essentially
spec housing for the rich. Although there seems
to be a strong predilection for the Neo-
Classical, all styles exist here. Everything is so
out of scale as to form a kind of unity.

27. Commercial Building, circa 1935
 9169 Sunset Boulevard
Rather elegant Streamline Moderne.

28a. Clarke House, 1950
 Whitney R. Smith and Wayne R. Williams
 1557 Oriole Lane
Not much can be seen of this house except the
garage with exposed rafters and a little plywood sheathing.

28b. Sale House, 1949
 Whitney R. Smith and Wayne R. Williams
 1455 Oriole Drive
The last house was planted out of sight. This
one is fenced, but you can see some of Smith's
ideas from above. Simplicity in wood, beautifully crafted.

29. Sierra Mar House, 1991
 Michael W. Folonis and Associates
 9443 Sierra Mar Drive
The building is composed of two parts: the
lower floor covered by a low-pitched shed roof
and the upper floor whose curved forms suggest the bridge of an ocean liner. Though the
new upper level has a strong visual presence, it
certainly fulfilled the architects' goal of
acknowledging "the character of the existing
structure in scale and style." The new second
floor was made possible by a steel frame which
was inserted into the existing wood frame
dwelling.

30. Parker House, 1951
 Paul Sterling Hoag
 959 North Alpine Drive
A house sheathed in stone and wood, in an
abstract way reminiscent of Pennsylvania
Dutch houses of the eighteenth century.

31. Hawthorne School, 1929
 Ralph C. Flewelling
 624 N. Rexford Drive
This exposed concrete building, with the
impression of the board forms retained, is
Spanish Colonial Revival. The tower, capped
with a dome of glazed colored tiles, and the
two-story entrance portico off the courtyard are
the focal points.

32. Howland House, 1933–34
 Lloyd Wright
 502 Crescent Drive
This house is a radical remodeling of a simple
stucco box. The exterior is as restrained as the
interior is flamboyant.

33. All Saints Episcopal Church, 1925
 Roland E. Coate
 Northeast corner of Santa Monica
 Boulevard and Camden Drive
The extensive areas of plain, uninterrupted
walls and the restrained historical detail of this
church show how close some aspects of the
Spanish Colonial Revival were to the "new"
architecture then developing in Europe and
America.

34. Kritzer House, 1966
Rex Lotery
1030 Woodland Drive
Looking up from the road, one sees the low, hovering roof of the house, below which is the white stucco face of a projecting balcony deck. The aesthetic feel of the house is Frank Lloyd Wright abstracted, including the tentlike ceiling of the living room.

35. Schacker House, 1956
Rex Lotery
917 North Foothill Drive
The centerpiece of this dwelling is a story-and-a-half glass volume which houses the entrance and principal living space. Off of this projected the secondary wings of the house, including the garage. The recent remodeling by the architect (1992–93) has both changed and brought the house back to its original condition. Walls have now been stuccoed, and a low wall separates the dwelling from the street.

36. Pendleton House, 1942
John Woolf
1032 Beverly Drive
A mansard-roofed Regency Moderne house with urns in niches at each side of the colonnaded entrance, this is a fine example of what John Chase calls "exterior decoration."

37. Imerman House, 1936
Wallace Neff
1143 Tower Road
Like so many major and minor houses in Beverly Hills and Bel Air, the Imerman house is not easy to see from the public road, but it is a Neff gem. The impression of the house is that a drawing from a children's storybook of the 1920s has been enlarged and made real. An immense, hipped roof bears down on thin, low walls, and small dormers pop out of the roof surface. At the entrance, the dominant note are two of Neff's very tall trademark chimneys.

38. House, 1983–84
Kamran Khauakani
1081 Laurel Way
Paired Ionic columns grace this large testimony to the fact that Beverly Hills will always remain the same.

1. Wells Fargo Bank, 1973
Sidney Eisenstadt
9600 Little Santa Monica Boulevard
The architect's unusual way with glass creates the illusion that each floor of his multistory building is cantilevered over the one below. Note also the entrance court with fountain supporting Jack Zajac's Swan IV (1971–73).

2. Barclay Bank and Shops Building, 1973
Kahn, Kappe, and Lotery
Northeast corner of Brighton Way and Bedford Drive
It is fascinating to find Kappe's ideas, which are usually seen in domestic building, applied to downtown architecture. The result is a pleasant relief from the usually bland Modernism of the late International style.

3. Manufacturers Bank Building, 1973
Daniel, Mann, Johnson, and Mendenhall
Northwest corner of Wilshire Boulevard and Roxbury Drive
A very large building encased in a curtain of black glass undulates around the corner. It has won much applause from people whose taste was jaded by the dry International Style Moderne tradition.

4. Perpetual Savings Bank Building, 1962
Edward D. Stone
Southwest corner of Wilshire Boulevard and McCarty Drive
A steel-caged high-rise encased in a shell of vaguely Oriental arches. The result, with window-boxes trailing real vine, might best be described as "Venetian Modern."

5. Nieman-Marcus Store Building, 1981
John Carl Warnecke Associates
9700 Wilshire Boulevard
Both the travertine monolith exterior and the spatially elegant interior completely express the essence of the Beverly Hills grand manner—and by a Frisco firm at that.

6. Creative Artist Agency Building, 1989
Pei, Cobb Freed and Partners (I. M. Pei);
Langdon and Wilson, associate architects
Southeast corner of Santa Monica Boulevard
and Lasky Drive
Three separate modernist fragments confront

viewers as they drive by on Santa Monica
Boulevard. The focal point of Pei's design is
the impressive semicircular glass-roofed
atrium. Both inside and externally the detailing
is elegant and expensive. Unquestionably the
whole affair adds up to the excessively precious

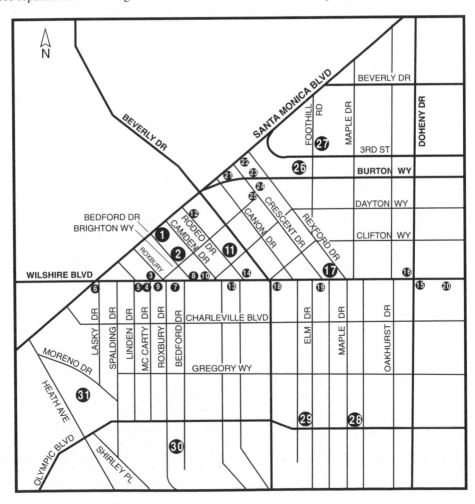

side. The most lively element one will encounter is a huge mural by Roy Lichtenstein, which dominates the 57-foot-high travertine wall of the atrium.

7. I. Magnin and Company Store Building, 1939
Myron Hunt and H. C. Chambers
Southwest corner of Wilshire Boulevard and Bedford Drive

Classical Moderne and very refined.

8. Security Pacific Place, 1969
Craig Ellwood Associates
Northeast corner of Wilshire Boulevard and Bedford Drive

Black Miesian austerity softened somewhat by a plaza and sculpture. The small matching **State Savings Bank** (1972–73) is also by Ellwood.

9. Saks Fifth Avenue Store Building, circa 1936–37
John and Donald B. Parkinson; Paul R. Williams
9600 Wilshire Boulevard

Elegant Hollywood Regency with enough curved surface to suggest that the 1930s Streamline Moderne could be elegant.

10. Frank Perls Gallery Building (now Shaxted), circa 1948
Alvin Lustig
350 N. Camden Drive

The International Style Modern given Beverly Hills classiness by a talented designer of the post-war years.

11. Anderton Court Building, 1953–54
Frank Lloyd Wright
328 Rodeo Drive

Said not to have been carried out precisely according to Wright's plans. It is as if the Guggenheim ramp had been zigzagged and shops put along it. This building by The Master has received little publicity, probably because it is one of his zaniest productions. The ramp winds its way around a central metal mast; somewhat nautical and Streamline Moderne are the groupings of round windows. Across the street (number 339) is a fancy **Gallery**

Building (1972–73) sheathed in polished black marble by Marvin Beck and Societe d'Etudes Santini Bouchard.

12. Rodeo Collection, 1980–82
Le Sopha Group/Environmetrics, Inc. (Olivier Vidal)
421 N. Rodeo Drive

A collection of stores perhaps more notable for its opulence than good taste. Tall arches and oversized round windows face Rodeo Drive; within, the shops are arranged around a sunken courtyard. The architectural theme seems to wander from Classicism to the Art Deco and the Modern, incoherent but rich.

13. Beverly-Wilshire Hotel, 1926
Walker and Eisen
Southwest corner of Rodeo Drive and Wilshire Boulevard

The Italian Renaissance strained through Beaux Arts ideas by a very productive Los Angeles firm.

14. Two Rodeo Drive, 1989–90
Kaplin, McLaughlin and Diaz
Northeast corner of Rodeo Drive and Wilshire Boulevard

You need not go all the way to London to experience a British retail street. The curved street of Two Rodeo Drive, lined by twenty-six two- and three-story buildings, provides visitors with a much-improved version of what they would encounter in England. Each of the stores are different and are meant to reflect not only different styles but also different moments of the past. The curved street rises abruptly from Rodeo Drive. Underneath is an extensive layered parking garage. At the Wilshire end of the street, formal steps lead down to a fountain. Proponents of serious architecture have called it a theme park in the manner of Disneyland, but then most architecture (especially when directed to the rich) exhibits that quality.

15. Coast Savings Office Building, 1987
Weltonshire Boulevard

Perhaps late fifteenth-century buildings of the Florentine Renaissance were on the architect's mind when he designed this building. All of these historic fragments have been wonderfully enlarged and marvelously misconstrued.

16. Kate Mantilini Restaurant,
1985
Morphosis (Thom Mayne and Michael Rotundi)
9101 Wilshire Boulevard
Mostly light gray with darker gray accents, this well-proportioned pavilion seems to be a parody (of sorts) on Mies. The interior plays a wonderful and lighthearted game of high tech. The interior and the facade is, of course, the result of a remodel.

17. Commercial Building,
circa 1928
9441 Wilshire Boulevard
Art Deco (Zigzag) Moderne.

18. Pacific Theater, 1931
B. Marcus Priteca
9404 Wilshire Boulevard
Late 1920s Art Deco with a Mexican flourish.

19. Columbia Savings and Loan Building, (I), 1987
Skidmore, Owings and Merrill/ Los Angeles
(Richard Keating)
Southeast corner Wilshire Boulevard and Elm Drive
This three-story building poses as an elegant modernist stage set. Richard Keating, who designed the building, commented that this building and the La Peer Drive Building up the way on Wilshire, " . . . are meant to read scenographically, as floating facades, skin-deep movie-set 'flats' over which the eye may slide in passing."

20. Columbia Savings and Loan Building, (II), 1987
Skidmore, Owings and Merrill/Los Angeles
(Richard Keating)
8942 Wilshire Boulevard
Another elegant modernist stage set. The facade is organized around a group of three

21. Beverly Hills Post Office Building, 1932–33

metal drums that suggest a space station. Beyond the drums is a courtyard which exhibits what, to a degree, is an excess of over-refined, machinelike detailing.

21. Beverly Hills Post Office Building,
1932–33
Ralph C. Flewelling; Allison and Allison
Southeast corner of Canon Drive and Santa Monica Boulevard
Although the building was much admired when completed, some civic leaders felt that it was too domestic and not public and monumental enough. A beautiful rendition of the Italian Renaissance in terra-cotta and brick. Inside the post office are mural lunette paintings by the artist Charles Kassler II (1935–36). These depict the "Pony Express" in one mural and "Air Mail" in another.

22. Beverly Hills City Hall, 1932

22. Beverly Hills City Hall, 1932
William J. Gage
East side of Crescent Drive between Santa
    Monica and Little Santa Monica boulevards
Spanish Renaissance magnificence built significantly at the beginning of the depression when
the people in this vicinity felt little pain. The
scheme of the building—that of a low, classical
base (symbolizing government) surmounted by
a tower (signifying business)—was frequently
employed for public buildings in the United
States from the teens through the 1930s.

23. Beverly Hills Civic Center, 1981–92
Charles Moore/Urban Innovations; Albert
    Martin Associates; Campbell and
    Campbell, landscape architects
In 1981 a competition was announced by the
city council for an expansion of the Civic
Center. Six architectural firms were selected to
present architectural plans: Frank O. Gehry and
Associates, Arthur Erickson
Architects, Gwathmey Siegel
and Associates, Moshe
Safdie and Associates, and
Charles Moore/Urban
Innovations Group. The winning design was that of
Charles Moore/Urban
Innovations Group.
    The winning design
exhibited a Spanish flavor,
enriched by references to the
Art Deco. The final design
carries the Art Deco one or
two steps further, making it
the dominant theme. The
buildings are organized
around a public promenade
which slices diagonally
through the project, with the
existing City Hall forming
part of the north side promenade terminating to the
northeast at the parking
garage. While a number of
features of the landscape
design were eliminated, the
planting which was carried
out is already bringing all the
elements together. The crown of the project is
the wonderful library, especially the children's
section with its row of arches converging at the
reception desk.

24. Music Corporation of America Building
(now **Litton Industries**), 1940, 1968–72
Paul R. Williams; Phil Shipley and
    Associates, landscape architects
Burton Way between Crescent and Rexford
    drives
The former Music Corporation of America
building, with its gardens, marks *the* high point
of traditional image architecture in Los
Angeles. The building is a formal, but still
somewhat rambling, version of the work of the
late eighteenth-century English Georgian tradition. (Robert Adam, et al.) The building's
architect, Paul R. Williams, fully understood
the Georgian mode, and he maneuvered it so

24. Music Corporation of America Building (now **Litton Industries**), *1940, 1968–72*

that it read traditional, modern, and California. Note not only the two-story porticoed entrance to the northeast, but also the garden facing toward the southwest. The garden in the plaza was designed in 1972 by the landscape architect Phil Shipley.

25. Parking Structure for Litton Industries, 1968–72
Paul R. Williams and Associate
South corner of Crescent Drive and Burton Way

To tie the parking structure into the existing building across the street, Williams clothed it in Georgian garb.

26. Burton-Hill Town Houses, 1974
Widon-Wein and Associates
9323 Burton Way

Twenty-four units, extremely sophisticated and understated 1970s Modern in wood and brick.

27. Virgin Records, 1991
Franklin D. Israel Design Associates
338 North Foothill Road

A beautifully proportioned bright red wall gently curves into the canopied entrance. On going inside you are in a miniature city with streets and buildings inside of buildings.

28. Volkswagen Showroom Building, circa 1937
Northwest corner of Maple Drive and Olympic Boulevard

Here it is again. Los Angeles would seem to have more monuments to the Streamline Moderne than any other city in the United States.

29. Cañon Court, 1930
J. Raymond
9379 Olympic Boulevard at northeast corner of Cañon Drive

This lovely Spanish Colonial garden-court apartment seems out of place on this now noisy street.

30. Wosk House, 1981–84
Frank O. Gehry and Associates
440 S. Roxbury Drive

As with his own house in Santa Monica, Gehry took an existing four-story apartment building, and in this case, transformed its top floor into what amounts to a new series of spaces and forms. Gehry's approach to the new fourth floor was to "rebuild [it] as a series of objects set back from the existing building's perimeter. The dense rooftop composition of 'appropriated' forms is suggestive of a miniature city and evokes the scale, details, and eclecticism of its surroundings." At the request of the client, the lower portions of the building were refinished in pink stucco.

31. Swimming Pool Building, Beverly Hills High School, circa 1937
Stiles O. Clements
Between Heath Avenue and Moreno Drive above Olympic Boulevard

This elliptical-facaded building with its barrel-vaulted, skylighted interior contrasts with the knife-sharp Yamasaki towers behind it. The single-story entrance pavilion with rounded corners and rows of deep horizontal bands makes the building Streamline Moderne.

CENTURY CITY

I n what, to an easterner, would seem easy walking distance of the Beverly Hills business district is Century City, built on what used to be the Twentieth Century-Fox movie lot. This is a totally new complex of high- and medium-rise buildings, some by distinguished name-brand American architects. There is, however, none of the intimacy and human scale that characterize the buildings of Beverly Hills. In fact, the governing idea seems to have been to inspire awe of corporate America via wide avenues and overscaled architecture. If you accept the effort to impress, then the attempt, even at this stage, has been successful. But there are problems. Except around the Century Plaza Hotel and a few theaters doing business, the place is pretty spooky on weekdays and downright frightening on Sundays. There is no on-street parking. In fact, there are few crosswalks. Pedestrians are forced to go under streets. One has the strange feeling that this city was planned not for people but for architectural photography. We have included only the buildings that we feel cannot be ignored, either because of their size or, in a few instances, because of their architectural importance.

1. Century City Medical Plaza, 1969
Daniel, Mann, Johnson, and Mendenhall
(Lumsden and Pelli; P. I. Jacobson)
Northeast corner of Olympic Boulevard and
Century Park East

Both major architects have since gone off into attacks on the International Style Modern. This complex, a seventeen-story office tower and a ten-story hospital, stands at the turning point in their reaction.

2. Fox Plaza, 1985–87
William Pereira Assoc.
Robert Herrick Carter Assoc., landscape
architects

This pink and gray, thirty-four-story behemoth with its six-story parking structure is most notable for its size. Perhaps, in an odd moment, H. G. Wells might have loved it.

3. Century Plaza Hotel, 1966
Minoru Yamasaki
Robert Herrick Carter, landscape architect
2025 Avenue of the Stars

A huge, high-rise ellipse enlivened by delicate detail.

4. ABC Entertainment Center, 1972
Henry George Greene
2040 Avenue of the Stars

Big and dull—mildly Brutal below, crisper above.

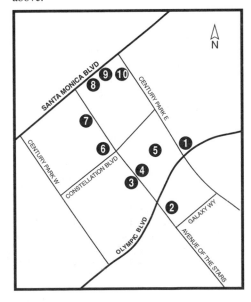

5. Century Plaza Towers, 1969-75
   Minoru Yamasaki
   Robert Herrick Carter, landscape architect
   East of ABC Entertainment Center
These two soaring towers, identical in height
and triangular floor plan, are the focal point of
Century City. They are truly stunning when
viewed nearby and play strange optical tricks
from the distant Santa Monica Freeway.

6. First Los Angeles Bank Building, 1975
   Maxwell Starkman and Associates
   Northwest corner of Avenue of the Stars and
   Constellation Boulevard
An extraordinarily fine building of brown brick
and black glass tilted to give the effect of the
skylight in an artist's studio.

7. 1900 Avenue of the Stars Building, 1969
   Albert C. Martin and Associates
   1900 Avenue of the Stars
A twenty-seven-story building of aluminum
and tinted glass.

8. ABI Tower, 1971
   Skidmore, Owings, and Merrill (E. Charles
   Bassett)
   10100 Santa Monica Boulevard
A twenty-six-story building of light aluminum
and black glass.

**9. San Diego Savings and Loan Association
   Building,** 1972
   Daniel, Mann, Johnson, and Mendenhall
   (Lumsden; P. I. Jacobson)
   Southwest corner of Santa Monica
   Boulevard and Century Park East
A squarish, twenty-story building set at a diagonal to the corner. The mitered corners which
line up with the street indicate that the designer
was perhaps trying to make some sort of statement. Or was he simply being playful? The
building nevertheless seems askew and unre-
lated to anything else.

10. Northrop Complex, 1982–83
   Welton Becket and Associates
   1800 Century Park East
A nineteen-story Corporate International Style
tower. An equally dull twenty-three-story tower
is underway.

CARTHAY CIRCLE

Carthay Circle was planned in 1921
by the landscape architects Cook
and Hill. The area is bounded by
Fairfax Avenue to the east,
Olympic Boulevard to the south
and Wilshire Boulevard to the north. It is
bisected by San Vicente Boulevard. The
founder of the 136-acre, mainly Spanish
Colonial Revival community, was the developer J. Harvey McCarthy. It was originally
planned around its own shopping center.
Originally the main buildings and many of the
lesser ones were designed by Alfred W. Eichler
and H. W. Bishop. Several of the spec houses
were designed by Irving J. Gill while he was
working for Bishop. The chief feature of
Carthay Circle was the theater, now long gone.
No major monuments remain—only a pleasan-
ter-than-usual community.

SOUTH CARTHAY

WEST HOLLYWOOD

This area just southeast of Beverly Hills and bounded by Olympic, Crescent Heights, Pico, and La Cienega boulevards was developed in the 1930s by a builder named Ponti. It is really all of one piece, mainly Spanish Colonial Revival, but also exhibits the other period revivals as well as the Moderne. It is mostly single-family dwellings, all in the same scale, except for the fringes on Olympic and Crescent Heights where small apartment houses in the same 1930s styles appear. There are very few intrusions from the succeeding decades, and where they do appear they are not liked. The sense of an organic community of period architecture caused the Los Angeles Cultural Heritage Board to recommend to the Planning Commission and the City Council that South Carthay be recognized as a cultural-historic district, or in officialese, a Historic Preservation Overlay Zone remarkable for its consistent good design.

For many years West Hollywood was unincorporated, i.e., located in the county, not in the city of Los Angeles. This had tax advantages and is one reason that it attracted small businesses such as interior design. It also drew a group of unusual human beings, some of them of great significance, who ended up living in the area: the writers Theodore Dreiser and Aldous Huxley, the architect R. M. Schindler, and the patent medicine czar Walter Dodge, who in 1916 commissioned Irving J. Gill to design a house that came to be considered one of the great monuments of modern architecture. In fact, the loose organization of government of the unincorporated area without many ordinances, especially in historic preservation, helped to make it possible for a developer to destroy the famed Dodge House and replace it with hideous condominiums.

Since that time, West Hollywood has become a city with a strong historic preservation ordinance and a real sense of place. It has helped to restore Schindler's own house on Kings Road and has protected many other monuments such as Lloyd Wright's house on Doheny Drive.

The Grand Palais for interior designers has been the Pacific Design Center at the corner of San Vicente Boulevard and Melrose Avenue—"The Blue Whale"—that houses the most prestigious wholesalers. But small shops, the mainstay of an earlier day, still abound. And not far from them are acres of bungalows, many being literally transformed by their designers-owners into miniature villas in a congeries of taste that stretches the imagination to the point that John Chase has written a book about them—*Exterior Decoration* (Los Angeles, 1982).

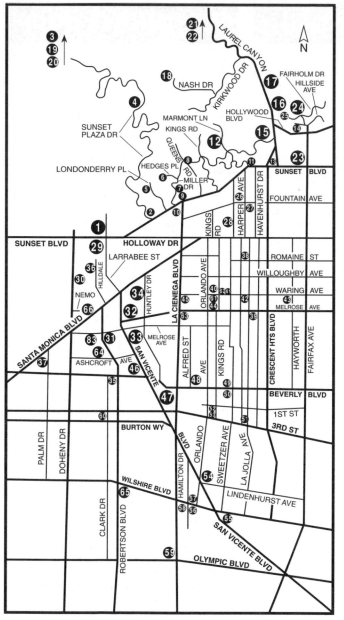

The questionable part of Sunset Boulevard that is called "The Strip" is also in the area, as are some wonderful garden apartments of the 1920s and 1930s. The hills above Sunset Boulevard are in Los Angeles proper and are full of excellent Period Revival houses as well as outstanding avant-garde work by Carl S. Maston, Raphael Soriano, Richard J. Neutra, John Lautner, Gregory Ain, Pierre Koenig, and R. M. Schindler. This is a wonderful part of the world.

We have taken the liberty of extending West Hollywood into these hills to the north and have pushed its southern boundary to Olympic Boulevard. At the same time we have observed the conventional western and eastern boundaries at Doheny Drive and Fairfax Avenue.

1. Sunrise Plaza Apartment Building, 1982
John Siebel Associates
1201 Larrabee Street
High Tech with all of its cliches.

2. Sunset Plaza, 1934–36
Charles Selkirk;
Honnold and Russell
8578–8623 Sunset Boulevard
Clustered near the intersection with Sunset Plaza Drive, most of these shops were designed by Charles

2. Sunset Plaza, 1934–36

Selkirk. Some are now being restored and rebuilt in their original Neoclassical, Regency, and Colonial Revival styles. Advanced respectability on the Sunset Strip! The crown jewel of them all is the shimmering white Ionic temple (1936) at 8619 Sunset Boulevard.

3. Muller House, 1990
Allyn E. Morris
2221 Sunset Plaza Drive

A carrying on of Schindler's modernist work of the late 1930s. The theme of layered horizontality asserts itself in a strong fashion, especially on the south elevation of the house. Numerous decks, some open, some covered, provide out-of-door living space on a steep hillside lot.

4. Lomax House, 1970–71
Lomax/Mills Associates
1995 Sunset Plaza Drive

An elegant cut-into stucco box, a reminder in the Modernist tradition that architecture can be minimal sculpture on a grand scale.

5. Wayne House, 1950
Alvin Lustig
1365 Londonderry Place

You can catch only a glimpse of this International Style Modern house.

6. Wolff House, 1963
John Lautner
8530 Hedges Place

This steep hillside house is a characteristically dramatic statement of its architect. It is made of dressed boulders, concrete, and jutting glass. Its most salient feature from the street is the greatly extended lip of the carport.

7. Reis House, 1950
R. M. Schindler
1404 Miller Drive

In this single-floor dwelling Schindler hovered a thin roof plane over a set of quite fragile stucco planes. As in all of his work, and especially in his post-1945 designs, there are many ideas going on in this small dwelling. But here the roof planes hold everything together.

8. Polito House, 1939
Raphael S. Soriano
1650 Queens Road

A two-story, Modernist box characterized by the abstract composition of stucco walls, horizontal banks of windows, and cantilevered balconies.

9. Carney's Restaurant Building
8361 Sunset Boulevard

A Union Pacific dining car brought to the site in the 1970s.

10. Sunset Tower Apartment Building, 1929–31
Leland A. Bryant
18358 Sunset Boulevard at Kings Road

The lower part of the tower is a first-class monument of the Zigzag Moderne while the upper portion anticipates the 1930s Streamline Moderne. The building has long been as much an emblem of Hollywood as the Hollywood Sign. Drive to the rear and note the stylized automobile radiator grills incorporated into the decoration of the garage.

10. Sunset Tower Apartment Building, 1929–31

15. Storer House, 1923

11. Chateau Marmont, 1928
Arnold Weitzman
8225 Marmont Lane near Sunset Boulevard
Perhaps more important historically than architecturally, this Norman pile was a favorite of the screen stars . . . still is.

12. Maston House, 1948
Carl Louis Maston
1657 Marmont Lane
Rather surprising to find this partisan of the "less-is-more" aesthetic practicing here in what would seem to be a late Craftsman technique—lots of wood.

13. Store and Office Building, circa 1925
Morgan, Walls, and Clements
Northwest corner of Laurel Canyon and
Sunset boulevards
Somewhat defaced but still recognizable as these architects' brand of the Churrigueresque, realized in cast concrete.

14. Mace House, 1958
Lloyd Wright
8292 Hollywood Boulevard
The facade right on the street is very private looking.

15. Storer House, 1923
Frank Lloyd Wright
Lloyd Wright, landscape architect
8161 Hollywood Boulevard
Wright's romantic creation of decorated concrete block, wonderfully fitted into the hillside. The interior space of this house is dominated by a central, two-story living room which opens onto terraces, both front and rear. The house was purchased by the producer Joel Silver, and it was partially restored in the 1970s by Lloyd Wright. More extensive renovation has taken place more recently under the direction of Eric Wright, Martin Eli Weil, and Linda Marder.

16. House, circa 1925
1808 Laurel Canyon Boulevard (actually a spur which veers off about 100 yards above Hollywood Boulevard)
A beautiful tribute to the Spanish Colonial Revival.

17. House, circa 1910
Paul Arnold Needham
2044 Laurel Canyon Boulevard (spur)
A horizontal, one-story house raised above the street level by the garage below. It is an example of the West Coast adaptation of the Midwestern Prairie School aesthetic.

20. Case Study House #21, 1958

18. Jones House and Studio, 1938
A. Quincy Jones
8661 Nash Drive (Laurel Canyon
Boulevard, then left on Kirkwood Drive,
right on Ridpath Drive to Nash Drive)
The influence in these buildings with broad
eaves is Wright filtered through the San
Francisco Bay tradition of the 1930s.

A little farther up Laurel Canyon
Boulevard, again jutting off to the left (west), is
Lookout Mountain Avenue, which you will rec-
ognize by a suitable log cabin at the entrance.
Lookout Mountain Avenue leads to some
important houses.

19. Janson House, 1949
R. M. Schindler
8704 Skyline Drive (Lookout Mountain
Avenue to Wonderland Avenue to
Greenvalley to Skyline Drive)
A house on a scanty budget. It looks as if it
were made of sticks. It is amazing to return to
this house after many years and discover that,
where in the 1950s it could easily be photographed, now it is almost invisible amid foliage
and new neighbors. A number of changes also
have been made to the house in recent years. If
you look closely at this dwelling and then at the
recent designs of Frank O. Gehry, you may be
able to see the connection.

20. Case Study House #21, 1958
Pierre Koenig
9038 Wonderland Park Avenue (Lookout
Mountain Avenue to Wonderland Avenue
to Wonderland Park Avenue. House on left,
just above Burroughs)
Koenig carried the elegance of the metal post-
and-beam aesthetic to the point that it almost
seems related to the popular Hollywood
Regency of the 1930s. Another example of this
refined approach can be seen in his **Case Study
House #22** (1959), located at 1635 Woods
Drive. In #22 the idea of the glass pavilion is
fully realized.

This elegant, precisely detailed Modernist
house of vertical wood panels is still very
smart.

21. De Bretteville-Simon Houses, 1976
Peter de Bretteville
8067–8071 Willow Glen Road off Laurel
Canyon Road
The image of the twentieth-century dwelling as
a machine. A spin-off from Charles Eames's
own house in Santa Monica Canyon.

22. Ain House, 1941
Gregory Ain
7964 Willow Glen Road
A narrow, room-in-a-line plan with all the
major spaces opening toward a terrace and the

26a. Patio del Moro, 1925

view, the whole covered with a low-pitched, hipped roof.

23. Sunset Car Wash, 1972
Robert Barnett
7955 Sunset Boulevard

A monumental, almost Egyptian, object in concrete.

24. Kun Houses, 1938 and 1950
Richard J. Neutra; Gregory Ain, collaborator
7947 Fareholm Drive

Two adjoining machine-image, International Style Modern houses on a precipitous hillside. The 1938 stucco-and-steel-windows dwelling was advertised as an "all-electric house." From the street you see only the top level. The rear elevation reveals that it is actually three levels.

25. Tucker House, 1950
R. M. Schindler
8010 Fareholm Drive

A two-story stucco frame design whose planes project and recede in a complex pattern.

26. Garden Apartments
Mainly on north/south streets between Sunset Boulevard and Fountain Avenue

Usually, as the name suggests, these are two- or three-story apartments in some way arranged around a garden, often elaborately landscaped with palms and other tall trees. A swimming pool is not usually a part of the ensemble, although it may exist on some other part of the property or may have been added to the sacred precinct more recently. They are at their best in the Spanish Colonial Revival mode and are generally charming if not great architecture. A recent visitor from Canada was heard to say, "Why don't all the people in Los Angeles live this way?" For a discussion of these garden apartments see Stefanos Polyzoides, Roger Sherwood, James Tice, and Julius Shulman, *Courtyard Housing in Los Angeles* (Berkeley, 1982).

Here is a group of apartments that are within easy walking distance of each other:

a. Patio del Moro, 1925
Arthur B. and Nina W. Zwebell
8225 Fountain Avenue

Although not the first designer/builder to hit upon the garden court, Zwebell was certainly a very active pioneer. This Spanish design has a gorgeous entrance and an interesting garden.

b. The Ronda, 1927
Arthur B. and Nina W. Zwebell
1400 Havenhurst Drive

From the street all you can see is the three-story facade with a garage entrance to the side and a small garden entrance to the north. Within this complex are two courtyard gardens.

c. The Andalusia, 1927
Arthur B. and Nina W. Zwebell
1475 Havenhurst Drive

Two garage buildings to each side form a forecourt beyond which a large arch leads into the inner court. Cantilevered balconies, a round tower, and a loggia complete the composition.

d. The Romanesque Villa Apartments, 1928
  Leland Bryant
  1301–1309 N. Harper Avenue

This three- and four-story garden courtyard apartment was produced by Leland Bryant, who also designed the Moderne Sunset Towers. His image in this case was Spanish Churrigueresque, notwithstanding its name, "Romanesque." Do note the Spanish Galleon weather vane, which tops the square and octagonal tower at the northeast corner.

26f. Villa d'Este, 1928

e. Villa Sevilla, 1931
  Elwood Houseman
  1338 N. Harper Avenue

An Andalusian village scene set on the hillside. A narrow interior garden court contains the entrances and stairways.

f. Villa d'Este, 1928
  Pierpont and Walter S. Davis
  1355 Laurel Avenue

Vaguely modeled on the not-so-famous Villa d'Este on Lake Maggiore, not on the famous one at Tivoli. This apartment house with garage as a forecourt on the street is surely the most beautiful of these wonderful garden courtyard apartments of the 1920s. Beyond the entrance and pool lies the main courtyard. Each of the two-story units has its own private patio.

Actually, to have settled on the garden apartment house may seem perverse. Look around at the other delightful apartments in this area. The nearby **Chateau Marmont** is only the most conspicuous of these.

27. "Villa de Malaga" Apartments, 1988
  Miguel Angelo Flores and Associates
  8228 Fountain Avenue (Southeast corner Fountain Avenue and Harper Avenue)

A seven-unit apartment, well carried out in the Andalusian mode. This architect also designed the Spanish-inspired 1982–83 "Villa de

Malaga" town houses in Santa Monica

28. Coral Gables Bungalow Court, circa 1932
  1233–1239 Sweetzer Avenue

A two-story Spanish Colonial Revival complex.

29. Modern Creators Store Building for W. Lingenbrink, 1937
  R. M. Schindler
  8750 Holloway Drive

Schindler supervised additions in 1947. Since then many remodelings have been made so that one can grasp Schindler's ideas only through illustrations in books. Oh, there is still a skyline.

30. Wright House, 1928
  Lloyd Wright
  858 N. Doheny Drive

The house is of stuccoed frame with elaborate precast concrete block decoration within and without, suggested by the Joshua tree. It is easily missed under its pine tree, which acts as an insulating device. No more romantic scene could be imagined than when Mr. Wright lighted a fire on the hearth of the "great hall" and opened the canvas drapery which separates the room from the small patio over which the huge tree sprawls.

30. Wright House, 1928

31. Office and Showroom Building, 1982
Tom Roberts Associates
638–642 North Robertson Boulevard
Three low towers identify this small wood and stucco complex. The towers are open frame, and the two to the side are placed at forty-five degree angles to their buildings. A Post Modern building which does not employ the usual language of that mode.

32. Pacific Design Center ("Blue Whale"),
1975; 1985–88
Victor Gruen Associates (Cesar Pelli)
Northeast corner of Melrose Avenue and
San Vicente Boulevard
Controversial to say the least. Some critics have damned "The Blue Whale," usually because it obviously contradicts the scale of the area, which is mainly small shops and houses. Others have praised it for its break with high-rise. The Center is vast and, on its San Vicente side, reminds you of London's Crystal Palace in its roofline. With the exception of the top floor, its interiors are just big spaces, possibly because the architect expected them to be filled with color and people by the designer tenants. A

grand exception is the **Sunar Showroom** (#206) designed by Michael Graves in 1981.

A decade after the original structure, Pelli designed two new buildings and a plaza for the complex. The two new structures are also sheathed in glass, one in green and one in maroon. Pelli commented about the two new structures in 1985: "The first building was conceived as a large fragment of overscaled elements in an unusual bright color; the added elements also are conceived as separate overscaled fragments in strong contrasting colors."

33. William S. Beckett Office Building (now Honnold, Riebsamen, and Rex), 1950
William Beckett
9026 Melrose Avenue
International Style Modern elegance now almost hidden in foliage.

34. Center for Early Education Building,
1968
Kurt Meyer and Associates
536 N. Alfred Street
Very Spartan in red brick but with Athenian blue doors.

35. Herman Miller Showroom Building, 1949
Charles Eames
8806 Beverly Boulevard

Although no longer used by Herman Miller, the glass street facade of this small building still looks as delicate, crisp, and bright as when it was built.

36. Margo Leavin Gallery Building, 1989
Claes Oldenburg and Coosje van Bruggen, sculptors
817 North Hilldale Avenue

A six-by-twelve-foot stainless-steel knife blade cuts down through the parapet of a nondescript, stucco-sheathed L.A. building. The stroke of the knife cuts into the center of the facade with such force that the adjoining plaster surfaces arc curled back.

37. Rapid Transit District Bus Maintenance Facility, 1982
Ralph Parsons Company (Engineering)
Santa Monica Boulevard at Palm Drive

About as Brutalist as we go in Southern California.

38. Duplexes, 1922
R. M. Schindler
Northeast corner of Harper Avenue and Romaine Street; northwest corner of La Jolla Avenue and Romaine Street

These two identical, low-budget structures were built as spec investments. Their style is close to Art Deco Moderne.

39. Service Station, circa 1935
8176 Melrose Avenue

Streamline Moderne.

40. Schindler Studio House, 1921–22
R. M. Schindler
833 N. Kings Road

Actually a double house, with guest quarters and a common kitchen, built for the Schindlers and R. M.'s engineer colleague Clyde Chase. In this studio house, Schindler experimented with tilt-slab concrete walls, the vertical space between each slab being filled with glass. In a sense, the house follows historic precedent. The interiors are in the woodsy do-it-yourself Craftsman style. The plan, which opens all rooms to courtyards, suggests both the Hispanic and Japanese traditions. It is a *classic* in modern architecture—and we use the word sparingly. God preserve it! It is owned and

40. Schindler Studio House, 1921–22

administered by the nonprofit Friends of the Schindler House, and the house and garden have been restored. The studio house is open to the public and often presents architectural and design exhibitions. It is open 11A.M.–4 P.M. on Saturdays, 1–4 P.M. on Sundays.

41. Apartment Building, circa 1925
    Carl Kay
    Northwest corner of Sweetzer and Waring avenues
An Islamic Revival complex, beautiful to behold.

42. Duplex, 1936
    William P. Kesling
    754–756 Harper Avenue
Splendid Streamline Moderne, coming close to International Style Modern.

43. El Greco Apartment Building, 1929
    Pierpont and Walter S. Davis
    West side of Hayworth Avenue, north of Melrose Avenue
You entered into this 1920s garden apartment building through an arched opening. The central courtyard is furnished with plants, potted plants, and a central pool. A projecting second-floor balcony overlooks the courtyard of this Andalusian design. This apartment building was originally located at 1028 Tiverton in Westwood. It was moved in 1986 by the architectural firm of de Bretteville and Polyzoides.

44. Gemini Studio Building, 1976
    Frank O. Gehry and Associates
    8365 W. Melrose Avenue
A remodeling and addition to an older single-story commercial structure, this is so understated that you do not notice the subtle relationship of the new facade and the huge sign on its roof. High Art successfully commenting on the common and everyday building behind.

45. Gerwin-Ostrow Office Building, 1960
    Craig Ellwood Associates
    Southeast corner of La Cienega Boulevard and Waring Avenue
Less glass than usual, the building still shows the influence of Mies.

46. Tail-O-the-Pup, 1946
    West side of N. San Vicente Boulevard, just north of Beverly Boulevard
A programmatic hot dog stand in the shape of a hot dog in a bun. The structure was moved from its former location on the northwest corner of La Cienega and Beverly Boulevards.

47. Beverly Center, 1982
    Welton Becket Associates
    8500 Beverly Boulevard
Just behind the Tail-O-the-Pup, so to speak, this monstrous shopping center with its department stores and shops is a sort of unintended joke on the Pompidou Center in Paris.

48. Los Angeles Free Clinic (Selick Ostrow Building), 1989–90
    Morphosis (Thom Mayne and Michael Rotundi)
    8405 Beverly Boulevard
A steel frame box provides the entrance to this three-story clinic building. Juxtaposition of volumes is the game with this structure. Forms at the base are of concrete block (including bands of split-faced block) and then are stucco sheathed above. The building houses the nation's oldest no-cost health clinic.

49. Janus Gallery, circa 1928
    Northwest corner of Beverly Boulevard and Sweetzer Avenue
Art Deco (Zigzag) Moderne.

50. Carson-Roberts Building, 1958–60
    Craig Ellwood
    8322 Beverly Boulevard
This building stands on stilts, providing a garage below. The front is made of glass panels extended beyond the real walls. These give extra privacy from the busy street.

51. Crescent Professional Building, 1959
    Richard J. Neutra
    8105 W. 3rd Street
White marble, unfenestrated to the street, the architecture is asserted by a stainless-steel canopy extended over the side walls.

52. Apartment Building, circa 1940
    Southwest corner of 1st Street and South Kings Road
A late version of the Streamline Moderne.

50. Carson-Roberts Building, 1958–60

53. House, 1936
  Milton J. Black
  127 S. Kings Road
As we have noted, this area is practically the
home of the Streamline Moderne.

54. Marshall House, 1948
  Konrad Wachsmann and Walter Gropius
  6643 Lindenhurst Avenue (rear)
You cannot easily see it from the street, but we
had to put it in because the prefabricated "panel
houses" by these famous architects are rarities.

55. Century Bank Building, 1972
  Daniel, Mann, Johnson, and Mendenhall
  (A. Lumsden)
  6420 Wilshire Boulevard
A well-designed medium-rise with much attention toward a break with 1960s Modern, but it
does inspire us to feel like whipping whoever it
was that invented black glass.

56. Fox Wilshire Theater, 1929
  S. Charles Lee
  8440 Wilshire Boulevard
A wonderful creation in Art Deco (Zigzag)
Moderne.

57. Shopping Center (now **Porsche-Audi**),
  circa 1928
  Northeast corner of Wilshire Boulevard and
  Hamilton Drive
A specimen of Spanish Colonial Revival archi-
tecture. Corner L-shaped shopping centers of
this vintage are rapidly fading from the scene.
It is good to find one in this area.

58. Great Western Savings Center Building,
  1972
  William Pereira Associates
  Southeast corner of Wilshire and La
  Cienega boulevards
This huge, black glass building with an oval
floor plan certainly makes a break with
International Style Modern sermonizing.

**59. Beverly Hills Water Department
  Building** (now: **Center for Motion
  Picture Study),** 1927
  Salisbury, Bradshaw, and Taylor (Arthur
  Taylor)
  Northwest corner of Olympic and La
  Cienega boulevards
You will at first think that this huge, poured-
concrete structure with Romanesque detail and
reasonably accurate facsimile of "La Giralda"
is a cathedral. And so it is in Los Angeles

County where water is sacred. In 1988 the building was taken over by the Academy of Motion Picture Arts and Science. In the hands of the architect Francis Offenhauser, the existing building was extensively remodeled and a new wing, sympathetic in character to the original building, was added.

60. Temple Emmanuel and School, 1954
  Sidney Eisenstadt
  300 N. Clark Drive
The temple is not as dramatic as much of Eisenstadt's work, but it contains a mural by Joseph Young, who designed the Triforium in downtown Los Angeles. The school, comprised of very low arches with brick and glass above, reminds us in some ways of the Frank Lloyd Wright civic building at San Raphael.

61. Orlando/Waring Condominiums, 1974
  Kenneth Dillon
  8380 Waring Avenue at Orlando Avenue
A large complex in the cut-into box idiom. Not great architecture, but the planting around it is magnificent.

62. Senior Citizens Housing Project, 1978-80
  Bobrow, Thomas and Associates; Charles
  W. Moore/Urban Innovation Group
  Northwest and northeast corners of Kings
  Road at Waring Avenue
These 106 one- to three-story units in stucco and tile spell Spanish Colonial. Several existing Spanish Colonial Revival houses of the 1920s have been incorporated in the project and help to tie the present to the past. The new buildings have been scaled and sited so as to continue the low residential character of Kings Road before the advent of apartment houses in the 1960s.

63. Woolf Studio Building, 1946–47
  John Woolf
  8450 Melrose Place
A one-story building, its outsize Pullman door surround has been greatly admired by the interior designers in West Hollywood.

64. House Remodeling, 1961
  Lawrence Limolti
  8937 Ashcroft Avenue
A tiny, originally Spanish Colonial Revival bungalow entirely rejuvenated with mansard roof, complete with bust in the tower and topiary work in the front yard.

65. Owl Drug Store Building, circa 1930
  Southwest corner of Wilshire and
  Robertson boulevards.
A version of the Art Deco (Zigzag) Moderne. Between fluted engaged columns on the upper floor are small, highly decorated columns and spandrels and rich relief ornamentation.

66. Click Agency Building, 1991–92
  Hodgetts + Fung Design Associates
  9057 Nemo Street
Modernist, rectilinear geometry is handsomely realized in a series of three contrasting volumes which compose this small office building. These distant volumes are in turn countered by a gentle curved wall of the mezzanine, and by the segment of an oval volume which arrives at the rear. The interior spaces end up being both conventional in certain ways and highly unconventional (spaces countering one another) in others.

CENTRAL HOLLYWOOD

ince everything about Central Hollywood is supposed to be fabulous, it is worth noting that the name may have been chosen by the developers, Mr. and Mrs. Horace Wilcox of Topeka, because Father Junipero Serra may have once said the Mass of the Holy Wood of the Cross near the site. Unfortunately, a much more prosaic explanation of the derivation is probable. But it is

significant that the Wilcoxes were determined when they platted the community in the late 1880s that it would be a center of high culture and morality, however contradictory these might be. They offered a free lot to any church that would build there. Their high tone was evidently contagious, for when movies were first developed in New York, they were banned in Hollywood, as were liquor and other forms of vice.

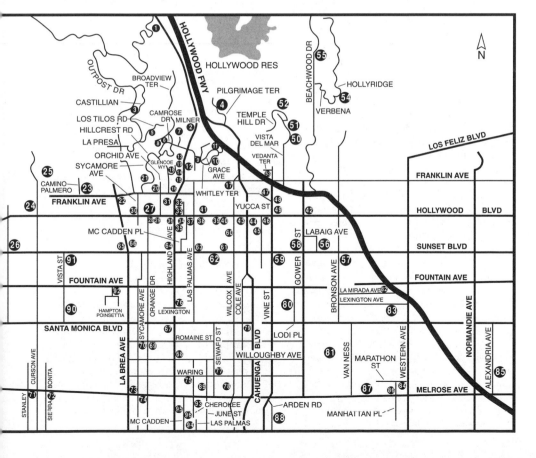

Needless to say, this happy condition did not last very far into the twentieth century. Whatever its present resemblance to Sodom and Gomorrah, Hollywood is conspicuously a city of churches, the First Presbyterian being the largest of that denomination in the world. But the movies came seeking the sun like everything else that came to California. The result may still be noted on the map in the form of large areas devoted to movie studios which, incidentally, may be converted eventually to new uses, as in Universal City to the north and Century City to the west. Also, the city acquired some of the most spectacular moving picture palaces that were built anywhere in the world in the 1920s and 1930s. Grauman's (now Mann's) Chinese is the most famous, but the Hollywood Pantages is the most magnificent.

The effect of movie madness on domestic architecture, or perhaps on the world of the interior decorator, can be seen in many remodels in the West Hollywood area. John Chase aptly labeled this approach "exterior decoration," the turning of nondescript small bungalows into miniature Versailles. In the earlier decades the taste of the stars and moguls, whatever their quest for opulence, was generally channeled into the Spanish, the Tudor, and the Anglo-Colonial. Nevertheless, the imaginative atmosphere did encourage a taste for the exotic in some citizens—the Egyptian, Islamic, Hansel and Gretel, Medieval, and Mayan traditions finding much favor. On the other hand, the same atmosphere seems to have encouraged other residents to employ some of the early Modernists—Gregory Ain, Richard J. Neutra, R. M. Schindler, Harwell H. Harris, Raphael S. Soriano, Pierre Koenig, and the Wrights, father and son. As a matter of fact, Hollywood Hills, though full of commonplace architecture, is an area that no student of twentieth-century traditional or avant-garde architecture can ignore.

If you are such a student, be sure to have your car and your patience in prime condition. We have done our best to make the maps accurate, but they can forecast only a few of the steep, tortuous roads and barely suggest the many opportunities to get lost. Persevere! "Civilization" is always nearby.

We begin at the north in Cahuenga Pass:

1. Maston Architectural Office Building, 1967
Carl Maston
2811 Cahuenga Boulevard (west side of Hollywood Freeway)
An ideal Modern design—an austere, horizontal brick wall, as an abstract plane is all that meets the eye from the street. Behind this wall is the glass facade of the building.

2. Hollywood Bowl, 1924 to present
2301 N. Highland Avenue
The first performance in the originally natural amphitheater was in 1922. In 1924 it was decided to improve the carrying power of the sound by building a shell, and Lloyd Wright was chosen as the designer. The result was a wood shell that was successful both visually and acoustically. In 1928 Wright was again employed to design a second shell which was elliptical in shape. In 1931 the Allied Architects of Los Angeles replaced that shell with a more pretentious one in concrete that never worked, in spite of almost continual remodeling. The latest shell (1982) is by Frank O. Gehry and Associates. Now the complaint is about the quality of the amplification system. The best thing at the Bowl is the gate on Highland Avenue. Three Federal Arts Project sculptures representing music, drama, and dance were sculpted by George Stanley (circa 1935). Very inspirational, especially at night, when lighted (although the original colored lights were a nice touch).

3. Goldberg/Bean House, 1991
Frank D. Israel Design Associates
2029 Castilian Drive
If you look closely, you can make out that the building we now see is a remodeling of a California Ranch house. The architect has tied the existing dwelling to the new via red and yellow colored stucco and natural wood walls. The new addition plays with both volumes and structure. Added to the exterior sheathing of wood and stucco are walls of concrete block and others covered with galvanized metal.

4. House, circa 1928
  2403 Pilgrimage Terrace
At first this seems to be a Queen Anne house, but closer inspection suggests a later date, perhaps even later than our guess.

5. Myers House, 1928, 1985
  Barton Myers Associates
  6900 Los Tilos Road
The architect acquired a modest, but spectacularly sited Spanish Colonial Revival dwelling of the late 1920s and transformed and added elements which bring this revival up-to-date. A small tower is now situated at the entrance, and Moorish-inspired tile walls enclose a new Franklin fireplace.

6. Hollywood Duplex, 1990
  Koning/Eisenberg Architecture
  6947–6949 Camrose Drive
These units appear from the street as two very separate towers, placed over their ground level garages. In plan each is L-shaped; between the L's are small terraces. The street fronts are rectangular stucco boxes, while the rear wing is covered by a low-pitched barrel roof and cut-out sections, which suggest or in fact are the stud structure of the buildings.

7. The High Tower, circa 1920
  North end of High Tower Road
Even if you do not decide to go up on the elevator, you will certainly want to admire this bit of whimsy, a small-scale version of the extravagances at Bologna. The two flanking Moderne houses are by Carl Kay (circa 1937).

8. Otto Bollman House, 1922
  Lloyd Wright
  2200 Broadview Terrace (reached by elevator from High Tower Drive below or by footpath nearby)
Architectural Expressionism at its height. This stuccoed frame house has pyramidal roofs covered by a pattern of horizontal and vertical boards. The boards have been removed, but you can get the idea from the unaltered garden house visible from the public walkway.

9. House, circa 1928
  Southwest corner of Milner Road and Las Palmas Avenue
A charming Hansel and Gretel in a storybook area. This area near the corner of Highland and Hollywood boulevards is one of the few in Los Angeles where you can actually park your car and walk to dozens of things. Of course, the natives will think you are mad!

10. Pike House, 1952
  George Vernon Russell
  6675 Whitley Terrace
A characteristic, rather delicate version of post-World War II Moderne, now painted brown. You can see this better than most of Russell's domestic work.

11. Lingenbrink House, 1930
  Jock Peters
  2000 Grace Avenue
Like other L.A. designers, Jock Peters used both Moderne and International Style Modern images. They are here in this house. In fact, Lingenbrink published several small books on both images in Los Angeles. Later in the 1930s he was a major patron of R. M. Schindler.

12. The Roman Gardens, 1926
  Pierpont and Walter S. Davis
  2000 N. Highland Avenue
The tower that you see does not look Roman (it could be from Moorish Spain or North Africa), but this is one of the more elaborate of Los Angeles's garden court apartment houses.

13. American Legion Headquarters Building, 1929
  Weston and Weston (Eugene Weston, Jr.)
  2035 Highland Avenue
Goodhue's Los Angeles Public Library certainly was on the architect's mind when he designed this modern Classical spectacle; its glittering tile ornamentation is still very fresh. The building is of reinforced concrete with the board pattern of the forms left exposed.

14. Shrader House, circa 1915
  Mead and Requa
  1927 Highland Avenue
Spanish Colonial Revival via Gill by an important San Diego firm. It is amazing that it still exists.

17. Montecito Apartment Building, 1931

16. First United Methodist Church, 1929

15. Duplex for De Keysor, 1935
　R. M. Schindler
　1911 Highland Avenue
The walls and sloped roofs of this hillside
house are covered with roll roofing material in
a manner similar to the original condition of the
Packard House (1924) in Pasadena.

16. First United Methodist Church, 1929
　Thomas B. Barber
　Northwest corner of Highland and Franklin
　avenues
English Gothic in revealed reinforced concrete;
it is a marvelous focal point at the curve of
Highland Avenue. Nearby, at the southeast corner of Selma Avenue and Las Palmas Avenue,
is the **First Baptist Church** (1935; Douglas
McLellan and Allen McGill), which illustrated
the broad popularity of the Anglo-Colonial
revival of the 1930s.

17. Montecito Apartment Building, 1931
　Marcus Miller
　6650 Franklin Avenue
The architect looked to the Art Deco skyscraper
when he produced this ten-story apartment
building. As with most Art Deco structures, the
windows are arranged in vertical bands, and
classic Art Deco ornament enriches the base
and the top of the building. In 1987 the building
was carefully restored for use as moderate-rent
apartments.

18. Koosis House, 1940
　Raphael S. Soriano
　1941 Glencoe Way
A delightful building because it does not seem
to take the International Style Modern too seriously.

19. Freeman House, 1924
　Frank Lloyd Wright
　1962 Glencoe Way
Another of Wright's concrete "knit-block"
houses which seems to begin Mayan and end
Islamic. To have seen the Freeman House
above the Methodist Church is to have reached
Mecca! Much of the built-in and freestanding
furniture was designed by R. M. Schindler in
1927. While Wright's other concrete block

19. Freeman House, 1924   *19. Freeman House, 1924 detail*

houses of the 1920s in L.A. are larger, the Freeman house is the most picturesque in its siting. The house was given by the Freemans to the University of Southern California, which has restored the dwelling.

20. Lane House (now Magic Castle), 1909
Dennis and Farwell
7001 Franklin Avenue at Orchid Avenue
This "French Chateau" has been transformed into a private club for magicians. Lucky are you if you get a chance to hear invisible Irma at her magic piano.

21. Bernheimer Bungalow (now Yamashiro Restaurant), 1913
Franklin M. Small; Walter Webber
1999 N. Sycamore Avenue
A stunning Japanese mountain palace and garden (with a real 600-year-old pagoda), built by two importers of oriental art, Adolphe L. and Eugene Bernheimer.

22. Crippled Children's Society Regional Office Building, 1969
Ladd and Kelsey
Southeast corner of Franklin and La Brea avenues
A sleek brick edifice in the late International Style version of Modern.

23. Fuller House, 1924
Arthur S. Heineman (Alfred Heineman, designer)
Northeast corner of Franklin Avenue and Camino Palmero
A strange mixture of Anglo-Colonial Revival and Italianate forms.

24. Erlik House, 1952
R. M. Schindler
1757 N. Curson Avenue
One of Schindler's last houses—an essay on how to use the typical Los Angeles stucco box. The interior of this single-floor house contains mirrored halls and much built-in furniture.

25. Wattles House and Gardens, 1905
Myron Hunt and Elmer Grey
1824 N. Curson Avenue
This large Mission Revival house was one of several designed by this Pasadena partnership. A pair of two-story wings enclose a three-arch arcade, which looks out over the valley. To the rear, adjoining the garden, is a two-story porch. Originally the house was entered via the south arcaded porch; later a new entrance with a porte cochere was added to the west. The detailing of the house hints both at the aesthetic of the late nineteenth century and the then popular

25. Wattles House, 1905

Craftsman movement. Originally it was almost entirely furnished in Craftsman fumed oak furniture.

The fame of the house rests on its terraced gardens to the rear and the plantings and winding pergola which ascend the steep hillside. The gardens were frequently publicized in the architectural journals and upper-middle-class shelter magazines of the times. Originally the gardens extended down to Hollywood Boulevard. The lower section is now used for the community's small garden plots. The gardens around the house were continually being changed and enlarged over the years. In 1911 Elmer Grey added walls and new handrails to the garden as well as a two-story reinforced concrete garage. The house and the garden are owned by the City of Hollywood. The house and the lower portions of the garden are administered by Hollywood Heritage. This organization has extensively restored both the house and its garden. The house and garden are open by appointment by calling Hollywood Heritage.

26. Henry Bollman House, 1922
    Lloyd Wright
    1530 N. Ogden Drive
An early use of textured "knit-block" construction combined with a wood stud frame covered with stucco. Lloyd Wright maintained that this was the first actual use of the concrete block "knit-block" system, which his father was to use in such later Los Angeles designs as the Storer House (1923), the Freeman House (1924), and the Ennis House (1924).

27. Grauman's Chinese Theater (now **Mann's**), 1927
    Meyer and Holler
    6925 Hollywood Boulevard
This giant tourist attraction surely must be familiar to everyone. Fortunately, nobody has tried to "modernize" it. The same cannot be said at the moment for Grauman's Egyptian theater down the street.

27. Grauman's Chinese Theater (now Mann's), 1927

28. Hollywood Masonic Temple, 1922
Austin, Field, and Fry
Intersection of Hollywood Boulevard and
Orchid Avenue
A magnificent Classical pile pushed up against
the wildly Churrigueresque Paramount Theater.

29. El Capitan Theater Building (now
Paramount), 1926
Morgan, Walls, and Clements; G. Albert
Lansburgh, theater designer
6834 Hollywood Boulevard
At first a combination theater and furniture
store, the store (six stories) has pulled out, leaving the theater to make ends meet. The South
Sea interior by Lansburgh was removed years
ago, but it has been recreated. Extensive
restoration was completed in 1991 under the
direction of Fields and Devereaux Architects.

30. El Cadiz Apartment Building, 1936
Milton J. Black
1731 Sycamore Avenue
A large Spanish Colonial Revival garden apartment with nice tile trim and art glass. Notice
that the garage is in the basement. A much
smaller Hispanic charmer is **El Cabrillo** (1928;
Arthur and Nina Zwebell), 1832 Grace Avenue
at the corner of Franklin.

31. U.S. Post Office, Osbourne Station,
circa 1928
1767 Highland Avenue
Art Deco in extremely colorful tile.

32. Don the Beachcomber Restaurant,
circa 1937
1727 N. McCadden Place
Although far from eye-catching today, this
restaurant was one of the first to employ openly
the South Sea Island motif so popular today.

**33. Los Angeles First National Bank
Building** (now **Security Pacific**), 1927
Meyer and Holler
6777 Hollywood Boulevard
A strange but effective Gothic and Spanish
Colonial goulash.

35. Max Factor Building, 1931

34. Bank of America Building, 1914
Ellet Parcher
Classical facade added in 1920s.
Remodeling 1935; Morgan, Walls, and
Clements
6870 Hollywood Boulevard
This originally was a four-story building. It was
cut down to its present one-story size by MWC,
who added the tile roof.

35. Max Factor Building, 1931
(Remodeling) S. Charles Lee
1659–1666 Highland Avenue
Lee was a fashionable theater designer, e.g., the
Los Angeles Theater in downtown Los
Angeles. He chose Regency Moderne (with his
usual side-glances at the Art Deco) to clothe
this old warehouse, giving it delicate and
sophisticated cosmetic richness with the use of
pink and white marble. Take a look inside. The
building now houses the Max Factor Museum
of Beauty.

36. Rexall Drug Company Building (now **Lee
Drug**), 1935
B. D. Bixby
6800–6804 Hollywood Boulevard at south-
west corner of Highland Avenue
Not as zappy Streamline Moderne as the nearby
Owl Drug Store at the corner of Cahuenga and
Hollywood boulevards, but it has its moments,
such as the neon Coca-Cola signs under frosted

glass in the pavement of the entrance. At risk of didacticism, it should be pointed out that this intersection of Highland and Hollywood is one of the few areas in Los Angeles where there is a real sense of place. This is the result of the immediate architecture all around it, but also the more distant Methodist Church to the north at a curve in Franklin and Highland. As we move east along Hollywood Boulevard, a generally grungy look has covered some good to outstanding architecture.

37. Egyptian Theater, 1922
Meyer and Holler
6712 Hollywood Boulevard
Here is an example of the grungy look, although it is a result of remodeling rather than signage and filth. As noted earlier, the wonderful Egyptian facade is completely gone and most of the interior madness has perished. Strangely, if you go down McCadden, at the west side of the theater you will find some very fresh looking restoration of the original decoration. Recently (1993) it was announced that the entire theater, including its forecourt, would be restored.

38. Shane Building (now **Hollywood Center**), 1930
S. Norton; F. Wallis
6652–6654 Hollywood Boulevard on the southwest corner of Cherokee Avenue
A marvelous Art Deco marquee on Cherokee Avenue calls attention to an equally distinguished lobby, almost completely intact.

39. Kress and Company Building (now **Frederick's**), 1935
Edward F. Sibbert
6606–6612 Hollywood Boulevard
It is very tempting to leave out this lavender and purple horror, but behind the recent color scheme is a good late Art Deco building by the New York-based architect who designed Kress stores across the country. Note the setbacks; try to ignore the window displays.

40. J. J. Newberry Company Building, 1928
Newberry Company
6600–6604 Hollywood Boulevard
The most colorful Art Deco on Hollywood

Boulevard, but it is upstaged by Frederick's next door.

41. Baine Building (now **U.T.B.**), 1926
Gogerty and Weyl
6601–6609 Hollywood Boulevard
Very lovely Spanish Colonial Revival above the "modernized" first floor.

42. Janes House, 1903
Dennis and Farwell
6541 Hollywood Boulevard
By a miracle this late Queen Anne house remains on this otherwise commercial boulevard. Farwell worked in the New York office of McKim, Mead, and White before he came to California.

43. Warner Theater Building (now **Pacific Hollywood**), 1926–27
G. Albert Lansburgh
6423–6445 Hollywood Boulevard
Somehow the architect combined Renaissance, Rococo, Moorish, and Art Deco ornamentation to produce a very effective piece of architecture.

44. Owl Drug Company Building (now **Julian Medical**), 1934
Morgan, Walls, and Clements
6380–6384 Hollywood Boulevard, on the southwest corner of Cahuenga Boulevard
Surely this must be one of the crowning achievements of the Streamline Moderne, to be rated in the same class as Robert Derrah's Coca-Cola Bottling Plant.

45. Francis Howard Regional Branch Library, 1985
Frank O. Gehry Associates
1623 Ivar Avenue
The old Hollywood Public Library burned in 1982 and was replaced by this present Gehry building. Internally, it is a pleasant and functional building, although the single, small circular staircase is inadequate for public traffic. What is really disturbing is the exterior, which has no public presence at all. From a distance, this structure could be a small office building; close up, the stairs leading down to the confining small forecourt hardly hint that this is a

public building. A few classic palms might have at least hinted that this is a public building.

46. Corner of Hollywood Boulevard and Vine Street
  a. Taft Building, 1923
  Walker and Eisen
  6290 Hollywood Boulevard
  b. B. H. Dyas Company Building
  (now **Broadway**), 1927
  6300 Hollywood Boulevard
  c. Hollywood Equitable Building, 1929
  Aleck Curlett
  6253 Hollywood Boulevard

These buildings are not great or even outstanding architecture. But for their time they were notable for their height—150 feet, the limit in the 1920s. They, therefore, represented a visible center for Hollywood. The Dyas (Broadway) Building has recently closed. Ironically, two lower buildings on the northwest corner were more notable—the **Laemmle Building** (1933) by Richard J. Neutra and **Sardi's Restaurant** Building (1932-34) by R. M. Schindler. Because of extravagant remodeling, neither has a sign of its architect's style.

47. Yucca-Vine Tower Building, circa 1928
  Gogerty and Weyl
  Northwest corner of Yucca and
  Vine streets

French curvilinear ornament mixed with Art Deco (Zigzag) Moderne.

48. Capitol Records Tower Building,
  1954–56
  Welton Becket Associates
  1750 Vine Street

Symbolic architecture. What could be more appropriate for the headquarters of a recording company than for the building to look like a stack of records! The twelve-story tower is constructed of reinforced concrete. Across the street at 1735 Vine Street is the old Hollywood Playhouse (later refurbished as The Hollywood Palace), a Churrigueresque dream designed (1926) by Gogerty and Weyl.

49. Pantages Theater Building, 1929
  B. Marcus Priteca
  6233 Hollywood Boulevard

On the exterior this theater building does not have the sensational quality of Mann's Chinese theater down the street, but go inside. It is one of the most dramatic Baroque statements ever made.

50. Krotona Court (now **Goldwater Patio Villa**), 1912–13
  Mead and Requa
  2130 Vista del Mar Avenue

Originally built for the Theosophical Society, this complex is properly exotic, although its exoticism is played off against the purity of Irving J. Gill (Mead had been a partner of Gill in San Diego for a few years). The aura of the mystical East is suggested in the Islamic domes and the horseshoe and cusped arches.

51. "Hansel and Gretel Cottages", circa 1925
  2234 and 2244 Vista del Mar Avenue

These two cottages look to the medieval rural English cottage. The double cottage with its central drive-through and folk paintings on its exterior walls, located at 6114–6116 Scenic Avenue, hints at the French rural cottage. Across the street, at 6111 Scenic Avenue, is a delightful French Norman cottage with a small tower attached to the hillside garage.

52. House, circa 1920
  6147 Temple Hill Drive

Islamic, with dome and all. A smaller **Islamic cottage** is situated nearby at 6106 Temple Hill Drive.

53. Vedanta Temple, 1938
  1946 Vedanta Terrace

The onion dome of this Islamic-image complex is visible from various points of the eastern Hollywood Hills.

54. Mosk House, 1933
  Richard J. Neutra
  2742 Hollyridge Drive

The image of the Mosk House is intended to be machine repeatable. The living room serves as a focal point for the lower wings at each side. This house was meant to be the first of a colony of Neutra houses to be built on this site.

55. Hollywoodland Gates, 1923

55. Hollywoodland Gates, Hollywood Sign, 1923
The Gates are located on Beachwood Drive at Westshire Drive

The sign is situated off Mount Lee Drive
These sandstone, somewhat Gothic fairy-tale picturesque gates were built to tell you that you were entering a very prestigious part of Hollywood, on the lowest slopes of Mount Lee. The subdivision was advertised by the famous Hollywood Sign still standing high on Mount Lee. When constructed, the sign read "Hollywoodland," and it was a grand, lighted billboard for that most time-honored activity in Los Angeles, the sale of real estate. The sign and the gates were constructed to promote five-hundred-acre subdivisions. The letters forming "land" were dropped off in 1945, and only "Hollywood" was left. The sign has been restored and restored, a reminder that beneath the facade of materialism, Los Angeles hides a strain of sentiment. Both the gate and the sign are cultural-historic monuments of the city. The last major restoration of the fifty-foot-long sign, lighted by more than 4,000 bulbs, took place in 1979. The suburban area

above the gates is fascinating for the student of period revivals. Note the tiny English cottage on the north side of Beachwood Drive at Ledgewood Drive. This was originally the real estate office for the development.

56. Courtyard Apartments, 1952
Craig Ellwood
1570 Labaig Avenue
A Miesian complex in a strange area for "less is more" architecture to appear.

57. Warner Brothers West Coast Studios, 1922
Southeast corner of Sunset Boulevard and Bronson Avenue
A long, low building which salutes the street with a magnificent set of Doric columns.

58. Columbia Broadcasting System Building, 1937–38
William Lescaze and E. T. Heitschmidt
6121 Sunset Boulevard
A classic, well-publicized example of the early (for America) International Style Modern, now badly remodelled. You can still sense Lescaze's design if you erase the present walls behind the pilotis.

59. Sunset-Vine Tower, 1964
Honnold, Reibsamen, and Rex
Corner of Sunset and Vine streets
Thin, late International Style Modern emphasizing the vertical.

60. U.S. Post Office, Hollywood Branch, 1937
Claude Beelman; Allison and Allison
1615 Wilcox Avenue
A small but impressive expression of the Classical PWA Moderne.

61. Retail Commercial Building, ca. 1928
6607 Sunset Boulevard
Lively Churrigueresque ornament around the entrance. We wonder how long such romantic buildings will last.

62. Hollywood Chamber of Commerce Building, 1925
Morgan, Walls, and Clements
Just west of Hudson Street on Sunset Boulevard

These architects always seem to treat their cast-stone Churrigueresque ornament in a light-hearted manner. The building was more charming, however, with the large pepper trees which used to stand in front.

63. Crossroads of the World, 1936
Robert V. Derrah
6671 Sunset Boulevard

The theme is set by a Streamline Moderne ship sailing into Sunset Boulevard with a tall, open tower (supporting a lighted globe) on its prow. Go to the stern and you will find shops in the Spanish Colonial, Tudor, and French Provincial modes. The architect has carried the concept of the 1920s pedestrian mall into the new stream-line age of the mid-1930s. It is perhaps signifi-cant that Derrah is one of the few architects to have two of his buildings declared cultural-his-toric landmarks by the Los Angeles Cultural Heritage Board. The other is the equally remarkable Coca-Cola Bottling Plant near downtown Los Angeles.

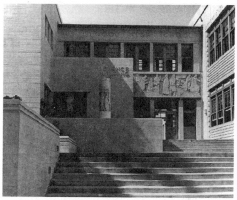

64. Hollywood High School Science Building, 1934–35

64. Hollywood High School Science Building, 1934–35
Marsh, Smith, and Powell
Northwest corner of Sunset Boulevard and Highland Avenue

Monumental Streamline Moderne given juice by high-minded slogans at appropriate places and a characteristic Federal Arts Project bas-relief by Bartolo Mako over the door. In the school library is a mural, *Education*, by Haldine Douglas. This was painted in 1934.

65. Tiny Naylor's Drive-in Restaurant, 1950
Douglas Honnold
7101 Sunset Boulevard, at the northwest corner of La Brea Avenue

A jutting angle of a roof made one of the most famous (and probably the last) of the drive-in restau-rants, where you were waited upon in your car. This "great" L.A. institution has now been demolished.

63. Crossroads of the World, 1936

66. Carolina Motel Building, 1959
Armet and Davis
East side of La Brea Avenue, just north of
Sunset Boulevard

A pure Southern California project of the 1950s, designed by a firm that produced a wide array of popular automobile-oriented restaurants and other buildings. With the exception of the lobby, a two-story perforated metal screen covers the entire front of the building. Behind this linear surface is the two-story motel, with underground garage and, of course, a pool-patio area.

67. Toberman Storage Warehouse
(now **Bekins**), 1925
Morgan, Walls, and Clements
1025 North Highland Avenue

This is an illustration of how a small skyscraper could be clothed in the Spanish Colonial Revival mode and at the same time appear as an excellent example of the 1920s "American Vertical style." The building has lost some of its zest in remodeling.

68. Community Laundry Building
(now **American Linen Supply**), 1927
W. J. Saunders
Northeast corner of Highland and
Willoughby avenues

The piers of this Spanish Colonial Revival building are covered with shields. When the sun rakes over them about midday, the effect is that of the Casa de las Conchas in Salamanca. We never exaggerate.

69. Aaron Brothers Building, circa 1928
East side of Orange Drive between
Romaine Street and Willoughby Avenue

Spanish Colonial Revival with some good ornament. But its salient feature is its present unearthly color.

70. Producers Film Center, circa 1928
Southeast corner of Romaine Street and
Sycamore Avenue

A little gem of the Art Deco (Zigzag) Moderne.

71. The Burger that Ate L.A., 1989

73. Danziger Studio, 1965

72. Claudia Grau Building, 1990

71. The Burger that Ate L.A., 1989
Solberg and Lowe
Southeast corner of Melrose Boulevard and
Stanley Avenue
Certainly this structure which consists of the
L.A. City Hall being eaten by a great burger is
one of L.A.'s great new programmatic build-
ings. The L-shaped building opens onto a pleas-
ant outdoor eating area.

72. Claudia Grau Building, 1990
South side of Melrose Boulevard, east of
Sierra Bonita Avenue
A wonderful shop front in tile (including the
sign), inspired by the turn-of-the-century
designs of Antonio Gaudi in Barcelona.

73. Danziger Studio, 1965
Frank O. Gehry and Associates
7001 Melrose at Sycamore Avenue
This small studio building was one of Frank
Gehry's first buildings to be highly publicized.
Though restrained compared to his current
work, the Danziger Studio building indicates
how he was moving from the world of traditional architecture to sculpture as architecture.

Minimal architecture at its best; a common
stucco box whose composition has raised it to
High Art.

74. Telesound Studio, circa 1945
6926 Melrose Avenue
The architect of this late Streamline Moderne
building curved the corners into the entrance,
leaving a single column in the middle. This
one, with its glass brick, is certainly not
minimal!

75. Propaganda Films Building, 1988
Franklin D. Israel Design Associates
Corner of Waring Avenue and Mansfield
Avenue
The nonassertive stucco facade of this 10,000-
square-foot warehouse building hides inside a
constructivist village. In the center is a boat-
shaped enclosure of rooms. Independent
"houses" define the other side of the streets as
they wander around the lozenge-shaped centerpiece.

76. Limelight Productions, 1991
Franklin D. Israel Design Associates
Corner of Highland Avenue and Lexington
Avenue
Like the Propaganda Films design, this is a
small village within a wood-roofed warehouse
building. The principal "street" plays with different, inexpensive materials, deep colors, and
natural and artificial light. With some of the
enclosures, the structure of the walls are

revealed; in others, a painted skin of plywood and other materials establishes either planes or entire volumes.

77. EVCO Film Library Building, 1968
    Leroy B. Miller
    838 Seward Street
Minimal Modern architecture in brick.

78. Apartment Building, 1926
    J. M. Close
    747 N. Wilcox Avenue
It is amusing to speculate upon what on earth was in this developer-builder-architect's mind when he conceived of buildings such as this, only one of several essays in the Egyptian Revival which he erected around Hollywood and elsewhere. J. M. Close designed, built, and then marketed many of these apartment buildings. In his advertisements, he encouraged prospective buyers to "pyramid your dollars." As you would expect, that which is Egyptian is only the pylon and colonnaded frontispiece. The rest is pure L.A. stucco box.

79. Film Exchange, Inc. Building, circa 1928
    Southeast corner of Santa Monica
    Boulevard and Cole Avenue
A tiny relic of the Regency Moderne. There is a key on top of the tower which may someday release something.

80. Hollywood Studio Club Building,
    1925–26
    Julia Morgan
    1215 Lodi Place
A mildly Italian Renaissance design; the second-floor loggia and the painted, decorated walls are carried out with delicacy.

81a. Hollywood Cemetery, 1900, and later
    Morgan, Walls and Clements, and others
    5950 Santa Monica Boulevard
With its mausoleums and ornate sculpture, not to mention the quantity of famous people buried here, this cemetery seems to be an annex of the Paramount Studio at the other end of the block. Probably the most distinguished architecture is the Classical mausoleum of William Andrews Clark designed (1922) by Robert Farquhar, although Egypt and other exotic sources are present in other monuments and

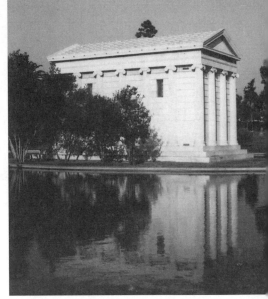

81a. William Andrews Clark Mausoleum, 1922

mausoleums. A more recent addition to the major monuments of the cemetery is the tombstone of Carl Morgan Bigsby (1959) which confronts us with a tall rocket ready to take us quickly to heaven.

81b. Paramount Studio Lot
    5500 Melrose Avenue
Off-limits to the public, but the main attraction is the old iron gate (circa 1928) at the end of Bronson Avenue at Marathon Street. Here a Spanish Renaissance gate is posed between two white stucco, tile-roofed, Hispanic buildings. The script sign "Paramount Pictures" is as much a delightful period piece as the gate.

82. Karnak Apartment Building, 1925
    J. M. Close
    5617 La Mirada Avenue
Since there is another Egyptian Revival apartment house just a block from here, we suggest that urban renewalists investigate the possibility of building a pyramid in honor of J. M. Close. They could do (and have done) worse.

85. House, 1939

84. Jardinette Apartment Building, 1927

83. Ahmed Apartment Building, 1925
J. M. Close
5616 Lexington Avenue

Almost a duplicate of the Karnak, this apartment house has been refitted with the original murals, which have been restored with considerable verve.

84. Jardinette Apartment Building, 1927
Richard J. Neutra
5128 W. Marathon Street, at southeast corner of Manhattan Place

This project began as a joint Schindler-Neutra venture, with Neutra finally doing it as an independent commission. Neutra provided bands of black (now painted over) between the windows that gave the illusion that this concrete building was composed of strongly contrasting horizontal bands of glass and projecting balconies. Henry Russell Hitchcock in his classic volume written with Philip Johnson (*The International Style, Architecture Since 1922*, New York, 1932), asserted that this coloristic effect of banding was "dishonest" and that it compromised the building.

85. House, 1939
Edward Richard Lind
822 Alexandria Avenue

Lind was in Schindler's office in the mid-1930s. Here you can see how creatively he applied the lessons of the master to a small, one-story stucco dwelling.

86. Service Station, circa 1928
5125 Melrose Avenue

Art Deco (Zigzag) Moderne.

87. Hollywood-Wilshire Health Center, 1968
Honnold, Reibsamen, and Rex
5505 Melrose Avenue

Some may write off this low, concrete building as 1960s Brutalist. We think it has class.

88. Morgan House, 1917
Irving J. Gill
626 North Arden Road

A variation by Gill of his small prototype, single-family dwelling. As with most of his buildings, its walls are of hollow tile covered with stucco. The building has recently (1989–90) been carefully restored by Roy McMakin and Andie Zelnio. For those interested in Gill's architecture, this building is a must.

91. Bungalow, circa 1920

96. Banning Houses, #s 2 & 3, 1929

89. House, circa 1925
   717 June Street
A tiny mosque.

90. Four Apartment Buildings, circa 1928
   1128–1144 S. Vista Street, just above Santa
   Monica Boulevard
A whole row of Andalusian treasures.

91. Bungalow, circa 1920
   1127–1129 Vista Street
A modest bungalow that poses as a miniaturized Egyptian temple.

92. Normandie Towers, 1924
   7219 Hampton Avenue
An apartment complex of twenty-three units
which is designed to suggest a fragment of a
French Norman village. Towers, turrets, and
balconies are enshrouded within a heavily
planted garden.

93. Lamy/Newton House, 1988
   Franklin D. Israel Design Associates
   620 North Cherokee Avenue
An addition to an existing house. This pavilion
comes close to being a cube, clothed in deep
colors—maroon, mustard, and blue. It seems to
float on a thin wood shelf extended over the
pool.

94. Gabriel Duque House, 1932
   Paul R. Williams
   340 North Las Palmas Avenue
As with other L.A. architects, Paul Williams's
version of the French Provincial dwelling
became increasingly delicate in its detailing and
at the same time more classical. These houses
are still Country French, but they seem to have
more to do with the then-popular Anglo-
Colonial Revival.

95. Banning House #1, 1929
   Paul R. Williams
   425 North McCadden Place
This Banning house is clothed in a version of
the French Provincial, in this case, stucco; the
design is intimate in scale and well adapted to
its suburban siting.

96. Banning Houses, #3, 1929
   Paul R. Williams
   426 and 432 North McCadden Place
For these two upper-middle-class suburban
dwellings, Williams turned to the late
eighteenth-century American Georgian, in
these two instances, brick. Note the handsome
recessed entrance at 426 with its pair of
classical columns.

HOLLYWOOD HILLS

lthough the roads were laid out in the 1920s, the summit of this section of the Santa Monica Mountains did not begin to be developed until the 1930s. Schindler's Fitzpatrick House (1936), which is so prominent when you finally twist to the top of Laurel Canyon Boulevard, was built as a real estate come-on to attract buyers to the area. The development of the summit before and after World War II is a dramatic illustration of how a landscape, even a rugged one, can be trans-

formed by energy and water. Indeed, the vegetation is now far more significant than most of the housing.

There are a remarkable number of important houses located in the Hollywood Hills. Regrettably only a dozen or so are really visible from a distance or from a public road. Even those that are visible are often difficult to find because of the bewildering pattern of meandering streets. These are all indicated on our map, but it might be advisable to plan your journey beforehand with a Thomas Bros. map in hand.

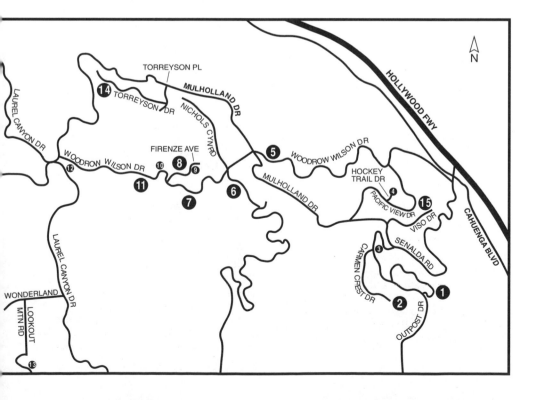

We have set this section apart from central
Hollywood simply because when you are up
this high, you might as well stay up.
Incidentally, there are other things on and just
off Mulholland Drive, a road that sticks with
determination to the top of the hills almost as
far as the ocean, many miles to the west.

1. Johnson House, 1963
　Lloyd Wright
　7017 Senalda Drive
Nothing more nor less than ancient Mayan
made Moderne. If the lavender hue isn't
original, it should be.

2. Wolff House, 1960
　Ladd and Kelsey
　2400 Carmen Crest Drive
A sheer stucco wall and metal door seal this
purist house from the curious.

3. Druckman House, 1941
　R. M. Schindler
　2764 Outpost Drive
A two-story house covered with one of
Schindler's unique gable roofs. Now it's almost
impossible to see, but we thought you would be
happy to know that it's there.

4. Carling House, 1950
　John Lautner
　Pacific View and Hockey Trail drives
One of Lautner's most dramatic gestures, raised
above your view.

5. Garred House, 1949
　Milton H. Caughey
　7445 Woodrow Wilson Drive
International Style Modern simplicity, almost
completely screened from the street.

6. General Panel House, 1950
　Konrad Wachsmann and Walter Gropius
　2861 Nichols Canyon Road
Of the four such houses by these famous architects in the Los Angeles area, this is the most
easily seen. This single-story design exudes
logic and dullness.

7. Bell House, 1940
　John Lautner
　7714 Woodrow Wilson Drive
Set far from Woodrow Wilson Drive on a very
private road, the house can nevertheless be seen
from certain points to the east. Like Lautner's
own house in the Silver Lake district, the pre-
World War II Bell House shares stylistic similar-
ities with the works of Harris, Ain, and Wurster.

8. Branch House, 1942
　Richard J. Neutra
　7716 Firenze Avenue
About all you see from the street is the carport
and some white clapboards. This house has
been altered extensively.

9. House, 1937–39
　Barcume and King
　7777 Firenze Avenue
A mixture of Monterey and Moderne.

10. Shulman House and Studio, 1950
　Raphael S. Soriano
　7875 Woodrow Wilson Drive
The distinguished architectural photographer's
studio is connected to the main house by a
small pergola and courtyard. He has landscaped
the grounds so magnificently (including a
Redwood grove!) that you cannot see the house
from the street.

11. Granstedt House, 1938
　Harwell H. Harris
　7922 Woodrow Wilson Drive
We are pleased that this beautiful house can be
seen easily from the street. A drive-through
garage runs parallel to the street. Also, here you
can see how Harris worked with his roof to create clerestory and other high sources of lighting.

12. Fitzpatrick House, 1936
　R. M. Schindler
　8078 Woodrow Wilson Drive
The de Stijl composition of overlaid volumes of
horizontal stucco surfaces can best be seen
from below on Laurel Canyon before it joins
Mulholland and Woodrow Wilson. The front
has been altered, but the southwest facade and
the sunken garden to the west are still intact.

10. Shulman House and Studio, 1950

13. Margaret Shelby Fillmore House
   (Edward A. Bailey), 1929
   Roy Sheldon Price
   Benjamin Morton Purdy, landscape
   architect
   8818 Lookout Mt. Avenue

Roy Sheldon Price was one of the most gifted of Los Angeles Period Revival architects of the 1920s. He really understood what the "picturesque" meant for his Los Angeles clients. His most famous residence, the extensive Spanish Colonial Revival house in Beverly Hills for the film director Thomas H. Ince, is regrettably now gone. Though small by comparison to the Ince House, the Margaret Fillmore House is one of the City's gems of traditionalist architecture. When it was completed, the editors of *Arts and Decoration* wrote of its style, "Though rural in effect, there is a suggestion of Medieval Italy in the doorway and wrought iron stair rails." In fact, its image has much more to do with the provincial cottage architecture of England and France. Countering this cultivated provincial image (in the manner of Edwin Lutyens) is an expansive Classical main entrance with pilasters supporting a pair of broken volutes, which serve as a porch roof. The play between the Medieval and the Classical continues on the interior. The rooms of the Fillmore house are oriented around an inner court, while to the rear looking over a view of the city and far distant ocean is a large, pillared, circular garden structure with a fireplace.

14. Leonard J. Malin House
   ("Chemosphere"), 1960
   John Lautner
   776 Torreyson Drive

At first it seems to be a flying saucer, but then you see that it is on a pedestal firmly riveted to the hill. The house is at the end of a private drive, but there are many places to view it on Torreyson Drive and Woodrow Wilson Drive. The owner/builder of the house commented that "there are a great number of very normal, intelligent people who do not specially enjoy doing yard work on Saturday afternoon. I am one of these. I will be very happy, sitting, looking down at the tops of trees, which do not have to be mowed."

15. Viso House, 1989
   Hodgetts + Fung Design Associates
   2911 Viso Drive

The vernacular tradition of Schindler is taken into the late 1980s in this stucco-sheathed hillside dwelling. The design centers on an internal cylinder, which is sliced through by an angled axis. To the rear you can experience the play of the layered volumes.

EAST HOLLYWOOD; LOS FELIZ; GRIFFITH PARK

In a characteristic L.A. fashion we have let the Hollywood Freeway (Highway 101) act as a dividing line between central Hollywood, east Hollywood and the Los Feliz district. To the north, Griffith Park provided a hilly backdrop to the area. The 3,015-acre park was given to the City in 1896 by Col. Griffith J. Griffith, though its development for public use had to wait until the twentieth century.

The meandering array of winding streets which make up east Hollywood (including Griffith Park and the Los Feliz district) were annexed to the City of Los Angeles in 1910. Through the early 1920s there were a number

of large houses and estates built in the Los Feliz area. The only one of these still standing is the Earl C. Anthony house, designed by Bernard Maybeck. In the teens, 1920s, and later, middle- and upper-middle-class houses were built in the hilly section north of Los Feliz Boulevard. Below Los Feliz Boulevard, reaching down to Hollywood Boulevard, land use was more mixed. Single family housing (dating from the turn of the century on through the early 1940s) was, generally, more modest in size, and there were a good number of duplexes and apartments built. Strip commercial development occurred along several of the north/south streets, and along portions of

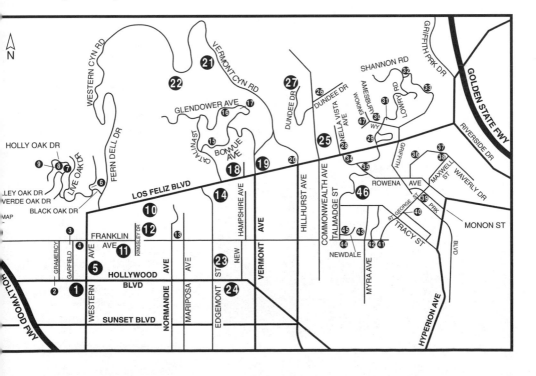

Franklin Avenue and Hollywood Boulevard.

Griffith Park: The original park consisted of 3,015 acres of mountainous terrain. This was slowly increased to its present area of 4,063.87 acres. Thus, in size it is in the league of New York's Central Park, Philadelphia's Fairmount Park, or San Francisco's Golden Gate Park. But, for a variety of reasons, this great park functions not as an urban park but more like a distant regional park. Its steep hilly terrain does not easily lend itself to the easygoing pleasures which Frederick Law Olmsted had in mind when he laid out Central Park in New York or Prospect Park in Brooklyn. Added to this limitation is the fact that the park really has no meaningful connection to the city proper. Its one major connection to the city is via Vermont Canyon Road, but even though this is a handsome winding boulevard, it creates the feeling of an upper-middle-class suburbia, not the entrance to the city's major park. As is generally the case with most of America's urban parks, Griffith Park has had to battle off the believers in hardscape—ranging from the incursion of freeways to the location of buildings constructed within it. One suspects that if Griffith Park is ever able to figure in the minds of most Angelinos, the whole idea of a public urban park and what it can provide for its citizens will have to be rethought.

6. Taggart House, 1922–24

1. MPA Office Building, 1928
S. Charles Lee
Southwest corner of Hollywood Boulevard and Western Avenue
Art Deco (Zigzag) Moderne—but the great effect is in the high relief sculpture on the balcony fronts.

2. Hollywood Christian Church, 1922
Robert H. Orr
1717 North Gramercy Place
A great Ionic pile.

Kleihauer Memorial Chapel, 1967
Carleton M. Winslow, Jr., and Warren Waltz
Austerely exotic, this building has no relationship to the older building.

3. Garfield Court Apartments, 1927
A. J. Waid
1833 Garfield Place
A really grand Spanish Colonial court with beautiful trees. Even the fire escapes are beautifully designed and crafted.

The twenty units of this two- and three-story garden court apartment are organized around a large courtyard. Below parts of the complex is an underground garage.

4. Security Pacific Bank Building, 1972–73
Craig Ellwood Associates
1811 N. Western Avenue
"Less is more" at a 45-degree angle to the street.

5. Bungalow Court, circa 1915
1742–1752 N. Western Avenue
An Oriental complex, complete with entrance gate.

6. Taggart House, 1922–24
Lloyd Wright
5423 Live Oak Drive
One of Lloyd Wright's simplest and most picturesque stucco and wood buildings, carefully related to the hill to which it clings. Incidentally, Ferndell Park just below the house is one of the loveliest parks in Los Angeles.

7. Samuels-Navarro House, 1926–28
  Lloyd Wright
  5609 Valley Oak Drive
Here Lloyd Wright translates the textured, pre-cast concrete Mayanesque block into pressed metal. The result hints at pre-Columbian Revival and Art Deco (Zigzag) Moderne composition. The main (top) floor is cross-axial, with one arm terminating in an open court with swimming pool. In 1990–91 Schweitzer BIM (Josh Schweitzer) provided a sophisticated remodeling of the interior spaces. This sort of remodel of a major historic monument always creates an inherent conflict between preservation and the desire of new owners to express themselves. The Schweitzer firm has sought to play a close game between their new work and a respect for Lloyd Wright's design, an approach that in this case is probably for the best.

8. Ernest House, 1937
  Gregory Ain
  5670 Holly Oak Drive
Using large areas of glass in this house, Ain emphasizes the relationship between indoors and out. Some details of the house indicate his admiration for Schindler's designs of the late 1920s and early 1930s.

9. Edwards House, 1936
  Gregory Ain
  5642 Holly Oak Drive
This single-story house comprises a series of walled enclosures that give each space complete privacy.

10. Vinmont House, 1926
  Roland E. Coate
  5136 Los Feliz Boulevard
A characteristic Mediterranean/Spanish Colonial Revival two-story house by an architect who specialized in this mode but who also did equally well in the Tudor and Colonial Revival styles.

11. The Casa Laguna, 1928
  Arthur B. and Nina W. Zwebell
  Southwest corner of Franklin Avenue and
  Kingsley Drive
A twelve-unit Spanish Andalusian garden court apartment by the pair who designed many of

11. The Casa Laguna, 1928

the most successful examples in Los Angeles. Behind a pair of palm trees is the balconied two-story building. Entrances to the individual apartments are off the large central courtyard. Within the courtyard is a large fountain and an out-of-doors fireplace. To the rear, a sunken row of garages supports a south-facing terrace.

12. Sowden House, 1926
  Lloyd Wright
  5121 Franklin Avenue
Built around an inner court which originally contained an elaborate fountain and Mayan-inspired stele, the building is entered through a door at the lower level, almost hidden under a huge, cavelike window framed in decorative concrete blocks.

13. Apartment Building, circa 1938
  Carl Kay
  1941–43 Mariposa Avenue
A two-story Streamline Moderne composition.

14. House, circa 1925
  David J. Witmer
  2020 Edgemont Street
An unusual example of a reinforced concrete house with the wide board marks of the forms strongly showing. Its image and detailing are Tudor.

15. Moore House, 1964
Craig Ellwood and Associates
4791 Bonvue Avenue
Here Ellwood applies his personal Miesian aesthetic to a structure that exhibits even more wood than the Kubly House, which he was building in Pasadena at the same time.

16. Skolnik House, 1952
R. M. Schindler
2567 Glendower Avenue
In several of his late works Schindler concentrated on simple, stucco-covered volumes, roofs extending over clerestory windows, and thin linear wood members. All are present in the Skolnik House. Later additions were made by Gregory Ain (1960).

17. Ennis House, 1924
Frank Lloyd Wright
2607 Glendower Avenue
Variously called a mausoleum, a Mayan temple, and a palace, this is without a doubt the most monumental of Wright's experiments with "knit-block" construction. It is being carefully restored by the owner.

18. House, circa 1924
Northwest corner of Los Feliz Boulevard and New Hampshire Avenue
A striking openly revealed concrete house best viewed from New Hampshire Avenue.

19. Los Feliz Manor Apartment Building, 1929
Jack Grundfor
4643 Los Feliz Boulevard
One of L.A.'s highly effective examples of the Art Deco. It still retains the contrast of white surfaces and green trim.

20. Barcelona and Coruna Apartments, 1932
George Fosayke
Northwest corner Los Feliz Boulevard and Hillhurst Avenue
A pair of Spanish apartments share a common interior court. Each has an arched entrance for the driveway, and both boast cantilevered wood balconies.

21. Greek Theater 1913, 1929–30
S. Tilden Norton and F. H. Wallis; Heath and Gore of Tacoma, Washington Department of Parks
Vermont Canyon Road
Heath and Gore were brought into the planning of the theater because they were considered "experts on Greek theaters." A flat Doric facade masks an open theater seating four thousand people. It isn't much as architecture, but you will certainlẙ notice it on the way up Vermont Canyon.

17. Ennis House, 1924

20. Barcelona and Coruna Apartments, 1932

22. Griffith Park Observatory and Planetarium, 1935
John C. Austin and F. M. Ashley; **Obelisk and bas-reliefs** (Galileo, Copernicus, etc.), 1934, Archibald Garner; **Interior Murals,** 1935, Hugo Ballin
Western Canyon Road
PWA Classical Moderne in exposed reinforced concrete. A fine achievement of the depression years. High on the hill, it is a very romantic object, completing many vistas in Los Angeles like a huge eighteenth-century English garden. Its siting and entrance are pure axial Beaux Arts.

23. Thirteenth Church of Christ, Scientist, 1930
Allison and Allison
1750 N. Edgemont Street
A very sophisticated Italian Renaissance ensemble.

24. Barnsdall Park
Entrance on Hollywood Boulevard about 100 yards west of intersection with Vermont Avenue.
Barnsdall ("Hollyhock") House, 1917–20
Frank Lloyd Wright

Studio-Residence A, 1920
R. M. Schindler, under Wright's supervision
Garden Wall and Landscaping, 1924
R. M. Schindler
Wading Pool and Pergola, 1925
R. M. Schindler and Richard J. Neutra
Junior Arts Center, 1967
Paul Hunter, Walter Benedict, Herbert Kahn, Edward Tarrell
Municipal Art Gallery, 1971
Wehmueller and Stephens
Aline Barnsdall, like another oil millionaire Gaylord Wilshire, toyed with Marxist ideas. She envisioned a veritable "people park" when she gave her estate to the city. In the years that have followed, the fringes of her estate on Vermont and Sunset have been inundated with commercial buildings and a medical complex that do nothing for the spirit of the place, to say the least. But go up the drive and you are almost out of this skulchpile. The first important building that you see is Studio-Residence

22. Griffith Park Observatory and Planetarium, 1935

24. Barnsdall ("Hollyhock") House, 1917–20

A, now called the **Arts and Crafts Center.** This was to be the first of several such artists' residences in the manner of the MacDowell Colony in New Hampshire. Even though designed by Schindler, the building is very beholden to the Prairie style of Frank Lloyd Wright, for whom Schindler acted as supervisor of the main house construction while the Master was in Japan. Studio-Residence B was razed in the 1950s. **The main Barnsdall House,** with its pre-Columbian air and stylized hollyhock ornamentation, is in good condition. Needless to say, even with time's changes, the interior, particularly in the entrance, living room, and dining areas, displays Frank Lloyd Wright's magical spatial concepts. All is drama. The principal interior spaces have been restored, and examples of Wright's original furniture for the house have been reproduced.

Wright constructed a temporary gallery between the main house and the pre-Columbian-style dog kennels in 1956. This gallery was intended to house a major showing of his own drawings, but was used as the municipal art gallery until the late 1960s, when a new gallery was designed and constructed by another firm and the old gallery was torn down. No loss, except that Wright had several interesting

designs for a new museum. Suffice it to say that the present building, while not great architecture, has exhibition spaces that, though small, are better adapted to the viewing of art than those found in several other public museums around town.

The Junior Art Center is a much-needed facility in a light Wrightian manner. The garden structures were designed by Schindler and Neutra.

25. House, 1924
   Alfred Heineman
   2234 Commonwealth Avenue
Important because with its roof swooping into the eaves and Hansel and Gretel ornament, it demonstrates a tendency of the Arts and Crafts movement toward sentimentality.

26. Schrage-Hallauer House, 1951
   Raphael S. Soriano
   2648 Commonwealth Avenue
Almost invisible, but it is here. A two-story, International Style Modern design in stucco, glass, and steel.

27. Lovell House, 1929
   Richard J. Neutra
   4616 Dundee Drive
Without question, this house and Schindler's house for the same clients in Newport Beach are the greatest monuments of the early International Style Modern in Southern California. The Lovell House, with its open, free-flowing plan, its modern machine-age materials, and its structural form, firmly established Neutra's world reputation. Today, more than fifty years after its construction and in spite of slight alterations, the Lovell House looks new—the highest compliment.

28. Apartment House, 1935
   Northeast corner of Los Feliz Boulevard
   and Nella Vista Avenue
Regency Moderne.

29. Johnstone House, 1935
   W. P. Kesling
   3311 Lowry Road
Streamline Moderne, of course. We emphasize this style because it took an act of moderate courage to flout the conventions of the time.

27. Lovell House, *1929*

30. Ulm House, 1937

30. Ulm House, 1937
   Milton Black
   3606 Amesbury Road
We are sounding one note. Just the same, this
Streamline Moderne two-story house, with its
dramatic curved staircase encased in glass
brick, simply stands out.

31. Cole House, 1948
   Ain, Johnson, and Day
   3642 Lowry Road
A regional version of International Style
Modern in stucco and wood.

32. House, circa 1928
   End of Lowry Road at Shannon Road
Ye olde English cottage.

33. Griffith Park Girl's Camp, 1949
   Smith, Jones, and Contini
   North end of Griffith Park Boulevard
A wood post-and-beam structure which is more
of an open shelter than a building.

34. Farrell House, 1926
   Lloyd Wright
   3209 Lowry Road
An ordinary Spanish Colonial Revival bungalow of the 1920s becomes pre-Columbian with
a facing of textured concrete blocks.

35. Carr House, 1925
   Lloyd Wright
   Southeast corner of Lowry
   Road and Rowena
   Avenue
Originally this still-unusual
house had a tent room at the
side (overlooking Rowena)
and a bent pattern of fine canvas awnings, which provided
privacy and kept the west sun
off the side of the house.
Portions of the exterior stucco
walls were stenciled to suggest an ornamented concrete
block pattern.

36. Anthony House, 1927
   Bernard Maybeck
Mark Daniels, landscape architect; Lutah
M. Riggs (1956–66)
   3412 Waverly Drive
Now a Roman Catholic retreat, this is almost
impossible to see unless you want to retreat,
which might be a good idea. We include it
because it is the only well-authenticated building by Maybeck in the Los Angeles area. It is
one of the architect's most romantic houses,
which is saying a lot. The general effect is
Medieval, but of course Maybeck thought nothing of bringing in elements of other styles in
order to get desired effects. It is fascinating to
compare Maybeck's spatial explosions with
Frank Lloyd Wright's equally dramatic but
more integrated volumes. Between 1956 and
1966 impressive formal gardens and walled terraces were laid out by Lutah M. Riggs (she also
added a **Studio Building** in 1967). These landscape additions represent the most extensive
formal gardens realized in Southern California
in the post-World War II years.

37. McAlmon House, 1935–36
   R. M. Schindler
   2721 Waverly Drive
The house is a piece of architectural sculpture
embracing the complete range of Schindler's de
Stijl aesthetic. Actually you get two for the
price of one. The house, with garage at street
level, is an old bungalow which Schindler

moved down the hill and clothed in modern dress.

38. Schapiro House, 1949
   J. R. Davidson
   Northwest corner of
   Waverly Drive and
   Maxwell Street
Almost all of Davidson's houses are hard to see, but here enough of the jutting roof is visible to make your trip worthwhile.

39. Bungalow Court, circa 1925
   2906–2912 Griffith Park
   Boulevard
Each of these eight units is a miniature Norman cottage. A matching tower stands at the rear to give visual focus. Certainly this is one of the outstanding bungalow courts in the Los Angeles area!

35. Carr House, 1925

40. John Marshall High School, 1930–31
   George M. Lindsey
   Northeast corner of Tracy and Saint George
   streets
Collegiate Gothic. After the 1971 earthquake the School Board said that it had to come down. But the neighborhood, after a fine battle, convinced the board that the shell could be stabilized and the interior remodeled.

41. Franklin Avenue ("Shakespeare")
   Bridge, 1926
   J. C. Wright for City Engineer's Office
   Built over Monon Street between St.
   George Street and Myra Avenue
A great, open spandrel arch is laced by long Gothic arches. At both ends of the bridge are pairs of Gothic aedicules which cry out for sculptured saints.

42. Apartment Building for Dr. F. Haight,
   circa 1937
   Wesley Eager
   4116 Franklin Avenue
The lines of this Streamline Moderne complex are muted in comparison to those of the spectacular bridge next to it.

43. Schlesinger House, 1952
   R. M. Schindler
   1901 Myra Avenue
From the street this dwelling is a deceptively plain design for Schindler, yet the interiors and his method of providing natural lighting for them are as successful and complex as the interiors of any of his other houses.

44. Apartment House, 1939
   J. Knauer
   4230–4234 Franklin Avenue
Part of the fine effect of this Streamline Moderne building is the result of its being sited on the crest of a hill.

45. Elliot House, 1930
   R. M. Schindler
   4237 Newdale Drive
Schindler set the house far back on the site in order to allow a view of the valley. On the street level is a garage and entrance, both covered by a pergola. The house is also partially covered by a second level which opens to terraces, both front and rear.

45. Elliot House, 1930

46. Gogol House, 1938–39
  Raphael S. Soriano
  2190 Talmadge Street
Only a single floor is visible on the Talmadge Street side of the house. A deck and patio face toward the view. The style: purist International Style Modern.

47. Walt Disney House, 1932
  F. Scott Crowhurst
  4053 Woking Way
As one would expect, this house is an enlarged Hansel and Gretel cottage. A large, squat, round tower with a high-pitched conical roof houses the entrance.

48. Rajagopal House, 1983
  Paul Sterling Hoag
  2122 North Gower Street
A curved wall, almost Baroque in character, leads one to the deep arched front door. The porch to the rear has the feeling of being a Baroque piece of furniture. Within this Baroque framework is a modernist composition of rectangles of walls and glass.

49. The Gene Autry Western Heritage Museum, 1987–89
  Widom, Wein and Cohen (Charles A. Widom and Michael Heinrich)
  Zoo Drive, Griffith Park
A mild-mannered version of Post Modern architecture. The banded tower with its tile roof and the various courtyards and other details suggest, but do not directly re-create, California's Hispanic architectural tradition. While you are in the eastern reaches of the park you might also wish to visit the **Los Angeles World Zoo,** which was designed in 1963 by Charles Luckman, with Robert Herrick Carter and Associates as landscape architects.
  While you are now well around the northeast side of the Park and are adjacent to Burbank, you might as well continue to the **Griffith Park Equestrian Center** (located north of the Ventura Freeway off of Victoria Boulevard). This complex was designed in 1963 by George Vernon Russell and Associates, and the image, as would be expected, is woodsy California ranch—well and sophisticatedly carried out.

SILVER LAKE

For so small a district, the Silver Lake area has a high concentration of first-rate architecture, making it one of the most important places to visit in the city. The most interesting work is by the best Los Angeles Modernists: Schindler, Neutra, Ain, Soriano, Harris, Lautner. These works stand side by side with houses designed in the Period Revivals of the 1920s and 1930s. It is essentially this latter work which gives Silver Lake its special character. In fact, looking from Schindler's ingenious **Walker House** down over the flood of tile roofs to the lake below reminds you, well, of Los Angeles's

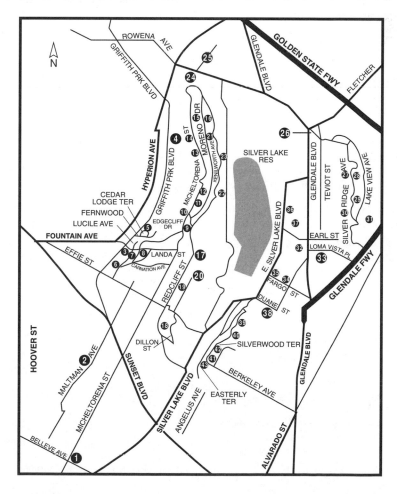

version of Urbino. Obviously the view (of hills and the reservoir) was the attraction, and the architects have played up to it. Along the eastern section of Sunset Boulevard running through the area is a sprinkling of Spanish Colonial Revival and Moderne commercial relics. There are also a few delightful exotics scattered hither and yon. For example, at 933 Parkman Avenue is a two-story **garden apartment** (circa 1920) which declares its allegiance to Islam through its minarets, dome, and arches. Here are our choices of the most representative architectural finds in Silver Lake:

1. Holy Virgin Mary Russian Orthodox Cathedral, 1928
658 Micheltorena Street

A lovely Russian village church, the cathedral is even more attractive inside. It reflects the taste of the emigrés from the Revolution—Russian intellectuals of the Count Tolstoy school. Great simplicity with patches of opulence.

2. McIntosh House, 1939
Richard J. Neutra
1317 Maltman Avenue

One of the earliest of Neutra's wood-sheathed houses. The narrow plan with the garage, sleeping, and service areas in front and living area to the rear takes full advantage of the narrow lot and view over the city.

3. Landa Apartment Building, 1966
A. E. Morris
Southeast corner of Griffith Park Boulevard and Landa Street

A stepped design of connected stucco boxes certainly inspired by the earlier work of R. M. Schindler. This architect is even more Expressionistic than Schindler.

4. Bubeshko Apartment Building, 1938 and 1941
R. M. Schindler
Southeast corner of Griffith Park Boulevard and Lyric Avenue

A dramatic setback of each level allows the building to hug the hillside and at the same time to continue internal spaces of each apartment outward to roof terraces and patios.

5. CDLT 1, 2 House, 1987–92
Michael Rotundi
1955 Cedar Lodge Terrace

The architect has written of this house, "No working drawings were made for this project. Sketches were made for the contractor to work from each morning. At the end of the day the contractor would leave lights pointed at the areas that needed to be resolved by the following morning." Though, as the architect has said, "The element of surprise was a major component of this house," its design turns out to be composed—composed to be sure of discordant elements, but then this is the language which he has employed in this design. The resulting house is certainly one of L.A.'s most important buildings of the early 1990s.

6. Falk Apartments, 1939
R. M. Schindler
Northeast corner of Lucile and Carnation avenues

Working with an extremely difficult hillside site, Schindler twists and turns the building so that each living unit has its own garden and roof terrace.

7. Manola Court (Sachs) Apartment Building, 1926–40
R. M. Schindler
1811–1813 Edgecliff Drive

These apartments, designed for the artist/designer Herman Sachs, are examples of the studied abstraction which Schindler was beginning to develop. They are designed as steps leading from the lower street up the steep hillside to the next.

8. Westby House, 1938
R. M. Schindler
1805 Maltman Avenue

Schindler's late de Stijl aesthetic at work in a two-story house.

9. Daniels House, 1939
Gregory Ain
1856 Micheltorena Street

The stucco box as a fragile container, masterfully detailed and imaginatively planned. The architect angled the house on a steep hillside in order to allow for a private patio and garden.

9. Daniels House, 1939

and gable roofs on the garden and view side. As a result, the interior is a syncopation of ceiling heights and changing axes. The living room, with its built-in furniture, is one of Schindler's most handsome.

13. Alexander House, 1941
Harwell H. Harris
2265 Micheltorena Street
Harris had learned a great deal from Frank Lloyd Wright about composition. Here he simplified Wright's Usonian concept. The low, hipped roof and simple walls seem to have as much to do with Wright as with the traditional California Ranch house.

10. Lautner House, 1939
John Lautner
2007 Micheltorena Street
Since World War II, Lautner has become one of the leading Expressionist architects in the country. Here we see him working in a subdued, controlled manner with redwood and concrete.

11. "Silvertop" House and Garden, 1957
John Lautner
2138 Micheltorena Street
Here's what we have just been talking about! This structure gets a high grade for exotic form. The total design includes the cantilevered driveway and swimming pool, the house, and, of course, the landscaping. Actually it can be seen better from a rear entrance near 2134 Redcliff Street and best (with binoculars) from across the lake on East Silver Lake Boulevard.

12. Olive House, 1933
R. M. Schindler
2236 Micheltorena Street
A house full of Schindler's wonderful contradictions. The house seems flat-roof International Style from the street, but it is all shed

14. Tierman House, 1938–39
Gregory Ain; Visscher Boyd, collaborator
2323 Micheltorena Street
A very ingenious house on two levels, pivoting around a central core lighted by a skylight. Essentially, the Tierman House is a stucco box with an attached garage, one-story on the street, two-story on the garden side.

15. Orans House, 1941
Gregory Ain
2404 Micheltorena Street
The living room is covered by a gently sloping shed roof that floats above bands of glass.

16. Van Patten House, 1934–35
R. M. Schindler
2320 Moreno Drive
This dramatic hillside house has been fenced in and the garages with their overlapping shed roofs have been converted to living space, but basically, Schindler's ideas have been maintained.

16. Van Patten House, 1934–35

17. Wilson House, 1938
  R. M. Schindler
  2090 Redcliff Street
Here, in another of his hillside houses, Schindler cantilevered three floors of projecting and receding boxes out to the rear and then connected them with projecting balconies at the side.

18. Hopmans House, 1951
  Harwell H. Harris
  1727 N. Dillon Street
A subtle touch revealed in a wood pavilion, the house has been modified a bit since it was built.

19. Lipetz House, 1935
  Raphael S. Soriano
  1843 Dillon Street
The living room is in the form of a Streamline Moderne ship's bridge. Bands of horizontal steel windows and metal railings extend the nautical theme, now somewhat altered.

20. House, circa 1930
  1824 San Jacinto Street (beyond the turn of Dillon Street)
A dollhouse of a mosque with flashing tiles on its lovely tower.

21. Droste House, 1940
  R. M. Schindler
  2025 Kenilworth Avenue
As this house was being finished, Schindler asked the owners to sit where their dining table would be on the second floor, so he could adjust the lintel of the picture window so that the owners wouldn't miss anything in the view.

22. Walker House, 1936
  R. M. Schindler
  2100 Kenilworth Avenue
The closed-in street facade reveals nothing of the glass and projecting-balconied, three-level drama to the rear inside.

23. Hansen House, 1951
  Harwell H. Harris
  2305 W. Silver Lake Boulevard
This stucco and wood beauty is rather surprising amid the relatively conventional suburbia on this street.

24. Kenngott-Brossmer Design Studio Building, 1968
  Carl Maston
  2840 Rowena Avenue
A gray brick street facade almost hides a court beautifully articulated with much use of wood.

25. Avenel Housing, 1948
  Ain, Johnson, and Day
  Katharine Bashford and Fred Barlow, Jr., landscape architects
  2839 Avenel Street
This is now painted pink, but the raking angle of the roof marks it as early Los Angeles International style mixed with L.A.'s tradition of the common stucco box and enclosed gardens.

26. Conrad's Drive-In, (now **Astro's**), 1958
  Louis Armet and Eldon Davis
  Southeast corner of Glendale Boulevard and Fletcher Drive
A striking example of People's Moderne of the 1950s with its angled roof. Other examples of

the designs of Armet and Davis are **Romeo's, Times Square** (1955; now **Johnie's**), at the corner of Fairfax Avenue and Wilshire Boulevard; **Pann's** (1956), at the corner of La Cienega Boulevard, Centinela Avenue, and La Tijera Boulevard in Inglewood; and **Norm's** (1957), at the corner of Overhill Drive and Slauson Avenue.

27. Hawk House, 1939
    Harwell H. Harris
    2421 Silver Ridge Avenue
Although very close to the road, this house is easy to miss. It is in dense foliage, but you can still see enough of this horizontal board house with its low, hovering roof to recognize the work of a consummate artist. The serene Oriental interior has always been beautifully maintained.

28. Howe House, 1925
    R. M. Schindler
    2422 Silver Ridge Avenue
The exterior is horizontal board and batten and concrete, very boxy. The house was originally flat-roofed. The interior is a tour de force in interlocking spaces. Incidentally Eads Howe was known as the "King of the Hoboes." The floor of the house below street level was, according to legend, a sort of dormitory for tramps who would come up from the railroad below. We cannot vouch for this, but it should be true.

29. Duplexes, 1958–62
    A. E. Morris
    2378–2390 Silver Ridge Avenue
Morris is sort of a Schindler undisciplined by Loos, who was a great disciplinarian. These two-story buildings shoot out blocky stucco volumes with apparent abandon. Number 2390 is Morris's own Studio Building (1957). The studio has a Wrightian flavor, realized in steel, glass, and brick. Equally theatrical is Morris's **Murakakami House** (1962) at 2378 Silver Lake.

30. Sabsay House, 1940
    J. R. Davidson
    2351 Silver Ridge Avenue
Rather quiet and bulky looking from the street, this is one of the few works by Davidson that you can actually see.

31. Duplexes, 1964
    A. E. Morris
    2330–2350 Silver Ridge Avenue
Another group of Morris's stucco box duplexes, similar to those nearby.

32. Bungalow Court, circa 1926
    Glendale Boulevard at Loma Vista Place
A lovely grouping of Hansel and Gretel Medieval bungalows.

33. House, circa 1965
    2384 Loma Vista Place
One of the most conscious imitations of Antonio Gaudi in America. It is most strange to see the Barcelona architect's special style coupled with louvered windows.

34. Eltinge House, 1921
    Pierpont and Walter Davis
    Charles G. Adams, landscape architect
    2327 Fargo Street (reached from Apex Street)
A Spanish Colonial garage plus garden walls are about all you can see of this extensive Mediterranean villa and its terraced Italian gardens. The Eltinge House was one of L.A.'s first major essays in the Mediterranean style.

35. Presley House, 1946
    Gordon Drake
    2114 Fargo Street
Drake was one of California's gifted young architects in the immediate post-World War II years. His early death cut short a promising career. Unfortunately there are few of his houses in existence, and none of them remains unaltered. This is one of the least changed.

36. Neutra House, 1964
  Richard J. Neutra and Dion Neutra
  (principal)
  2300 E. Silver Lake Boulevard
The original pure International Style Modern
(Research) house, built in 1933, was partially
burned in 1963. The present structure, though
far from having the experimental quality of the
first, is late, romantic Neutra. It steps in three
stages away from Silver Lake, and each layer
has its own tiny rooftop lake.

37. "Colony" of Neutra Houses
  Richard J. Neutra, Dion Neutra
  Intersection of Earl Street with Silver Lake
  Boulevard and Argent Place
It is rare that you have the chance to survey the
work of a major Modernist in such a concen-
trated form, particularly in Los Angeles.

a. Yew House, 1957
  2226 E. Silver Lake Boulevard
b. Kambara House, 1960
  2232 E. Silver Lake Boulevard
c. Inadomi House, 1960
  2238 E. Silver Lake Boulevard
d. Sokol House, 1948
  2242 E. Silver Lake Boulevard
e. Treweek House, 1948
  2250 E. Silver Lake Boulevard
f. Reunion House, 1949
  (Remodeled by Dion Neutra 1966 and later)
  2240 Earl Street
g. Flavin House, 1958
  2218 Argent Place
h. Ohara House, 1961
  2210 Argent Place
i. Akai House, 1961
  2200 Argent Place

38. Silverview Condominiums, 1983
  EDC, Inc. Architects (Walter Abronson and
  Ko Kiyohara)
  2330 Duane Street
A suitable neighbor for the Neutras, but the
architects should have had Neutra's sensitivity
to landscape architecture in order to tone down
the white walls. Maybe the landscaping will
come in time.

39. Koblick House, 1937
  Richard J. Neutra
  1816–1818 Silverwood Terrace
A three-story, beautifully sited house with windows ranked around the third-floor living room,
which has a sensational view of the lake and
mountains.

40. Walther House, 1937
  Harwell H. Harris
  1742 Silverwood Terrace
It is very interesting to see the two very different design philosophies of Neutra (the dwelling
as an art-object machine) and of Harris (the
dwelling as a romantic shelter) on the same
street.

41. Feldman House, 1953
  Gregory Ain
  1607 Angelus Avenue
The facade is mainly bands of windows. The
setback of the second story makes the house
almost classically composed.

42. Silverwood Duplex, 1965
  A. E. Morris
  1611 Silverwood Terrace
Nice, white, with Schindleresque interlocking
volumes and details.

43. Three Houses, 1935–38
  William Kesling
  1530–1536 Easterly Terrace
  2808 W. Effie Street
Balanced somewhere between High Art
Modern and Streamline Moderne. Kesling
designed other Streamline Moderne houses in
this area, but they have been altered.

Angelino Heights, Echo Park, Elysian Park

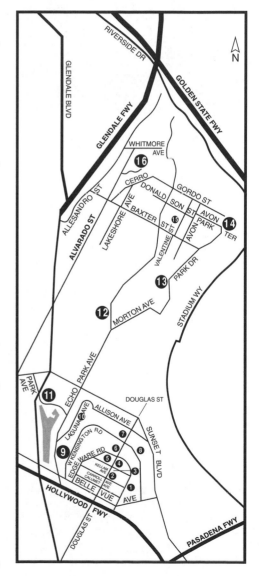

This area is now cut off by freeway from the Silver Lake area to which it is atmospherically related. The northern part has some funky things as well as high art. The district around Echo Park is much older. In fact, the 1300 block of Carroll Avenue in Angelino Heights has the highest concentration of Victorian houses still remaining in Los Angeles—not many in comparison with San Francisco, but very choice—including two by Joseph Cather Newsom.

Don't miss the lake in Echo Park (1894), reminiscent, if you please, of the Public Garden in Boston, with peddle boats for rent and the most magnificent lotus plants you will find anywhere.

1. Betsford House, circa 1890
801 E. Edgeware Road
The mansard tower, with original iron balustrade, deserves mention.

2. Carroll Avenue
This was once an esteemed residential district with a nice view of the city, previously reached by streetcar. It has been coming back in the last decade, due mainly to attempts by its proud residents to improve the surroundings. Three Victorian houses have even been moved in to take the place of ones demolished long ago. We begin at the east end of the block.

a. Philips House, 1887
1300 Carroll Avenue
Almost pure Queen Anne with just a little Eastlake decoration here and there.

b. Russell House, 1887–88
1316 Carroll Avenue
Again, Queen Anne, but this time with pronounced Stick-style features.

c. Heim House, 1887–88
1320 Carroll Avenue
This time Queen Anne combines with Italianate brackets in the cornice and a wonderful round tower.

2h. Sessions House, 1888

d. Scheerer House, 1887–88
  1324 Carroll Avenue
A Queen Anne cottage.

e. House, circa 1887
  1321 Carroll Avenue
Both this house and the next, number 1325, were once on Court Street—1145 and 1123 respectively. They were moved to Carroll Avenue in 1981. Both are late Eastlake, working into the Queen Anne.

f. House, circa 1887
  1325 Carroll Avenue
Eastlake/Queen Anne.

g. Foy House, 1873
  1325 Carroll Avenue
The Foy House was moved in 1993 from its original location at 633 South Witmer Avenue. As with many other California cities and towns, Los Angeles once had a tremendous number of late Italianate houses built during the years 1865 through the early 1880s. Regrettably, only a few of these houses still remain in the Los Angeles area. This house exhibits the usual high entablature accompanied by extended paired brackets. The house will be completely restored at its new site. The restoration is under the direction of Jai Pol Vhalsa; the preservation consultant is Lawrence E. Winans.

h. Sessions House, 1888
  Joseph Cather Newsom
  1330 Carroll Avenue

A fine Newsom creation recognized as such by the architect, who illustrated and described it in his *Picturesque and Artistic Homes and Buildings of California* (No. 3), (San Francisco, 1890). The predominant Queen Anne theme of Carroll Avenue is here sustained and embellished by Moorish (Chinese?) detail, including "Moongate" openings on the second-floor porch.

i. Innes House, 1887–88
  1329 Carroll Avenue
Built for a shoe store magnate, this house illustrates the peculiar California wedding of Queen Anne and Eastlake styles.

j. Haskin House, circa 1888
  1344 Carroll Avenue
Some authorities have dated this house in the 1890s, but it is such a pure example of Queen Anne expansiveness (much spool-work and no Eastlake ornament) that we suspect it was done about the same time as the other houses (if not earlier). It is immaculately maintained and constantly being used as a subject for painters and a backdrop for TV commercials.

k. Sanders House, 1887
  1345 Carroll Avenue
Good Queen Anne with wrought-iron railing still crowning the roof.

l. Pinney House, 1887
  1355 Carroll Avenue
Similar in style and scale to the **Sanders House** next door, this house is still in the Pinney Family. It seems to be in its original colors.

m. Cohn House, circa 1887
  1443 Carroll Avenue
A two-story Queen Anne house with an unusual corner bay tower.

n. Cottage, 1889
  Joseph Cather Newsom
  1407 Carroll Avenue
This story-and-a-half cottage falls basically into the Queen Anne style, though some portions, such as the angled bay and the roof, have an Eastlake quality. This was one of several spec houses built from Newsom's published "El Capitan" plan.

Other houses on Carroll Avenue are worthy of preservation and restoration. In fact, the whole of Angelino Heights is a delight to anyone who can, in the mind's eye, see these houses and their gardens restored to their original condition.

3. House, circa 1890
1334 Kelham Avenue
A very late Queen Anne/Colonial Revival cottage.

4. Houses, 1890
1347, 1343, and 1341 Kelham Avenue
Obviously designed by the same Queen Anne-inspired architect (builder?). Number 1341 has the most ornament.

5. House, circa 1905
1405 Kelham Avenue
A large Mission Revival dwelling. This suggests that the Angelino Heights area is important for other styles besides the Victorian ones.

6. House, circa 1887
917 Douglas Street
A rare, almost pure, example of the Eastlake style.

7. House, circa 1896
1101 Douglas Street
A merging of the Queen Anne and Colonial revivals.

8. Weller House, 1887
824 Kensington Road
Certainly this Queen Anne gem is worthy of its neighbors on Carroll Avenue. The spindly porches and open belvedere tower add to its fairy-tale quality.

9. St. Athanasius Episcopal Church, circa 1890
Northeast corner of Echo Park and Laguna avenues
This mixture of Shingle style with diminutive Gothicism suggests the work of Ernest Coxhead, but it lacks the strong mannerist quality that usually marks his work.

10. Lacey Duplex, 1922
R. M. Schindler
830–832 Laguna Avenue
A remodeling of an older house, Schindler's design suggests both the Spanish Colonial Revival and the early Moderne.

11. Angelus Temple, 1925
A. F. Leicht
Northeast corner of Glendale Boulevard and Park Avenue
The architect of this concrete, classical-styled temple must have been inspired by the Mormon Tabernacle in Salt Lake City. Strange, since the egg shape is hardly symbolic of the Four Square Gospel once preached by the Temple's Aimee Semple McPherson.

12. Apartment Building, circa 1928
1650 Echo Park Avenue
A four-story Art Deco Moderne structure further enlivened by a vivid floral motif.

13. Southhall House, 1938
R. M. Schindler
1855 Park Drive
As so often happens in avant-garde houses of this period, the garage is right on the street with the house secluded behind it. The plan of the house is a large rectangle from which three bayed spaces project. The whole is sheathed in plywood.

14. Atwater Bungalows, 1931, and later
Robert Stacy-Judd
1431 and 1433 Avon Park Terrace
Northwest corner of Park Drive and Avon Park Terrace (best following northerly route along Park Drive as indicated)
This architect, who was best known for his advocacy of the pre-Columbian Revival, here shows himself equally the master of the Pueblo Revival in a most romantic rendering.

15. Ross House, 1938
Raphael S. Soriano
2123 Valentine Street
Again, a garage stands almost in front of one of Soriano's handsome early International Style Modern designs. The two-story glass and stucco house is one of Soriano's best works.

16. Meier House, 1942
Harwell H. Harris
2240 Lakeshore Avenue
You can't see it, but Harris is so rare that we thought we should include it.

WILSHIRE BOULEVARD DISTRICT; HANCOCK PARK

As the map and dates of the following buildings suggest, Wilshire Boulevard, named for an oil millionaire who was also a Marxist, has had several spurts of growth. In the 1920s it had already started its march west to Santa Monica and the Pacific, the complete apotheosis of the linear city. It was commercial about as far as Western Avenue. Beyond that, a great region of bungalows proliferated. Still farther, starting near Crenshaw Boulevard, the rich took up their abodes north

and south of Wilshire with a little commercial building here and there. The buildings on Wilshire Boulevard itself gradually began rising in height and ostentation until the beginning of the "Miracle Mile" at Hauser Avenue, where ten-story or so office buildings and luxury shops were built at the end of the 1920s and on into the 1930s, and where a great deal of building has occurred since World War II. To the north and south of Wilshire Boulevard are multiple housing units and an array of upper-middle-class suburban housing. In the area around

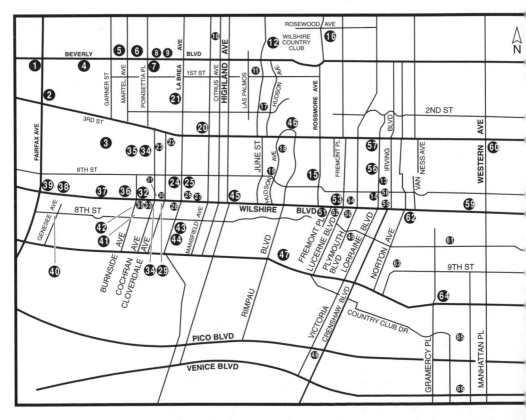

Hancock Park, there are larger apartment buildings, then fourplexes and duplexes, and finally single-family housing. Most of this housing was built before 1942, and thus it provides a wonderful look at architectural styles from the early 1920s through the late 1930s. Drive north on Cochran, Cloverdale, or Detroit avenues to see how successful this housing was. You will also note how intrusive and unfortunate most of the multiple housing in this area turns out to be.

In fact, it is greatly fascinating to drive the length from Number One Wilshire in downtown Los Angeles to the sea in an open car. In its own way it is as overwhelming as a similar drive along the length of Park Avenue in New York. Strangely, if you go off Wilshire on the streets above and below it, you will still find residential areas sometimes only a block away.

1. CBS Television City, 1952
Pereira and Luckman; major addition 1976, Gin Wong Associates
Southeast corner of Beverly Boulevard and Fairfax Avenue

A 1950s low modern cube, big and bland but not without distinction. The addition is in exactly the style of the original.

2. Farmer's Market, 1934–37 and later
Northeast corner of Fairfax Avenue and 3rd Street

Built by Roger Dahljolm to show off Southern California's great ability to grow magnificent fruits and vegetables, this complex of buildings is more an institution than it is architecture. Its only pretension is the somewhat Colonial Revival tower which replaced a wonderful windmill advertising the name of the building on a blade. The place was Colonialized (Anglo, that is) even more in 1941 with additions and changes by the Beverly Hills architect J. E. Dolena.

Behind Farmer's Market on Gilmore Lane (cuts between 3rd Street and Beverly Boulevard) is the Gilmore Adobe that Antonio Jose Rocha built on the Rancho La Brea in 1828–30. This L-shaped adobe (the present south and west wings) originally had a flat, tar-covered roof. In the 1920s it was remodeled by John Byers and Edla Muir. They added the

2. Farmer's Market, 1934–37 and later

north wing and built a low second story over a portion of the original adobe. They also added pitched gable roofs covered with tile. As we see the adobe today, it reflects the 1920s ideal more than what it actually looked like in 1830.

3. Park La Brea Housing (Metropolitan Life Housing Development), 1941–42; **Towers,** 1948–49
Leonard Schultze and Son and E. T. Heitschmidt; Tommy Tomson, landscape architect
Tower complex designed by Leonard Schultze and Associates of New York, and by J. E. Stanton and Gordon Kaufmann (the 1948–49 landscape design by Thomas Church)
A 10 ½-acre development bounded by 3rd Street, Cochran Avenue, 6th Street, and Fairfax Avenue.

The first thing that strikes your eye from a distance is that Carcassonne has been transported to L.A.—the 1948 towers merge to appear to be a medieval wall. From a shorter range the more interesting features are the earlier, two-story housing units which are in a sort of stripped Regency Moderne mode.

3. Park La Brea Housing (Metropolitan Life Housing Development), 1941–42; Towers, 1948–49

4. Pan-Pacific Auditorium, 1935–38
  Wurdeman and Becket (Wurdeman)
  7600 Beverly Boulevard
This was a major L.A. expression of the Streamline Moderne, probably the city's most photographed and painted monument. For a number of years various proposals were made as to how the building could be restored and used, but all of this became meaningless when the building burned in 1989. Now if you wish to see it, you must go to Disneyland in Florida.

5. A. J. Heinsbergen Decorating Company, 1925
  Claude Beelman with A. B. Heinsbergen; details by Willard White
  7415–7421 Beverly Boulevard
The general impression of this brick building is English Medieval with a little Baroque added here and there. Very picturesque and old world in a strange area for that to happen.

6. Spanish Kitchen Building, circa 1925
  Northeast corner of Beverly Boulevard and Martel Avenue
Not great Spanish Colonial, but the windows appear to have the original 1920s paintings of caballeros and señoritas. As of this writing the building has no tenant, social change making it

a derelict, but the 1920s chairs are still piled on the 1920s tables, needing only to be dusted off before a good meal.

7. Commercial Building, 1930
  J. R. Horns
  Southeast corner of Poinsettia Place and Beverly Boulevard
Art Deco (Zigzag) Moderne.

8. Commercial Building, 1929
  L. Mulgreen
  7223 Beverly Boulevard
Art Deco (Zigzag) Moderne.

9. Service Station, circa 1925
  7201 Beverly Boulevard
Mission Revival with a dome!

10. Beckman House, 1938
  Gregory Ain
  357 N. Citrus Avenue
An immaculately maintained Los Angeles conception of the International Style Modern. In plan the house is narrow, and the principal rooms open to small terraces and enclosed courts.

11. Churchill House, 1928; 1982
  Pierpont and Walter S. Davis; Tedesco Architects (Lorenzo C. Tedesco)
  108 North Las Palmas Drive
One of the Davis's excellent examples of the Mediterranean type. Low-pitched tile roofs, thinly detailed at the eaves, shelter carefully fenestrated stucco walls. The Tedesco firm added a new contextual wing and remodeled portions of the existing house.

12. Meade House ("La Casa de las Campanas"), circa 1927
  Lester Scherer
  350 June Street
Needless to say, you are among the swells. This immense Spanish Colonial Revival house on this gently winding street has real distinction. The Meade house and the now destroyed Ince house were the two most lively versions of the Spanish Colonial Revival to be built in the 1920s in the Los Angeles area. Note the

12. Meade House ("La Casa de las Campanas"), circa 1927

impressive formal entrance, the ironwork in
the entrance gates, and the projecting wood
balcony at the north end of the house.

13. Leistikow House, 1923

13. Leistikow House, 1923
Paul R. Williams
554 South Lorraine Boulevard
1923 was the first full year of independent practice for Paul Williams. The Leistikow house is an English Cottage design, realized in brick. Note the large stair window to the left of the entrance.

15. Rothman House, 1926

14. Collins House, 1932
Paul R. Williams
601 South Lorraine Boulevard
Now somewhat hidden by trees, but you can still see this painted brick example of the French Provincial style. Much of the design is treated as a story-and-a-half house.

15. Rothman House, 1926
Paul R. Williams
541 Rossmore Avenue
This brick and half-timber English-type dwelling reads as a story-and-a-half house. A pair of picturesque tall English chimneys hold the house to its site. A low walled, formal garden lies to the west of the house.

16. Apartment Building, circa 1928
Southeast corner of Rossmore and
Rosewood avenues
This huge, somewhat Spanish pile and the **Ravenwood,** an Art Deco Moderne structure with Assyrian inclinations (at 570 Rossmore Avenue), and a few rather nondescript lesser monsters nearby are among the few large Los Angeles apartment complexes which would compare in size to those of the apartment house craze in New York during the same period.

17. Smith House, 1929–30
J. C. Smale
Northwest corner of 2nd Street and Hudson Avenue
One of the few concrete Art Deco (Zigzag) Moderne houses in the Los Angeles area and probably the greatest. It is very elegant in an extremely elegant neighborhood. Paris would be proud of it.

18. Bowen House, 1925
Elmer Grey
Florence Yoch, landscape architect
336 Hudson Avenue
Grey, in an English mood. As the editors of *Southwest Building and Contractor* commented late in 1925 in reference to this house, "English types of

17. Smith House, 1929–30

residence architecture fit beautifully into many California settings, and just now they are very much in vogue." This large English Tudor house has a lower floor of brick and then a variety of half-timber, gable-roofed bays on the second floor. As befitted a house of this size, "a garage with space for four machines" was included. Florence Yoch provided a formal garden, enclosed in part behind a blue brick wall. Note that this block contains a number of splendid examples of the English Tudor mode.

19. Sisson House, 1926
Robert B. Stacy-Judd
Northwest corner 6th Street and Hudson Avenue

Although we generally associate Stacy-Judd with the pre-Columbian Revival, he designed a number of Medieval French and English houses in Southern California. The Sisson's house, with its central three-story round tower, was described as "Norman English." An article in the magazine *Arts and Decoration* (April 1928), which illustrated this design, stated "how delightful the English Norman architecture suits these same flower-covered lands and vivid Sky [of Los Angeles]." As with all of this architect's designs, there are many odd moments to be encountered in this house.

20. Apartment Building, circa 1928
Northwest corner of 3rd Street and Mansfield Avenue

This two-story Art Deco Moderne building is a typical Los Angeles flat.

21. Retail Shop, circa 1930
153 La Brea Avenue

La Brea was once a rich feast for the connoisseur of the Moderne in its various ramifications and permutations. Today almost all the shops in this mode have been demolished or refaced. This one seems pretty well tuckered out.

22. Apartment Building, 1930
J. C. Smale
364 S. Cloverdale Avenue

Another Art Deco Moderne flat.

23. Apartment Building, 1938
Milton J. Black and R. Borman
462 S. Cochran Avenue

A two-story Streamline Moderne structure. Black, who designed well in the Spanish Colonial Revival style in the 1920s, has here kept up with the times.

24. Automobile Showroom, circa 1927
Morgan, Walls, and Clements
611 La Brea Avenue

Probably intended to be Moorish, this tiny building must have been very swanky in its day.

25. Courtyard Retail and Office Building, circa 1926
Roy Selden Price
624 La Brea Avenue

A U-shaped Spanish building with Moorish arches.

26. Wilson Building, 1929
Meyer and Holler
Northeast corner of Wilshire Boulevard and La Brea Avenue

You know this firm for their Grauman's Chinese and Egyptian theaters in Hollywood. For them, this Art Deco (Zigzag) Moderne tower is really straight.

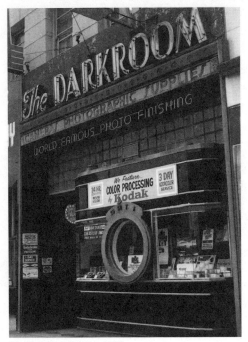

28. The Dark Room, 1938

27. Security First National Bank of Los Angeles (now **Security Pacific Bank Building**), 1929
    Morgan, Walls, and Clements
    5209 Wilshire Boulevard
A single-story, glazed, black-and-gold terra-cotta-sheathed building similar to this firm's famous Richfield Building, which was destroyed in 1968.

28. The Dark Room, 1938
    Marcus P. Miller
    5370 Wilshire Boulevard
A Programmatic building clothed in black vitrolite with silver trim. Streamline Moderne, the conventional nautical porthole in this case is placed in the middle of a plate glass window and thus becomes the lens of a camera. The new tenant has maintained the Streamline image but not, of course, the sign.

29. Dominguez-Wilshire Building, 1930
    Morgan, Walls, and Clements
    5410 Wilshire Boulevard
An eight-story Art Deco (Zigzag) Moderne tower placed on a two-story base. The detail is sharp and brittle.

30. Chandler's Shoe Store, circa 1938
    Marcus P. Miller
    Northwest corner of Wilshire Boulevard
    and Cloverdale Avenue
One of the busiest buildings ever done in the Streamline Moderne idiom, this building is actually a remodeling of a Spanish Colonial Revival structure of the 1920s.

31. Roman's Food Mart, circa 1935
    5413 Wilshire Boulevard
Streamline Moderne with a matching small tower at one end.

32. El Rey Theater, circa 1928
    W. Cliff Balch
    5519 Wilshire Boulevard
A small, angular Art Deco Moderne gem with marvelous box office and original signage, a king's head etched in neon.

33. Commercial Building, 1927
    Frank M. Tyler
    5464 Wilshire Boulevard
Art Deco (Zigzag) Moderne framed by two small, and quite mad, towers.

34. Cochran Avenue Court, circa 1928
    Charles Gault
    Just south of Wilshire Boulevard on
    Cochran Avenue
Small Spanish Colonial court covered with dense foliage.

35. Desmonds Department Store Building, 1928–29
    Gilbert Stanley Underwood
    5514 Wilshire Boulevard
Art Deco (Zigzag) Moderne with flamboyant ornament; an eight-story tower placed on a two-story base with enormous rounded corners.

36. Ralph's Supermarket Building, 1927–28
    Morgan, Walls, and Clements
    5623 Wilshire Boulevard

Once this was typical of the firm's work—a simulated cut-stone facade with Spanish Gothic arches and Churrigueresque ornament. It has been almost completely ruined by "modernization," but its proud tower still stands above the mess.

37. Prudential Building, 1948
Wurdeman and Becket
Ruth Shellhorn, landscape architect
5757 Wilshire Boulevard

A large office and commercial building in the International Style Modern, affected more by Gropius than by Mies. It thus shows its age stylistically, but well.

38a. Los Angeles County Museum of Art, 1964; 1982–83
Pereira and Associates; Hardy, Holzman and Pfeiffer
Wilshire Boulevard at Genesee Avenue in Hancock Park

38a. Pavilion for Japanese Art (The Price Museum of Oriental Art), 1988

38a. Los Angeles County Museum of Art, 1982–83

The original 1964 complex of buildings was that of a group of pavilions, set on a podium in a park. The buildings were reflected in a surrounding moat of water and fountains—all very 1960s modern. While it could be argued that the architecture was not much, still there was a certain relationship between the park and the museum buildings. This has all been lost in the new entrance building (the Robert O. Anderson Building), which brings the complex right up to the street. As with much of H.H.&P.'s work the theme is their usual multistory glass and metal shopping mall atrium. The facade facing Wilshire Boulevard tried to be urbane, but fails—the feeling is again that of an upscale shopping mall.

Off to the side, hovering over the park's famed tar pits is the **Pavilion for Japanese Art (The Price Museum of Oriental Art)**, designed by Bruce Goff before his death in 1982. Goff started the design in 1978, and the building was completed in 1988 under the direction of the New Mexico architect Bart Prince. Although the relationship of the new building to the adjacent tar pits is questionable, the quality of the interior space with its ramps and open lighting is highly successful.

38b. A Discovery of La Brea Museum, 1976
Thornton and Fagan Associates
Hancock Park

Hancock Park gets its name from the family that bought the Rancho La Brea (essentially our Wilshire District) in 1860, and, after having tapped it for almost all of its crude oil (brea), gave the tar pits to the city and sold off the rest to other rich people. In drilling for oil, Major Henry Hancock began digging up large bones but thought little of it until in 1906 Professor J. C. Merriman of the University of California recognized that these pits had trapped large numbers of prehistoric animals. Many of their skeletons can now be seen at the County Museum of Natural History in Exposition Park. The new museum, a sort of mound, celebrates this major scientific discovery, but we are sorry to say that in spite of the planners' good intentions, it makes further inroads on valuable open space.

39. May Company Department Store Building, 1940
   Albert C. Martin and S. A. Marx
   Northeast corner of Fairfax Avenue and
   Wilshire Boulevard
Streamline Moderne. The corner gold tower (really a sort of elegant perfume bottle) with its sign is the architecture of the building, especially when lighted at night. This also marks an entrance, but the main entrance is characteristically at the parking lot connected to the building. The adjoining multi-level parking structure was designed by Albert C. Martin and

39. May Company Department Store Building, 1940

Associates in 1953. The May Company left the building at the end of the 1980s, and for some time it has been in doubt as to what might happen to the structure. In August of 1993 it was announced that the building would be saved, and it would become a part of a large-scale development consisting of a 3.5-acre park, 1,597 apartments, a twenty-three-story and a fifteen-story set of office buildings, plus a ten-story hotel. One is delighted that the May Company building will remain, but the proposed development is much too intense for the site.

40. Buck House, 1934
   R. M. Schindler
   Southwest corner of 8th Street and Genesee
   Avenue
All privacy on the exterior with just a touch of Streamline Moderne. The interior spaces open through great panels of glass into the south garden area. One of Schindler's finest houses.

41. The Monterey Apartments, 1925
   C. K. Smithley
   754 Burnside Avenue
Extremely austere and absolutely impregnable Spanish Colonial garden apartments.

42. Apartment Building, circa 1928
   741 ½ Burnside Avenue
French Norman and very happy.

43. Firestone Garage, 1937
   R. E. Ward, engineer
   800 S. La Brea Avenue
Difficult to describe! A huge streamlined shell cantilevered over the corner.

44. Cedu Foundation Building, circa 1928
   842 La Brea Avenue
A very lovely Spanish Colonial Revival assemblage that has survived the change on La Brea.

45. AVCO Savings Building (now **Imperial Savings**), 1973
   Burke, Kober, Nicolais, and Archuleta
   4929 Wilshire Boulevard
This ten-story building is one great cube of bronze-hued glass. At least it's bronze and not black.

40. Buck House, 1934

46. Reynolds House, 1958
 John Woolf
 200 Rimpau Street (cul-de-sac north of 3rd
 Street)
A tall, arched door, looking very much like a
paper clip, cuts through a high mansard roof—
one of Woolf's most imitated designs.

47. Memorial Library, 1930
 Austin and Ashley
 4625 W. Olympic Boulevard
Submerged in vines is this Tudor and Gothic
branch library obviously intended to go with
the old Collegiate Gothic Los Angeles High
School, now replaced by repressed Brutalism.
The fine art glass window with heraldic
emblems on it was fashioned by the Judson
Studios.

48. Paul R. Williams House, 1951
 Paul R. Williams and Associates
 1690 South Victoria Avenue
When completed the house was described as
"California Modern." Its design entails traditional proportions coupled with modernist
devices such as cantilevered balconies, thin,
hovering roofs, and a dominant semicircular
bay. The principal interior space is a lanai that
opens out to an enclosed courtyard/garden.

Leaping deer in brass line the brass railing of
the circular staircase. The informality of the
lanai is countered by the formality of the dining
room and the living room with its fireplace in
green Swedish marble.

49. Apartment Building, circa 1935
 814 Plymouth Boulevard
Streamline, then squared off.

50. Wilshire United Methodist Church, 1924
 Allison and Allison
 4350 Wilshire Boulevard
Quite Romanesque on the exterior, this exposed
reinforced concrete church turns Gothic inside.
To top that, it has another of those free interpretations of the "La Giralda" that were so popular, whether in New York or in Florida and
Southern California.

51. Fremont Place Entrance Gates, 1911
 Martyn Haenke
 South corner of Wilshire Boulevard and
 Fremont Place
This pair of cast stone entrance gates was one
of several built along the Hancock Park section
of Wilshire Boulevard. One has to look twice to
know that these classical design pylons flanked
by colonnades are in fact concrete made to look
like stone. They were produced by the

California Ornamental Stone Company, which produced a wide array of concrete products that look like stone. Fremont Place is regrettably a private street. Within this enclave Martyn Haenke designed a number of classical-inspired residences (1911), including three for members of the Janss family.

52. Ebell Club, 1924
Hunt and Burns
4400 Wilshire Boulevard
The club building, auditorium, and garden are a very sedate, respectable version of Beaux Arts classicism mixed with the Spanish.

53. Verbeck Mansion, circa 1897
637 Lucerne Boulevard
A huge, 2 ½-story Queen Anne Revival house with Colonial Revival touches. It was moved here in the 1920s.

54. Gless House, 1916
Arthur S. Heineman (Alfred Heineman, associate)
Southwest corner of Plymouth Boulevard and 6th Street
Although rather late for the Craftsman style, this house has all the trappings. The faintly Tudor exterior shows traces of Frank Lloyd Wright, and the magnificent interiors of teak reflect the ideas of Charles Greene. The art glass, designed by Alfred and carried out by the Judson Studios in Garvanza, is especially fine. Incidentally, it was moved to this area in the 1930s, though it looks as if it had always been on this corner. It is one of the Heinemans' most important structures outside Pasadena.

55. Lytton Building (now **Great Western Savings**), 1968
William Pereira and Associates
4333 Wilshire Boulevard
Cleaned up Brutalism, there is a cocked-hat attitude to the roof.

56. Donovan House ("Sunshine Hill"), circa 1910
Theodore Eisen
419 S. Lorraine Boulevard
A Classical giant portico disguises a house that is strongly Adamesque inside.

57. Van Nuys House, 1898
Frederick L. Roehrig
357 S. Lorraine Boulevard
A magnificent example of the emergence of the Colonial Revival Shingle style from the earlier Queen Anne style.

58. House, circa 1915
Southwest corner of Irving Boulevard and 6th Street
A Tudor effort betraying the peculiar attitude of the early twentieth century toward that style. This entire area is very strongly Tudor.

59. Wilshire Professional Building, 1929
Arthur E. Harvey
3875 Wilshire Boulevard
Unfortunately, the first floor of the nine-story-plus-penthouse Art Deco (Zigzag) Moderne building has been spoiled.

60. Commercial Building, circa 1928
356 S. Western Avenue
Art Deco Moderne with a tall tower and urn.

61. Apartment House, circa 1935
3919 W. 8th Street
This three-story-plus-penthouse Streamline Moderne structure with a large parking area in the basement is premonitory of present systems.

62. INA-PEG Building, 1960
Charles Luckman and Associates
Southeast corner of Wilshire Boulevard and Norton Avenue
This building, except for a little unnecessary detail, would pass for a Skidmore, Owings, and Merrill interpretation of Mies.

63. Weber House, 1921

63. Weber House, 1921
  Lloyd Wright
  3923 W. 9th Street, at 4th Avenue
Lloyd Wright's first realized building in Los
Angeles. It is a two-story modified Prairie-style
building, including art glass in geometrical patterns resembling those developed by his father.

64. House, circa 1915
  965 Gramercy Place
This has to be the supreme act of misunderstood Orientalism in America. Gable after
gable protrudes, shaming the Greene brothers
into insignificance.

65. House, circa 1910
  G. Lawrence Stimson
  3340 Country Club Drive
Mission style mixed with Beaux Arts details.

66. Apartment Building, 1936
  Earl D. Stonerod
  1554–1560 S. Saint Andrews Place
A symmetrical Streamline Moderne building.

MACARTHUR PARK, WEST

This section of the city, west of downtown, developed early as a desirable place for middle-class dwellings. At first it was the modestly hilly area just west of the present Harbor Freeway which became a fashionable neighborhood. The grouping of houses on South Bonnie Brae Street and on Alvarado Terrace provides a glimpse of what this section of Los Angeles was like in the 1890s and early 1900s. The single-family residential nature of the area continued throughout the First World War, but the1920s introduced a strong pattern of auto-oriented strip commercialism along such streets as Venice, Pico, Washington, and Olympic boulevards, and along Western Avenue and other north/south streets. Multiple housing also became more frequent—at first bungalow courts, and two- and three-story apartment buildings. Later, in the 1920s, a number of six- to eight-story apartment buildings were built. Generally the mixed use of the region—retail, commercial, and single and multiple housing—has continued right on down to the present day. Since the 1950s high-rise buildings of the downtown area have slowly spread into the area.

Two major public spaces occur in the midst of this area. **MacArthur Park** (at first named Westlake Park) with its small, picturesque lake provides thirty-two acres. **Lafayette Park** to the west has eleven acres. MacArthur Park was laid out in the 1880s and Lafayette Park was donated to the city in 1899. Wilshire Boulevard, which formerly went around MacArthur Park, was rerouted to slice through the middle of it in 1934, an advantage for the auto and the boulevard, but hardly for the park.

The glory of the area has been and is Wilshire Boulevard, the "Champs Elysees of Los Angeles" as it was characterized in the 1920s. Beginning in the 1920s, major churches, retail stores, and office buildings were built along it. Since the early 1950s new and even higher office towers have been added, so that Wilshire Boulevard as the prototype linear city is as vigorous today as it was in the 1920s.

1. United Church of Christ, Scientist, 1945
South end of Oxford Avenue just north of the Santa Monica Freeway
A small but impressive Spanish Colonial Revival church building, whose tower is visible from the Santa Monica Freeway. The Hispanic borrowings on the design are varied. The tower is from the Mission Revival, the entrance of cast stone suggests the Churrigueresque, and the central rose window relates to the late Gothic in Spain. All of this mixture of sources has been carried out well. Originally the building was located where the freeway now stands and it was moved to its present site in 1963.

2. House, circa 1905
2068 Hobart Boulevard
Mission Revival with a wonderful entrance porch supported by stout, "primitive," cylindrical columns.

3. House, 1908
2091 Harvard Boulevard
A commodious box becomes picturesque and Mission by the addition of parapeted end wall gables, quatrefoil windows, and above all by the delightful, second-floor arcade with its cusped, Moorish arches.

4. Scott House, circa 1906
Frank M. Tyler
1910 S. Harvard Boulevard
When built it was described as "an Italian design with the qualities of Moorish architecture incorporated." This all adds up to Southern California Mission Revival with a Moorish touch.

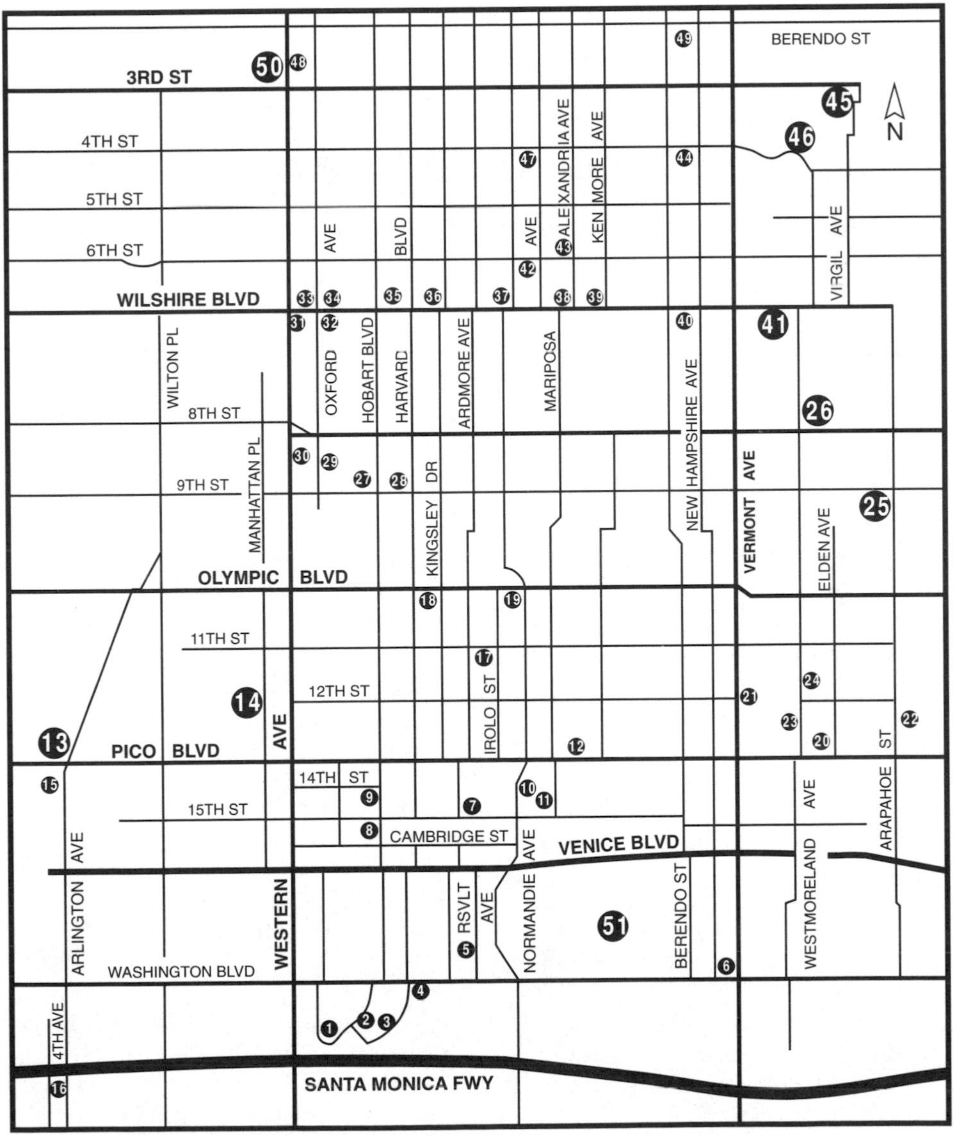

BERENDO ST

3RD ST 50 48

4TH ST

5TH ST

6TH ST

WILSHIRE BLVD

4TH ST

5TH ST

6TH ST

ALEXANDRIA AVE

KENMORE AVE

VIRGIL AVE

45

46

47 44

43

42

33 34 35 36 37 39 39

49

N

AVE

BLVD

AVE

WILTON PL

OXFORD

HOBART BLVD

HARVARD

ARDMORE AVE

MARIPOSA

NEW HAMPSHIRE AVE

VERMONT AVE

ELDEN AVE

31 32 40 41

26

25

8TH ST

9TH ST

MANHATTAN PL

30 29

27 28

KINGSLEY DR

OLYMPIC   BLVD

18 19

11TH ST

12TH ST

14

IROLO ST

17

12TH ST

13 PICO   BLVD

AVE

21 24

23

20

22

ARAPAHOE ST

14TH   ST

9

15TH ST

8

CAMBRIDGE ST

7

10 11

15

ARLINGTON AVE

WESTERN AVE

RSVLT AVE

NORMANDIE AVE

VENICE BLVD

BERENDO ST

WESTMORELAND AVE

5

51

6

WASHINGTON BLVD

4TH AVE

1 2 3

4

16

SANTA MONICA FWY

5. Apartment Building, circa 1925
1817–19 ½ Roosevelt Avenue
Spanish Colonial Revival with a peculiar entrance.

6. Boulevard Theater (now **Innercity Repertory**), 1925
Albert C. Martin
1615 W. Washington Boulevard
Spanish Colonial Revival with a penthouse on top.

7. Pacific Telephone Company Building,
circa 1926
Northeast corner of Ardmore Avenue and 15th Street
A Churrigueresque dress for a utilitarian building.

8. Wheeler House, 1905
Charles and Henry Greene
2175 Cambridge Street
A modest, two-story Craftsman bungalow. The broad, cantilevered roof dramatically projects its rafter ends. The low attic gable is entirely vented, and sticklike posts and rails articulate the entrance porch.

9. Bungalow, circa 1910
Henry L. Wilson
Southwest corner of Hobart Boulevard and 14th Street
A classic California bungalow which was published in Wilson's *Bungalow Magazine*. Note the front door which goes right through the middle of the chimney.

10. St. Sophia's Greek Orthodox Cathedral,
1948
Gus Kalionzes, Charles A. Klingerman, and Albert R. Walker
1324 S. Normandie Avenue
Anyone who has seen a Byzantine church in Greece will come away from this building wondering where all of these inventive ideas came from. Even though the elements are often in the wrong traditional place, the design still does manage to read as Byzantine.

11. St. Thomas the Apostle Roman Catholic Church, 1905
Maginnis, Walsh, and Sullivan
1321 S. Mariposa Avenue

This church illustrates the inventiveness of these Boston architects who employed the Mission Revival image. The building conveys a strong primitive quality, and its towers and upper roofed arcade never occurred in this manner in original Mission architecture of the late eighteenth/early nineteenth centuries.

12. Retail Store/Apartment Building,
circa 1925
2713 W. Pico Boulevard
A three-story store and apartment block has been taken out of the ordinary by being clothed in a rectangular pattern of glazed and unglazed tile.

13. Arlington Avenue Christian Church,
1926
Harold Cross and A. F. Wicker
Northwest corner of Pico Boulevard and Arlington Avenue
A concrete church which employs detailing derived from the Spanish Renaissance. The gable roof has been highly simplified, with the tile pulled out to the edges of the walls. The tower is undecorated until the belfry, where cast concrete ornament provides decorative relief.

14. Wilshire Ward Chapel, Church of Jesus Christ of Latter-day Saints (Mormon),
1928
Harold W. Burton
1209 S. Manhattan Place
A Goodhuesque abstraction of Medieval architecture—a little Gothic mixed with the Byzantine and the Romanesque. The dome's octagonal tower is impressive. The structure is of reinforced concrete with the form board pattern exposed.

15. Forum Theater Building (now a church),
1921–24
Edward J. Borgmeyer
Southwest corner of Pico Boulevard and Norton Avenue (6th Street)
The most refined example of a Beaux Arts theater still standing in Los Angeles. Two pedimented porticoes enclose a six-columned entrance porch. The fluted Corinthian columns, the cornices, entablatures, and the engaged piers are all richly decorated.

14. Wilshire Ward Chapel, Church of Jesus Christ of Latter-day Saints (Mormon), 1928

16. Alice Lynch House, 1922–23
   Harwood Hewitt
   2414 Fourth Avenue South
The Lynch house was one of those early 1920s dwellings which firmly established the popularity of the Spanish Colonial Revival in Southern California. The style of the house is derived from Andalusian farm houses of southern Spain. Facing the street is a story-and-a-half wing which houses the living room; the rest of the house behind is arranged around a small patio. The house is of adobe construction, with the adobes being made on the site. The architect, Harwood Hewitt, was a major figure in the Mediterranean/Hispanic revival of the 1920s.

17. Bungalow Court, circa 1920
   1038–1044 S. Ardmore Avenue
A single-story, narrow bungalow court in the guise of the Islamic. A sloped and painted archway leads from the street into the narrow entrance court. To the side, pairs of small towers adorn each of the two wings.

**18. Apartment
Building,** circa 1922
1020 South Kingsley Drive
A typical L.A. stucco box apartment with an Egyptian Revival street facade.

**19. VIP Palace
Restaurant
Building,** circa 1973
Southeast corner of Olympic Boulevard and Irolo Street
A return to the romanticism of the Orient. Not, of course, the real Orient, but one that must exist somewhere in a story book.

20. House, circa 1912
   1223 S. Elden Avenue
A one-and-half-story, shingle-and-stone, Colonial Revival dwelling.

**21. American National Red Cross Chapter
Building,** 1939
   Spaulding and Rex
   1200 S. Vermont Avenue

17. Bungalow Court, circa 1920

A late-1930s, flat-roofed, California Modern house somewhat enlarged to serve as a small, one-story office building set in a garden. The atmosphere is woodsy and suburban.

22. Double House, circa 1900
  Attributed to Joseph Cather Newsom
  1214 S. Arapahoe Street
A central driveway entrance goes right through the 1 ½-story double bungalow. The main gable and the front dormers, which are now enclosed, were originally open sleeping porches.

23. House, circa 1910
  1229 S. Westmoreland Avenue
A large number of upper-middle-class suburban houses built in L.A. between 1900 and 1917 are clothed in respectable English Tudor, as is this one.

24. Apartment Building, 1936
  1146–1152 S. Westmoreland Avenue
Streamline Moderne with the usual strong nod to the nautical with portholes and steel railings.

25. House, circa 1900
  Attributed to Joseph Cather Newsom
  957 S. Arapahoe Street
Since Newsom invented terms to indicate style, he would most likely have labeled this stucco, wood-detailed, and high-pitched-roof dwelling as "Rhenish."

26. First Unitarian Church, 1930
  Allison and Allison
  2936 W. 8th Street
One suspects that the architects had cast a quick glance at northern Italian churches of the early sixteenth century when they designed this exposed concrete church. They also included a small, pointed dome on the tower, which seems somewhat Islamic. The sanctuary and the cloisters enclose a charming courtyard.

27. Apartment Building, 1936
  Milton J. Black
  Northwest corner of Hobart Boulevard and 9th Street
A Streamline Moderne apartment building of four units, designed by one of L.A.'s masters of the style. A horizontal bay with a row of fins dominates the street facade. The fins have unfortunately been removed.

28. Harvard Apartments, 1992–93
  Kanner Architects (Stephen Kanner)
  9th Street at Harvard Boulevard
At first glance this three-story stucco apartment (it contains thirteen one-bedroom units) appears as an updating of a late 1920s European International Style building. Insistent horizontal bands of windows are carried around the corners, with round windows suggesting the nautical. But a second look reveals that this International Style stage set projects from a "Swiss Cheese" section (in bright yellow stucco), which in turn backs up to a long, red-painted volume. The round windows (some real, some not) turn out to give the feeling of being casually placed here and there on the building. In contrast, the rear red volume has square windows, set hither and yon, some on edge, others not.

29. Val d'Amour Apartment Building, 1928
  G. W. Powers
  854 S. Oxford Avenue
Art Deco (Zigzag) Moderne. At the street entrance, kneeling male figures somehow manage to hold up the five concrete stories above. Cast concrete figures stand guard along the parapet and alternate with Moderne relief ornament.

30. Parking Garage Building, circa 1926
  824 Western Avenue
The plan is that of an L-shaped structure with an open (on three sides) drive-in entrance facing onto Western Avenue. This automobile entrance is surrounded by a rich array of cast concrete Churrigueresque ornament. It all adds up to a remarkable composition in reinforced concrete. Note the stepped pattern of the walls, like the garage's ramp. Do not miss the building (circa 1939) directly to the south. It is a sophisticated exercise in the Art Deco Moderne.

**31. Warner Brothers Western Theater;
Pellissier Building** (now **Wiltern Theater**), 1930–31
  Morgan, Walls, and Clements, G. A. Lansburgh, and Anthony B. Heinsbergen
  Southeast corner of Wilshire Boulevard and Western Avenue

A fully intact Art Deco (Zigzag) Moderne theater and office tower building. The narrowness of the vertical recessed band windows and spandrels removes any reference to scale, so that from a distance you would think you were looking at a large skyscraper (in reality it is only twelve stories high). In 1985 the extraordinary auditorium and the exterior were restored by Brenda Levin Associates, for the developer, Wayne Ratkovitch.

32. Beneficial Plaza, 1967
Skidmore, Owings, and Merrill
3700 Wilshire Boulevard

An eleven-story ice-cube tray set on end (it must have been cut out of graph paper), situated in a late 1960s non-pedestrian plaza.

33. McKinley Building, 1923
Morgan, Walls, and Clements
Northwest corner of Wilshire Boulevard and Oxford Avenue

Morgan, Walls, and Clements developed their own version of the Spanish Churrigueresque, of which this is one example. The upper portion of the corner tower is encrusted with cast concrete ornament. Although the building has been modified over the years, the original courtyard remains within the building.

34. Ahmanson Center Building, 1970
Edward D. Stone Associates
3701 Wilshire Boulevard

Ten floors plus a penthouse, this building is rather neutral Modern in spite of the curves.

35. Wilshire Boulevard Temple, 1922–29
Abraham A. Adelman, S. Tilden Norton, and David C. Allison
Northeast corner of Wilshire and Hobart boulevards

The mystery and the opulence of the Near East are suggested in this luxurious, Byzantine-inspired edifice. Black marble, inlaid gold, brilliant multi colored mosaics, and rare woods were used throughout the interior. Hugo Ballin's murals add the final touch of richness to the interior.

36. St. Basil's Roman Catholic Church, 1974
Albert C. Martin and Associates
Emmet L. Wemple and Associates, landscape architects
Northwest corner of Wilshire Boulevard and Kingsley Drive

A forest of vertical concrete volumes creates an illusion through fuzzy, dark glass of a medieval northern Italian town, perhaps with Sir Basil Spence's Coventry Cathedral in mind. Herb Goldman did the interior sculpture of the Stations of the Cross and also other sculpture in the side altars.

37. Wilshire Boulevard Christian Church, 1922–23
Robert H. Orr
Northeast corner of Wilshire Boulevard and Normandie Avenue

Northern Italian Romanesque, which was so popular in Southern California in the teens and twenties, was used for this church. The campanile and other features of the church are Italian, while the great rose window is French. The building is of reinforced concrete with the pattern of the form boards revealed.

38. Office Building, 1936
Walker and Eisen
Northwest corner of Wilshire Boulevard and Alexandria Avenue

Behind all sorts of odds and ends on the street level you will find an excellent version of a four-story Art Deco Moderne office building. Wide, fluted piers encase a row of double, narrow piers. Above, double spirals provide the needed ornament.

39. Tishman Building, 1956
Victor Gruen and Associates
3325 Wilshire Boulevard

A characteristic mid-1950s Corporate International Style Modern building—dull and dry. Now it is a real period piece of its time. Perhaps we will eventually come to respond to it in a positive fashion.

40. One Park Plaza, 1971–72
Daniel, Mann, Johnson, and Mendenhall (Anthony J. Lumsden)
3250 Wilshire Boulevard

A twenty-two-story skyscraper clad in a thin, fragile glass skin set with a light metal frame. The form of the building, with the secondary towers projecting from each of the corners, suggests the shape of a Richardsonian Romanesque tower.

41. Bullocks-Wilshire Department Store Building, 1928
John and Donald Parkinson; Feil and Paradice; Jock Peters
3050 Wilshire Boulevard

Bullocks-Wilshire is a remarkable building, a treasure trove of late 1920s Moderne design. The store's management engaged some of the most notable L.A. artists of the time to design the interior of the building. The principal figure involved with the interior was the architect-designer Jock Peters. His hand can be seen most forcibly in the sportswear shop as well as in the center foyer at ground level. Art abounds. If you go through the parking lot entrance, you will pass through Art Deco (Zigzag) Moderne gates (expressing the theme "Times Fly"). On the ceiling of the porte cochere is a mural by Herman Sachs. A relief sculpture, *The Spirit of Sports,* by Gjura Stojano adorns the walls of the sports shop. Other decorations are by Mayer

43. Chapman Building 1928–29

Krieg, David Colins, George De Winter, and John Weaver. This store was one of the first on Wilshire Boulevard to provide a dual frontage, one (traditional) on Wilshire Boulevard (for advertising purposes) and the other facing on the extensive, well-landscaped parking lot to the rear (this is, of course, the real entrance in the store). The building is sheathed in light tan terra-cotta and trimmed with brown copper. As we see it today (five floors plus the tower), it was to have been the first phase of a ten-story structure. What is remarkable about the building today is that so much of its original Art Deco interior design remains and is so beautifully maintained.

The building was damaged in the 1992 riots, but was restored. Regrettably, because of financial problems of its parent company, the store was closed in 1993.

42. Commercial Garage, 1927
Robert H. Orr
South side of 6th Street between Normandie and Mariposa avenues

The design concept for this five-story reinforced concrete garage structure, was to disguise its use. When the garage opened, it was noted that "The site is in a high class district, amid residences, hotels and apartments, yet so unobtrusively does it blend into the surrounding buildings that it is often mistaken for a residential structure of some sort." In style it is Mediterranean; it is detailed in a crisp, abstract fashion that we associated with the Post Modernist mode of the 1980s. The client/owners of the garage were the Chapman Brothers, who also commissioned Chapman Park Market down 6th Street.

43. Chapman Park Market, 1928–29
Morgan, Walls, and Clements
Northwest corner of West 6th Street and Alexandria Avenue

A Spanish Colonial Revival shopping center which occupies the entire block between Alexandria and Kenmore avenues. The central court was an auto park with the surrounding retail stores facing both onto the parking lot and onto the adjoining streets. Across Alexandria Avenue at the northwest corner of West 6th

46. Shatto Recreation Center, 1991

patterns occur on the inside walls of the large gymnasium.

47. Ninth Church of Christ, Scientist, 1924–27
Robert H. Orr
433 S. Normandie Avenue

This Classical English brick building lightly suggests the turn-of-the-century work of Sir Edwin Lutyens. In contrast, drive over to South Alvarado Street and see Elmer Grey's handling of the Romanesque in a highly traditional but vigorous manner in his 1912 **First Church of Christ, Scientist.**

Street is the **Chapman Building** (Morgan, Walls, and Clements, 1928), a two-story Spanish Colonial Revival retail store and office building. In 1991 the complex was restored by Brenda Levin Associates.

44. Temple Sinai East (now **Korean Royal Church**), 1926
S. Tilden Norton
407 S. New Hampshire Avenue

A mixture from the Eastern Mediterranean area—Byzantine, Islamic, plus other odds and ends. A central dome dominates both the interior and the exterior, and hand-cut bricks of varied color create a rich tactile surface.

45. Virgil Apartment Building, 1950
Carl L. Maston
315 S. Virgil Avenue

A two-story building whose image is light post-World War II Modern. Each of the living units faces out onto an enclosed small patio.

46. Shatto Recreation Center, 1991
Steven Ehrlich Architects
3191 W. 4th Street

The intent of the architect was to suggest the curved form of a Pacific wave in his building. For the vertical surface of the wave, Ehrlich and the artist Ed Moses created a broken-up abstract pattern of sandstone-colored split-faced concrete block, black glazed concrete block, along with red clay bricks. Similar geometric

48. Kentucky Fried Chicken, 1990
Grinstein/Daniels
340 North Western Avenue

Hardly a normal image for a fast-food establishment. The building ranges from a suggestion of the Programmatic, in the chicken bucketlike form of the main section of the building, to the suggestion of the commonplace turned into high art in walls of corrugated metal. Above all of this is a white cube with the face of the Colonel on four sides.

49. Automotive Garage Building, circa 1926
248 S. Berendo Street

A single-story Spanish Colonial Revival automobile garage, luxurious enough in its cast concrete ornate facade to accommodate Franklins, Packards, and Pierce Arrows.

50. Selig Retail Store Building
(now **Crocker-Citizens National Bank Branch Offices**), 1931
Arthur E. Harvey
Northwest corner of Western Avenue and West 3rd Street

Though modest in size, this is one of L.A.'s most vigorous examples of the use of glazed terra-cotta tile of the late 1920s/early 1930s. The gold ornament is dramatically set off against the rich black tile background. The rich ornament is pure Art Deco (Zigzag) Moderne. The sheathing of this building will give you some indication of what the famous Richfield Building in downtown L.A. looked like.

51. Rosedale Cemetery

West Venice Boulevard between Normandie Avenue and Catalina Street
Rosedale Cemetery exhibits a number of monuments and buildings well worth a visit. One of the most interesting of these is the **Chapel of the Pines,** 1903. The chapel itself is a round, low, domed building. It is approached through a classical Greek Doric temple front, the proportions of which are quite "correct." Another major monument is the **Emma and Lewis Grigsby Mausoleum,** in the form of a miniature Egyptian pyramid, sheathed in smooth black slate.

51. Grigsby Mausoleum,

MacArthur Park, North

1. Bungalows, circa 1910–25

Arthur Heineman (Alfred Heineman, Associate)
The Heinemans designed a number of bungalows in the northern part of the MacArthur Park district, including a group on South Ardmore Avenue. Those that are authenticated are situated at 110, 179, 201, and 228. The Heinemans also designed two "Oriental" bungalows at 720 and 741 S. Irolo Street. The bungalow at 228 S. Ardmore Avenue is also Oriental, while the one at number 201 is Colonial Revival with a sandstone base and columns.

2. Studio Court, circa 1925

4350 Beverly Boulevard
The French Norman mode was particularly popular in Los Angeles in the 1920s for small cottagelike commercial complexes and bungalow courts. With the continual intensification of land use in the west Los Angeles region, most of these have unfortunately disappeared. Here is a good remaining example—a fairy tale-scaled group of buildings.

3. Mount Vernon Office, Pacific Savings Building (now California Federal Savings)

1960
Rick Farver Associates
270 N. Vermont Avenue
This lighthearted version of George Washington's Mount Vernon was originally built at 400 N. Vermont Avenue where one could readily see it from the Hollywood Freeway. It has now been moved down the street where you will have to search it out.

4. KFL (KEHE) Radio Station Building,
   1936
   Morgan, Walls, and Clements
   133–141 N. Vermont Avenue
Though altered, this radio station building is
still one of Los Angeles's forceful examples of
the 1930s Streamline Moderne. The central
pylon tower, designed for the display of the
station's call letters, was originally surmounted
by an open metal vertical tower 475 feet high.

5. Multipurpose and Classroom Building,
   Commonwealth Avenue Elementary
   School, 1992–93
   Siegel Diamond Architects (Katherine
   Diamond)
   215 South Commonwealth Avenue
The architect mentioned that this addition to an
older school building was "based on children's
building blocks, playfully breaking down the

scale of the building through colors and materials." Some of the boxes are of wire and mesh,
making them light and airy and also permitting
one to see into the various staircases. The
building encompasses multipurpose/audito-
rium, food service area, six classrooms, plus
three kindergarten rooms with their adjacent
play areas.

6. American Storage Company Building
   (now **Yellow Pages Building**), 1928–29
   Arthur E. Harvey
   3639 Beverly Boulevard
A fourteen-story (supposedly ten stories to
meet the restriction on height) Los Angeles
landmark. The thin verticality of the tower creates the illusion of great soaring height. In contrast to the Art Deco (Zigzag) Moderne tower,
the base of the building exhibits a rich vocabulary of the Spanish Colonial Revival.

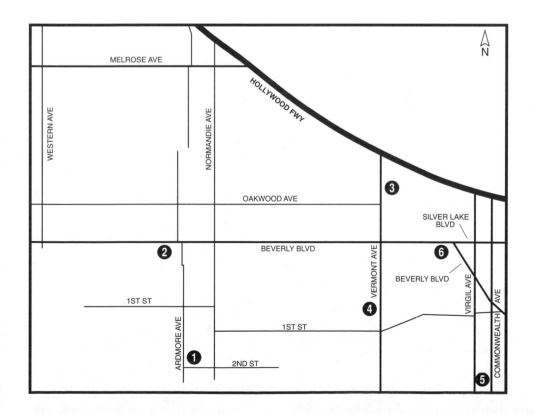

MACARTHUR PARK, EAST

1. Ponce de Leon Apartment Building,
circa 1905
1136 S. Alvarado Street
Compared with most other American cities,
Los Angeles did not use the Classical Beaux
Arts style of the years 1895 through the teens
as frequently. The Ponce de Leon Apartment
Building, though, is an exception. The building
is correctly dignified, and exhibits an elaborate
columned entrance that provides the appropriate formal entry into this three-story building.

2. Cottage, circa 1895
1805 12th Place
A small Queen Anne cottage.

3. Dora Apartments, 1906
1600 W. Pico Boulevard
Between 1900 and 1915 a good number of
three-story Mission Revival apartment buildings were built in the area west and south of the
downtown. In the Dora Apartment Building a
corner bay emerges above the tile roof as a low,
octagonal tower. Gabled parapets, arched openings, and stucco walls help to create the needed
Mission image. Apartment buildings with retail
stores on the ground level, such as this one,
were common.

4. Pico Union Villa Building, 1980
John Mutlow
1200 S. Union Avenue
A three-story, multiple-housing building for the
elderly. It is in the form of a square with an
interior courtyard. A diagonal passage pierces
through the two opposite corners of the complex. Freestanding pylons in the courtyard and
at the entrance are, one assumes, to contradict
visually the square and its diagonals. The idea
of the interior courtyard comes from the traditional courts found within the Mediterranean
tradition—though in this case its design suggests a prison exercise yard. The saving grace

of the building (as art, not as a dwelling) is the
excellent use of colors on the walls.

5. Alvarado Terrace Houses, Southwest of
Pico Boulevard and Bonnie Brae Street
Alvarado Terrace, laid out as a gentle, curved,
upper-middle-class residential street, was
planned in the early 1900s by Pomery Powers,
who was at the time president of the Los
Angeles City Council. The development was at
first called Windmill Links—named after the
landmark of a nearby windmill and tank. The
seven remaining houses on the north side of the
street provide us with a good glimpse of L.A.'s
suburban streets from about 1900 through the
mid-teens. These houses indicate the wide
smorgasbord of images employed by architects
and clients.

a. Barmore House, circa 1902
1317 Alvarado Terrace
English and Germanic Medieval styles establish the character of this suburban dwelling.
b. Cohan House, circa 1902
Hudson and Munsell
1325 Alvarado Terrace
Late Queen Anne in concept, but simplified and
made more classical with references to the
Shingle Colonial Revival.
c. Gilbert House, circa 1902
1333 Alvarado Terrace
A late Queen Anne Shingle dwelling with the
usual hint of the Colonial Revival. The building
with the round corner bay tower is sheathed in
Santa Barbara sandstone below and shingles
above. There is an abundance of ornament,
both inside and out.
d. Powers House, 1903
A. L. Haley
1345 Alvarado Terrace
This is the house which the developer of
Alvarado Terrace laid out for himself—an exuberant Mission Revival piece (one of the best

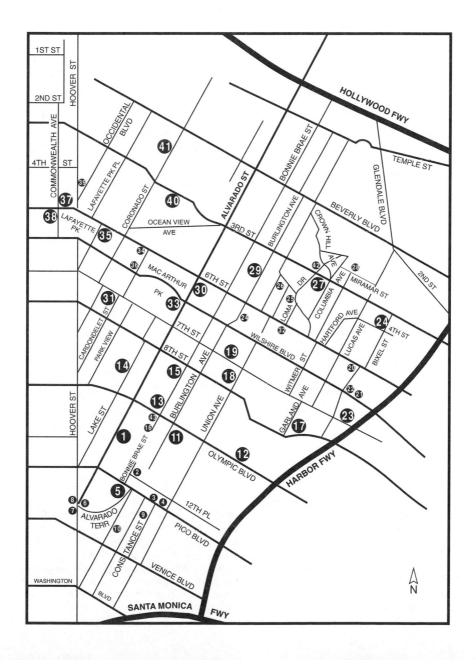

examples still standing in Los Angeles). The house was designed by A. L. Haley whose extensive practice was primarily in the realm of spec apartments and other commercial buildings. The front porch of the Powers House exhibits an arcade supported by short, thick, fat, "primitive" columns, and the roof presents a picturesque assembly of open and closed towers, scalloped parapets, and quatrefoil windows.

e. Raphael House, circa 1902
    Hunt and Eager
    1353 Alvarado Terrace
A good-sized, two-story English Tudor dwelling. Note the beautiful entrance with its windows of beveled glass.

f. Evanardy-Kinney House, 1902
    Hunt and Eager
    1401 Alvarado Terrace
Late Queen Anne modified by Colonial Revival details. The house is sheathed in sandstone and stucco below, and shingles above.

g. House, circa 1905
    1406 Alvarado Terrace
A good example of Los Angeles turn-of-the-century attachment to Anglo fashions, here in a Colonial Revival dwelling.

h. Milner Apartment Building, circa 1925
    1415 Alvarado Terrace
A multiple-housing unit intrudes in this single-family enclave. This apartment building utilizes an elaborate English Gothic image.

6. First Church of Christ, Scientist, 1912
    Elmer Grey
    1366 S. Alvarado Street
Northern Italian Romanesque as a source, but strongly abstracted. A high, semicircular temple porch with Corinthian columns looks out toward the street intersection. Another more delicately detailed porch faces east, and the tower has been reduced to a single rectangular volume, with a grouping of three vertical windows on each of its surfaces.

7. House, circa 1897
    1519 S. Hoover Street
A late Queen Anne dwelling.

8. House, circa 1900
    1515 S. Hoover Street

Another late Queen Anne dwelling, this time modified with classical American Colonial Revival detailing.

9. House, circa 1900
    1346 W. Constance Street
This imaginative composition, using seemingly all of the current imagery of the period, could well be labeled as the Bavarian Hunting Lodge style.

10. Bungalow Court, 1925
    Edwin W. Willit
    1428 S. Bonnie Brae Street
A miniaturized pylon gateway with relief sculpture establishes the Egyptian theme for this single-story, double-row bungalow court (the Hollywood film set brought into the world of "real" architecture).

11. House, circa 1898
    1030 Burlington Avenue
An unbelievable array of Islamic details cover this simple wood building.

12. Loyola University Law School Building,
    1981–84, and later
    Frank O. Gehry and Associates
    1441 W. Olympic Boulevard
One of Los Angeles's really important buildings of the early 1980s. Here we can see Gehry and his associates at their best, in both planning and design. The main building is broken in the middle by a greenhouse-like gabled roof temple, which is approached from below by a long, narrow staircase. The smaller, single-story buildings in the court in front of the large building are rendered as small, abstracted classical temples.

13. Houses
    South Bonnie Brae Street
Bonnie Brae Street was one of a series of fashionable suburban streets situated west of downtown Los Angeles. Most of the single-family upper-middle-class dwellings which lined these north/south streets were built between 1890 and 1910. As one would expect, much has been lost. Still enough remains so that we can gain a sense of suburban Los Angeles at the turn of the century.

13d. House, circa 1895

e. House, circa 1897
1047 S. Bonnie Brae Street
A two-story, simplified, late Queen Anne house.

f. House, circa 1905
1053 S. Bonnie Brae Street
A boxy Colonial Revival dwelling with some imaginative touches, including a small Gothic window set in a frame with tiny columns, and a Romanesque window placed below. Fluted pilasters terminate the corners of the building.

14. Marlinex Apartment Building, circa 1930
938 S. Lake Street
A seven-story Art Deco (Zigzag) Moderne apartment building. Perhaps its most impressive detail is the "Modernistic" lettering.

15. 800 Block of south Bonnie Brae Street
Another of Bonnie Brae's turn-of-the-century streetscapes.

a. Wright-Mooers House, 1894
818 S. Bonnie Brae Street
This house is one which is often illustrated in discussions of West Coast Victorian architecture. The open plan and the overall general design of the building are Queen Anne. The arched street entrance (in wood) with its two pairs of small columns is Richardsonian Romanesque, while the tower with its elongated domed roof and ogee dormers appears Islamic. And there are other suggestions, as well, of the French Chateauesque, and of the American Colonial Revival. Note especially the stair hall landing window on the north side of the house.

a. House, circa 1897
1026 S. Bonnie Brae Street
"Palladian" (perhaps). Really a Queen Anne design with American Colonial Revival frosting.

b. House, circa 1896
1032 S. Bonnie Brae Street
An additional example of the late Queen Anne open plan, with many American Colonial Revival references.

c. House, circa 1898
1035 S. Bonnie Brae Street
Shingled late Queen Anne/Colonial Revival.

d. House, circa 1895
1036–1038 S. Bonnie Brae Street
One of the remaining architectural gems of the Avenue, this dwelling is French Chateauesque accomplished in wood, with small corner turrets and a low balcony between.

15a. Wright-Mooers House, 1894

designs is the dramatic stair landing bay which projects from the north side of the house. This house was one of many illustrated in Joseph Cather Newsom's *Artistic Buildings and Homes of Los Angeles* (1888).

16. House, circa 1902
    Attributed to Joseph Cather Newsom
    1011 Beacon Street
Newsom employed a combination of images in all of his work in Los Angeles and elsewhere. He would probably have labeled this dwelling as an example of the "Bavarian Hunting Lodge Style." This meant a combination of a Queen Anne floor plan with medieval vernacular detailing from central Europe.

17. Dennis House, 1910
    Dennis and Farwell
    767 S. Garland Avenue
The architectural firm of Oliver P. Dennis and Lyman Farwell was one of Los Angeles's most productive offices from around 1896 through the mid-teens. A good number of their designs tend towards the Beaux Arts Classical and to the American Colonial Revival. (Farwell had worked in the New York office of McKim, Mead, and White.) Here in Dennis's own house we can see a Colonial Revival dwelling with a few leftovers from the earlier Queen Anne.

b. House, circa 1897
    824 S. Bonnie Brae Street
A Colonial Revival design accompanied by a wide veranda, which is wrapped around the corner bay tower. The tower is capped by an Islamic domed roof.

c. Flint House, 1888
    Joseph Cather Newsom
    842 S. Bonnie Brae Street
The Flint House illustrates one of the many variations of the Queen Anne side-hall plan worked out by the Newsoms. A square bay projects off the southwest corner of the house, and above on the second floor is an open, spindled porch (now enclosed). A hallmark of their

18. House, circa 1905
    740 S. Union Avenue
Colonial Revival of the stately type with a temple front, large-scale Corinthian columns and all.

19. Young's Market Building (now **Andrews Hardware and Metal Company**), 1924
Charles F. Plummer
1010 W. 7th Street

A Maybeckish romantic version of the Beaux Arts tradition. A row of classical columns supports the upper arcade. Between them is a "life-size frieze of genuine della Robbia style." The interior is decorated in a "Pompeiian" fashion with marble and antique mosaics. The Market was damaged in the 1992 riots, but it now has been restored and is open to the public.

20. Wilshire Financial Building, 1985–86
Albert C. Martin and Associates
Southwest corner of Wilshire Boulevard and Bixel Street

The opinion that the downtown core should leap over the Harbor Freeway to the west has long been in the minds of planners and business interests. The thirty-eight-story Wilshire Financial Building was conceived as an important step in that westward march of high-rises. Although it is on Wilshire Boulevard, it does not make itself an element within the Wilshire corridor. It, like most urban downtown buildings, exists in and of itself. The unique aspect of its design is that the building becomes a triangle above its twelfth story.

21. Office Tower for the Signal Oil Company, 1958
Pereira and Luckman; remodeled in 1973–74 by Craig Ellwood and Associates
1010 Wilshire Boulevard

Ellwood resheathed a rather dull, 1950s Modern tower of seventeen floors into his own version of the Miesian aesthetic.

22. Woodbury College Building, 1937
Claude Beelman
1027 Wilshire Boulevard

A monumental Streamline Moderne building. The grand entrance and the basic symmetrical facade suggest the dignity of an institution.

23. Arco Center Building, 1988–89
Gin Wong Associates
1055 W. 7th Street

Another high-rise, like the Wilshire Financial Building, which hopes to establish the

26. Osiris Apartment Building, 1926

downtown connections of the "West Bank," i.e., west of the Harbor Freeway. There is not much to say about this dark clad thirty-three-story high-rise other than its form is reserved.

24. Scholts Advertising Company Building, 1937
Richard J. Neutra
1201 W. 4th Street

On the street side the one-story facade is divided into three extended horizontal bands of stucco with the windows carried up to the soffit of the flat roof and finally the thin fascia line of the roof itself. The principal offices face north away from the street and out onto a landscaped court.

25. Loma Court, circa 1925
380–388 Loma Drive

One of Los Angeles's many Mediterranean-styled bungalow courts.

26. Osiris Apartment Building, 1926
J. M. Close
430 S. Union Avenue

J. M. Close, who acted as both architect and builder, designed a number of Egyptian Revival apartment buildings in the area west of the downtown. As in the Osiris Apartment Building, that which is Egyptian (and it works well) is the pylon street facade. The rest of the building is a typical Los Angeles stucco box.

27. Mary Andrews Clark Memorial Home (YWCA), 1912–13
Arthur B. Benton
306 Loma Drive
The master of the Mission Revival here turned his hand to the French Chateauesque. The building seems most satisfactory from a distance, where the towers and high roofs emerge out of the surrounding trees. Inside, the more public spaces exhibit exotic woods and some splendid leaded and colored art glass.

28. Lewis House, 1889
attrib. Joseph Cather Newsom
1425 Miramar Street
The Newsom brothers, Samuel and Joseph Cather Newsom, best known for their often-illustrated Carson House in Eureka, California, produced some of the wonderful inventive if not slightly "mad" Victorian houses in Los Angeles during the Great Boom of the 1880s. Regrettably, most of these houses have disappeared one by one over the years. The Lewis House is a delightful but subdued example of one of their Queen Anne designs. The effectiveness of their design would be more apparent if the second-floor porch above the entrance were not enclosed.

29. Bungalow Court, circa 1937
428–432 S. Burlington Avenue
A Streamline Moderne bungalow court. Other nearby courts are to be found at 445 S. Burlington Avenue (Mission Revival, circa 1914) and at 470–478 S. Burlington Avenue (a bit of Dutch Cottage imagery, circa 1922).

30. Westlake Theater, 1926
Richard M. Bates, Jr.
638 S. Alvarado Street
The interior was originally Adamesque, but both the interior and the exterior have continually been updated over the years. The interior is still worth a visit.

31. Hite Building, 1923–24
Morgan, Walls, and Clements
Southwest corner of Carondelet Street and West 7th Street
The firm of Morgan, Walls, and Clements designed well over a dozen small retail/commercial buildings in the MacArthur Park area. They utilized a Spanish image, but maneuvered it into something which always read as a pure 1920s design. Ornament inspired by Spain and Mexico—the Plateresque, the Churrigueresque, and of the Renaissance—was placed as accent marks on simple stucco volumes. In the Hite Building the street elevation of the single-story section boasts a composition of a six-columned arcade balanced on each side by entrances with cast-concrete ornamented panels above. Two other Morgan, Walls, and Clements buildings nearby are the **Thorpe Building** (1924) at the northwest corner of Parkview and West 7th streets and the **Studio and Shop Building** for Mrs. Olive J. Cobb at 2861 W. 7th Street (1924).

32. Carl's Supermarket Building, 1933
Morgan, Walls, and Clements
1530–1536 W. 6th Street
An early supermarket building. Its image is transitional between the Art Deco Moderne and the then-emerging Streamline Moderne. Note the composition of the pylons to each side, which sprout three layers of plantlike spirals at their tops.

33. Prometheus, 1935
Nina Saemundsson
MacArthur Park (near the southwest corner of Wilshire Boulevard and Alvarado Street).
An eight-foot-high cast-concrete figure placed on a wonderful high base with sunrays and other Moderne patterns. This is a Federal Arts Project sculpture which well sums up the aesthetic qualities of public art of the 1930s.

34. The Elks Building, (now **Park Plaza Hotel,**) 1923–24
Curlett and Beelman
607 S. Park View Street
A monumental Goodhuesque composition with its prime reference being to the early

Romanesque. The glory of the building externally lies in the groupings of large-scale sculptured figures at the upper ends of each of the wings of the building and the eight, larger-than-life-size figures near the parapet of the high central section of the building. The interiors were decorated by Anthony Heinsbergen.

35. Granada Building, 1927
  Franklin Harper
  627 S. Lafayette Park Place
A full block of retail stores, offices, and studio apartments designed as a single Spanish village. Inner paseos, balconies, and courts create a series of pleasing, small-scaled spaces.

36. The Town House (now **Sheraton-Town House),** 1928
  Norman W. Alpaugh
  1600 Wilshire Boulevard.
A thirteen-story brick-and-stone trimmed Beaux Arts hotel of the twenties. Designs such as this were common across the country, but there were never a great number built in L.A. in the teens and 1920s. This hotel makes its nod to the Southland in its garden enclosed within the L of the building. This is one of the few examples still left in L.A. In the spring of 1993 it was declared a Cultural/Historic Monument by the city.

37. First Congregational Church, 1930–32
  Allison and Allison (Austin Whittlesey)
  Northwest corner of Commonwealth Avenue and West 6th Street
A concrete structure with revealed horizontal, form board patterns on its wall surfaces. One assumes that the design was derived from English late Gothic, especially the central tower.

38. CNA Building, 1972
  Langdon and Wilson
  Emmet L. Wemple and Associates, landscape architect
  Southwest corner of Commonwealth Avenue and West 6th Street
A mirrored glass cube—it works well as long as there is something around worth reflecting.

39. Church of the Precious Blood, circa 1932
  Henry C. Newton and Robert D. Murray
  North corner of Hoover Street and Occidental Boulevard
Italian Romanesque in reinforced concrete, beautifully sited in relation to the joining of the two major streets.

40. Charles Croze Studio, 1948
  Harwell H. Harris
  2340 W. 3rd Street
If only the MacArthur Park area could have developed after World War II with buildings and landscaping of this quality, it would have maintained the Arcadian image of Los Angeles. Here, within a grove of blue gum eucalyptus trees, Harris has placed his beautiful L-shaped building with its dramatic cantilevered balcony and its forecourt of low planting and brick paving.

41. Hill House, circa 1911
  Walker and Vawter
  201 S. Coronado Street
This Craftsman dwelling was frequently illustrated as the typical Los Angeles bungalow. The principal rooms of this bungalow open through glass doors to a terrace surrounded by a clinker brick wall. Long, heavy shingles cover the walls, and the Japanese exposed roof beams lend an oriental feeling.

42. Bungalow Court, circa 1925
  West corner of Loma Drive and Crown Hill Avenue
Hillsides were often used to advantage throughout Los Angeles for stepped patterns of bungalow courts. This example displays a Spanish Colonial Revival image.

43. House, circa 1900
  Southwest corner of Bonnie Brae Street and West Olympic Boulevard
A Chateauesque dwelling with the characteristic dominant round tower surmounted by a conical roof.

DOWNTOWN

Yes, Virginia, there is a downtown Los Angeles, although you may continue, to this day, to wonder why. The present-day central city lies southeast of the fabled multi-level interchange of the Hollywood, Santa Ana, Pasadena, and Harbor freeways. The northern section of this area, occupying what remains of Bunker Hill, is devoted to public buildings and spaces—symbolic, cultural, and bureaucratic. The remainder of Bunker Hill and south into the flatlands is given over to commerce (with some more recent high-density housing).

Downtown L.A. is the product of three major building booms. The first was in the years 1900–1917; the second was from the early 1920s through 1931; and the last started in the late 1960s and is still very much with us. The first two booms utilized the imagery of the Classical Beaux Arts, and it is amazing how many ten- to twelve-story office buildings were built, especially on South Broadway and on South Spring Street. The second expansion moved toward the west from South Broadway to South Flower Street and was clothed in variations of the Art Deco (Zigzag) Moderne and the PWA Moderne.

In the late 1930s a few Streamline Moderne buildings were constructed and a number of street level frontages were remodeled. Little building activity occurred from 1945 through the early 1960s, so there are only a few examples of post-World War II Corporate Modern buildings. The high-rise buildings constructed since the late 1960s are much more varied in form, running the gamut from smooth-skin modernism to outright Post Modernism. Many, even the Modernist buildings, convey a Post-Modernist stance by clothing the building in skins of stone (usually much too thin, to be sure) rather than in the usual metal and glass

sheathing which we associate with Modernist products.

Since the early 1920s, downtown L.A. has been a disappointment for those who feel that a city should have a primary high-density urban core, with the necessary cityscape of skyscrapers. Even today, downtown Los Angeles finds itself doing battle as the city's center with other urban cores and strips.

During the 1930s the view that downtown should only be one among many urban centers was officially codified in the regional plan for the L.A. Basin. It was in the late 1930s, too, that the freeway system was planned, and as soon as World War II was over, work commenced on completing the Hollywood Freeway. A short time later, the Santa Ana and Harbor freeways were built. In the 1950s, these freeways and the pre-World War II Pasadena Freeway (1934–41) were connected by the famous multilevel interchange known as "The Stack."

So far, downtown L.A. has followed the classic approach to urban renewal, namely the bulldozing away of the past and starting anew. The greatest losses were the wonderful residences on Bunker Hill which were swept away in Charles Luckman's plan for the area. Many of the buildings which were situated on Bunker Hill could have been revamped and reused, but they are all gone now. With the exception of several restored nineteenth-century buildings near the Plaza (and of course the Bradbury Building at Broadway and Third Street), little or no evidence of nineteenth-century Victorianism remains in downtown Los Angeles. The number of major buildings lost in the past ten to twelve years is, if nothing else, impressive. Included among the major lost monuments are the great black and gold 1928 Richfield Building (Morgan, Walls, and

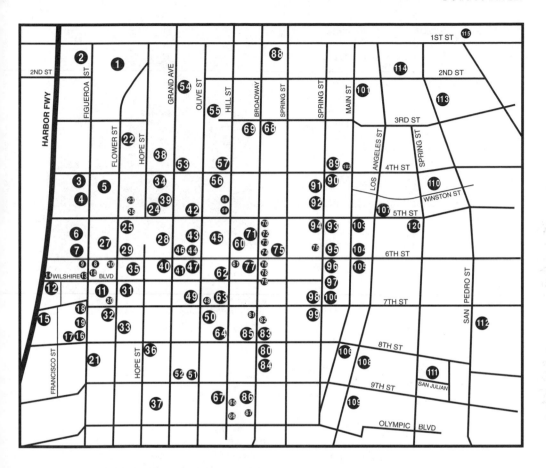

Clements) and the 1935 Sunkist Building (Walker and Eisen), with its roof gardens and abundance of sculpture and paintings, and more recently the Sullivanesque Philharmonic Auditorium Building by Charles F. Whittlesey. We have also lost through remodeling the wonderful Moderne-style Clifton's Cafeteria, and more recently Saint Paul's Cathedral, the Hotel Cordova, the Abbey Building, the Bath Building, the Municipal Water and Power Building, and others.

Through urban renewal, the houses of Bunker Hill were bulldozed, and replaced bit by bit with the big-city illusion of high-rise towers. On the whole these towers are

competent exercises, but they in no way address the specifics of Bunker Hill as a hill or the climate and geography of Los Angeles. The streets adjacent to these high-rises are for the automobile, and they are not on the whole a pleasant experience for pedestrians, notwithstanding a few very handsome ground-level plazas.

In 1980 five developer/architect teams were invited to submit their proposals for the last remaining large parcels of Bunker Hill, an eleven-acre site. The B.H.A. Associates with Arthur Erickson were finally chosen, though even a casual look at the proposal of the Maguire Partners (which included a star-studded cast composed of Cesar Pelli, Lawrence Halprin, Charles W. Moore, Robert Kennard, Hardy, Holzman, and Pfeiffer, Richard Legoretta, Frank O. Gehry, Paul Krueger, Barton Myers, Harvey S. Perloff, and Edgardo Contini) would indicate that their proposal was far superior. Many of Erickson's proposals have been carried out. You can form a judgment of the projected whole by looking at what has been built (hardly inspiring).

1. Bunker Hill Towers, 1968
    Robert E. Alexander
    Northeast corner of Figueroa and West 1st
    streets
Three high-rise towers which are supposed to introduce mixed use (residential living) into downtown. In style and concept they are marginally respectable.

2. Promenade Towers, 1985
    Kamnitzer and Cotton; Abraham Shapiro
    Fong and Associates, landscape architects
    West side of Figueroa Street, between 1st
    and 2nd streets.
The idea of providing downtown living accommodations is perhaps fine, but the buildings are bland. The garden between them with palms and exotic planning is the best part of the project.

3. Sheraton Grande Hotel, 1978–83
    Archsystems
    Southwest corner of Figueroa and West 4th
    streets
A fifteen-story structure which plays off curvilinear and angular shapes. Like the Bonaventure Hotel, it is best when experienced from the freeway. The thick planting of palms at the entrance is the high point of the design.

4. Union Bank Building, 1968
    Albert C. Martin and Associates
    Figueroa Street between West 4th and West
    5th streets
A typical example of the late 1960s Corporate International Style Modern, here is a vertical box set on a low podium. It is notable for being the first high-rise in central Los Angeles since the 1920s.

5. Bonaventure Hotel, 1974–76

5. Bonaventure Hotel, 1974–76
    John Portman and Associates
    Northeast corner of Figueroa and West 5th
    streets
The science-fiction world of Buck Rogers and the twenty-first century have not left us. Five bronze-clad glass towers rise from their podium base, just like one of the 1940s drawings by Frank R. Paul for *Amazing Stories*. As a contribution to downtown L.A., they work best when seen from one of the freeways. Portman was quoted as saying of L.A. and his hotel, "Put cars in their place, put people on their feet, and put the city in order" (1973). Obviously his view of putting people on their feet meant inside of his building, not on the adjoining streets. As with many other recent downtown L.A. projects, the streetscape of the Bonaventure is grim; the public sidewalk alongside the adjoining streets is not for pedestrians. And this is reinforced by four pedestrian bridges which connect the upper level of the Bonaventure Hotel with adjoining buildings. As

seems typical of the design of skyways across America, all of these are dull, both for their users and as objects within the streetscape. The atrium space within Portman's hotel is visually exciting, but maddening when you try to find your way around. As a partial answer to the criticism that the hotel ignored the street, a new entrance has been added on Flower Street (1985–86; designed by John Portman and Associates). To a degree, this change helps the hotel and the street, but this section of Flower represents the world of the automobile, not, regrettably, the pedestrian.

6. Manulife Plaza, 1981–82
Albert C. Martin and Associates
515 S. Figueroa Street

Another vertical reflective box, in this case blue-green glass with a step-back facade. A suggestion of luxury is added to this twenty-story skyscraper by the use of green granite both externally and in the lobby. Below the shaft of the building are four levels of parking. The usual stage-set plaza is provided, adorned by a sculpture of a family of bears fishing for salmon, the work of Christopher Keene.

7. Jonathan Club, 1924
Schultze and Weaver
545 S. Figueroa Street

A restrained, low-rise building realized in a Beaux Arts version of early-sixteenth-century Italian Renaissance architecture.

8. Linder Plaza, 1973–74
Honnold, Reibsamen, and Rex
888 W. 6th Street (at Figueroa Street)

A fifteen-story triangular skyscraper whose fragile skin is sheathed in silver and gray steel and glass. The fine and expensive machine-image detailing of the building is impressive.

9. Nicola Restaurant, 1992–93
Michael Rotundi
601 S. Figueroa Street

The design of this restaurant was meant to take into account the space allotted to it and to counter that space. A linear pattern composed of thin sections of wood and metal creates its own spiderweb pattern. These tied-together patterns create the unified visual theme of the space.

10. Engine Company #28 Building, 1912
John Parkinson
644 S. Figueroa Street

This three-story brick and stone-trimmed firehouse was restored in 1989 by the architectural firm of Altoon and Porter.

11. Fine Arts Building, 1925
Walker and Eisen
811 W. 7th Street

The street facade of this twelve-story building displays a highly original use of Romanesque (the Cathedral at Lucca comes to mind). Twisted columns, sculptured corbeling, heavy arched windows, and elongated columns were all employed. The tripartite division of the facade has taken into account how the building is viewed; it is subtle close up at the street level, large and bold at the top so that it will make an impact from a distance. The tour-de-force of the building (and a must to see) is the two-story, arcaded main lobby with its rich surfaces and ornament produced by the tile-maker Ernest Batchelder.

11. Fine Arts Building, 1925

14. 1000 Wilshire Building, 1984–87

12. Office Building, 1978–80
Skidmore, Owings, and Merrill (Chicago Office)
911 Wilshire Boulevard
One more horizontal-grid skyscraper, twenty-three stories high. This is a familiar type unfortunately found in urban environments across the U.S.

13. Sanwa Bank Plaza (Mitsui Fudosan Building), 1986–89
Albert C. Martin and Associates
Northwest corner of Figueroa Street and Wilshire Boulevard
The architect's design is that of a 760-foot-high, 50-story skyscraper which exhibits slightly layered setbacks and clipped corners. Its principal walls are of coral-colored granite contrasted with bronze panels and green glazing. Within, one will discover an impressive 75-foot-high atrium. Before you glance at this high-rise, bear in mind that this was until a few years ago the site of Saint Paul's Episcopal Cathedral, a major Los Angeles landmark.

14. 1000 Wilshire Building, 1984–87
Kohn Peterson Fox
Wilshire Boulevard, just east of the Harbor Freeway
The 1000 Wilshire Building is downtown Los Angeles's most assertive Post Modern Building. Though by no means as tall as other downtown skyscrapers (it contains 21 stories), it really stands out when viewed from the Harbor Freeway. The building exhibits gabled ends, enlarged/overscaled windows, contrasting banding, and frequent references to Art Deco designs of the late 1920s. The best way to experience the building is from the south at 7th Street; you go up formal staircases, through a gateway onto a plaza, and then into the building. At the north side of the building you enter through a 34-foot-high gatehouse. There is no question that as long as it is around, this building will dominate the western sections of downtown Los Angeles.

15. *Harbor Freeway Overtone*, 1991–93
Kent Twitchell, artist
On the Citicorp Plaza Parking Structure facing the Harbor Freeway;
8th Street and the Harbor Freeway.
Players of the Los Angeles Chamber Orchestra greet you as you go by on the freeway. Twitchell really understands how a large-scale public mural can function. Often they are far more important than the buildings around. Other downtown examples of this artist's public murals are: *Ed Ruscha Monument,* (1978–87) on the exterior of the Job Center Building, 1031 South Hill Street; and *The Bride and Groom,* (1972–76) on the exterior of Victor Clothing Company Building, 240 South Broadway. Twitchell's most well-known public mural is *The Freeway Lady*, located on the exterior of the Prince Hotel at 1255 West Temple Street (visible from the Hollywood Freeway). This work was painted in 1974; in 1981 a new building was constructed which partially obscured the mural, and then in 1986 it was painted over. A legal settlement was made between the owner of the property and the artist (1992), and it has now been repainted (with a few changes and extensions).

16. 865 South Figueroa Tower, 1985–87
    Albert C. Martin and Associates
    865 S. Figueroa
A 36-story skyscraper, rendered in polished red granite and bronze windows. The building's surfaces are layered à la skyscrapers of the late 1920s and early 1930s.

17. Hotel Figueroa, 1925
    Stanton, Reed, and Hibbard
    939 S. Figueroa Street
A learned Beaux Arts interpretation of northern Italian Renaissance town houses.

18. Citicorp Plaza 777 Tower, 1988–90
    Cesar Pelli and Associates; Langdon Wilson Mumper
    Southwest corner Figueroa and 7th streets
A reflective-skinned fifty-three-story tower, its form a layered series of cylinders. The structure, and especially the lobby, reveal the sophisticated detailing one associates with Pelli's work.

19. Seventh Market Place (Bullocks Department Store), 1985–86
    Skidmore, Owings and Merrill (Chicago Office)
    925 W. 8th Street

19. Seventh Market Place (Bullocks Department Store), 1985–86

Essentially this is a posh shopping center arranged around a sunken court. The court boasts plenty of exposed ironwork, fountains and trees. The project is colorful, with use of a varied scheme of mauve, peach, light blue and celadon. Bullocks itself has the feel that its designer was inspired by one of Otto Wagner's metal-frame-and-paneled railroad stations in Vienna. It all seems light and festive; good for shopping.

20. Home Savings of America Tower,
    1988–89
    Albert C. Martin and Associates (Tim Vreeland)
    Northeast corner of Figueroa and 7th streets
Another odd Post Modernist high-rise. Tim Vreeland, who was responsible for the design of this twenty-eight-story building, noted that he looked to the turn-of-the-century New York versions of the French Chateauesque style. The most dramatic space in the building is the domed and barrel-vaulted sixth-floor "Sky Lobby." While the reference to the

18. Citicorp Plaza 777 Tower, 1988–90

20. Home Savings of America Tower, 1988–89

Chateauesque mode is apparent, the proportions and detailing needed to carry out this historic mode are only partially apparent in the building.

21. Friday Morning Club Building, 1923–24
Allison and Allison
938–940 S. Figueroa Street
A Beaux Arts formula; in this instance there seems to be a suggestion of Byzantine or Romanesque.

22. Security Pacific Plaza, 1973–74
Albert C. Martin and Associates
Southeast corner of South Flower and West 3rd streets
The return of the Beaux Arts (as a set of classical design principles, not the usual vocabulary): the tower is fifty-five stories high and its facades are accentuated by thirty-six vertical piers sheathed in light gray granite from Ponteverde, Spain. The gardens and their fountains are quite formal. A large arched sculpture in steel (painted red) by Alexander Calder is placed near the entrance to the tower. Across South Figueroa Street to the west is the full-block **World Trade Center** (1974–76; Conrad Associates) which, notwithstanding its twin eight-story towers, poses as an urban non-space.

23. Wells Fargo Building (444 Plaza Building), 1979
Albert C. Martin and Associates
Northeast corner of South Flower and West 5th streets
When one considers that this forty-eight-story skyscraper replaced the handsome Sunkist Building (1935; Walker and Eisen), the demand for a building whose design would be far above the normal was to be expected. The emphasized horizontality of its stepped-back rectangular volume is well carried out, but hardly distinguished. The plaza with its palm trees heads in the right direction, but it does not save the composition. Equally mixed is the sense of meaningful public sculpture by Michael Hiezer, Bruce Nauman, Robert Rauschenberg, Frank Stella, and Mark di Suvero.

24. First Interstate World Center, 1988–90
I. M. Pei and Partners
North side of 5th Street, west of Grand Avenue
A round high-rise which in a slablike fashion reduces its diameter as it nears the top. This tower comes off as one of the best of the newer downtown L.A. skyscrapers.

24. First Interstate World Center, 1988–90

25. Los Angeles Public Library, addition 1983–93

25. Los Angeles Public Library, 1922–26
Bertram G. Goodhue and Carleton M.
Winslow
Southeast corner of South Flower and West
5th streets

This building and the Nebraska State Capitol at Lincoln are Goodhue's two most significant works and also two of his most influential designs. In both, Goodhue sought to bring the past and present together in a single, readable image. From the past he borrowed far and wide, from Egypt, Rome, Byzantium, and various Islamic civilizations. He also continued the tradition of monumental construction and the extensive use of sculpture, painting and mosaics. He implied the new age of the twentieth century in his hint at the skyscraper (modern business), his utilitarian planning, the expression of undecorated surfaces, and the use of twentieth-century materials, here reinforced concrete.

As with several of his important designs, Goodhue originally started out with a rather elaborate building, with domes and much ornament in the Spanish Colonial Revival style, one which he himself had done so much to popularize at the 1915 San Diego Exposition. He simplified and abstracted his original design to produce, as it was referred to in those years, a design which was "modified Spanish Colonial style." As in his design for the Nebraska State Capitol Building, Goodhue created an abbreviated skyscraper as the exterior focal point of his design, but inside he retained his traditional dome, vaulting, and arches.

Operating within a Beaux Arts tradition, he introduced a wide array of art: exterior sculpture by Lee Lawrie, the twelve murals in the second floor of the rotunda by Dean Cornwall, the thirteen murals in the History Room by Albert Herter. In the Children's Room, the fresco *Stampeding Buffalo* was by Charles M. Kassler, and the scenes by Julian Garnsey and A. W. Parsons convey episodes from Sir Walter Scott's novels. "Sculpture here," wrote Lee Lawrie, "is not sculpture, but a branch grafted on to the architectural trunk; forms that portray animated life, emerge from blocks of stone and terminate in historical expression." As with the Nebraska State Capitol Building, Goodhue and Lawrie worked closely with the philosopher Hartley B. Alexander in drawing up the ideological program of decoration for the library. Their theme was "centered in the illuminated book, symbolized by the torch of knowledge which is handed on from one age to another by the great literary figures of all ages." In a way the design of the landscape provided by Goodhue and Winslow was to pass on historic symbols (in the plants used and the design of the landscape) and to see that they were regenerated and made meaningful for the present. The east garden pointed to the informality of the English Picturesque tradition; the west garden looked to the ancient Mediterranean world and the Islamic gardens of the Near East. His view that the library was a building in a park was integral to his design.

Los Angeles's initial discussion (in the 1960s and 1970s) as to what should be done with its central library was to suggest that the site be sold for development, and the library facility be moved somewhere else. As if to hurry on that event, an arsonist (who has never been found to this day) set the building on fire in 1986. A second fire occurred a few years later, augmented by damage suffered in the 1987 earthquake.

Earlier, in 1983, the city had finally decided that the approach to the library should be a complicated affair of restoration, expansion of the building to the east, granting of air rights to surrounding development, etc. This led to the development of the Library Square project, with the library building being surrounded, and to a considerable degree dwarfed, by a ring of high-rise towers. The Los Angeles office of the New York firm of Hardy, Holzman and Pfeiffer was selected to guide the renovation and design the additions. They initially proposed a new wing, which was to dominate the Goodhue building. After much public review, this design was modified to be lower than the massing of the original building. In the meantime, Brenda Levin and Associates was engaged to supervise the restoration, and Lawrence Halprin together with Campbell and Campbell were brought in to redesign the remaining parkland around the building.

In mid-1993 all of this work was finished and the building is once more open for library patrons and visitors. What of the results? On the good side is the wonderful and sensitive restoration of the building, particularly its great interior public spaces. Another plus is the relandscaping of the west garden, though this has some problems with the injection of new structures and an underground parking garage. But it has been replanted, perhaps even overplanted, an approach perhaps needed in the world of the surrounding hardscape of streets, sidewalks, and buildings. A number of new works of art have entered into the building and its landscape, including sculptures and inscriptions by Jud Fine for the "Spine," which leads up to the building's west entrance. On the negative side is the loss of the charmingly scaled Children's Wing and the east park. As to Hardy, Holzman and Pfeiffer's addition, it may work functionally, but aesthetically it is at best

26. Bunker Hill Steps, 1989–90

unfortunate. They have reverted to their usual theme of a central skylighted atrium (if it works for a shopping mall, why not a library, or a museum?). The verticality of the eight-story atrium space suggests the Gothic, whereas Goodhue's design is fully within the tradition of horizontality associated with Classical architecture. Externally, their efforts in massing and detailing to slightly mimic Goodhue has little substance to it. Whether the splendid restoration was worth the price of an uninspired and inappropriate addition, the loss of the Children's Wing, and the elimination of a much-needed public parkland is something history will have to decide.

26. Bunker Hill Steps, 1989–90
Lawrence Halprin

Los Angeles's own version of Rome's Spanish Steps meanders up the hillside from 5th Street to Hope Street, 103 steps in all. The steps are divided by a raised water channel whose water course seems to suggest a natural rock-bedded stream. Terraced planting occurs on each side. At the top of the stairs and water course is an impressive small-scaled sculptured figure by Robert Graham (1992).

27. "Double Ascension," Atlantic Richfield Plaza, 1973

27. Atlantic Richfield Plaza, 1972
   Albert C. Martin and Associates
   West side of South Flower Street between
   West 5th and West 6th streets.
These two, thin, fifty-two-story towers (one of
which houses the Atlantic Richfield Oil
Company offices, the other the Bank of
America) replace one of L.A.'s major monuments, the 1928–29 Art Deco (Zigzag)
Moderne, black and gold, terra-cotta Richfield
Building (Morgan, Walls, and Clements). The
dark, polished-stone-sheathed twin towers of
the new buildings are formal, dignified, and reticent. The plaza between the towers contains a
fountain sculpture, *Double Ascension* (1973) by
Herbert Bayer. Below the plaza are two levels
of an underground mall, which in color and
design is more self-consciously fashionable
than the towers (Bielski and Associates, design
consultants for the mall).

28. Mayflower Hotel (Checkers Hotel), 1927
   Charles F. Whittlesey
   535 South Grand Avenue
A small hotel built in the Spanish
mode. Its elaborate facade contains sculptures of gargoyles and
ships (including the *Santa Maria*
and the *Mayflower*). In 1989 the
building was remodeled and
restored by Holtsmark Architects,
Kaplan/McLaughlin/Diaz.

29. The California Club,
   1929–30
   Robert D. Farquhar
   238 S. Flower Street
The classical tradition via the
Beaux Arts in an eight-story structure. The architect carried out his
instructions "to use the best materials without elaboration and to
provide an atmosphere of the
finest type of American Club life."
The exterior is of warm brown
Roman brick with a thin tufa trim.

30. Security Pacific Building, 1973
   William L. Pereira Associates
   Southwest corner of South Flower and
   West 6th streets
The picturesque aspects of Louis Kahn's
Richards Medical Towers at the University of
Pennsylvania are applied to a seventeen-story
office tower, all a bit thin and of a decorative
nature.

31. The Broadway Plaza, 1972–73
   Charles Luckman and Associates
   Southeast corner of South Flower and West
   7th streets
This square block project contains the Hyatt
Regency Hotel with its round revolving restaurant on top, a thirty-two-story office tower, the
downtown Broadway Department Store, and
the open-atrium Broadway Plaza Galleria. The
two-story Galleria is pleasant, but the ground
floor level of the building creates a grim experience for both pedestrians and passengers in
cars.

32. 801 Tower, 1991
Architects Collaborative (John Hayes)
801 S. Flower Street
The high-rise tower sits somewhere between
early 1970s modern, and the Post Modernism
of the mid-1980s. The real plus of this project
is the Zanja Madre Plaza to the west of the
building. This plaza was designed by Andrew
Leicester working closely with the architect.
Though somewhat on the hefty side as far as
hardscape is concerned, it makes wonderful use
of water and its metal, tile, and stone abstraction of plant forms.

**33. Southern Counties Gas Company
Building,** 1939–40
Robert V. Derrah
820 S. Flower Street
Forget the ground floor of the building. It has
been hopelessly remodeled. But the five floors
above indicate how well Derrah (who designed
the Coca-Cola Building and the Crossroads of
the World) could work with the Streamline
Moderne. The slightly recessed center is of
glass, and the two concrete side sections curve
into the center.

34. O'Melveny and Myers Office Building,
1982
Welton Becket Associates (Robert Taylor)
The SWA Group, landscape architects
South side of 4th Street between South
Hope Street and South Grand Avenue
A twenty-six-story tower of six sides, sheathed
horizontally in alternating bands of tinted
reflective glass and polished brown granite.
The tower is set at an angle on its site, and at
ground level there is an ample plaza with a
double row of sixty-eight Italian cypress trees.
The lobby of the tower is composed of a fifty-
foot-high greenhouse. The building's most distinguished feature from afar is its thirty-degree
slope roof, suggesting that it is either a minimal
piece of sculpture or that solar collectors are in
use.

35. United California Bank Building, 1973
Charles Luckman and Associates
Northwest corner of South Hope Street and
Wilshire Boulevard

29. The California Club, 1929–30

A nondescript vertical shaft, sixty-two-stories
high; characteristic not only of the work of this
firm, but of American high-rise architecture of
the late 1960s to early 1970s.

36. Grand Hope Park, 1989–93
Lawrence Halprin
Southeast corner South Hope Street and 9th
Street
This small 2 ½-acre site was set aside for a park
in 1975. The theme of the park was described
as "bringing functional art and nature to an
urban setting." Grand Hope Park suffers from
the same problem as Pershing Square, too little
nature and too many hardscape structures. In
this tiny piece of land Halprin has provided a
53-foot-high yellow and red clock tower (somewhat Post Modernist in design), a pair of fountains, and pergolas, but even with this amount
of hardscape, nature will probably predominate.
The planting is rich, with the introduction of
good-sized palms, sycamores, California oaks,
Italian cypresses, and ficus trees. The snake
fountain was designed by Raul Guerrero, and
Halprin and Lita Albuquerque designed the
other fountain. Added late in the project is an

39. Southern California Edison Building (now One Bunker Hill), 1930–31

polished brown granite and tinted glass. In the space between the two towers is a glass-atrium garden court with an exotic garden designed by Lawrence Halprin. In it are pieces of sculpture by Jean Dubuffet, Robert Graham, Juan Miro, and Louise Nevelson.

39. Southern California Edison Building (now One Bunker Hill), 1930–31
Allison and Allison (Austin Whittlesey)
Northwest corner of South Grand Avenue and West 5th Street

The slope of the two streets made it logical to place the main entrance of this twelve-story Art Deco office building at the corner. Over the entrance are three relief panels by Merrell Gage: Hydro Electric Energy, Light, and Power. Once in the formal entrance, go on to the elevators, and there you will find a mural *Apotheosis of Power* by Hugo Ballin. The tower portion of the building is basically classical and massive, but the deep-cut vertical window/spandrel units create a strong vertical pattern.

eight-foot-high wrought iron fence with seven gates; this addition has provoked extensive controversy.

37. Standard Oil Company Office Building, 1923–24
George W. Kelham
605 W. Olympic Boulevard between South Hope Street and South Grand Avenue

The San Francisco architect George W. Kelham utilized a rusticated, late fifteenth-century northern Italian "Palazzo" scheme for this urbane eight-story building. The Los Angeles building is similar to the 1921 office building, which he designed for Standard Oil in San Francisco.

38. Crocker Center, 1982–83
Skidmore, Owings, and Merrill
Southwest corner of South Grand Avenue and West 3rd Street

Two 760-foot-high prismatic towers of

40. Edwards and Wildey Building (California Pacific National Bank Building), 1925
Walker and Eisen
603 South Grand Avenue

Another example of the wide range of images used within the Beaux Arts tradition in downtown Los Angeles, in this case a thirteen-story office block imprints a Romanesque image on a classical frame. The building is sheathed in "Granitex," a terra-cotta surfacing which reads as stone. Cast iron was used for the arched openings of the first floor.

41. One Wilshire Building, 1964
Skidmore, Owings, and Merrill (San
Francisco)
East side of South Grand Avenue and
Wilshire Boulevard
A big, bulky box with a stamped-out facade.
Recent renovations have helped a bit.

42. The Gas Company Towers, 1988–91
Skidmore, Owings and Merrill (Los
Angeles Office; Richard Keating)
555 W. 5th Street (Northwest corner Olive
Street and 5th Street)
A 52-story high-rise with an impressive 300-
foot abstract mural by Frank Stella at its base.
The towers seem to refer back to SOM's classi-
cal modernist work of the late 1950s/early
1960s (modular and thin-skinned) coupled with
the concept of layered slabs associated with
Rockefeller Center in New York.

43. Biltmore Hotel, 1922–23 and 1928
Schultze and Weaver
Southwest corner of South Olive and W.
5th streets
Designed by the New York firm which produced in the teens and 1920s many of
America's major hotels. Its composition and
much of its detailing are faithful Beaux Arts,
called at the time "Renaissance." But if you
look closely, you will find that much of the
brickwork and terra-cotta detailing are sixteenth century Italian. Internally, a variety of
moods are created, including the Spanish
Churrigueresque. The two interior spaces that
should attract your attention are the lobby, with
its dramatic staircase, and the interior shopping
street, labeled "El Camino." Many of the ceilings were painted by Giovanni Smeraldi, who
also did the designed plasterwork and sculpture. After Smeraldi's death much of the work
was finished by Anthony B. Heinsbergen. In
the mid-1970s the hotel was renovated and
handsomely restored (Gene Summers and
Phyllis Lambert). The building was remodeled
once again in late 1986 by Barnett and Schorr,
and the painted ceilings were restored by
Anthony T. Heinsbergen, the son of Anthony
B. Heinsbergen.

44. Biltmore Place, 1985–87
Landau Partnership
Olive Street, south side of the
Biltmore Hotel
A twenty-four-story copper-roofed office tower
which is, at least on the surface, contextual to
the adjoining hotel. The scale of the upper stories and the vertical bays are regrettably overscaled in relation to the original hotel.

45. Pershing Square (formerly **La Plaza
Abaja, Public Square,** and **Central Park**)
Langdon and Wilson
Between South Olive, South Hill, W. 5th,
and W. 6th streets
This 5.02-acre park was part of the original
public land of the Pueblo of Los Angeles. It
was set aside as a public park in 1866. Over the
decades the park fell into disuse several times,
and each time was rescued. The most successful of these revampings was the 1910 scheme
of Parkinson and Bergstrom. They introduced a
grand-scaled central fountain and four
entrances provided with balustrades. They also
replanted the park with lush foliage and introduced underground comfort stations.
   Up until the early 1950s the park was best
known for its vegetation, among which was a
wide variety of palm trees. All of this went out
when Stiles Clements (1950–51) dug it all up to
provide an underground parking garage in the
manner of Union Square in San Francisco. The
idea of a multilayered parking structure under a
park is an attractive one. Seemingly it is the
best of both worlds, a park and a place for
autos. But the difficulty is always how to get
the cars in and out; it always results in reducing
the size of the park and then destroying the
pedestrian perimeter of the park.
   In 1985–86 a competition was held for a
new design for the park. This was won by SITE
of New York (the jury was chaired by Charles
W. Moore). For a variety of reasons (much taking place behind the scenes), the SITE scheme
(titled The Magic Carpet) was put aside in the
next few years and a new team was selected.
This team consisted of the Mexican architect,
Ricardo Legorreta, and the landscape architect
Laurie Olin. In 1991 work began on their plan,
and it was finished at the end of 1993.

The theme of their approach was to provide a symbolic bridge between Los Angeles's Hispanic and Anglo communities; in fact the design almost divides the park in half, each section supposedly addressing one of these constituencies. The dominant note in this design is a 120-foot-high purple-colored campanile and what seems like acres of hard surface pavement, low walls, and other structures, including restaurants. The overall effect is that of a miniature city realized primarily in hardscape. The Olmstedian idea that an urban park should provide a natural oasis within a city is obviously thrown aside in this design. Olmsted wanted us to experience nature so that we could collect and calm ourselves. Though handsome in many ways, Legorreta and Olin's design of this park projects the staccato liveliness one associates with Magic Mountain or Knotts Berry Farm.

46. Pacific Mutual Building, 1912, 1922,
    1926, 1937, and 1974
    523 W. 6th at S. Olive Street
The original Pacific Mutual Building was a close-to-unbelievable, six-story, glazed, white terra-cotta Corinthian temple (1908; designed by John Parkinson and Edwin Bergstrom). In 1922, a new twelve-story building was constructed next door (designed by Dodd and Richards). In 1926 a three-story parking garage was added, and in 1937 Parkinson and Parkinson remodeled their Corinthian temple into a lukewarm Moderne building. Dodd and Richards's 1922 twelve-story building is a typical example, well done, of a Beaux Arts office tower. The H-plan building has an arcaded base which embraces three stories, then a seven-story shaft, and finally two floors hidden behind a colonnade and capped by a heavily-bracketed overhanging roof. The vaulted ceiling and engaged piers which line the walls of the ground-floor elevator lobby are more impressive. The building was restored in 1974 by Wendell Mounce and Associates using Bond and Steward as design consultants.

47. Oviatt Building, 1927–28
    Walker and Eisen
    617 S. Olive Street
Though the building's design is essentially Italian Romanesque, it is the Art Deco (Zigzag) Moderne details of the building which attracted attention when it was built; it was described as "Ultra Modern." Extensive use was made of Lalique glass in the external store front, marquee, interior lobby, and salesroom. According to publications of the time, the shop front, marquee, and all of the other interior decorative work were designed and produced in France and were then shipped to Los Angeles accompanied by five French engineers and architects who had "come over especially to supervise the installation of the fixtures." It was also noted at the time that "Mr. Oviatt had built a bungalow on the roof for his use." The two-story bungalow was no bungalow at all, but a sophisticated Art Deco apartment with "Modern" French furniture and decorative arts. The building has been recently revamped and restored as a restaurant and office building by Brenda Levin Associates.

48. Los Angeles Athletic Club, 1911–12
    John Parkinson and Edwin Bergstrom
    Northeast corner of South Olive and West
    7th streets
This steel-frame, twelve-story building is certainly a knowing display of Beaux Arts principles of design. The exterior of the building is pressed brick with terra-cotta trim and a projecting iron cornice.

49. Clifton's Silver Spoon Cafeteria
    (originally **Brock and Company Jewelry
    Store**), 1922
    Dodd and Richards
    515 W. 7th Street
A small, four-story building with a theatrical parapet, almost Sullivanesque in feeling. The three upper floors of the building are treated as a picture within a frame.

**50. Los Angeles Pacific Telephone Company
Building,** 1911
Morgan and Walls
716 S. Olive Street
This is one instance where a recent renovation
has enhanced an earlier design. The circa 1930
remodelling of this building by Morgan, Walls,
and Clements produced a good, but textbook,
example of the Art Deco (Zigzag) Moderne.
Timothy Walker and Associates brightened it
all up in 1979 so that its facade is more force-
fully Art Deco today than it was in 1930.

**51. Los Angeles Branch, Federal Reserve
Bank of San Francisco,** 1930
John and Donald Parkinson
Northwest corner of S. Olive Street and
W. Olympic Boulevard
One's image of a Federal Reserve Bank build-
ing is that it should look like a vault, a cold,
impersonal fortress. And that is just what the
Parkinsons provided. The severe exterior is
Moderne Beaux Arts. Over the entrance is a
relief sculpture composed of a spread-wing
eagle placed between two kneeling figures (by
Edgar Walter). To the rear of the building is a
vaultlike door opening to a ramp which winds
down to the basement level so that armored
cars can safely enter the building.

**52. (new) Los Angeles Branch, Federal
Reserve Bank of San Francisco,** 1985–87
Dworsky Associates
950 S. Grand Avenue
The new building is situated adjacent to the
1930 structure, so one can compare the current
architectural response with the 1930s older
building. In general, the new building conveys
the impression of an office building in a park (it
is only five and six stories high) rather than an
urban building; the landscape of trees and other
horticultural materials is important. The design
of the new building is composed of two parts, a
formal granite-clad building towards the front
and a layered glass-wall building behind. The
bowed entrance with its high doorway suggests
the monumental and public use. Through the
entrance, one will discover a four-story atrium
lighted by a glass skylight. The walls of the
lobby are of granite and marble.

53. California Plaza and **Two California
Plaza,** 1983-
Arthur Erickson Architects, Kamnitzer and
Cotton, Gruen Associates
Northeast corner of Grand Avenue and 4th
Street
A pair of metal-and-glass-clad forty-two-story
towers, with the southwest corner rounded off
in each tower.

54. Museum of Contemporary Art (MOCA),
1983–87
Arata Isozaki; Gruen Associates
Southeast corner of Grand Avenue and
Kosciuszko Way
The MOCA is unquestionably one of the most
beautiful buildings erected in Los Angeles during the past four or five decades. Its wonderful
surface of red Indian stone clothes a grouping
of forms which suggests both the delight of the
modernist in three-dimensional geometric
forms and an interest (in this case) in traditional
architecture. The museum consists of two separate pavilions, separated by a slightly raised
court. What appears to be the entrance (for the
public this leads only to the museum shop) is
placed under a raised section of the north pavilion, which is covered by an elegant barrel-
vaulted roof. The south pavilion exhibits two
small and one large pyramidal skylights.
Though very handsome, the layout of the
museum seems at times a bit strange. The large
barrel-vaulted wing should be the natural public
entrance to the building. It is not. It houses
offices. The public galleries are approached
down a flight of stairs that lead into the south
pavilion. From the street, these stairs are hardly
apparent. It almost seems as if the architect
wished to make the museum embody a religious ritual. Do not overlook the
Moorish/Spanish garden to the east of the
Museum, which seems much in keeping with
the building. It was designed by Arthur
Erickson Architects.

54. Museum of Contemporary Art (MOCA), 1983–87

55. Angelus Plaza, 1981
  Daniel Dworsky and Associates
  Southwest corner of South Hill and West
  2nd streets
A group of three sixteen-story, concrete,
medium-rise apartment units for the elderly,
with an accompanying parking structure to the
east.

56. Subway Terminal Building, 1924–26
  Schultze and Weaver
  417 S. Hill Street
According to the architects, this large twelve-
story building was based upon a sixteenth-cen-

tury Italian prototype. From the street the four-
bay division of the building makes it appear as
four individual buildings. Rusticated masonry
is used on the lower two floors, and the upper
portion of the building is treated as a two-story
Palazzo. Far below the ground level, five subway tracks enter the building. Trains entered
the building from such faraway destinations as
Santa Monica and San Fernando in the valley.
The subway tunnel, which was a mile in length,
brought trains in from the west. It was in operation from 1925 through 1955. The columned
entrance lobby of the building was restored in
the early 1980s by Bernard Judge.

In 1986 Brenda Levin designed a trompe l'oeil for the side wall of the building; one has to look twice to know that the windows, pilaster, and cornice of her painting are not real.

57. Angels Flight, 1900
    Northwest corner of Hill Street and 4th
    Street
This funicular railroad was built in 1900 to carry passengers from Hill Street up to Olive Street, then a fashionable residential district of Bunker Hill. It continued in operation until 1969 when it was purchased by the Community Redevelopment Agency, with a promise that it would be rebuilt in the near future. In 1993, funds were appropriated by the CRA, with a completion date set for late 1994.

58. The National Bank of Commerce,
    1929–30
    Walker and Eisen
    439 S. Hill Street
Art Deco (Zigzag) Moderne as the language for a Beaux Arts design. The building's forte is the entrance and the three high-relief panels above. Please take note of the message of the right-hand panel: "Wealth means power, it means leisure, it means liberty."

59. Title Guarantee Building (Guarantee
    Trust), 1929–31
    John and Donald Parkinson
    Northwest corner of South Hill and West
    5th streets
A twelve-story Art Deco (Zigzag) Moderne skyscraper, sheathed in light buff terra-cotta with a granite base. A suggestion of the Gothic is conveyed in the upper reaches of the building with its tower and flying buttresses. The building's verticality was accentuated at night by dramatic exterior lighting. In the lobby is a mural, *The Treaty of Cahuenga,* by Hugo Ballin.

60. International Jewelry Center, 1979–81
    Skidmore, Owings, and Merrill (Los
    Angeles)
    Northeast corner of South Hill and West
    6th streets
A horizontal, ribbon-windowed, sixteen-story building with a faceted Sienna granite and

reflective glass facade. The building occupies approximately half of the east side of Pershing Square, and though its facade is broken up above its lower street level, it is somewhat overbearing for the scale of the park. If one looks to the west side of the Square at the Biltmore Hotel and the Pacific Mutual Building (on South Olive Street), one can sense how much more satisfactory their contribution is to the public space of the Park.

61. William Fox Building, circa 1929
    S. Tilden Norton
    608 S. Hill Street
A mild Art Deco (Zigzag) Moderne office tower with an excellent black and gold vestibule and lobby.

62. Bankers Building (now **International**
    Center), 1930
    Claude Beelman
    629 S. Hill Street
The late 1920s Moderne, leaning towards the verticality of the Gothic. Unfortunately, the Moderne marquee has been removed, but the entrance/elevator lobby retains its Moderne elegance.

63. Warner Brothers Downtown Building
    and **Pantages Theater** (now **Jewelry**
    Center Building), 1920
    B. Marcus Priteca
    Northwest corner of South Hill and West
    7th streets
A Beaux Arts composition of the late teens, much more French than the typical designs of American architects of the 1920s. Heavy piers accent the corners and divide the two street facades into three vertical window bays. The corner of the building is rounded, forming an impressive bay surmounted by a Baroque Revival dome.

64. Garfield Building, 1928–30
    Claude Beelman
    408 W. 8th Street (northwest corner of
    South Hill Street)
The exterior is bland, but the Art Deco (Zigzag) Moderne entrance/elevator lobby is a gem with its dark marble walls and detailing in German silver and gold leaf.

65. Mayan Theater,1926–27

65. Mayan Theater,1926–27
Morgan, Walls, and Clements
1040 S. Hill Street

Seven "Mayan" warrior-priests look down on you as you enter the theater, and within you are a participant in a 1920s Hollywood film recreating a pre-Columbian world as it should have been. The cast concrete sculptured facade of the building (by Francisco Comeja) has been brightly painted (originally it was left a light gray concrete color that suggested an aged quality). In 1989 the theater was refurbished and opened as a nightclub.

66. Belasco Theater (now Metropolitan Community Church), 1926
Morgan, Walls, and Clements
1050 S. Hill Street

Morgan, Walls, and Clements going forward at full steam, with the Spanish Churrigueresque realized in concrete. The ground level of the street facade has been remodeled, so concentrate your gaze above. The ceiling of the theater and the asbestos curtain were painted by Anthony Heinsbergen.

67. White Log Coffee Shop (now Tony's Burger), 1932
Kenneth Bemis
1061 S. Hill Street

Here the best of the past and present are combined: time-honored American theme of the rustic, non-urban world of the log cabin coupled with its white, steel frame and concrete logs, which signify the hygienic present as well as the Colonial past. By the end of the 1930s Kenneth Bemis had created sixty-two imitation log cabins on the Pacific Coast. The building is now painted brown, and the original roof sign (of steel) in imitation of logs has been replaced by an excellent sign typical of the late 1950s.

68. Bradbury Building, 1893
George H. Wyman
304 S. Broadway

You would hardly believe that this dull exterior (mildly Romanesque) hides one of the most beautiful interior spaces to be found in L.A. The iron and glass-skylighted court contains open balconies, staircases, and elevators. The lacy quality of the metal work in the inner court plays off against its glazed brick walls. The building was restored in 1991 by Brenda Levin Associates. Levin also added a new south entrance to the building which connects the building to Biddy Mason Park and to the Broadway Spring Center Parking garage.

69. Million Dollar Theater, 1918
Albert C. Martin; William L. Woollett
307 S. Broadway

A lush, Churrigueresque exterior is complemented by an equally sumptuous and rather mysterious Baroque interior (now much simplified) designed by William L. Woollett. Symbolism abounds in Woollett's sculptured and painted decoration. What is needed is a Nancy Drew to figure it all out. The lobby has been altered, but the Baroque auditorium remains as built. This theater, together with the nearby **Grand Central Market Building,** the **Homer Laughlin Building,** and the **Lyons Building,** is to be renovated for housing and office use. This renovation, named **Grand Central Square,** is to be carried out (1994) by private developers and the city's Community Development Agency.

70. Roxie Theater, 1932
John M. Cooper
518 S. Broadway

68. Bradbury Building, 1893

Here the Art Deco (Zigzag) Moderne eases over into the Streamline Moderne. This was the last major theater to be built in the downtown theater district.

71. Reed Jewelers, circa 1929
533 S. Broadway

Art Deco Moderne with an impressive bas-relief on the front. Don't miss **Hartfells** next door, which is equally committed to the Moderne.

72. Pantages Theater (now **Arcade**), 1911
Morgan and Walls
534 S. Broadway

An early Beaux Arts theater building.

73. Broadway Arcade Building, 1922–23
MacDonald and Couchot
542 S. Broadway

The lower three floors of this twelve-story building are wholeheartedly Spanish Renaissance while the upper nine floors are Beaux Arts. An open, skylighted shopping arcade runs through the building from Broadway to Spring Street.

74. Clunes Broadway Theater (now **Cameo Theater**), 1910
Alfred F. Rosenheim
528 S. Broadway

A nickelodeon with its interior fully intact, including the silk canopy over the auditorium ceiling.

75. The Dutch Chocolate Shop, 1914
Plummer and Feil (remodeling)
217 W. 6th Street (northwest of South Broadway)

Inside you will discover a world of Ernest Batchelder tile, representing the designs and colors he used during his Craftsman years.

76. Story Building and Garage, 1916 and 1934
Morgan, Walls, and Clements
Southwest corner of South Broadway at West 6th Street

The often-repeated Beaux Arts formula of stacking one horizontal volume on top of another, here successfully realized in white terra-cotta. The upper zone uses arcaded openings, an attic story, and a heavy projecting cornice to terminate the composition effectively. On West 6th Street is a garage whose entrance was designed in 1934 by Stiles Clements. This entrance with its gates represents a high point of the Moderne in L.A.

77. Los Angeles Theater, 1931
S. Charles Lee
615 S. Broadway

A Baroque motion-picture palace. Twin Corinthian columns frame the central notched arch. Above, a varied skyscraper is provided with pinnacles and other sculptured forms. The interior grand staircases and rich decoration is as French Second Empire as the street facade. Probably the finest theater building in Los Angeles.

78. Schauber's Cafeteria, 1927
Charles F. Plummer
620 S. Broadway

A Spanish Colonial Revival eating establishment, badly mauled by the riots.

79. Orpheum Theater and Office Building
(now **Palace Theater**), 1911
G. Albert Landsburgh
630 S. Broadway

A French Second Empire theater, reserved on the outside and exuberant on the inside (with sculpture by Domingo Mora). Note the use of multicolored terra-cotta decoration throughout the building. The San Francisco architect G. Albert Landsburgh was the principal designer of theaters on the West Coast during the decades 1900 through 1930. In 1927 two wall panels were added to the auditorium, painted by Anthony Heinsbergen.

80. Tower Theater, 1925–26
S. Charles Lee
Southeast corner of South Broadway and West 8th Street

A Spanish composition with Romanesque and Moorish details. The small but highly effective tower which rises from the corner of the building is quite Goodhuesque. This was one of the earliest theater designs by S. Charles Lee, who was to emerge in the 1930s and 1940s as L.A.'s principal designer of motion-picture theaters. As with most of the older theaters, the present marquee was added after the end of World War II.

81. State Theater, 1921
Weeks and Day
703 S. Broadway

One can assume that the Beaux Arts-educated Charles P. Weeks of San Francisco was thinking of the Mediterranean when he designed this building.

82. Globe Theater, 1921
Morgan and Walls
744 S. Broadway

A classical Beaux Arts design. The interior reflects the influence of nineteenth-century Paris.

83. Charles E. Chapman Building, circa 1923
756 S. Broadway

A twelve-story Beaux Arts office block, large Ionic columns gracing the ground-floor level.

84. Ninth and Broadway Building, 1929
Claude Beelman
850 S. Broadway

A thirteen-story Art Deco (Zigzag) Moderne office block with an emphasis on the vertical. The lobby is especially worth a visit.

85. The Eastern Columbia Building
(now **849 Building**), 1929
Claude Beelman
849 S. Broadway

Now that the Richfield Building is gone, the Eastern Columbia Building assumes the mantle of being L.A.'s major Art Deco Moderne building of the 1920s. In this stepped-back design, vertical piers and shafts extend close to the top of the tower, which houses four faces of a clock (neon-lighted). The exterior terra-cotta sheathing is in gold and blue-green. The building originally housed two retail stores: Columbia and Eastern Outfitting. An L-shaped arcade, with entrances on South Broadway and on West 8th Street, separated the two stores. Above the entrances are pierced grills forming a sunburst pattern, and these are stippled in gold.

86. Texaco/United Artists Building, 1927
Walker and Eisen; C. Howard Crane
929 S. Broadway

It is surprising that in Los Angeles the 1920s rage for Spanish (and Mediterranean architecture in general) was not employed frequently for commercial building. As this building indicates, it is a shame that the style was not used more often. Terra-cotta and cast stone readily lend themselves to the style, and its richness can be fully expressed. In this building the style is Spanish Gothic. The lobby is modeled after the nave of a Spanish church, richly decorated with vaulting and murals.

87. Women's Athletic Club, 1924
Allison and Allison
1031 S. Broadway

Described when built as an example of Italian Renaissance architecture. The most interesting aspects of the design are the courtyarded roof garden, with its plantings, loggia, and stairs.

88. Times-Mirror Building, 1931–35
    Gordon B. Kaufmann
    Southwest corner of South Spring and West
    1st streets
American newspapers have a fondness for
assuming official governmental garb and,
whenever possible, locating themselves so as to
imply that they and the government are one.
The *L.A. Times* building fulfills this image very
well. The original building is monumental
PWA Moderne, and its siting, just across the
street from the buildings of the Civic Center,
makes it seem as if it belongs. There are some
wonderful spaces inside the Kaufmann building, if you can arrange to get inside. Above all,
see the Rotunda with Hugo Ballin's mural
Newspaper. In 1948 Rowland H. Crawford
designed a ten-story addition at the northwest
corner of South Spring Street and West 3rd
Street. It too is PWA Moderne, but in this case
the classical monumentality has been mellowed
quite a bit. Nevertheless the sculpture at the
central parapet still helps the building to read
with authority. To the west of the older building, William L. Pereira and Associates added a
six-story addition in 1970–73 consisting of two
horizontal boxes hovering over various vertical
boxes below. The marriage of the old and new
is not a happy one, but then it seldom is in the
hands of a "Modern" architect.

89. Hellman Building (now **Banco Popular
    Center**), 1903
    Alfred F. Rosenheim
    Northeast corner of South Spring and West
    4th streets
A typically respectable turn-of-the-century
Beaux Arts office building, similar to others
erected across the country.

90. Brady Block (later **Hibernian Building**),
    1904
    John Parkinson
    Southeast corner of South Spring and West
    4th streets
This building has often been cited as L.A.'s
first skyscraper. It is a twelve-story Beaux Arts
office block which has an elaborately decorated
attic with a colonnade in the Corinthian order.

91. Stowell Hotel Building
    (now **Hotel El Dorado**), 1913
    Frederick Noonan
    416 S. Spring Street
A sort of Neo-Gothic treatment of the facade,
including extensive cantilevered canopies. The
walls, sheathed in glazed green brick, contrast
with the light tan, cast stone ornament.

**92. Title Insurance and Trust Company
    Building** (now **Los Angeles Design
    Center**), 1928
    Walker and Eisen
    433 S. Spring Street
Lightly Art Deco (Zigzag) Moderne. There are
mosaic panels above the entrance and murals
by Hugo Ballin. The lobby was decorated by
Herman Sachs. Note the elevator doors.

**93. Security Trust and Savings Bank
    Building,** 1907
    John Parkinson and Edwin Bergstrom
    Security National Bank Building, 1916
    John Parkinson
    Southeast corner of South Spring and West
    5th streets
The office building is textbook Beaux Arts with
a pronounced cornice. The two-story bank is
quite elegant, with its four pairs of Ionic
columns behind which are windows that light
the main banking room. In 1982–85 the bank
building was converted into **Los Angeles
Theater Center** by John Sergio Fisher. To the
side of the old bank facade (which was left
intact), a new deep-set entrance has been
created. This leads into modernist 35-foot-high
skylighted space. Off this central lobby are four
theaters.

94. Alexandria Hotel, 1906
    John Parkinson
    Southwest corner of South Spring and West
    5th streets
What counts in this building is the interior palm
court with its stained-glass ceiling. The palm
court was refurbished in 1967–70 when the
lobby was drastically remodeled in order to
look Victorian rather than retain its original
Baroque magnificence.

238 / *Los Angeles Architectural Guide*

95. Merchants National Bank Building
(now **Lloyd's Bank,**) 1915
William Curlett and Son
Northeast corner of South Spring and West
6th streets
Another squarish, but well-designed, Beaux
Arts office block.

96. Pacific Coast Stock Exchange, 1929–30
Samuel E. Lunden; John and Donald
Parkinson, consulting architects.
618 S. Spring Street
Monumental PWA Moderne (in somber gray
granite) as an appropriately solid fortress. Four
large-scaled fluted pilasters articulate the street
elevation. Under the flat entablature are three
panels symbolizing modern industry (by
Salvatore Cartaino Scarpitta). Inside is sculpture from the Wilson studio and murals by
Julian Ellsworth Garnsey. Next door at 626
S. Spring Street is a handsome six-story Beaux
Arts building with the space between the
engaged piers now filled with glass.

97. Banks-Huntly Building, 1929–31
John and Donald Parkinson
632 S. Spring Street
A vertical Art Deco (Zigzag) Moderne twelve-
story building with its upper facade treated as a
tower with vertical panels of chevrons.

98. Union Oil Building (now **Security Pacific
National Bank**), circa 1911
John Parkinson and Edwin Bergstrom
Northwest corner of South Spring and West
7th streets
An eleven-story Beaux Arts office block in
white terra-cotta.

99. I. N. Van Nuys Building, 1910–11
Morgan and Walls
Southwest corner of South Spring and West
7th streets
Another eleven-story white terra-cotta exercise
in the Beaux Arts tradition, with engaged Ionic
columns at the street level. Next door at number
719 is a four-story Beaux Arts Annex (designed
by Morgan, Walls, and Clements, 1929–30)
with an office space in the center and a garage
door to each side. The north garage entrance
still retains its original classical metal gates.

**100. Hellman Commercial Trust and Savings
Bank Building** (now **Bank of America**),
1924
Schultze and Weaver
Northeast corner of South Spring and
West 7th streets
Four two-story Ionic columns bring dignity to
the ground floor of this Beaux Arts office
block.

101. St. Vibiana's Cathedral, 1871–76
Ezra F. Kysor; W. J. Mathews
114 E. 2nd Street
This cruciform-plan church was supposedly
modeled after the church of San Miguel del
Mar in Barcelona. In 1922 John C. Austin
added the present "more correct" entrance
facade in stone. The rear elevation and the
interior are, in spite of heavy remodeling,
basically mid-nineteenth-century Italianate.

102. Van Nuys Hotel (now **Barclay Hotel
Building**), 1896
Morgan and Walls
103 W. 4th Street
A six-story Beaux Arts composition of repeated
bays separated by four-story-high pilasters.

103. Charnock Block (now **Pershing Hotel**),
1888
Southeast corner of South Main and West
5th streets
A rare late-nineteenth-century commercial
building. As usual, forget the remodeled first
floor and look at the second floor of this brick
building. Five classical decorated oriel bays
and a corner bay tower punctuate the facade.

104. Kerkhoff Building (now **Santa Fe
Building,**) 1907 and 1911
Morgan and Walls
Northeast corner of South Main and East
6th streets
A ten-story Beaux Arts office block.

105. Pacific Electric Building, 1903–5
Thornton Fitzhugh
610 S. Main Street
The often encountered turn-of-the-century combination of Richardsonian Romanesque and the
Beaux Arts. In this case huge pilasters with
exaggerated Ionic capitals separate the major

bays, while small arched bays occur within. A pergola garden with wonderful views was placed on top of this ten-story building.

106. California Theater, 1918
Alfred B. Rosenthal
810 S. Main Street
The sculptured French Third Empire facade looks down (with disgust) at its modernized marquee and lobby.

107. Fire Station No. 29, 1910
Hudson and Munsell
225 E. 5th Street
Small, mild classicism in concrete.

108. Gray Company Building (now **824 Building**), 1928
Morgan, Walls, and Clements
824 S. Los Angeles Street
Stiles Clements convincingly demonstrated in this five-story building how well the Spanish Colonial Revival vocabulary could be used for a commercial structure. Here he used thin vertical piers which terminated in an entablature of cast concrete ornament.

109. Gerry Building, 1947
Maurice Fleischman
910 S. Los Angeles Street
A 1930s Streamline Moderne design built in the years immediately after the Second World War. The center of the facade, which is almost entirely of glass, curves inward on each side.

110. Wolfer Printing Company Building, 1929
Edward Cray Taylor and Ellis Wing Taylor
416 Wall Street
A Tudor Revival commercial building.

111. Simone Hotel, 1989
Koning/Eisenberg Architecture
520 San Julian Street
This five-story, 123-room hotel was designed to provide inexpensive single rooms. Each room is equipped with a sink, closet, small refrigerator, desk, and bed. Common bathrooms are located on each floor. The rooms, though small, enjoy good-sized windows. Externally, the building looks to some of the turn of the

century designs in Vienna of Adolf Loos and Otto Wagner. The trademark of this firm's work is the curved parapet of the building.

112. Commercial Block, circa 1889
740–748 S. San Pedro Street
A two-story brick Queen Anne commercial building with a cast-iron street front.

113. Japanese American Cultural and Community Center
San Pedro Street between Azusa and East 3rd streets
The area of Little Tokyo has been experiencing intensified building activity in the late 1970s and now into the 1980s. Note should be made of the theme tower of wood (1978; David Hyun) and now more recently Isamu Noguchi's stone sculpture *To Issei* (1983) placed in the Plaza of the Center. Close by is the **Japan American Theater** (244 S. San Pedro; 1982; by Kajima Associates, George Shinno), a gracefully curve-facaded building which looks out onto the Plaza.

The Japanese American National Museum at the northwest corner of Central Avenue and 1st Street is a remodeling by Knusu Joint Venture Architects (James R. McElwain, historic preservation architect) of a Buddhist Temple (1925; Edgar Kline) to provide a museum featuring the Japanese-American contribution to the American culture. In 1993 its efforts at adaptive reuse received honor awards from both the Los Angeles Conservancy and the National Trust for Historic Preservation.

114. Weller Court, 1982
Kajima Associates, George Shinno
123 Weller Street
The ground-level section of this building with its flat and curved volumes, together with the plaza and its fountain and planting, provide a pleasant Modernist pedestrian space (but more planting and less hard surfaces would have helped).

115. "The Temporary Contemporary" Museum, Los Angeles Museum of Contemporary Art, 1982–83
Frank O. Gehry and Associates
134–152 Central Avenue

An extensive warehouse complex (partially of wood and partially of concrete) which has been remodeled to serve as an extra exhibition space for the new Museum of Contemporary Art on Bunker Hill. The interior spaces work well. As of the writing of this Guide "The Temporary Contemporary" is closed.

116. 1st Street Viaduct Bridge, 1928
   H. P. Cortelyon, engineer
   East 1st Street, east of Santa Fe Avenue
Concrete homage to the classical tradition of Rome.

117. 4th Street Viaduct Bridge, 1930–31
   Louis L. Hunt, architect; Merrill Butler, engineer
   East of Santa Fe Avenue
Mildly Medieval forms in concrete.

118. 6th Street Viaduct Bridge (Whittier Boulevard Bridge), 1932
   Louis Blume and Merrill Butler, engineers
   Between Alameda Street and Soto Street
The Art Deco is the dominant theme in the 3,446-foot-long 6th Street bridge. It was the largest concrete bridge built in California before World War II.

Three other Viaduct bridges to the south which also cross over the railroad yards and the river are the **7th Street Viaduct Bridge,** the **Olympic Boulevard Viaduct Bridge,** and the **Washington Boulevard Viaduct Bridge.** The Washington Boulevard Viaduct Bridge boasts a colorful frieze depicting various bridge-building activities.

119. Palmetto Construction Headquarters, Department of Water and Power, 1991–92
   Neil Stanton Palmer Architects (Walter Scott Perry)
   Palmetto Street, east of Alameda Street
A high-tech steel framed and sheathed object, somewhat reminiscent of the Streamline Moderne of the 1930s. The bent, curved metal sheathing is white, while the glazed window-walls are Post Modern green.

120. Florence Hotel, 1911; 1986
   Urban Innovations (Rex Lotery)
   310 E. 5th Street
This is one of a series of renovations of small older hotels which provide living spaces for the homeless. Urban Innovations' work on this 1911 three-story hotel was essentially to refurbish the interior, add bathrooms, and to bring the building up to current seismic codes. Urban Innovation has also revamped a number of other small hotels, including the **Carleton Hotel** of 1924, located at 47 Wall Street (Their work on the Carleton Hotel was completed in 1992).

116. 1st Street Viaduct Bridge, 1928

DOWNTOWN, CIVIC CENTER

A s early as 1900 there were discussions of creating a "City Beautiful" Civic Center for the City and County of Los Angeles. In 1905 a Municipal Arts Commission was appointed, and this group in turn engaged the pioneer city planner Charles Mulford Robinson to prepare a plan, which it formally published in 1909. Robinson's report did suggest the loose grouping of civic buildings but not really a characteristic City Beautiful Civic Center. The task of carrying forth the then-highly-popular idea of a City Beautiful Civic Center fell into the hands of a newly formed City Planning Association, formed in 1913. The Southern California Chapter of the A.I.A. advocated that a national competition should be held to select an architect/planner to design a civic center for the city.

The first comprehensive proposal for a City Beautiful Civic Center was made early in 1917 by the landscape architect and engineer J. S. Rankin who argued for the present site of the center. In 1918 a commission was appointed to select a site. They recommended setting aside the location, which is now occupied by the various buildings of the present Civic Center.

Immediately after World War I in 1919, a Civic Center Plan Committee, chaired by the engineer William Mulholland (the builder of the Los Angeles Aqueduct), was appointed to carry out this scheme. The majority of this committee recommended the present site of the Civic Center; the minority advocated the location at Pershing Square. Various specific proposals were put on the table, one of the most interesting being labeled the "Dodge Civic

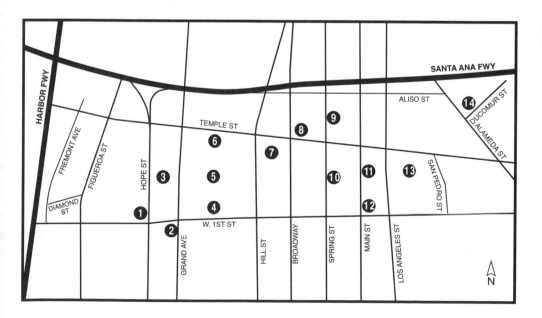

Center Plan," named for Jonathan S. Dodge, chairman of the Los Angeles County Board of Supervisors. This plan, devised by the architect Lyman Farwell, contemplated among other things, a seven-story reinforced concrete City Hall, together with a five-story building for the Board of Public Service.

The planning and landscape firm of Cook and Hall was commissioned to plan the details of the site. In 1923 the firm submitted a scheme which called for a Beaux Arts axial plan, with the major buildings grouped around Broadway and Main Street. The existing pattern of streets was essentially left intact, but provision was made for subways and extensive auto parking. One of the most interesting aspects of these various schemes was that the public-oriented Civic Center was seen as one component within the downtown area. The other three components were to the north—the historic old Plaza area and a projected new railroad passenger station; to the south the modern high-rise downtown was to develop (slowing spreading to the south and to the west).

The following year (1924) the Allied Architects of Los Angeles proposed its own scheme—a much more grandiose cross-axis Beaux Arts plan. The principal figures involved in this plan were Edwin Bergstrom and Harwood Hewitt. Out of these two schemes finally emerged the "adopted plan" of 1927, which was as dull and unimaginative as one could ask and which seemed to combine the worst portions of both plans. Other architects also tried their hands at schemes. William L. Woollett had projected a design as early as 1921, and Lloyd Wright submitted his own "futuristic" cross-axial plan in 1925, composed of skyscrapers, airports, layers of streets, and an integrated rapid transit system and freeways.

In 1939, Sumner Spaulding, together with Myron Hunt, John C. Austin, Stiles Clements, William Schuchardt, Palmer Sabin, David C. Allison, Earl C. Heitschmidt, and Ralph Flewelling, proposed a return to the basic concept of the 1924 Allied Architects plan, but, like the plans of the 1920s, Spaulding's plan, while accepted by the county and the city, was never fully realized. During and immediately

after the Second World War, the Civic Center Authority drew up detailed plans relating to streets, parking, and building locations. In addition, the 1920s' suggestion was again advanced that the center of Bunker Hill be cleared and transformed into a large urban park with streets going under it.

After World War II, the planning and construction of the Civic Center became closely involved with urban renewal, and the razing of the historic buildings on Bunker Hill took place. The August 12, 1949 issue of the *Southwest Builder and Contractor* proudly announced "L.A.'s Historic Fort Moore Hill disappearing in quiet, nighttime engineering feat." Construction also was begun on the depressed Santa Ana Freeway, which divided the Civic Center complex from the old Plaza area. At first it was proposed that this six-block section of the freeway be completely covered, by both parkland and buildings, but this was abandoned for the much more economical scheme of simply bridging over the north/south city streets.

A proposal very much on the minds of those involved with the post-World War II Civic Center was the construction of both an Auditorium and an Opera House. A constellation of local and national architects was engaged to prepare designs for the proposed opera house and the auditorium. Head of this consortium of architects was New Yorker Wallace K. Harrison. Other architects included were William W. Wurster, Eero Saarinen, Henry Dreyfuss, Reginald D. Johnson, Gordon B. Kaufmann, William Pereira, and Charles O. Matchem. The theme of their modernist sketches was that of a "tropical motif."

The idea of wasting good profitable land on a park on Bunker Hill was abandoned, and Pereira and Luckman and Welton Becket devised a scheme with high-rise towers for housing, accompanied at its eastern side by a "cultural" trade center with civic auditorium, exposition buildings, and music hall, with plenty of underground parking.

In 1946–47 the Los Angeles Civic Authority engaged the architect Burnett C. Turner to revise and formalize the late 1930s' scheme of

Spaulding and others. This plan was accepted by the Authority in 1947, and it constituted the plan which was basically followed over the next two decades.

What we have today is something in the way of a ghost of Spaulding's 1939 scheme. An east/west axis runs from the Water and Power Building at the west end to the City Hall on the east. Lining the axis are the buildings of the Music Center; then, to the north, the Hall of Administration, the Hall of Records, and the Criminal Court Building; to the south, the Courthouse, Law Library, and State Building. The City Hall was to have been the termination of this major axis and to have been the center of a north/south axis. The latter idea never was achieved. Somewhat off-center, the Department of Water and Power building forms a sort-of termination of the major east/west axis. By the end of the 1960s the formal portion of the terraced mall with its underground parking garages was completed (designed by Ralph Cornell and his associates).

The major planning addition to the Civic Center in the 1970s was the Los Angeles Mall Shopping Center between the City Hall South and the L.A. Children's Museum to the north. This 1974–75 mall combined space for retail stores, plus a park well planted in palms. A bridge over Temple Street connected the two sections of the mall. It was designed by William Stockwell and the landscape architects Cornell, Bridgers and Troller (Howard Troller).

The grand City Beautiful vision which continued to underlie the development of the Civic Center, even as late as the 1960s, has bit by bit been abandoned in recent years. Public buildings continue to be built, particularly at the east end of the Civic Center from Los Angeles Street to Alameda Street. But they are not in any way

Civic Center

sited to contribute to, or become part of, the Civic Center. These buildings and their surrounding spaces pose as commercial buildings casually lining the streets. Frank O. Gehry's new Walt Disney Hall may well add a major jewel to the Civic Center, but much more will be needed to make it aesthetically distinguished.

The criticism which Allied Architects leveled at the Cook and Hall plan—that retention of north/south streets would destroy the unity of the Civic Center—has proved to be absolutely correct. Today, there is simply no feeling of coherence or unity. Parts do work, like the plaza of the Music Center and the space between the Hall of Administration and the Courthouse, but they only function as fragments. As to the individual buildings themselves, none is great. But the following are worth a real look (working from west to east):

1. Los Angeles Department of Water and Power Building, 1963–64

1. Los Angeles Department of Water and Power Building, 1963–64
Albert C. Martin and Associates
Northwest corner of South Hope and West 1st streets
Best seen at night from the Harbor Freeway to the north with all of its lights on. At this time the solidity of the building melts, and all that is left are thin vertical and horizontal lines of

support, the floors, and the sunscreen. Note the forest of fountains around its base; they may be on or off depending on the availability of water.

2. Disney Concert Hall, 1988–94
Frank O. Gehry and Associates
Southwest corner of Grand Avenue and 1st Street
The four finalists announced in 1988 to be considered to design the Disney Concert Hall were Gottfried Bohm of Germany, Hans Hollein of Austria, James Stirling of England, and Frank O. Gehry. Gehry's "Pop-modernist" scheme was selected. Gehry's submission was seen as a symbolic garden placed in front of a series of oddly placed, layered boxes. Numerous changes were made in this initial design, and in truth it has become more adventuresome as it has gone along, especially the exterior of the building. It should not be surprising that Gehry's design provoked praise, criticism, and bewilderment. Some writers to the *Los Angeles Times* called it "space trash," others thought it indicated that the "whole world has gone mad." At long last the building is (1993) under construction, and it should be finished in a year or two.

3. Los Angeles Music Center, 1964–69
Welton Becket and Associates; Cornell, Bridgers and Troller, landscape architects
North of West 1st Street between South Hope and South Grand streets
The building located within a seven-acre park

2. Disney Concert Hall, 1988–94

faces onto an east/west plaza with a central pool dominated by a 1969 Jacques Lipschitz sculpture. A new addition to the plaza at the head of the east stairs (from Grand Avenue) is Robert Graham's "Dance Door." To the south is the largest of the three buildings, the **Dorothy Chandler Pavilion;** to the north, enclosed by a free-standing colonnade, is the circular **Mark Taper Forum** and the **Ahmanson Center** (Theater). Under all of this is the essential

Dorothy Chandler Pavilion, 1964-69

multilayered parking garage. Aesthetically, the most forceful of these buildings is the circular Mark Taper Forum. It rises from a pool of water, and the walls are composed of an abstract 378-foot-long, cast concrete, low-relief panel. These three buildings and their siting characterize the accommodations then being made between modernism and the continuing Beaux Arts-Classical tradition. The whole composition is light, fragile, but elegant. However, it should be noted that, like most 1960s modern designs, it is not growing better with age. Functionally, it all appears to be working very well.

3. Los Angeles Music Center, 1964–69

4. Los Angeles County Courthouse, 1958
J. E. Stanton; Paul R. Williams; Adrian Wilson; Austin, Field and Fry

Northwest corner of Hill and First streets
In 1944 a competition was announced for the new courts building. A consortium of architects was finally selected to provide the design. The result was a late 1950s Modern design making, at least, a halfhearted effort to be classical and public. The building does go public with some sculpture. Note the higher portion of the building to the north which exhibits a clock face and the east facade which is windowless and divided into squares and has an overlay of relief sculpture.

4. Los Angeles County Courthouse, 1958

9. Federal Building and Post Office (now U.S. Federal Courthouse), 1938–40

5. Paseo de los Pobladores, 1961–
J. E. Stanton, W. F. Stockwell, Adrian Wilson, and Austin, Field and Fry
East of Grand Avenue between the County Courthouse and the Hall of Administration
A series of terraces, pools, and steps lead up the hill from Broadway to Grand Avenue. Though formal, but with modernist tricks, the design is somewhat heavy in the realm of hardscape.

6. Hall of Administration Building,
1956–61
Stanton, Stockwell, Williams and Wilson; Austin, Field and Fry
Southeast corner of Grand Avenue and Temple Street
The best section of this eight-story building is the west facade which somewhat carries on the PWA Moderne of the 1930s. The best one can say about the design of this building is that it is reticent.

7. Hall of Records Building, 1961–62
Richard J. Neutra, Robert Alexander; Honnold and Rex; Herman Charles Light and James Friend
320 West Temple Street

A rare, realized Neutra high-rise. Functionally it seems to fulfill its task, but its design seems confused, and it ends up neither a distinguished example of Modernism nor making any strong contribution to the Civic Center. Note the large 80-foot glass mosaic mural *Water Sources in L.A. County* by Joseph Young (1962).

8. Hall of Justice Building, 1925
Allied Architects of Los Angeles
Northeast corner of South Broadway and West Temple Street
This fourteen-story building in the Italian style indicates what the Allied Architects had in mind for the buildings of the Civic Center— pure Beaux Arts classicism of the early 1920s. The building is sheathed in gray granite with highly polished granite columns. The building has been abandoned and is in danger of demolition.

9. Federal Building and Post Office
(now **U.S. Federal Courthouse**), 1938–40
Louis A. Simon; Gilbert Stanley Underwood
Northeast corner of South Spring and West Temple streets
PWA Moderne of the late 1930s, beautifully and convincingly carried out. When the *Architectural Record* in 1940 asked a number of Los Angeles citizens to cite their favorite buildings, the then-new Federal Building was one of them. Though seventeen stories high (on South Spring Street) the building manages to remain snugly within the classical tradition, albeit in an abstracted manner. Within, luxury and formalism are evident, ranging from rose marble and Sienna travertine to James L. Hauser's larger-than-life-size sculpture *The Young Lincoln,* to Archibald Garner's eight-foot-high sculpture in stone, *Law.*

10. Los Angeles City Hall, 1926–28
John C. Austin, John and Donald Parkinson, and Albert C. Martin; Austin Whittlesey, interiors.
Southeast corner of South Spring and West Temple streets
The approach which the architects took was Goodhuesque, combining the traditional classical temple as a base with the symbol of a

10. Los Angeles City Hall, 1926–28

skyscraper, commenting on the prowess of American business. In its presentation of the design, the consortium of architects noted that "the first story of the City Hall would be of monumental character," and that the skyscraper tower "was necessary to cut the skyline." The tower, with its sloping walls, turned out to be monumental as well, and the top of the tower seems to be a 1920s interpretation of what the ancient Mausoleum at Halicarnassus should have looked like (although it should be noted that when the building was built it was referred to as "Italian Classic"). Following in the footsteps of Goodhue, Hartley Burr Alexander of the University of Nebraska furnished the inscriptions for the building. ("The city came into being to preserve life, it exists for the good life.")

In the interior public spaces, especially in the central rotunda, the mood is Byzantine, with the floor, wall, and ceiling decoration by Austin Whittlesey, who worked closely with Herman Sachs and Anthony Heinsbergen. It was fitting that when the building was dedicated in April of 1928, the three-day affair was under the direction of Sid Grauman, the moving-picture-palace tycoon.

Until the 1950s the twenty-eight-story tower was the only structure allowed to exceed the 150-foot height limitation. Now its tower is only one among many.

From 1989–93 the City Hall, both inside and out, has been restored, including much of its decoration, artwork, and furnishings.

11. Los Angeles Mall, 1973–74
Stanton and Stockwell; Cornell, Bridgers, Troller and Hazlett, landscape architects
East side of South Spring Street between West First and Aliso streets

This civic addition consists of a six-level mall, a four-level underground garage, and two buildings: **City Hall East,** and a small **Children's Museum.** The skyway, which connects the mall to the original City Hall, is as dull as the other buildings. The two objects which make a noble, but vain, attempt to lift all of this out of the mundane is Millard Sheet's wonderful mural at the Spring Street entrance to City Hall East (1973–74; Stanton and Stockwell) and Joseph Young's Triforium (1975), a sixty-foot fountain of light and music. The landscaping is well carried out, but now ten years after it was finished, it is all beginning to look a bit tired. Even the fountains run only intermittently.

12. Health Administration Building (now City Hall South), 1953–54
Lunden, Hayward and O'Conner; Tommy Tomson, landscape architect
Northeast corner of Main Street and 1st Street

An eight-story modernist exercise with its commitment to horizontal bands of windows. The best part of the design is the south entrance, whose steps are lined by parapet walls of polished opal pink granite.

13. Parker Center, 1955
Welton Becket and Associates, and J. E. Stanton
Southeast corner of Temple Street and Los Angeles Street

As with most Corporate Modern buildings of the 1950s and 1960s, this building has not aged well. When built, it was a good example of where Modernism was taking us.

14. Los Angeles Department of Water and Power Central District Headquarters, Phase II, 1988–92
Barton Phelps and Associates, Clements and Clements/Benito A. Sinclair and Associates,
444 East Ducommun Street (corner Alameda Street and East Ducommun Street)

A handsome addition to the group of recent public buildings erected at the east end of the Civic Center. Geometry of volumes dominates the design. Groups of four rectangular volumes arise from a horizontal base. Phelps described his design approach as "mantel over a base." The upper section of the building is sheathed in white and light green metal panels while the lower section is of concrete.

Other recent buildings in the area are the **Federal Building** at the northeast corner of Temple Street and Los Angeles Street, the **Federal Center** and the **Metropolitan Detention Center,** both behind (to the east) of the Federal Center. (Go into the courtyard behind the Federal Building to see the curved pergola and its sculpture, designed by Tom Otterness, 1992–93). At the northwest corner of Temple Street and Alameda Street is the **V.A. Outpatient Clinic,** a well-scaled cornerpiece for this end of the Civic Center.

DOWNTOWN, PLAZA AND NORTHEAST

The section around the Old Plaza and east towards the present course of the Los Angeles River was the center of Los Angeles from 1781 through the mid-nineteenth century. The first public plaza, which lay to the northeast near Sunset Boulevard, was gradually filled in by early settlers. The present Plaza, which was essentially the church/government plaza, has continued to remain open and public,

though some of the buildings to the north have extended into the public space (especially after it was "improved" in the 1840s). In 1862, the Plaza was replanned and replanted, this time with topiary work.

By the 1870s the business center of Los Angeles had moved south, and the Plaza area remained a low-density backwash. In the early 1900s, the area was somewhat rejuvenated by a renewed interest in things Hispanic, and during

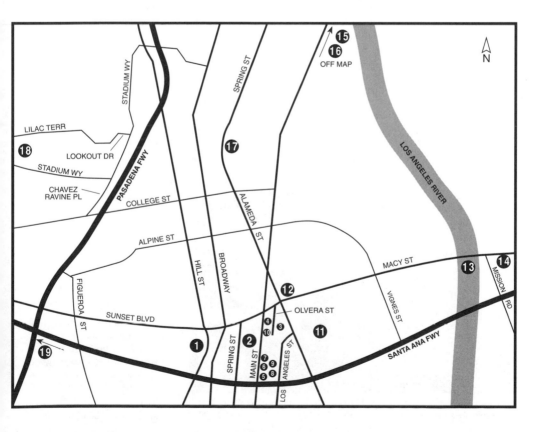

the 1920s Olvera Street and several of its adjoining buildings were restored. The plaza area has just missed extinction on two occasions: in the early 1920s it was proposed that the area be incorporated into the projected civic center, and in 1949–50 the plaza narrowly missed being devoured by the construction of the Santa Ana Freeway. Since the 1950s, and especially since it was made a state park, the Plaza area has increasingly become a tourist spot amid restored historic buildings.

Chinatown originally developed in the 1870s where the Union Passenger Terminal now stands. New Chinatown lies in and around North Broadway and Alpine Street and was built after 1933 when clearing was begun for the Terminal.

1. Fort Moore Pioneer Memorial, 1949–57
Kazumi Adaori and Dike Naggana, architects; Albert Stewart, Art Advisor
Department of Water and Power
North side of Hill Street, between the Santa Ana Freeway and Sunset Boulevard
An L.A. extravaganza, dedicated to the importation of water which made L.A. possible. This block-long concrete memorial contains (when it is running) a 77-foot-long, 50-foot-high sheet of water. When it was built, it was noted that it was "probably the most spectacular man-made waterfall in the United States," and it probably still is. The inscription on the glazed ceramic wall reads, "May those who live in our naturally arid land be thankful for the vision and good works of the pioneer leaders of Los Angeles, and may all in their time ever provide for its citizens water and power for life and energy."

As a historical note on L.A. glorification of water, the **Fort Moore Pioneer Memorial** hardly can hold a candle to the proposal made in 1913 for an "art marvel" to honor the completion of the Owens Rivers Aqueduct. This 800-foot-high monument (designed by the architect George A. Howard, Jr.), centered on a gigantic Grecian Doric column, was to be L.A.'s answer to Paris' Eiffel Tower, New York's Statue of Liberty, and Washington, D.C.'s Washington Monument. It was to have been lavishly lighted, and "a truly remarkable and novel scintillating effect will be gained by the use of water, trickling down the sides of the 220-foot column." This exotic monument was to have been built in Exposition Park, but at the last moment the needed funds were not raised.

Although modest in comparison, the sheer sense of gross overuse of water so effectively conveyed by the 1954–55 monument serves as an all-too-effective reminder of our casual tendency to overexploit our natural resources.

2. La Iglesia de Nuestra Señora la Reina de Los Angeles (The Church of Our Lady the Queen of the Angels), 1818–22; 1861–62; 1875; 1912; 1923
535 N. Main Street

2. La Iglesia de Nuestra Señora la Reina de Los Angeles (The Church of Our Lady the Queen of the Angels), 1818–22; 1861–62; 1875; 1912; 1923

The simple, gable-roofed adobe church was rebuilt and received a new facade in 1861. A bell tower was added in 1875. In 1912 the church was once more restored and enlarged, making it more "Mission" Spanish than it had been before. In 1923 a tile roof replaced the late-nineteenth-century shingle roof. As originally built, the facade of the church had a single arched entrance placed within a molded rectangle. Above was a single window which lighted the choir and nave. Above a horizontal molding which followed the parapet molding of the sides of the building was a single *espadaña* (belfry wall). To the south of the facade was a *campanario* (bell tower) which had a single opening (not a double opening as we now see it). The church was at first flat-roofed. Thus, what we see today (internally and externally) is a modest village church which essentially dates from 1861 onward.

6-7. Merced Theater, and Pico House, 1869–70

3. Avila Adobe, circa 1818
10 Olvera Street

This once was the oldest original dwelling standing in Los Angeles. As with most late-eighteenth/early-nineteenth-century adobes it is not clear what it originally looked like. By the 1830s the dwelling consisted of a traditional double row of rooms, one set facing a porch looking out on the street; to the rear was a second porch facing toward the court. The house is now covered with a tile roof, but it is unlikely this was part of the original building. The adobe was damaged in an earthquake in 1971, and it has now been rebuilt in concrete.

4. La Casa Pelanconi, 1855
33–35 Olvera Street

This two-story house was the first brick dwelling in Los Angeles. A winery occupied the ground floor; the living quarters were above. Note the wood balcony and the main fireplace on the ground level. Although not strong in character, the house is basically very late Greek Revival in style.

5. Masonic Temple, 1858
416 N. Main Street

A cast-iron balcony poses over the triple-arched street opening below. The Italianate style shows up in the widely projecting cornice.

6. Merced Theater, 1870
Attributed to Ezra F. Kysor
420–422 N. Main Street

A three-story masonry building, Italianate in style. The second and third floors boast arched openings inset between simple pilasters. A cast-iron balcony projects off the third floor. The ground level was planned as a retail store, the second floor as a 400-seat theater, and the third floor as an apartment.

7. Pico House, 1869–70
Ezra F. Kysor
430 N. Main Street

This Italianate hotel was the first three-story masonry building constructed in Los Angeles. The openings are all arched and set between vertical pilasters and projecting horizontal cornices. The street elevations of the building were stuccoed over and then painted to imitate light blue granite. The building has been completely rebuilt and has awaited use for a number of years.

11. Union Passenger Terminal, 1934–39

10. Sepulveda House, 1887
624 N. Main Street
This two-story red brick building was constructed as a hotel and a restaurant. The upper bay window balconies suggest the Eastlake style.

11. Union Passenger Terminal, 1934–39
John and Donald B. Parkinson; J. H. Christie, H. L. Gilman, R. J. Wirth; Herman Sachs, color consultant
Tommy Tomson, landscape architect
East side of North Alameda Street between Aliso and Macy streets
The last of the large metropolitan passenger depots to be built in the U.S. The terminal provided for sixteen tracks and for extensive parking (120 cars underground and 400 in front of the building). Landscaped grounds and courtyards convey an indoor-outdoor sense of space seldom encountered in large-scale public buildings. The design successfully merged the Streamline Moderne and the Spanish. The 135-foot-high observation and clock tower, the principal interior spaces, and the patios manage to convey both modernity and tradition.

8. Garnier Block, 1890
415 N. Los Angeles Street
What we now see of this restored building is only half of the original block. The south half went in 1950 when the Santa Ana Freeway was built. The building is a two-story brick and stone structure, mildly Romanesque in style.

9. Old Plaza Firehouse, 1884
Southwest corner of Old Plaza and North Los Angeles Street
A two-story brick building with an Eastlake balcony over the high entrance.

12. Terminal Annex Post Office, 1937–38
Northeast corner of Macy Street and Alameda Street
A late version of the Spanish Colonial Revival, realized in exposed concrete. Note the two drums and domes which dominate the building.

13. Macy Street Viaduct, 1926
Macy Street between Keller Street and Mission Road
The most northern of the series of viaduct/bridges which were built to cross over railroad tracks and the Los Angeles River. The reinforced concrete Macy Street Viaduct is Spanish Renaissance with Ionic and Doric columns.

14. Macy Street Residence, circa 1890
1030 Macy Street
A brick Queen Anne dwelling.

15. Carlson Studio-House, 1993
Michael Rotundi
600 Moulton Avenue
The architect has added a gallery and living area to a 1920s industrial building. The ground floor has been designed as a gallery, while the living area, including a garden and swimming pool, occurs at the upper level. Exposed structure is transformed into the complex geometry of art.

16. Fuller Paint Company Warehouse, 1924–25
Morgan, Walls, and Clements
290 San Fernando Road
One of Morgan, Walls, and Clements creative exercises in the Spanish Colonial Revival for a five-story reinforced concrete warehouse building. The facade is a classical tripartite division; the base is decorated with low relief cast in stone (with a wonderful three-unit entry); above is a row of piers for three floors; and then there is an attic with perforated openings.

17. Capital Mill, 1884
1231 N. Spring Street
The Capital Mill is the oldest existing flour mill in the city. The utilitarian building is of brick. Sections of it are as high as four stories. The 1884 building incorporates parts of an even earlier brick building, constructed circa 1855.

18. U.S. Naval and Marine Corps Armory, 1939–40

18. U.S. Naval and Marine Corps Armory, 1939–40
Stiles Clements
North side of Stadium Way, southeast of Lilac Terrace
Late PWA Moderne terra-cotta-sheathed design with engaged fluted piers and panels of relief sculpture. The Armory is a little-known late-1930s L.A. monument which is well worth a visit. Do not miss the wonderful eagles.

19. Bank Americard Building (Bank of America Computer Center), 1979
Skidmore, Owings, and Merrill
Beaudry Avenue between West Temple and Mignonette streets
An eleven-story box, highly visible from the freeway interchange. It seems purposely to be a non-building which contributes nothing to one's experience, either from the freeway or close-up.

DOWNTOWN, SOUTH

1. Los Angeles Herald-Examiner Building,
1912
Julia Morgan
1111 S. Broadway
From time to time one comes across buildings
which could, as far as design authorship is concerned, provide a perfect theme for a Nancy
Drew mystery. The Herald-Examiner Building
is one of these. Over the years Julia Morgan has
always been credited with the design of the
Herald-Examiner Building. The production of
this building becomes a little more complex
when one looks into the Los Angeles contrac-
tual and building records. Surprisingly, these
records indicate that the building was
"designed" by J. Martyn Haenke (Haenke and
Dodd), and strangely these records do not mention Julia Morgan at all. On April 5, 1913, it
was announced that Haenke had "been commissioned to prepare plans" for the building. On

April 10 it was mentioned that he was "prepar-
ing preliminary plans," and on April 17
"Preliminary sketches prepared by architects
Haenke and Dodd . . . have been approved by
Mr. Hearst." The July 5 issue of the *Southwest
Contractor and Manufacturer* announced that
the contract had been let to the Alta Planning
Mill Company, with Haenke and Dodd super-
vising the construction of the building. Several
additional contracts were let by Haenke and
Dodd for such things as the tile for the domes.
The building was open and in use by late
1914.

Considering the distance from the Bay
region to Los Angeles, it seems reasonable to
assume that Julia Morgan designed the building, and that Haenke and Dodd produced the
working drawings and supervised its construction. Whether there was ever any give-and-take
between Morgan and Haenke remains open,

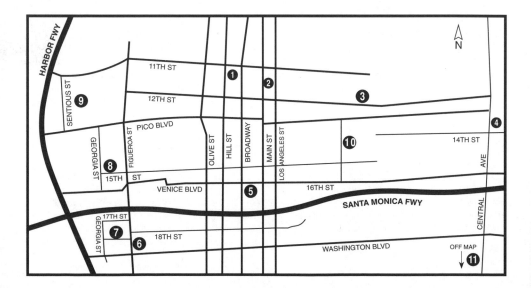

though it should be noted that Haenke, in his own work, was not an exponent of the Mission revival.

The Mission-revival image of the Los Angeles Herald-Examiner Building with its central square drum and dome certainly looks back to A. Page Brown's California Building at the 1893 World Columbian Exposition in Chicago. The Mission theme had been used in a number of Julia Morgan's early works, and she was to use it again in her 1932–36 "Las Milpitas," the ranch house adjacent to the Mission San Antonio for William Randolph Hearst. One gathers from the pages of the *Los Angeles Examiner* that the urge to use the Mission style was one shared by both architect and client. Julia Morgan is quoted as commenting on the design of the building in the December 22, 1914, issue of the *Los Angeles Examiner:* "There has been so much wasted architectural opportunity in this South Land, when public and commercial buildings might well be a part with their environment, and where the rich colors and contrasts and rich shadows could be allowed to play such an invaluable part in the design."

At the time it was built, the local L.A. press (including the *Examiner*) did not refer to the design as Mission, but as an example of the Spanish Renaissance style. The Herald-Examiner Building is certainly one of California's distinguished Hispanic-inspired buildings, with its colorful domes, tile roofs, white walls, and base with a row of arched openings. The richly decorated lobby with its staircases really poses as a domestic baronial hall, not what one would ever expect as an entrance to a commercial newspaper plant. This luxurious, almost Baroque space is one that we can be quite certain no Mission father would recognize as being in Alta California. Morgan made some alterations in the building in 1921, and more alterations and an annex was built from her designs in 1930–31. As one looks at the building today, the one appreciable external change has been the removal of the windows between the ground level arches and the closing in of these spaces. It was through the windows of this arcade that one could see the great printing

presses at work (à la Charlie Chaplin in *Modern Times*). With the closing of the newspaper, the building is now vacant, and one can only hope that a new use will be quickly found for it, and that it will then be restored.

2. Morgenstern Warehouse, 1978
Moss and Stafford
1140–1146 S. Main Street
This is an instance where even strong, exuberant architecture is having a difficult time maintaining itself against use, in this case the need for signage. The low stucco boxes with their cylinder end adjacent to the street are now on the tawdry side. Still it is a delightful, if somewhat self-indulgent, design.

3. Cohn-Goldwater Building, 1909
525 E. 12th Street
This was supposedly the first Modern "Class A" steel-reinforced concrete building erected in the city.

4. Coca-Cola Bottling Company Plant, 1936–37
Robert V. Derrah
1334 S. Central Avenue
The Streamline Moderne posing as ocean liner is one of the most frequently illustrated buildings in the Los Angeles area. This reinforced concrete building is equipped with a ship's bridge, metal railings of a nautical feeling, porthole windows, ship doors, and suggestions of metal rivets. "What, therefore, could more aptly express the bottling method of the Coca-Cola Company than a ship motif . . ." The interiors were originally as nautical as the exterior of the stucco and concrete flagship. The suggestion of a ship is still present internally, but not the way it used to be. The 1936–37 two-story ship is, in fact, a remodeling and addition to several older structures which were on the site.

5. Illing of California, 1946–47
Paul Laszlo
1600 S. Broadway
Most of Laszlo's work was domestic. Here you can see how the master of the Moderne created a classic statement.

4. Coca-Cola Bottling Company Plant, 1936–37

6. Patriotic Hall, 1926
  Allied Architects
  1816 S. Figueroa Street
The impressive Beaux Arts facade works equally
well from the street or from the Harbor or Santa
Monica freeways. The west street elevation of
the ten-story concrete building is Italian
Renaissance. The sides and back are just there.

7. Forthmann House, circa 1887
  Burgess J. Reeve
  629 W. 18th Street
This elegant Victorian house boasts Eastlake
details with Italianate brackets, plus a mansard-
roofed tower.

8. Fifteenth Street Residence, circa 1895
  633 W. 15th Street
A late Queen Anne dwelling in the Caribbean
Style.

9. Los Angeles Convention Center, 1972,
  1980, 1993
  Charles Luckman Associates (1972); Pei
  Cobb Freed & Partners (James Ingo Freed);
  Gruen Associates (Ki Suh Park)
  1201 S. Figueroa Street
A classic and highly successful example of an
L.A. building geared to the auto and the freeway. The center is located close to the interchange of the Harbor and Santa Monica
freeways. The slightly formal building sits on a
podium with its parking structure situated
across Sentous Street to the west. The new
addition more than doubles the size of the

original building. Like other buildings by the Pei firm, the new addition turns its back on the old and
proceeds in its own way to reflect
the latest in fashion—in this
instance, glass roofs and exposed
structure. Though Freed is quoted as
saying he wished to create a major
architectural statement for downtown L.A., the result, like his
Holocaust Museum in Washington,
D.C., is reasonable, but hardly brilliant. Strangely, even though the
structure is large, it does not establish any presence when seen from
the freeways.

**10. Central Distribution Center, Department
of Water and Power,** 1988–89
  Ellerbe Becket (Mehrdad Yazdani); Fong
  and Associates, landscape architects
  Maple Avenue, between Pico Boulevard
  and 15th Street
A group of rectangular volumes are attached to,
or project above, a twelve-foot-high concrete
block security wall. This may not sound like an
impressive composition of buildings, but it is,
notwithstanding the neighborhood. The dominant focus of the design is the projecting semicircular bay—with the building's entrance to
the side, and then a glass-sheathed volumetric
box on top of the bay (the box houses an
assembly room).

**11. Second Baptist Church (First A.M.E.
Church),** 1924
  Paul R. Williams; Norman F. Marsh
  2412 Griffith Avenue (corner 24th Street
  and Griffith Avenue)
This church was the young architect's first
major public commission (he also designed
several public schools at this time); and it was
also one of his few commissions for the black
community. In design the building reflects the
then-very-popular northern Italian Lombardian
Romanesque. Entrances occur to each side of
the principal gabled facade, and a high
Lombardian tower is situated to the right. The
building is of ruffled-face brick along with
cast-stone trim.

BOYLE HEIGHTS

B y the late 1880s Boyle Heights, which lies just east of the Los Angeles River, was connected with downtown Los Angeles by two street railroads which crossed the river on the East First Street and on the East Alison Street bridges. Boyle Heights itself is centered around Hollenbeck Park (acquired in 1892) and its lake, while Brooklyn Heights to the north has a similar center in and around the oval form of Prospect Park. By the time of the First World War, the area had declined as a home for artisans and the middle class. In the 1950s four freeways cut huge swathes through the area; the worst and the most unbelievably thoughtless was the Golden State Freeway,

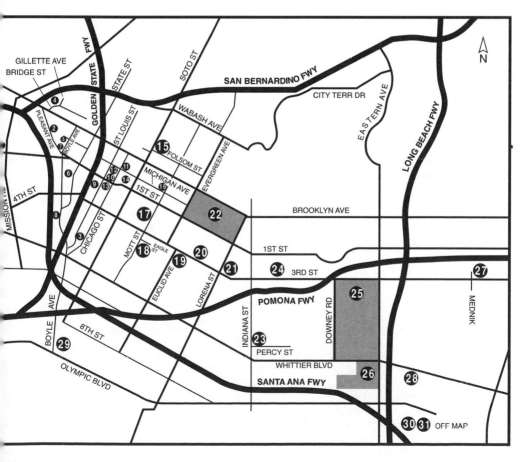

placed adjacent to the once-quiet Hollenbeck Park. The past twenty years present a mixed picture of decay, restoration, well-kept yards and gardens, high, protective, chain-link fences, and formidable watch dogs. In August of 1993 it was announced that Pico Gardens Apartments and Aliso Apartments would be demolished and rebuilt.

The fame of East Los Angeles in the late 1960s and through much of the 1970s rested on the ever-changing street murals. A number of these can be seen on Whittier Boulevard from Soto Street east to Atlantic Boulevard. Others are situated on First Street between Lorena and Indiana streets, on Brooklyn Avenue at Gage Avenue. Some of these murals are by professional artists, others are by self-taught painters and children.

1. Public Housing Projects, 1941–42
Several of these housing projects were started as low-cost developments of the later Great Depression years, and then with the approach of the Second World War they became War Housing Projects.

1a. Aliso Village, 1941–53
  George G. Adams, Walter S. Davis, Ralph C. Flewelling; Eugene Weston, Jr., Lewis E. Weston, Lloyd Wright;
  Katherine Bashford and Fred Barlow, Jr., landscape architects
  Northwest corner of First and Mission streets
This housing project consists of thirty-three two-story, masonry/stucco/wood-framed, flat-roofed boxes. It was planned to house 2,975 persons on the 34.3-acre site. As is true of many public projects in Los Angeles, the site plan and the landscape design ended up being far more imaginative than the architecture.

1b. Rosehill Courts Public Housing, 1942
  W. F. Ruck and Claude Beelman
  Northeast on Huntington Drive to Esmeralda Rose Hill Drive and Amethyst Street
A small World War II housing project of one hundred living units contained in fifteen two-story frame and stucco-sheathed buildings. Existing eucalyptus trees were retained, which helps.

1c. William Mead Homes, 1941–42
  T. A. Elisen; A. R. Walker, Norman R. Marsh, David D. Smith, Herbert J. Powell, and Armand Monaco
  1300 N. Cardinal Street (North Main Street to Elmyra Street, east on Elmyra Street to Cardinal Street)
These 449 living units were built on a site of 15.2 acres. Corner windows, horizontal balconies, and other details slightly suggest the late 1930s Moderne.

1d. Pico Gardens Public Housing, 1941–42
  John C. Austin, Sumner Spaulding, Earl Heitschmidt, and Henry C. Newton
  500 S. Pecan Street (south on Pecan Street off East First Street)
This project contains 250 living units in thirty-seven two-story buildings.

2. Mount Pleasant Bakery Building, circa 1885
  1418 Pleasant Avenue
This small, false-fronted wooden building is supposedly the oldest bakery building still standing in Los Angeles. It is essentially Queen Anne in style with some older elements of the Italianate.

3. House, circa 1900
  706 S. Chicago Street
What appears to be a late Queen Anne two-story dwelling moves on to suggest either the Richardsonian Romanesque or, more likely, the Mission Revival. Note the two rows of cobblestone arches.

4. House, circa 1905
  603 Gillette Street
A boxy, hip-roofed, turn-of-the-century Colonial Revival dwelling is yanked from the normal by the injection of a pointed Gothic window in the center of the street facade. And this feature is "balanced" on one side by an oversized round window. The design is a perfect one-upmanship of the current fashion of Post Modernism.

5. Cottage, circa 1885
  914 E. Michigan Avenue
A rare (for Los Angeles) surviving example of a Second Empire mansard-roofed cottage. This

story-and-a-half cottage exhibits a traditional
street elevation which includes a small porch
placed between two bay windows.

6. Cottage, circa 1889
  327 S. State Street
A story-and-a-half Queen Anne cottage with
original chimney still present (which in Los
Angeles is rare because of frequent earthquakes). Sunburst patterns occur in the gable
ends, and jigsaw work is present on the
entrance porch.

7. House (now a neighborhood center),
  circa 1895
  358 S. Boyle Street
A two-story Queen Anne/Colonial Revival
dwelling with both first- and second-floor
porches sporting an abundance of turned woodwork.

8. Hollenbeck Home for the Aged,
  1896; 1908; 1923
  Morgan and Walls; Morgan, Walls, and
  Clements
  573 S. Boyle Avenue
Pure Mission Revival, though as often happens
in that style, many design elements, proportions, and details came directly from the
Richardsonian Romanesque style of the 1880s.
One can see this in the entrance arcade, in the
corbeling below the extended eaves, and in the
engaged columns employed around openings.

9. Cottage, circa 1885
  2018 E. Second Street
Compared to cities of the East and Midwest,
there were few Eastlake houses and cottages
built in and around Los Angeles. And of these,
very few remain. This small cottage displays a
wide array of wood surfaces and sawed work
which we associate with this style. The exterior
surfaces include forty-five-degree shiplap,
tongue-and-groove horizontal boards, and a
small bit of fish-scale shingles.

10. Grace Methodist Episcopal Church,
  (now **Free Methodist Church**), 1906
  John C. Austin
  200 N. Saint Louis Avenue
A shingled Craftsman Gothic church building
with lead glass windows. The high point of this

11. First Hebrew Christian Church, 1905

picturesque composition are the two miniature
towers over the side entrance.

11. First Hebrew Christian Church, 1905
  Northeast corner of North Chicago Street
  and East Michigan Avenue
Here you will find a New Yorker's idea of
architecture in Los Angeles: a stucco Austrian
Secessionist/Islamic facade (with a corner
dome) placed in front of a plain clapboard box.
The culmination of the design is a large roof
sign in the form of an open Near Eastern scroll.

12. Hollenbeck Presbyterian Church (now
  Iglesia Bautista Unida), 1884
  East side of North Chicago Street south of
  Michigan Avenue
A wood Craftsman church building with both
Gothic and Romanesque details. The design
displays an assortment of different window
shapes, including pointed Gothic windows. One
is not certain whether we are to respond to the
entrance porch as Richardsonian Romanesque
or Mission. The tower is almost worthy of the
Episcopalian Ernest Coxhead. It is one of the
oldest church buildings remaining near central
Los Angeles, and it is still imposing, even
behind its chain-link fence. Incidentally, it is
the place where Occidental College was
founded in 1887.

13. House, circa 1887
2123 E. 2nd Street
Shingled arches are supported by turned wood columns on the entrance porch of this Queen Anne cottage. Across the street at number 2126 is another, larger, **cottage** (circa 1890) which represents more of the typical Los Angeles builder's spec cottage (Queen Anne in style).

14. Los Angeles Jewish Community Center, 1937
Raphael S. Soriano
2317 E. Michigan Avenue
Pre-World War II International Style Modern. A stucco-sheathed rectangular box with a strong emphasis placed on horizontality via bands of windows, the usual thin roof fascia, and then the horizontal bands of the stucco itself.

15. Apartment Building, circa 1925
East side of North Soto Street, north of East Folsom Street
A common man's do-it-yourself version of Austrian Secessionism just emerging into the 1920s Art Deco Moderne.

16. Cottage, circa 1890
2533 E. Michigan Avenue
A many-gabled Queen Anne cottage. It could be right out of any number of late-nineteenth-century architectural pattern books.

17. House, circa 1895
South side of East Second Street West of Mott Street
A two-story Queen Anne/Colonial Revival dwelling. A round corner bay tower is covered with a conical domed roof.

18. House, circa 1895
2700 East Eagle Street
Another Queen Anne dwelling with the traditional corner bay-tower.

19. House, circa 1890
2922 Euclid Avenue
A two-story Queen Anne dwelling with emphatic projecting boxed windows.

20. Cottage, circa 1889
3059 E. Fourth Street
Clapboard, fish-scale shingles, flush tongue-and-groove boarding, and board and batten form the surfaces of this Queen Anne cottage. The cottage is now partially hidden from the street by a later, single-floor commercial building.

21. Cottage, circa 1887
3407 E. Fourth Street
A picturesque tower roof projects above the bay and porch of this Eastlake/Queen Anne cottage.

22. Evergreen Cemetery, 1877
Southwest corner of Brooklyn Avenue and Lorena Street
Evergreen Cemetery is one of the oldest cemeteries in the city of Los Angeles, and it contains some interesting nineteenth-century tombs and sculpture. Architecturally, the important object within the cemetery is **Ivy Chapel,** designed by Arthur B. Benton in 1903. The chapel is a medieval stone structure with a handsome front composed of four pointed windows along with a long, narrow porch.

23. Bungalow, circa 1910
3672 E. Percy Street
The porch of this modest bungalow establishes it as something almost regal. Four flat arches with stuccoed brackets are supported by thick, primitive columns. Above the eave a curved pediment marks the principal entrance.

24. Our Lady of Lourdes Roman Catholic Church, 1930
L. R. Scherer
3773 E. 3rd Street
An imaginative and forceful mixture of the Art Deco (Zigzag) Moderne and the Spanish Colonial Revival of the 1920s (plus hints of the Mission Revival and the Gothic). All of this imagery has been realized in a reinforced concrete church building.

25. New Calvary Cemetery and Mausoleum, 1927
Ross Montgomery
4201 E. Whittier Boulevard
Ross Montgomery's **Mausoleum of the Golden West** is a concrete building in the same league as the Los Angeles Public Library and the Los Angeles City Hall. It is a major but

25. Mausoleum, New Calvary Cemetery, 1927

little-known monument. The architect has beautifully succeeded in creating a picturesque and memorable building by combing the past and choosing references (it would seem) to Babylonia, to the Hindu architecture of India, to the Mausoleum at Halicarnassus, to Italian and Spanish architecture, and finally to the then-developing Art Deco Moderne of the late 1920s. Inside the Mausoleum are paintings of California scenes and a great deal of art glass fabricated by the Judson Studios. Also within the cemetery is **Grace Chapel** (circa 1900). The **entrance gates** off Whittier Boulevard were designed in 1923 by Albert C. Martin.

26. Home of Peace Cemetery, 1931
4334 Whittier Boulevard
The **Chapel** is somewhat Byzantine in feeling, enriched by what appear to be a pair of Islamic minarets. The major monument of the place is the 1931 **Hamburger Mausoleum,** which is a perfect example of the monumental Art Deco.

27. David Wark Griffith Junior High School, 1978
Fernando Juarez
4765 East 3rd Street (at Mednik Avenue)
The architect has been able to suggest the atmosphere of a northern Mexico adobe church through a wonderful grouping of the arched bays which project from the entrance front of the building.

28. Boulevard Theater,
circa 1937
Balch and Stanberry
4549 E. Whittier Boulevard
A Moderne motion-picture theater, more angular than streamlined. The nine letters of *Boulevard* project separately off the horizontally lighted tower.

29. Wyvern Wood Housing Project, 1938–39
David J. Wetmore and Loyal Watson
Between East 8th Street and East Olympic Boulevard, south of South Soto Street and South GrandeVista Avenue

26. Hamburger Mausoleum, Home of Peace Cemetery, 1931

29. Wyvern Wood Housing Project, 1938–39

The first low-cost public housing project to be built in Los Angeles (built with private, not public, funds). The seventy-acre site was designed with curved streets and open courts. The site included retail stores which face Olympic Boulevard and Soto Street and a school and playground which adjoin Grande Vista Avenue. The loosely Colonial Monterey-style buildings are two-story stucco, some with projecting balconies.

30. Samson Tyre and Rubber Company Building (The Citadel), 1929–30
Morgan, Walls, and Clements
5675 Telegraph Road, City of Commerce (take the Santa Ana Freeway to the South Washington Boulevard exit, then northeast on Telegraph Road)
An architectural wonder of Los Angeles, and a startling experience as you travel up or down the Santa Ana Freeway. This industrial office and manufacturing plant was built as a walled Babylonian (or is it Assyrian?) city, right out of a 1920s Hollywood movie set. After carefully consulting the published archaeological reports, architects modeled the building after the famous ziggurats and fortified walls of the

ancient city of Khorsabad, to which they added features from other ancient Assyrian and Babylonian cities. Priest-kings and other creatures adorn the walls and add prestige to the production of automobile tires. The name Samson is associated with the Near East, as is Babylon. So now you don't have to travel to the Tigris and Euphrates rivers (with the somewhat difficult problems these days of visiting Iraq) to see Babylon, for here it is—improved upon in Los Angeles.

The factory closed in 1978, and the buildings remained vacant for a decade. In 1990–91 the site was transformed into a shopping center (**The Citadel Outlet Center**). The metal factory buildings were removed, and the stage set of the 1,700-foot Assyrian wall was left. New buildings were grouped around a central allée which runs through the wall. The glory of the place is the new landscape, especially the new forest of palm trees. The master plan for the site was developed by landscape architect Martha Schwartz of San Francisco (Schwartz/Smith/Meyer). The specific design of the project was by Sussman/Prejza Inc., and by Peridian Irving.

31. Lever Brothers Office and Soap Company Building, 1951
Welton Becket and Associates
6300 Sheila Street, City of Commerce (take the Santa Ana Freeway to East Washington Boulevard exit, then to Sheila Street)
A period piece of the 1950s Modern, very well done. The most assertive element of the design is the glass penthouse placed on top of the principal building.

EXPOSITION PARK, WEST; LEIMERT PARK

Before and after the turn of the century, the northeast part of this section of Los Angeles was a prestigious residential area. This was especially true of the district around Chester Place and St. James Park. The great residential street of the 1900s was West Adams Boulevard extending from South Figueroa Street to South Arlington Avenue. Though individual enclaves of upper-middle-class exclusiveness were laid out in the 1920s, much of the eastern section in and around Adams Boulevard began to decay.

South of Adams Boulevard a number of subdivisions were laid out in the 1920s. One of the most successful of these was Leimert Park, planned in 1927 by Olmsted and Olmsted. Their centerpiece for the community was Leimert Plaza (at the junction of Leimert Parkway, Crenshaw Boulevard, and Vernon Avenue). They connected the Plaza with a narrow park strip extending up Leimert

Parkway to the northeast, and to the south on Crenshaw Boulevard (as far as 60th Street). The hilly area southwest of the Plaza exhibits the usual winding streets which one associates with upper-middle-class enclaves.

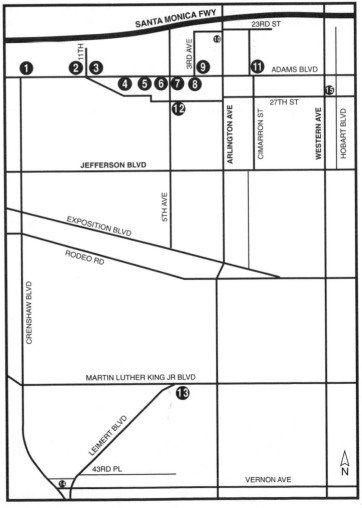

It has in part become commercialized or has been turned into various types of multiple housing. The extensive flat plain south of Exposition Boulevard developed in the usual strip commercial fashion along major thoroughfares (South Western and South Vermont avenues, South Figueroa Street), with an infill primarily made of modest artisan bungalows and some small-scale multiple housing.

Though Exposition Park and adjacent USC to the north provided open space, those two enterprises really had very little to do with residential neighbors nearby. The 1960s redevelopment has torn down a number of blocks of houses and stores west of USC and replaced them with new commercial buildings (oriented around the auto), and now multiple housing. The streets north of USC used to have many examples of late-nineteenth- and early-twentieth-century residential architecture (ranging from the Queen Anne through the Mission Revival and adaptations of English Medieval), but now there are few examples left.

A number of the late-nineteenth-century Victorian houses around USC have been renovated and a handful of others have been moved—even as far away as Pasadena. Probably the greatest loss has occurred and is occurring along West Adams Boulevard. One of L.A.'s great formal Italian gardens with a hillside water staircase used to surround the Beaux Arts classical **Murphy House** (circa 1906; Hudson and Munsell) at 2079 West Adams (landscaped, revised and enlarged in 1931 by A. E. Hanson and Lutah Maria Riggs), but only a few of the larger trees now remain. And more recently, the Colonial Revival **Childs House** at 3100 West Adams Boulevard was demolished.

1. Church of the Advent, 1925
Arthur B. Benton
4976 West Adams Boulevard
This was one of Benton's last major commissions (he died in 1927). It follows the form of the rural English Gothic churches which he had so often used (with wonderful results) from the 1890s on throughout Southern California. There were several important houses of his built on

West Adams Boulevard, but these are all now demolished.

2. McCarty Memorial Christian Church, 1931
4101 West Adams Boulevard (Northwest corner of West Adams Boulevard and 1st Avenue)
An excellent example of one of L.A.'s reinforced concrete churches of the late 1920s. The style in this instance is Gothic, partially English and partially French.

3. Apartment Building, circa 1955
4025 W. Adams Boulevard
A post-World War II L.A. stucco box which emerges as something exotic because of its Japan-esque roof details.

4. Louise Denkin House, 1912
B. Cooper Corbett
3820 W. Adams Boulevard
By 1910 there were over half a dozen Beaux Arts villas on West Adams. This one, somewhat eighteenth-century French, is one of the few still remaining.

5. Mary L. Briggs House, 1912
Hudson and Munsell
3734 West Adams Boulevard
The firm of Hudson and Munsell produced a number of houses on West Adams Boulevard. Regrettably, few are left. Their architectural vocabulary went the rounds from Beaux Arts classicism to Tudor/Craftsman dwellings such as this. Somewhat more in the Craftsman vogue is the nearby **MacGowan House** of 1912, at 3726 Adams Boulevard.

6. Gusti Villa (Busby Berkeley Estate), 1910
Hudson and Munsell
3500 West Adams Boulevard
One of the few examples of this firm's work in the Beaux Arts classical imagery. This one has the atmosphere of a late-eighteenth-century French country house.

7. Lindsay House, 1908
Charles F. Whittlesey
3424 W. Adams Boulevard
This massive stone house comes close in spirit to Secessionist work from Vienna,

though its arches and other elements help it to read as Mission as well. Two balls balance on projecting pinnacles at each side of the west front dormer. A heavy, arcaded balcony projects over the entrance porch. The house, which is of hollow terra-cotta tile, was built by the Western Art Tile Works of Los Angeles.

Whittlesey was one of L.A.'s gifted architects at the turn of the century. He, along with Irving J. Gill, was one of many Southern California architects who were fascinated with the possibilities of reinforced concrete for small as well as large buildings. Regrettably, most of Whittlesey's work has been demolished or defaced.

8. Walker House (now **Seventh-Day Adventist Building**), 1905– 6
Charles F. Whittlesey
3300 West Adams Boulevard
Whittlesey's designs were always original, and the Walker House is no exception. Half-timbering suggests the Medieval, but basically the stucco volumes and tile roofs are Mission Revival. Generous terraces face toward the street and the rear (south), overlooking the hillside and garden.

9. Fitzgerald House, 1903
Joseph Cather Newsom
3115 W. Adams Boulevard
Whatever Newsom touched, he transformed. This design is as inventively outrageous as any of his earlier Queen Anne or Eastlake designs. If you wonder what style it is, the architect labeled it Italian Gothic. While it is Medieval in spirit, none of the details are handled traditionally. The tour de force is the elaborate entrance and large clinker brick chimney with an arched window punctured through it. Fortunately, the house has recently been restored.

10. House, circa 1902
2301 W. 24th Street
"South Seas Edwardian"—a little bit of the Medieval coupled with the Colonial Revival and even a little Queen Anne.

11. William Andrews Clark Memorial Library (UCLA), 1924–26
Robert Farquhar
Ralph D. Cornell, landscape architect
2520 S. Cimarron Street
According to the literature, this building was "designed in the style of the Italian Renaissance." A more obvious source was Wren's addition to Hampton Court Palace, though for some reason Farquhar omitted the orange colors from Wren's symbolic decoration and substituted yellow brick for his lovely pink. One might also add that the design has the classical calmness which one associates with Farquhar's work. At the time the library was built, the landscape architect Ralph Cornell introduced the more formal garden which we now see. The villa (library) was undoubtedly more successful when the walled and hedged formal gardens which surround the building were well planted and maintained. The interior is "correct" and elegant. The rooms are decorated with a number of murals painted by Allyn Cox.

When built, the Library was one of several buildings within the walled block-sized estate. An observatory on the grounds was removed in 1954, and the main house itself in 1971. In addition to the Library building, the only remains of the former estate was the service building at the northwest corner of the property. In 1989–90 the architect Barton Phelps and Associates was commissioned to design buildings at the north side of the property. This narrow band of a building, named **North Range** was designed to house a variety of needs ranging from offices to conference rooms. Phelps's approach was to keep it all low-keyed, modern, but in sympathy with the main building. His design consists of a series of brick-sheathed boxes attached by a single brick wall. A metal pergola stands in front, and eventually will provide a screen in front of the structure.

Arrangements to visit can be made by calling the library (731-8529).

14. Leimert Theater, 1931–32

12. Lukens House, 1940
Raphael S. Soriano
3425 W. 27th Street
The single-floor dwelling is arranged around an enclosed patio in a design much less insistently International Style Modern than most of Soriano's pre-World War II plans.

13. Touriel Medical Building, 1950
Raphael S. Soriano
2608–2610 W. Martin Luther King, Jr., Boulevard
A steel-frame, post-and-beam building with a small entrance courtyard which carries the *Arts and Architecture* Case Study House aesthetic into the commercial realm (it all seems inter-changeable).

14. Leimert Theater (now **Jehovah's Witness Hall**), 1931–32
Morgan, Walls, and Clements
3300 43rd Place

This reinforced concrete theater building is, except for the ornamental open-work oil derrick tower and signage, a direct result of the Paris Exposition of 1925. The interior ceiling of the oval-shaped auditorium still retains its Moderne patterns. Also, note the murals in the lobby. The theater, which faces onto **Leimert Park,** was a major element in this L.A. suburban development.

15. Fire Engine House No. 18, 1904
John Parkinson
2616 South Hobart Boulevard
A small, delightful, twin-towered Mission Revival building.

EXPOSITION PARK, EAST

1. Stimson House, 1891
    Carroll H. Brown
    2421 S. Figueroa Street
The Richardsonian Romanesque in stone never enjoyed as great a popularity in California for residences as it did in the Midwest and East. The Stimson House was one of the largest and most elaborate examples built in Los Angeles. In plan, with its great living hall, it is really Queen Anne. Externally the four-story octagonal tower with crenelated battlements is picturesque.

2. St. Vincent de Paul Roman Catholic Church, 1923–25
    Albert C. Martin
    Northwest corner of South Figueroa Street
    and West Adams Boulevard
Certainly one of the principal landmarks of L.A. and of the Spanish Colonial Revival in California. The Spanish Churrigueresque of Mexico was used as a design source for this church, certainly inspired by Bertram G. Goodhue's California Building at the 1915 San Diego Exposition. A richly decorated screen made of Indiana limestone dominates the entrance, and brightly colored tile covers the forty-five-foot-diameter dome. The interior ceiling decoration is by John B. Smeraldi.

3. Automobile Club of Southern California, 1921–23
    Hunt and Burns; Roland E. Coate
    Aurele Vermeulen, landscape architect
    2601 S. Figueroa Street
The corner of this building, with its octagonal tower surmounted by a domed cupola, and the Baroque entrance screen, are forceful elements of the Spanish Colonial Revival. Equally impressive is the interior, especially the public entrance and lobby space.

2. St. Vincent de Paul Roman Catholic Church, 1923–25

4. St. John's Episcopal Church, 1922–23
    Pierpont and Walter S. Davis
    514 W. Adams Boulevard
The design for this church was the result of a competition juried by Ernest Coxhead of San Francisco, William Templeton Johnson of San Diego, and the Rev. George A. Davidson of Los Angeles. The historic source for the design was northern Italian Romanesque. The interior ceiling was modeled after the Church of San Miniato in Florence. The bas-reliefs around the rose window were designed by S. Cartaino Scarpitta. The surfaces of this reinforced concrete church reveal the horizontal board pattern of the forms.

5. House, circa 1900
    426–428 E. Adams Boulevard
Medieval imagery of a sort, with a remarkable composition of connected dormers.

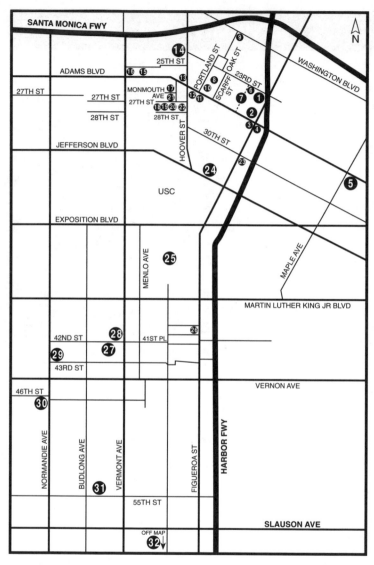

was one of the most frequently illustrated. While for a Newsom design it looks reasonably calm from the street, it is anything but sedate behind and, above all, inside.

7. Chester Place
Between West 23rd Street and West Adams Boulevard, west of South Figueroa Street Chester Place was a private enclave of twenty acres which originally contained thirteen large dwellings. It was laid out as a residential park in 1895. The various houses within the park were built just before and after 1900. Of the houses that still remain, the two most interesting are the **Doheny House** at number 8 and the **Wilson House** across the street at number 7. The Wilson House was designed by Dennis and Farwell in 1916 and is somewhat Mission/Islamic in style. Its cast ornament was certainly inspired by the work

6. Severance House, 1904
Joseph Cather Newsom
650 W. 23rd Street
Joseph Cather Newsom designed a number of Mission Revival buildings during his second period of active practice in Los Angeles. Of these, the story-and-a-half Severance House

of Louis H. Sullivan. The Doheny (originally Posey) House was built in 1898–1900 and was designed by Theodore A. Eisen and Sumner P. Hunt. Externally, the house is rather neutral (could it be called Chateauesque?). Internally, its most famous space is the Pompeiian Room, designed by Alfred F. Rosenheim and built in 1906. Other additions and alterations (including the main entrance) were also made by Alfred F. Rosenheim in 1913. Much of the interior was remodeled in the French rococo style in 1933–34.

8. Apartment House, circa 1905
   2342 Scarff Street
An authoritative Beaux Arts frontispiece set in front of a conventional apartment house.

9. Odd Fellows Temple Building, 1924
   Morgan, Walls, and Clements
   1828–1834 Oak Street
A reinforced concrete building with cast concrete ornament, in this instance more Spanish Renaissance than Churrigueresque.

10. House, circa 1875–79
   2624 Portland Street
One of the once-many modest Italianate dwellings which formerly lined many Los Angeles streets from the late 1860s through the early 1880s.

11. Casa de Rosas (Froebel Institute), 1894
   Sumner P. Hunt
   950 W. Adams Boulevard
Charles F. Lummis labeled this as Mission and so it must be. It was stuccoed and had an arcade supported by short Tuscan columns. And above all it had a patio. Historically it was important as one of the very early instances of the self-conscious cultivation of the myth of the Mission in a new building.

12. Second Church of Christ, Scientist, 1905–10
   Alfred F. Rosenheim
   948 W. Adams Boulevard
This Beaux Arts classical design was inspired by the Mother Church in Boston. The concrete dome is sheathed in copper. An authoritative bank of six Corinthian columns faces Adams Boulevard.

13. House, 1892
   1140 W. Adams Boulevard
A two-story Queen Anne dwelling.

9. Odd Fellows Temple Building, 1924

14. Rindge House, 1900
   Frederick L. Roehrig
   2263 S. Hoover Boulevard
An imposing Chateauesque dwelling with fat corner towers between which is a Richardsonian Romanesque porch.

15. Kerckhoff House, 1900
   1325 W. Adams Boulevard
A shingled Queen Anne/Colonial Revival dwelling.

16. Cottage, circa 1889
   1308 W. 25th Street
This small wood cottage was moved in 1981 and handsomely restored. In style it exhibits both Eastlake and Queen Anne features.

17. Adlai E. Stevenson House, 1895
   2639 S. Monmouth Avenue
A late, simplified Queen Anne dwelling, characteristic of many built in the Exposition Park area.

24. Shrine Civic Auditorium (Al Malaikah Temple), 1920-26

18. Kiefer House, 1895
    Sumner P. Hunt and Theodore A. Eisen
    1204 W. 27th Street
Queen Anne in concept, but with a turn-of-the-century nod to the Colonial Revival.

19. House, 1904–5
    John C. Austin
    1194 W. 27th Street
A Craftsman dwelling given Tudor roots and respectability.

20. House, circa 1890
    1160 W. 27th Street
A Queen Anne dwelling. Of special interest are the long, horizontal windows in the gable ends.

21. House, 1890
    Bradbeer and Ferris
    1163 W. 27th Street
A Queen Anne with a touch of the Colonial Revival. Its commanding feature is the third-floor tower set on the thin posts of the second-floor porch.

22. House, 1891
    Bradbeer and Ferris
    2703 S. Hoover Street
Queen Anne with an extensive, curved, wrap-around veranda, plus the obligatory palm trees.

23. Bungalow Court, circa 1920
    627 W. 30th Street
A late Craftsman bungalow court. A group of clapboard bungalows faces onto a long, narrow, open court.

24. Shrine Civic Auditorium (Al Malaikah Temple), 1920-26
    John C. Austin, A. M. Edelman, G. Albert Lansburgh
    665 W. Jefferson Boulevard
Islamic imagery from somewhere (the Hollywood stage sets?) was employed externally and internally. The pair of domed cupolas and balcony loggia are the strongest features of the design. The auditorium seats 6,400 and a large ballroom pavilion adjoins at the north.

25. Exposition Park
    Between Menlo Avenue, South Figueroa Street, Exposition, and Martin Luther King, Jr., boulevards
This site was established in 1872 as a privately operated fairgrounds and racetrack. The Southern District Agricultural Society, which owned the park, went bankrupt in 1880. In 1898 the land was purchased jointly by the state, county, and city. The fanatically Beaux Arts **Los Angeles County Historical and Art Museum,** now a small part of the County Museum of Natural History, was designed in 1910 by Hudson and Munsell and opened in 1913. It was thought of as being an example of Spanish Renaissance architecture. In 1911 the landscape architect Wilbur D. Cook, Jr., laid out the grounds of the park.

    In 1923 the park was the site of the Monroe Centennial Exposition. The buildings designed for this temporary exhibition are now gone, but they constituted an impressive continuation of the abstract approach taken to Spanish architecture by Irving J. Gill (although they were referred to at the time as Pueblo). They were designed by Charles H. Kyson. One wonders if

25. *Los Angeles County Historical and Art Museum, 1910-13*

Irving J. Gill might also have been involved in the design, for they are very similar to his 1919–22 Clark House in Santa Fe Springs.

The **Memorial Coliseum** was designed in 1921–23 by John and Donald B. Parkinson. This was the central sports facility for the 1932 Olympic Games in Los Angeles. In 1992 Howard Needles Tammen and Bergendoff, Sports Architectural Group, with HNTB and Walter Moore Company, developed a scheme to dramatically increase the seating and other facilities within the Coliseum. With the difficult economic times being experienced in the early 1990s, this grand plan was put aside, probably for the good, and small modifications are currently being made. One of the high points of the park is the seven acres of sunken **Rose Gardens** which run parallel to Exposition Boulevard and to the east of the Natural History Museum. One of the latest additions to the buildings in Exposition Park is the **California Aerospace Museum** (1982–84) designed by Frank O. Gehry and Associates. This complex design, resplendent with references to technology, flight, and high art, contains spaces which enhance and dramatize the objects on exhibition.

29. St. Cecilia's Roman Catholic Church, 1927

Two other buildings were completed in 1984–85. These are the Museum of **Afro-American History** (designed by Jack Haywood and Vincent J. Proby, 1983–84) and the **Multi-cultural Center** (designed by Barton Myers, 1983-84). For the 1984 Olympic Games, the sculptor Robert Graham designed the *Olympic Gateway* composed of two bronze piers supporting two figures, one male and the other female, both headless and nude. The most current proposal (1993) for the park is a new California Museum of Science and Industry building to be located south of the Rose Garden and for which the Zimmer Gunsul Frasca Partnership has provided a play between space frame elements and thin enclosed volumes.

26. Van de Kamp Building, circa 1930
    Northwest corner of South Figueroa Street and 41st Place
A windmill tower, sadly lacking its blades, brings attention to this corner. The suggestion of shingles, with their V-shaped forms, hints at the Art Deco (Zigzag) Moderne.

27. Apartment Buildings, circa 1915
    1016–1018, 1020–1022, and 1040–1042 W. 42nd Street
A group of typical L.A. Craftsman apartment houses.

28. Manual Arts High School, 1934–35
    John and Donald B. Parkinson
    Northwest corner of South Vermont Avenue and West 42nd Street
A two-story, exposed concrete, PWA Moderne building, in this case Streamline. Don't miss the relief sculpture over the entrance to the auditorium, and of course the dramatically rounded corners of this concrete building.

29. St. Cecilia's Roman Catholic Church, 1927
    Ross Montgomery
    Northeast corner of South Normandie Avenue and West 43rd Street
An impressive version of the Italian Romanesque order. A low, highly effective tower dominates the crossing. Sections of the exposed concrete walls were originally tinted in reds, yellows, and tans.

30. Pilgrim Congregational Church, circa 1905
    West side of South Normandie Avenue at West 46th Street
A shingled Craftsman church with some Gothic detailing.

31. Two Bungalows, circa 1910
    1102 and 1156 W. 55th Street
Two characteristic L.A. Craftsman bungalows. Nearby on West 54th Street east of South Normandie Avenue are other spec Craftsman bungalows.

32. Mount Carmel High School Building, 1934
    7011 S. Hoover Street
Here, in a mid-1930s building, one can sense how the Spanish Colonial Revival tradition was being continually and creatively modified.

UNIVERSITY OF SOUTHERN CALIFORNIA

USC was established in 1880 on an eighteen-acre site located adjacent to Exposition Park. In 1910 the architectural firm of Train and Williams prepared a general plan for the campus, followed in 1920 by a strong axial plan prepared by John Parkinson. The Parkinson plan projected the major axis—University Avenue—as being lined with three- and four-story northern Italian Romanesque buildings. The avenue itself was to be bridged

at various points by Venice-like foot bridges. During the 1920s a number of these buildings were constructed along University Avenue.

At the end of the 1930s, the strict adherence to the vocabulary of the northern Italian Romanesque was modified and modernized in the **Hancock Foundation Building** and in the **Harris Hall/Fisher Gallery Building**. After World War II, Marsh, Smith, and Powell prepared (in 1949–50) a revised master plan, but

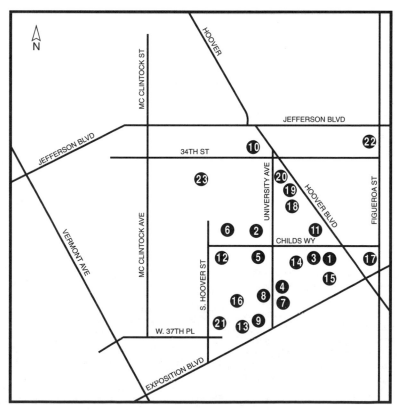

this was never really carried out. In 1961 William L. Pereira and Associates were engaged to provide still another master plan with additional changes in 1966. One ingredient of this last plan was the gradual closing off of all the streets which cut through the campus, replacing them with pedestrian walkways. Another element was to intensify the density of the campus by introducing high-rise buildings.

From the early 1950s to the present, the tendency has been to infill the campus's older green spaces with new buildings, and also to slowly expand the campus into the residential area to the north. The newer high-rise buildings—some of which are up to fourteen stories high, do not fit in very well with the older buildings, and now there is not much open green space left (although some of the more recent landscaping has been handsomely carried out). USC's architectural image since 1945 has been self-consciously Modern, and, as is true in the case of most of America's academic architecture after World War II, the structures built during these years are, as a group, hardly distinguished. During this time the University has engaged an impressive array of national and regional name-brand architects and architectural firms, including I. M. Pei, Albert C. Martin and Associates, Stanton and Stockwell, Robert E. Alexander, and others. But the overall results have, on the whole, been disappointing.

We wish that the situation had improved since we last wrote about the campus in the mid-1980s, but such has not been the case. The fourteen-story **Webb Tower** and the adjacent eleven-story **Flour Tower** are as mindless as the earlier high-rise designs. Competent, but disappointing, are such recent buildings as the **Pertusati Bookstore** (1987; Grillias Pirc Rosier), and the **Law Center Addition** (1987; Albert C. Martin Associates). Several smaller projects have turned out quite successful. These include the **Helen Topping Architecture and Fine Arts Library Addition** (1989) by Ellerbe Becket (Graeme Morland), where the task was to introduce natural light into a basement structure; and **The Forthman House** which is an 1880s house that was moved to the campus from the site of the Los Angeles Convention Center. The renovation of the house took place in 1988, and was by De Bretteville and Polyzoides. It is possible, as has been the case at the UCLA campus, that a distinguished landscape architectural program might rescue it all, but this will be a formidable task to carry out.

1. Widney (Alumni House) Hall, 1880
   Attributed to Ezra F. Kysor and Octavius Morgan

This two-story wood structure reads as an early example of the Colonial Revival, though it was in fact an Italianate dwelling when it was originally built. It was moved to its present site in 1958 and transformed into a Colonial revival dwelling by Lawrence Test. Among his Colonializing additions were green shutters and a widow's walk on the roof.

2. George Finley Bovard Administration Building, 1920–21
   John and Donald Parkinson

The first of this architect's brick northern Italian Romanesque designs to be built on the campus. It is interesting to note that the reactions to the building's architectural images varied. In the 1920s it was described as a fine example of the Spanish Renaissance, while others labeled it Lombardian. The building's large square tower (which was built as a bell tower), with eight heroic sculptured figures (by Casper Gruenfeld, who also did the sculpture on the south front)) at each corner, was meant to dominate the new center of the campus. If one compares USC's version of the northern Italian Romanesque with that of UCLA's, it is apparent that Parkinson and others produced a group of buildings which were more inventive, playful, and lively. Even the most distinguished of the northern Italian Romanesque designs at UCLA, Royce Hall, cannot be compared in quality of design and detailing to the Wilson Student Union Building, the Doheny Library, or the Mudd Hall of Philosophy at USC.

By the southeast corner of Bovard Administration building is the sculpture *Tommy Trojan*. This eight-foot-high warrior is supposed to look warlike; instead it is delightful camp. It was designed by Roger Noble Burnham and was dedicated in 1930.

3. Elizabeth Von Kleinsmid Hall (now **Student Administrative Services Building**), 1925
William Lee Woollett
A low brick complex which meanders over its site, similar in feeling to an English medieval collegiate building.

4. Law School Building (now **School of Social Work**), 1926
John and Donald Parkinson
Northern Italian Romanesque, with some excellent cast stone detailing around the windows and the main entrance.

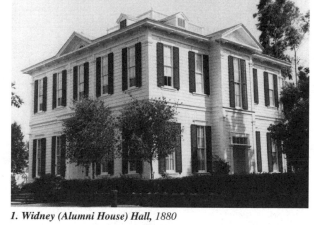

1. Widney (Alumni House) Hall, 1880

5. Gwynn Wilson Student Union Building, 1927–28
John and Donald Parkinson
This version of the northern Italian Romanesque exhibits a first floor treated as an enclosed loggia and two upper floors which are rich in cast-stone ornament. The southeast and the southwest corners of the building are particularly successful in their imaginative use of cast-stone ornament and low- and high-relief sculpture.

6. Physical Education Building, 1928
John and Donald Parkinson
The centerpiece of this northern Italian Romanesque design is the west entrance, with its single large arch and extensive use of cast-stone detailing.

7. Bridge Hall, 1928
John and Donald Parkinson
A four-story interpretation of the nave of a northern Italian Romanesque church.

8. Science Building, 1928
John and Donald Parkinson
A deep entrance passageway from the east leads through a pair of wrought-iron gates to a ceramic tile panel depicting four figures captivated by the world of science (by Jean Goodman, 1937).

9. Colonel Seeley Wintersmith Mudd Memorial Hall of Philosophy, 1928–29
Ralph C. Flewelling
The high campanile of this complex was the dominant vertical element of the campus until it was supplanted in 1966 by the Carillon Tower of the Von Kleinsmid Center. Though the Parkinson buildings are very good examples of the northern Italian Romanesque, they do not come up to the quality of the Lombardy Romanesque entailed in this design. Its high point is the cloisters at the east side of the building.

10. Methodist Episcopal University Church (now **United University Church**), 1931
C. Raimond Johnson
Another important, but often neglected, monument of the campus. One enters this northern Italian Romanesque church through a partial cloister situated on the southeast side of the building. The building's picturesque skyline is enlivened by a pair of buttress towers surmounted by twisted, cast-stone roofs.

11. Edward L. Doheny, Jr. Memorial Library, 1932
Cram and Ferguson (Ralph Adams Cram); Samuel Lunden
The Doheny Library is certainly the most

10. Methodist Episcopal University Church (now United University Church), 1931

luxuriant of the northern Italian Romanesque buildings on the USC campus. Cram modeled its design closely on the buildings which he and Bertram G. Goodhue had designed in 1910 for Rice University in Houston. The centerpiece of the building is the two-story-plus, square entrance hall with stained-glass windows. Other interior spaces are impressive, especially the reading rooms. The Library Building to the east and Bovard Hall to the west create the central open space of the campus with its fountain and planting of sycamores.

North of the Doheny Library, is the **Thomas and Dorothy Leavey Library,** completed in the late fall of 1993.

12. Harris Hall of Architecture and Fine Arts (including the Fisher Art Gallery), 1939
Ralph C. Flewelling

The architect sought to modernize both the vocabulary of the Italian Romanesque and that of the Beaux Arts, and he succeeded admirably. The brick and cast-stone walls and the scale of the building closely match his earlier Mudd Hall of Philosophy to the east. And the

rambling character of the building is admirably played against the more formal classical elements, such as the two splendid entrances on the south side of the building.

13. Alan Hancock Foundation and Memorial Museum, 1940
Cram and Ferguson; C. Raimond Johnson; Samuel E. Lunden

Although its scale is compatible with the older 1920s northern Italian Romanesque buildings around it, the four-story Hancock Building is in reality a version of the classical PWA Moderne. An abstracted portico is presented at the center of the west facade. The sculpture (by Merrell Gage) used around the building consists, as was so much the practice in the 1930s, of figures which float out in front of the wall surface. Do not miss the delightful group of animals and other forms (dominated by an elephant) cast into the exposed concrete wall of the auditorium on the north side of the building. Also see Alan Hitchcock's yacht sculptured above the south entrance door.

Within the Museum are rooms and the furnishings from the no-longer-standing Hancock house of 1907 (that stood on the corner of Wilshire Boulevard and Vermont Avenue). In addition, there are four rooms and their furnishings rescued from Empire Maximilian's Palace in Mexico City (which was demolished in 1936)

14. Faculty Center, 1960
Jones and Emmons

A modest, non-assertive design by one of L.A.'s important early modernists.

15. Ahmanson Center for Biological Research, 1964
William L. Pereira and Associates

The dominant note of these connected, boxlike, five- and six-story buildings is a surface pattern of cast-concrete hooded windows—the same on the north as well as on the south.

16. Registration Building, 1964
Ladd and Kelsey
A delicate pavilion set on a low podium which employs the Miesian post-and-beam system.

17. Von Kleinsmid Center of International and Public Affairs, 1966
Edward D. Stone Associates
The block of the campus which contains the Von Kleinsmid Center to the north, the Social Science Building in the center, and the Phillips Hall of Education (all by Edward D. Stone Associates) is the finest of the post-World War II group of buildings on the USC campus. The U-shaped Von Kleinsmid Center is composed of three low, rectangular volumes placed on a podium and surmounted by a projecting roof. A four-sided, concave-surfaced Carillon Tower is situated to one side of the courtyard. The brick work and the general exterior detailing enhance the polished feeling of the design.

18. Social Science Building, 1968
Edward D. Stone Associates
The square Social Science Building has been carefully sited and designed to be related to the Von Kleinsmid Center to the south and the tower of the Phillips Hall of Education to the north. The facade of the Social Science Building is arcaded, and the building looks out to the west upon a sunken courtyard with a central fountain.

19. Waite Phillips Hall of Education, 1968
Edward D. Stone Associates
The architect has articulated the four facades of his tower into thin, vertical, brick piers with narrow, intervening spandrels and windows. The building rises from a freestanding arcaded brick wall.

20. Ray and Nadine Watt Hall of Architecture and Fine Arts, 1973
Killingsworth, Brady, and Associates; Sam T. Hurst
A heavy, exposed concrete, savings and loan pavilion which does battle with the 1939 Harris Hall to the west (note that Harris Hall easily wins). The interior public areas of Watt Hall

22. Arnold Schoenberg Institute, 1978

convey a funereal atmosphere—a rather strange environment in which to educate future architects and artists.

21. Charlotte S. and Davre Davidson Conference Center, 1975
Edward D. Stone, Inc.
A characteristic Stone pavilion, with the east and west facades centering on a recessed, three-arch loggia. The building stands on a podium, its brick walls held in place by a thinly detailed projection roof. There is a handsome sunken garden to the south of the building.

22. Arnold Schoenberg Institute, 1978
Adrian Wilson and Associates
The Center is unquestionably an impressive piece of complex angular sculpture of exposed concrete walls and metal and glass windows and roofs. The whole composition is set above a really fine garden of ferns and trees.

23. Cinema-Television Center, 1983
A. Quincy Jones and Associates
Not one of A. Quincy Jones firm's great buildings; the well-developed landscape helps it.

24. Zohrab A. Kaprielian Hall, 1989
Abbott Marshall Partners
Post-Modern enters the USC campus.

VERNON, COMMERCE, HUNTINGTON PARK, SOUTH GATE, BELL, MAYWOOD

The southern section of the Los Angeles plain, west of the Los Angeles River, was the scene of extensive speculation during the great land boom of the 1880s. Some residential and commercial growth took place in the late 1880s and early 1890s, but basically the area was devoted to agriculture. The development of the communities of Vernon, Huntington Park, Maywood, Bell, and South Gate came after 1900. Huntington Park was incorporated in 1903, Vernon in 1905, and South Gate as late as 1923. In the teens and later, this section of Los Angeles County emerged as the industrial region of the basin, though it should be noted that the industrialization was accompanied by quite a bit of spec single-family housing. There are a few examples of turn-of-the-century housing to be found in Huntington Park, but almost all of the dwellings to be found today date from after 1920. These communities do contain several of L.A.'s major architectural monuments—the murals of **Farmer Johns, Watts Towers**, and several wonderful 1930s Streamline Moderne office and industrial buildings.

1. Pueblo del Rio Public Housing, 1941–42
   Paul R. Williams, Chief Architect; Adrian
   Wilson, Gordon B. Kaufmann, Wurdeman
   and Becket, Richard J. Neutra
   Ralph Cornell, landscape architect
   1801 E. 53rd Street, Vernon

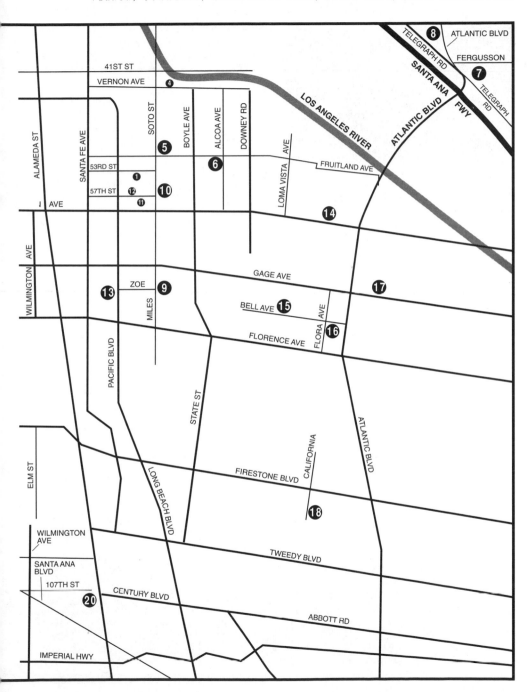

3. Hacienda Village, 1941–42

Pueblo del Rio still stands as a beautiful oasis within this section of Los Angeles. The grounds are well kept up, as are the buildings. This project consisted of fifty-seven two-story units placed on a 17.5 acre site within which the architect provided 400 living units. These brick and reinforced concrete buildings, with their horizontal banding of windows, walls, and roofs are mildly but not instantly Modern in style. As part of the project, individual garden plots and fruit trees were provided.

2. Avalon Gardens, 1941–42
Carleton M. Winslow, Chief Architect; Roland E. Coate; Samuel Lunden Katherine Bashford and Fred Barlow, landscape architects
Avalon Boulevard at 88th Place (south of Manchester Avenue)

Another of the city's well-preserved war-time housing projects. The successful approach to planning was stated in a 1942 article in the *Architect and Engineer:* "By planning the site as a whole there will be dwellings for one hundred and sixty families in sixty-two buildings, each placed at the proper angle to obtain the best exposure to the sun and each surrounded by generous open space of attractively landscaped gardens and recreation areas for children and adults."

Although the site is not large (14.9 acres), its design does realize these goals. Fourteen of these wood-frame buildings are two stories; the rest pose as California Ranch houses.

3. Hacienda Village, 1941–42,
Paul R. Williams, Chief Architect; Adrian Wilson, Richard J. Neutra, Walter Wurdeman and Welton Becket
1515 E. 105th Street. (103rd Street at Compton Boulevard)

Hacienda Village is in excellent condition, notwithstanding some half century of use. It is the most suburban of the public housing projects of these years. The site of 17.63 acres has 72 one-story buildings, which contain 184 units that convey the feeling of modest California Ranch houses of the late 1930s.

4. Farmer John's (Cloughtan Packing Company), 1953 and later
3049 E. Vernon Avenue, Vernon

Farmer John's expresses a high point in the use of painted illusionism to create its own world, despite what goes on within. Here you will find little pigs right out of an illustrated children's storybook romping along with nineteenth-century Tom Sawyer farm boys. The painted scenes continue along the fences, along the street walls of the buildings, and here and there the pigs become three-dimensional and climb onto or over the roofs. If you drive along Vernon Boulevard at thirty-five miles per hour,

4. Farmer John's (Cloughtan Packing Company), 1953 and later

the small boulevard trees become a part of the scene. The fences and walls were painted in this public-scaled *trompe l'oeil* by Leslie A. Grimes, and since his death (he fell from a scaffold while painting), they have been repainted by Arco Sign Company.

5. Owens-Illinois Pacific Building, 1937
H. H. Brunnier
Northeast corner of East Fruitland Avenue and South Soto Street, Vernon

As you would expect from this company, this is an ode to the glory of glass brick. Best of all is the Streamline Moderne corner bay. As with well-designed glass-brick walls, the ones on this building work well both in the day and at night.

6. Aluminum Company of America Building, 1938
Gordon B. Kaufmann
Southwest corner of Fruitland and Alcoa avenues, Vernon

Aluminum used as one of the new materials for Modern architecture. In style it is Streamline Moderne, except for the angular bay on the north side, which is reminiscent of the turn-of-the-century work in Glasgow of Charles Rennie Mackintosh. Be sure to see the lobby with its Moderne lights, and also the two cast-aluminum spandrels which depict the virtue of hard work.

7. East Los Angeles Union Pacific Railroad Passenger Station, 1928
Gilbert Stanley Underwood
Southeast corner Atlantic Boulevard and Ferguson Drive

The architect, Gilbert Stanley Underwood, designed a number of stations for the Union Pacific Railroad. The East Los Angeles Station was one of his late designs wherein he utilized the Spanish Colonial Revival style. The dual frontispieces of this hollow tile building were the two entrances, one facing the parking lot, the other the train platform. These convey in their cast-stone ornament a strong Mexican Churrigueresque feeling. Heavy ornate ironwork was used for window and door grills. Inside, the exposed wood-beam ceiling was sumptuously

7. East Los Angeles Union Pacific Railroad Passenger Station, 1928

stenciled and painted. At present the station is abandoned, and one can only hope that it will not only be preserved but also restored.

8. Lees Market Building, c. 1929
1247 Atlantic Boulevard

This narrow fronted two-story commercial building plays at being much larger by suggesting that it is composed of two side pavilions, enclosing a recessed center. Vertical pilasters climb up the front of the building, and then project beyond the parapet as finials.

9. Huntington Park Civic Center, 1945–51
Hugh R. Davies

East corner Miles Avenue and Zoe Avenue

Planning for the Civic Center started in 1939, but the occurrence of the Second World War stopped any activity. In 1947 Hugh R. Davies prepared a Spanish Colonial Revival scheme which organized the buildings around a courtyard. The principal point of interest in this plan was a large auditorium to the rear of the courtyard and a high domed Spanish tower to the south. Modifications of this scheme were made. The first unit built was the City Hall which was dedicated in December, 1947. Other buildings were added to the complex, including the 1951 Justice Building. Davies's tower in the courtyard was joined by an even larger tower placed to the front at the north end of the enclosing arched corridor. Other buildings were added,

9. Huntington Park Civic Center, 1945–51

following the architect's original scheme. The most important of these was the 1951 Justice Building. In 1970 the firm of Williamson and Norris turned (with only marginal success) to the imagery of late Modern for the Regional Library Building.

10. Lane-Wells Company Building (now **Winnie and Sutch Company**), 1938–39
    William E. Myer
    5610 S. Soto Street, Huntington Park
This and the adjoining buildings to the north (now **W. W. Henry Company**) represent one of L.A.'s really impressive Streamline Moderne buildings. "Rounded corners and three large continuous glass areas give the building a strong horizontal feeling, but the tall pylons provide interesting contrasts at the entrances," wrote the architect shortly after this reinforced concrete building was completed. Essentially, the buildings were placed in a parklike setting "so that when one enters the plant nothing

reminds him of manufacturing, for beautiful flowers and shrubs, well-kept grounds and distinctive buildings have removed the stigma of the old-fashioned factory."

11. Apartment Building,
    circa 1925
    2802 E. 57th Street,
    Huntington Park
A near-perfect solution (especially with the budget in mind) to bring history and fashion into an L.A. stucco box: Place a stucco-relief mission bell within a panel and then give a slight indication at the entrance of columns and an entablature. By magic it all becomes Mission Revival.

12. Cottage, circa 1889
    2735 E. 57th Street,
    Huntington Park
A spec Queen Anne cottage. Farther west on 57th Street at the southwest corner of Malabar Street, the bungalow court devotee will discover one which is attired in a Missionesque design.

13. Warner Brothers Theater, 1930
    B. Marcus Priteca
    6714 S. Pacific Boulevard,
    Huntington Park
An Art Deco (Zigzag) Moderne motion picture theater. The auditorium is still intact and has a multilayered ceiling and hidden lights.

14. Maywood City Hall, 1938
    Wilson, Merrill, and Alexander
    4319 E. Slauson Avenue, Maywood
A two-story PWA Streamline Moderne public building. If you look closely as you drive along Slauson Boulevard from Maywood west to Baldwin Hills, you will find the remains of a good number of late 1930s Streamline Moderne buildings.

15. Bell Avenue School (Corona School),
1935
Richard J. Neutra
3835 Bell Avenue, Bell
Neutra continued the early California tradition of the open-air school in this building. Each of the classrooms opens through sliding glass walls to its own enclosed out-of-doors court. An open exterior corridor runs along the other side, and high clerestory windows balance the interior light of the classrooms. This stucco and wood-frame building is an excellent example of pre-World War II High Art Modern.

16. Bell High School, 1935
Robert F. Train
Southeast corner of Bell and Flora avenues
This building, and especially its central section, is a characteristic example of the PWA Moderne in reinforced concrete.

17. Vicente Lugo Adobe (El Viejo Lugo Adobe), 1844
6360 E. Gage Avenue, Bell Gardens
An extensive, two-story Monterey adobe surrounded by a two-story wood-railed porch, and covered by a low-pitched, hipped roof, extended at a lower pitch over the porches. The Lugo Adobe indicates how universal the two-story Monterey adobe was in California. This adobe burned (1984). It will either be restored on the site or moved and restored.

18. South Gate Civic Center, 1941–42
William Allen and W. George Lutzi
Southeast corner California Avenue and Ardmore Avenue
Rather than use the prevailing Spanish Colonial style or that of the Art Deco, the architects and the community settled on a version of the Anglo Colonial Revival. When the building was dedicated the editors of the *Southwest Builder and Contractor* wrote, "The architectural style is a modified Georgian with a pitched roof, an imposing pediment at the main entrance and a graceful cupola surmounting the main section." The structure is of reinforced concrete, with the surface treated with a buff color. In the lobby are two murals by Frank Bowers. They depict the history of South Gate.

18. South Gate Civic Center, 1941–42

Within the porticoed entrance of the Civic Center Community Building (formerly the City Library) is a tile mosaic by Stanton McDonald Wright (1938). This mosaic was produced through the Federal Art Project, and the subject is "Evolution of Writing."

19. Watts Towers, 1921–45
Simon Rodia
1765 E. 107th Street, Watts
L.A.'s most notable contribution to the architecture of folk fantasy, accomplished on a grand scale, which fits the image of Los Angeles and Southern California. Broken tile, china, soda pop bottles, plaster, concrete, steel, and iron form the colorful lacework of these towers. Rodia said that he wished to do something big and memorable, and here it is: L.A.'s rival to Paris and its Eiffel Tower, and Barcelona and its Sagrada Familia Cathedral.

20. Dominguez Ranch House, 1826
18127 S. Alameda Street, Compton
The front of this house, as we see it today, is pure Mission Revival, circa 1910. The long, open corridor with its simple, square, wood posts and Greek Revival double-hung windows is characteristic of Spanish-Anglo adobes from the mid-1830s on.

21. Green Dog and Cat Hospital, circa 1936
1514 W. Slauson Avenue, Los Angeles
A sharp, angular, 1930s Moderne building which merges into a spectacular central tower-sign.

22. Bethlehem Baptist Church, 1944

22. Bethlehem Baptist Church, 1944
R. M. Schindler
4900 S. Compton Avenue, Los Angeles

This is Schindler's only built church, and it is a must to see, although it is not in the best condition. The street front on busy Compton Avenue is composed of a series of wide overlapping stucco bands, closing off the main building effectively from the street and its noises. The principal natural light for the auditorium is introduced by skylights placed at the base of the cruciform tower.

23. Thomas Jefferson High School, 1936
Stiles O. Clements
319 E. 41st Street, Los Angeles

Here is monumental PWA Streamline Moderne at its best. Horizontality asserts itself everywhere via moldings, bands of windows, and horizontal fins. The tour de force is the concave wall of the entrance with its band of dramatic lettering.

24. Root Beer Barrel Restaurant, circa 1932
1000 E. Slauson Avenue

A drive-in restaurant in the form of the container of its product.

23. Thomas Jefferson High School, 1936

HIGHLAND PARK

This community, still discernible in spite of merging with Los Angeles, was once one of the famous "suburbs in search of a city." Situated on the road to Pasadena (Figueroa Street in this area was once Pasadena Avenue), it was perhaps the first of the suburbs. By the turn of the century it had many fine homes and even exhibited a high cultural tone—Charles Fletcher Lummis, William Lees Judson, Clyde Browne, Mary Austin, and other luminaries lived there. It was the home of Occidental College until 1914. It must also be noted that near what is now Sycamore Grove Park was one of the most notorious red-light districts in Los Angeles County.

No more! The Sycamore Grove area, once the site of many dalliances, is now quite respectable. Occidental College flourishes today in nearby Eagle Rock. Most of the artists are gone (many younger ones are on Mount Washington nearby), as are most of the Victorian houses (one of them moved across the Arroyo Seco to Heritage Square). A sad note: the pre-Columbian Revival buildings that once composed Luther Burbank Junior High School have been leveled.

But do not despair. Much fascinating material remains.

1. Robert Williams House (now **Hathaway Home for Children**), circa 1905
Train and Williams
840 Avenue 66
A huge, boulder-based, Craftsman piece, now painted but having some good interiors including a stair-hall with a large panel of stained glass designed by Judson Studios. Train and Williams's work was featured in the one and only issue of the *Arroyo Craftsman* (October, 1909).

3. Bungalow, circa 1905

2. McClure House, 1889
James H. Bradbeer
432 Avenue 66
Queen Anne, Eastlake, and Italianate styles have been merged here. The house has been altered but it still shows what the architect intended.

3. Bungalow, circa 1905
201 Avenue 66
This is a true California bungalow, with strong Swiss Chalet influence and even a little Orientalism in its slightly upswept eaves. The vertical board and batten siding suggests the early date.

4. Judson Studios, 1901
200 Avenue 66
Originally, before the roof burned off in 1910, this was a three-story building in Islamic Revival style. It was the home of the Los Angeles College of Fine Arts founded by William Lees Judson, a prominent regional painter who came to the area in 1893. When the College became a part of the University of Southern California, the building was converted into a Guild Hall for the Arroyo Guild of Fellow

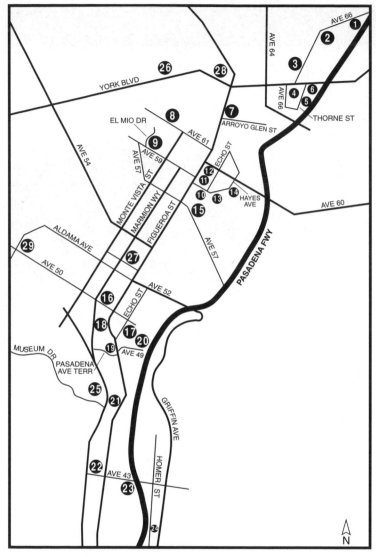

5. Judson House, circa 1895
William Lees Judson
216 Thorne Street
Judson's interpretation of the Shingle style is a real curiosity.

6. Fargo House, 1908
Harry Grey
206 Thorne Street
The elevation is remarkably similar to a number of designs by the Greenes. The house is most picturesque viewed from the Pasadena Freeway behind it.

7. Abbey San Encino, 1909–25
Clyde Browne
6211 Arroyo Glen Street
A miniaturized stone abbey which reads as a child's medieval castle. Browne was a printer who, like his hero William Morris, collected the literati of the area in his living room. The house begins with Mission Revival and ends with Spanish Colonial.

Craftsmen, a group of workers inspired by Judson and George Wharton James, an editor of *The Craftsman,* to emulate William Morris and Gustav Stickley. Note the logo of the Guild, an arm and hammer and the motto "We Can" over the entrance. Still later it became the Judson Studios, the "Tiffany of the West," fabricating fine art glass—as it still does.

8. Bungalow Court, circa 1915
337 Avenue 61
Big, independent units along the court with a two-story duplex at the end. A Craftsman ensemble with Oriental flourishes.

9. House, 1890
5905 El Mio Drive at Avenue 59
A Queen Anne mansion with a great view in every direction.

10. Yoakum House, circa 1900
140–145 Avenue 59
Rather rare Tudor Revival.

11. House, circa 1905
5903 Echo Street at northwest corner of Avenue 59
Colonial Revival.

12. House, circa 1910
5915 Echo Street
Colonial Revival again but this time made Californian with Islamic arches!

13. Duplex, circa 1900
5960–5962 Hayes Avenue
Mission Revival with holly leaves in leaded glass.

14. House, circa 1895
6028 Hayes Avenue
A one-story Queen Anne reminiscent of some of the simpler southern plantation houses.

15. Ebell Club, 1912
Sumner Hunt and Silas Burns
127 Avenue 57
Ever since this building was constructed it has been the civic, educational, and social center of Highland Park. The style is Mission Revival with Italianate brackets, but the broad overhanging eaves suggest the Midwestern Prairie style.

16. Hall of Letters, 1904–5
G. A. Howard, Jr.
Old Campus, Occidental College
Northwest corner of Figueroa Street and Avenue 50
In this red brick, now nondescript but once vaguely French Renaissance building, Robinson Jeffers studied English literature. Incidentally, the architect was the son of the Chairman of the Occidental Board of Trustees.

17. Three Duplexes, circa 1900
Echo Street at southeast corner of Avenue 50

Exactly alike, the adjoining buildings resemble Neo-Classical city houses of 1870s London.

18. Professor's Row, 1911–12
Milwaukee Building Company (Meyer and Holler)
4967–4985 Figueroa Street
Until recently there were five of these excellent Craftsman houses in the manner Gustav Stickley would have approved (there are now only three left). They were all supposedly built for professors at the nearby old campus of Occidental College.

19. Hiner House and Sousa Nook, 1922
Archibald Dixon Pechey
4757 Figueroa Street at Pasadena Avenue Terrace
This was the house of Edwin M. Hiner, the director of the most popular brass band in the Los Angeles area. He founded the music department at the old Los Angeles Normal School, now UCLA. The Tudor house done in boulders is unusual. The nook is more conventional Craftsman bungalow style, but John Philip Sousa slept here!

20. Bent House, circa 1909
Hunt, Eager, and Burns
End of Avenue 49 next to Pasadena Freeway
Another (but very different) flat-roofed Craftsman/Tudor house whose picturesque oak and boulder-strewn garden once wandered down into the Arroyo Seco.

21. "Casa de Adobe," 1917
Theodore Eisen
4603 N. Figueroa Street
An interesting effort (because it is early) to re-create an authentic hacienda of the Spanish-Mexican period. It is, in spite of a few modernisms, completely successful. It houses a museum of materials from the late Mexican and early Anglo periods in Los Angeles history and is administered by the Southwest Museum on the hill above it.

24. Heritage Square

22. Mount Washington Cable Car Station,
1909
Fred R. Dorn
200 West Avenue 43

A small Mission Revival building that housed a waiting room for people riding the funicular railway to their homes on Mount Washington. The operation was closed down in 1919, apparently a victim of the automobile.

23. Lummis House ("El Alisal"), 1895–1910
Sumner Hunt and Theodore Eisen; Charles F. Lummis
200 East Avenue 43

Lummis, a graduate of Harvard who had taken courses from Charles Eliot Norton, an authority on the Greek culture, a friend of Ruskin and first president of the Boston Society of Arts and Crafts, built this house of boulders from the Arroyo and named it for the huge sycamore in the patio. Little of the original furniture exists, but there is a great deal about the place that evokes the presence of this amazing man whom his friend Charles Keeler called "William Morris turned into a [New] Mexican Indian."

Lummis was the founder of the Southwest Museum, one of the important repositories of Native American art in the United States. You can see Lummis's admiration of the Indian culture in the magnificent pottery that was left after the 1971 earthquake dashed most of his personal collection to pieces and also in the lantern slides fixed in one window showing Indian dances. The doors and some built-in furniture were designed by Maynard Dixon, as was the magnificent hardware on the main door on the garden side. And there is even an Art Nouveau fireplace designed by Charles Walter Stetson, a prominent painter and an important figure in the local Arts and Crafts movement. Be sure to notice the Mission-style gable on the dining room wing with a bell given to Lummis by the King of Spain. This reminds us that, among his many other contributions to the culture of Southern California, Lummis founded (1894) the California Landmarks Club that, in its efforts to save the California missions, was one of the first preservation organizations in the United States.

24. Heritage Square
End of Homer Street, south of Avenue 43
(Pasadena Freeway off-ramp)

Whatever you may think of such projects, it is quite clear that none of the buildings moved here in the last two decades would exist if some enterprising people had not decided to do something about retaining these disjointed shards of the Victorian culture. Ruskinian purists in preservation do not like to see buildings moved from sites to which they were meant to relate (in some cases). But what do you do when buildings of the obvious quality of these are being vandalized and would otherwise be demolished? The obvious solution: move them. And it may be significant for the image of Los Angeles that two of these buildings had been moved before—one of them twice! The site has been described as "a freeway-isolated arroyo littoral" (Nathan Weinberg, *Preservation in American Towns and Cities,* p. 63). It is not ideal, but with landscaping the problems of the site are being diminished. And then it has the advantage that you can take it all in as you travel on the Pasadena Freeway.

Listed from north to south:

a. Palms Railroad Station, circa 1886
An Eastlake building brought from Palms near Century City.

b. Perry House ("Mount Pleasant"), 1876
Ezra F. Kysor
An Italian villa being restored by the Colonial Dames. Probably it was the finest house in Los Angeles when it was built by William Hayes Perry in Boyle Heights.

c. Hale ("C. M.") House, circa 1885
W. F. Norton
Queen Anne proportions with Eastlake and Queen Anne details. Restoration is almost complete inside and outside. Although named for the Hale family that was its longest resident, high in the front gable are the letters "C. M." carved in a shield, the initials of Charles Morgan, the original owner.

d. Shaw ("Valley Knudson Memorial") House, circa 1877
A French Second Empire (Mansard) cottage built originally for Richard E. Shaw in East Los Angeles. The restoration has been liberally endowed by the Bel Air Garden Club of which Mrs. Knudsen was a founder and president.

e. Ford ("Beaudry Street") House, circa 1885
Queen Anne, Eastlake, and Italianate mixed. But the style is not so important as the elaborate decoration on such a small house. The first owner, John J. Ford, was a wood carver of extraordinary imagination and talent. The house was moved from Beaudry Street where a computer center now stands.

f. Lincoln Avenue Methodist Church, 1898–99
George W. Kramer; W. A. Benshoff, supervising architect
Moved from Pasadena to make way for a new and strikingly hideous post office, this is a good Eastlake Gothic building that will make a good meeting place at the Square. The door, with its pilasters and pediment, is at the corner suggesting that the interior is laid out on the famous Methodist "Akron Plan"—the pulpit at the opposite corner with the pews in arcs around it.

24f. Lincoln Avenue Methodist Church, 1898–99

25. Entrance, Southwest Museum, 1919

g. Longfellow-Hastings (Octagonal House), 1893

Before being moved to Heritage Square, this house was situated on South Allen Avenue in Pasadena (where it had been moved from a previous site). The Longfellow-Hastings house is closely modeled after the octagonal designs published in the mid-nineteenth century by the phrenologist O. S. Fowler in his often published *A Home for All or the Gravel Wall and Octagonal Mode of Building.* The nationwide rage for the octagonal house was in the 1850s and early 1860s. California came late on the scene and only a few were built in the north and south. The Longfellow-Hastings House is the only example still standing in the southland. Its interior with the central staircase lighted by the cupola is fascinating. The house is currently under restoration, and the surrounding porches and other details will be returned to their original locations.

25. Southwest Museum, 1910–14, and later
   Sumner Hunt and Silas R. Burns
   Northwest corner of Museum Drive and
   Marmion Way

A monument of the Mission Revival with definite references to the siting and exterior of the Alhambra and its hilltop site. This building houses a fine collection of Native American art. Its specialty is, of course, Southwestern, but there are some excellent California, Plains, and Alaskan things. One of the thrills of visiting the museum is to enter through the 1919 **Mayan Entrance** (Hunt and Burns) at the base of the hill, and then proceed through a 240-foot-long tunnel lined with dioramas to an elevator, which after 108 feet brings you to the building on the hilltop. Nowadays, you drive up the steep road to the top of the hill.

26. Northeast Police Station, 1925
   City of Los Angeles Building Department
   6045 York Boulevard

A buff-colored brick building in the Beaux Arts style, too sophisticated, perhaps, for its surroundings.

27. Morrell House, 1906
   Charles E. Shattuck
   215 North Avenue 53

A handsome brick Arts and Crafts bungalow. It was illustrated and discussed in *The Craftsman* magazine in 1909.

28. Arroyo Seco Bank Building, 1926
   Austin and Ashley
   6301 North Figueroa Street

A rather odd interpretation of Beaux Arts classicism, with an elegant Churrigueresque entrance situated at the corner.

29. Aldama Apartments, 1961
   A. E. Morris
   5030–5038 Aldama Avenue near
   Avenue 50

These stepped stucco boxes clinging to the hill evoke the spirit of Schindler's apartment houses of the 1920s and 1930s but are more openly mannered than their ancestors.

MOUNT WASHINGTON

Artists' nests abound in this area above Highland Park and the real world. When you get to the top of San Rafael Avenue, you realize that Mount Washington was invaded in the early twentieth century and people have been building ever since. It is said that Mount Washington is above the smog. Not true. But it does, in spite of the winding streets, give a sense of neighborhood as few places in Southern California do. Incidentally, we are sorry that Jack Smith's house cannot be viewed properly, and we have thus been forced to leave out this fabled structure. Perhaps it is best left to legend.

1. Elmer and Marion Cavanaugh Wachtel House and Studio, 1906
Elmer Wachtel
315 West
Avenue 43
A pleasant Arts and Crafts cottage that is remarkable because it was the home of two excellent *plein air* painters. The interior, all paneled in wood, is very fine.

2. Birtcher-Share House, 1942
Harwell H. Harris
4234 Seaview Lane (between Seaview Drive and Seaview Avenue)
Influenced by Wright's Usonian houses, Harris

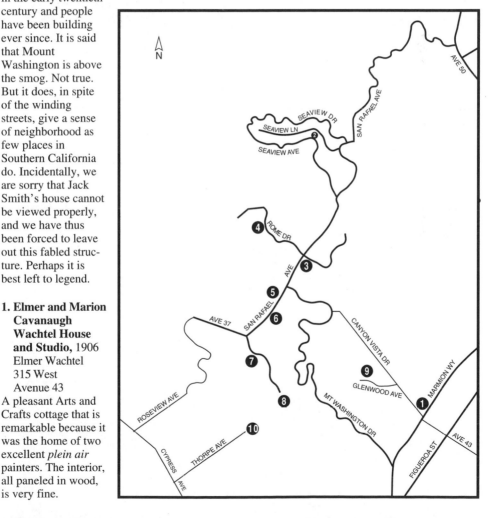

nevertheless seems to straighten the Master out. This large, one-story wood house is one of his masterpieces. Another small view of it can be obtained from Seaview Avenue unless the bushes have grown too high.

3. Hinds House, 1947
  Richard J. Neutra
  3941 San Rafael Avenue
Yes, you can see the house if you get out of your car. The number is on the lower part of the small cliff. It is one of Neutra's few wood-sheathed houses.

4. Mauer House, 1949
  John Lautner
  932 Rome Drive
Subdued for this architect, the derivation from Frank Lloyd Wright's Usonian houses of the 1930s is clear.

5. House, circa 1910
  3855 San Rafael Avenue
A great Mission Revival structure with massive columns. While here you will want to look at the large house across the street now owned by the Vedanta Society. Although big, it is not distinguished architecture.

6. House, circa 1925
  3820 San Rafael Avenue
An adobe structure with adobe wall and gate. In spite of its late date it is much more convincing than most of the nineteenth-century adobes. Across the street is a good Craftsman house often attributed to the Greenes but apparently mistakenly.

7. Byler House, 1937
  Gregory Ain
  914 Avenue 37
Vertical boards stained brown and looking very Craftsman. It is amazing how many Ain houses have weathered the years and come out looking as if they were brand new. The architect must have satisfied the owners.

8. House, 1941
  Raphael S. Soriano
  End of Avenue 37
This is a big, unfinished house which is impressive here but even more impressive from the Golden State Freeway far below.

9. Williams House, 1948
  Smith and Williams
  4211 Glenwood Avenue
From the street this house is a simple box with huge protruding eaves.

10. Jeffries House, circa 1905
  End of Thorpe Avenue east of Cypress
  Avenue
It is significant that Jim Jeffries, the famous pugilist, would build a refined Classical Revival house as his ideal in life. Ah, that someone would see his intelligence and restore it!

EAGLE ROCK

When Occidental College moved from Highland Park to Eagle Rock in 1914, the town was a crossroads whose only other real ornament was a huge rock with a naturally-formed image of a spread-winged eagle on its face. The rock and the area around it had been a significant Indian site at the beginning of the nineteenth century and earlier. Later it was a favorite picnic site for city folk who rode the old trolley line out Figueroa Street.

In the 1920s the town grew, as is evidenced by the thousands of bungalows that cover the

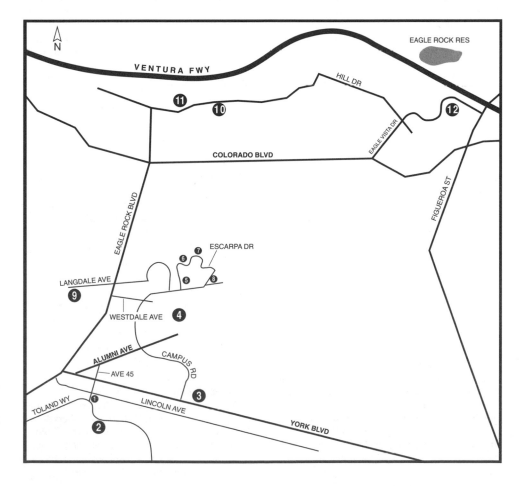

land between Glendale and Pasadena. Few of these small dwellings have claims to aesthetic significance, but as a whole they signify a pleasant and respectable way of life in the American tradition of single-family housing. More expensive houses were erected on the hills, but again the architectural talent displayed is not outstanding. Two Schindler houses, the Lowe House #1 (1923), and the Lowe House #2 (1937), were demolished when the Ventura Freeway was constructed. The old buildings that stood at the corners of Colorado and Eagle Rock boulevards, and that once gave a kind of Midwestern charm to the place, have been demolished or remodeled beyond recognition. Eagle Rock Boulevard has somehow managed to become even more hideous than it was when our first architectural guide came out.

1. Sparkletts Drinking Water Corporation, 1925–29
   Attributed to a "Mr. King"
   4500 Lincoln Avenue
A mosque of the first water. Unfortunately the 1971 earthquake so shook its minarets that they had to be removed.

2. Kapin House, 1935
   George Kapin
   4512 Toland Way
Situated above the Sparkletts plant, this house seems to be related to it.

3. Motels R Us, 1983
   4855 York Boulevard
This building defies all canons of taste and must be mentioned for its sheer horror, impossible to experience in black and white.

4. Occidental College, 1911–13
   Myron Hunt
   Beatrix Farrand, landscape architect
   1600 Campus Road
The architecture of the college contrasts sharply with that of the community. It seems, in spite of its many tile-roofed buildings, to have been transplanted from New England, so orderly and understated is its campus style, a kind of regionalized Palladianism. Jarring intrusions, such as the chapel, are all the more irritating because of the overall unity throughout the

campus that was achieved by hiring Myron Hunt and H. C. Chambers to design almost all the buildings right up to the mid-1930s.

We have listed only the most interesting buildings:

a. Swan, Johnson, and Fowler halls, 1914
   Myron Hunt
   These buildings were the college until a modest flurry of building in the 1920s transformed the campus. Indeed, they set the tone for future building. Hunt originally designed a columned hall to connect Johnson and Fowler, but this part of his plan was never carried out. In 1968 the **Coons Administrative Center,** designed by William Pereira Associates, was placed where Hunt envisioned a colonnade. Most of the building is invisible but not quite underground. The second level is almost entirely sheathed in glass so that it has, perhaps unkindly, been dubbed "the Chrysler Showroom."

b. Clapp Library, 1924
   Myron Hunt and H. C. Chambers
   Extensions at each side of the original tiny Mediterranean-style building doubled its size in 1954. Then in 1969 an addition in "State College Modern" was made by Neptune and Thomas, again doubling the size of the building. Except for the fact that the old book stacks are separated from the new ones, the entire building functions well.

c. Herrick Chapel, 1964
   Ladd and Kelsey
   Distinguished by its slip-form concrete construction—marvelous to view when construction was underway but unremarkable when finished—and its magnificent stained-glass windows by Perli Pelzig.

d. Freeman Union, 1928
   Myron Hunt and H. C. Chambers
   The charming, double-arcaded entrance patio is good for dancing. In 1956 Chambers and Hubbard added a large extension to the old building. The extension is efficient but not charming. It is currently planned that the building will be recycled and enlarged by

Brenda Levin Associates. Levin will also be restoring Myron Hunt's Art Barn (originally the Women's Gymnasium), as an annex of the student union.

e. Thorne Hall (Auditorium), 1938
Myron Hunt and H. C. Chambers
The last of Hunt's major designs for Occidental. The incidents surrounding its construction figure prominently in Aldous Huxley's *After Many a Summer Dies the Swan,* in which Occidental is "Tarzana College." The firm of Brenda Levin Associates has extensively refurbished this building, continuing an Occidental tradition of revamping and reusing the twenty-two original Myron Hunt buildings rather than destroying them.

f. Booth Music-Speech Center, 1929
Myron Hunt and H. C. Chambers
The old building comprises studios and a small recital hall around an arcaded court. A large classroom, office, and theater addition was made by Charles Luckman Associates in 1960. Brenda Levin has recently remodeled this building to house the Education Department and a new Music Library.

g. Orr Hall (now Weingart Center for the Arts), 1925
Myron Hunt and H. C. Chambers
Originally built as the first women's dormitory on the campus, it is also one of the loveliest of Hunt's buildings. Unfortunately it was discovered to have serious seismic problems. It was completely gutted and its walls were reinforced (under the supervision of the architectural firm of Neptune and Thomas). It now houses the Art Department and the offices of the Core Curriculum.

h. Erdman Hall, 1927
Myron Hunt and H. C. Chambers
Another example of civilized student housing.

i. Faculty Club (originally **President's House**), 1922
Myron Hunt and H. C. Chambers
Eastern Colonial Revival at its best.

j. Dean of Students' (now **Advising Center**) **House,** 1951
Smith and Williams
Unassuming rationality with a hint of Orientalism.

k. Comptroller's House (now **Public Policy Center**), 1932
Myron Hunt and H. C. Chambers
Monterey style. Well planned for entertaining.

l. Dean of the Faculty House (now **Alumni Center**), 1932
Myron Hunt and H. C. Chambers
Monterey Revival again, bigger than the Dean's House but not so well planned—or seen.

m. Bird Hillside Theater, 1925
Myron Hunt and H. C. Chambers
Very Greek, this amphitheater is used for commencement exercises, recreation, and excellent summer drama. A beautiful place to watch the sun set through eucalyptus trees.

n. Norris Residence Hall, 1966
Pereira and Associates
Bay Area style plastered on Harvard-inspired clustered apartments around stairs. The scale is too small for active students.

o. Keck Theater, 1987–88
Kamnitzer and Cotton
After experimenting with the Modernist Movement in the 1950s, 1960s, and 1970s the college, like many institutions, adopted the contextual approach in the 1980s Kamnitzer has made a strong statement placing the apse of a Spanish church over the volume of the auditorium—red tile roof and all. If you think that the exterior is too Brutal, go inside. The architect has treated the theater as a rococo hall worthy of staging a Mozart opera. It all cost a great deal of money and even agony to build, but it is simply a lovely place, without doubt acoustically and aesthetically one of the finest modern theaters in the city.

12. Eagle Rock Playground Clubhouse, 1953

5. Chambers House, 1923
    2068 Escarpa Drive
The Chambers were enthusiasts for American Indian designs and thus had their house built in the style of the Pueblo Revival. A Hopi symbol for happiness is used again and again in details as well as in the floor plan.

6. Martin House, 1966
    Donald Martin
    2039 Escarpa Drive
Designed by the architect for his parents, this house shows the influence of Richard J. Neutra.

7. Four Houses, 1962–68
    Oakley Norton
    2003, 2009, and 2026 Escarpa Drive
These neo-Craftsman houses cling to the hill for a view of Mount Verdugo and, though they didn't ask for it, the Ventura Freeway.

8. Paxson House, 1971
    Buff and Hensman (Conrad Buff)
    1911 Campus Road
The Craftsman tradition revived.

9. Mason House, 1916
    2434 Langdale Avenue
This house has often been attributed to Irving J. Gill although few of the details suggest his work.

10. House, circa 1925
    2403 Hill Drive
Hill Drive has some very good Spanish Colonial Revival houses. This is one of the best.

11. Brauch House, 1923
    Egasse and Brauch (J. L. Egasse)
    2327 Hill Drive
The general impression is medieval (of some sort) until you see the drooping swags of stucco at the point of the front gable. Hansel and Gretel appear. The architects said of his house that "In this particular instance, Norman lines, such as were left by the descendants of the Vikings, following their peregrination of an ante-medieval period, were the main source of inspiration." (*California Southland,* Dec., 1923). A double stone archway (one for people, one for autos) provides entrance to the garden. As one ascends the hill, one passes through a series of arches leading to the front terrace.

12. Eagle Rock Playground Clubhouse, 1953
    Richard J. Neutra and Associates (Dion Neutra)
    1100 Eagle Vista Drive
A Neutra house enlarged, an unexpected International Style Modern building in this area.

LINCOLN HEIGHTS

ortheast Los Angeles is now bisected by the east/west San Bernardino Freeway and the north/south Golden State Freeway. The section west of the Golden State Freeway is industrial/railroad, with some modest residential sections to the north. There is a smattering of modest late nineteenth-century Queen Anne cottages and houses still standing in and around Workman and Griffin streets. Equally nineteenth century in feeling is Lincoln Park with its small lake. Lincoln Park (or as it was then called East Lake Park) contains a conservatory building designed in 1913 by Franklin M. Small of New York, with Walter Webber being the resident architect. The major visible monument in the Mission Road area is the Los Angeles County

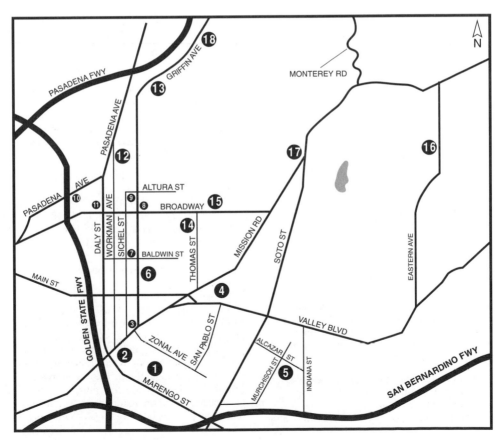

5. Ramona Gardens Public Housing, 1940–41

Hospital, but the real architectural gem is Ernest Coxhead's Epiphany Chapel of 1888–89.

1. Los Angeles County/USC Medical Center,
1928–33 and later
Allied Architects of Los Angeles: Edwin Bergstom, Myron Hunt, Pierpont Davis, Sumner P. Hunt, and William Richards
1200 N. State Street

The twenty-story central concrete-and-steel unit of the hospital has remained as the landmark in eastern Los Angeles. Its basic form is PWA monumental Moderne—with more than a slight hint of the influence of Bertram G. Goodhue. Its design of sculptural volumes and heavy arches slightly suggests early Romanesque. High relief sculpture on a grand scale adorns the major entrance from the west. This entrance, which is still partially preserved, has an axial walkway and garden leading up to the building. Not much can be said of the many later additions to the building except that they look as if they were put up quickly and cheaply (which they probably were not).

2. Administration Building, Los Angeles County Hospital, circa 1912
1100 N. Mission Road
An Austrian/German Secessionist design in the classical manner. The center of the building exhibits a low dome.

3. University of Southern California School of Medicine, Administration Building,
circa 1920
Northwest corner of Mission Road and Griffith Avenue

The rows of arches, stucco walls, and the Mission bells leave no one in doubt that this is a Mission Revival Building, though when we look closer we will find that the low tower is in fact Spanish Colonial Revival. The arcade to the north of the building (with Mission bells) is a freestanding wall—really a screen which encloses a small garden.

4. Lincoln Park (formerly East Lake Park),
1874
East corner of Mission Road and Valley Boulevard

This forty-five-acre park contains a picturesque lake (man-made, of course) and until recently a wonderful carousel (which burned). The park's first carousel now resides in Golden Gate Park in San Francisco. In the late nineteenth century and through the early years of the twentieth century, the park was widely known for its exotic planting, its ostrich farm, and its alligator farm. Alas, it is all quite tame nowadays.

5. Ramona Gardens Public Housing,
1940–41
George G. Adams, Walter S. Davis, Ralph C. Flewelling, Eugene Weston, Jr., Lewis Eugene Weston, and Lloyd Wright
Katherine Bashford and Fred Barlow, Jr., landscape architects
Between Alcazar, Murchison, and Indiana streets

In this public housing project, 102 concrete units of two stories provide 610 living units on a thirty-two-acre site. The hilly location of the project with its meandering streets seems well planned. The housing units themselves are simple and straightforward, with a minimal sense of architecture about them. The contemporary (of the last twenty years) wall murals which have been painted on a number of the housing units may perhaps be ideologically satisfying,

but they add little to the
homelike atmosphere of
the project.

6. House, circa 1890
   2054 Griffin Avenue
A modest two-story Queen
Anne (most likely spec)
dwelling.

**7. Sacred Heart Roman
   Catholic Church,**
   circa 1900
   2210 Sichel Street
A late Victorian Gothic
brick church, with a traditional square corner tower
but without its original
high spire.

10. Engine Company No. 1 Fire Station, 1940

8. Federal Bank Building
   (now **El Pollo Loco
   Restaurant),** 1910
   Otto Neher and C. F. Skilling
   2201 N. Broadway
A V-shaped building with a semi-circular pavilion where the angled streets come together. The
public banking room is covered by a delightful,
quite small glass dome. In August 1993, **El
Pollo Loco Restaurant** opened in this building, the first example in Los Angeles of a fast-
food restaurant opening in an important
landmark building. It looks great, both inside
and out.

9. Epiphany Chapel, 1888–89
   Ernest Coxhead
   2808 Altura Street (Southeast corner of
   Sichel and Altura streets)
The small gable-roofed chapel to the left is a
really fine, small Coxhead design. Low stone
walls support a slightly projecting single gable
with an overscaled round window. As usual,
Coxhead maneuvers the shingles across the surface in a highly original fashion. The building
has most fortunately been recently restored.
The rest of the church complex, including the
Sanctuary (now much remodeled), was
designed by Arthur B. Benton in 1913.

10. Engine Company No. 1 Fire Station, 1940
   2230 Pasadena Avenue
A Streamline Moderne design, its rear more
Modern than Moderne. The street elevation of
this two-story building comes close to being
pure two-dimensional design, with the windows
and entrance door as an L-shaped form articulated in the lower section with horizontal fins,
the lettering treated as a horizontal line, and
then the two fire truck entrances as two deep
rectangles.

**11. Department of Water and Power
   Building,** circa 1937
   S. Charles Lee
   2417 Daly Street
Regency Moderne. The slightly convex facade
of glass suggests the product which this public
department sells. The marquee with its projecting letters can be seen best at night when the
glass behind is lighted.

12. Cottage, circa 1889
   2652 Workman Avenue
A well-preserved Queen Anne cottage. The
gable end over the front bay and the entrance
porch are decorated with sawed relief work.

13. House, circa 1890
  Attributed to Joseph Cather Newsom
  3537 Griffin Avenue
A two-story Queen Anne dwelling with a number of sharp angular Eastlake details in wood. Especially unusual is the double-gabled dormer on the third floor.

14. Sturgis House, 1889–90
  Ernest Coxhead
  2345 Thomas Street
One suspects that this design is supposed to evoke the feeling of the Anglo Colonial Revival. As with a good number of Coxhead's designs of the 1890s, the Sturgis House seems to be a composition of architectural fragments, each of which strongly stands on its own. The street elevation of the entrance porch sits as a screen with its paired columns and independent entablature. Above, the arched opening of the small second floor porch contrasts with the pair of high, vertical, transomed windows to the side.

15. Abraham Lincoln High School, 1937–38
  Albert C. Martin
  3501 N. Broadway
A formal axis leads up from the street. The concrete buildings fit within the PWA Moderne, but in their scale, and some of their details, they point to the Spanish Colonial Revival.

16. Farmdale School Building, 1889
  2839 N. Eastern Avenue (at the rear of the
  school grounds)
An unusually elaborate Queen Anne Revival-style schoolhouse with a large, open, square bell tower.

17. Lunch Pail Restaurant Building,
  circa 1930
  4067 Mission Road
A small fast-food restaurant which suggests a pail with perhaps a milk bottle on top.

18. Group of Spec Bungalows, circa 1910
  4000 block of Griffin Avenue
This group of spec Craftsman bungalows provides an excellent glimpse of what many of the residential streets of Los Angeles looked like by the mid-teens.

One of the oldest suburbs of Los Angeles, this town was set out (1873) in five- to ten-acre lots by Benjamin D. Wilson (who later became mayor of Los Angeles) between the Arroyo San Pasqual and the Old Mill Wash. He called it Alhambra because his wife was rather belatedly reading Washington Irving's *Tales of the Alhambra.* The shrewd land speculator had found a theme and named the streets after incidents and characters in the romance. The present Main Street was, for instance, called Boabdil for the last king of Granada, who wept as he surveyed his beloved city seized from him by Ferdinand and Isabella in 1492. The name was soon changed because the residents found it impossible to pronounce. Unfortunately, almost every evidence of the world of Don Benito has been erased, some fairly recently. As usual, most of the old buildings were situated in the town center where urban renewal, early and late, got them.

The main commercial street dates from the 1950s with a little decoration from the 1920s interspersed. The local urban conservationists have wisely decided to restore each building to its original state, even if it has the fifties blahs. A strong element in the design of the entrances to these buildings is often a terrazzo floor, sometimes elaborately designed in pastels. Alhambra has other good things, some on the outskirts. Unfortunately one of Alhambra's gems, the 1907 Japanesque Cajal house, has been demolished.

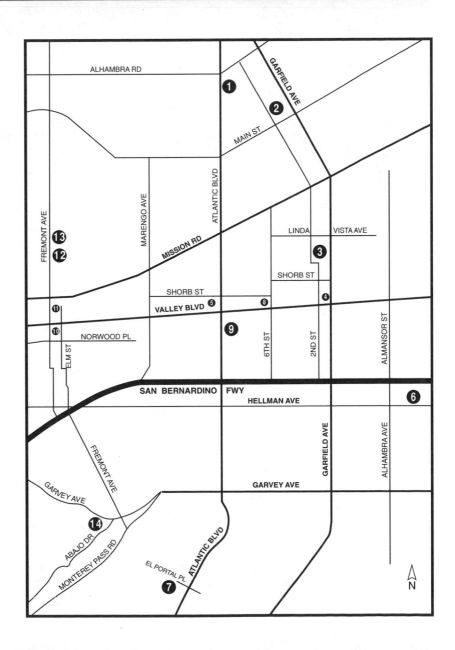

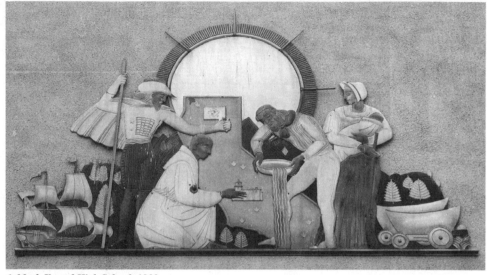

6. Mark Keppel High School, 1939

1. Descanso Court, circa 1915
   509 Atlantic Boulevard
Eight Oriental bungalow units.

2. Alhambra Women's Club, circa 1910
   204 S. Second Street
A good Craftsman building with interiors
intact.

3. House, circa 1937
   Southeast corner of Second Street and Linda
   Vista Avenue
A Streamline Moderne structure—a ship's
bridge sailing into Second Street.

4. Service Station, circa 1938
   Northwest corner of Valley Boulevard and
   Garfield Avenue
This is bigger than the last entry, but the inspi-
ration is the same Streamline Moderne.

5. "Crawford's Corner" Shopping Center,
   circa 1965
   Northwest corner of Valley and Atlantic
   boulevards
Victoriana again raises its head.

6. Mark Keppel High School, 1939
   Marston and Maybury
   501 E. Hellman Avenue
A huge Streamline Moderne structure. The
brick base is vaguely pre-Columbian while still
being Moderne. The high point of the design is
the monolithic curved corner auditorium which
contains two stainless steel and enamel murals
by Millard Sheets. One panel depicts the early
history of California; the other contains a map
of California.

7. Cascades Park, circa 1928
   Cook, Hill, and Cornell (Ralph D. Cornell),
   landscape architects
   Atlantic Boulevard and El Portal Place,
   Monterey Park (South of Alhambra)
Here is a real estate developer's dream if there
ever was one! At the west end of El Portal
Place a small hill rises on which has been con-
structed an elaborate tile fountain with cascade.
At the other end is a Spanish Colonial Revival
building with the original "El Encanto" sign in
place, apparently once a restaurant and offices.
It faces El Mercado, a commercial district that
never developed. Across the street from El

Encanto is an adobe bungalow court which
looks early. The whole area was finally built up
in the 1950s.

**8. Fire Station and City Administration
Building,** circa 1938
Sixth Street north of Valley Boulevard
The complex is extremely picturesque, but the
most attention has been given to the fire station.
The buildings are sheathed in pink brick,
painted white and allowed to weather.

**9. Church of St. Simon and Jude (Episcopal
Home for the Aged),** 1926
Reginald D. Johnson
1428 Marengo Avenue
Spanish Colonial Revival on an almost
medieval dollhouse scale by the son of the
(then) Episcopal Bishop of Los Angeles. The
church is dedicated to the two saints.

10. Fire Station No. 4, circa 1938
Northwest corner of Norwood Place and
Elm Street near Fremont Avenue
A Spanish Gothic surprise.

11. C. F. Braun and Company, circa 1929–37
Marston and Maybury
1000 S. Fremont Avenue
We mean no sneer when we say that these
buildings are comparable to the best work of
Albert Speer in the Germany of the 1930s
Austere red brick with almost peep-hole fenes-
tration, they owe nothing to the International
Style Modern.

12. Sears Complex, 1971
Albert C. Martin and Associates
900 S. Fremont Avenue
This group of buildings set within a landscaped
site is dominated by a great mirrored glass box.

**13. St. Steven's Serbian Orthodox
Cathedral,** 1949–52
North side of Garvey Avenue west of intersection with Abajo Drive
Serbian Romanesque with two glistening tile
domes, the church is done in California's
favorite ecclesiastical material—concrete with
the impression of the forms still showing.

MONTEBELLO, PICO RIVERA

This Italian name was once applied to a large section of the Repetto Ranch which the Anglo pioneer Harrison Newmark purchased in 1887. When he subdivided a portion of the ranch and established a town, he, of course, called it "Newmark." In 1920 the town's name was changed to Montebello. Notwithstanding its poetic name, Montebello and the regions to the south and west are now basically industrial, spawned by the discovery of oil shortly after 1900. As a commercial retail strip Whittier Boulevard is well worth a cruise (though do note that it is often closed at night to automobiles because of drag racing and other social problems). The facades of many of the one-story (and a few two-story) commercial buildings along Whittier Boulevard exhibit a number of variations on the late 1930s Streamline Moderne, plus a sprinkling of other exotic images.

Montebello Park, south of Whittier Boulevard between Gerhart and Vail avenues, was laid out in 1925 by the planning and landscape architectural firm of Cook and Hill. On paper the plan looks fine, but in actuality there is little of great inspiration to be found in either the landscaping or the modest houses which line the streets.

Montebello marks the beginning of what is a great industrial park (the City of Industry sprawls nearby). Huge complexes of factories and warehouses are erected in an anonymous architecture that might best be called "Computer Moderne," a style that is even more salient in the Irvine area.

Pico Rivera, which lies to the east of Montebello between the Rio Hondo and San Gabriel rivers, is a recent creation (1958), when the towns of Pico and Rivera were combined. Like Montebello, it is an industrial city whose principal architectural glory is the commercial strip of Whittier Boulevard.

1. The Tamale, 1928
6420 Whittier Boulevard, East Los Angeles
An often-illustrated example of California's programmatic architecture, we have here a small roadside restaurant in the form of one of its products—a tamale. The poor little structure is now pressed in by buildings on both sides, and it is no longer painted or signed as it was when built, but we should be happy that it is still with us.

2. Marcel and Jeanne French Cafe,
circa 1930
Southeast corner of Whittier Boulevard and 22nd Street, Montebello
A dollhouse-scaled French Norman cottage right out of a children's storybook. Do not miss the final mark of France—a small version of the Eiffel Tower as the restaurant's sign.

3. House, circa 1915
Southeast corner of Montebello Boulevard and Los Angeles Avenue, Montebello
A clapboard dwelling, of modest size, which almost succeeds in being Moorish.

4. Juan Matias Sanchez Adobe, 1845,
mid–1850s, and later
945 N. Adobe Avenue (off Lincoln Boulevard), Montebello
Here on the west bank of the Rio Hondo River is an impressive story-and-a-half adobe. The oldest section of the adobe runs parallel to the river, while the mid-1880s wing was extended at a right angle to the original house. The wide, hipped roof with dormer windows and much of the woodwork are twentieth century. Nonetheless, the adobe and its site do an excellent job of conveying what Southern California was like in the 1840s and 1850s. It is now used as a museum by the City of Montebello and is open to the public on Wednesdays, Saturdays, and Sundays, 1:00–4:00 P.M.

5. Mount Baldy Inn, 1927
9608 Whittier Boulevard, Pico Rivera

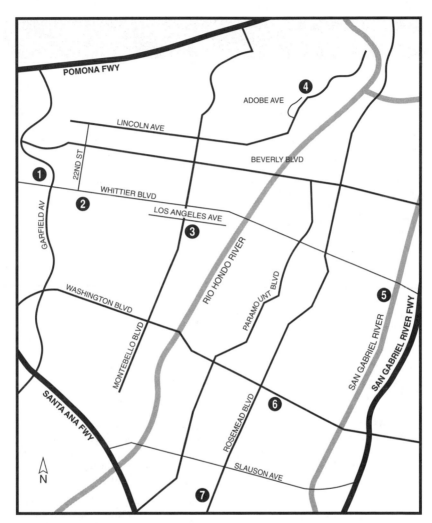

A good-sized programmatic roadside restaurant in the form of the snow-capped peak of Mount Baldy. At this writing the restaurant is no longer in use, so see it quickly while it is still around.

6. Santa Fe Passenger Station (now **Pico Rivera Chamber of Commerce**), circa 1880
9122 E. Washington Boulevard, Pico Rivera
This early, Eastlake style railroad station has been moved, restored, and converted into offices for the Chamber of Commerce.

7. United Auto Workers Union Building, 1961
Neutra and Alexander (Dion Neutra)
8503 S. Rosemead Boulevard, Pico Rivera
A Neutra Modern machine image, indoors and out, with courtyards, pools, plantings, and covered walkways. When you walk in and out and through a building of this quality, you sense how unusual it was in the era of the 1960s that produced little really good commercial design.

WHITTIER

A Quaker organization, the Pickering Land and Water Company, founded the community of Whittier in 1887. A college was formed in 1887 but succumbed in the bust of 1888 and was reorganized as the Whittier Academy in 1891. Though the extensive orange, lemon, avocado, and walnut orchards are now gone, the city still retains a pleasant, small-town atmosphere, quite separate from the rest of the valley to the south and west. The community has done reasonably well at preserving its historic buildings. The two unfortunate losses in the last few years are David S. Bushnell's 1928 Whittier Theater, which combined a motion picture theater with a forecourt of shops, and the rather mad, but delightful Harvey Apartments of 1913.

1. El Rancho High School, 1954–55
William A. Harrison
West corner of Norwalk Boulevard and Orange Grove Avenue
The post-World War II years experienced a renaissance in public school construction across California. The El Rancho High School won an Award of Merit in a 1955 awards program of the A.I.A. and the American Association of School Administrators. The plan is that of a characteristic finger scheme of one- and two-story buildings, with exterior corridors. These are carefully arranged over the thirty-nine-acre site.

2. Whittier Union High School, 1939–40
William H. Harrison
Northeast corner of Philadelphia Street and Whittier Avenue
PWA Moderne structures, the best of which is the auditorium with its lettering high on each corner and its undulating facade, which comes close to the then-popular Hollywood Regency.

3. Santa Fe Railroad Passenger Station,
circa 1889
South of the corner of Philadelphia Street and Lindley Avenue
This wooden Eastlake Style station has been temporarily moved to this site. It will eventually be relocated and restored.

4. Lincoln School, circa 1935
Attributed to William H. Harrison
Southwest corner of Broadway and Newlin Avenue
PWA Moderne, more classically monumental than the nearby high school building. One wall of the kindergarten classroom wing folds aside to combine garden with classroom.

5. First Christian Church, 1923
Northwest corner of Greenleaf Avenue and Hadley Street
A nice minor effort in Beaux Arts Neo-Classicism.

6. C. W. Harvey House, 1888
Northeast corner of Painter Avenue and Beverly Boulevard
This two-story Queen Anne dwelling was one of the first substantial houses built in the community. It is picturesquely located on a hillside, and it has been carefully restored.

7. Bailey House (The Old Ranch House), 1887
North side of Camilla Street, between Painter and Haviland avenues
A one-story, gable-roofed, wood ranch house, with the usual porch across the front.

8. Lou Henry Hoover School, 1938
William H. Harrison
East end of Camilla Street at Alta Avenue
The severity of this Regency Moderne building is lightened by the concave central bay with a handsome Wedgewood-like curved relief panel depicting the *Pageant of Education* by Bartolo Mako.

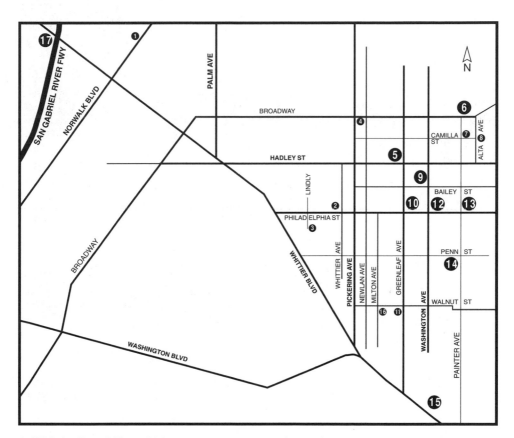

9. Whittier Post Office, 1935
  Louis A. Simon
  Northwest corner of Washington Avenue and
  Bailey Street
A single-story, rather mild PWA Moderne
building which fits well into the streetscape of
downtown Whittier.

10. National Trust and Savings Building,
  circa 1935
  William H. Harrison
  Northeast corner of Philadelphia Street and
  Greenleaf Avenue

An impressive example of the PWA Moderne.
Bunched, fluted pilasters to each side of the
entrance terminate in four large, highly stylized
eagles.

11. Wardman Theater, 1932
  David Bushnell
  7038 Greenleaf Avenue
An Art Deco theater accompanied by seven
adjoining stores. The building was damaged in
the 1987 earthquake. The exterior facade and
the lobby of the theater have since been
restored.

8. Lou Henry Hoover School, 1938

12. Charles House, 1893
6537 S. Washington Avenue
A simple, well-maintained, two-story Queen Anne.

13. Whittier College, (founded as **Whittier Academy** in 1887)
Corner of Philadelphia Street and Painter Avenue
The college has been situated on its present site since 1896. Much of the building activities took place in the 1920s, resulting in a group of white-walled, red-tile-roofed Spanish Colonial Revival buildings. A 1990 Post Modern version of the Spanish Colonial Revival is the Ruth Shannon Center designed by Albert C. Martin Associates. The traditional Hispanic details are scattered as fragments throughout the project—it is almost a ruin, or perhaps a catalogue of parts.

14. Whittier Civic Center, 1955–59
William H. Harrison
13230 Penn Street

City Hall, 1955
In this building the architect looked at the Modern through the eyes of Eliel Saarinen. A tower with a stone base surmounted by two cylinders dominates the north side of the building. The editors of the *Southwest Builder and Contractor* (1959) wrote that "The Kaibab stone-faced tower at the entrance of the city hall is topped by a beacon symbolizing enlightened good government, and terminates in an

illuminated super-structure of concrete and aluminum which can be seen many miles away." Next to the tower is the two-story lobby, equipped with a floating concrete stairway. The lobby has glass walls at both ends; those to the south open out onto a terrace and garden. To the west of the City Hall is the 1988 Bicentennial Garden (celebrating Whittier's one-hundredth birthday), which in essence is a miniature English garden. In the garden, sitting on a rock by the pool, is Tita Hupp's 1988 sculpture *The Barefoot Boy,* derived from the poem by Whittier.

Whittier Public Library, 1959
The architect has in this building turned to the pavilion forms we associated with Edward D. Stone in the 1950s and 1960s. A curved concrete ramp leads up to the glass entrance, which is covered by a cantilevered thin slab roof. The Stone-like design (very well carried out) also boasts the usual precast open concrete grills.

15. Krause House, 1950–52
    Raphael S. Soriano
    8513 La Sierra Avenue (Whittier Boulevard to Catalina Avenue, left on Mar Vista Street, right to Sierra Vista Avenue, then right)
A large, single-story steel modular post-and-beam house, with most of the walls being infilled with glass, masonry, and corrugated fiberglass. The front wall facing the auto court has a narrow band of windows carried just below the roof. The precise geometry of the house contrasts with the luxurious planting of the grounds.

16. Cottage, circa 1900
    7602 Milton Avenue
A late Queen Anne cottage composed of parts which somehow remain separate from one another. Two low gable wings press in on a central, hipped-roof pavilion. It all adds up to a delightful architectural oddity.

17. Governor Pio Pico Adobe, 1842, 1882; restored 1913, 1946
    Pioneer and Whittier boulevards just west of San Gabriel River Freeway (Whittier Boulevard off-ramp)
According to some accounts, this adobe was once two stories in height and contained thirty-three rooms. Hard to believe, but Pio Pico, the last of the Mexican governors of California, was a very successful manager of real estate until financial problems in the 1880s forced him into bankruptcy. The house was flooded in 1867 and rebuilt on a more modest scale, and then restored three more times! Nevertheless it remains one of the most credible of the adobes because the present curators have kept the early Victorian furnishings good but sparse, as they probably were in Pico's day. It is a state historic park and is normally open to the public, Wednesday–Sunday, 10:00 A.M.–5:00 P.M., but it should be noted that the adobe was damaged in the 1987 earthquake and is at the moment closed. Its exterior can be seen, but it will be some time before the building is restored and open to the public.

SANTA FE SPRINGS

This community was founded in 1873 when J. E. Fulton established the Fulton Sulfur Springs and Health Resort. The town was renamed **Santa Fe Springs** in 1886 and, as was true of much of this area of Los Angeles County, it remained agricultural until oil wells were brought in during the early 1920s. The city was incorporated in 1957, and the basic impression one has is that it is all quite new. While there are a number of recent office and commercial buildings located around Telegraph Road, the real point of architectural interest is the handsome, small-scaled Santa Fe Springs Town Center.

The site of the Santa Fe Springs Civic Center is the northern portion of the Clarke Estate, the lower section of which contains the **Clarke House** designed by Irving J. Gill. Within a beautifully landscaped park are located a group of one-story, concrete-block public buildings. While none of these buildings is architecturally assertive, they do seem to work well with one another, and within the context of the park. These buildings are:

1. Fire Station, 1959
Marson and Varner (Marion J. Varner)
This red brick "warm" modernist building was the first in the civic center, and it does reflect a somewhat different architectural image from the others. But because of its scale and the planting around it, it seems compatible with the other structures.

2. City Hall, 1967
William L. Pereira and Associates
In a traditional California fashion, the covered walkway around the building is in fact the corridor for the interior spaces.

3. Library, 1976
Anthony and Langford
A very pleasant building within. Do stop and see the ceramic mural at the entrance. By Raul Esparza, it depicts events in the history of the community.

4. Town Center Hall, 1971
William L. Pereira and Associates
Another of the Civic Centers small scaled Modernist buildings.

5. Santa Fe Springs Post Office Building, 1969
William L. Pereira and Associates
Like the other structures in the Civic Center, this building is of concrete block, and is well sited within its immediate landscape.

6. Marie and Chauncey Clarke House (1919–22)
Gill and Pearson (Irving J. Gill)
The sixty-two-acre site of the **Clarke House** was purchased by the Clarke's in 1914, and they developed it into orange groves. In 1919 they engaged Gill to design this large two-story country house. But with the discovery of oil on the land, they abandoned the idea of using the house as a country retreat.

It is organized around a central patio. The pavement of the patio contains a pattern of Maya hieroglyphs, and several wall planters exhibit pre-Columbian motifs. On the second floor miniaturized Italian balconies look out over the patio. Sections of the exterior walls contain the imprint of various species of leaves, and somewhere along in its existence fake vigas were added to the upper reaches of the building. One suspects that the pre-Columbian elements, as well as the leaf patterns, reflect the interests of Marie Rankin Clarke. She was intensely interested in plants and landscape

DOWNEY

gardening and was one of those responsible for the development of the Hollywood Bowl.

The Clarke House is not only the largest of Gill's houses that is still standing, but also matches in its quality of design his famous Scripps house at La Jolla (now extensively remodeled), and the destroyed Dodge house in Hollywood. After its purchase by the City of Santa Fe Springs, the house was extensively restored. It is open to the public by making arrangements with the Recreation Services Division of the Department of Community Services, the City of Santa Fe Springs.

The Santa Fe Springs Town Center and Irving J. Gill's Clarke House are located on the south side of Telegraph Road between Alburtis Street and Pioneer Boulevard.

7. Heritage Park (Opened in 1987)
12100 Mora Drive
This six-acre park recreates portions of the historic horticulturist ranch of Harvey Hawkins (which dated from the 1880s). One can see the ruins of the ranch house and its accompanying English-style gardens. The Carriage Barn and the tank house/windmill have been rebuilt.

Although the city was subdivided as early as 1865 by Governor John G. Downey, it, like the neighboring communities, is essentially a product of the post-World War II years. At the southwest corner of Lakewood Boulevard and Florence Avenue is a monument of roadside architecture, America's first **McDonald's** drive-in restaurant (1953), the first restaurant established before the chain itself developed. It preceded by one year the McDonald's at 563 E. Foothill Boulevard in Azusa, and it was also earlier than the one often mentioned in the Midwest. The design consists of two neon-lighted elliptical arches, which plunge through the typical 1950s shed-roofed restaurant building. Architecturally, this design, in contrast to the later classic McDonald's Restaurant buildings, poses somewhat mid-way between popular and serious architecture. Also take note (as if you could avoid it) of the impressive, well-lighted sign at the corner. It is part and parcel of the entire composition of sign, parking lot, and building.

NORWALK

ARTESIA

Norwalk was founded in 1877, and two years later a post office was established. The early commercial center of the community was laid out around Front Street, which parallels the Southern Pacific tracks. A few of the older commercial buildings, including a turn-of-the-century Beaux Arts **bank building,** still remain on Front Street, although most of these have been remodeled over the years. At the northwest corner of Pioneer Boulevard and Rosecrans Avenue is one of Southern California's greatest free-standing signs, which announces the **Norwalk Square Shopping Center.** The very high sign is composed of an inverted open metal triangle topped by an open metal rectangle (upon which the letters are placed), and finally a series of four upward-reaching loops—it is all similar in feeling to the central spaceship restaurant at the Los Angeles International Airport. This extravaganza was designed between 1951 and 1954 by Stiles Clements for the Pacific Mutual Life Insurance Company, which sponsored the shopping center as an investment. Farther to the north on the northeast corner of San Antonio Drive and Sproul Street is an excellent Art Deco Moderne former **auto show room** (now used for the sale of auto parts). The building is designed around a low, squat, square tower, and it is ornamented (in cast concrete) with horizontal bands of connected chevrons. It dates from about 1930. In **Norwalk Park** (at Sproul Street and Norwalk Avenue) you will find an Eastlake cottage (circa 1889), the **Gilbert Sproul House.** It is now maintained as a house museum by the city and is open Wednesday, Thursday, and Friday, 10:00 A.M.–2:00 P.M.; and Saturday and Sunday, 1:00–5:00 P.M.

This town, located south of Norwalk, was set out in the 1870s by the Artesian Water Company, although nothing really remains from these early years. The character of the community is primarily post-World War II, both in its commercial buildings and in its housing. Like Bellflower to the northeast, the town is located on the Southern Pacific Railroad tracks and it is adjacent to the San Gabriel River. The architectural gem of Artesia is the former **First National Bank Building** (1925), on the northwest corner of Pioneer Boulevard and 187th Street, designed by the Los Angeles architect Henry Withey. This Mediterranean building is a simple rectangular box with an elegant, three-arched loggia resplendent with doubled twisted Saracenic columns. The community has also done much better than most with its new **Post Office Building** (1970–71; Donald M. Forker), located at the northeast corner of 183rd Street and Alburtus Avenue. The post office is a low-adobe-appearing (it is of slumpstone) building with deeply-splayed recessed windows, a low-pitched tiled roof, and a wide and cool portal.

This community is situated on the west bank of the lower San Gabriel River. It was founded in 1906, but most of its growth occurred in the 1960s and 1970s. Its older commercial core is located in and around Bellflower Boulevard just north of the San Gabriel Freeway (Highway 91). The commercial center is dominated close up and from afar by the now-unused marquee and the expansive sign of the **Holiday Theater** (located on the west side of Bellflower Boulevard north of Flower Avenue). This theater was built at the end of the 1920s, although the wondrous curved and open theater sign dates from the post-World War II years (circa 1950). South of the theater on Bellflower Boulevard, at the northeast corner of Arkansas Avenue, is a programmatic fast-food establishment, the **Taco Hour.** This is composed of a huge doughnut on the rooftop with the hands of a clock contained within the doughnut (circa 1960). At the southeast corner of Woodruff Avenue and South Street is the **Dutch Village Shopping Center** (circa 1960 and later). A shingled Dutch windmill proclaims the principal entrance to the complex, and north across South Street, another smaller windmill marks the Dutch Mill Bowling building.

East of Bellflower and Artesia, not far from the Los Angeles/Orange County line, are two new "wonders" of the Southern California architectural scene. One of these is a pure programmatic building, the **Bear Tree** (1982–83; Bea de Armond with Jason and Michelle Walker), and the other is the **Doll and Toy Museum** (1979; "created by" Jay and Bea de Armond). The Bear Tree is in the form of a huge tree stump, with you and me as the little people who inhabit it. The Doll and Toy Museum is, according to the building's legend, a half-scale replica of the White House in Washington, D. C. Both of these structures form a part of **Hobby City,** which is located at 1238 South Beach Boulevard.

SAN FERNANDO VALLEY

Charles Lummis wrote that the Franciscans "unerringly chose from the California wilderness the garden spots, and a hundred years of experiment have failed to find anything better than their first judgment." Early pictures show the San Fernando Mission in pasture land, dependent on the winter rains for life. But the Franciscans dammed the springs near the mission (the dam is its oldest fragment) and then the Los Angeles River in the rainy season. The fertile land bloomed.

Heavy settlement waited for the Yankees, who carved up the former Mexican holdings. In the early 1870s a Bavarian immigrant, Isaac Lankershim, and his friend, I. N. Van Nuys, both large landholders in northern California, set out the southern part of the valley to sheep ranches and to wheat dry farming. Charles Maclay, a Methodist minister turned land speculator, bought the northern valley a few years later thanks to a loan of $60,000 from Leland Stanford, who seems to have trusted Methodists.

Stanford sustained his interest. He made San Fernando the northern terminus of his Southern Pacific Railroad and shipped some railroad equipment there to make the designation look realistic. In fact, Maclay's deal determined the route of the line that in 1876 broke through the mountains and linked San Francisco and Los Angeles, leaving San Fernando a way station between two great cities.

The railroad brought more people to the Valley. They settled in old towns such as Calabasas and Chatsworth, both of which had been stagecoach stations, and, of course, San Fernando. But there were new settlements at Zelzah (now Northridge), Reseda, Pacoima, Roscoe (now Stonehurst), Sunland, Lankershim, Burbank, and Glendale. These

towns, like the railroad, serviced a magnificent agricultural area, made more magnificent by the completion in 1913 of Mulholland's aqueduct bringing what at that time seemed unlimited water from the High Sierra 250 miles to the north.

Then, gradually at first, began the transformation of the landscape from wheat and citrus to what has been called "L.A.'s bedroom." Hollywood spread across the Santa Monica Mountains to form North Hollywood. Glendale oozed northwest. Although the scent of orange blossoms filled the air until World War II and even after, the rural idyll was then approaching the transformation into miles of dull tract housing, streets of apartment buildings, shopping centers, and commercial strips that mark it today. Ventura Boulevard was the great commercial strip to the south and the beginning of the main inland route to Ventura and Santa Barbara until the Ventura Freeway took its place in the mid-1960s. The immediate effect of the freeway was to further disintegrate the community, but, as in so many cases, the long-term effect has been to renew it, especially at Sherman Oaks and Encino, where mediocre high-rise is beginning to obscure the mountains.

Yes, the Valley became super-respectable in places. In fact, it has been denounced too often. The stately rows of trees on east/west streets such as Sherman Way and the dry winds that sweep through them near sunset are as much of the present as they are of the past.

315

GLENDALE

L ong inhabited by Mexican
rancheros, the huge Rancho San
Rafael was, before the Yankees
came, mainly grazing land interspersed with a few farms which
raised wheat, corn, beans and hay. After the
Gringo conquest, the land was subdivided, the
southern half comprising what is now Glendale
as well as Eagle Rock and part of Pasadena.

With the extension of the Southern Pacific
Railroad north in 1873, the town (originally
called Riverdale), was planned. Then in 1876,
when the railroad was completed to San
Francisco, and with Los Angeles County thus
open to transcontinental immigration, the community now called Glendale began to grow. It
was supposed to grow wildly in the land boom
of the 1880s. The obligatory extravagant hotel

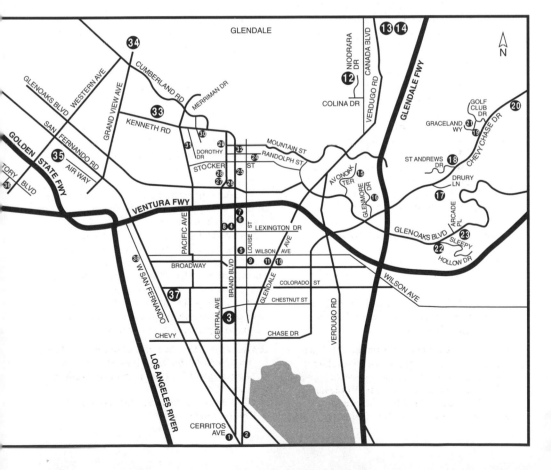

designed by Joseph Cather Newsom was built, but when the boom collapsed in 1888, the hotel stood finished but empty. After serving as a girls' school and then a tuberculosis sanitarium, it was demolished in the 1920s.

Significantly, it is very difficult to find anything left of Glendale's Victorian past. Its real history begins with the early twentieth century when the Pacific Electric Railroad (Interurban) extended its tracks from Central Los Angeles to Glendale (1904). The city is thus well-bungalowed, and in its upper reaches and along its main street (Brand Boulevard) well-stocked with the architecture of the 1920s, which is either being spruced up or demolished, and in some cases replaced with architecture that looks as if it came from the 1920s or wished it had. Most of the newest buildings are cliches derived from old issues of *Progressive Architecture*—banal reformatory hives in concrete, or glass aviaries punctured with angular extrusions à la James Stirling. These, along with pretentious street lights at corners and brick pedestrian walkways across streets, make Glendale super-Mod. Oh yes, it has a galleria (shopping mall), that is so successful that it appears that it eventually will consume the entire business district. During the late 1980s a rash of high-rises with their accompanying huge parking garages have been built in and around the freeway and upper Brand Avenue. As with most groupings of recent high-rise buildings, these work best at night.

1. Southern Pacific Railroad Station,
circa 1922
MacDonald and Couchot
Southwest end of Cerritos Avenue at
Railroad Avenue
If there ever was a stage set, this is it! The Spanish Colonial Revival appears here at its most cloying. But it still works.

2. Forest Lawn Memorial Park, 1917–present
Frederick A. Hansen, landscape architect
Entrance just north of the intersection of San Fernando Road and Glendale Boulevard.
Map of grounds available at Information Booth near entrance and "Art Guide" at

Administration Building near Information Booth.

The man behind this famed Southern California inspiration was Dr. Hubert L. Eaton, who planned it as "a great park, devoid of misshapen monuments . . . a place where lovers new and old shall love to stroll." In other words, Forest Lawn was calculated to be something more than an architectural experience.

But architecture resides here. Behind the Tudor **Administration Building** (1918 and later), designed by Charles Kyson and given ornamental enrichment by Austin Whittlesey (who also designed the Kerckhoff Monument), is the **Church of the Flowers** adapted (1918) by A. Patterson Ross from the church at Stoke Poges about whose cemetery Thomas Gray composed his "Elegy." It is the best piece of architecture at Forest Lawn and is often missed. F. A. Hansen's inexact copy of the **Wee Kirk of the Heather** is here, as is Paul O. Davis's **Church of the Recessional,** which is supposed to be an exact copy of Rudyard Kipling's home church at Rottingdean. It isn't. Everyone, we assume, will want to see the enormous painting "Calvary" by the Polish artist Jan Styka, with its accompanying light show and music from Wagner's *Parsifal*. It is housed in the **Cathedral/Auditorium** designed in 1950 by Roy W. Donlay, with David S. Allison as consulting architect.

The main program here is, of course, sculptural, with more copies of Michelangelo's work than exist anywhere else on earth. Also an awful lot of modern Italian stuff, the most arresting being E. Gazzeri's *The Mystery of Life* in the Court of Memory. Just as interesting for other reasons is *The Dream of Peace* by Gutzon Borghlum in his Art Nouveau phase.

We could go on, but will add only that in spite of all the generally execrable art, Forest Lawn does preserve a lot of open space.

3. Glendale Chamber of Commerce Building
(now **Sons of the American Revolution Genealogical Library and Patio Gallery**),
circa 1925
600 Central Avenue, at southeast corner of Chestnut Street

A one-story Spanish Colonial Revival building whose walls preserve their original burnt umber coloring.

4. Glendale Federal Savings Building, 1959
Bank Building and Equipment Company
Northwest corner Brand Boulevard and Lexington Drive

When this office building was erected, it was the biggest, tallest structure on Brand Boulevard; pure 1950s razzle-dazzle. Now look north and you encounter nothing but mediocre to ugly behemoths, that are an insult to the magnificent site at the foot of the mountains. Look about you, and no matter how hard you may work at it, you will see no monuments.

5. Alex Theater, 1924–25
Arthur G. Lindley and Charles R. Selkirk; front added 1939.
268 N. Brand Boulevard

An Art Deco Moderne piece that puts the more recent architecture on Brand Boulevard to shame. The central pylon erupting out of curved forms gives dramatic emphasis to the fact that the silver screen is inside. Probably the most salient feature of the building is its lobby, which combines Greek Doric columns with chandeliers that resemble giant heliotrope blossoms.

6. The American Savings Bank Building, 1986
Skidmore, Owings and Merrill
Northwest corner Brand Avenue and Milford Street

The white marble walls and red window trim of this high-rise assault the eye with awful intensity.

2. Forest Lawn Memorial Park, 1917–present

7. 550 North Brand Building, 1987
Hellmuth, Obata and Kassebaum
550 North Brand Avenue

Post Modern of a sort; a white marble whopper crowned with a gigantic Palladian arch.

8. First American Title Company of Los Angeles Building, 1987
Leason/Pomeroy Associates
520 Central Avenue

In some lights this high-rise appears to be greenish, in others violet, with blue glass trim around the edges of the windows.

9. Glendale Post Office, 1933–34
George M. Lindsay; J. A. Wetmore
313 E. Broadway

Italian Renaissance with a good interior.

10. Glendale City Hall, 1940–42
Albert E. Hansen
Northwest corner of Broadway and Howard Street

Crisp Classical Moderne with a clock tower.

12. Rodriguez House, 1941

A woodsy, late Craftsman bungalow all on one floor. Variations on the same theme are to be seen at 3068 Chevy Chase Drive and at 1709 Golf Club Drive (see entry number 20 below).

15. House, 1980
    950 Avonoak Terrace, north of Glenoaks Boulevard
It is encouraging to see that fantasy is still with us. A small castle.

16. House, circa 1920
    680 Glenmore Drive, off Chevy Chase Drive
The stone facade of the house and the garden layout are similar to those at Tujunga, which is one of Southern California's meccas of boulder architecture.

17. House, 1929
    2322 Drury Lane, at Chevy Chase Drive
Unsophisticated but very romantic Spanish Colonial Revival, almost Hansel and Gretel. Quantities of such houses abound in Glendale, especially in the area above the Ventura Freeway.

18. Derby House, 1926
    Lloyd Wright
    2535 Chevy Chase Drive, at Saint Andrew's Drive
Built mainly in what Wright's father, Frank Lloyd Wright, called his "textile block" construction, Lloyd claimed it as his own invention. The design of the concrete blocks was inspired by pre-Columbian ornament, but the general effect of the house is Islamic. Since the road has been widened practically to the front door, there is no problem in seeing the house.

19. Calori House, 1926
    Lloyd Wright
    3021 Chevy Chase Drive
An abstract arrangement of shed and gable roofs hovers incongruously over the volumes

11. Glendale Municipal Services Building, 1965
    Albert C. Martin and Associates (Merrill W. Baird)
    Northwest corner of Broadway and Glendale
Toned-down concrete Brutalism hovering on stilts over a plaza with fountain.

12. Rodriguez House, 1941
    R. M. Schindler
    1845 Niodrara Drive
The angled roof with its wooden projections protects the rectangular de Stijl composition below. Unfortunately, the extraordinary structural gymnastics of the house are largely screened from public view by fences and planting.

13. Paietta House, 1928
    Southeast corner of Verdugo Road and Sparr Boulevard
A hillside Spanish Colonial Revival extravaganza thrown together by a builder with a lot of money and even more spirit.

14. Leavitt House, 1948
    A. Quincy Jones and Frederick E. Emmons
    1919 Bayberry Drive

below, while two massive brackets, supporting a small enclosed balcony, create a cavelike entrance to the house. A very free interpretation of the Spanish Colonial Revival.

20. Fuller House, 1948–49
A. Quincy Jones and
Frederick E. Emmons
3068 Chevy Chase Drive
As noted in entry number 14, this house was a variation on a theme established by the architects for several houses. Nearby at 1709 Golf Club Drive the **Kett House** (1948–49) preserves its woodsy, Craftsman exterior.

21. Lewis House, 1926
Lloyd Wright
2948 Graceland Way
This stucco structure has been modified, but the south elevation is similar to the strong vertical components of the Millard House by Wright's father. (Lloyd was just finishing the studio for Mrs. Millard at this time.)

22. House, circa 1927
2414 E. Glenoaks Boulevard, at Sleepy Hollow Terrace
A rare use of the Zigzag Moderne in domestic architecture.

23. Bauer House, 1938
Harwell H. Harris
2528 E. Glenoaks Boulevard, at Arcade Place
A fence screens this house from the street, but what can be seen is good late Craftsman in style.

24. House, circa 1905
Southwest corner of Randolph and Louise streets
A Mission Revival house which once was a famous Mexican restaurant, Casa Verdugo, at the end of the Pacific Electric Line.

25. St. Mark's Episcopal Church, 1948
Carleton M. Winslow; Louis A. Thomas
1020 North Brand Boulevard
Poured concrete construction with the wooden forms indented in the exterior surface, this large Gothic image building shows the strength of the Episcopalians in Glendale. This church was

18. Derby House, 1926

the last one designed by Winslow before his death. It was completed by Louis A. Thomas. Take note of the Nativity window and the triple lancet window "The Te Deum," designed in 1949 for the church by Judson Studios.

26. Church of the Incarnation Roman Catholic Church, 1951
Northwest corner of Brand and Glenoaks boulevards
Both inside and out, this is a superb period piece of late Classical Moderne. This building and its adjacent school, along with the Methodist church down the block and the Mormon church nearby (next two entries), form a shrine for the Moderne enthusiast.

27. North Glendale Methodist Church, 1941
Harry W. Pierce
Northwest corner of Glenoaks Boulevard and Central Avenue
Gothic Moderne. One of the parishioners said she liked it because it wasn't "this far-out stuff."

28. Glendale Second Ward, Church of Jesus Christ of Latter-day Saints (Mormon), 1937
Georgius Y. Cannon
Northwest corner of Dryden Street and Central Avenue

Rather dry and somewhat academic but still a good example of abstracted Art Deco of the 1930s.

29. House, circa 1927
 Southwest corner of Central Avenue and
 Spencer Street
A fairy-tale castle with a lovely tile band wrapped around the tower.

30. House, circa 1905
 Southeast corner of Merriman Drive and
 Kenneth Road
A two-story tribute to the eastern Colonial tradition.

31. Adobe San Rafael, 1865 (restored 1932)
 1330 Dorothy Drive
A one-story, beautifully maintained structure with Monterey style porch. It is notable that such buildings evoke New England as much as they do the West. The house and gardens are open to the public Sunday and Wednesday afternoons, 1:00–4:00 P.M.

32. First Church of Christ, Scientist, 1989
 Moore, Ruble and Yudell (Charles W.
 Moore)
 1320 North Brand Boulevard
Here, as in his St. Matthew's Episcopal Church in Pacific Palisades, Moore catches the spirit of the denomination—in this case a kind of Christian Science smile. When you go into the pristine white sanctuary, you have a feeling that no problems really exist. Although the complex is raised up above the boulevard, and is fenced, one still feels that all is open and inviting.

33. Senator Madison Jones House, 1902
 727 Kenneth Road
A two-story Ionic portico with Adamesque front door is the pride of this house. Tradition has it that Senator Jones's brother was the architect.

34. Brand House ("El Miradero"), 1902–04
 Nathaniel Dryden
 1601 W. Mountain Street, at north end of
 Grandview Avenue
Certainly worth a trip to Glendale. This Islamic folly is supposed to have been inspired by the East Indian Pavilion at the World's Columbian Exposition in Chicago in 1893. It was the home of Leslie C. Brand, the Glendale booster who brought the Pacific Electric to Glendale in 1904. He gave his estate to the city on the condition that it be a public library and park, and so it is. In 1955 "Brand Castle" was converted into a cultural library by Raymond Jones. This firm also added a harmonious addition in 1969 (Jones and Walton). It is currently used as an art library and cultural center. The grounds are beautiful. Since the publication of our last Guide, the Queen Anne **Doctor's House** (circa 1887), formerly at Wilson Avenue and Belmont Street, has been moved into the park and is being restored.

35. Grand Central Air Terminal, 1928
 Henry L. Gogerty
 1310 Air Way
A surviving Spanish Colonial Revival curiosity, since the airport has disappeared and has been replaced by factories and warehouses.

36. Two Bungalows, 1935
 246 and 248 Jesse Avenue, at Victory
 Boulevard
Tiny treasures of the Streamline Moderne with glass brick and portholes.

37. Joy Company, 1972–73
 Craig Ellwood Associates
 4565 Colorado Street
One Miesian box cantilevered over another, this fine example of Ellwood's taste can be viewed best from the Golden State Freeway across the Los Angeles River channel (paved, of course). Traveling north on the freeway in this area you will also get a good view of public art of a sort: huge cat faces that have been painted around drainage ducts emptying into the river.

38. Aeroscopic Building, circa 1935
 5245 West San Fernando Road
A dynamic version of the Streamline Modern, with special pizazz over the main entrance.

BURBANK

C ontrary to popular assumption, this city was not named for Luther Burbank, the horticulturist, but for a typical Angelino, Dr. David Burbank, a dentist who was one of the happy subdividers in 1887. Too much fun has been made of "beautiful downtown Burbank." It has a shopping mall that seems to work, i.e., where you see people. It is amusing that almost everything worth seeing is on or just off Olive Avenue, a street that cuts diagonally southwest through the conventional grid which lines up on the Los Angeles River, of all things.

We begin, however, in the northwest, near the very busy Burbank Airport:

1. Memorial Rotunda, 1927
   Kenneth MacDonald, Jr.
   End of Valhalla Drive just off Hollywood Way, south of the main runway of the airport.
One of L.A.'s extravagant gems; an open-domed temple richly embellished with cast concrete ornament almost worthy of San Francisco's Bernard Maybeck. This was to have been the entrance to a sumptuous memorial park.

2. Public Service Department Building, 1945
   Daniel A. Elliot
   Northeast Corner Magnolia Boulevard and Lake Street
If your interest is in modernist architecture after World War II, then this building is worth a visit. Bland, not assertive, but it was read as modern in the late 1940s.

3. House, circa 1955
   7630 Glenoaks Boulevard, near Cabrini Drive (just outside the Burbank boundary)
The house seems to be a takeoff on the brittle Neo-Classicism of Sir John Soane. But the real sight is the front garden, alive with old street lights. A local wag has dubbed it, therefore, the "Villa Luminaria."

4. Adolph's Office Building, 1951–53
   Raphael S. Soriano
   1800 Magnolia Boulevard, at Parish Place
The post-and-lintel modular system taken to the point where it almost becomes an anonymous building.

5. Bungalow, circa 1920
   Southwest corner of Olive Avenue and Ninth Street
One of the handsomest and most characteristic "airplane" bungalows in the region.

6. Two bungalows, circa 1920
   Northeast corner of Olive Avenue and Ninth Street
Indigenous boulder architecture.

7. St. Robert Bellarmine Complex
   Northwest and southwest corners of Olive Avenue and Fifth Street
Monsignor Martin Cody Keating, the priest who envisioned this, deserves some kind of medal. Next to God, his hero was Thomas Jefferson. The **Jefferson-Bellarmine Elementary School,** a rebuilding in the 1930s of the old Holy Trinity Church, is thus partly Neo-Classical, supposedly based on Jefferson's stables at Monticello, and partly Moderne. It was designed by Paul Kingsford. The nearby **St. Robert Bellarmine Church** (1939; George Adams), at the southeast corner of Fifth Street and Orange Grove, is similarly Neo-Classical with its portico modeled on the south front of Monticello. Then back on Olive Avenue is the **Jefferson-Bellarmine High School** (1945; Barker and Ott), a facsimile of Independence Hall with a splendid facsimile of

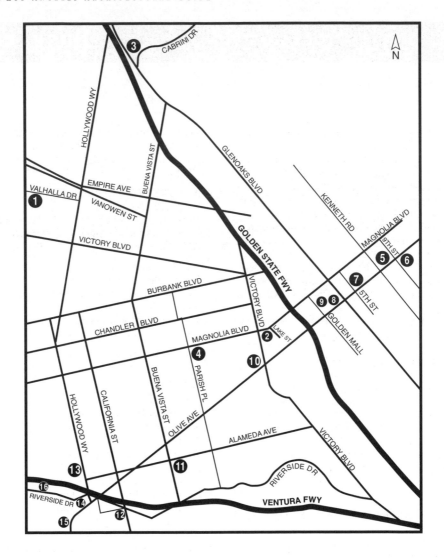

the Liberty Bell in the entrance hall under the tower. All this is followed by a Classical Roman **auditorium** (1952; Barker and Ott), inspired by Jefferson's Library at the University of Virginia. Three cheers for the architect(s) and the priest who conceived of (and for the church who endorsed) this Fourth of July celebration.

8. Burbank City Hall, 1940–41
  William Allen and George Lutzi
  Southwest corner of Olive Avenue and Third Street

A reinforced concrete classic of the PWA Moderne with matching fountain decorated with WPA bas-relief (by Bartolo Mako) on the Third Street side, the whole carried out with

6. Two bungalows, circa 1920

great delicacy. The lobby has retained all of its original pizzazz. Within the two-story lobby (at the stair landing) and in the council chambers are large murals by Hugo Ballin.

9. The Golden Mall, 1967
Simon Eisener and Lyle Stewart
San Fernando Road from San Jose Avenue to Tujunga Avenue
Eisener and Stewart were major figures in the planning world of Southern California in the years after 1945. In this instance they created a wonderful tree-lined pedestrian way.

10. Grist Mill Restaurant, circa 1950
Southwest corner of Olive Avenue and Victory Boulevard
A skirted windmill whose slats, edged with lights, actually twirl and make you nostalgic for those old blue Van de Kamp's bake shops of the 1920s and 1930s.

11. Disney Studio Buildings
Southeast Corner of Buena Vista Street and Alameda Avenue

a. Studio Buildings, 1939–40
Kem Weber

The original set of buildings: their interiors and much of their furnishings were designed by one of America's leading industrial designers of the 1920s and 1930s, Kem Weber (including Walt Disney's own offices and bedroom suite). Weber's buildings were reticent, somewhat of a play between art Modernism and industrial architecture. The only outright playful elements were things such as street signs with one or another of Disney's characters on them. Unfortunately, one can see these buildings only from a distance, and behind a high fence, but they are there.

b. Disney Studio Office Building, 1992
Michael Graves
Graves has provided one of his usual classical-inspired buildings, in certain ways, terribly ponderous. He has sought to make it program-matic and playful by using the five dwarfs from Snow White as caryatid figures to support its low gable roof. One could only wish that some-how this design had succeeded in restoring what Freud called "the lost laughter of inno-cence," but such was not its fate. Equally pre-tentious is the formal plaza in front of the

building. Southern California landscape can, at times be playful and childlike, but this space does not help the situation. As with the Weber buildings, the Graves building must be viewed from the street behind a metal fence.

12. Warner Brothers Records Building, 1975
   A. Quincy Jones Associates
   South side of Riverside Drive at junction of
   Warner Boulevard and California Street
Natural wood framed in metal softens the International Style Modern building.

13. Bungalows, circa 1930
   300 Block of Hollywood Way
A block-long row of tiny, terribly quaint, Hansel and Gretel cottages with some "intrusions."

**14. Warner/Elektra/Atlantic Corporation
   Building,** 1981
   Gibbs and Gibbs
   Northwest corner of Olive Avenue and
   Hollywood Way
The building appears to be a vast assemblage of huge Tinker Toy beams, perhaps as a comment on the early Craftsman movement.

15. Warner Brothers Office Building, 1979
   Charles Luckman Partnership
   Northeast corner of Olive Avenue and
   Maple Street
A Post-Modern and very conscious revival of the Streamline Moderne of the 1930s by the firm whose head once ironically participated in the design of New York's International Style Modern Lever House that pioneered the Miesian aesthetic in post-World War II America. In every way the new building is monumental!

16. Bob's Big Boy Restaurant, 1949
   Wayne McAllister
   4211 Riverside Drive
The design of a fast-food restaurant as a sign, in this case thirty-five feet high. This Big Boy was one of the first group of six built in the Los Angeles area; the others have been torn down. In 1992, over the objection of its owner, the building was recommended for historic designation by the State of California.

UNIVERSAL CITY

Tucked in below Toluca Lake and the Los Angeles River to the north and the Hollywood Freeway to the south at the intersection of Cahuenga and Lankershim boulevards is the old lot of Universal Studios, now turned into an amusement park with a fringe on Lankershim Boulevard of elegant **office buildings** by Skidmore, Owings, and Merrill (1970–present). It all began with a black glass tower and three lower volumes, also black glass boxes. Then, as if the architects had changed their minds, huge horizontal, brown, travertine marble slabs began appearing as if the fragments of a long-lost Schindler design had developed elephantiasis. The latest is a new tower, the headquarters (1984) of the **Getty Oil Company Building** (Skidmore, Owings, and Merrill). One of the most recent additions to Universal City is the **Ivan Reitman Productions Building** (1993), at 100 Universal City Plaza, designed by Barton Myers Associates. As with a number of contemporary modernist buildings, this one creates a small townscape within its large open space. From the entrance, a long curved wall leads one through the space. Externally, the Ivan Reitman Production Building strongly expresses its modular steel frame construction.

Oh yes, we should mention the restaurants. **The Victoria Station** (1980; Swinerton and Walberg Company) and **Fung Lum's** (1981; Tracey Price) are architecturally the most sensational.

The latest addition to entertainment shopping is Universal City's **City Walk,** designed in 1992 by Jerde Partnership. It is located off Lankershim Boulevard on Universal Terrace Parkway. This is the cleaned-up retail strip as it should be. It is excellent stage-set architecture, lively and well carried out. Within City Walk are a few assertions that read as "real" buildings. One of these is the **Panasonic Building** (1991) by Hodgetts + Fung Design Associates. This small-scaled building provides the visitor with a good case study of what many contemporary L.A. architects are about. It is a classic Post Modernist design: the theme of "logical" modernism asserted, and then countered by seemingly irrational elements. The whole of City Walk poses somewhere between the shopping area of Disneyland in Anaheim, and Two Rodeo Drive in Beverly Hills. While some critics have reservations about the antiseptic nature of the place, it does work well, and some of the shops are well worth a visit.

NORTH HOLLYWOOD

North Hollywood, the sister of the Hollywood over the hill, owes its existence to the film industry that found the valley photogenic and less hazy than the L.A. Basin. Not the faintest trace of Isaac Lankershim's wheat barony remains except for his name attached to a street that has the gall to cut diagonally across a grid firmly based on north/south, east/west axes. North Hollywood had an unusual number of parks and other spaces, but the freeway engineers have taken advantage of almost all of them in order to put through their great works easily. So much for parks.

Not much really exotic or monumental architecture exists in the acre upon acre of tract housing, apartments, and condominiums. But North Hollywood is far from a total loss:

1. North Hollywood Pump Station, Department of Water and Power, 1989–92
Barton Phelps and Associates
11803 Vanowen Street
The street facade of this long concrete building acts as a billboard, containing an abstract map of California and of the three aqueducts which feed Los Angeles. A low arched window at the ground provides a view into the station so that one can see the pumps at work. A long, low, glass-and-metal clerestory projects out over the concrete box below.

2. St. Charles Boromeo Roman Catholic Church, 1959
J. Earl Trudeau
Parish Hall, 1938
Laurence Viole
Southwest corner of Moorpark Street and Lankershim Boulevard
The original church was designed in 1938 by M. L. Barker and G. L. Ott. This complex is impressive when viewed from the Ventura Freeway, but the Spanish Colonial Revival

2. St. Charles Boromeo Roman Catholic Church,
1959

church itself is not as bold when closely inspected. The ascetic Mission Revival **Parish Hall** adjoining it is more impressive architecturally.

3. La Caña Restaurant Building, circa 1935
Near northeast corner of Lankershim Boulevard and Vineland Avenue
An enlarged root beer barrel, a Programmatic image that enlivens an otherwise dreadful area.

4. DWP Building, 1939
Attributed to S. Charles Lee
5108 Lankershim Boulevard
A tasteful exposition of the fragile Streamline Moderne.

5. Methodist Church, 1949
Northeast corner of Riverside Drive and Tujunga Avenue
A Spanish Colonial Revival building with a

sort of Mudejar tower ending in two stages that might have been designed by Asher Benjamin.

6. Masonic Temple (North Hollywood Temple Association), 1946–51
   Robert B. Stacy-Judd; J. Aleck Murrey
   5122 Tujunga Avenue
Egypto-Mayan (with a small dose of 1930s Moderne), by California's most passionate pre-Columbian exponent. This structure maintains the tradition of off-beat architecture established by the Freemasons in early California. Although Stacy-Judd did design a number of Mayan Revival buildings after World War II, this structure was his last realized design in this style.

7. Los Angeles County Regional Branch Library, circa 1929
   Weston and Weston
   Near northwest corner of Magnolia Boulevard and Tujunga Avenue
Spanish Colonial Revival with strange, non-functional porch.

8. DWP, Distribution Headquarters, 1992
   Ellerbe Becket (Mehrdad Yazdani)
   11847 Vose Street (off of Laurel Canyon Boulevard)
What a strange place to find a piece of good architecture! But the DWP historically has done well over the decades in the buildings arts. Do note the pumping station next door. Not great, but it tries.

9. "The Great Wall," (murals), 1974–83
   Judy Baca
   Northwest corner of Coldwater Canyon Avenue and Burbank Boulevard
In 1972 the Army Corps of Engineers was inspired to commission Judy Baca, a professor of art at U. C. Irvine, to supervise the painting of a mural on the history of California that would cover the west concrete wall of the Tujunga Wash. She began the project by sketching out plans that members of street gangs would carry out in a series of panels. These were then touched up by trained artists. The murals strike a note of celebration in an otherwise lackluster area.

TOLUCA LAKE

This lovely residential section, roughly bordered by the Ventura Freeway, the Los Angeles River, Cahuenga Boulevard, and the border with Burbank, is a real surprise in the Valley. The drawing card for the well-heeled gentry coming in the 1930s and later was the lake and the country club. The winding, tree-lined streets are up to Pasadena standards. Yet, as in so many parts of beautifully land-scaped Los Angeles County, very little note-worthy architecture exists in the shade of the trees.

The mildly International Style Modern **MacFadden House** (1948) at 1052 Toluca Lake Avenue near the intersection with Tolofa Avenue was designed by J. R. Davidson as, one would like to think, a foil for its "traditional" neighbors. The **Elliott House** (1951) at 10443 Woodbridge Street, near Strohm Avenue, is one of Harwell H. Harris's late Craftsman master-pieces. Rather unexpectedly at 4217 Navajo Street near the corner of Valley Spring Lane you will find a large **Streamline Moderne house** whose roof is adorned with a huge antenna obviously tuned to "Buck Rogers in the Twenty-fifth Century." The house was designed by Kenneth Worthen, Sr., in 1935. A more recent addition to Toluca Lake's small trove of outstanding architecture is Frank O. Gehry and Associates' **World Savings Building** (1982) at 10064 Riverside Drive (intersection with Mariota Avenue). It is definitely Post-Modern with its false walls, including fenestration.

1. King's Castle Restaurant, circa 1986
   Northeast corner of Riverside Drive and Vallet Street
A "real" castle is most welcome in the dullness that prevails in the nearby modernist architecture.

2. Dick Powell House, 1934–35

2. Dick Powell House, 1934–35
 Richard Frederick King
 17 Toluca Estate Road (private), near Valley Springs Lane.
The image is Anglo Colonial Revival, but the U-shaped plan centering on the swimming pool entails the ideal of the California Ranch house. The walls are of white painted brick, and the plan is informal, although many of the rooms (as well as sections of the garden) are formally arranged.

I t is difficult to distinguish Studio City from North Hollywood except that its heart (the word seems inappropriate) is south of the Los Angeles River and along Ventura Boulevard which begins here. In fact, this section of Ventura marks one of the earliest (1930s) commercial strips in the Valley. Its remains can still be seen.

 Also, Studio City is blessed with a considerable amount of good to excellent architecture, much of it by R. M. Schindler.

1. Condominiums, 1975
 Tom Roberts
 12024 Kling Street
Originally this High Tech-image multiple housing unit, with the second floor served by exterior spiral staircases, was painted white. Appropriately, solar panels now occupy the roof.

2. Ward House, 1939
 Richard J. Neutra
 3156 Lake Hollywood Drive
Low, sleek, private, its inner complexities are masked by an International Style Moderne facade.

3. Hay House, 1939
 Gregory Ain
 3432 Oakcrest Drive
This modular box, done mainly in wood, looks as if it had just been finished. The International Style Modern at its most beautiful.

4. Showboat Restaurant, 1968
 Cahuenga Boulevard near Bennett Drive at Hollywood Freeway ramp.
Well, part of a Mississippi showboat with its pair of metal smokestacks appropriately situated near the Los Angeles River.

5. Centrum Office Building,
1982
Johannes Van Tilburg and
Partners
3575 Cahuenga Boulevard,
near Multiview Drive
Described as "futuristic," this
vast hulk seems somewhat
old-fashioned—brutal at the
bottom moving into Stirling-
like tipped glass panels at the
top. Nevertheless, it acts as a
nice foil for the "less-is-more"
of Universal City directly
across the freeway.

3. Hay House, 1939

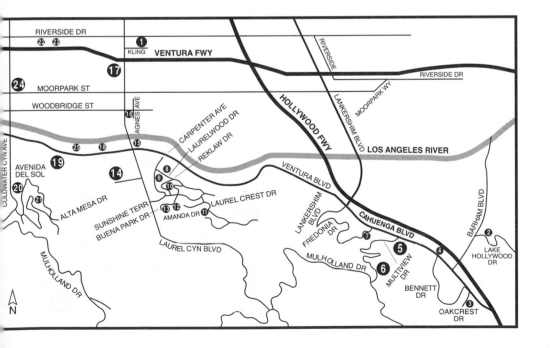

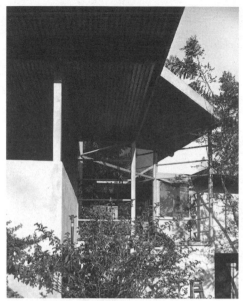

11. Lechner House, 1948

6. Kallis House, 1947
    R. M. Schindler
    3580 Multiview Drive
This angular cliff-hanger, now sequestered in foliage, is one of Schindler's most dramatic houses.

7. Fredonia Apartment Building, 1964
    Raymond L. Kappe
    3625 Fredonia Drive, off Ventura Boulevard
An ellipse of glass and stucco set into the hill, this small but luxurious building commands a magnificent view of the valley.

8. Laurelwood Apartment Building, 1948
    R. M. Schindler
    11833–11837 Laurelwood Drive
Two rows of simple, stucco box, de Stijl designs step up the small rise of land. At the time of this writing they are somewhat the worse for the wear, but we should rejoice in the fact that at least they are still here.

9. Goodwin House, 1940
    R. M. Schindler
    3807 Reklaw Drive

Not much can be seen of this small-scaled de Stijl composition from the street.

10. Gold House, 1945
    R. M. Schindler
    3758 Reklaw Drive
From the gate you will get a good view of Schindler's imaginative maneuvering, both vertically and horizontally, of light stucco volumes.

11. Lechner House, 1948
    R. M. Schindler
    11606 Amanda Drive
Actually, the best view is from Laurelvale Drive below. Schindler gives conventional builders' forms the stamp of his genius in this tentlike structure. The house was extensively remodeled in 1985 by Paul Sterling Hoag.

12. Waxman House, 1964
    J. Barry Moffat
    3644 Buena Park Drive
A theatrical essay in vertical and horizontal thrusts.

8. Laurelwood Apartment Building, 1948

6. Kallis House,
1947

13. Roth House, 1945
   R. M. Schindler
   3624 Buena Park Drive
Another "builder's house" whose flaring porch
at the curve of the road is a major exterior
feature.

14. Rodgers House, 1937
   Arthur S. Herbergon, Jr.
   12045 Maxwellton Road

A handsome brown clapboard Anglo Colonial
revival dwelling. It is difficult to photograph
because of the close-up trees, but it can be seen
easily if you walk past it.

15. Home Savings and Loan Building, 1968
   Millard Sheets
   Northeast corner of Ventura and Laurel
   Canyon boulevards
Sheets's huge mosaic over the door adds zest to
an area that needs it.

19. Lingenbrink Shops, 1939–42

16. Presburger House, 1945
R. M. Schindler
4255 Agnes Avenue
Not much can be seen, but this house with its high clerestory window running full length was imitated many times by contractors in the L.A. area.

17. Campbell Hall School, 1951
Jones and Emmons
4533 Laurel Canyon Boulevard
Modest International Style Modern on a small, shaded campus.

18. Medical Arts Building, 1945
R. M. Schindler
12307 Ventura Boulevard
Very chaste, this structure remains almost exactly as Schindler designed it, which is more than we can say for the next entry.

19. Lingenbrink Shops, 1939–42
R. M. Schindler
12632–12668 Ventura Boulevard
A complex of ten small offices and shops compromised by modernization. But there are recognizable fragments, as well as the wonderful

jagged roof line, mauled to be sure by signage.

To the east at 12601 Ventura Boulevard, note the two Southern Pacific Railroad cars that have been turned into **Carney's Express Restaurant** (circa 1978).

20. Saint Savior's Chapel, Harvard School, 1914
Reginald D. Johnson
3700 Coldwater Canyon Avenue
In 1937 this building was moved from the old campus at Venice Boulevard and Western Avenue in Central Los Angeles. It is mildly Gothic inside—supposedly based on a chapel at Rugby. The exterior suggests rural Spanish models.

21. Stevens House, 1941
Rodney Walker
3642 Altamesa Drive
All you can see are some Mexican pots hanging from a pergola, but this view is suggestive of Walker's romanticism.

22. Dorman/Winthrop Clothiers Building, 1966
Pulliam, Zimmerman, and Matthews (Bernard Zimmerman)
12640 Riverside Drive
A glistening International Style Modern glass box pushed up against the Ventura Freeway; its street front is almost a classical temple.

23. Riverside Law Building, 1972
Goldman/Brandt (Ron Goldman)
12650 Riverside Drive
Brownstone and wood, this two-story office building is designed around a small court. It looks fine and the lawyers say that it works.

24. Office Building, 1983
Ebbe Videriksen
4400 Coldwater Canyon Avenue
Twenty-eight thousand square feet of English Queen Anne.

25. Kinsey Office Building, 1978
Pulliam, Matthews, and Associates
12345 Ventura Boulevard
A beautifully articulated, brick, cut-into box with the front covered with plates of glass set behind metal columns.

PACOIMA

SHERMAN OAKS

This section of the valley is not rich in architecture, but until recently it had two houses designed by Joseph Cather Newsom. One has been moved to Mission Hills, and the other (1887) at 13204 Judd Street has had its fine Queen Anne lines covered with stucco. A good river-boulder **stone house** of the 1920s is at 13333 Fillmore Street.

A residential development of the 1930s with a commercial strip along Ventura Boulevard, Sherman Oaks was changed by the intersection here of the Ventura and San Diego freeways in the early 1960s. Sherman Oaks is now exposed to medium high-rise, all of it boring. The process has continued to the present with the same results. Nowhere is the aphorism "change and decay" more apt. In the last few years Smith and Williams's Goldman Medical Building (1948) has been demolished and an awful thing put in its place. The "dazzling scraffito work" on the Fiore d'Italia Restaurant has been painted over, though the exciting facade remains. The best here is elderly.

1. "Model House," 1935
H. Roy Kelley, Edgar F. Bissantz, and H. G. Spielman
14211 Valley Vista Boulevard
This Model House was erected at the first housing exhibition held at the Pan Pacific Auditorium in West Los Angeles. The house was raffled off and moved to this hillside site in the San Fernando Valley. As was the case with a number of 1930s L.A. designs, this one is essentially a California Ranch house which has been brought up-to-date by elements (such as portholes), which we associate with the Streamline Moderne. There have been a few changes to the dwelling, but its essential design is still apparent.

2. Notre Dame High School Building,
circa 1938
Northeast corner of Woodman Avenue and Riverside Drive
Mission style of the 1930s for the building facing Woodman Avenue and Riverside Drive. It is difficult to say what was the model for the

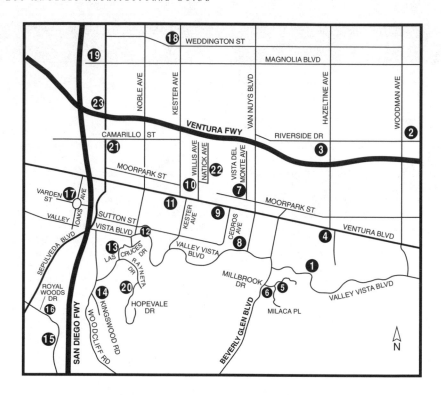

depression-period, Churrigueresque-style
gymnasium that makes a diagonal behind the
corner.

3. Sunkist Headquarters Building, 1969
   Albert C. Martin and Associates
   14130 Riverside Drive
A huge, four-square wine crate on stilts, all in
concrete; it works well from the freeway.

4. Bungalow Court, circa 1930
   South side of Ventura Boulevard just west of
   Hazeltine Avenue
A conversion of the Craftsman staple of the
Southern California diet to a restaurant and
shops. Well done.

5. Schwenck House, 1940
   Harwell H. Harris
   14239 Millbrook Drive
A barely-visible "Brown and Brown" clinging
to the hillside.

6. Dyer House, 1980
   Paul Sterling Hoag
   4009 Milaca Place
A steep-gabled roof, redwood house, with the
fenestration playing between the vertical and
the horizontal. The living room is two stories
high with a small balcony library.

7. Bungalow, circa 1935
   Northwest corner of Moorpark Street and
   Vista del Monte Avenue
A tiny stucco cottage exhibiting a good check-
list of all elements of Streamline Moderne.

8. Mesner House, 1951 and later
   Gregory Ain (Ain, Johnson, and Day)
   14571 Valley Vista Boulevard
Everything but the jutting roof is swamped in
foliage.

9. La Reina Theater, 1939
  S. Charles Lee
  Southwest corner of Ventura Boulevard and
  Cedros Avenue
A small Moderne structure with multi-sided
marquee supporting a crown. A little of the
etched glass is left in the otherwise disappoint-
ing interior.

10. Esplanade Apartment Building, 1967
  Kamnitzer, Marks, and Vreeland
  4617 Willis Avenue
International style Modern with a bit of color.

11. Fiore d'Italia Restaurant Building,
  circa 1965
  14928 Ventura Boulevard
Formerly, the general tone of this area was
Wild West, to which this once marvelously
decorated building served as a foil. Now the
scraffito work is gone and even the restaurant
has become Wild West. Ironically, the
Disneyland neighbors have almost disappeared
in new building.

12. Bernstein House, 1985
  Rebecca Bender
  15119 Valley Vista Boulevard
A highly inventive and imaginative remodeling
of a post-World War II ranch house.

13. Foster House, 1950
  John Lautner
  4235 Las Cruces Road
Anyone who remembers the fine Julius
Shulman photograph of this house in our 1965
Guide will now have difficulty seeing what was
intended before nature took over.

14. Elterman house, 1961
  Gregory Ain
  15301 Kingswood Lane
Spartan sophistication. Again, little can be
seen.

15. Barsha House, 1959
  Raymond Kappe
  3515 Royal Woods Drive
A modernist version of the Craftsman aesthetics. Note the three stepped-up clerestories on
the roof.

16. Handman House, 1963
  Raymond Kappe
  3872 Royal Woods Drive
A late Constructivist-Craftsman piece lost in
foliage.

17. Smith House, 1948
  Rodney Walker
  15435 Varden Street
Designed in International Style Modern simplicity before the architect developed his strong
tendency toward romanticism.

**18. Kester Avenue Elementary School
  Building,** 1951
  Richard J. Neutra; addition 1957;
  Dion Neutra
  Northwest corner of Kester Avenue and
  Weddington Street
A refinement of the finger-plan open-air
school, for which Neutra is famous.

19. Tower of Wooden Pallets, 1951
  Daniel Van Meter
  15357 Magnolia Boulevard
Daniel Van Meter built this folk folly of
wooden pallets, which he had obtained from the
Schiltz Brewery. Since 1978 it has been an offi-
cial historical landmark of the city of Los
Angeles.

20. Willheim House, 1978-79
  Charles W. Moore (Urban Innovations
  Group); with Elias Torres and John Rubel
  3944 Hopevale Drive
A plaster-and-wood castle clinging to a
hillside.

21. Sherman Oaks Galleria, 1980
  Albert C. Martin and Associates; Interior
  mall, Charles Kober Associates
  Southeast corner of Sepulveda Boulevard
  and Camarillo Street
A vast assemblage of white, late International
Style forms stretching for a long city block.

22. Zimbalist Apartment Building, 1973
  B. H. Bosworth
  4520 Natick Avenue
This L.A. Post-Modern endeavor consists of a
large ellipse of classical columns and pediments.

23. Castle Miniature Golf Course, circa 1976

23. Castle Miniature Golf Course
5000 Block, Sepulveda Boulevard
Begun in the late 1960s, this elaborate development of Hansel and Gretel forms and fantasy fountains is a nice stage-set for the off-ramp from the Ventura to the San Diego freeway.

The Portola expedition (1769) referred to what we now call the San Fernando Valley as "Santa Catalina de Bononia de los Encinos" for the many great oaks found in the area. The development of Encino, beginning with the introduction of an alternate route of the Southern Pacific Railroad in 1890, did not banish the oaks, many of which still exist. Significantly one of the oldest (1000 years) oaks in the state is on Louise Avenue just below Ventura Boulevard.

If you continue on Louise Avenue and then turn west on Rancho Street, you will have a pleasant drive back to Ventura Boulevard, where at 16661 you will see the **Travelers Insurance Building** (1966) designed by Howard Lane in a Neo-Streamline Moderne mode. Not far away and just off Ventura Boulevard (turn north on Petit Avenue) at 16756 Moorpark Street is the two-story masonry Greek Revival house (1849) of the **Rancho de los Encinos,** a state monument of California, open 1:00–4:00 P.M., Wednesday through Sunday. The southern hillside of Encino contains a number of large country houses, almost all of which cannot be seen from a public road. It is possible to catch a few brief glances at **Welbourne House** at 17128 Rancho Street. This house, including a free-standing mirador tower, plus other outbuildings, was designed in 1940–41 by Myron Hunt and H. C. Chambers. Hunt and Chambers produced, in this complex, one of their really elegant versions of the Spanish Colonial Revival, abstracted to a marked degree. Back on Ventura Boulevard at the northwest corner of Genesta Avenue is an intriguing row of **Tudor shops** that seems to hail from the 1920s.

When you drive on either the Ventura Freeway west of its interchange with the San Diego Freeway or on the San Diego Freeway north of the Ventura Freeway, you will see off to the northwest the spillway of the **Sepulveda**

Flood Control Dam. This rock-faced dam was built between the years 1939 and 1941 as a flood control point on the Los Angeles River. The dam was designed by the U.S. District Engineer, War Department, in Los Angeles. The total length of the earth-fill dam is 15,444 feet. The spillway and outlet works are an impressive 550 feet long, and 50 feet in height. The central concrete flood gates and tower are one of the most impressive examples of the PWA Moderne to be found in the Los Angeles Basin. As with so many of the dams and similar utilitarian constructions of the 1930s, the spillway section of the dam was designed through the eyes of the Streamline Moderne—beautiful, curved surfaces for the water channels, and even round porthole windows for the concrete control tower. In order to reach the dam you must park at its north end, just off Burbank Boulevard, north of Sepulveda Boulevard, and then put on your jogging shorts and prepare for a long run to the spillway and tower which are off limits, but you can wander around in the basin and below the basin to obtain a close view of its design.

Rancho de los Encinos, 1849

Since the basin is a vast area of open land, proposals have been and are continually being made as to how it might be further developed. Fortunately, most of these proposals have not taken place, since the area after all is a flood control basin. One project which was created and adds much to the area is the **Donald C. Tillman Japanese Gardens,** designed in 1983 by Koichi Kawana of UCLA. The theme is traditional Japanese, yes, but the resultant landscape has a strong modernist tinge. This is a very handsome garden, and well worth a visit. These gardens are located at 6100 Woodley

Avenue. They are not always open to the public, so you had better inquire beforehand about their hours.

Adjacent to the Japanese Gardens is the 1984 **Sepulveda Flood Control Basin Reclamation Building,** designed by Anthony Lumsden. While this is a strong modernist assertion, somewhat on the futuristic side in its design, its beautiful scale and detailing relate it to the Japanese Garden, which flows in and around it.

Sepulveda Flood Control Dam, 1939-41

TARZANA, WOODLAND HILLS

There is really no distinguishing these bedroom communities along the Ventura strip. Tarzana has the more colorful name given it by express permission of Edgar Rice Burroughs whose ranch covered much of the area. Two modernist buildings of the 1970s worth a visit are the **Barclays Bank Building** (1971) by Honnold, Reibsamen, and Rex at 18321 Ventura Boulevard, and the **Medical Center of Tarzana** (1973) just north of it (via Etiwanda Avenue and Clark Street) by Rochlin and Baran and Associates.

1. Fleetwood Center, 1987

1. Fleetwood Center, 1987
  Martin and Dovretzky
  19611 Ventura Boulevard
A continuation into the 1980s of L.A.'s tradition of Programmatic architecture. In this instance a huge, pink automobile radiator front with double headlights. We suppose that it is Post-Modern?

2. Wilbur Medical Plaza, 1986
  Albert C. Martin Associates
  5620 Wilbur Avenue
It's nice to see that Tarzana is really getting with it. This Post-Modernism is a study in lavender and white. We especially like the planting of palm trees.

3. Shopping Center, 1987
  18711–18743 Ventura Boulevard
Very nifty version of the Spanish Colonial Revival with plenty of room to park in the central courtyard. Everything is right except the scale.

4. Wall Street Plaza,
  circa 1988
  Robert and Lillian Wall
  (the owners)
A lot of gables suggest the Tudor was on the minds of the designers, but where is the black-and-white work? As a matter of fact the predominant color is a sort of turquoise and very unnerving. Will this building weather well?

5. Apartment House,
  1976
  Tom Roberts
  6350 Reseda Boulevard
Though this is perhaps not Robert's best work, this mildly High Tech assemblage stands for quality on a street of the tackiest apartments you have ever seen. Incidentally, if you have a taste for tract housing of the 1950s, try the streets east and west of Reseda Boulevard.

  In Woodland Hills, R. M. Schindler's **Van Dekker House** (1940) may be viewed from a distance at 5230 Penfield Avenue. It is sited on

Griffith Ranch House (1936)

the slope of a small hill. A dramatic shed roof corners the living room and is intersected by layers of low horizontal roofs; the walls are made of wood, stucco, and stone.

An exotic addition in 1984 to the Woodland Hills landscape is the **Struckus House** (1982–84) just northwest of the corner of Saltillo Street and Canoga Avenue. It plays off several quite different images—that of a delightful eighteenth-century bird cage strung between four oak trees, while its round windows have the feeling of Captain Nemo's submarine. It was designed by Bruce Goff (his only house in Southern California) just before his death in 1983.

The **Griffith Ranch House** (1936) by Lloyd Wright is almost invisible at 4900 Dunman Avenue. In this dwelling, Wright took the theme of the late 1930s California Ranch house and imposed a Prairie cruciform plan upon it.

As the Freeway (Highway 101 west) ascends the hill west of Winneka Avenue, one is treated to a characteristic varied world of Southern California's architectural images.

To the east on the hillside at the northwest corner of Ventura Boulevard and Del Moreno Drive is a three-story Spanish Colonial Revival **Office Building** (1983). From the Ventura Freeway its large round tower, tile roofs, and white walls look romantic; but unfortunately it is not as impressive close up. Then as you proceed up the hill, Georgian London suddenly comes into view via the **Chateau Office Building**. This 1985 building located at 20501 Ventura Boulevard was designed by Siegel, Skarek and Diamond. It is in every way a grand and perfect Hollywood stage set which visually works best from a distance, not close up. Rows of great Corinthian Columns are matched by classical pediments and balustrades. It looks best at night when it is brilliantly lighted. Still farther along to the west on the Ventura Freeway you encounter yet another architectural image, in this case what appears to be a half-timbered **Medieval building.** This structure, located behind 20631 Ventura Boulevard was an addition to what was a small, two-story restaurant building (circa 1970). The restaurant is now an accounting office, and the new building to the rear (circa 1980) contains a ground-level garage and two floors of additional offices. Next door to the east is one of the **Victoria Station** Restaurants—in the usual form of a railroad car.

Chateau Office Building, 1985

CALABASAS

One of the oldest settlements in the valley, Calabasas was a stagecoach stop on the Camino Real route from Santa Barbara to Los Angeles. Only a few simple brick buildings remain from the late nineteenth-century commercial district and these have been Disneyized in order to create an image of the Wild West that will amuse if not edify. A touch of reality at 23400 Calabasas Road is the beautifully restored two-story **Leonis Adobe** (circa 1850) with its wooden Queen Anne gingerbread added by Miguel Leonis when he moved there in the 1870s. The back lawn, shaded by one of California's greatest oaks, helps to create a nineteenth-century atmosphere even with the freeway only a hundred yards away. Thanks to the late Catharine S. Beachey and her family this may be one of the best endowed house museums in the country. Open to the public Wednesday, Saturday, and Sunday, 1:00–4:00 P.M., no admission charge.

About a mile southwest of Calabasas (via Calabasas Road and Park Granada Boulevard) is a new subdivision called **Calabasas Park.** The landscape of the lake area was designed in 1972 by Julian George. The Country Club (1972) was laid out by Robert Trent Jones. The surrounding condominiums and town houses (1974–later) were designed by Dorman/Munselle Associates who chose the Spanish Colonial Revival image. Along with the provision of a multitude of trees, the whole enterprise fits well into the landscape.

Almost directly south of Calabasas (Mulholland Drive, then Val Mar Road to Bluebird Drive) are the remnants of the **Park Moderne,** conceived by L.A.'s early patron of the Moderne and Modern, William Lingenbrink, in 1929 (see **Lingenbrink Shops,** Studio City) for "Lovers of Modernistic Art," meaning both the de Stijl and Art Deco phases

of that passion. He employed European-educated R. M. Schindler and Jock Peters to design houses "along Modern lines." Due to the depression, few of these houses were built. We don't want to encourage you to make a desperate effort to see what is left (for there is little left today) but thought it our duty to record the facts:

1. House, 1931
   Jock Peters
   Northeast corner of Bluebird Drive and
   Meadowlark Drive
Art Deco (Zigzag) Moderne transformed by later hands into an English Cottage.

2. Community Building (now a private residence), 1931
   Jock Peters
   23031 Bluebird Drive
Close to European Modern of the 1920s with a strong contrast between the horizontal corner windows and the vertical fins and piers.

3. Fountain, 1930
   Jock Peters
   South side of Blackbird Way, south of
   Meadowlark Drive
Art Deco (Zigzag) Moderne in concrete.

4. House, circa 1931
   South side of Blackbird Way, south of
   Meadowlark Drive
Remodeled Art Deco (Zigzag) Moderne.

5. House, 1929
   R. M. Schindler
   3978 Blackbird Way
Of the three houses Schindler designed for Lingenbrink at Park Moderne, one remained a project, a second was built and subsequently demolished. Only this one remains. In scale it is a single-floor cabin, dominated by strong horizontals—projecting flat roofs and narrow bands of clerestory windows.

6. Well-house, 1931
  Attributed to Jock Peters
  Opposite 22959 Hummingbird Way
Angular Art Deco (Zigzag) Moderne in cast
concrete.

7. Andy Anderson House, 1937–38
  Andy Anderson
  22912 Bluebird Way
The best-preserved house of this early period,
and Pueblo Revival to boot. Except for the
Southern California vegetation, it seems to be
in Santa Fe. It was designed and built by its
owner, the craftsman Andy Anderson. Because
of the building codes of the time, it employed
wood frame construction to imitate adobe.

8. Benson House (1981–84)
  Frank O. Gehry and Associates.
From the small, narrow road, you can see two
volumetric boxes toppling over a steep hillside.
Both of these connected boxes are sheathed in
different colored and patterned asphalt shingles—even the entrance door is shingled. The
house is located at 23638 Clover Trail (do consult your maps carefully to find this one—proceed up Mulholland Highway to Canyon Drive,
then keep a close lookout for Clover Trail
which is off of Summit Drive).

HIGHWAY 101 WEST

MALIBU CANYON AREA

1. King C. Gillette Ranch (presently Soka
  University), 1929
  Wallace Neff
  26812 West Mulholland Hwy (just off of Las
  Virgenes Road)
This ranch complex represents one of the high
points of the Spanish Colonial Revival. Neff in
this house fully captured the spirit of a rural
Cortijo which one might come across in southern Spain. One enters the complex through a
ceremonial arch into the auto court. The house
itself (constructed of adobe) is centered around
a central fountained courtyard. Over the years
there have been some insensitive remodelings
and additions, but the strength of Neff's
abstraction of the Hispanic remains.

2. Sree Venkateswara Temple, 1982–88
  S. M. Ganapathi
  East side Las Virgenes Road north of its
  junction with Mulholland Highway
Towered Hindu temples peer out from the trees
and shrubs of a small southern California
canyon. The temples with their stepped towers
were built by Hindu craftsmen from India. The
structures are of concrete and brick, and are
covered with carvings of elephants, lions, drag-
ons, and lotus flowers. Their white surfaces
gleam in the sunlight.

SIMI VALLEY

1. Ulmar House, 1939–later
  Terry Ulmar
  4986 Cochran Street
One of Southern California's Folk Follies. The
owner/builder has wrought his composition out
of concrete block to create something which at
one moment is medieval, the other pre-
Columbian.

2. Grandma Prisbrey's Bottle Village,
1959–74
Tressa Prisbrey
4595 Cochran Street

When the Walker Art Center of Minneapolis in 1974 organized its exhibition "Naives and Visionaries" the Bottle Village was selected as an important national example of America's folk tradition (see Esther McCoy's chapter on Grandma Prisbrey's Bottle Village in the catalogue for this exhibition). A miniature Simi Valley folk village, with buildings of glass bottle walls, dolls (whole and parts), automobile headlights, a fountain of old fluorescent tubes, and so on. The buildings include a schoolhouse, a chapel, a thatched house, the "Leaning Tower of Pisa," and "Cleopatra's Bedroom." Each year when we return to the village, less is preserved, and one wonders how long it will be with us. Needless to say, this is a monument like Simon Rodia's Watts Towers, which should be preserved for future generations to enjoy.

WESTLAKE VILLAGE

In the classic relationship of freeways and suburban development, a number of communities began to develop in western Los Angeles County as Highway 101 was transformed from a two-lane affair to the present six and eight lanes. Hidden Hills, a horse-oriented community, was laid out after World War II by the landscape architect/developer, A. E. Hanson (California Ranch houses, rail fences, horse corrals, and guarded gates). The most impressive single development was Westlake Village, "A new city in the country." The American-Hawaiian Land Company purchased the 12,000 acre Albertson Ranch, and engaged Bechtel Corp. in 1966 to draw up the initial master plan. This plan was revised the following year by Albert C. Martin and Associates, and it was once again revised in 1967 by Jack Bevash. The planning ideal of Westlake Village was that it would not be a bedroom suburb, rather it would be a small city within which most of its inhabitants would work, live, shop and have their own recreational activities.

While there was no strong aesthetic style laid down, the general guidelines looked to Spanish, and specifically to variations on the California Ranch House. These were later loosened up to include some modern and some other traditional styles. Now after a quarter of a century (the city officially opened in 1966), you can see the results. It is upper-middle-class, pleasant, and it seems to work well, but it does not project a strong personality. The best aspect of the project is the landscape architecture; the thick trees and other plants have really taken over, and everything is very well maintained.

While Westlake Village has continued, in a loose way, to maintain its stucco/tile roof Hispanic image, there are some inroads. There is a Frank Gehry house in the hills (unfortunately not visible from a public road), and then for those enamored of the Anglo Colonial tradition, there is the **Sherwood Country Club** (1991–92) at 320 West Stafford Road, Thousand Oaks. (This is a gated community, but you can see some of the buildings from the public road). In the way of public visibility, certainly the most interesting building in Westlake Village is the **Prudential Building** designed by Albert C. Martin and Associates (1978–80). This late modernist building angles itself in an organic fashion between two knolls, so that all you see from the freeway is a series of three horizontal bands looking out over a typical landscape of wild grassland studded by native California oaks. The heavy eyebrows over the strip windows do function, for this side faces to the south and west. To the rear, that is to the northeast, you can see the multi-storied atrium space of the building. The **Prudential Building** is located north of Highway 101, on Thousand Oaks Boulevard, between Lindero Canyon Road and Westlake Boulevard.

As long as you have gone as far as Westlake Village you might be interested in traveling on a few minutes more on Highway 101, and go on to Thousand Oaks—to see at least two recent modern "monuments." These are the new **Thousand Oaks Art and Civic Center** now being completed (1994). This has been designed by Antoine Predock. The Civic Center is located north of Highway 101, off of

Prudential Building, 1978-80

Thousand Oaks Boulevard. Further north on
Highway 101, off of the Lynn Road interchange is the **Sirmai-Peterson house**
(1983–88) designed by Frank O. Gehry and
Associates. Because of the high planting you
can only see a few tantalizing fragments of this
house, such as the metal sheathed tower. The
house is located at 970 Calle Arroyo.

CANOGA PARK

The early seat of the Orcutts and the Workmans, this area is really Valley—meaning that it is given over to tract housing that was the subject of cartoons in the 1950s. If you wish to view this phenomenon, it is best to take the north/south streets off the main boulevards—Roscoe, Saticoy, Sherman Way (magnificent lines of Imperial palms) and Vanowen. You should also see these same areas from the air, for the glint of the sun off the unused swimming pools is quite charming. Some good things on the ground:

1. Canoga Mission Gallery Building, 1934–36
Francis Lederer
23130 Sherman Way

Lederer, the famous cinema idol of yesteryear, designed this building as stables in the simple, very late Mission mode. But when the city decided to cut through his estate in order to extend Sherman Way, the road led right past the stable. Mrs. Lederer, sensing an opportunity, remodeled the stables to serve as a gift shop selling Mexican and Californian crafts. In fact, it also serves as a kind of social hall for this part of the Valley.

2. W. W. Orcutt House ("Rancho Sombra del Roble"), circa 1930
23555 Justice Street
Orcutt was an early oil baron who bought this property that had years before provided the timber used in firing the kilns producing bricks for the San Fernando Mission. His Spanish

1. Canoga Mission Gallery Building, 1934–36

Colonial Revival house is rarely open to the public and is barely visible from the street.

3. Workman House ("Shadow Ranch"),
1869–72; remodeling 1935–36
Lawrence Test
Charles Gibbs Adams, landscape architect
22633 Vanowen Street

The original board and batten two-story ranch house was the center of a 23,000 acre ranch. At the time of its mid–1930s remodeling the site had been reduced to ten acres. Lawrence Test retained much of the original informal quality of the original building. But he did add to and revamp the exterior, moving the old carriage house and attaching it to the main house with a long low garage and dog trot. The radical changes came about inside where

(with the exception of the "Adobe Room") all looked to the Anglo Colonial Revival of these years. Eighteenth-century wide floorboards were shipped from Connecticut, and the eighteenth-century fireplace in the dining room came from a house in Fredericksburg, Virginia.

In 1961 the house and its site were acquired by the City of Los Angeles, and the grounds were somewhat altered for public use by the landscape architect Arthur G. Barton. The house is really lovely, set in a public park with some of the oldest eucalyptus groves in the state.

4. Great Western Savings Building, 1966
Kurt Meyer and Associates
6601 Topanga Canyon Boulevard
A huge, Neo-Brutalist temple in exposed concrete and glass. The projecting roof is supported on both sides of the entrance by two sets of double columns.

5. Bullock's Woodland Hills, 1972–73
Welton Becket and Associates
Promenade Shopping Center, 6000 block,
Topanga Canyon Boulevard (actually in
Canoga Park)
The sparingly-fenestrated, white slumpstone facade evokes the image of the walls of a Mexican village—on a very large scale, to be sure.

3. Workman House ("Shadow Ranch"), 1869-72

8. Platt Office Building, 1981

6. Canoga Park Post Office, 1938
  Louis A. Simon, supervising architect
  Northwest corner of Sherman Way and
  Jordan Avenue
The building is simple Spanish Colonial
Revival with Moderne tendencies. Inside is a
fine Federal Arts Project (WPA) mural,
Palomino Ponies, painted by Maynard Dixon in
1942.

**7. Crippled Children Society ("Rancho del
Valle"), Main Building,** 1979
  John Lautner
  6530 Winnetka Avenue

A wing of this radially planned, one-story
building has been erected. It has all the drama
that we have come to expect of Lautner
designs.

8. Platt Office Building, 1981
  T. W. Layman
  19725 Sherman Way (just west of Corbin
  Avenue)
Parts of buildings, formerly on Bunker Hill,
have been assembled here to give us something
more than a new Victorian (Queen Anne) commercial building. This is a bona fide and very
welcome folly.

CHATSWORTH

In our last Guide we noted that "This old town has, in spite of growth, managed to avoid being submerged." Well, the deluge has made horrible inroads since then, mainly in the form of vast, tasteless "mansions" that are a monument to the self-centered culture.

Chatsworth began its Anglo life as a small settlement at the southeast end of the Santa Susana Pass, where it was a stop on the inland stagecoach route opened in 1861 between San Francisco and provincial Los Angeles. The trail down the pass (parts are still visible) was so steep that the wheels of the coaches were locked and timbers hauled behind in order to control the descent. Harried travelers were relieved when the stagecoach line was relocated (1874) along the Camino Real (see Calabasas), but the trail was used by travelers to and from the Simi Valley until the railroad tunnels were built in 1904. Now a freeway to the north of the town communicates with Simi.

The great outcrop of rock known as **Stony Point** has often been used as scenery in Wild West movies. Earlier it marked the site of Indian settlements. The very active Chatsworth Historical Society is an excellent source of information on Indian lore. It is also the agency chiefly responsible for moving the picturesque Eastlake-Gothic **Methodist Church** (1904) to the **Oakland Cemetery** (10000 block of Valley Circle Boulevard) when the church was threatened by progress.

Methodist Church (1904)

NORTHRIDGE

First named Zelzah (in 1908), the settlement's current respectable name was suggested in 1935 by Carl S. Dentzel, a founding member of the Los Angeles Cultural Board. Immediately after World War II this part of the valley was sparsely settled, agricultural land planted with orange groves and truck crops. In the 1950s a little **Modern tract housing** (Smith and Williams, 1954) was tried near Reseda Boulevard. The block bounded by Chase Street, Darby Avenue, and Rathburn Avenue contains the highest proportion of original, relatively unremodeled examples. Obviously, builders' tract housing took off from there.

Also, in the early 1960s Northridge became the seat of **San Fernando Valley State College** ("Valley State") which in a few years raised itself to a university (California State University, Northridge) that is roughly bounded by Reseda Boulevard, Lassen Street, Zelzah Avenue, and Nordhoff Street (where there is a little visitor parking). The architect Richard Neutra (with Robert E. Alexander), whose nearby Streamline landship, the Von Sternberg House (1935), now destroyed, may have suggested him to the trustees, designed the **Fine Arts Building** (1959). The architects of several other buildings have tried to imitate his design featuring elongated sunshades, but they have succeeded only in reproducing State College Modern dullness.

In places, Reseda Boulevard retains memories of its strip development in the 1930s. In fact, just off Reseda Boulevard at 18448 Saticoy Street is a Streamline Moderne diner, **Brown's Burger Bar** (circa 1940). North of Saticoy Street are several of the now-plentiful stucco box **apartments.** The variety of images possible in this medium is suggested by 7923 Reseda Boulevard, which is Polynesian (circa

1958), and the one at the northwest corner of Reseda Boulevard and Strathern Street, where a large corner mosaic of a winged bull proclaims its Assyrian heritage (circa 1960).

Farther west, on and off Tampa Avenue, are some equally interesting developments. **Bullock's Northridge** (1972), designed by Welton Becket and Associates, is in the Northridge Plaza near the southwest corner of Plummer Street and Tampa Avenue. It is all roof with its two ends resembling sawed-off pyramids. Southwest of it at 190601 Nordhoff Street (northeast corner of Corbin Avenue) is the black, sophisticated **Teledyne Systems Company** (1968) that Cesar Pelli designed for Daniel, Mann, Johnson, and Mendenhall before Post-Modern tendencies struck him. At the Corbin Avenue corner is a tiny grove of orange trees, and across the street is a large wood lot with green fields behind it. South on Tampa Avenue at the west end of Cantara Street there is actually a large barn. But this arcadian bliss is passing, as the large **Northridge Hospital** (1968–later) by Rochlin and Baran and Associates attests. This complex, just east of the intersection of Roscoe Boulevard and Reseda Boulevard, is superficially a spin-off from Louis Kahn's Richards Medical Center in Philadelphia.

GRANADA HILLS, MISSION HILLS

VAN NUYS, PANORAMA CITY, SEPULVEDA

This area of the northern San Fernando Valley began its residential development in the late 1950s, and the newer tracts reach right up to the Santa Susana Mountains. Its green space has been enhanced by golf courses and parks in a manner very uncharacteristic of the normal tendencies in Southern California. To be sure, some of these spaces are cemeteries.

Most of the housing is conventional middle-class stuff, a better-than-average tract being reached by driving north on Balboa Boulevard to Westbury Drive and then west to Jimeno Avenue. Jimeno Avenue, Lisette Street, Nanette Street, and Darla Avenue were developed by Joseph Eichler. The housing was designed by Jones and Emmons (1963–64) around courtyards.

Mission Hills has as its great claim to fame a Victorian Queen Anne house (1887) moved there from Pacoima. It was designed by Joseph Cather Newsom as one of a group of spec houses. The house, moved to 17410 Meyerling Street (between Shoshone and Andasol Avenues), has a two-story, side-hall plan and exhibits the usual array of Newsom's ornament in sawed and turned wood.

The name Van Nuys is the only thing that memorializes the great wheat rancher. The area has not seen wheat for years. It is dignified by having a branch of the Los Angeles City Hall around which some urban renewal is going on. Otherwise, there is not much to distinguish it from its neighbors, Panorama City and Sepulveda, to the north. Thus, if you get off the freeway here, you might as well see them all.

1. Post Office, circa 1926
14540 Sylvan Street
Modest Spanish Colonial Revival, but worth protecting against urban renewal. Next door at 14550 is one of those charming Moderne **gas stations** (Richfield) of the 1930s and next to it is a small, dumpy Classical Revival **office building.** An imaginative urban designer could give great interest to this group.

1. Post Office, circa 1926

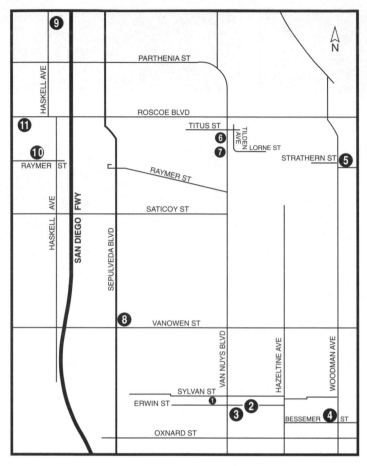

classicism in white
brick and concrete is
ultra-sophisticated for
the valley. In case there
is a misunderstanding
of the relationship
between architecture
and art, the building's
cornerstone bears the
following: "Federal Art
in Architecture
Program."

4. House, 1935
Just behind apart-
ments at northwest
corner of Woodman
Avenue and
Bessemer Street
At least the extremely
picturesque Spanish
Colonial Revival house
was preserved when the
front yard was taken
over by progress.
Incidentally, George
Brent once lived here—
before progress.

**5. The Taos West
Apartments,** 1972
7924 Woodman
Avenue
Pueblo Revival that no
resident of Taos would
recognize as home, but

2. Valley Municipal Building, 1932
Peter K. Schabarum
14410 Sylvan Street
An eight-story Art Deco/(Zigzag) Moderne
office building which certainly stands out in
this area of the Valley. According to rumor, it
may not be with us much longer.

3. U.S. General Services Administration,
1974
Lyman Kipp
Southeast corner of Van Nuys Boulevard and
Erwin Street
This long, sleek, four-story example of modern

which gets some points for its outrageous parody of folk architecture.

6. Great Western Savings Bank, circa 1970
Northwest corner of Van Nuys Boulevard
and Titus Street, Panorama City
We admire bankers who have the nerve to go
so deeply into the architecture of fantasy. This
is not great architecture, but it certainly pokes
convention in the nose.

7. Carnation Research Building, 1952–53
8015 Van Nuys Boulevard at Lorne Street
An understated, post-World War II Streamline
Moderne building, if such is possible.

8. Valley Presbyterian Hospital, 1983–84
  Thomas, Bobrow, and Associates
  Northeast corner of Sepulveda Boulevard
  and Vanowen Street
The nondescript 1950s buildings have been
included in a new site plan of Bobrow and
Thomas. The first phase of their plan has provided a new entrance at the center of the complex which joins two of the older buildings
together. Also, new parking facilities have been
added. The entrance and the other new additions express a reserved, sophisticated version
of the late Modern mode, realized in exposed
concrete and glass.

9. Greer House, 1940
  Lloyd Wright
  9200 Haskell Avenue
Some touches of Streamline Moderne (portholes) adorn this building, now easily accessible since it has been incorporated with the
church next door.

**10. Ninety-fourth Aero Squadron
  Headquarters Restaurant,** 1973
  Lynne, Paxton, Paxton, and Cole
  16320 Raymer Street
French Provincial with a vengeance, this large
farmhouse at the Van Nuys Airport even has
bales of hay apparently ready to be pulled into
the loft. The only thing that is missing is the
pile of manure that would give this marvelous
creation the sense of complete authenticity.

**11. The Torrington Manufacturing
  Company,** 1953
  Marcel Breuer (Craig Ellwood, supervising
  architect)
  16300 Roscoe Boulevard
Incredibly close (a few blocks) to the previous
entry, this long, two-story monument to
Bauhaus modularism stands (perhaps as it
should considering its attack on history) in a
visual wasteland. In spite of its age, it looks just
fine—one of the things that should slow you up
on your way to Bakersfield.

MISSION SAN FERNANDO REY DE ESPAÑA

Iglesia, 1974 (based on church of 1804–6)
  15151 San Fernando Mission Boulevard, just
  east of Sepulveda Boulevard and the Golden
  State Freeway. (A map of the Mission complex is given to you when you buy your
  ticket to the grounds.)
The Mission was founded by Padre Fermin
Lasuen in 1797. Nothing architectural remains
from this period except the ruins of the dam
that provided a water supply for the acres of
wheat and corn. The church looks and is new.
The earthquake of 1971 shook the old building
so badly that it had to be demolished. The 1974
building, while in concrete, is faithful to the
former one, but it must be noted that the previous church was in its turn a rather imaginative
reconstruction (1935) by M. R. Harrington of
the original. With few hints as to the details of
the first building, Harrington set out to investigate the decoration of other missions and imitated what he found in order to give romantic
appeal to the new church, an appeal which the
good fathers have attempted to render in the
1974 building.
  The **Convento** (1810–22), the first thing that
you see when you approach the entrance, is old.
It used to look old until the 1974 restoration,
which spread from the church to the outbuildings. Stucco was swished over everything
(especially exposed adobe bricks) and painted
so that the Mission complex looks brand new.
  The **cemetery,** containing the graves of
Indian converts and early white settlers, is just
north of the church. Across the street from the
Convento is a lovely park which, with its fountain, gardens, and statue of Junipero Serra,
almost makes you forget the follies of contemporary restoration projects.

*The **Convento**, San Fernando Mission (1810–22)*

By jogging south on Columbus just west of the mission, you will encounter, amid a trailer court and other skulch, the **Andres Pico Adobe.** Its address is 10940 Sepulveda, well marked. The house was the home of the Mexican who in 1845 leased the entire San Fernando Valley and began its development. In 1873, after the American occupation, Pico decided to remodel the adobe (begun in 1834) in American style, adding Yankee sash, a second story, and other fashionable details. The house has been remodeled and enlarged many times, particularly by Dr. M. R. Harrington in the 1930s when the Spanish Colonial porch was added. It is, in the mess of the valley, an oasis of civilization.

***Andres Pico Adobe** (1834; 1873)*

This town is the oldest in the valley. It was settled northeast of the Mission which is, by a fluke of politicking, in Los Angeles and not in separately incorporated San Fernando. Its short boom began in 1874 when the Southern Pacific Railroad, coming up from the south, reached it. The one remaining shred of this Victorian period is the **Geronimo Lopez Adobe** (1878) at the northwest corner of Pico Street and Maclay Avenue. It is two-story Monterey style with some pretty Queen Anne sawed gingerbread across the gallery. Otherwise all signs of the old town have disappeared, except for the railroad.

Some attempts to invent a Spanish Colonial past have been made in the new buildings by the use of stucco walls and tile roofs, but the effect is not as successful as the similar effort at Santa Barbara. An exception is **St. Ferdinand's Roman Catholic Church** (1949) just across Maclay Avenue from the Lopez Adobe. The church takes its sculptural forms from the simple mission churches, even going as far away as Taos, New Mexico, for its inspiration.

A typical **stone house** of the 1920s, so evocative of the picturesque image of the valley, appears on the northeast side of Laurel Canyon Boulevard near Brand Boulevard. The **Municipal Light, Water, and Power Building** (circa 1937) at 313 S. Brand Boulevard near the corner of Pico Street is a semiprecious gem of the Streamline Moderne. But don't go out of your way to see the oldest town in the valley.

SAN FERNANDO

Geronimo Lopez Adobe (1878)

St. Ferdinand's Roman Catholic Church (1949)

NEWHALL; SAUGUS; VALENCIA

In your eagerness either to enter or to leave Los Angeles you may forget that a good deal of history, mainly transportation and engineering, took place in this area. Beside you on the Golden State Freeway is The Cascade that in 1913 marked the termination of William Mulholland's Los Angeles Aqueduct that brought water from the Owens River Valley so that Los Angelenos would never be thirsty—or so it seemed at the time. Near this place is an off-ramp marked "The Old Road," meaning the famous Ridge Route that was opened in 1915 and that, in spite of its curves, cut off many miles between Los Angeles and San Francisco. Much of the concrete is still there, but the roadhouses and gas stations are all gone.

By turning northeast on the Antelope Valley Freeway you will soon come to the **Placerita Canyon State Park and Nature Study Center.** Here you can see the "Oak of the Golden Dream" under which Francisco Lopez discovered in 1842 the first gold to be found in California in commercial quantities. Architecturally the award-winning **Nature Center** (1973), a collection of low, hipped-roof buildings designed by Richard L. Dorman and Associates, is more rewarding.

Turn back (west) on the Sierra Highway, then north on San Fernando Road. In a few hundred yards you will see a State Landmark sign directing you to the first commercial **oil refinery** (1876) in California, a plausibly restored group of buildings in a strangely picturesque setting. Continue north on San Fernando Road to the **William S. Hart Park,** once the estate of the famous cowboy movie star. The original ranch house (circa 1910) is a log cabin, but by climbing the hill you will come upon the mansion (Arthur Kelly, 1925),

which will delight followers of the Spanish Colonial Revival.

Back to San Fernando Road and north again at Drayton Street you will come to the site of the bracketed **Southern Pacific Railroad Station** (circa 1900) that unfortunately burned a few years ago. This site should remind you that in 1876, about ten miles east of this place, the last section of track was completed on the railroad link between Los Angeles and San Francisco, thus joining with the transcontinental railroad to bring thousands of people to Southern California, eventually transforming Los Angeles from a sleepy village into questionable urbanity.

Heading north again on San Fernando Road, you will almost immediately see Magic Mountain Parkway. Turn left on it and then left again on Valencia Boulevard and then again on Newhall Avenue, which becomes McBean Parkway. To the south of this road is the community of **Valencia** which you may wish to visit because it was planned (1966) by Thomas L. Sutton, Jr., and Victor Gruen Associates as a New Town (like Westlake Village and Irvine). It will be, according to the descriptive literature, "a semi-contained urban element" with its own industry as well as retail centers and housing. The promoters expect a town of 150,000 people by the year 2020. The housing (designed by Barry Berkus, Maxwell Starkman and Associates; Edward C. Malon, and others) ranges from garden apartments to single-family dwellings and, in spite of its essential dullness, works out better than most project housing because of excellent planning and landscaping. Parks, greenbelts, and bike paths were provided.

Near the intersection of the McBean Parkway with the Golden State Freeway, you will see the entrance to the **California Institute**

William S. Hart
House (1910)

of the Arts whose main buildings were designed by Ladd and Kelsey (1969–70) in brown slumpstone and concrete. One would expect better architecture considering the competence of the architects and the wherewithal of the Walt Disney estate that is behind it financially, but the architecture is only a cut above that of the tract housing nearby.

After looking around Valencia, cross under the Golden State Freeway (Highway 5) to Magic Mountain Parkway. Go to the end (west), and you will arrive at the **Magic Mountain Amusement Park** (now **Six Flags Magic Mountain**) designed in 1970 by Thomas L. Sutton for the Newhall Land and Farming Company, the developer of Valencia. After establishing clearly where you have parked your car in relation to the "auto gate," go on to the ticket counter and entrance. Until 1982 you entered through the gates of a French chateau and moved ahead into a formal garden with a fountain and geometrical planting. Visually this arrangement helped to bring a sense of order before you plunged into the

exuberance of the park. Unfortunately this has all been changed. A new entrance designed in serious High Modern-High Tech provides no joy or tone of fantasy.

The same seriousness pervades the High Tech image of the **Texas Instruments Computer Discovery Center** (1982). Notwithstanding these recent movements away from the original lightheartedness of Magic Mountain, its glory remains its landscaping designed by Emmet Wemple and Associates, who also designed the old French forecourt. The architecture runs the full range from the Oriental (perhaps it is Japanese, but who can be sure?) to German, Swiss, and English Medieval to American Colonial and Victorian. And California's own tradition of the Mission Revival can be seen in the Forecourt of the Revolution. The Monterey style is featured in the Holiday Bazaar. Magic Mountain is far more informal and easygoing than the highly organized environment of Disneyland, its rival to the south.

PALMDALE; LANCASTER

LA CRESCENTA VALLEY

This country is hardly an architectural oasis. Lancaster's Western Hotel (1874), a plain, two-story building with columned porch at 557 W. Lancaster Boulevard, is a remnant of pioneer days. There are several PWA Moderne public buildings in Lancaster, including the Post Office Building (1940, Louis A. Simon; Neal A. Melick) at 567 West Lancaster Boulevard, and the former School Building (circa 1937) now used for the Lincoln School District. The Post Office Building, together with the other mildly PWA Moderne civic buildings, has been placed (1993) on the National Register of Historic Places. The school is located on Cedar Street, between New Grove Street and Lancaster Boulevard. Beyond Palmdale, about fifteen miles along Avenue O, you will come to Avenue 170 East. Go north on it and then west on Avenue M. Almost immediately you will come upon the Antelope Valley Indian Museum (1928), a simple wooden building intended by its creator, H. Arden Edwards, to embody elements of Indian design, but tending to look more like a Swiss chalet than any example we know of Native American architecture. The collection of Indian artifacts, particularly Southwestern rugs, is excellent. The Kachina Hall will attract the Craftsman enthusiast. Open only on weekends and Monday holidays.

If you have visited Newhall, Valencia, and Magic Mountain and wish to return to Los Angeles by a different route, exit from the Golden State Freeway (Highway 5) onto the Foothill Freeway (Highway 210) (Pasadena signs!). You thus skirt the eastern side of San Fernando and eventually, after some beautiful, lonely, and almost desert landscape, enter Sunland, from which you can make an amusing diversion south on Sunland Boulevard to Sun Valley.

Actually, Sun Valley is closer to the Golden State Freeway, so you can make your choice between the Golden State Freeway and the Foothill Freeway. If you choose the former, exit at Sunland Boulevard and go north to the city of Sunland. Thereafter, you should probably stay on Foothill Boulevard visiting the towns as we have listed them. You will come out at Pasadena, as you will if you take the Foothill Freeway.

A general map of the area will make all this clear and also, we believe, make you sympathize with our problems of establishing a rational plan for visiting the Los Angeles area.

If you want to get the feel of working-class Southern California in the 1920s and 1930s, you cannot get it anymore in Hollywood. The epicenter of "Old Wide-open Southern California" is in the Sunland-Tujunga area. It is hot, dusty, occasionally smog-ridden, but with exceptions which you must learn to cancel out (especially along Foothill Boulevard); here are almost the last of the freewheeling communities with close ties to nature, golden hills, and monuments to dreams. For instance, the **Villa Rotunda** (circa 1955) at 8618 La Tuna Canyon Road. What is it? Why is it round?

The delight of the area is the quantity of its

Hansen Dam, 1938-40

boulder ("cobblestone" out here) architecture. The **house** (circa 1922) at 8642 Sunland Boulevard near Olinda Street is a good introduction. But the mecca for boulder enthusiasts is the old town of Roscoe (now Stonehurst). Here forty or so stone bungalows were built, according to the story, for $100 apiece, some say by Indian labor. You can see that we are hedging on facts. There is disagreement about them as there is about the English colony that is supposed to have lived here and the movie stars that are supposed to have vacationed in Roscoe with the idea of "roughing it." Stick to what you see along Stonehurst Avenue and Sheldon, Thelma, Allegheny, and Wicks streets.

Going east along Sunland and Foothill boulevards you will encounter more delights, although, we are sorry to say, a great many have disappeared in recent years. But venture into the side streets. Try going north on Orovista Avenue to Hillrose Circle. The whole area is delightful, but it is simply preparing you for Tujunga.

One major relic remains in the area. This is **Old Vienna Gardens** (now the Villa Cinzano Restaurant) located at 9955 Sunland Boulevard. It is an unexpected Hansel and Gretel house in this seeming wasteland. It was built over a period from 1928 to 1937. Also notice the **August Furst Castle,** situated high above the restaurant (at 9983 Johanna Avenue). The one major public monument of La Crescenta Valley

area is the **Hansen Dam** and its flood basin, behind which is a large parklike recreation area. The dam was designed by the U. S. Engineering Department, and was constructed between 1938 and 1940. At the time it was built, the compact earth structure was the "largest of its type in the world." The centerpiece of the dam is the handsome streamline spillway and outlet works. This monolithic concrete structure of spillway, gates, and tower is 285 feet in length. From a purely aesthetic point of view this dam and the nearby Sepulveda Dam are two of the most impressive structures in the valley. To reach Hansen Dam and its spillway take the Osbourne Street off-ramp and proceed southwest to the parking and picnic area. Then prepare yourself for an enjoyable, but long, hike along the top of the dam to the spillway.

TUJUNGA

P arts of the Tejunga and La Canada ranchos were subdivided in the boom of the 1880s, and it was thought that the picturesque acreage which now constitutes Sunland and Tujunga would take off economically. Soon, however, most of the town plots were "sold for taxes." Another try at building came in 1907 when M. V. Hartranft, whose family had speculated in land in other parts of Los Angeles County, attracted a little group of Socialists with his slogan, "A Little Land and a Lot of Living," thus settling "La Ciudad de los Terrenitos" or the "Little Landers." Their boulder **Clubhouse,** whose cornerstone was laid on April 12, 1913, is still at 10116 Commerce Avenue and has been restored. The **boulder houses,** which until the 1971 earthquake made the town very picturesque, dated from the 1920s. Some remain, along with their wonderful boulder retaining walls. Several of them are spectacular. We have tried to list the best, but we have undoubtedly missed some. The town is best seen by walking along Commerce, Samoa, Pinewood, and Fairgrove avenues. It is easily as funky as Venice West. But see it soon; slummy apartment houses are rapidly taking the place

of stone follies. The end of camp ambience is near.

1. McGroarty House, 1923
   Arthur B. Benton
   7570 McGroarty Terrace, south of Foothill
   Boulevard at end of Plainview Avenue
The architecture is not much, even with the leaded art glass windows given to John Steven McGroarty, once Poet Laureate of California, by Frank Miller, the host of the Mission Inn at Riverside where McGroarty wrote his once-famous Mission Play (the inspiration, inciden-

*3. Bolton Hall (now known as **Tujunga City Hall**), 1913*

tally, for the building of the Mission Playhouse in San Gabriel). This house took the place of an earlier house which burned. The original furniture that survived is as delightfully bombastic as the play.

2. Harris House,
circa 1910
George Harris
7320 Foothill Boulevard, east of Mount Air Avenue

Perched just below street level, this bungalow is remarkable for still existing on a street which has gone honky-tonk commercial. Harris came west as a representative of an eastern publishing house. He doffed his Prince Albert, donned corduroy vest and knickers, and began

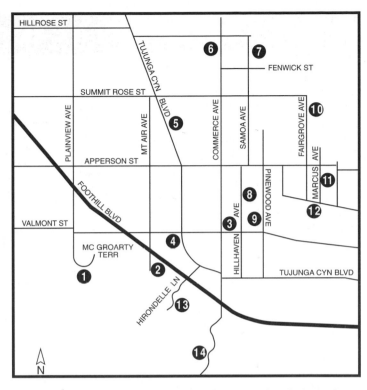

making curious garden furniture in what must be called the "Rustic Baroque" style. A suggestion of this is the concrete railing along the walk (bridge) to his house. His most important piece of architecture is the next entry.

3. Bolton Hall (now known as **Tujunga City Hall**), 1913
George Harris
10116 Commerce Avenue

If you think that the exterior of this boulder, Mission-style-influenced building is extraordinary, you should see the wood-beamed interior! It was originally the clubhouse for the "Little Landers" and was called Bolton Hall for the New York Socialist of the same name.

4. "Blarney Castle," circa 1925
10217 Tujunga Canyon Road, at southwest corner of Valmont Street

A stucco two-story house with a round tower

that now guards the parking lot of a large shopping center.

5. House, circa 1925
10428 Tujunga Canyon Boulevard, south of Summitrose Street

A long, low, boulder house enhanced by new boulder walls in the front.

6. Weatherwolde Castle, 1928
Dumas
10633 Commerce Avenue, near southwest corner of Hillrose Street

A stucco suggestion of Normandy.

7. Reavis House, 1923
10620 Samoa Avenue, north off Fenwick Street

A boulder gem built for a blind man who was attracted to Tujunga by McGroarty's Mission Play.

8. House, circa 1925
  10142 Samoa Avenue
A fine boulder house in the Craftsman tradition.

9. Tujunga American Legion Hall, circa 1928
  10039 Pinewood Avenue
Egyptoid and Art Deco Moderne combined. A
real surprise in bungalow-land.

10. House, circa 1925
  10420 Fairgrove Avenue
A very tidy Craftsman boulder structure.

11. House, circa 1925
  10226 Marcus Avenue
This towered boulder house with its matching
garage is really delightful; apparently it was
originally a schoolhouse.

12. House, circa 1915
  6915 Day Street
Not one of the best boulders (upper clapboard
story added) but interesting because it is supposed to have been a Wells Fargo station. Hard
to believe, but it's part of local lore.

13. Park House ("The Rock of Ages House"),
  circa 1925
  D. M. Denton
  9920 Hirondelle Lane
Self-explanatory; very nicely designed.

14. Newcomb House "El Roble," 1910, 1922
  J. J. Blick; The Postle Company
  9725 Hillhaven Avenue
A good Craftsman house beautifully sited on a
hillside.

LA CRESCENTA

This community, settled in the 1880s, is still unincorporated. It continues the commercial strip along Foothill Boulevard with fine residential areas on each side. Try Briggs Avenue and the streets east of it. Orange Cove Avenue with its shingle and boulder Craftsman architecture (numbers 2301, 2321, and 2346) is good.

La Crescenta also has an extremely pic-turesque boulder church—**St. Luke's of the Mountains** (1924; S. Seymour Thomas)—at the northeast corner of Foothill Boulevard and Rosemont Avenue. La Crescenta's high-toned ruggedness is nowhere better asserted than in this church, all done up in boulders.

Significantly, the idea for it was sketched by a plein air painter, S. Seymour Thomas, and then in 1924 the plans were drawn by an archi-tect, Harry Peters. The effect of the building, even today when much of the area has become suburbanized, is a picture-postcard evocation of the rural idyll.

St. Luke's of the Mountains (1924)

LA CANADA-FLINTRIDGE

lintridge and La Canada, both subdivided in 1920, were joined and became incorporated as a city in 1976. Both parts are very upper-middle-class. Montrose to the south is a step lower on the social ladder.

1. House, circa 1927
2143 Montrose Avenue at Rincon Avenue
The Craftsman house is all right but the tile is better.

2. Egyptian Gardens,
circa 1935
2254 Foothill Boulevard
near Ocean View
Boulevard
Two sphinxes guard the gate.

**3. Wallace House
("El Nido"),** 1911
Arthur B. Benton
End of Castle Knoll
Road
A vaguely Medieval Venetian folly built as a summer home for a lieutenant governor. It is known locally as the "Pink Castle."

4. Lewin House, 1962
Gregory Ain
15310 Jessen Drive
Very simple International Style Modern, barely visible from the street.

**5. Lutheran Church in
the Foothills,** 1965
Culver Heaton
Foothill Boulevard on
southeast corner of El
Camino Corto

It is the campanile rather than the church that is visually striking. The bland shaft is topped by a huge sculpture characterizing the people looking towards the foothills. The sculpture is by Perle Pelzig.

6. House, circa 1927
Southeast corner of Alta Canyada Boulevard
and Hacienda Drive
This splendid Spanish Colonial Revival house has the quality of a John Byers design, though it is not by him. There is a splendid Byers

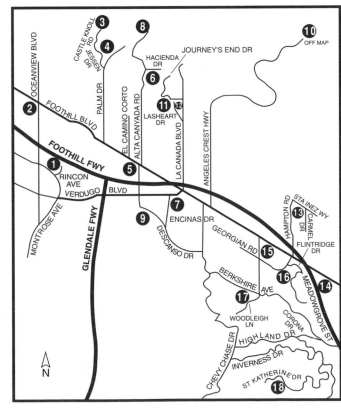

5. Lutheran Church in the Foothills, 1965

house, the **Robbins House,** at 717 Hillcrest Avenue (1931), but it is very difficult to see from the road. Note the fine garden. In fact, almost all of Alta Canyada is beautifully landscaped.

7. Lanterman House ("El Retiro"), 1915
   Arthur L. Haley
   4420 Encinas Drive
A two-story Craftsman house that will soon become a museum honoring a California legislator from this area.

8. Degnan House, 1927
   Paul R. Williams
   5200 Alta Canyada Road
The Degnan house is one of Paul R. William's really fine versions of the Mediterranean—part Spanish, part Italian. The main block of the house is quite formal, though modest in scale. This formality is countered by the picturesque siting of the building on the hillside and by low pergolas and walls to each side. For those enticed by California's Spanish Colonial Revival of the 1920s, this house is a must.

9. Descanso Gardens,
   1937, 1941–later
   1418 Descanso Drive
In 1937, E. Manchester Boddy, editor of the old *Los Angeles Daily News,* bought the 165 acres on which the gardens are now situated and began setting out camelias in a forest of live oaks. When in 1941 Japanese-American nurserymen and their families were sent to relocation camps, Boddy was able to acquire thousands of camelias and azaleas. The county bought the gardens in 1953, and they are now a branch of the County Arboretum. In 1966 the Descanso Guild commissioned Whitney Smith and Wayne Williams to design a Japanese-inspired teahouse. Here you may sip tea while you take in the natural beauty and listen to the mockingbirds sing their hearts out. Open year round during daylight hours.

10. Mount Wilson Observatory, 1913
   Daniel H. Burnham and Company
   Mount Wilson Road off Angeles Crest Highway
One of the last buildings designed by Burnham, completed after his death.

11. House, 1945–48
   J. R. Davidson
   4756 Lasheart Drive
The Moderne lamps on the gate posts are about all that you can see.

12. Gainsburg House, 1946
   Lloyd Wright
   1210 Journey's End Drive
A variation on the Usonian houses, but more theatrical than his father's work.

13. Cottage, circa 1925
   Southwest corner of Santa Inez Way and Carmel Road

A rustic hunting lodge gone bungalow. Notice the magnificent planting. In fact, the streets in this area have been planted with a variety of trees, all of which have flourished. The houses, mostly small, have a great deal of charm.

14. Flintridge Country Club (now St. Francis High School), 1921
Myron Hunt and H. C. Chambers
Just east of off-ramp of Foothill Freeway at intersection with Daleridge Road
The hacienda section, more Mexican than Spanish, of the Club still exists with its long portal.

15. La Canada Thursday Club, circa 1930
Henry Newton and Robert Murray
4440 Woodleigh Lane
Beautifully scaled Spanish Colonial Revival.

16. House, 1928
Myron Hunt and H. C. Chambers
535 Meadow Grove Street

Georgian Revival and livelier than most of Hunt's work. Important houses by Hunt, Paul Williams, Wallace Neff, and the rest of the Pasadena crowd are in this section of town but, as in Bel Air, they have been landscaped out of sight.

17. Mitchell House, 1924
Paul R. Williams
640 Berkshire Avenue
Paul R. Williams designed a number of the houses built in Flintridge/La Canada in the early 1920s. He employed three different images for these houses: the English Tudor, the Spanish, and the Anglo Colonial. The Mitchell house is Anglo Colonial, a white clapboard dwelling, picturesquely situated on a gentle hill looking to the north.

18. The Flintridge Biltmore (now Flintridge Sacred Heart High School), 1927
Myron Hunt and H. C. Chambers
Saint Katharine Drive (take Corona Drive off Highland Drive and follow signs)
More impressive from the valley of the Arroyo Seco than up close, this is an ample but dry building in Hunt's usual Spanish Colonial manner. The Biltmore saw a few good years. Then the Great Depression and the building's remoteness from anything did it in, but not before the management had commissioned two huge pictures (1929) for the lobby by George Fisher and Desmund Rushton. One is rather strange (considering the context): a group of Plains Indians on horseback. The other depicts a highly diverse procession of people in their national costumes moving toward the then-new Los Angeles City Hall.

8. Degnan House, 1927

A NOTE ON ROUTE 66—SAN GABRIEL VALLEY

PASADENA

Thehe Main Street of America" of old still plies its way east along Colorado Boulevard through Pasadena and Arcadia connecting with Huntington Drive, which becomes Route 66 until Huntington suddenly becomes Foothill Boulevard just west of Azusa, when it then joins Alosta Avenue. When Alosta runs into the City of San Dimas, it becomes Foothill Boulevard again and with that name continues to Claremont and on through Cucamonga, beyond the L.A. County line. For many years the camp ambience of roadhouses, gas stations, and motels seemed to have passed, but the nearby Foothill Freeway that should have been the final blow to America's Main Street has ironically brought Route 66 back, not as a highway but as an access road. Almost every single building dating from as far back as the 1920s has been spruced up and in some cases recycled. In fact, it is fun to try to pick out the old places from the cheap, modern horror that surrounds them.

Significantly, it is where the Foothill Freeway now stops at San Dimas that you easily begin to pick up the forlorn monuments to the early days of transcontinental driving. If the freeway is completed as proposed, it will veer north and leave the old roadside civilization along Foothill decaying as it is at present.

It is said that Pasadena means "Crown of the Valley" in the language of the Chippewas, an Indian tribe that never set foot in the area. The land on which the city was built was first occupied by Gabrielino Indians and then by the Spanish and the Mexicans who built several adobes. (One, **Adobe Flores,** still exists in South Pasadena.) The history of Yankee settlement really began in 1874 when the San Gabriel Orange Grove Association acquired most of the land of the old Rancho San Pasqual east of the Arroyo Seco to the present Fair Oaks Avenue and sold it to prospective citrus growers from Indiana.

The Indiana Colony, as it was called, flourished in the gently rolling land dotted with clumps of oaks and sycamores and later orange and olive groves. But the surge of growth came in the 1980s and 1990s when the Southern Pacific and Santa Fe railroads entered the town, and, with the aid of local boosters, the farming community turned into a fashionable winter resort with large hotels on the scale of those at Atlantic City, Miami, and the White Mountains of New Hampshire. The grandest hotel was the Raymond, on a small hill just inside the South Pasadena boundary. But the Green Hotel near the Santa Fe station, whose location was not as picturesque, was so popular that it had to be enlarged three times, the second time to a site on the other side of the street and connected to the older building by a picturesque "Bridge of Sighs." The Maryland, the Wentworth (now Ritz Carlton-Huntington), and the Vista del Arroyo were other hotels patronized into the 1920s and beyond. (The Huntington is still a very popular Pasadena institution.)

The resort atmosphere was of great significance for Pasadena's architectural history. It drew conservative and often very rich immigrants, some of whom eventually decided to become permanent residents of a city that could provide plenty of sun and a cog-railroad up past the Echo Mountain House to Mount Lowe. A local legend has it that in 1900 there were fifteen millionaires on Orange Grove Avenue (now Boulevard). Naturally these people desired mansions in the latest eastern styles and especially those that easterners thought most suitable for the West. Architects such as Harry Ridgeway, A. B. Parkes, and Frederick L. Roehrig made sure that supply kept up with demand. Lawrence Test, an architect who grew up in this environment of building, answered when he was asked how he happened to go into architecture: "Why, there was never any other thought in my mind about my profession. With so much building going on, how could I think of anything else but architecture?" And he added slyly, "I wonder what would have become of me if I had been raised in Glendale or Monrovia!"

From the beginning, Pasadenans were partisans of cultural uplift. The Orange Grove crowd was drawn to the Valley Hunt Club, from which they set out to catch more coyotes than foxes. They founded that excessively famous Pasadena institution, the Tournament of Roses, whose parade once ended with a chariot race à la Ben Hur rather than the present football game. Another group, highly educated and usually residents of the area around the picturesque Arroyo Seco, created the Coleman Chamber Music Association (1904) and the Pasadena Playhouse Association (1917), two pillars of Pasadena culture—both, having experienced vicissitudes, are now alive and well.

The abundance of money meant that Pasadenans would have expensive homes. What is just as interesting is that on Orange Grove these people would engage in an elaborate Victorian Baroque street planning with traffic circles at major intersections and a parkway in the center in the shape of two giant lozenges linked together. Apparently part of this 1874 plan was carried out. The pattern east of Orange Grove was the usual grid with the business center at Fair Oaks Avenue and

Colorado Boulevard. By the 1990s the commercial district was already moving east along Colorado with an array of business blocks designed in Victorian styles whose boldness should shame the fainthearted efforts of modern architects. In the 1920s Colorado Boulevard was widened and all of these buildings lost their fanciful facades. Most were then refaced with Art Deco and Spanish fronts, so that Colorado as far as Euclid Avenue, in spite of recent encroachments, still has 1920s-era fronts and Victorian red brick in the alleys to the rear.

In the old residential districts many Queen Anne cottages remain. The grand Victorians on Orange Grove have been completely eliminated and replaced by garden apartments, now mainly condominiums. Elsewhere a few pretentious gingerbreads have stood up against change. But, in spite of the fact that Barney Williams's **"Hillmont"** has one of the finest ensembles of nineteenth-century interiors in America, Pasadena is not strong in Victoriana. Its great treasury of building (and great it is!) comes from the period 1900 to 1940, the first years dominated by the woodsy Arts and Crafts aesthetic, so much appreciated by Gustav Stickley in *The Craftsman* magazine (1901–1916), and the later years devoted to the period revivals. The Arts and Crafts or Craftsman style, a kind of amalgam of Swiss Chalet, Tudor, and Oriental forms, can best be savored on the eastern side of the Arroyo Seco. There, just north of the Ventura Freeway, the greatest concentration of work by the now-famous architects Charles and Henry Greene still stands. South of the freeway important houses by less familiar names such as Louis B. Easton, Arthur and Alfred Heineman, G. Lawrence Stimson, and Jeffrey, Van Trees, and Millar, provide the finest collection of Craftsman architecture outside Berkeley.

Pasadena's architectural heritage of the 1920s and 1930s, on the other hand, parallels the accomplishments of Santa Barbara. In fact, the two cities often used the same architects. Besides Bertram G. Goodhue and George Washington Smith, and J. Wilmer Hershey, all of whom worked in both places, Pasadena residents employed Roland E. Coate, Reginald D. Johnson, Garrett Van Pelt, Gordon B. Kaufmann, and Wallace Neff—the last coming closest to Smith in originality and assurance within the forms of the Spanish Colonial Revival. Their work is most magnificent on the western edge of the Arroyo Seco and best viewed from Arroyo Boulevard on the eastern side. Smaller but still ambitious Period Revival architecture is more easily seen in the Oak Knoll district. Lombardy Road is particularly rich.

As in most of Los Angeles County, the greatest amount of fine architecture is domestic, but Pasadena is ahead of most of her neighbors in public architecture. The **Civic Center** is one of the few successes of the "City Beautiful" movement. The 1923 general plan was designed by the Chicago firm of Bennett, Parson, Frost, and Thomas. The same year a competition was announced for the design of the main buildings. The winners were Myron Hunt for the Library, Edwin Bergstrom of the firm of Bennett and Haskell for the Auditorium, and Bakewell and Brown (San Francisco) for the City Hall whose proposed facade was an incredible enlargement of the campanario of the San Gabriel Mission. This design was eventually discarded in favor of the present, more respectable triumphal arch and dome. The imagery of all three of these buildings was Classical Mediterranean.

The result of this planning is magnificent. The major axis running along Holly Street toward City Hall begins with the **YMCA** designed by the important Pasadena firm of Marston and Maybury and the **YWCA** by Julia Morgan. Neither is among these architects' best buildings, but both illustrate Pasadena's historic mission to wed ethics and aesthetics. Bakewell and Brown's **City Hall** is a wonderful stage set, or better, a wedding cake, less elaborate than the same firm's San Francisco City Hall, but much more entertaining. In front of it runs Garfield Street, the minor axis of the Beaux Arts plan. At its north end is Hunt and Chamber's **Public Library.** The south end of the axis was once closed by Bergstrom's **Civic Auditorium** on Green Street. Now up front on

Colorado is the stupid arch designed by Kober Associates as a supposed link between the two extremities of the **Plaza Pasadena.** Other horrors have intruded, such as the vertically-striped court building near the library, but the grand plan is still evident and effective especially since it stands aside from Colorado Boulevard, the main commercial artery, and thus does not interfere with traffic and business. It is in every sense a triumph of California's own version of Beaux Arts ideas.

The skyline of the city should be viewed from the steps of the **Norton Simon Museum** or even better from the campus of **Ambassador College** to the south. Besides the dome of City Hall, church spires appear at just the right places. Unfortunately, the cityscape is marred by the tasteless, out-of-scale **Parsons Tower** and out-buildings, which cannot be landscaped out of sight. It is sad to say that even greater blemishes were erected in the 1980s, particularly along Lake Avenue.

Like most California cities, Pasadena has not invested in many parks. Its high moral tone has never interfered with real-estate values. Partial compensation for the paucity of open spaces is the very large park in the valley of the Arroyo Seco that runs in a southerly direction through the western part of the city. When visiting the site in 1911 Teddy Roosevelt is supposed to have said, "The Arroyo would make one of the greatest parks in the world." It is not quite that great, but it is Pasadena's greatest natural treasure besides its view of the mountains, often clouded with smog. The northern part of the Arroyo is broad and includes a golf course and an exhibition area as well as the famous **Rose Bowl,** which is used more often for flea markets than for athletic endeavors. At a narrowing of the gorge is a new freeway bridge modeled as closely as possible on the lines of the old **Colorado Street Bridge** (1912–13) alongside it. The huge concrete arches of both bridges are spectacular, especially when seen from Arroyo Boulevard which cuts through them. Unfortunately the stream bed has been paved with a concrete channel, but the palisades on both sides are covered with trees and are very picturesque.

Nature and architects were, until the 1950s, very good to Pasadena. Modern architecture has not fared so well. Certainly the city continues the tradition of rearing and attracting excellent architects, but their work tends to be elsewhere. The business district is full of new buildings, mostly mediocre and designed by outsiders. Single-family dwellings of distinction are now rarely built and, needless to say, the quality of most apartment houses and condominiums is undistinguished. Naturally there are exceptions to these observations, and we have tried to include them.

UPPER ARROYO SECO

This area north of the Ventura Freeway is one of the richest architectural districts in the West. The Linda Vista Avenue (western) side is hilly, exclusive, and well guarded. Some beautiful architecture is there, but it can best be viewed in the pages of the sumptuous *Architectural Digest* of the 1920s and 1930s. The east side is even richer in art if not in banknotes. It contains two monuments of American architecture—the **Millard House** (**"La Miniatura"**) by Frank Lloyd Wright, and the **Gamble House** by the Pasadena architects Charles and Henry Greene. In fact, one whole street, Arroyo Terrace, was designed by the Greenes and another, Grand Avenue, has works by them, by Myron Hunt, and by other architects of equal talents.

The entire Arroyo Seco should be declared a national monument. The architecture is as important as that of Charleston, South Carolina, and the scenery is much better.

1. Matthews House, 1966
Mortimer Matthews (Pulliam, Matthews, and Associates)
1435 Lindaridge Road
The arresting roof line of this house can best be seen from the curve below it.

2. Ralphs House, 1950
Ain, Johnson, and Day (C. Raymond Johnson)
1350 Lindaridge Road
One of Ain's largest houses, it has been well maintained over the years.

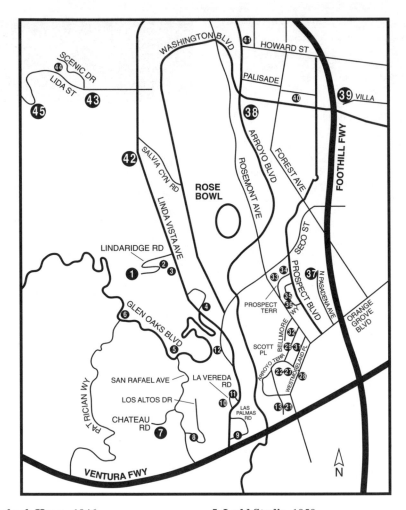

3. Schonbach House, 1946
  Leland Evison
  701 Linda Vista Avenue
A modular post-and-beam system in which the frames are made of asbestos; concrete panels exposed.

4. House, 1946
  Henry Eggers
  1043 Pine Oak Lane
A brick house of extreme simplicity.

5. Ladd Studio, 1950
  Thornton Ladd
  1085 Glen Oaks Boulevard
Pasadena's own version of the house as a glass box. The house (actually a studio for the architect's own use), is an elegant 900-square-foot enclosure of steel frame, glass, and sliding canvas sunscreens. It perches at the edge of a cliff, with an extensive garden to the rear. The studio building won an A.I.A. Award of Honor. You catch a glimpse of this International Style Modern building from the street below. This small studio, is without doubt, one of the great

classics of post-World War II Modern architecture in Southern California. One wishes that Ladd had had the opportunity to design one of the *Arts and Architecture* Case Study houses.

6. Ladd House, 1956
Thornton Ladd
1280 Glen Oaks Boulevard, at Patrician Way

7. Kelsey House, 1961
Ladd and Kelsey (John Kelsey)
1160 Chateau Road
The architect's own house is a beautifully articulated Miesian structure. This is all accomplished via wood and glass. The house is very private on the street side. Perched just below the crest of a hill, this low-lying, modular structure is as handsome as when it was built.

8. Wilbur House, 1928
Gordon B. Kaufmann
25 Los Altos Drive
This Mediterranean-style house peers through trees at the Annandale Golf Club. It is on a private road but can be seen from San Rafael Avenue.

9. Fowler House, 1927
Edward W. Fowler
825 Las Palmas Road
Apparently Fowler got his ideas from magazine illustrations. This **Andalusian house,** the **Basque house** around the corner on El Circulo Drive, and the **Majorcan house** at 95 El Circulo were all designed by him and certainly seem to have come out of a picture book, all the more incredible since now the enormous arches of the freeway bridge tower over this quaint assemblage.

10. Smith House, 1929
David A. Ogilvie
181 La Vereda Road
A Tudor villa on a pleasant street.

11. Kubly House, 1964
Craig Ellwood and Associates
215 La Vereda Road
Ellwood in his Miesian phase. This is one of his most elegantly detailed houses, gaining strength of character from its exposed timber framing.

12. Two Houses, circa 1924
Train and Williams
373 and 405 Mira Vista Terrace
Both are Bavarian hunting lodges, especially significant because they were designed by the only architectural firm to be directly affiliated with the Arroyo Guild of Fellow Craftsmen.

13. Halsted House, 1905
Charles and Henry Greene
90 N. Grand Avenue
The Greenes were just finding their way here, but this is a fine Craftsman house in spite of frequent alterations during the teens and 1920s.

14. Park House, 1904
130 N. Grand Avenue
An awkward but fascinating example of turn-of-the-century Colonial Federal Revival.

15. Newcomb House, 1910, 1922
141 N. Grand Avenue
A Tudor mansion complete with necessary gatehouse and servants' quarters. Just around the corner is **"200–236,"** a group of condominiums designed (1980) by Buff and Hensman. We mention them because they are good examples of the currently fashionable Neo-Craftsman mode.

16. Myron Hunt House, 1905
Myron Hunt
200 N. Grand Avenue
Simplified Doric columns mark the entrance of this otherwise Craftsman house.

17. House, circa 1887
202 N. Grand Avenue
A Queen Anne pearl that was moved from the site (across the street) of the present Culbertson House. This must have been one of the first houses in this area. Notice the original carriage house in the rear.

18. Van Rossem House, 1904
Charles and Henry Greene
210 N. Grand Avenue
Josephine Van Rossem, a real estate speculator, built this brown, barnlike Craftsman house just after having built another Greene and Greene around the corner on Arroyo Terrace.

19. Speirs House, 1904
Hunt and Grey
230 N. Grand Avenue
A good, early example of the Dutch Colonial Revival.

20. Duncan-Irwin House, 1900, 1906
Charles and Henry Greene
240 N. Grand Avenue
One of the largest and finest houses by Greene and Greene, this house began its history as a single-story bungalow which was incorporated in the Irwins' 1906 extension that we see today. The composition of the facade is more beautiful than the much more elegant Gamble House.

21. James A. Culbertson House, 1902, 1914
Charles and Henry Greene
235 N. Grand Avenue
Little of the original, very important house is left. Only the bay window, the front door with its Tiffany glass, and the magnificent pergola and wall along Grand were designed by the Greenes. These items would also have been demolished except for the protests of the architects Smith and Williams, who remodeled the house in 1953.

22. Charles Sumner Greene House, 1901,
1906, 1912, 1914
Charles and Henry Greene
368 Arroyo Terrace
Charles was naturally mainly responsible for the design of this house and its additions. It is not as richly appointed as the nearby Gamble House, but its Craftsman details are just as fine.

23. White Sisters House, 1903
Charles and Henry Greene
370 Arroyo Terrace
Charles Greene's sisters-in-law lived in this once completely shingled house. Notice the crescendo of the retaining wall made of clinker brick and Arroyo Seco boulders.

24. Van Rossem-Neill House, 1903, 1906
Charles and Henry Greene
400 Arroyo Terrace
Carefully restored, this shingled house looks very much as it did when it was pictured in *The Craftsman* magazine in 1915.

25. Hawks House, 1906
Charles and Henry Greene
408 Arroyo Terrace
Almost identical to the contemporaneous **Bentz House** on Prospect Boulevard.

26. Willet House, 1905
Charles and Henry Greene
424 Arroyo Terrace
A Craftsman house completely remodeled on the exterior by another architect who chose the Spanish Colonial Revival mode.

27. Ranney House, 1907
Charles and Henry Greene
440 Arroyo Terrace
Another Oriental Craftsman, two-story house, recently beautifully restored. This completes the row of Greene and Greene houses but, of course, there are many more nearby.

28. Fenyes House, 1906
Robert Farquhar
170 N. Orange Grove Boulevard
Neo-Classical, expensive, but not Farquhar at his best (see **Clark Library** on West Adams and the **California Club** in Central Los Angeles). This design nevertheless suggests the high style of living that once characterized Orange Grove Avenue. It can be visited Tuesday and Thursday afternoons courtesy of the Pasadena Historical Society whose headquarters are here.

29. Neighborhood Church, 1972
Whitney R. Smith
1 Westmoreland Place
Modern Shingle style evoking memories of the old Neighborhood Church on California Street. The pines and other trees are beginning to give the area the parklike atmosphere that the architect had in mind.

30. Cole House, 1906
Charles and Henry Greene
2 Westmoreland Place
The Greenes hit their stride here. The interior has been remodeled for use as church parlors, but the exterior is almost precisely as the Greenes designed it. Notice the monumental boulder chimney to the south, which emerges from the ground like a tree trunk.

31. Gamble House, 1908

31. Gamble House, 1908
Charles and Henry Greene
4 Westmoreland Place

Certainly this is the masterpiece of these master architects, not because of its facade or its plan (which is conservative even by late Victorian standards) but for the rich interiors, unmatched for loving attention to detail. Like most architects, the Greenes were happiest when they had a rich client who gave them an open purse. But what is remarkable is that the intricate teak interiors that they designed could be carried out with such incredible craftsmanship, forget the price. Containing almost all of the original Greene-designed furniture, this is probably one of the five finest house museums in America. Thanks to the Gamble family, and to the City of Pasadena and the University of Southern California who jointly administer it, this house is open to the public. For tour hours and admission fees, call the Gamble House (818-793-3334 or 213-681-6427).

Note as well, the stone gateposts and wrought-iron gates (1913) at the Rosemont Avenue entrance to Westmoreland Place.

32. Dickinson House, 1941
Lawrence Test (Woodbridge Dickinson, associate)
429 Bellmore Way

An understated, dark wood house in the Craftsman tradition. This is the best house on a

36. Millard House, 1923

street of good houses built during and just after World War II.

33. McMurran House, 1911
Frederick L. Roehrig
499 Prospect Terrace

Roehrig could and did design in every style. This house shows him expansive in the Mission style.

34. Hindry House, 1909
Arthur S. Heineman (Alfred Heineman, associate)
781 Prospect Boulevard

A huge Mission-style mansion overlooking the Arroyo Seco. Arthur Heineman saw the clients and worked out the floor plans. His brother Alfred, who had just joined the firm, had a hand in designing the details as he continued to do until the firm broke up in the 1930s. The leaded glass in the dining room was carried out to Alfred's designs by the Judson Studios in Garvanza. The fireplace in the hall may have been designed by Charles Greene.

35. Bentz House, 1906
Charles and Henry Greene
657 Prospect Boulevard

The architects at their most restrained. The house is perfectly maintained.

Prospect Boulevard deserves special praise. The houses on it are comfortable and some are of high quality. But the real attraction is the cork oak, camphor, and small palm trees that line it—one of the loveliest sights in Pasadena.

36. Millard House ("La Miniatura"), 1923
Frank Lloyd Wright
645 Prospect Crescent

The first of Wright's "textile block" constructions, La Miniatura has the feeling of a Mayan ruin set in a jungle ravine. The famous view of it is from a gate on Rosemont. The studio at the west side of the pond is by Lloyd Wright (1926). While the studio is related to the house in scale and materials, it does reveal the differences of approach between father and son. The house and its garden play a fascinating environmental game. It all appears natural, but the ravine (arroyo) is in fact filled in, and of course most of the shrubs and trees are not native to the place.

45. Art Center College of Design, 1977

37. Gartz Court, 1910
Architect unknown; De Bretteville and
Polyzoides, restoration architects
745 North Pasadena Avenue

These six half-timber and stucco bungalows
(actually four and a duplex) were moved from
Madison Avenue near central Pasadena. The
restoration is immaculate. De Bretteville and
Polyzoides also designed complementary
garages and rear patios that you would swear
were original. More than that the court looks
better here than it did on Madison Avenue; so
good, in fact, that in spite of being moved, it
was kept on the National Register.

38. Franks House, 1932
Palmer Sabin
1260 N. Arroyo Boulevard

A well-turned Monterey Revival house overlooking the Arroyo.

39. Charlotte Perkins Gilman House,
circa 1900
Architect unknown
Southeast Corner of Villa Street and Cyprus
Avenue

A turn-of-the-century Colonial Revival house
of no great architectural distinction, but it was
the home of the great American feminist, the
author of *Yellow Wallpaper* and many other
books. It was moved into this neighborhood
from across town and is presently (1993) being
restored.

40. Grover Cleveland
Elementary School,
1934
Robert H. Ainsworth
524 Palisade Street

PWA Moderne with a
direct message bas-relief of
a child reading.

41. Byles and Weston
House, 1950
H. Douglas Byles and
Eugene Weston III
1611 Kenneth Way

An understated vertical
batten house.

42. Wadsworth House,
1925
1145 Linda Vista
Avenue

The supreme Craftsman statement—a two-story
log cabin.

43. House, circa 1887
1360 Lida Street

This Queen Anne cottage is a relic of the tiny
hamlet of Linda Vista.

44. Hernly House, 1949
Lawrence Test
1475 Scenic Drive

The siding is three-quarter-inch plywood with
the inside face exposed in rooms. The skilled
workmanship is an echo of the Craftsman era.
The use of unusual materials is representative
of the experimental work that was done just
before and after World War II.

45. Art Center College of Design, 1977
Craig Ellwood and Associates
1700 Lida Street

Every follower of Mies must have wanted to
design a bridge that was also a building. Here
Ellwood had his opportunity. This is a very
striking building, and yet notice how it is sited
so as to avoid spoiling the natural landscape.
The mess of equipment on the roof was not
designed by the architect.

LOWER ARROYO SECO, NORTH

O n a map, the Lower Arroyo seems to be cut off from the upper by the freeway, but in reality Arroyo Boulevard connects the two areas as it always has. It is a lovely drive and is favored by bicyclists, joggers, and people who like to stroll. In fact, it is one of the few residential sections in Southern California where you see people walking because there is something to experience—lovely scenery and interesting to distinguished architecture set in well-kept gardens.

In the nineteenth century, the edges of the Arroyo were not considered desirable places to build. Too many vapors! The Arroyo itself was used as a wood lot by the millionaires on Orange Grove Boulevard and also for picnics and the collecting of wild flowers. The western bank pitched abruptly into the stream bed, but the eastern side was moderated by two natural terraces before it too dropped into the valley. This land provided the locale for elaborate gardens, the most extensive being that of Adolphus Busch, the beer tycoon. The Busch Gardens, in fact, ran into the Arroyo. They were open to the public until they were subdivided in the late 1930s.

As the gardens disappeared, so did most of the Orange Grove mansions that were eventually replaced by pleasant but unremarkable garden apartments. But the lower slopes had, beginning around 1900, become attractive to people of moderate means and often of intellectual and artistic pretension. Many of them built bungalows and larger houses in the "ostentatious simplicity" of the Arts and Crafts (Craftsman) movement. Almost all of these brown, woodsy houses remain, many in almost pristine condition. There are even a few new ones. It is for this reason that we have included so many entries for this section.

3. Perkins House, 1955

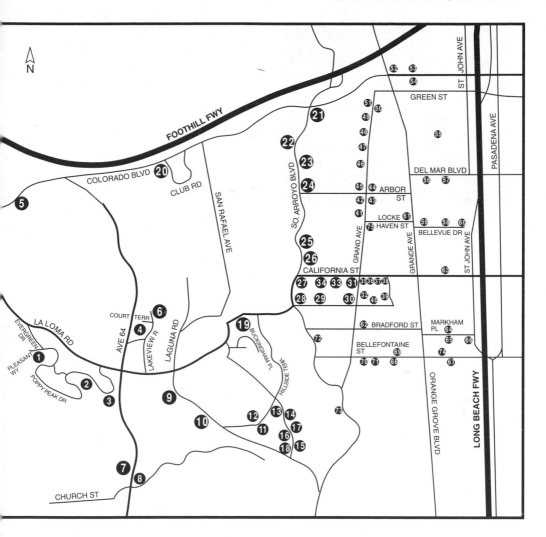

1. Laing House, 1935
   Harwell H. Harris
   1642 Pleasant Way
Simplified Wright, but Harris understood the
Orient much better than the master.

2. Kempton House, 1961
   Lyman Ennis
   1685 Poppy Peak Drive
Austere stucco with even more austere slit windows. A late rendering of the Pueblo Revival.

3. Perkins House, 1955
   Richard J. Neutra
   1540 Poppy Peak Drive
Neutra's ability to make a small space seem
large by turning it into the outdoors is seen here
at its best.

8. Church of the Angels, 1889

4. Harris House, 1939
    Harwell H. Harris
    410 N. Avenue 64
An unpretentious example of this architect's
sophistication. Again, Harris evokes Wright but
simplifies.

5. John Carr Real Estate Company Building,
    1950
    John Carr
    1400 W. Colorado Boulevard
A Spanish Colonial Revival office building
with pergola in rear. The design was supposedly based on details taken from the Santa
Barbara County Courthouse.

6. Clark House, 1968
    Alson Clark
    430 Lakeview Road
Recent Spanish Colonial Revival with
Georgian and other highly innovative touches.

7. Greenshaw House, 1907
    Joseph Cather Newsom
    1102 Lantana Drive
An awkward version of the Mission Revival by
an architect who, with his brother Samuel,
designed the famed Carson House in Eureka,
California. Both of the Newsom brothers kept
up with the latest fashion, so it is not surprising
to find J. Cather designing Mission Revival
buildings in the early 1900s.

8. Church of the Angels, 1889
    Arthur Edmund Street; Ernest A. Coxhead
    1100 Avenue 64
This church was erected as a memorial to
Alexander Campbell-Johnston, a Scot who
bought most of Rancho San Rafael and developed it. His wife went to England to order plans
and chose Street, the son of the famous
Victorian architect George E. Street, whose
Holmbury Saint Mary's in Dorking was the
model. Street's drawings were then given to
another Britisher, Ernest A. Coxhead, who was
living in Los Angeles at the time and who was
semi-official architect for the Episcopal church
in California. Coxhead took great liberties with
the design, the result being one of his several
masterpieces. The interior is almost precisely
the way it was in the nineteenth century, and so
is the exterior. The 1971 earthquake knocked
off the belfry with its Saxon columns, but this
has now been beautifully restored (1992, by
Richard Rose Associates).

9. Gould House ("Villa Evarno"), 1911–later
    Raymond Gould (?)
    945 Ellington Lane
This building (the main house is now gone) is
essentially a garden pavilion that one can live
in. The English gardener, Marion Cran, in her
Gardens in America (1931) describes the garden pavilion which was built in the mid-1920s:
"We breakfasted over the lake on the terrace of
the 'temple' which is a spacious room, very
Italian in manner. A beautifully furnished room
in the woods; in it his friends take tea and hear
music looking over his lake and the valley of
blossoms."

10. Puelicher House, 1960
    Boyd Georgi
    901 Laguna Road
An International Style Modern box with an
unusual amount of color in its bank of louvers.

11. House, 1927
    L. C. Brockway
    976 Hillside Terrace
A comfortable-looking shingled English
Colonial.

12. Tabor House, 1950
Paul Haynes
969 Hillside Terrace
The horizontality of this
International Style Modern
house is carried through with
real assurance.

13. Case Study House #10,
1947
Kemper Nomland and
Kemper Nomland, Jr.
711 S. San Rafael Avenue
Beautifully sited International
Style Modern.

14. Young House, 1927
George Washington Smith;
A. E. Hanson, landscape
architect
808 S. San Rafael Avenue
A two-story Andalusian house
of which you can only gain
glimpses. Notice the entrance
wall, gate, and the south facade
overlooking one of A. E.
Hanson's splendid Andalusian
gardens. Regrettably, the gardens no longer remain intact.

15. Martindale House, 1924
Joseph Kucera
1000 S. San Rafael Avenue
Spanish Colonial walled off from the street.

16. Crowell House, 1952
Smith and Williams (Whitney R. Smith)
949 S. San Rafael Avenue
The architects working in a Japanese mood;
one of Pasadena's best 1950s houses.

17. Jevne House, 1913
Eager and Eager
910 S. San Rafael Avenue
A sort of Danish country home in dressed
stone.

18. Gallion House, 1956
Arthur B. Gallion
1055 S. San Rafael Avenue
Japanese-style Modern by a city planner and
former dean of the USC School of Architecture.

16. Crowell House, 1952

19. Cunningham House, 1980
Pulliam, Matthews, and Associates
969 Buckingham Place
A large cut-into box house with vertical wood
sheathing.

Something must be said about the array of
houses on **San Rafael Avenue** north of the
intersection with La Loma Road. They are
large, private (behind their security systems),
and some are fine works of art by Marston and
Maybury, Morgan, Walls, and Clements, Paul
R. Williams, Reginald D. Johnson, Gordon B.
Kaufmann, and other distinguished architects.
Almost none can be even vaguely glimpsed
from San Rafael Avenue, though there is a tantalizing view of them from Arroyo Boulevard
across the Arroyo Seco. All we can say is that

we hope that you will watch for house tours, particularly those put on by Pasadena Heritage. Often the San Rafael mansions are the backdrops for movies and television shows and commercials. Naturally the credits never indicate the location.

20. Messler House, circa 1950
    Paul Haynes
    126 Club Road
A clapboarded house in the Harwell H. Harris tradition.

21. Colorado Street Bridge, 1912–13
    Waddell and Harrington (John Alexander
    Low Waddell, designer and engineer);
    Mercereau Bridge and Construction
    Company (John Drake Mercereau, contractor)
Waddell, of the engineering firm of Waddell and Harrington of Kansas City, pioneered reinforced concrete in this monument which he designed to connect Colorado Street in Pasadena to the county road that ran east/west through Eagle Rock. The 1,467.5-foot-long reinforced-concrete bridge has a roadway which is 28 feet wide, and 48 lamp clusters lighted the bridge. This long, high concrete bridge spanning the Arroyo was curved so that it would get solid footing. The aesthetic result has been compared to that achieved by the aqueduct in Segovia, Spain. The community became so fond of their monument that, when the bridge needed radical repairs a few years ago, the people of Pasadena demanded that it should be rebuilt and restored as closely as possible to its original appearance. This restoration was completed in late 1993.

22. La Casita del Arroyo, 1934
    Myron Hunt
    177 S. Arroyo Boulevard
Very uncharacteristic Hunt, this small meetinghouse was inspired by the Pasadena Garden Club's interest in spurring employment during the depression. The main funds came from the PWA. Hunt donated his services and designed this structure using boulders and sand from the Arroyo, fallen trees from higher up the canyon, and even parts of the bicycle track abandoned after its use in the 1932 Olympics.

23. Barber House, 1925
    Roland E. Coate
    270 S. Arroyo Boulevard
An attractive Cape Cod Colonial in brick, accompanied by a California version of what a New England garden should be. The landscape architect was Katharine Bashford.

24. House, 1983
    Buff and Hensman
    Northeast corner of South Arroyo
    Boulevard and Arbor Street
An elaborate Craftsman bungalow.

25. Cheesewright House #2, 1912
    Jeffrey, Van Trees, and Millar
    490 S. Arroyo Boulevard
A beautifully sited Craftsman house.

26. Mannheim House, 1913
    Jean Mannheim (?)
    500 S. Arroyo Boulevard
Mannheim, a distinguished regional painter, had earlier been associated with Frank Brangwyn, one of the few painters in the English Arts and Crafts movement. Although Mannheim is usually given credit for the design of his house, the quality of the design and its detailing suggests that he must have had an architect friend.

27. Batchelder House, 1909, 1913
    Ernest A. Batchelder
    626 S. Arroyo Boulevard
A shingled Craftsman house with a brick-terrace entrance and a large, second-floor sleeping porch. Batchelder was, by the 1920s, one of the country's most successful producers of decorative tile. It all began in the backyard of this house, where his kiln house still stands. He was also a frequent contributor of articles on design and aspects of the Arts and Crafts movement for *The Craftsman* magazine. His wife, a professional pianist, founded the Coleman Chamber Music Association, the oldest such organization in the United States.

28. Clark House, circa 1910
    George A. Clark
    648 S. Arroyo Boulevard
Another Swiss chalet, well publicized in the periodicals of the time and featured in H. von

Holst's *Modern American Homes* (1915). Incidentally, Clark was a haberdasher!

29. Wright House, circa 1909
    Timothy Walsh
    691 La Loma Avenue
Craftsman with classical touches, illustrated and discussed in *The Craftsman* of January 1910. Walsh was a Boston architect who came out to Los Angeles to do the new Roman Catholic cathedral. The church never got off the drawing boards, but Walsh was quickly converted to the Pasadena style.

30. Austin House, 1909
    Grable and Austin, contractors
    629 S. Grand Avenue
The architectural historian Clay Lancaster believes that this true (i.e. one-story) bungalow was based on an ancient Lycian house illustrated in the *American Architect and Building News* in 1908. If he is correct, Grable and Austin followed through quickly since this house was published in the *Western Architect* in 1909. An almost identical twin is at 990 Vermont in Oakland.

31. House, circa 1910
    Timothy Walsh
    619 S. Grand Avenue
A Craftsman chalet; or better, a Bavarian hunting lodge.

32. Volney-Craig House, 1908
    Louis B. Easton
    620 S. Grand Avenue
A simple Rocky Mountain cabin on the outside, this house exhibits all the Craftsman paraphernalia on the interior—redwood framing and paneling, inglenook, and even a burnt-wood sideboard.

33. Williams House, 1911
    Grable and Austin, contractors/designers
    638 W. California Boulevard
A fine bungalow in mint condition.

    In spite of our heavy coverage of this area, we are mentioning only what we consider to be the best examples of the Craftsman architecture here. You should plan to walk Grand Avenue, California Street, Arroyo Boulevard, La Loma Avenue, and Bradford Street.

34. Cheesewright House #1, 1909–10
    Jeffrey, Van Trees, and Millar
    686 W. California Boulevard
E. J. Cheesewright, an Englishman, was one of the leading interior designers in Southern California. Perhaps he suggested the feeling of a thatched-roof Cotswold cottage for this otherwise Craftsman house. When drawings of the proposed house were first published in 1909, it was described as "the English cottage type."

35. House, 1910
    Attributed to Louis B. Easton
    550 W. California Boulevard
A fine California bungalow in the Craftsman tradition. In 1990 the house was completely refurbished. Tim Andersen was the restoration architect.

36. Norton House, 1905
    Alfred Heineman
    540 W. California Boulevard
This is not a very imposing work of art, but it is significant for having been designed by Alfred Heineman, a major Arts and Crafts designer, before he joined his brother's firm (Arthur S. Heineman).

37. De Forest House, 1906
    Charles and Henry Greene
    530 W. California Boulevard
A large Craftsman house; one of the best-preserved specimens of the Greenes' early work.

38. House, 1905
    Grable and Austin, contractors/designers
    520 W. California Boulevard
A handsome Craftsman design, worthy of comparison with the Greene and Greene next door. Obviously this contracting firm either brought in an architect or had an architect in their office in order to produce a design of this quality.

39. Noble House, circa 1910
    475 La Loma Avenue
The Tudor Craftsman mode.

40. Clapp House, 1874
    549 La Loma Avenue
A simple but refined Italianate dwelling. One of the oldest buildings in Pasadena, it housed the city's first school. It was moved before the turn

of the century from the southwest corner of Orange Grove Boulevard and California Street.

41. Francis House, 1929
Reginald D. Johnson
415 S. Grand Avenue
One of Johnson's best Georgian efforts.

42. Bolt House ("Cobbleoak"), 1893
Seymour Locke and Jasper
Newton Preston
395 S. Grand Avenue
A large cobblestone and shingle house. Another strongly Richardsonian house (1895) by the same firm is at 325 S. Grand Avenue.

43. House, 1910
G. Lawrence Stimson
390 S. Grand Avenue
Dressed-up Craftsman, this house is similar in style to **Myron Hunt's house** at 200 N. Grand Avenue.

44. Post House #2, 1903
Joseph J. Blick
360 S. Grand Avenue
A late Shingle-style structure with Richardsonian touches.

45. Staats House, 1924
Marston and Van Pelt
293 S. Grand Avenue
A French provincial mansion.

46. Tod Ford House, 1919
Reginald D. Johnson
257 S. Grand Avenue
A grand Mediterranean-style mansion with beautifully landscaped forecourt and impressive gardens terraced into the valley of the Arroyo Seco.

47. Freeman Ford House, 1907
Charles and Henry Greene
215 S. Grand Avenue
This house cannot be seen from the street, but it is one of the Greenes' major works and must be mentioned. The gardens were set out by Robert Gordon Fraser, the landscape architect for the Busch Gardens.

48. Robinson House, 1905
Charles and Henry Greene
195 S. Grand Avenue
The gates have Oriental lanterns, but the house, with its suggestion of half-timbering, seems Tudor.

49. Shakespeare Club, circa 1925
Marston, Van Pelt, and Maybury (Sylvanus Marston)
171 S. Grand Avenue
A severe Florentine villa.

50. Vista Grande Townhouses, 1981
Buff and Hensman
72–108 S. Grand Avenue
This linked-together stucco and wood style has become very popular in this area thanks, in large part, to this firm. See also the similar and impressive condominiums by Harrison, Beckhart, and Mill just around the corner at 1 S. Orange Grove Boulevard.

51. Vista del Arroyo Hotel, 1920
Marston and Van Pelt
Tower, 1930
George Wiemeyer
125 S. Grand Avenue
This hotel began its life in 1882 as Mrs. Bang's boarding house. Needless to say it prospered, only to suffer a loss of patronage in the 1930s. It was taken over by the federal government during World War II. Today it has been converted for use as an appellate court building. The so-called bungalows in the extensive gardens are mostly by Marston and also Myron Hunt.

52. Memorial Flagpole, 1927
Bertram G. Goodhue
Northeast corner of Orange Grove Boulevard and Colorado Boulevard
The sculpture at the base is by Lee Lawrie, who worked with Goodhue on many buildings, including the Nebraska State Capitol and the Los Angeles Public Library.

53. Pasadena Museum of Art (now **Norton Simon Museum**), 1969
Ladd and Kelsey
411 W. Colorado Boulevard
To a degree this building, with its curved forms,

draws upon the Streamline Moderne of the 1930s, but of course it has a formal classic quality as to its plan, proportions, and use of materials. The collection it houses is superb. The hours are Thursday–Sunday, Noon–6:00 P.M.

54. Elks Club Building, 1911
Myron Hunt and H. C. Chambers
400 W. Colorado Boulevard
A pleasing variation on Mount Vernon.

55. Ambassador Foundation Campus
Between Green Street, West Colorado and Del Mar boulevards, and Saint John Avenue
The administration of the Ambassador Foundation deserves special praise for its efforts to preserve and use the old houses which remained on the land it purchased in the 1950s. More than that, the Foundation has demolished fences in order to develop old backyards into a magnificent park with views of the city through palms and oaks. The new buildings are flamboyant Modern, some deserving attention. A tour, including some interiors, may be arranged at the Information and Administrative Center on Green Street. The buildings that follow are some highlights:

a. Scofield House, 1909
Frederick L. Roehrig
280 S. Orange Grove Boulevard
A merging of the styles of Harvey Ellis as illustrated in *The Craftsman* and of Will Bradley (who, incidentally, lived for a time in South Pasadena). There is more than a little of Frank Lloyd Wright, too, especially in the entrance hall.

b. Sprague House, 1903
A. A. Sprague
Behind Scofield House
A vast, half-timbered Tudor pile.

c. Merritt House, 1905–6
W. F. Thompson
An Italian Renaissance palace set between two large wafflelike grills near the corner of Green Street and Orange Grove Boulevard.

d. Information and Administrative Center, 1969
Peter Holstock (for O. K. Earl Corporation)
Influenced by early Yamasaki.

e. Student Center, 1966
Gerd Ernst (for Daniel, Mann, Johnson, and Mendenhall)
A pleasing pavilion.

f. Auditorium, 1974
Daniel, Mann, Johnson, and Mendenhall
This building is already famous for its opulence and good acoustics.

56. Mead House, 1910
Louis B. Easton
380 W. Del Mar Boulevard
A monument of the Craftsman movement by a brother-in-law of Elbert Hubbard. The house was restored in 1979, and a porte-cochere was added by the restoration architect, Tim Andersen.

57. Bolton House, 1906
Charles and Henry Greene
370 W. Del Mar Boulevard
The shingle exterior shows only a few signs of the Orientalism which was to emerge full-blown in the Greenes' work two years later. The staircase bulge was added by Garrett Van Pelt in 1918. The house has gone through many interior changes but is was restored in 1982 by the restoration architect, Tim Andersen.

58. Rhodes House, 1906
W. J. Saunders
365 W. Bellevue Drive
Worthy of Maybeck, this huge Bavarian hunting lodge deserves study.

59. Condominium, 1982
Batey-Mack
371–379 W. Bellevue Drive
Clear stucco abstraction worthy of Irving J. Gill.

60. Jacobs House, 1992
Gilbert S. Hershberger
335 W. Bellevue Drive
A really distinguished monument of the current Arts and Crafts revival. This new dwelling and

its gardens replace a nondescript house of the 1950s. Particularly noteworthy is the retention of the enormous Moreton Bay fig tree that completes the picture.

61. Wrigley House, 1911
G. Lawrence Stimson
391 S. Orange Grove Boulevard

Mission Revival with delusions of Beaux Arts grandeur, this mansion, though itself of no great quality, is set in ample gardens that give an idea of the high style once common on Orange Grove Boulevard. It is now the headquarters of the Tournament of Roses Association.

62. Fitzpatrick House, 1980
Gilbert L. Hershberger
549 Bradford Street

Craftsman Revival in an area that is worthy of it. Certainly special credit goes to Rodger Whipple, the master carpenter, along with the architect and the imaginative owner.

63. Apartment Building, 1926
Robert H. Ainsworth
339–353 W. California Boulevard

Andalusian Spanish Colonial Revival giving variety of design within the uniformity of the U-shaped plan.

64. MacPherson House, 1894
Henry Ridgeway
337 Markham Place

A Georgian Revival dwelling.

65. Blankenhorn-Lamphear House, 1893
Bradbeer and Ferris
346 Markham Place

A beautiful and typical example of the Queen Anne style.

66. McCarthy House, 1937
Donald McMurray
762 Saint John Avenue

If the Long Beach Freeway is completed, this fine Monterey Revival house will be demolished.

66. McCarthy House, 1937

67. Hollister House, 1899
  Charles and Henry Greene
  310 Bellefontaine Street
Early Greene. They tried out the English
Colonial Revival and showed their allegiance to
the vogues of the eastern seaboard, particularly
the work of McKim, Mead, and White.

68. Ware House, 1913
  Charles and Henry Greene
  460 Bellefontaine Street
Here the Greenes seem to be moving away
from their Swiss and Oriental influences. The
house looks more like their early work, for
example, the Hollister House.

69. Phillips House, 1906
  Charles and Henry Greene
  459 Bellefontaine Street
A large, very characteristic, brown chalet. The
only Greene and Greene style that you do not
experience in these Bellefontaine houses is,
strangely enough, the Japanese.

70. Thomas House, 1911
  Sylvanus Marston
  574 Bellefontaine Street
Tudor Craftsman.

71. Marshall-Eagle House (now **Mayfield
  School**), 1917
  Frederick L. Roehrig
  500 Bellefontaine Street
A huge Beaux Arts mansion whose grounds
have been well maintained.

72. Swift House, 1927
  Donald McMurray
  850 S. Arroyo Boulevard
One of the finest Monterey Revival houses in
Pasadena.

73. Pergola House, circa 1910
  Attributed to Robert Gordon Fraser
  1025 S. Arroyo Boulevard
This remains among only a few relics of the
Busch Gardens begun in 1903 under Fraser's
direction. He had trained at the great
Horticultural Gardens in his native Edinburgh.
So far as is known, he had no architectural
background, but the idea of a platform from
which to view Camel's Hump must have been

his. Now the circular building has been incorporated in a relatively modern house.

74. Buckingham House, 1918-19
  Sylvanus Marston
  325 Bellefontaine Street
A handsome example of the late Queen Anne
Style that Vincent Scully has called the Shingle
style. Two more examples are located nearby at
707 and 721 Saint John Avenue. They date
from 1890 and 1897, respectively (Frederick L.
Roehrig). Both will be demolished if the Long
Beach Freeway is completed.

75. Three Houses
  Southeast corner of South Grand Avenue
  and Lockhaven Street
These houses have been moved to the property
once occupied by the La Solana Inn. The one
on Lockehaven is a marvelous Queen Anne
extravaganza (1887, Merithew and Ferris) that
was originally at 626 W. 30th Street near the
USC campus. Tim Andersen was the restoration architect for the Lockehaven house. He
also designed the "Victorian" carriage house,
and a turret at the back of the house. On the
corner of 440 South Grand is a Shingle style,
two-story house designed by W. B. Edwards
(1903). It has an inordinate amount of pizazz as
the result of an imaginative paint job. Just south
of this house is an early two-story twentieth-
century Colonial Revival dwelling which was
also moved to this new site and restored.

LOWER ARROYO SECO, SOUTH

When the city of South Pasadena was laid out in 1886, there was a movement to incorporate it with Pasadena. But the good people of this area held out against "the diabolical traffic" in liquor, tolerated by the Presbyterians to the north. South Pasadena was, in the words of the historian Hiram Reid, "compelled by sheer necessity for self-protection to incur the expense and trouble of forming a city corporation." The town fought alcohol well into this century. Perhaps that is the reason that it is not so rich in architecture as its northern neighbor.

But the tradition of otherwise-mindedness also has its rewards. More recently South Pasadena has taken a gallant stand against the Long Beach Freeway that would cut down Meridian Avenue, the old main street of South Pasadena, demolishing old commercial buildings and a fine residential district which includes important Victorian houses, two houses by Greene and Greene, and one by R. M. Schindler.

We do not mean to create ironies, but the simple fact is that freeways, while often destroying major and minor monuments, do not, when properly constructed, divide cities as they seem to do on maps. If elevated, or especially if depressed and bridged, they may actually reduce the traffic flow on surface streets and preserve neighborhoods. The Pasadena Freeway, in spite of its dangerous on and off ramps, is almost invisible as it bends out of the Arroyo and through the northern part of South Pasadena. Thus, at the risk of inflaming the passions of people in both Pasadena and South Pasadena, we have included a part of South Pasadena in the following section and then in a later section rather courageously gone on to

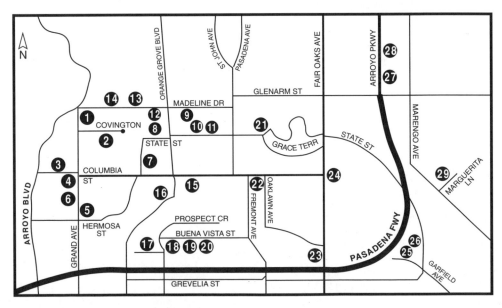

move east through the main part of South Pasadena. We do this not to confuse, but to help the knowledgeable admirer of architecture who cares nothing for political boundaries, particularly since they were drawn on the principles of the Anti-Saloon League.

7. Davis House, 1936–37

1. House, 1938
Donald McMurray
Southeast corner of Grand Avenue and Madeline Drive, Pasadena
A Spanish urban house of great quality. Its model was a seventeenth-century house in Antigua, Guatemala.

2. House, 1950
Leland Evison
520 Covington Place, Pasadena
Good conservative Modern with oiled-redwood exterior.

3. Jeffries House, 1922
Bertram G. Goodhue
695 Columbia Street, Pasadena
Unfortunately, when this once-huge house was divided a few years ago, the wonderful Churrigueresque entrance was removed. But we are told that it is stored somewhere on the grounds. It is still possible to see some of the architect's intentions from a gate on Columbia Street.

4. Tanner-Behr House, 1917
Reginald D. Johnson
Southwest corner of Columbia Street and Grand Avenue, South Pasadena
A rather formidable essay in the Mediterranean style, now best viewed from the gate on Grand Avenue. The two Roman busts at the tops of the gate posts always have wreaths around them at Christmastime. Notice also the lovely antique pink wall.

5. Koebig House, 1927
H. Roy Kelley
Northeast corner of Hermosa Street and Grand Avenue, South Pasadena
A compact Tudor villa in brick. This house was frequently published at the time, and in 1928 it "won the first prize for a 5-8 room house" in a competition sponsored by *House Beautiful*.

6. House, circa 1925
Donald McMurray
309 N. Grand Avenue, South Pasadena
With its scalloped wall and beautiful maintenance, this Spanish Colonial Revival house is almost too good to be true.

7. Davis House, 1936–37
Roland E. Coate
1230 Hillside Road, Pasadena
Federal Revival in painted brick. Note the arcaded office on the one-story wing to the south.

8. Perrin House, 1926
Garvin Hodson
415 West State Street, Pasadena
Monterey Revival with mannered touches strongly suggesting the influence of George Washington Smith.

9. Westridge School, 1906–80
   324 Madeline Drive, Pasadena
The campus, most of whose buildings can easily be seen from the street, is a veritable museum of the works of Pasadena's architectural worthies. Remember that the school is private property. Buildings are listed in clockwise fashion.

a. Administration Building, 1923
   Marston, Van Pelt, and Maybury (Sylvanus Marston)
A modest Tudor Revival structure by a firm that was more at home with the congeries of Mediterranean.

b. Performing Arts Building, 1909
   Frederick L. Roehrig
   1932, North wing added; Bennett and Haskell
   1958, Stage designed; Henry Dreyfuss
Most of the Roehrig design has been covered up or remodeled. The later wing harmonizes with the Tudor Administration Building. The stage is, of course, the product of one of the world's greatest industrial designers, who incidentally lived a few blocks away.

c. Hoffman Gymnasium-Auditorium, 1980
   Whitney R. Smith
A shingled box reminiscent of Smith's Neighborhood church.

d. Pitcairn House (now **Fine Arts Building**), 1906
   Charles and Henry Greene
   Interior remodeled 1973 by Roland E. Coate, Jr.; Tim Andersen, associate
The Greenes in beautiful form. This building is now a good example of recycling. The interior retains many of the old features; the exterior, with its wonderful stepped windows reflecting the interior staircase, remains exactly as built.

e. Laurie and Susan Frank Art Studio, 1978
   Whitney R. Smith

   Seeley G. Mudd Science Building, 1978
   Whitney R. Smith
How do you design new buildings next to a major work by the Greenes? Smith chose shingles but wisely understated the design, though

the Art Studio may have been modeled on the Gamble House garage—a good model.
   The landscaping of the south half of the campus is by Yosh Kuromiya.

f. Ranney House Classrooms, 1962
   Henry Eggers and Walter W. Wilkman

Gladys Peterson Building, 1962
   Henry Eggers and Walter W. Wilkman

Library (south wing of Administration Building), 1962
   Henry Eggers and Walter W. Wilkman
The most "modern" looking buildings on the campus.

g. Gertrude Hall Building and Classrooms, 1955
   George Vernon Russell
Barely visible from the street (Madeline Drive), these buildings are compromises between Modern architecture and the Tudor Revival Administration Building nearby.

10. Mervin House, 1904
   Charles and Henry Greene
   267 W. State Street
A columned porch identifies this otherwise Craftsman house.

11. Rolland House, 1903
   Charles and Henry Greene
   225 W. State Street
A Craftsman bungalow (now painted white) with a recessed window in the middle of the roof. Incidentally, Henry Green's own house (demolished) once was across the street.

12. Cravens House, circa 1929
   Lewis P. Hobart
   430 Madeline Drive
In spite of its present address, this French chateau by a San Francisco architect is the best remaining example of the Orange Grove style of life. It is now Pasadena's Red Cross Headquarters and can be visited from 8:30 A.M.–5 P.M. on weekdays. The gardens, designed by the Olmsted Brothers, have been subdivided and lost.

13. Old Mill of Banbury Cross, circa 1907;
   additions later, especially in the 1920s
   Attributed to Robert Gordon Fraser
   485 Madeline Drive
The Hansel and Gretel mill was the teahouse in
the old Busch Gardens. It cannot be seen from
the street but the lich-gate entrance is a fine
piece of street furniture.

14. Dunham House, 1956
   Carl L. Maston
   495 Madeline Drive
The best view of this International Style
Modern structure is from Stoneridge Drive.

15. House, circa 1885
   919 Columbia Street, South Pasadena
Professor Thaddeus Lowe lived in this expansive Queen Anne villa while his own great
house, now demolished, was being built on
Orange Grove Boulevard.

16. Porter House, 1875
   215 N. Orange Grove Boulevard, South
   Pasadena
A Queen Anne cottage built by one of the
founders of the San Gabriel Orange Grove
Association that sold the first 84 lots to the
Hoosier settlers of Pasadena.

17. Prospect Houses, 1948
   Van E. Bailey and William Gray Purcell
   543–545 Prospect Lane, alley just north of
   Pasadena Freeway and off Prospect Circle,
   South Pasadena
Rare examples of Purcell's late work. Simple
slip-form concrete structures with wide, over-
hanging eaves; somewhat reminiscent of
Wright's Usonian houses.

18. House, circa 1895
   929 Buena Vista Street, South Pasadena
Huge turn-of-the-century Tudor with lots of
shingles. Note also the fine, shingled mansion
next door at number 917.

19. Garfield House, 1904
   Charles and Henry Greene
   1001 Buena Vista Street, South Pasadena
The Greenes designed this modest but
respectable house for the widow of President
James A. Garfield. It is a Craftsman Swiss

chalet without the Oriental touches that they
were beginning to display in other commissions.

20. Longley House, 1897, 1910
   Charles and Henry Greene
   1005 Buena Vista Street, South Pasadena
This is a strange but significant work. Here the
Greenes were trying their wings in architec-
ture—and they seem to have tried almost
everything. It includes Mission-style, Moorish,
Richardsonian Romanesque, Oriental, and even
Georgian Revival elements.
   These Buena Vista houses are all in the
path of the proposed extension of the Long
Beach Freeway and may be demolished in spite
of the fact that the Greene and Greene houses
are on the National Register.

21. House, circa 1900
   135–137 Grace Terrace, South Pasadena
A shingled Mission Revival building constructed as a chauffeur's dwelling for the
William Stanton estate. The first floor was once
a garage where Pierce Arrows were parked.

Oaklawn Avenue, dating from the early 1900s,
has many handsome Craftsman houses. See
especially numbers 216, 217, 304, 309, 317,
and 325.

22. Oaklawn Gates, 1905
   Charles and Henry Greene
   On Columbia Street at Oaklawn Avenue
A Craftsman redwood fence ends in boulder
pillars supporting beautiful tile roofs.

23. Oaklawn Bridge and Waiting Station,
   1906
   Charles and Henry Greene
   Oaklawn Avenue at Fair Oaks Avenue,
   South Pasadena
The bridge across the tracks of the Southern
Pacific and Santa Fe railroads was an unsuc-
cessful but amusing sally of the Greenes into
engineering. The waiting station is an amazing
concoction of redwood beams with tile roof.

24. Waiting Station and Cobblestone Wall,
   circa 1902
   Attributed to T. W. Parkes
   Southeast corner of Fair Oaks Avenue and
   Raymond Hill Road, South Pasadena

A fine Craftsman shelter where guests of the Raymond Hotel, once on the hill above, used to wait for the "Big Red Cars" on the Pacific Electric line—a branch of what was once one of the greatest rapid transit systems in the country.

25. Casa de Jose Perez, "Adobe Flores,"
1839; 1849–50
1804 Foothill Street, South Pasadena
A single-floor, L-shaped adobe, now covered with a tile roof. The Mexican Army headquarters during the Mexican-American War, this adobe was restored and "enhanced" in 1919 by the well-known exponent of the Spanish Colonial Revival, Carleton M. Winslow, Sr. In the 1920s it was a teahouse with a high cultural tone. It is now a private residence.

26. Group of Adobes, 1925–27
Carleton M. Winslow, Sr.
West side of Garfield Avenue north of Foothill Street, South Pasadena
In spite of their late date, these are much more "convincing" structures than the previous entry.

27. Royal Building, 1968
Nyberg and Bissner
East side of Arroyo Parkway north of Glenarm Street
A stilted pavilion related to Edward D. Stone's projects but without his Moorish screens.

28. Grieger Building, 1972
Daniel, Mann, Johnson, and Mendenhall
900 S. Arroyo Parkway
A strong Streamline Moderne building of almost monumental proportions.

29. Spanish Colonial Revival Village,
circa 1928
Marguerita Lane on curve of Marengo Avenue below Glenarm Street
A group of very pretty cottages—actually a bungalow court.

Besides Pasadena proper there were other real estate ventures aimed at appeasing the voracious appetites of Midwesterners for paradise. The Oak Knoll area, now a part of Pasadena but in the 1880s a separate subdivision, was bought by a Mr. Rosenbaum, a New York speculator, and was laid out by the R. R. Staats Realty Company. Land contours (some determined by earthquake faults!) and native oaks were preserved by curving streets. Oak Knoll was, from the beginning, an area of fine houses on estates originally almost as extensive as those on Orange Grove Boulevard. All of these were broken up in the 1920s so that houses in the Craftsman idiom are cheek to jowl with period revivals.

1. "Bubble House," Experimental Dome House, 1946
Wallace Neff
1097 S. Los Robles Avenue
A thin-shell concrete dome by this famous exponent of the Spanish Colonial Revival. Like many other architects of the World War II years, Neff was looking for a practical, low-cost structure that would replace the balloon frame. He started his design exploration for the "Bubble House" in 1934. His first extensive use of this new form of structure was a colony of 20 units built at Falls Church, Virginia, in 1941.

2. House, circa 1887
Southwest corner of Oakland Avenue and Miles Street
A colorful Queen Anne two-story with picket fence.

3. Flintoft House, circa 1910
G. S. Bliss, contractor
800 S. Oakland Avenue
A two-story Craftsman house. Fine Craftsman

OAK KNOLL

houses, some bungalows, pop up elsewhere on this street. See especially numbers 755, 903, 911, and 1315. Bliss constructed many bungalows in Pasadena.

4. Toleston House, 1913
  E. P. Zimmerman
  965 S. Oakland Avenue
American Georgian with Dutch and Federal elements.

5. House, 1915
  Rossiter-Banfield Company
  1205 S. Oakland Avenue
A Pueblo Revival house, unusual in this area.

6. Rochester House, circa 1910
  T. Beverly Keim
  1365 S. Oakland Avenue
The Rochesters chose a Los Angeles architect to design this magnificent Beaux Arts mansion for them.

7. Grey House, 1911
  Elmer Grey
  1372 S. El Molino Avenue
Although touches of Italian influence appear in the architect's own house, the broad circular front porch is very Californian. The composition of the rough stucco walls reminds you of Voysey or even Mackintosh. The house is beautifully sited on the hillside.

8. Van Pelt House, 1926
  Garrett Van Pelt
  1212 S. El Molino Avenue
This important architect chose a variation on a French provincial theme for his own house.

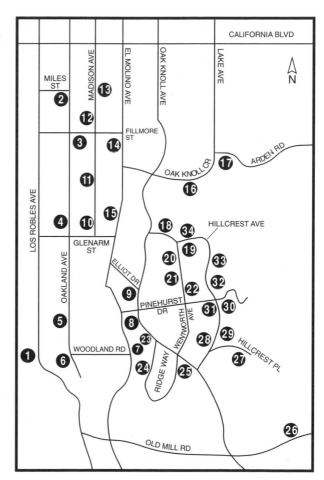

9. Ross House, 1911
  Arthur S. Heineman (Alfred Heineman, associate)
  674 Elliott Drive
The Craftsman aesthetic in its later stage, this house is often mistaken for a work by the Greenes.

10. House, 1910
    Sylvanus Marston
    1011 S. Madison Avenue
West Coast Prairie style.

11. Ioannes House, 1911
    Louis B. Easton
    885 S. Madison Avenue
A rather well-turned effort in Mission-style
stucco by an architect who usually used wood.

12. E. J. Blacker House, 1912
    Charles and Henry Greene
    675 S. Madison Avenue
Obviously this house does not bear comparison
with the one that the Greenes had built earlier
for another Blacker (see entry **#19**). It is, nevertheless, a good Craftsman design as is the one
(1907) at 805 S. Madison Avenue by Frederick
L. Roehrig.

13. Blood House, 1911
    654 S. Madison Avenue
An excellent U-plan Craftsman bungalow
painted yellow in the latter day.

14. House, circa 1911
    Arthur S. Heineman (Alfred Heineman,
    associate)
    885 S. El Molino Avenue
Although painted, this two-story house still
shows its Craftsman origins.

15. Crow-Crocker House, 1909
    Charles and Henry Greene
    979 S. El Molino Avenue
Actually, this Craftsman masterpiece was
designed entirely by Henry Greene.

16. McDonald House, circa 1927
    W. F. Staunton
    800 Oak Knoll Circle
A good Monterey Revival two-story.

17. "Tara West," 1978
    Thornton and Fagan Associates
    Southeast corner of Lake Avenue and
    Arden Road
A folly if there ever was one! It is supposed to
be modeled on Scarlet O'Hara's mansion in the
late-1930s film *Gone with the Wind.*

18. Garford House, 1919
    Marston and Van Pelt
    1126 Hillcrest Avenue
A rather dry but dignified version of the
Spanish Colonial Revival. Just north of it and
running along Oak Knoll Avenue is an
Orientalized Gunite wall designed by the
Greenes.

19. R. R. Blacker House, 1907
    Charles and Henry Greene
    1177 Hillcrest Avenue
Like the Gamble House across town, this is one
of the very finest of the Greenes' Craftsman-
Japanese designs. Its magnificent gardens have
been subdivided and built upon. The chauffeur's and gardener's houses, now separate
dwellings on Wentworth Avenue, give an idea
of the grandeur of the ensemble.

20. Lunkenheimer House, 1906
    Joseph J. Blick
    1215 Wentworth Avenue
Mission Revival, very similar to the work of
Lester S. Moore.

21. House, circa 1913
    Arthur S. Heineman (Alfred Heineman,
    associate)
    1233 Wentworth Avenue
The Craftsman aesthetic, moving directly into a
version of Cotswold Hansel and Gretel.

22. Campbell House, 1924
    Roland E. Coate
    1244 Wentworth Avenue
One of this architect's best Spanish Colonial
Revival houses.

23. O'Brien House, 1912
    Arthur S. Heineman (Alfred Heineman,
    associate)
    1327 S. Oak Knoll Avenue corner of Ridge
    Way
A beautifully crafted house in the Heineman's
special fusion of Oriental details with the feeling of a Cotswold cottage.

24. Ledyard House, "Idyllwild," 1909
    1361 Ridge Way
An extraordinary Craftsman house framed in
logs.

*19. R. R. Blacker
House, 1907*

25. Wentworth Hotel (now **Ritz Carleton-
Huntington Hotel**), 1906, 1913, 1991
Charles F. Whittlesey; 1913, Myron Hunt;
1991 rebuilding: McClellan, Cruz, Gaylord
and Associates; DeBretteville and
Polyzoides, historic architecture consultants
The Peridian Group, landscape architects
1401 S. Oak Knoll Avenue
Whittlesey, well known for his Mission Revival
railroad stations and hotels in the Southwest,
continued the tradition here in this great hotel,
catering to Easterners and Midwesterners trying
to escape wretched winters back home. Henry
Huntington, of Southern Pacific Railroad fame,
took over operation and in 1913 commissioned
Myron Hunt to expand the central section
upward. The result was a rather ungainly
facade, but it became beloved by Pasadenans,
many of whom claim to have been married in
its gardens.

By the 1980s a series of post-World War II
remodelings, reflecting changing ownership
and management, left the interiors a mess and
many of the rooms were sub-standard. Finally,
on the grounds that the building was an earthquake hazard, the great central tower was
demolished and rebuilt in the Mission Revival
style, but in a bit more coherent version than
had hitherto been encountered. The beautiful
Whittlesey-designed public rooms—the
Venetian and the Georgian—were saved from
the wrecking ball and have been restored to
their original grandeur, the Venetian being
more interesting since it displays the architect's
fondness for the ornamental designs of Louis
Sullivan. Also salvaged was a rustic bridge
with murals painted in 1933 by Frank M.
Moore.

26. El Molino Viejo, 1816
1120 Old Mill Road, San Marino
Built under the direction of Father Zalvidea on
the outer limits of the San Gabriel Mission
property, it served as a flour mill until the
"new" and presumably more efficient mill put
it out of service. It moldered until the 1920s,
when it was refurbished and used as a house
with painted decoration added to interior walls.
Both Myron Hunt and Carleton M. Winslow,
Sr. were involved in the restoration of the
building, and the gardens were restored by
Katherine Bashford. Certainly it is one of the
most picturesque of the old adobe structures
remaining in Los Angeles County.

27. Hamish House, 1951
Henry Eggers and Walter W. Wilkman
940 Hillcrest Place (watch the bumps in the
road)
Actually, all you can see is one wall of the
house, but it is a beautiful wall.

28. Landreth House, circa 1918
　　Reginald D. Johnson
　　1385 Hillcrest Avenue
A grand American Classical Revival mansion.

29. Spinks House, 1909
　　Charles and Henry Greene
　　1344 Hillcrest Avenue
A blend of barn and Swiss Chalet, with
Japanese details. The grounds, recently restored
by Isabelle Greene, the architect's grand-
daughter, are magnificent.

30. Freeman House, 1913
　　Arthur S. Heineman (Alfred Heineman,
　　associate)
　　1330 Hillcrest Avenue
The once-rolled eaves have now been clipped,
but this is still a great Craftsman house. Notice
the extensive use of Batchelder tile. There is
more inside.

31. Prindle House, 1926, 1928
　　George Washington Smith
　　1311 Hillcrest Avenue
Bold Spanish Colonial Revival forms mark this
house; its tour de force is the loggia garden to
the rear.

32. Elliott House, 1925
　　Wallace Neff
　　1290 Hillcrest Avenue
Extremely dignified Spanish Colonial Revival.

33. Griffith House, 1924
　　Johnson, Kaufman, and Coate
　　1275 Hillcrest Avenue
Spanish Colonial Revival. See also the house in
the same style next door.

34. Cordelia Culbertson House, 1911
　　Charles and Henry Greene
　　1188 Hillcrest Avenue
This Gunite-sheathed house with green tile roof
seems more Chinese than Japanese. It is
roughly U-shaped with a Moorish fountain in
the central court. The back of the house, which
once looked down on extensive terraced gardens, is almost pure Segovia. Only a suggestion
of the extensive gardens remains.

The commercial heart of nineteenth-
century Pasadena was at Fair Oaks
Avenue and Colorado Boulevard,
mostly on Fair Oaks. Indeed, a small
and precious fragment remains. But,
contrary to early expectations, the main business developed along Colorado Boulevard and
the result was a congeries of taste that we have
already described. Spanish and Art Deco
Moderne facades hooked to Victorian structures line the street from Delacey to El Molino
avenues with an interruption on the south side
between Arroyo Parkway and Los Robles
Avenue where the new **Plaza Pasadena,** a
commercial success but an architectural disaster, appears like a yellow brick fortress. It has
been suggested that the intersection at Garfield
Avenue be renamed the Place d'la Bastille.

As in most California communities,
Colorado Boulevard (Pasadena's main street)
was, until the 1950s, pretty much a commercial
strip with single-family residential areas
spreading behind almost within the same block
both north and south. Recently this pattern has
changed with the building of hotels, banks, and
condominiums to the south of Colorado and the
development of the Parsons Engineering firm to
the northwest. This new growth has wiped out
many neighborhoods and several landmarks,
but it has been accompanied by a growing
awareness of the importance of old buildings,
an awareness that is visible in the restoration of
storefronts, the cleaning of the brick backs and
alleys, and restrictions on signage. Other indi-
cations of responsibility are an extremely active
urban conservation program emanating from
city hall and a resourceful private support organization, Pasadena Heritage.

PASADENA, CENTRAL BUSINESS DISTRICT

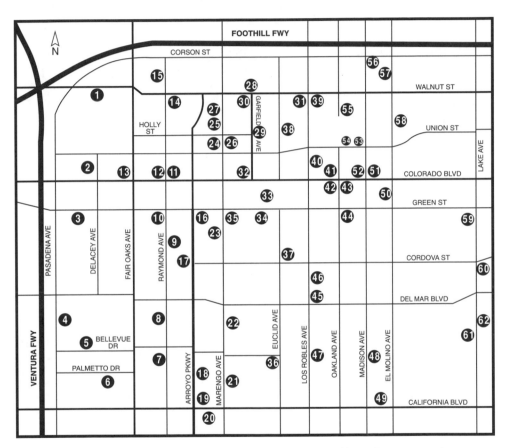

1. Ralph M. Parsons Company, Office Tower, 1974
William Pereira Associates
100 W. Walnut Street
Two almost identical **office buildings,**
1979, 1981
Skidmore, Owings, and Merrill

Sorry to begin this section on a negative note, but the tower in particular is something that should stand as a monument to what should be avoided. Architecturally dull, its bulk is an insult to the fine scale of the older buildings on the skyline. The other two major buildings, designed in Skidmore, Owings, and Merrill's wrap-around style, are not much better, though there is a rather striking view of the older one from the picturesque alley to the south of it.

2. Pennsylvania Oil and Tire Warehouse, 1930
Bennett and Haskell
33 Delacey Avenue
The lower portion of the structure has been remodeled, but the tower remains pretty much as it was envisioned by the architects—Art Deco (Zigzag) Moderne with a programmatic frieze of automobile wheels.

3. Friend Paper Company, 1965
Smith and Williams
100 W. Green Street
A surprising place for this sophisticated, typically regionalized (softened), International Style Modern design to have been erected. The deep bays were landscaped by Eckbo, Dean, and Associates.

4. Stahlhuth House, 1907
Charles and Henry Greene
380 S. Pasadena Avenue
Originally you would be unable to distinguish this bungalow from the hundreds of others that once surrounded it. It now has a fine view of the uncompleted Long Beach Freeway.

5. House, 1893
Wood Taylor
101 Bellevue Drive
A charming two-story Queen Anne dwelling with characteristic ornament in the gable. You have to imagine it in its orange grove.

6. Palmetto Court, 1915
A. C. Parlee, builder
100 Palmetto Drive
Fourteen tiny Craftsman bungalows.

7. Royal Laundry Building, 1927, addition, circa 1935
Gordon B. Kaufmann
443 S. Raymond Avenue
Restrained Spanish Colonial Revival enhanced by a fine tile doorway almost Art Deco Moderne in design. The later addition is in Streamline Moderne. All this is on the site of the once-sensational Moorish Revival Lowe's Opera House.

8. Pasadena Humane Society Building, 1932
Robert H. Ainsworth
361 S. Raymond Avenue
A fine Mediterranean-style building. The new (1993) addition is by Kurt Meyer Associates.

9. Santa Fe (AMTRAK) Railroad Passenger Station, 1935
H. L. Gilman
222 S. Raymond Avenue
The *Chief* (demoted from *Superchief*) still stops at this colorful Spanish Colonial Revival depot. Note the magnificent Batchelder tiles in the waiting room.

10. Hotel Green (now **Castle Green Apartments** and **Hotel Green Apartments**), 1898, 1903
Frederick L. Roehrig
50 E. Green Street at southwest corner of Raymond Avenue
The Hotel Green, once one of the great resort hotels, has now been converted into apartments and condominiums. Both are very private but quite often the owners of the Castle Green play host to Pasadena Heritage, and it is possible to see the public rooms, almost completely intact with even some of the Moorish furniture in place. These buildings are late additions to an older hotel that was on the other side of Raymond Avenue, but demolished in the 1930s. Thus the "Bridge of Sighs" that once connected the newer buildings to the old is now cut off at the sidewalk. The Staats Company is partly housed in what is left of the old hotel which was designed by Strange and Carnicle (southeast corner of Raymond and Green). Note the original curved entrance at the corner.

11. United California Bank (now **Bank Theater Building**), 1929
Bennett and Haskell
Northeast corner of North Raymond Avenue and East Colorado Boulevard
A crisp brick essay in Art Deco (Zigzag) Moderne.

12. Kinney-Kendall Building, 1897, and
remodeled 1925
Charles and Henry Greene; remodeled by
Bennett and Haskell
65 E. Colorado Boulevard at northwest corner of North Raymond Avenue
As a result of the 1920s set-back and the strip-
ping away of almost all ornament, this rare
example of the Greenes' commercial work
bears little resemblance to their original ideas.
While it was never a great building, the Greene
and Greene cult should take it in hand and
restore it.

13. Old Pasadena
Fair Oaks and Raymond avenues two
blocks north and south of Colorado
Boulevard
Here is the commercial heart of old Pasadena.
It has been pretty badly handled by time,
neglect, and remodeling, but the **White Block**
(1887), at one time the city hall, at the southwest corner of Union Street and Fair Oaks
Avenue, the **Slavin Block** next door on Fair
Oaks, the **Venetian Revival Building** (1887,
Harry Ridgeway), and further down the street at
number 9–17 are presently being restored and
recycled. A good example of what can be
accomplished is the **Renaissance Revival
Block** (1894, Frank Hudson) at 32 S. Raymond
Avenue, and there are other good refurbishings
all around. Best of all are the brick alleys that
are gradually being drawn upon for their highly
picturesque quality.

**14. Entrance to Old Pasadena Public
Library,** 1887
C. W. Buchanan
Southeast corner of Walnut Street and
Raymond Avenue
This relic of the Richardsonian Romanesque
library remains as a garden ruin at the corner of
a small park. Across the street at 145 N.
Raymond Avenue is the stunning PWA
Moderne **California State Armory,** now the
Armory Gallery. It was designed by Bennett
and Haskell and built in 1932. Notice also the
rare group of clapboard **row houses** (1901) at
the opposite corner.

*10. Hotel Green (now Castle Green Apartments and
Hotel Green Apartments), 1898, 1903*

15. St. Andrew's Roman Catholic Church,
1927
Ross Montgomery
311 N. Raymond Avenue
Early Christian fabric with Romanesque campanile right out of old Ravenna. The rich interior is as marvelous as the contribution of the
outlines of the church to the cityscape. Best
seen from the Foothill Freeway going east at
sunset. *The Stations of the Cross* and other
murals were painted by the Venetian artist,
Carlo Wostry.

16. Bankamericard Center Building, 1975
Edward D. Stone
Southeast corner of Green Street and
Arroyo Parkway
Late Stone, a huge pink marble block without
windows (presumably because computers do
not need light). One wag has suggested that it
looks like the box that the **Conference Center**
(across Marengo Avenue) came packaged in.

17. Pasadena Winter Garden (now **Storage Facility**), 1940
Cyril Bennett
Arroyo Parkway at west end of Cordova Street
Originally a skating rink, this Streamline Moderne mass evokes nostalgia for the FDR era.

18. Bryan's Cleaners, 1938
Eliot Construction Company
544 Arroyo Parkway
A well-turned essay in the Streamline Moderne.

19. Hunt Offices and Display Rooms, 1925
George Hunt
Northeast corner of Arroyo Parkway and California Boulevard
Hunt was the foremost furniture maker to the rich in the 1920s. This Monterey Style structure was good advertising.

20. Architect's Offices, 1929
Wallace Neff and Ernest Torrance
186 E. California Boulevard
Very picturesque, rural Andalusian Spanish, still so, in spite of its siting behind a new gas station.

21. Two Houses, 1905
Louis B. Easton
530 and 540 S. Marengo Avenue
Easton, Elbert Hubbard's brother-in-law, built number 540 improvising upon a plan he found in a book. But according to a legend, which should be true even if it isn't, in designing number 530, he cast away precedent and relied on his own best judgment. It is the better of the two, in the Swiss Chalet version of Craftsman architecture. It has been restored by Pasadena Heritage.

22. Don Carlos Court, 1927
Burrell and Company, builders
374–384 S. Marengo Avenue
A pleasant bungalow court in the Spanish Colonial Revival mode. South Marengo still has many bungalow courts. Some are being recycled as this street becomes commercial. Others are in limbo.

23. Stoutenburgh House, circa 1887
J. H. Bradbeer
255 S. Marengo Avenue
A lovely Queen Anne holding on for dear life against the tides of change. In 1980 it was converted to office use by Tim Andersen, restoration architect.

24. First Baptist Church, 1926
Carleton M. Winslow, Sr. and Frederick Kennedy
75 N. Marengo Avenue
Italian Romanesque in exposed concrete with a beautiful tower that adds to the cityscape.

25. Turner and Stevens Mortuary (now **Holly Street Grill**), 1922
Marston and Van Pelt
95 N. Marengo Avenue
A long, low brick structure in the English Gothic mode.

26. YWCA Building, 1920–22
Julia Morgan
Southeast corner of Marengo Avenue and Holly Street
A disappointing, very bland Mediterranean-style work by a major architect. The addition is, of course, not to be blamed on her.

27. American Legion Post, 1925
Marston and Van Pelt
131 N. Marengo Avenue
Spanish Renaissance. As the ranks of this once-active American institution dwindle, the future of such fine buildings as this and the even greater one in Hollywood is insecure.

28. Pasadena Public Library, 1927
Myron Hunt and H. C. Chambers
285 E. Walnut Street
Spanish Renaissance. The rich Plateresque entrance beyond the screen on the street is unusual for Hunt, whose works are often on the dry side. A new public entrance has been added on the north side of the building, and the interior has been elegantly restored.

29. Pasadena City Hall, 1925–27
John Bakewell, Jr. and Arthur Brown, Jr.
100 N. Garfield Avenue
One of several exceptions to the rule that

29. *Pasadena City Hall,* 1925–27

Pasadena's best buildings were designed by Pasadena architects, this giant wedding cake is by the San Francisco firm that is responsible for that city's marvelous headquarters. Pasadena was less generous so the interiors are not as opulent as the earlier San Francisco City Hall, but its central patio with fountain and beautiful garden makes up for the absence of all that marble. The Spanish Baroque dome and western facade are stunning in the late afternoon sun.

Notice also the handsome **Gas Company Building** (1929) at the northwest corner of Garfield Avenue and Ramona Street, and across Garfield on the northeast corner, the old **Court Buildings** (1952, Breo Freeman), the latter distinguished by being well-executed Spanish at so late a date and the former for its rare scraffito-work in the second story.

30. Pasadena Police Department Building, 1989–90
EKONA, planning architect; Robert A. M. Stern, design architect (Stern Ehrenkrantz Ramager) Campbell and Campbell, landscape architects; Robert Irwin, sculptor
Southwest corner Walnut and Garfield streets

The architects faced a difficult task in designing this building. The nearby City Hall, Library, and Gas Company Building are so strong in design that they had to choose between being self-effacing or salient. Being rather strong architects themselves, they naturally chose the latter stance, the volutes on the roof being their big statement. Except for anemic detailing, the building comes off rather well, especially when set off by the small garden and sculpture, not to mention the wall in shades of lavender.

31. Doubletree Inn, 1989–90
Moore, Ruble and Yudell; Lawrence Halprin, landscape architect; Joyce Kozloff, ceramic designer
Southwest corner Walnut and Los Robles streets

Set in the Plaza de las Fuentes (by Halprin) this monster is not the firm's best work. With its round arches, it seems to be playing off the

Mission Inn in Riverside. The plaza is much better, setting off the city hall beautifully. The large amount of colorful tile-work seems on the gaudy side for Pasadena (but note the old Batchelder tile fountain on the center of the wall).

32. Old Pasadena Post Office, 1913
Oscar Wenderoth; Marston and Maybury, 1938 addition
Northwest corner of Garfield Avenue and Colorado Boulevard

The Italian Renaissance palace is notable not only for its facade with light relief decoration but also for its interior space enclosed in colorful marble walls paid for by the people of Pasadena, mind you, and not the federal government. The electric blue walls in the rear are recent and lamentable. The building is now a branch of the downright hideous new Central Post Office at Lincoln Avenue and Orange Grove Boulevard.

33. Plaza Pasadena, 1980
Kober Associates
South side of Colorado Boulevard between Marengo and Los Robles avenues

We have already paid our respects to this monstrous cliche that photographs well, if the photographer gets the right angle (see *Progressive Architecture,* July 1981, 94–97, that gave it an award). Come, experience it, and you will go home shouting the praises of Frank O. Gehry's **Santa Monica Place** (1980).

34. Pasadena Civic Auditorium, 1932
Edwin Bergstrom; Bennett and Haskell; J. E. Stanton, decorator
300 E. Green Street

A low-silhouette, Italian Renaissance palace that was once the "City Beautiful" southern anchor of the minor Garfield Avenue axis dominated by City Hall and anchored at the north by the Public Library.

35. Pasadena Convention Center, 1975
John Carl Warnecke
300 E. Green Street

At both sides of the auditorium are what one little old Pasadena lady has called "The Pig Sties," low structures with most of their interior

30. Pasadena Police Department Building, 1989–90

spaces underground. The intention of the architect was to avoid competing with the auditorium. Very commendable except that he was in a Brutalist phase and the roofs do intrude, but thankfully not so much as the lines of the heavy-handed Plaza Pasadena across the street.

36. Condominiums, 1981
Eric Moss and John Stafford
475 S. Euclid Avenue

Really, in Pasadena? A Post-Modern extravaganza in stucco with window panels in stepped glass brick. A large ear appears on the roof of this object, so much in contrast with its Craftsman and Spanish Colonial neighbors.

37. Masonic Temple, 1926
Bennett and Haskell
200 S. Euclid Avenue

A Beaux Arts Renaissance structure of great dignity.

38. All Saints Episcopal Church, 1925
Johnson, Kaufman, and Coate (Roland E. Coate)
Parish House and Rectory, 1930
Bennett and Haskell
Interior of Parish House totally remodeled after fire, 1979
Warren Callister
132 N. Euclid Avenue

English country Gothic without and within, including Tiffany windows from an earlier church. The Episcopalians seem to have unfailing good taste. The observation applies to the new interiors of the Parish House; joyful is the best word to describe them. The sanctuary has been remodeled (1991) by Kurt Landberg Associates of St. Louis. In order to meet the needs of the modern service, parts of the rood screen were placed in the south transept, and the altar, choir stalls, and pulpit were brought forward. In doing this only a small area of the original Batchelder tile floor was removed. All in all an extremely sensitive transformation of a church that is in the vanguard of social action.

39. First Congregational Church, 1904, 1916
  Buchanan and Brockway
  Southeast corner of Walnut Street and Los Robles Avenue
A large English Gothic church that dignifies a rather forlorn commercial area.

40. Grace Nicholson Building (now **Pacific-Asia Museum**), 1924
  Marston, Van Pelt, and Maybury
  46 N. Los Robles Avenue
A real surprise—a Chinese palace. A dealer in Oriental art and books on the Orient, Ms. Nicholson built it as a shop and home. Later it became the Pasadena Museum of Art until that institution moved to new quarters. Now it is the Pacific-Asia Museum, which has done very well by it by giving unusually good exhibitions and building a lovely Chinese garden in the central court (1979, Erikson, Peters, Thomas, and Associates).

41. Warner Building, 1927
  Marston and Maybury; Jess Stanton, designer
  481 E. Colorado Boulevard
Most of the marvelous black and gold Art Deco seashell and flower ornament has been restored.

42. First United Methodist Church, 1926
  Thomas P. Barber
  Southwest corner of Oakland Avenue and Colorado Boulevard
On the outside, this English Gothic church is notable for the pleasant entrance court and the lovely tracery of the large east window, best viewed on a Sunday morning. The stained-glass windows throughout the church were fabricated by Roy C. Baillie Studios of Los Angeles. The interior has the usual Methodist central plan with curved pews and curved balcony surrounding the pulpit. But it is the fan vaulting of the ceiling that is remarkable. If you look closely, you will see that the intricate plaster work ingeniously encloses the ventilating system.

43. Singer Building, 1926
  Everett Phipps Babcock
  520 E. Colorado Boulevard
A good, as-yet-unspoiled example of Spanish Colonial Revival commercial work.

44. First Church of Christ Scientist, 1909
  F. P. Burnham
  Southeast corner of Oakland Avenue and Green Street
Like most churches of this denomination, this is a variation on the Neo-Classical "Mother Church" in Boston. It is one of the first large exposed concrete structures in the area.

45. Throop Memorial Unitarian-Universalist Church, 1923
  Frederick Kennedy
  Northeast corner of Los Robles Avenue and Del Mar Boulevard
An exposed concrete (now plastered over) Gothic design that gives sophistication to this area.

46. E. W. Smith House, 1910
  Charles and Henry Greene
  272 S. Los Robles Avenue, next door to Throop Church
A large, two-story Craftsman house that shows very little evidence of the Greenes' affair with the Orient. Converted to commercial use without damaging the integrity of the architecture, this building is a model of adaptive reuse.

47. Pages Victorian Court, 1981
  Thornton and Fagan Associates
  430 S. Los Robles Avenue
Talk about a protest against the Modern movement, this is it—a humorous, not too authentic but still recognizable Eastlake Revival extravaganza.

48. Pasadena Town Club, 1931
  Roland E. Coate
  378 S. Madison Avenue
This chaste, one-story Monterey-style building, with a good Greek Revival door, exudes respectability.

49. Casa Torre Garden Court, 1927
  Everett Phipps Babcock
  611–627 E. California Boulevard

A two-story, L-shaped Spanish Colonial Revival apartment building that looks as if it is about to be gobbled up by modernism.

50. Pasadena Playhouse, 1924–25
    Elmer Grey
    Interiors, Dwight Gibbs
    37 S. El Molino Avenue
Once the very heart of Pasadena culture, this theater and school came upon hard times in the 1950s and collapsed in the mid-1960s. The wonder is that it is still with us. The theater has been beautifully restored and has resumed its old spirit and ambience as an extremely successful, legitimate theater.

51. First Trust Building (now **Sanwa Bank**), 1928
    Bennett and Haskell
    595 E. Colorado Boulevard at Madison Avenue
This dignified Renaissance Revival building is most impressive inside. The banking room was decorated by Giovanni Smeraldi and is hung with four large paintings by Alson Clark. Also, this happens to be the first building in Pasadena built to resist earthquakes. In 1971 it met the test.

52. Pasadena Presbyterian Church, 1976
    Gougeon-Woodman
    Northwest corner of Colorado Boulevard and Madison Avenue
Architectural expressionism at its very height, this church replaces a Collegiate Gothic structure (1906) by F. L. Roehrig that was badly damaged in the 1971 earthquake.

53. Blaisdell Medical Building, 1952
    Smith and Williams (Whitney R. Smith)
    547 E. Union Street
A small reinforced concrete building with central patio. Smith was obviously influenced by Wrightian ideas. He did not design the wooden fence.

54. Earl Apartment House, 1912
    Charles and Henry Greene
    527 E. Union Street
The Greenes working in the Mission style, though they could not resist occasional Oriental touches.

55. Blinn House (now **Women's City Club**), 1905–6
    George W. Maher
    Oakland Avenue at Ford Place
So far as is known, this is the only house in the West designed by the well-known Chicago architect, friend of Sullivan and Wright. (Incidentally, Maher's only other western building is, of all things, a combined public library and water tower in Fresno.) Stylistically the Blinn House is distantly related to the Mission Revival, though it is hard to place the corner windows on the second floor. The interior, somewhat remodeled, is nevertheless still exciting, particularly the staircase and glazed-tile fireplace.

56. Bungalow Court, 1910
    Attributed to Hunt and Grey
    270 N. Madison Avenue
A handsome Tudor court.

57. Lukens House, 1886–88
    Harry Ridgeway
    267 N. El Molino Avenue
This beautifully restored house in its garden is one of the few vestiges of Victorianism left in this part of town. It is Queen Anne with dripping lath-work similar to that on Lucky Baldwin's Guest House in Arcadia.

58. Scottish Rite Cathedral, 1924
    Joseph J. Blick
    150 N. Madison Avenue
Pre-PWA Classical Moderne with guardian sphinxes.

59. First City Bank, 1961
    Ladd and Kelsey
    123 S. Lake Avenue
A beautifully articulated Miesian box.

60. Retail Shops, 1961
    Pulliam, Matthews, and Associates
    230 S. Lake Avenue
Very civilized International Style Modern, including an outdoor cafe.

61. Bullock's Pasadena, 1947
    Wurdeman and Becket; Ruth Shellhorn and Carl McElvy, landscape architects
    401 S. Lake Avenue

The design and siting of this posh upper-middle-class store is in many ways unique, even to the California scene. Essentially it appears from Lake Avenue as a building in a park. As was mentioned when the building opened in 1947, "Because the new store was planned to serve the people of Pasadena and the San Gabriel Valley, whose lives are spent in garden communities and whose homes express a marked degree of love of the out-of-doors, the architects designed a building in keeping with the garden theme so dear to the dwellers in those prosperous and progressive communities of cultivated estates." (*Southwest Builder and Contractor,* Sept. 26, 1947).

The building extends the Streamline Moderne idiom into the post-war era, but, as was becoming increasingly common in the late-1930s, the architects have combined the Streamline with delicate and sophisticated image of the Regency. The elegance of the interior craftsmanship, now beginning to show wear, evokes (in an elitist fashion) the Arts and Crafts tradition which one so closely associates with early Pasadena.

See also **Robinson's Pasadena** nearby at 777 E. Colorado Boulevard, designed in 1950 by Pereira and Luckman.

62. The Burlington Arcade, 1982
Symonds/Deenihan
380 S. Lake Avenue

A galleria of two, two-story tiers of shops facing each other, reminiscent of the original London building of the same name. These architects also designed **The Commons** (1982), a courtyard shopping center up the street at South Lake Avenue. This time they chose the mansard mode. You will find it impossible to keep from looking up Lake which is lined with medium high-rise commercial buildings, all of them without exception disappointing. It is incredible that the Design Review Commission for a city that has such a high reputation for good architecture could have allowed this to happen.

The section of the city east of Lake Avenue and south of the Foothill Freeway is fairly recent Pasadena with projects of the 1920s and 1930s appearing in the western portion. Then about Hill Avenue at Pasadena City College, shards of the 1950s begin to pop up, at first on commercial Colorado Boulevard and then south of it in the residential districts. It is easy to brush this stuff off as kitsch culture, but who knows what forthcoming Ph.D. candidate will pronounce it not just significant but profound!

1. House, circa 1915
71–75 Sierra Madre Boulevard

Midwest Prairie-style houses built in the Los Angeles area are rare, and of those built few remain. Here is an example of the style sheathed in tan-colored brick. It even exhibits Wrightian planters on the top of the columns that support the front pergola.

2. Trinity Lutheran Church, 1927
Frederick Kennedy, Jr.
997 E. Walnut Street at Catalina Avenue

Vaguely English Gothic in revealed concrete. Kennedy was a strong advocate of concrete construction in the Los Angeles area and his work deserves a careful study.

3. Sanborn House, 1903
Charles and Henry Greene
65 N. Catalina Avenue

This is a large, angular Craftsman structure, never very good and made worse by a nasty paint job. But it is by Greene and Greene and significant, for in 1903 they were on the brink of their great creative period.

EAST PASADENA

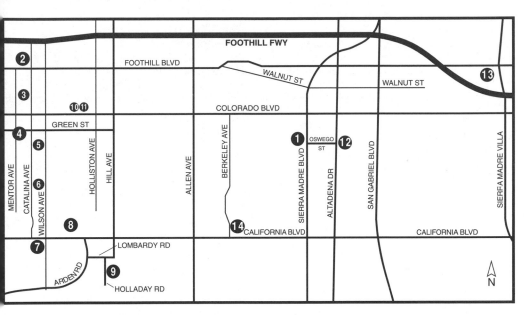

4. Thatcher Medical Center and other buildings, 1948–49
L. G. Scherer
960 E. Green Street at Mentor Avenue
A collection of offices, shops, and apartments in the New Orleans Mansard style, rather strange to encounter in Pasadena.

5. Apartment Building, 1963
Pulliam, Matthews, and Associates
241 S. Wilson Avenue
Elegant International Style Modern simplicity on a tree-lined street notable for apartments designed with less sophistication, to put it mildly.

6. House, circa 1915
Arthur S. Heineman (Alfred Heineman, associate)
516 S. Catalina Avenue

The rolled-eave treatment of this house is almost a trademark of Heineman's work in the teens.

7. Polytechnic School, 1907
Hunt and Grey
1030 E. California Street at Wilson Avenue
This is probably the first fully realized bungalow school. Not only does it manage to get all the classrooms on one floor, but it also opens these rooms with ranks of doors to the outside, pioneering the idea of the indoor-outdoor school that has won wide popularity in California and elsewhere. The old building has been remodeled, but the idea is still clear.

8. California Institute of Technology, 1908–present
California Boulevard between Wilson and Hill avenues

The first campus plan and buildings for Cal Tech were designed by the firm of Myron Hunt and Elmer Grey. Their scheme provided a Beaux Arts axial mall, open at one end and surrounded by two-story Mission Revival structures on the enclosed sides. Their principal building, which terminated the major axis, was **Throop Hall (Pasadena Hall)** of 1910. Hunt and Grey continued their work on the campus over a period of eight years, from 1908 through 1915. In 1915 they were replaced by Bertram G. Goodhue. Goodhue enlarged and elaborated on the original axial plan, making the landscape more Moorish and the buildings more Spanish Churrigueresque. After Goodhue's death in 1924, his firm, Goodhue Associates, continued to design buildings for the campus through the late 1930s. From 1928 through 1938 Beatrix Farrand was the consulting landscape architect for Cal Tech, and fragments of her various designs remain.

As with most American academic institutions after World War II, the Modern Movement entered the scene. The results have added little of merit, and they have done much to destroy the strong character of the original campus plan and its architecture.

The most interesting buildings that remain are:

a. Gates Chemistry Laboratory (now **Administration Building**), 1917
Bertram G. Goodhue and Elmer Grey
Its exterior is dominated by a fine Churrigueresque door. The interior has been recycled (1983) by Bobrow and Thomas; Peter de Bretteville and Stefanos Polyzoides. The **Gates Annex** (1927) is by the Goodhue Associates and is Spanish mixed with Art Deco Moderne.

b. Bridge Physics Laboratory, 1922
Bertram G. Goodhue
Again, rather severe Spanish with relief given by a Churrigueresque entrance.

c. West Court Buildings, 1928–30
Goodhue Associates
The main (Wilson Avenue) entrance to Cal Tech consists of two long, arcaded buildings

somewhat reminiscent of the Campo Santo at Pisa. The rows of Italian cypresses in front of them were recently cut down.

d. Athenaeum (now Faculty Club), 1930
Gordon B. Kaufmann
A marvelous, Mediterranean (Italian) style building without and within.

e. Dormitories, 1931
Gordon B. Kaufmann
Designed around three courtyards, these vaguely Spanish/Italian Romanesque buildings, with capitals in the cloisters featuring the heads of aviators and scientists, are real treasures.

f. Beckman Auditorium, 1963
Edward D. Stone
A fanciful Islamic image in Stone's World's Fair phase.

9. Hale Solar Laboratory, 1924
Johnson, Kaufmann and Coate (Roland E. Coate)
740 Holladay Road
Here is an oddity and a significant one. This was the private preserve of the astronomer, George Ellory Hale, who was one of the great cultural leaders in Pasadena, and who, as a Trustee of Caltech, was as responsible as Robert Millikan for bringing CalTech to national eminence. He was also a student of planning and architecture. In the case of this building, the style is Spanish Colonial with strong Egyptian overtones befitting the laboratory of an astronomer. No one seems to know who designed the bas-relief of Akhenaton with sun rays over the entrance. Another bas-relief over the mantle inside is by the nationally known sculptor, Lee Lawrie. The gardens were laid out by Beatrix Farrand in 1928, but little remains of her design.

California Boulevard east of Cal Tech
This street, extending into San Marino and San Pasqual, has fine houses in the period revivals of the 1920s and 1930s. It is a good place to walk. Even better is Lombardy Road, one block below California, but, since most of Lombardy is in San Marino, we have included it in our San Marino section.

10. Austin Automobile Showroom, circa 1927
Austin Company (Cleveland)
1285 E. Colorado Boulevard
Huge, gaping jaws full of plate glass are framed by cast-stone Plateresque ornament.

11. Holliston Avenue United Methodist Church, 1899
John C. Austin
Northwest corner of Holliston Avenue and Colorado Boulevard
This large Gothic structure (which looks Richardsonian) was moved stone by stone from its original site at Marengo Avenue and Colorado Boulevard where it had been First Methodist. It lost its tower in the 1971 earthquake, but it otherwise speaks of the late Victorian age. The interior is based on the Akron Plan with its semicircular seating oriented to the northwest corner pulpit area.

12. Pasadena Public Library, Lamanda Park Branch, 1966
Pulliam, Matthews, and Associates
140 S. Altadena Drive at Oswego Street
Though one-story, the massive concrete post-and-lintel frame makes this building seem monumental. The interior is well-planned for use and beauty.

13. Stuart Pharmaceutical Company, 1957–58
Edward D. Stone; Thomas D. Church, land-scape architect
3300 block of E. Foothill Boulevard near Sierra Madre Villa Avenue
This building and the American Embassy in New Delhi are Stone's best designs in the post-World War II era. Like the embassy, the Stuart Building poses as a delicate Islamic box set in an Oriental pond. "Despite its sparkling modernity," it was mentioned in the May 23, 1958 issue of the *Southwest Builder and Contractor,* "the Stuart building has been likened to the Taj Mahal for its beauty and its Asian influence."

8c. California Institute of Technology, West Court Buildings, 1928–30

Church's design for the garden fully acknowledges the mood that Stone was trying to convey. As one would rightly expect of an ideal working environment in Southern California, parking was provided for 300 cars, and Church designed a swimming pool for employees and guests. This impressive ensemble is a significant reminder of the days when industry saw itself as a major patron of the arts.

14. Ten Spec Houses, circa 1927
Wallace Neff
500 Block of S. Berkeley Avenue, San Marino
A delightful group of modest-sized Spanish Colonial revival houses by an architect who usually designed much larger ones.

North Pasadena

This area, bounded on the west and south by the Foothill Freeway, on the east by Michillinda Avenue, and on the north by the boundary with Altadena is listed from west to east, generally alternating streets south-north and north-south.

1. Savage House, 1924
   Henry Greene
   1299–1301 N. Marengo Avenue
A Spanish Colonial Revival duplex distinguished only by the name of its architect. It was done after his partnership with his brother, Charles, was dissolved.

2. House, 1891
   Frederick L. Roehrig
   1247 N. Garfield Avenue
The Anglo Colonial Revival at its best, this beautifully detailed house awaits restoration.

3. "Mansion Adena" (Lewis House), 1886
   Attributed to Eugene Getschell
   Northeast corner of Garfield Avenue and
   Adena Street
This otherwise Queen Anne house sports a mansard tower.

4. Rust-Smiley House, 1887
   E. W. Houghton
   730 N. Garfield Avenue
Another good Queen Anne well set back from the street.

5. Bowen Court, 1913
   Arthur S. Heineman
   (Alfred Heineman,
   associate)
   539 Villa Street
This is one of the first bungalow courts. It is set in tall trees and extends in an arc around to North Oakland Avenue. Note the rustic "playhouse" (now glassed in) which is toward the center of the court. **Two other bungalow courts** of the same period—one Mission style, the other Craftsman—are at 567, and 572–574 North Oakland Avenue respectively. The former is quite simple but retains marvelous Mission-style lanterns in the center of the court.

3. "Mansion Adena" (Lewis House), 1886

6. House, 1914
   Southwest corner of Orange Grove
   Boulevard and El Molino Avenue
A huge airplane bungalow on a boulder base.

7. Westminster Presbyterian Church, 1928
   Marston, Van Pelt, and Maybury (Sylvanus
   Marston)
   1757 N. Lake Avenue
Certainly a landmark as Lake Avenue rises
toward the mountains, this church seems
vaguely modeled on St. Maclou at Rouen.

8. St. Elizabeth's Roman Catholic Church,
   1924
   Wallace Neff
1849 N. Lake Avenue, north of Westminster
Presbyterian Church, Altadena

The monumental but simple facade of this
Spanish Colonial Revival church is marred only
by a bad sculpture of the saint over the door.

9. House, circa 1910
   Southwest corner of Michigan Avenue and
   Washington Boulevard
Mission style with red trim.

10. Houses, circa 1912
   800 N. Michigan Avenue
A number of Craftsman bungalows, not by the
Greenes, are to be found in almost mint condition in this area. See also from about the same
period number 885 and 1399 North Michigan
Avenue, 835 and 897 North Holliston Avenue,
and 1261 North Mar Vista Avenue.

11. Williams House, "Hillmont," 1887
 Harry Ridgeway
 Northwest corner of Hill Avenue and
 Mountain Street
This Queen Anne house of extraordinary quality is set in beautiful grounds. Ridgeway was
Pasadena's first professional architect. Hiram
Reid in his *History of Pasadena* (circa 1895)
wrote that Ridgeway "never wanted any man to
be able to point out any structure and say
'that's one of Ridgeway's designs—it shows
the earmarks of his style.' He sought and
achieved that ideal freedom from style called
the artlessness of art."
 Just west of the house at 1507 Mountain
Street is the utterly nondescript **Thum House**
(1925) by Henry Greene.

12. Gartz Duplex, 1921
 Irving J. Gill
 950 N. Oakland Avenue
Very simple stucco walls and an arch—very
characteristic of Gill in a highly puritanical
mood.

13. Craig Adobe, "The Hermitage,"
 circa 1880
 2121 Monte Vista Street, just west of Craig
 Avenue
Except for its walls, this is a Queen Anne cottage with fish-scale shingles in the gable. Most
of the "Victorian" details were added in a
remodeling (circa 1950) by Earl Hugens.

14. Pasadena Jewish Temple and Center,
 1957
 1434 N. Altadena Drive, just above
 Washington Boulevard
Classical Moderne.

15. St. Luke's Hospital, 1934
 Gene Verge, Sr.
 2632 E. Washington Boulevard near
 Altadena Drive
Classical Moderne with strong Spanish
Colonial Revival elements.

16. Hale House, circa 1910
 835 N. Holliston Avenue
A sturdy example of the Craftsman aesthetic in
a predominantly Swiss Chalet version.

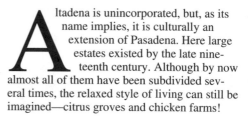

Altadena is unincorporated, but, as its
name implies, it is culturally an
extension of Pasadena. Here large
estates existed by the late nineteenth century. Although by now
almost all of them have been subdivided several times, the relaxed style of living can still be
imagined—citrus groves and chicken farms!

1. House, circa 1906
 Louis B. Easton
 403 W. Ventura Street, near Lincoln Avenue
By a miracle this Craftsman bunkhouse was not
torn down when the C. C. Curtis ranch house
was demolished. It is, along with the Volney-
Craig House in Pasadena, one of Easton's finest
designs, which is to say that it is one of the best
examples of the Craftsman aesthetic anywhere.
 The house across the street is also probably
by Easton. In 1925 additions were made to it by
Henry Greene.

2. McNally House, 1888
 Frederick L. Roehrig
 654 E. Mariposa
A towered, simplified Queen Anne (Shingle
style) building now almost obscured by later
building. A. N. McNally (of Rand-McNally)
was a commissioner of the World's Columbian
Exposition in Chicago in 1893. According to
the story, he liked the interior of the Turkish
display so much that when it was dismantled he
had parts of it crated and sent to Altadena
where, presumably with the aid of Roehrig,
they were added to the main house as a "smok-
ing room." In fact, remembering Roehrig's
Islamic pretensions, we rather imagine that he
was the instigator of this delightful enterprise.

3. Altadena Public Library, 1967
 Boyd Georgi
 600 E. Mariposa Street, southwest corner of
 Santa Rosa Avenue

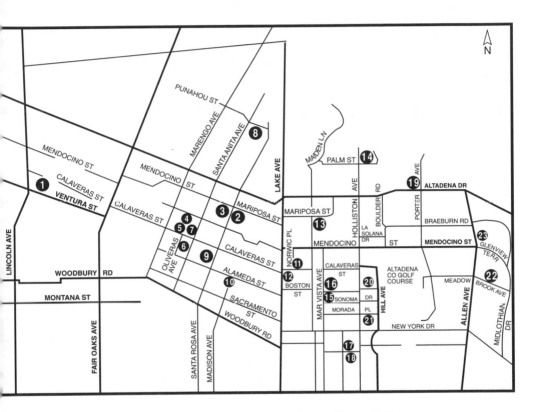

The International Style Modern box softened by Orientalism.

4. Hong House, 1917
Myron Hunt
396 E. Mendocino Street, east of Marengo Avenue
A stucco Anglo-Colonial Revival dwelling. Very gracious.

5. Griffith House, 1923
369 E. Calaveras Street
Egyptian Revival. This town has everything! This house was remodeled and enlarged in 1991.

6. Coates House, 1938
Whitney R. Smith
2320 N. Oliveras Avenue
A very simple Modern structure.

7. Bowen House, 1905
Charles and Henry Greene
443 E. Calaveras Street, at northwest corner of Santa Anita Avenue
One of the Greenes' best early bungalows, enlarged and almost totally changed at a later date.

8. Lowe House, 1934

8. Lowe House, 1934
  Harwell H. Harris (Carl Anderson, associate)
  596 E. Punahou Street, between Santa Anita
  and Santa Rosa avenues
An impressive classic of the 1930s. The garage
to the street and the L-shaped house enclose the
entrance court. Small wood-walled enclosures
extend from each bedroom so that it is possible
to sleep out-of-doors in privacy. The feeling is
Japanese but also very personally Harris.

9. Case Study House #20, 1958
  Buff, Straub, and Hensman
  2275 N. Santa Rosa Avenue
An elegant, small house set in bosky
("Christmas Tree Lane") surroundings.

10. Woodbury House, 1882
  Attributed to Harry Ridgeway; Ballroom by
  Frederick L. Roehrig, 1898
  2606 N. Madison Avenue, on cul-de-sac
  just north of Mariposa Street
An old ranch house in the Italianate manner.

11. "Little Normandy," 1925
  J. Wilmer Hershey
  Norwic Place just east of Lake Avenue and
  off Mendocino Street
A group of quaint dollhouse dwellings
intended to be reminiscent of rural France.
Unfortunately, there were some intrusions in
the early 1950s.

12. Eliot Junior High School, 1944
  Marston and Maybury
  2184 N. Lake Avenue
This is essentially a pre-World War II design,
realized immediately after the war. It is an
example of a stripped Gothic Revival, though
the buff-colored brick wall seems to draw it
into the warm Modern.

13. Brandt-Serrurier House, 1905
  Charles and Henry Greene
  1086 Mariposa Street, at southeast corner
  of Maiden Lane
A tiny Craftsman bungalow.

14. Gateposts, circa 1910
  Northeast corner of Holliston Avenue and
  Palm Street
An impressive boulder entrance to the old
Gillette ranch.

15. Williams House, 1915
  Charles and Henry Greene
  1145 Sonoma Drive at northeast corner of
  Mar Vista Avenue
The stuccoed house, with its green tile roof,
seems almost Spanish until you notice the oriental touches. It is interesting to compare it
with the Earl Apartments (1912) and the
Cordelia Culbertson House (1911) by the same
architects.

16. Mansfield House, 1916
> Northeast corner of Boston Street and Mar
> Vista Avenue

A Pueblo Revival bungalow with matching pergolas jutting from the central "upper room."

17. Dyment House, 1923
> Northeast corner of Woodbury Road and
> Michigan Avenue

A late example of the Mission style with corner
gate.

18. McClean House, 1929
> 1290 E. Woodbury Road

Mission-style simplicity placed on an almost
monumental rustic cobblestone base. Very
strange.

19. Parsons Bungalow, 1910
> Arthur S. Heineman (Alfred Heineman,
> associate)
> 1605 E. Altadena Drive at Porter Avenue

This is simply one of the finest, most characteristic California bungalows to be found anywhere. And its siting at a diagonal to the nearby
mountain is spectacular. In our 1977 *Guide to
Architecture in Los Angeles and Southern
California,* it was still at the corner of Los
Robles Avenue and California Street in
Pasadena. But times change. Incidentally, it
proved impossible to move the original cobblestone foundations and pillars, so they were
rebuilt by modern craftsmen. Tim Andersen
was the restoration architect when the house
was moved in 1980.

There are some fascinating neighborhoods
in this area. You will not believe **Boulder
Road,** just west of the previous entry, and
nearby **La Solana,** a street devoted to the
Spanish Colonial Revival. Farther south, **Mar
Vista Avenue** above and below New York
Drive is a very characteristic pre-World War I
street.

20. Keyes Bungalow, 1911
> 1337 E. Boston Street, west of Altadena
> Country Club

A first-rate example of the "airplane bungalow," called that for its wingspread. It is obvious that it once was surrounded with much
more open space.

21. Dorland House, 1949
> Lloyd Wright
> 1370 Morada Place, west of Altadena
> Country Club

A large glass prow accents the street facade.

22. Beard House, 1934
> Richard J. Neutra
> 1981 Meadowbrook Road, between Allen
> Avenue and Midlothian Drive

A small but elegant machine-image house with
walls and roof of H. H. Robertson ribbed steel
panels.

23. Gunther House, 1923
> D. E. Postle Co., designers
> 1960 Mendocino Lane, facing
> Allen Avenue

This is a striking sight—it is almost as if the
street were designed to show off this rather
unusual and large Mediterranean-style house
here at the east end of Mendocino.

SOUTH PASADENA, CENTRAL SECTION

We have already introduced South Pasadena under the Lower Arroyo, South section. The following listing covers the business district of South Pasadena and its immediate surroundings.

1. House, circa 1910
499 Monterey Road, at southwest corner of Indiana Court
A large Tudor-Craftsman chalet with Mission touches.

2. Bungalow, circa 1900
1102 Indiana Avenue, north of Monterey Road, near the Santa Fe Railroad tracks
A marvelous misinterpretation of Vitruvius on a very small scale.

3. Bilike House, 1905–6
Parkinson and Bergstrom
Entrance at 699 Monterey Road
An uphill drive takes you to this Mission Revival house that is now an educational center and church office for the nearby United Methodist Church. Also, the view of Pasadena and the mountains can be magnificent.

4. Two Bungalows, circa 1922
N.E. Corner of Monterey Road and Glendon Avenue
These two Period Revival stucco bungalows of the 1920s express the romantic exoticism of the Islamic.

5. Chiat House, 1967
Carl Maston
612 Camino Verde
In an area of pleasant but unremarkable houses, this vertically planked Miesian box stands out as one of the best pieces of architecture in South Pasadena.

6. Graham House, "Wynyate," 1887
W. F. Norton
851 Lyndon Street
This triumph of the Queen Anne style was a meeting place for such worthies as John Muir, Mary Austin, and Charles F. Lummis. Imagine it with its porte cochere and tall chimney restored!

7. Meridian Iron Works, circa 1890
913 Meridian Avenue
An example of the Pioneer False Front style, rare in this area.

8. Watering Trough and Wayside Station, 1905
Norman F. Marsh
On Meridian Avenue, just across the street from the Iron Works
This large boulder cairn was a rest stop for horses and their riders on their way between Los Angeles and Pasadena.

9. South Pasadena Public Library, 1930
Marsh, Smith, and Powell; Howard H. Morgridge and Associates, 1982 addition
1115 El Centro Street
Only the Renaissance Revival facade of the 1930 building has been retained in the new construction. All traces of the older (1907) Carnegie Library (with dome, of course) have been destroyed. But the new building is harmonious with the old as it now stands.

10. South Pasadena Presbyterian Church
(now **Grace United Brethren Church**), 1906
Northeast corner of Fremont Avenue and El Centro Street
Mission-style monumentality screening the apse of the much earlier (1886) Pasadena Presbyterian Church that was moved from the site at Colorado and Madison when the 1906 church by Frederick L. Roehrig was built.

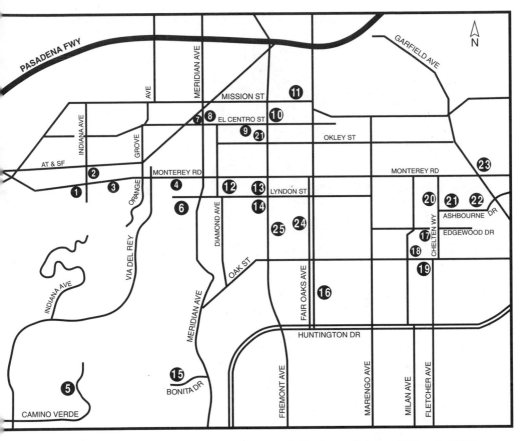

11. South Pasadena Civic Center, 1985–88
De Bretteville and Polyzoides
Northwest Corner Mission Street and
Mound Avenue

The commission required a complex of a police
station, jail, fire station, and a council chamber
being added to the existing City Hall. The
architects chose to organize these various elements around several courtyards and to clothe
them in good old Spanish Colonial Revival
garb with a little Post-Modern color thrown in.

12. Cottage, circa 1890
1103 Monterey Road, southeast corner of
Diamond Avenue

A Queen Anne relic.

13. St. James Episcopal Church, 1907
Cram, Goodhue, and Ferguson (Carleton
M. Winslow, Sr., associate)
Southwest corner of Monterey Road and
Fremont Avenue

Some points of similarity to the West Point
Chapel (by the same firm) on the outside—
heavy Gothic mixed with Romanesque—but
the interior is airy and elegant.

14. South Pasadena High School Auditorium, 1937
Marsh, Smith, and Powell; Millard Sheets,
murals; Merrill Gage,
sculptured panels
Southwest corner of Fremont Avenue and
Lyndon Street

15. Grokowsky House, 1928

PWA Classical Moderne rather delicately worked. South of the high school there are some good streets of bungalows; Ramona Street has some sophisticated designs; Diamond Avenue is another interesting street. East of Fair Oaks Avenue are more bungalows and other Craftsman houses; also, try Milan Avenue.

15. Grokowsky House, 1928
    R. M. Schindler
    816 Bonita Drive off Meridian Avenue
An excellent example of Schindler's early de Stijl phase.

16. 1414 Fair Oaks Building, 1959
    Smith and Williams; Eckbo, Dean, and Associates, landscape architects
    1414 Fair Oaks Avenue
A building as a sunscreen with gardens and enclosed spaces underneath. Some unfortunate alterations have been made by the new tenants.

17. Spears House, 1925
    Ernest Irving Freese
    1921 Edgewood Drive
A modest English-style bungalow pays its homage to the automobile through a dominant covered driveway and adjoining entrance porch.

18. Bungalow, circa 1910
    Northeast corner of Oak Street and Milan Avenue
Pictured in *Sweet's Bungalows* (circa 1911), the design may be by the Heinemans.

19. House, circa 1905
    Southwest corner of Oak Street and Fletcher Avenue
Mission style with Oriental touches.

20. Miltimore House, 1911
    Irving J. Gill
    1301 Chelten Way
This house is one of Gill's best; puritanical, based on Mission style. Note the extensive pergolas that provide the transition between house and garden. Also compare the houses nearby— very different in imagery but only a little earlier. This section around the intersection of Chelten Way and Ashbourne Drive was once called Ellerslie Park, full of ancient oaks. It was privately developed with many of the live oaks being saved by curving the streets around them, a perverse twist dear to the hearts of ecologists, old and young.

21. House, 1926
David A. Ogilvie
2000 Ashbourne Drive
The yellow brick walls of this Tudor villa give it a Cotswold feeling.

22. Baer House, 1930
Roland E. Coate
2040 Ashbourne Drive
Spanish Colonial Revival somewhat corrected by reference to the eastern Colonial. It is swamped in foliage.

23. Bixby House, 1925
Roland E. Coate
1148 S. Garfield Avenue, at northeast corner of Monterey Road
This house is one of the first in Southern California to employ the Monterey Revival style. Compared to later uses of this style by Coate, the Bixby House is more Hispanic than Anglo. It was often illustrated and mentioned in regional and national magazines in discussions of that revival in the 1920s and 1930s.

24. Rialto Theater, 1925
L. A. Smith
Northwest corner of Fair Oaks Avenue and Okley Street
The exterior, once mildly Plateresque with Baroque touches, is defaced. But the mainly Spanish interior is still intact. Note an Egyptian influence here and there.

25. South Pasadena Women's Improvement Association Clubhouse, 1913
Norman F. Marsh
Northeast corner Fremont Avenue and Rollin Street
A shingled Arts and Crafts building reminding us that the women's club and the Arts and Craft movements flourished at the same time.

SAN MARINO

It should be obvious from its architecture that this town, settled on the Henry E. Huntington estate of the same name, is largely inhabited by members of the moneyed class. Its "high tone" was set by Huntington, who put his house and then his library on a fine prominence with a distant view of the Pacific (still seen occasionally). In the 1920s and 1930s the would-be barons gathered around his regal estate. Even the subdividing of properties in recent years and the consequent building of houses closer and closer together has not really interfered with the picture of opulence. This is the way all people should be able to live even if they do not wish to do so. Try **Saint Albans Road** north of Huntington Drive to get a feeling for "the way of life."

A rule never boldly stated in this book but sometimes implied is that good architecture and a great deal of money are constant companions. In San Marino this rule often breaks down. It is not that there isn't a lot of beautiful building; it is just that the expenditure should have produced more, particularly since nearby Pasadena has always had excellent architects ready to cross the border. As a matter of fact, most of the best work is near Pasadena.

1. House, 1970
B. R. Offenhauser
1045 Oak Grove Place
An unusual and very knowing play on the Mediterranean style.

2. House, 1960
Lynn V. Maudlin
931 Canon Drive
A return to the Oriental Craftsman tradition. The setting is lovely.

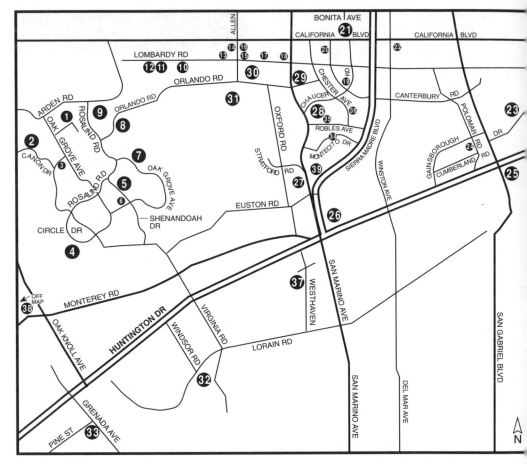

3. Thompson House, 1958
Buff, Straub and Hensman
1030 Canon Drive
A two-story villa in the firm's late Craftsman style.

4. House, 1932
Roland E. Coate
1435 Circle Drive
A turn at the Georgian Revival.

5. Schuyler Doane House, 1924
Wallace Neff
1180 Shenandoah Road
In part, as a result of the American experience in northern France, the vernacular Norman farmhouse image (or as it was referred to in those years, the "Norman type") came into great popularity. Even at this very early date, Neff mixes our remembrance of childhood fairy-tales with the reality of a building. Great expansive roofs come almost to the ground, and a central round tower contains its own exterior staircase.

6. House, 1929
John Atchinson
1215 Shenandoah Road
Tudor finery.

7. Romboz House, 1927
Weston and Weston
1762 Oak Grove Avenue
Spanish Colonial Revival Mudejar with a
gorgeous entrance.

8. House and Outbuildings, circa 1915
870 Orlando Road
A Mission Revival complex of great interest. It
is rare to be able to see all the main buildings
from the street. This is a picturesque ensemble
with Orientalized chimney and green tile roofs.

9. Mays House, 1927
Roland E. Coate
945 Orlando Road
New Orleans, Georgian, and Tudor styles
mixed very nicely.

10. Marlow House, 1981
B. R. Offenhauser
1556 Lombardy Road, Pasadena
Recent eastern Colonial Revival in the former
cutting garden of the Collins House next door.

11. Collins House, 1927
Wallace Neff
1550 Lombardy Road, Pasadena
A solid-looking, handsome, Mediterranean
house set in a well-kept garden.

12. Fong House, 1976
Miller Fong
1500 Lombardy Road, Pasadena
Airy International Style Modern. It fits in quite
well.

13. Ostoff House, 1924
George Washington Smith
1778 Lombardy Road
A beautiful abstraction of rural Andalusia transferred to opulent suburbia.

14. Baldwin House, 1925
George Washington Smith
665 S. Allen Avenue
Rid yourself of any reservation you may have
about the uses of historical imagery. In the hands
of an artist, it can produce great things, as this
romantic Spanish dwelling and garden attest.

15. Up de Graff House, circa 1927
Wallace Neff

Northeast corner of Lombardy Road and
Allen Avenue
Another Spanish Colonial Revival masterpiece
with a marvelous staircase in front.

16a. Milligan House, 1928
Roland E. Coate
1850 Lombardy Road
Monterey Revival with a trace of Regency.
Other nearby examples of Roland Coate's work
are:

b. Le Fens House, 1933
691 Holladay Road
A painted stone Monterey Revival dwelling
with an elegant Greek Revival entrance and
sidelights.

c. Pitner House, 1928
1138 Arden Road
A highly refined Monterey Revival.

d. Heath House, 1930
2080 Lombardy Road
A two-story Regency house with an unusual
use of fluted piers for the two-story porch.

17. House, 1948
R. H. Ainsworth
1910 Lombardy Road
A Classical Revival giant portico on a delicate
Federal (Adamesque) Revival fabric. See 1945
Lombardy Road for an almost identical twin
(1941) by the same architect.

18. Bourne House, 1927
Wallace Neff; Katherine Bashford, landscape architect
2035 Lombardy Road
One of the finest of Neff's Spanish Colonial
Revival houses. Here he enlarged the theme of
the white, stuccoed, Andalusian farmhouse to a
stately villa.

19. Jordan House, 1941
Whitney R. Smith
705 Canterbury Road
A good number of this architect's pre-World
War II designs fit into the then-popular
California Ranch house mode or that of the
Monterey Revival. The Jordan house is a well-
carried-out version of the two-story Monterey
style.

16a. Milligan House, 1928

20. House, circa 1940
   Whitney R. Smith
   705 Canterbury Road
Monterey style—and good—by an architect best known for his early Modern work.

21. House, circa 1910
   580 Bonita Avenue at northeast corner of California Street
A fine Craftsman house in an otherwise Mediterranean-style area.

22. Fitzgerald House, 1919
   Roland E. Coate
   708 Winston Avenue
Coate was, of course, always at home with the Monterey style.

23. Packard House, 1924
   R. M. Schindler
   931 N. Gainsborough Road
Maybeckian spaces and the tidy line of the early International Style Modern; Schindler was a master of both. The original rolled-composition roof has been shingled over. Three wings project out of the central-core kitchen.

24. Day House, 1932
   H. Roy Kelley
   2871 Cumberland Road
Compact Monterey style.

25. Carver Elementary School, 1947
   Marsh, Smith, and Powell
   1300 San Gabriel Boulevard at Huntington Drive
It is interesting to compare this brick, International Style Modern school (with its

continuation of the indoor-outdoor classroom tradition) with Hunt's and Grey's much earlier (1907) **Polytechnic School** in Pasadena.

26. Sobieski House, 1946
  Harwell H. Harris
  1420 Sierra Madre Boulevard, just north of Huntington Drive
The beautifully crafted, two-story shingle and wood garage is about all that can be seen from the street.

27. Haigh House, 1948
  Wallace Neff
  1173 San Marino Avenue
The architect in one of his French Norman moods.

28. House, 1933
  Rainer and Adams
  2170 Chaucer Road (visible only from San Marino Avenue gatehouse)
This fine Tudor Revival house with its extensive black-and-white work encourages great expectations for the almost invisible mansion behind it. Records are confused, but it would appear that the gatehouse came first, and that the mansion was designed (1937) by Girard R. Colcord.

29. Bertololli House, circa 1928
  Wallace Neff
  2115 Orlando Road
A characteristic Neff Tuscan villa, with an inset second-floor loggia placed above the front entrance.

30. Wallace Neff House, 1929
  Wallace Neff
  1883 Orlando Road
A larger version of entry number 29, this Tuscan house was even more impressive before the entrance court was changed and the fence added.

31. Henry E. Huntington Art Gallery, Library and Gardens
  Gallery (originally the house), 1910
  Myron Hunt and Elmer Grey
  Library, 1925
  Myron Hunt and H. C. Chambers
  Entrance is at end of Allen Avenue at Orlando Road

Public areas are open, free of charge (donation suggested!) 1:00–4:30 P.M. every afternoon except Monday. Reservations required on Sunday. Closed in October and on all major holidays.

You will enter through a mildly Beaux Arts gate and orientation building designed by Whitney Smith (1981). The main **Gallery** is reserved, academic, Beaux Arts Neo-Classicism. Architecturally, the salient points are the Palladian-like porch and the interior grand staircase. The treasure is the collection, assembled for the railroad magnate by Lord Joseph Duveen. English eighteenth-century painting may not turn you on, but the main gallery, with Lawrence's *Pinkie* on one side and Gainsborough's *Blue Boy* on the other and Reynold's *Mrs. Siddons as the Tragic Muse* at the end, is something to behold.

The later, separate **Library** building is also Beaux Arts with a decidedly French feeling. The main collections can be used only if you have a Ph.D. or similar credentials. But there is a large, recently renovated exhibition hall where you can gaze at such things as a Gutenberg Bible, Thoreau's manuscript of "Walden," or an architectural drawing by Thomas Jefferson.

The **gardens**—French, Shakespearian, Japanese, Cactus, etc.—begun in 1904 by William Hertrich and extended by Wilbur David Cook—are among the most beautiful in the world. The Japanese garden (begun 1911) is especially fine with a teahouse (1906), much changed, since it was taken from the Japanese Tea Garden that once stood at the northeast corner of California Boulevard and Fair Oaks Avenue in Pasadena. More recently, a Zen garden designed by Robert Watson has been added.

Do not miss the impressive **Huntington Mausoleum** (1933) designed by America's prominent Beaux Arts architect, John Russell Pope, the designer of the National Gallery in Washington, D.C. Here Pope explores the theme of the circular and domed Classical Temple, a theme he returned to again and again.

Nearby is the **Virginia Steele Scott Gallery of American Art** (1983–84) designed by Paul

30. Wallace Neff House, 1929

Gray (Warner and Gray). It is a sensitive and lively continuation of the Classical tradition of Pope with its principal space organized around an open dome.

32. Sheppard House, 1934
    Jock Peters
    1390 Lorain Road
A rare, executed example in Streamline Moderne of the work of the gifted architect who was the principal interior designer of Bullocks Wilshire in Los Angeles.

33. House, circa 1925
    Southwest corner of Pine
    Street and Granada
    Avenue, Alhambra
The strange Hansel and Gretel feeling of this building suggests that it was designed by the Heineman firm in Pasadena.

34. "The Mosque," 1980
    2250 Montecito Drive
This is the name that neighbors have aptly given this house—a little out of place in San Marino.

35. Rupple House, 1938
    Roland E. Coate
    2225 Robles Avenue
This small, single-floor, French-styled dwelling is organized around a central motor court. The design is on the stark side but very well carried out.

36. Phillips House, 1934
    H. Roy Kelley
    940 Chester Avenue
The Streamline Moderne style is neither frequent in this architect's work nor frequently encountered in San Marino. Kelley's handling of the scale, detailing, and landscape design allows this modernist house to fit in with the surrounding Period Revival dwellings.

39. Stanwyck House, 1940

37. Baird House, 1938
    H. Roy Kelley
    1745 Westhaven Road
One of the popular modes of the Anglo-Colonial Revival in the 1930s was the informal stone and wood Pennsylvania Colonial. The Baird house, which was one of several versions of this style by Kelley, was frequently published in the architectural journals and popular shelter magazines of the time.

38. Townley House, 1936
    Harold Saxsmith
    880 Winthrop Road
In this instance, the Anglo-Colonial image, is rendered with the simplicity of the early modern.

39. Stanwyck House, 1940
    William D. Holdredge
    1300 Sierra Madre Boulevard
The architect managed very well to combine a number of Anglo-Colonial revival traditions, ranging from Colonial Williamsburg, to the Cape Cod cottage. The house ends up being both formal and informal.

SAN GABRIEL VALLEY

The San Gabriel Valley is roughly bounded by the San Gabriel Mountains to the north, the desert on the east, the Whittier Hills to the south, and the Arroyo Seco to the west. Not all of it is covered here, because the Los Angeles County line cuts down the middle of it. It is an area of many towns, a large number founded by land speculators attached to the Southern Pacific and Santa Fe railroads. Some towns still show their nineteenth-century origins in their display of Victorian architecture, but instead of the citrus groves and vineyards that once surrounded them, you see acres and acres of tract housing, most of it tedious. It has come to resemble the San Fernando Valley except that you see few trees outside the boundaries of the old towns. Also, sadly, the San Gabriel Valley, particularly the eastern side, often gets the worst smog in the county.

San Gabriel

It all began with the founding of the San Gabriel Mission in 1771, near the present site of Montebello. When the Mission was relocated in 1776, the town also moved. What is left of this later settlement dates from 1791 to 1850, and there is precious little of it. Early photographs show, however, that in the 1890s, West Mission Road was a charming country town street with adobes and extended pitched roofs over the sidewalks. But in 1913 the residents voted for incorporation and progress. Their decision meant the absolute destruction of the visible past, a process which has continued until fairly recently, leaving few shards other than the Mission (itself in bad shape even today). The Mission, in spite of its woebegone appearance (and its gift shop, unmatched for its bad taste), is still considerably more convincing than the next in the chain—San Fernando—which has been restored beyond credibility.

1. Rose House, 1862
  7020 La Presa Drive, off
  Huntington Drive
Said to be the oldest frame house in the San Gabriel Valley, it looks the part. It is a simple house without style, but it is nevertheless picturesque in its beautiful garden.

2. Miller Water Garden, 1925–later
  Bill Miller
  6221 N. San Gabriel Boulevard
Driving by, you might think that this was just another nursery, but take time to muse. The garden furniture takes you back to early California. This is distributed among concrete grottoes, rustic concrete bridges, and rare aquatic plants and fish. There is even a concrete log cabin.

3. San Gabriel Union Church and School, 1936
  Northwest corner of Las Tunas Drive and Pine Street
Basically, this building is Classical PWA Moderne with an update of Streamline touches, such as a porch with chrome trim intact.

4. "The Alamo," circa 1929
  522 E. Broadway
Yes, this residence has an entrance that vaguely resembles that of The Alamo in San Antonio.

5. San Gabriel Village, circa 1938
  Percy Bitton Limited, developer
  Fairview Avenue west of Del Mar Avenue
This settlement was to have 840 units selling for around $4000 each. The houses are not much, but efforts at low-cost housing in the 1930s deserve mention.

6. Ortega-Vigare Adobe, 1792–1805
  616 S. Ramona Street
Only half of this one-story adobe remains, but it is old in spite of its restored appearance.

Originally, the roof was flat and the corridor was completely open.

**7. Mission San Gabriel
   Archangel,** 1791–1806,
   and later
   Mission and Junipero
   Serra drives

The Mission was established in 1771 and was moved to its present site in 1776. The stone church, begun in 1791, replaced an earlier small adobe church. When first built, the long nave of the church was covered with a barrel vault, but because of earthquake damage, this was replaced by a timber roof in 1804. The building was designed to receive stone vaulting thus explaining the rows of buttresses, which create the fortresslike quality of the church. The square tower which stood to the right of the entrance and much of the fabric of the church were severely damaged in the earthquake of 1812. The church was then partially rebuilt, although the present campanario was not added until 1828.

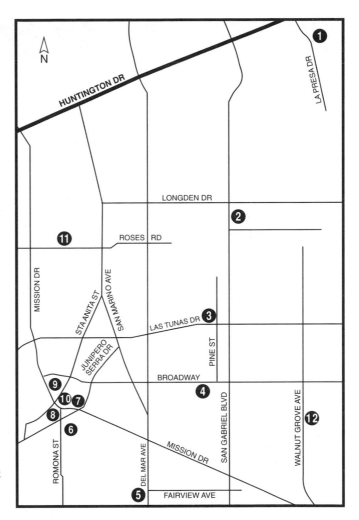

Over the years the church has gone through several major earthquakes, the last major one occurring in 1987. The church is now closed, and a controversy exists as to what should be done with the building. As usual, the conflict is between those who, as followers of William Morris, would either leave it as is or would simply restore it to its pre-1987 visage, and those, such as the well-known historic preservationist Norman Neuerburg, who would strongly argue in the tradition of Eugene Viollet-Le-Duc, for its restoration to its exis-

tence during the early Spanish Mission period. We hope that the latter view prevails.

**8. San Gabriel City Hall and Municipal
   Buildings,** 1923
   Walker and Eisen
   Southwest corner of Mission Drive and
   Ramona Street
Spanish Colonial Revival without zest.

9. San Gabriel Civic Auditorium, "Mission Playhouse," 1923–27
Arthur B. Benton; restored 1992 by
DeBretteville and Polyzoides
Northwest corner of Mission Drive and Santa
Anita Street

This huge Mission-style building (the prototype was the Mission of San Antonio de Padua near the present town of Jolon) was designed specifically for the production of John Steven McGroarty's *Mission Play* that between 1912 and 1933 presented 3200 performances. The emblems of Spanish provinces that adorn the interior were given by the King of Spain. The building also houses a fine theater organ.

10. Lopez de Lowther Adobe, 1792–1806
330 S. Santa Anita Street

This single-room-wide, gable-roofed adobe was probably one of the Mission outbuildings. It has escaped the wrecker by being on a side street. It is open to the public on Sunday afternoons, 1:00–4:00 P.M.

11. Church of Our Savior (Episcopal), 1872–later
535 W. Roses Road, near Rosemont
Boulevard

Only the portion of this rural English Gothic church behind the entrance is old, but it retains some good Tiffany windows.

12. Sorg House, 1926
R. M. Schindler
5204 N. Walnut Grove Avenue

A tight de Stijl composition, with pergola sunroof and garage. The rows of two-by-six supports suggest the wood-stud wall construction behind the stucco-covered walls.

N amed by its developer, Nathaniel C. Carter, in 1881, Sierra Madre was intended to be a boom town, but it never quite made it. It still evokes the image of a Midwestern crossroads village of the turn of the century. Its big industry was tuberculosis sanitariums, almost all of which have disappeared. But it attracted more than its share of distinguished architects—Ernest A. Coxhead, Joseph Cather Newsom, Charles and Henry Greene, Timothy Walsh, Irving J. Gill, Wallace Neff, Harwell H. Harris, and John Gougeon.

1. Mulvihill House, 1949
Harwell H. Harris
580 N. Hermosa Avenue

Although this house has been remodeled, it still bears comparison with the same architect's Johnson House in Bel Air of exactly the same year.

2. Sierra Madre Garden Apartment Houses (Lewis Courts,) 1910
Irving J. Gill
Northeast corner of Mountain Trail and
Alegria Avenue

In this project Gill provided an individual terrace and an enclosed porch or loggia for each of the small stucco-walled, two-bedroom bungalows. The open courtyard in the center contained a pergola and a croquet court. The complex is now changed almost beyond recognition and is threatened with demolition, but it is so famous that we felt that we had to include it.

3. Church of the Ascension, 1888
Ernest A. Coxhead
Northeast corner of Baldwin and Laurel
avenues

One of Coxhead's storybook churches. Some

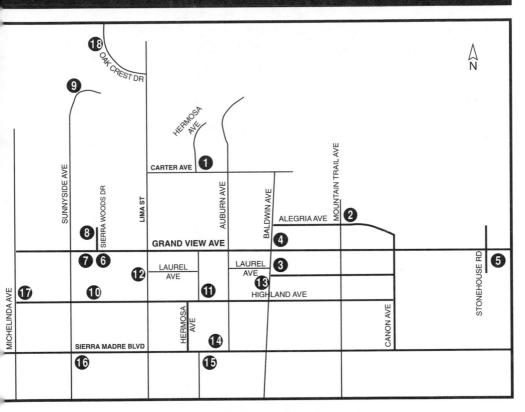

remodeling was done by Carleton M. Winslow, Jr. who also designed the parsonage.

4. Saint Rita's Church, 1969
John Gougeon
Northeast corner of Baldwin and Grand View avenues

Modern Expressionism with a slight Spanish flavor. Gougeon's later Pasadena Presbyterian Church goes even further.

5. House, circa 1890
Near southeast corner of Grand View Avenue and Stonehouse Road, Arcadia

A stone structure, originally built as a maintenance building for the northern section of E. J. "Lucky" Baldwin's extensive ranch.

6. Cabin, circa 1900
468 Grand View Avenue, east of Sierra Woods Drive

Tiny, vertical board-and-batten building that suggests the back-to-nature atmosphere that Sierra Madre once boasted.

7. Coldwell House, circa 1907
Louis B. Easton
649 Sierra Madre Boulevard

In 1908 a writer in *The Craftsman* magazine wrote that "This house is an admirable illustration of the adaptation of a dwelling to the climate and surroundings, and the preservation of harmony between exterior and interior of the house." It was recently saved from demolition.

1. Mulvihill House, 1949

8. Edgar Camp House, 1904
 Charles and Henry Greene
 327 Sierra Woods Drive
One of the Greenes' most picturesque bungalows with later additions. It is almost visible
from the street.

**9. Passionist Fathers Monastery and Retreat
 House,** 1928–31
 Timothy Walsh
 North end of Sunnyside Avenue
Two huge Spanish Colonial Revival piles with
very little ornament; large but on the dry side.
They were recently partly demolished due to
earthquake damage. Walsh had come west to
design a new Roman Catholic Cathedral of Our
Lady of Guadalupe in Los Angeles. The design
for the cathedral was richly Churrigueresque,
somewhat in the manner of the great cathedral
at Santiago de Campostella. It should have been
built, but financial problems struck even before
the depression.

10. House, circa 1910
 481 Highland Avenue
A long, two-story, shingled Craftsman house
with horizontality worthy of the Prairie School.

11. Sierra Madre School, circa 1930
 Marsh, Smith, and Powell
 North side of Highland Avenue between
 Hermosa and Auburn avenues
Spanish Colonial Revival in poured concrete.

12. Pinney House, 1886
 Joseph Cather Newsom
 225 Lima Street, west end of Laurel
 Avenue
Originally, this building was a large but rather
plain hotel on the order of the other Newsom
hotel still standing in San Dimas. Then in the
1930s, a movie company added the outsized
spindle work on the porch and the equally
mannerist swan's neck pediment, both from a
house being demolished on Wilshire
Boulevard in Los Angeles. The result is overwhelming.

13. House, 1911
171 N. Baldwin Avenue
A beautifully maintained shingled Craftsman
house.

14. Church of the Nazarene, 1890
191 W. Sierra Madre Boulevard
A Victorian Gothic structure in wood, somewhat botched around the entrance and, unfortunately, painted white.

15. Congregational Church, 1928
Marsh, Smith, and Powell
170 W. Sierra Madre Boulevard
Some parts of this church are said to date from
1886, but they do not show under the
Romanesque exterior.

16. Essick House, circa 1905
550 W. Sierra Madre Boulevard
A large, true bungalow (one-story) with flat
roof above a thin, horizontal, latticed attic for
ventilation.

17. Barlow House (now **Alverno School**),
1923–24
Wallace Neff
Northeast corner of Michillinda and
Highland avenues
This villa was built by Dr. James Barlow for his
wife, who had visited the Villa Collazzi (sometimes attributed to Michelangelo) outside
Florence and who wanted a house just like it.
Neff gave them what they desired and included
a superb southern cortile from which they had
magnificent views of the San Gabriel Valley
below them through Italian cypresses, palms,
and formal gardens.

**18. McKinney House ("The Pyramid
House"),** 1972–74
McKinney
751 Oak Crest Drive
Obviously the virtues of the geometric form of
the pyramid were discovered by McKinney a
number of years before I. M. Pei employed it at
the Louvre. This example is sheathed in metal
and glass. Unfortunately you can view the
house only from a distance.

ARCADIA

This small city is essentially a comfortable upper-middle-class residential community, but it is best known
for the **Santa Anita Racetrack,**
where Los Angelinos go to sin, and
the **Santa Anita Mall,** where they go to spend.
The acres of asphalt parking lots surround the
Santa Anita Racetrack are hardly much of a
drawing card. But what is a drawing card are
the wonderful grandstands designed in 1935 by
Gordon B. Kaufmann. Along the front of these,
as a frieze, are horses, riders, and the absolutely
necessary palm trees. The motifs of this frieze
are entirely two dimensional, being rendered in
thin sheets of steel. The original landscape was
designed by Tommy Thompson, and some of
these plantings remain.

The best thing in town—in fact one of the
high points in Los Angeles County—is the
County **Arboretum,** on what was once the old
Rancho Santa Anita, the estate of E. J. Baldwin,
one of the most eccentric millionaires that
California has ever produced. The Arboretum
was established in 1947 primarily through the
efforts of Dr. Samuel Ayres. Within some 127
acres the plants vary widely, from those coming
from a temperate zone, to the subtropical. One
of the interesting features of the park is the
Sunset magazine gardens, where landscape
solutions for the suburban house are presented.
In 1989 the small **Peacock Cafe,** its garden,
and terraces was restored and redesigned by
Campbell and Campbell.

The Santa Anita Ranch was granted during
the Mexican period to Hugo Reid in 1841.
Either just before that date or shortly thereafter,
he built an adobe on the ranch. From evidence
now available, we know this adobe was a single-floor dwelling with a corridor running
along one side, and it was covered by a flat
roof. This adobe was later incorporated into a

Santa Anita Racetrack, 1935

large house. Between 1948 and 1960, the **Hugo Reid Adobe** was rebuilt; this rebuilding has been recently updated by the California Conservations Corporation. A new garden of herbs and flowers characteristic of the Mexican period has been planted by the adobe.

In 1875, E. J. "Lucky" Baldwin purchased the Rancho, and over the years he extensively planted the area and dredged the picturesque lake. Baldwin was interested in horses, gold mines, real estate, and horticulture. In fact, he was interested in everything, and almost everything he touched turned into gold. Thus, his nickname "Lucky." Having literally struck pay dirt in Northern California, he bought the rancho east of Los Angeles, possibly with the idea of "roughing it," for he moved (1875) into the Hugo Reid Adobe and started raising horses—and money! He also planted a wide variety of trees, the nucleus of the Arboretum, though now it is much more lush than Lucky would have imagined possible. Incidentally, the early growth was the site of the filming of the first Tarzan movies.

Baldwin was also interested in architecture. Like many other Americans, he was excited by the Queen Anne buildings that the British

erected for their pavilions at the Philadelphia Centennial Exhibition in 1876. When he returned to California he hired Arthur A. Bennett, one of the architects of the Capitol Building at Sacramento, to design a **Queen Anne Cottage** (1881) as a guest house for the ranch. Although not closely related to the British pavilions and not really Queen Anne, it was and is pretentious both inside and out. The exterior has ornament extracted from Eastlake and is painted to suggest what Vincent Scully has called the "Stick style." There are also Islamic touches. The original features inside are Victorian Baroque with marble fireplaces and art-glass windows that would have been the pride of San Francisco, where they were probably made.

Perhaps more fascinating are the ample stables and dog house in the same style as the exterior of the guest house. Oh yes—a Queen Anne **railroad station** (1890) that Baldwin built on the Santa Fe right-of-way has now been moved to the grounds.

The California Arboretum Foundation took over the operation of the Arboretum in 1948, and it was opened to the public in 1955. The Arboretum may be visited every day except Christmas, from 8:30 A.M. to 4:30 P.M. for a small admission charge.

As if grateful for this architectural success, Baldwin married the architect's daughter. The marriage was not so fortunate and the couple soon separated. A previous marriage (there were four) had produced a beloved daughter, Anita, to whom he gave a large section of his ranch to the north. In 1910 she built a large but nondescript house. **Anoakia,** (designed by Arthur B. Benton), which she proceeded to furnish with large numbers of Tiffany chandeliers and some rather astonishing murals by Maynard Dixon. There is also a small Palladian temple in the gardens! All this Californiana at

429

the northwest corner of Baldwin Avenue and Foothill Boulevard is the well-maintained head-quarters of a developer. It is occasionally open, but is private property.

Anita Baldwin's estate has, of course, been subdivided and is now called Santa Anita Oaks. It is a pleasant piece of suburbia that exhibits acre after acre of the California Ranch houses of the 1930s and 1940s, as well as some impressive historic-image designs by H. Roy Kelley and others. One of the best of these is the **O'Bryan house** at 1225 Rodeo Road just north of Foothill Boulevard above Sycamore Avenue. It was designed by Wallace Neff, (1939) one of the greatest of the purveyors of the Mediterranean style, who here sheaths his familiar architectural forms in gray shingles. The rest of the area is genially soporific but lushly so.

Another architectural attraction of Arcadia is an excellent Art Deco Moderne **retail store building** (circa 1932) at 53 Huntington Drive. The relief sculpture on the building is by J. J. Mora. Another, more recent landmark is the **Great Scot Restaurant,** (circa 1967) at the northeast corner of Santa Anita Avenue and Wheeler Street. Its image is that of an English pub, not from England or Scotland, but from a Hollywood stage set.

Another gem is **Clearman's Village** at the southwest corner of Huntington Drive and Rosemead Boulevard. This is a large-scale, post-World War II drive-in of the early 1950s and later. At first the most striking thing about it is **Northwood Inn,** a make-believe log cabin with imitation snow on its roof. Deeper obser-vations soon catch other delights such as a restaurant in the shape of a ship, and many spe-cialty shops in a variety of arrays. See espe-cially, the Spanish Colonial revival gun shop with its tropical-tile roof merging nicely with a snow-covered roof next door.

MONROVIA

All of the towns in the shadow of the San Gabriel Mountains owe their existence to the Santa Fe Railroad, which came through the valley in the 1880s. This town is named for a construction engineer, William N. Monroe, who saw the opportunities of this beautiful spot and platted the town in 1886. Though now thoroughly built over, Monrovia still demonstrates its nineteenth-century origins better than most of the San Gabriel Valley com-munities. Its Victorian houses are sprinkled around town, usually at street corners—evi-dence of a land speculator's dream that did not materialize until the twentieth century. Old photographs show Queen Anne and Eastlake houses amid orange groves and vineyards. Monrovia must have been lovely.

Like its neighbor, Sierra Madre, Monrovia was a health resort with tuberculosis sanitaria distributed through the upper reaches of the city—a deep irony, for now it gets some of the worst smog in the county, both from friendly Los Angeles and from the industry miserably sprawled to the southwest. The Foothill Freeway which runs through the southern sec-tion does nothing to improve the atmosphere. But stop by, if only to see the **Aztec Hotel** (in the Mayan style!), one of the most exotic things that you will ever encounter.

1. Monrovia High School, 1928
John C. Austin and Frederic M. Ashley
(Austin Whittlesey)
Northeast corner of Madison Avenue and
Colorado Boulevard
A Palladian facade on an otherwise Spanish Colonial Revival building, Whittlesey, the designer, was well known for his books on Spanish architecture.

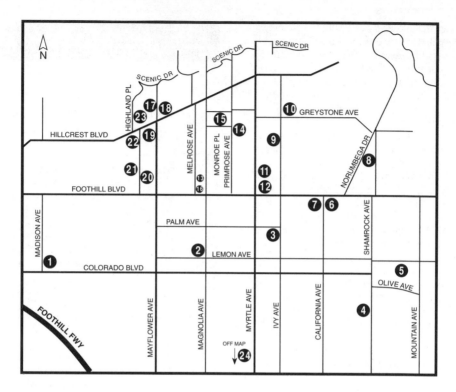

2. House, circa 1915
    423 S. Magnolia Avenue
This remodeled house has all the marks of an
Irving J. Gill design.

3. United Methodist Church, 1911,
    addition 1923
    Southwest corner of Ivy and Palm avenues
An imposing piece of early-twentieth-century
Beaux Arts Neo-Classicism.

4. Cottage, circa 1887
    823 S. Shamrock Avenue
It is conceivable that this one-and-a-half-story
Queen Anne building was designed by one or
both of the Newsoms.

5. Park, 1923
    Cook and Hill, landscape architects
    Between Shamrock and Mountain avenues,
    Olive and Lemon avenues
This is Monrovia's only park of any size—but,
of course, there are the mountains!

6. St. Luke's Episcopal Church, 1926
    Carleton M. Winslow
    Southeast corner of California Avenue and
    Foothill Boulevard
A very severe handling of Spanish Romanesque
and Gothic in poured concrete. The interior is
even more severe.

7. Four Bungalows, circa 1910
    Tifal Brothers, builders
    Southwest corner of California Avenue and
    Foothill Boulevard
A row of bungalows in mint condition.
Actually, there are more, apparently by the
same builders, on Wild Rose Avenue on the
south side of the same block.

8. Dumond House, circa 1925
    270 Norumbega Drive
Pure Hansel and Gretel, the house/studio of an
artist.

9. Watt Bungalow, circa 1910
231 N. Ivy Avenue
A flat-roofed, single-story house—right out of a "bungalow book."

10. Butts House, 1894
Arthur B. Benton
Northeast corner of Ivy and Greystone avenues
An angular example of the Shingle style with a first story of boulders and mannerist touches in the floor above.

11. Burr House, 1893
150 N. Myrtle Avenue
A two-story Queen Anne with a suggestion of the Colonial Revival.

12. United Presbyterian Church, circa 1926
Harry L. Pierce
Northeast corner of Myrtle Avenue and Foothill Boulevard
A Mission Revival tower, but otherwise rather academic Spanish Colonial Revival. The interior has hints of the Rococo.

13. Stewart House, circa 1887
117 N. Magnolia Avenue
A two-story Queen Anne dwelling.

14. House, circa 1887
Solon I. Haas
250 N. Primrose Avenue
Another Queen Anne, but this time with a tall, narrow, mansard tower, still crowned with iron railing and pinnacles.

15. Monroe House, 1887
225 Monroe Place
This is the Queen Anne house of William N. Monroe, who founded the town and for whom it was named.

16. Aztec Hotel, 1925
Robert Stacy-Judd
Northwest corner of Magnolia Avenue and Foothill Boulevard
Words fail. By the mid-1920s, Stacy-Judd had emerged as one of America's most flamboyant apologists for the pre-Columbian Revival, which he thought, since it was "Native American," should form the basis for a true American style in the future. Here he presents it in cast concrete and stucco.

17. Mills House, "Mills View," 1887
329 N. Melrose Avenue
It is possible that this house was designed by Joseph Cather Newsom. It has the mark of his outrageous aesthetics in its Queen Anne mass with mansard tower at the southwest corner.

18. Case House, 1887
Northeast corner of Hillcrest Boulevard and Mayflower Avenue
A Queen Anne/Colonial Shingle-style dwelling.

19. Pile House, "Idlewild," 1887–88
Joseph Cather Newsom
255 N. Mayflower Avenue near corner of Hillcrest Boulevard
A two-story Queen Anne with a strange bracket at the corner, the wonderful interiors are well preserved.

20. Mellenthin House, circa 1912
Frank O. Eager
168 Highland Place
A fine, shingled Craftsman house in the Swiss Chalet vein.

21. Everest House, circa 1912
Arthur Kelly
173 Highland Place
Another Craftsman two-story dwelling, almost worthy of Charles and Henry Greene. The **Daniels House** across the street (number 174) was *once* by Arthur Kelly.

22. Badger House, circa 1912
Attributed to Arthur Kelly
225 Highland Place
Craftsman shingles again.

23. Wood House, circa 1925
Herbert J. Gerhardt
338 Highland Place
Another evidence of the search for Native America, here realized through the Pueblo Revival.

24. Santa Fe Railroad Passenger Station,
circa 1925
William H. Mohr
Just above Duarte Road on west side of Myrtle Avenue
A small Hispanic building.

DUARTE

AZUSA

This community, founded in 1886 southeast of Monrovia, was once covered with rural estates dating mainly from the teens and twenties. After World War II these succumbed to the growth syndrome and were subdivided. A few good houses remain behind gates and high hedges, but your experience of the "better day" will be only the magnificent trees. Duarte does have a beautiful Mission Revival **school** (1908) by F. S. Allen at 1247 Buena Vista Street. Its paired towers and pedimented gables are easily visible from the nearby Foothill Freeway, so you won't really even need to slow down.

BRADBURY

Very exclusive, mostly behind locked gates. Everything is post-World War II. It does have the honor of having an excellent hilltop house by Frank Lloyd Wright—the **Pearce House** (1950)—situated, most unfortunately, behind guarded gates at 5 Bradbury Hills Road.

Any reader over fifty will remember this town, along with Cucamonga and Anaheim, as one of Jack Benny's stops on his imaginary railroad journeys around Southern California. It was founded in 1887. One of the city's sons, the eminent historian Robert Glass Cleland, wrote that Azusa had in the late nineteenth century "more saloons than Protestants." And he continued, "So, also, certain priceless gifts—freedom and space, simplicity and leisure, blue skies overhead, and unfailing kindness and friendship in the hearts of our neighbors."

The Civic Center buildings are good examples of the "City Beautiful" movement. The **City Hall** (1909) looks newer than the wings (1925) that flank it. The little gray stone **Iglesia Presbiteriana** (circa 1900) nearby at the northwest corner of Alameda Avenue and Foothill Boulevard is picturesque. And the **Wells Fargo Bank** at the northeast corner of Azusa Avenue and Foothill Boulevard, designed (1918) by Robert H. Orr in a mixture of Romanesque, Classical, and Moderne forms, adds interest to an otherwise uninspiring business district.

GLENDORA

SAN DIMAS

Whereas Azusa was Presbyterian in its early religious orientation, Glendora, also on the Santa Fe Railroad, was firmly Methodist, a saving grace of nearby Monrovia. Glendora had a strong Dixie element. As late as 1935 the local chapter of the United Daughters of the Confederacy would announce in the *Glendora Press* an essay contest in which "ten points will be deducted in judging any manuscript that uses the term 'Civil War' when speaking of the War Between the States." Today the sleepy southern crossroads town comes to mind particularly on Glendora Avenue. The northern part of Glendora has simply been taken over by developers for tract housing to the point that the town's original reason for being, its citrus industry, is gone. Surely Citrus College at the west end of town will change its name. In the foothills behind Glendora there is still some evidence of truck farming. Beautifully tended nurseries cling to the slopes of the hills, as do some Victorian houses, none of great architectural quality. The best work is early-twentieth-century Craftsman. In town the **Tudor two-stories** (circa 1920) at the northwest corner of Minnesota Avenue and Foothill Boulevard and at the northwest corner of Bennett and Vermont avenues, and the **bungalows** (circa 1915) at the northwest corner of Foothill Boulevard and Wabash Avenue and at the southeast corner of Bennett and Vermont avenues (beautiful beveled glass door) are cases in point. The modern work at **Citrus Junior College** by Neptune and Thomas is bland.

Another town inspired by the Santa Fe Railroad and the boom of the 1880s, San Dimas is almost exactly midway between Los Angeles and San Bernardino, to which the railroad had completed its tracks in 1885. As in other boom cities, the first building of consequence was a **hotel** (1885–87), designed by Joseph Cather Newsom in the Queen Anne style. Again paralleling the history of many such enterprises, the hotel was finished just as the boom collapsed and it never functioned as a hotel. In 1889 J. W. Walker bought this thirty-room structure and used it as his home. It has recently been purchased in order to turn it into a bed-and-breakfast inn. For the first time it will actually function as a hotel. Address: 121 N. San Dimas Avenue.

San Dimas's business street has been remodeled into someone's version of a Wild West town, but the residential streets, with their modest, late-nineteenth-century cottages and later bungalows, are pleasant.

Hotel San Dimas, 1885-87

La Verne

Temple City, El Monte

Originally named Lordsburg for I. W. Lord, who laid it out in 1888, La Verne was another of the Santa Fe Railroad enterprises based on health and citrus. It is the seat of **La Verne University** (formerly College) which never made it to Claremont as Pomona did. The college looks like the one in Sinclair Lewis's *Elmer Gantry,* which you couldn't distinguish from the county poorhouse except for the sign out front. The grand exception is the absolutely outlandish (and success-ful) **Student Center and Drama Laboratory** (1973), designed by the Shaver Partnership to resemble tents. In fact, the five large episodes *are* tents coated with Teflon! Otherwise the best building in town is the **Church of the Brethren** (1930) at the southwest corner of 5th and E streets. It is flamboyant Gothic with sug-gestions of the Moderne roughed out in rein-forced concrete and was designed by Orr, Strange, and Inslee.

On the west side of town below Foothill Boulevard at the intersection of Moreno Avenue and Gladstone Street is the **Water Filtration and Softening Plant** (1940), designed by Daniel A. Elliot with monumental Spanish forms in reinforced concrete. It is one of the substations on the 392-mile aqueduct that brings water to Los Angeles from the Colorado River.

La Verne may not have much to offer archi-tecturally, but it has some of the most beautiful trees of any town in the state.

Mostly depressing, but the **Security Savings Bank** (1976) by Pulliam, Matthews, and Associates slipped in at Las Tunas Drive and Cloverly Avenue in Temple City. To the south in El Monte, the **El Monte High School** (1938–39), designed by Marsh, Smith, and Powell through PWA funding at Tyler Avenue and Bodger Street, is a good Moderne work whose best effect is an impressive long, horizontal, cast-concrete bas-relief sculpture by Bartolo Mako on the Administration Building. It depicts *The End of the Santa Fe Trail* beginning with a cov-ered wagon and ending with a coed with tennis racket. There are other panels of relief sculp-ture, including four on the side of the audito-rium which depict industrial activities in El Monte. While in El Monte you may want to take a look at the **Busway Terminal** (1973), designed by Daniel, Mann, Johnson, and Mendenhall (at the west end of Romano Boulevard near Santa Anita Avenue) to encour-age people in the area to give up their cars at the parking lot and ride the buses into L.A. The attempt by architects to achieve absolutely anonymous architecture seems to have reached its complete fulfillment here.

COVINA, WEST COVINA, EL MONTE, IRWINDALE, GLENDORA

Covina, a product of land speculation in the late 1880s, has real presence in spite of the calculated designs of its political and commercial leaders to destroy it. The area around the intersection of Citrus Avenue with Badillo Street can be brought back in the mind's eye to a better day before modernization took over. How wonderful the broad-eaved Arcade Apartments must have been before their face-lifting! How majestic the Ionic beauty of the First National Bank before its new owners decided to block out its rich architrave with a concrete slab! Thank God for sparing Arthur B. Benton's Holy Trinity Episcopal Church (1910), a shard of a better day. A few Queen Anne cottages even remain around the town.

1. Holy Trinity Episcopal Church, 1910
Arthur B. Benton
Northeast corner of Badillo Street and 3rd Avenue, Covina

Benton has put aside his Mission style (Mission Inn, Riverside) for the Episcopalians' preferred Eastlake-Gothic. The strong tower and fabric of the church was made of stones dragged from the San Gabriel River. The interior is well-wooded and has good stained-glass windows.

2. First National Bank, circa 1918
Train and Williams
Northeast corner of Citrus Avenue and College Street
Covina

A well-proportioned Ionic pile, now somewhat altered.

3. Masonic Hall, circa 1900
Southwest corner of 2nd Avenue and School Street, Covina

A huge, Classical Revival, rather awkward building made of wood. The Masons have as many architectural pretensions as the Episcopalians, and we are glad of that.

4. St. Martha's Episcopal Church, 1956–62
Carleton M. Winslow, Jr.
Northeast corner of Lark Ellen Avenue and Service Street, West Covina

Very exotic, the facade is enriched by metal stars suspended a couple of feet in front of the walls and held in place by wires.

5. Subsistence Homestead Project, 1934–35
Joseph Weston
Lower Azusa Road, west of Peck Road, El Monte

One of eight early projects of the New Deal (Subsistence Homesteads, Resettlement Division of the Department of the Interior) was to relocate people into the country on plots where they could produce their own food. The El Monte Subsistence Homestead project was the one and only example realized in the Los Angeles area. Each of the one hundred houses was situated on three-quarters of an acre. It was noted in the August 9th, 1935, issue of the *Southwest Builder and Contractor* that "Seventeen different plans and architectural designs have been used for the houses, distrib-uted to avoid monotony of repetition . . ." In style, the houses range from the Anglo Colonial cottage to the California Ranch house. Needless to say, there have been many changes since these houses were built. But a careful drive through the area reveals a good number of the original houses, most added to, but nonetheless recognizable.

It was pointed out in the same issue of this magazine that this project "is not a 'subsistence homestead,' as that term has generally been understood, for the co-operative ideas, involved in other similar projects, is not applied here. Individual owners of homes in this project will provide for themselves independently, producing and utilizing whatever they may grow or raise on their land, as they elect."

6. First Presbyterian Church, circa 1900
  5116 Irwindale Avenue
  Irwindale
A late Shingle-style church. Boulders form the base of the building, and above this solid earthy base are thin shingle-covered walls for the sanctuary and the corner tower.

7. Our Lady of Guadalupe Church, 1917
  16239 Arrow Highway, at Morada Street,
  Irwindale
A miniature chapel constructed in a Craftsman fashion of river boulders (there are plenty of them in the nearby river beds).

8. Ruble house "The Rock Castle," 1985
  Michael Ruble
  844 Live Oaks Avenue, Irwindale
An 1980s folly; a parapeted castle of river boulders and cinder-block walls. What will capture your attention is the seventy-four-foot high clock and chimes tower.

I ndustry is what it says it is—an industrial park, although the word *park* hardly seems appropriate. Much of it is faceless, computerized buildings, eminently forgettable. La Puente seems to be inhabited but has very little else to offer. Here is what we turned up.

1. Puente Hills Mall, 1974
  Victor Gruen Associates
  Southeast corner of Pomona Freeway exit
  and Azusa Avenue
Nothing really holds this ninety-four-acre shopping center together except the parking lot. A few buildings, especially the **Sears** store, are noteworthy.

2. Francisco Grazide Adobe, circa 1875
  South of Puente Hills Mall (turn east on
  Colima Road, then south on Batson Avenue)
A single-floor adobe picturesquely situated on a tiny lake.

3. Workman Adobe ("Rancho La Puente"),
  1842; greatly altered 1872 by Ezra Kysor

Temple Hall, 1919–23
  Walker and Eisen
  15415 E. Don Julian Road (Hacienda
  Boulevard exit from Pomona Freeway, then
  north to Don Julian Road, then west to
  Rancho entrance)
William Workman ("Don Julian" to his contemporaries) led the first wagon train of Yankees into the Los Angeles area in 1841. Because he had a Mexican wife and thus had a right to claim land, he and his friend John Rowland received the enormous Rancho La Puente, which they shared in common for awhile. Finally the ranch was divided, Workman taking the western half. As his business ventures prospered in Los Angeles, he

decided to remodel his ranch
house to resemble what he
remembered an English
country house to look like.
The result was to Gothicize it
and remove almost all traces
of the simple adobe, at least
on the exterior.

Ironically, it was his
grandson, Walter P. Temple,
who revived the Spanish tradition by building Temple
Hall ("La Casa Nueva") next
door in the vigorous Spanish
Colonial Revival style—
with a Manueline
(Portuguese) front door!
Temple Hall has been
immaculately restored by
Raymond Gervigian and is a
veritable house museum of
the taste of the 1920s.

The grounds also con-
tain the oldest private cemetery in Los Angeles County.
In it among the graves of
other pioneers are those of
Pio Pico and his wife, Maria
Ygnacia. The houses and grounds are open
(free) to the public Tuesday through Friday,
1:00–4:00 P.M. and Saturday and Sunday 10:00
A.M.– 4:00 P.M. Groups by reservation.

Temple Hall, 1919–23

4. The Donut Hole, 1968
John Tindall, Ed McCreany, and Jesse Hood
Southeast corner of Elliott Avenue and Amar
Road, La Puente (near Hacienda Boulevard,
north of "Rancho La Puente")
The first of the Donut Hole establishments was
built in 1963 in Covina; by the end of the 1960s
there were five examples in Southern

California. In these programmatic buildings
you drive through the hole in the giant doughnut, pick up your sack of doughnuts, and then
exit through a large doughnut at the other end.
The whole experience is consummated without
your having to get out of your car.

POMONA

N amed for the Roman goddess of fruit trees, Pomona has exchanged the scent of orange blossoms for the stink of smog. It was founded in the 1880s, another railroad town—this time the Southern Pacific. It was the commercial center of a very large agricultural region in the east San Gabriel Valley until very recently when changing population and economic patterns turned the area toward housing and industry. Also, the smog, the worst in Southern California, quite literally has wiped out citrus groves and vineyards that would otherwise still be producing. Incidentally, much of this smog is not really caused by Los Angeles but by local industry. The economy being what it is, people are afraid to enforce rules that might drive industry elsewhere.

In truth, the business district, in spite of some good tries, looks terrible. In 1960 Gruen and Associates, with the best intentions, put in a pedestrian mall along 2nd Street between Gordon and Palomares streets. It didn't work. Business moved elsewhere. Several banks were built in the late 1960s and a new **city hall, public library,** and **post office** were constructed in the same period. While in some cases moderately good architecture, they nevertheless demonstrate all the problems of the "City Beautiful" movement that Jane Jacobs so eloquently deplored in her *Death and Life of Great American Cities.* However, there are some fascinating things in Pomona, especially from the turn of the century.

1. Xerox Corporation Manufacturing Facility, 1967
Craig Ellwood
800 E. Bonita Avenue, at southwest corner of Towne Avenue (just above Arrow Highway)

Miesian, large, but Spartan, this building just misses the look of having been turned out by a computer.

2. Palomares Adobe, circa 1850–54
491 E. Arrow Highway in Palomares Park
A single-story, L-shaped adobe with a shingle hipped roof. A corridor runs around the L, and originally a second corridor faced the patio. The adobe was substantially restored in 1939.

3. Bungalow, circa 1920
178 E. Arrow Highway
An example of the Boulder style much more plentiful in the communities to the north.

4. Los Angeles County Fairgrounds
Northwest corner of McKinley and White avenues
Most of the buildings date from the mid-1930s and thus have Moderne pretensions. Note particularly the sculpture (1939) near Gate 3—man's tribute to his equine friend done by Lawrence Tenney Stevens in the heroic style often associated with Nazi art. Remember that this style was not the product of dictatorship (though Mussolini and Hitler went for it) but a more general movement in the history of taste not yet completely analyzed. Everybody will love the **Santa Fe Railroad Station** (circa 1885) brought from Arcadia. It is a tight mixture of Queen Anne and Stick-style forms, almost dollhouse in scale. Why would Arcadia let this go?

5. La Casa Primera Adobe (Ygnacio Palomares Adobe), circa 1837–later
Southwest corner of McKinley and North Park avenues
A single-floor, five-rooms-in-a-line adobe with a corridor along the front and on one side. It is the headquarters of the Pomona Valley Historical Society.

6. House, circa 1887
Southwest corner of Garey
and Jefferson avenues
A big, angular, Queen Anne
house with intricate ornament.

**7. Pilgrim Congregational
Church,** 1911
Robert H. Orr
East side of Garey Avenue
between Pasadena and
Pearl streets
A large Gothic complex,
including cloister, offices,
parish house, etc., all in red
brick.

8. House, circa 1900
Southwest corner of Pearl
and Main streets
Classical Revival with a dou-
ble-columned, two-story portico.

9. Park Place, circa 1920
Park Avenue at Pearl Street
A highly unusual compound.
Four rows of two-story apart-
ment units all sheathed in
boulders.

10. House, circa 1887
Northeast corner of Holt
and Park avenues
Such Queen Anne houses
make you realize how mar-
velous Victorian Pomona
must have been. A hideous
little building has been
dumped in the front yard.

11. First Baptist Church,
1911
Norman F. Marsh
Garey and Holt avenues
A Beaux Arts design which would seem to
have escaped from one of the turn-of-the-century World's Fairs. A lot of Classical elements
have been strung across and around the facade
of this structure. The effect is challenging, even
unnerving.

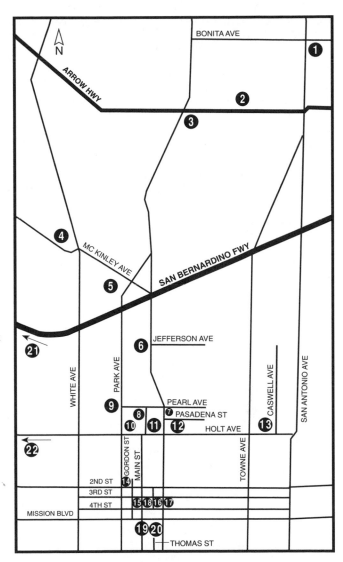

12. House, circa 1910
143 Holt Avenue
A two-story Classical Revival house set at a
respectable distance from the street.

13. Ebell Club, circa 1910
  Ferdinand Davis
  Northwest corner of Holt and Caswell
  avenues
This two-story, L-shaped building is a monument to the women's club movement of the turn of the century and to the sober, shingled Craftsman style.

**14. Great Western Savings and Loan
  Association,** 1965
  Kurt Meyer and Associates
  300 Pomona Mall West (2nd Street)
A big temple with concrete roof slab and concrete columns.

15. Seventh-Day Adventist Church,
  circa 1895
  Ferdinand Davis
  Southeast corner of 3rd and Gordon streets
A mad concoction of Queen Anne, Gothic, and Italianate forms mercifully preserved in the midst of progress.

16. Fox Theater, 1931
  Balch and Stanberry
  Southwest corner of Garey Avenue and 3rd
  Street
A late example of Art Deco Moderne. Presently much remodeled.

17. Wells Fargo Bank, 1972
  Northeast corner of Garey Avenue and 4th
  Street
Classical Moderne Revival.

18. Masonic Hall, circa 1900
  Ferdinand Davis
  Northwest corner of 4th and Thomas streets
A fancy building with mansard roof. Davis's work needs more study.

**19. Pomona City Hall and Council
  Chambers,** 1969
  Welton Becket and Associates (B. H.
  Anderson)
  South side of Mission Boulevard west of
  Garey Avenue
The City Hall is square; the Council Chambers building is round. Both are dull. They are included because they are testaments to the big try.

20. Pomona Central Library, 1965
  Welton Becket and Associates (Everett L.
  Tozier)
  Northwest corner of Garey Avenue and 6th
  Street
This fussy interpretation of the International style is not outstanding architecture, but it seems to work.

**21. California State Polytechnic University,
  Pomona**
  Valley Boulevard turn-off from San
  Bernardino Freeway
An agricultural college turned technical in the 1960s, Cal Poly has several interesting modern buildings.

The School of Environmental Design (1971) by Carl Maston is an asymmetrical massing of cubic forms. The **Student Health Center** (1976) designed by Mosher, Drew, Watson Associates of La Jolla is also well done. Probably the best building on the campus is the **Student Union** (1976) whose architects were Pulliam, Matthews, and Associates, proponents of the Cut-into Box style.

22. Phillips House, 1875
  2640 W. Pomona Boulevard, off Corona
  Freeway below Holt Avenue
An elegant French Second Empire house that seems dreadfully alone in this part of the world.

DIAMOND BAR

CLAREMONT

South Coast Air Quality Management District Headquarters, 1990–91

Meyer and Allen Associates
21865 East Copley Drive (off of the Golden Springs Drive Interchange)

A modernist image, for one of Southern California's major "official" environmental bodies. The building has been sensitively sited to take advantage of its orientation to the sun, and skylights have been carefully placed to introduce light internally. It also employs some advanced technology via fuel cells, etc. There are ironic twists to the siting of this building: this eastern section of L.A. County gathers more than its share of smog; the users of the building can (in their spare time) gaze out the windows at the conjunction of the Pomona Freeway; and of course the architect had to design a car park for 1,200 automobiles. As to the design of the building, it is well carried out with remembrances here and there of such great modern buildings of the 1920s as Gropius's Bauhaus at Dessau.

Claremont was named for its view and for Claremont, New Hampshire, the home town of one of the directors of the Pacific Land and Improvement Company that settled the property along the Santa Fe Railroad. It was platted in 1887, and by the next year a large hotel was rising to accommodate the visitors who, it was assumed, would soon be thronging the area. Then the "Boom of the Eighties" busted. At first it appeared that the town would also expire.

But every economic cloud has a silver lining. A college had been founded by the Congregationalists at Pomona in 1887. Then suddenly, no money! But there was the empty new hotel in nearby Claremont. Pomona College moved into the hotel during Christmas vacation in 1888–89 and named it Sumner Hall in honor of the wife of a Congregational minister. At first it was thought that with good times the college would move back to Pomona, but Claremont proved to be its permanent home. It became the nucleus of a group of "Associated Colleges"—Claremont Graduate School (1925), Scripps College (1926), Claremont Men's (now Claremont-McKenna) College (1946), Harvey Mudd College (1955), and Pitzer College (1963). The Southern California School of Theology, originally connected with the University of Southern California in Los Angeles, is also here, though not formally associated. All of these schools share faculty and libraries.

This is to indicate that even though founded by the Santa Fe Railroad, Claremont has always been a college town—and looks the part except for the area south of the tracks. In fact everything about the town is small and pleasant. The east side is devoted to the colleges and the west side (roughly west of Harvard Avenue) to housing

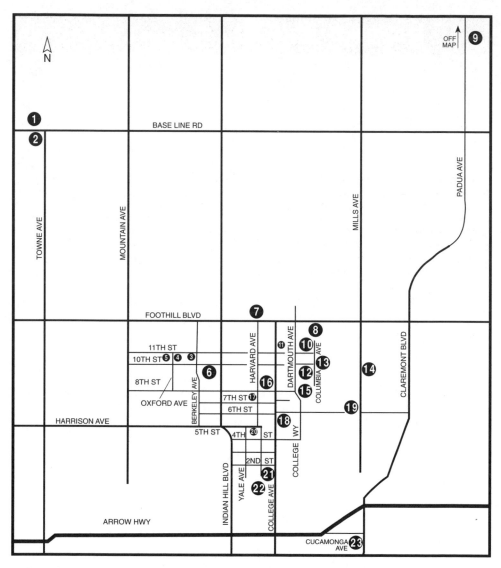

on beautiful tree-lined streets. Claremont is a lively and attractive place on a smog-free day. Like its neighbors, Upland and Ontario, it looks and is civilized.

A note on **Base Line Road:** this road, which begins in Azusa, gives up in Glendora and then picks up again in San Dimas, stretches in an almost straight east/west line out into the

desert. It is a fascinating route to explore. In L.A. County it runs through land that was once devoted to citrus and grapes, but now the pitiful orange groves and vineyards are interrupted repeatedly by intervals of tract housing. But it is still possible in places to conjure up an older California (1900–1930). Many Craftsman bungalows and Spanish Colonial Revival houses remain, as do a few Victorian efforts mainly of the vertical board-and-batten shack variety. The most interesting features of the machine-made landscape are the boulder (cobblestone) pump-houses and reservoirs and barns that remind us that this area was once green. Note especially the stone structures at Benson and Padua Avenue in the Claremont area.

1. Webb School, 1922–later
1175 W. Baseline Road
This boys' preparatory school was founded in 1922 by Thompson Webb, a native of Tennessee, and his California-born wife, Vivian. The aim was that the boys should live with nature in a gentlemanly manner. Except for Webb's late Craftsman house, the Spanish Colonial Revival was chosen as the style of the early buildings. Apparently Webb and the con-tractor worked together on these. The **gymna-sium** is extraordinarily picturesque both inside and out. Recent buildings are mainly by Allen Siple. The **Jones Dormitory** and the house next to it are by Roland E. Coate, Jr. the **Museum** was designed (1965) by Millard Sheets with one of his Neo-WPA murals over the door. The loveliest building on the campus is the **Vivian Webb Chapel** (1944) that Webb designed as a memorial to his wife. It is a tiny Mission church. Webb, the faculty, the student body, and friends in Claremont literally built it with their own hands. Even the adobe brick was made from the earth of the campus.

Back of the Webb School near the junction of Live Oak Canyon Road and Summit Road is a small collection of **houses** (1960s), designed by Foster Rhodes Jackson, a student of Frank Lloyd Wright. The few that can be seen from the road are impressive.

2. Pitzer House, 1910
Robert H. Orr
Southwest corner of Towne Avenue and Base Line Road
This house is tragically near the proposed extension of the Foothill Freeway. Pitzer hired Orr to design a bungalow that would reflect the rustic environment, which can still be sensed to the north. Orr chose to sheathe it in boulders. The plan is essentially a box almost split by an

interior patio whose walls are encased in boul-ders and whose ceiling is the sky. Although seemingly carefully calculated in floor plan, the effect of the arrangement seems very informal. As usual in a house of this kind, the most important rooms, besides the patio, are the liv-ing and dining rooms, the former having a boulder fireplace framed with art-glass win-dows depicting a Dutch boy and girl. The house and gardens have been carefully restored.

3. House, circa 1927
Southwest corner of Berkeley Avenue and 11th Street
Probably designed by Helen Wren, a local architect of talent who usually worked in the Anglo-Colonial Revival of which this Monterey Revival is an intended offshoot. The street planting is even better than the house. Praise water and the absence of Dutch elm disease!

4. House, circa 1965
Vincent Savoy
East side of Oxford Avenue between 10th and 11th streets
A sophisticated International-style essay in brick and glass.

5. Criley-Patterson House, circa 1965
Attributed to Vincent Savoy
782 W. 11th Street
Similar to the previous entry.

6. Lincoln House, circa 1927
Helen Wren
472 W. 10th Street
Monterey Revival in miniature.

7. Southern California School of Theology, 1960–61
Pereira and Luckman
Entrance is near the intersection of Harvard Avenue and Foothill Boulevard
This is not one of the firm's greatest works. What a shame at such a site! The only salient feature is the **Kresge Memorial Chapel** (1961), and it is by Edward D. Stone!

7. Southern California School of Theology, Kresge Memorial Chapel (1961)

8. Harvey Mudd College, 1957–later
Edward D. Stone; Heitschmidt and
Thompson, supervising architects
Between Columbia and Mills avenues
Stripped Neo-Classical in concrete blocks.

9. Padua Hills
At the northeastern boundary of Claremont is
the entrance to Padua Avenue. About three
miles north is a tiny community that grew up
around the Padua Hills Theater and Dining
Room, an institution in Claremont's culture
since the 1920s. Here the stage version of
Helen Hunt Jackson's *Ramona* was played. The
cluster of houses on Via Padova includes the
Hansch House (1955) by Richard J. Neutra at
number 4218, and a **house** (circa 1965) by
Foster Rhodes Jackson at number 4161.

10. Four College Science Center, 1970
Caudill, Rowlett, and Scott
Near northwest corner of 11th Street and
Columbia Avenue
Cleaned up Brutalism, especially effective set
off against the dullness of Harvey Mudd
College nearby.

11. Daggs House, circa 1910
1102 N. College Avenue
A beautifully sited Craftsman house with vertical board-and-batten siding.

12. Garrison Theater, 1963, addition 1970
Millard Sheets Associates and S. David
Underwood
Northeast corner of Dartmouth Avenue and
10th Street
Sheets, once a member of the faculty of the
Claremont Colleges, knew modern architecture.
He believed that the International Style was too
severe. Obvious solution: soften it by giving a
Saarinen-inspired classicism some hoopla in
the form of mosaics and sculpture. The result is
this drama center, strongly related to the Home
Savings and Loan Association buildings that he
designed or remodeled all over the county in
the 1950s and 1960s. There is one of these, in
fact, in downtown Claremont.

13. Scripps College, 1927–later
Gordon B. Kaufmann
Edward Huntsman-Trout,
landscape architect
Access at Columbia Avenue and
10th Street
Scripps has to be one of the prettiest colleges in
the country. It has a small and select student
body and looks that way largely thanks to
Kaufmann, who designed most of the buildings.
His **Denison Library** (1930) is especially well
done in the Spanish Colonial Revival style of
most of the campus. The **Balch
Administration Building** (1929) was designed
by Sumner Hunt and Silas R. Burns and fits in
beautifully. Note the Shakespearian bas-reliefs
by John Gregory that were the casts for those
ornamenting the Folger Library in Washington,
D.C. Other, more recent, buildings on the campus were designed by Smith and Williams,
Criley and McDowell, and Warnecke and
Associates. In the Margaret Fowler Garden of
the Scripps Fine Arts Foundation are nine panels painted by Alfredo Ramos Martinez. These
are worth a visit.

14. Pitzer College, 1964–and later
    Criley and McDowell
    Entrance at 9th Street off Mills Avenue

Not very distinguished in general except for the **McConnell Center** (1967), which was designed by Killingsworth, Brady, and Associates. Its projecting "rafters" suggest an attempt to break with the International style. See also the **Zetterberg House** (1906), a handsome, Orientalized Craftsman house that was moved (1977) to the Pitzer campus from 721 Harrison Avenue and restored by faculty and students.

15. Honnold Library, 1952
    J. E. Stanton. Addition 1956; Stanton and Stockwell
    College Way at intersection of Dartmouth and Columbia avenues

The facade is stripped Moderne so crisp that it has a Regency look. This is the main library of the Associated Colleges.

16. Darling House, 1903
    Charles and Henry Greene
    Northwest corner of College Avenue and 8th Street

A significant house in the Greenes' oeuvre, for it is one of the first of their houses in the true Craftsman mode—in this case Swiss Chalet, with Oriental touches.

17. Sugg House, circa 1930
    Helen Wren
    Northwest corner of 7th Street and Harvard Avenue

This large house is Anglo Colonial, Wren's favorite style.

18. Pomona College, 1887–and later
    Ralph Cornell, landscape architect
    Both sides of College Avenue between 2nd and 6th streets

This is the oldest and largest of the colleges with a congeries of styles and architects. The **gates** (1914) at Sixth Street and College Avenue are by Myron Hunt, as is the **Bridges Hall of Music** (1915). The latter, based on a Mannerist triumphal arch, is one of Hunt's best buildings. Just east of it is the **Harwood Garden** (1921) laid out by Ralph Cornell and

remaining close to his original ideas. Beyond it is **Sumner Hall,** the hotel that was Pomona's first building, but it has been so heavily remodeled that it is worth only a glance. Dating from 1908 and looking older is the **Carnegie Building** designed by Franklin P. Burnham. The **Bridges Auditorium** (1931) by San Diego architect William Templeton Johnson is vaguely Romanesque enlivened with a little Art Deco (Zigzag) Moderne. The interior, with its frescoed ceiling, is a period piece. Also notable is **Frary Hall** (1929), not for its architecture by Webber and Spaulding but for its murals. Just inside the entrance porch is a striking one by Rico Lebrun (assisted by James Pinto and William Ptaszynski) called *Genesis* (1960). In the dining hall you will find one of California's most famous murals, *Prometheus* (1930), by Jose Clemente Orozco. In 1960 Honnold and Rex designed a 125-foot-tall **Memorial Bell Tower.** The modernist form of this tower, composed of two solid slabs enclosing two surfaces of grill work, supposedly fitted into the existing Spanish Colonial Revival building tradition. It really doesn't accomplish this goal, but the effort was there. The grill work was designed by the Los Angeles sculptor Malcolm Lleland.

19. Claremont-McKenna (formerly Men's) College, 1948 and later
    Allison and Rible
    Mills Avenue and 6th Street

Not inspired architecture, but the two residential towers, **Fawcett Hall and Claremont Hall** (both 1966), designed by Ladd and Kelsey, are worth mentioning because high-rise, even medium high-rise, seems odd in Claremont. Also the scoops taken out of the corners of the buildings seem an obvious, planned dig at the International style.

20. Bungalow, circa 1910
    Southeast corner of Yale and Harrison avenues

Brown in color, of course, with vertical board-and-batten siding. Just behind this house at 428 N. Yale Avenue is another well-maintained Craftsman house.

21. Sumner House, 1887
105 N. College Avenue

A two-story Queen Anne mansion built just before the bust.

22. Santa Fe Railroad Passenger Station,
circa 1925
William H. Mohr
1st Street and railroad tracks, just west of the end of Harvard Avenue

This small-scaled Churrigueresque extravaganza has received a new lease on life. It has, since our last Guide, been beautifully restored.

23. Russian Village, 1928–later
South Mills Avenue (approached from the north by Claremont Avenue) just below Arrow Highway

Thirteen picturesque houses built of cast-off materials, such as concrete pavement torn up from Holt Avenue when it was being repaved. Its creator was Steve Stys, a Pole, who began with 290 S. Mills Avenue, rather conservatively fashioned by Stys from fieldstone and other materials that he had accumulated. He figured that it cost him $35 to build it. Later he went on to use broken concrete, boulders, and, after the Long Beach earthquake of 1933, marble and other parts of the ruins. He did not build all of the thirteen houses, but his imagination obviously dominated the project.

One can gain some idea of the mountains of literature published on Los Angeles by thumbing through Doyce B. Nunis, Jr.'s, *Los Angeles and Its Environs in the Twentieth Century* (now well over two decades old, 9,895 entries in 501 pages), and this bibliography covers only the years 1900 through 1973. While every state and every American city had its array of PR sales literature in the nineteenth century, no region or city comes close to equaling the output of literature on Southern California and Los Angeles. And the last quarter century has seen no letdown in the publishing of articles and books about Los Angeles.

The accompanying bibliography lists those writings which the authors have found most useful in forming our understanding of the built environment of Los Angeles. Though of real value in research, we have on the whole left out those ponderous "histories," mostly written in the early twentieth century. Periodicals that concern themselves at least in part with architecture in the Southland are *Sunset, Westways, Buzz,* and the *Los Angeles Magazine,* and occasional articles which occur in the *Magazine* section of the *Los Angeles Times.* Those specifically devoted to architecture which we have continually consulted are *Architectural Digest,* the *L. A. Architect,* and the *Newsletter* of The Los Angeles Forum for Architecture and Urban Design. Older publications are historically of value, such as the *Home Magazine* of the *Los Angeles Times,* and *California Arts and Architecture,* (later *Arts and Architecture*).

Other magazines no longer published but of great value to us have been: *Architect and Engineer, Southwest Builder and Contractor, California Home Owner, Bungalow Magazine, Land of Sunshine* (later *Outwest*), and the all-too-brief *West* magazine of the Sunday *Los Angeles Times.* The real-estate section of the Sunday *Los Angeles Times* has in the past provided revealing clues as to what was occurring in Los Angeles architecture (especially commercial and popular spec architecture), but this is regrettably no longer the case. Then there are those very valuable articles written by the architectural critics of the *Los Angeles Times* (John Pastier, John Dreyfus, Art Seidenbaum, Sam Hall Kaplan, and more recently Leon Whiteson, Michael Webb and Aaron Betsky) and those written by Joseph Giovannini for the *Los Angeles Examiner,* as well as other newspapers and magazines. The Southern California scene in general has been, and is, well presented in many of the national magazines such as *Architectural Digest, House and Home, House and Garden,* and *Metropolitan Home.* Also no longer published but very revealing of Los Angeles and its environs was the environmental planning magazine *Cry California.*

Institutions notable for their collections on Los Angeles architecture (books, runs of magazines, photographs and other documents) are the Huntington Library; the History Department of the Los Angeles Public Library; the History Division of the Los Angeles County Museum of Natural History; the Los Angeles Cultural Heritage Board; the Pasadena Urban Conservation Program; the UCLA Special Collection, Research Library, Art and Architectural Library; the Art and Architecture Library of the University of Southern California; and the Special Collections Library at the University of California, Santa Barbara.

Original architectural drawings and archives are of great value in the study of architecture in Los Angeles and the Southland. The largest single collection is contained in the Architectural Drawing Collection, University Art Museum, University of California, Santa Barbara. Other collections of drawings are to be found at the Huntington Library (including the Gamble House drawing collection of the University of Southern California) and at the Library, UCLA.

Earlier writings which have continually influenced us are Esther McCoy's *Five California Architects* (first published in 1960; republished in

1975) and Reyner Banham's *Los Angeles: The Architecture of Four Ecologies* (1974). More generally, Robert Venturi and Denise Scott Brown and Charles Moore have informed and inspired us. Their pioneering publications on Los Angeles and vernacular architecture have been continued by John Margolies, Jim Heiman, Rip George, John Chase, and John Beach. Los Angeles will never be the same.

Anonymous. "California's Contribution to a National Architecture." *The Craftsman* 22 (August 1912): 352–547.

_____. "Southern California: The Land of Heart's Desire: Its People, Homes and Pleasure: Art and Architecture." *Los Angeles Morning Herald*, 1912.

_____. *Handbook of Southern California, Los Angeles and San Diego*. New York: 1914.

_____. "The Los Angeles Civic Center." *Architect and Engineer* 73 (June 1923): 65–67.

_____. "Work of Some Contemporary Los Angeles Architects." *Pencil Points* 22 (May 1941): 306–33.

_____. "The Housing Authority of the City of Los Angeles Presents a Solution." *California Arts and Architecture* 60 (May 1943): 47–66.

_____. "Street Art Exploration in Los Angeles." *Sunset* 150 (April 1973): 110–13.

_____. "The Los Angeles 12." *Architectural Record* 160 (August 1976): 81–90.

Abeloe, William N., et al. *Historic Spots in California*. Stanford: 1966.

Allison, David C. "The Work of Myron Hunt." *Architect and Engineer* 53 (April 1918): 38–68.

Amos, Patrick. *At Home with Architecture*. La Jolla: 1983.

Atkinson, Janet Erene. *Historical Directory of Los Angeles County*. Jefferson, N.C.: rev. edition, 1987.

Avensleben, Ludolf von. *John Lautner Architect Los Angeles.* Vienna: 1991.

Andersen, Timothy J., Eudorah M. Moore, Robert Winter. 1974. *California Design 1910*. Reprint, Salt Lake City: 1980.

Andre, Herb. "John Byers: Domestic Architecture in Southern California 1919–1960." Master's thesis, University of California, Santa Barbara, 1971.

"Architectural Design Goes West." *Architectural Design* 43, no. 8 (1973).

Austin, John C. *Architecture in Southern California*. Los Angeles: 1905.

Austin, Mary. *Land of Little Rain*. Boston: 1903.

_____. *California: Land of the Sun*. London: 1914.

Baer, Kurt. *Architecture of the California Missions*. Berkeley: 1963.

Bangs, Jean Murray. "Greene and Greene." *Architectural Forum* 89 (October 1948): 80–82.

_____. "Los Angeles . . . Know Thyself." *Home Section, Los Angeles Times* (14 October 1961): 4–11.

Banham, Reyner. "L.A.: The Structure Behind the Scene." *Architectural Design* 41 (April 1971): 227–30.

_____. *Los Angeles: The Architecture of Four Ecologies*. London: 1974.

_____. "A London–L.A. Love Affair." *West Magazine, Los Angeles Times* (6 June 1974): 9–14.

Basten, Fred. *Santa Monica By the Bay: Its First 100 Years*. Los Angeles: 1974.

_____. *Portrait of a Fabled City*. Los Angeles: 1975.

Baum, Dwight James. "Ecclesiastical Architecture of California." *American Architect* 34 (July 1928): 71–78.

_____. "An Eastern Architect's Impression of Recent Work in Southern California." *Architecture* 38 (July 1918): 177–180.

Baum, George C. "The Spanish Mission Type." *Architectural Styles for Country Houses* by Henry H. Taylor. New York: 1919, pp. 67–74.

Baylis, Douglas and Joan Parry. *California Houses of Gordon Drake*. New York: 1956.

Beach, John. "Lloyd Wright's Sowden House." *Fine Home Building* (April/May 1983): 66–73.

Belloli, Jay, ed. *Wallace Neff 1895–1982. The Romance of Regional Architecture*. San Marino: 1989.

_____. *Johnson, Kaufmann, Coate: Partners in the California Style*. Claremont and Santa Barbara: 1992.

Benton, Arthur B. "Architecture for the Southwest." *Outwest* (*Land of Sunshine*) 4 (February 1896): 126–30.

_____. "The California Mission and Its Influence on Pacific Coast Architecture." *Architect and Engineer* 24 (February 1911): 35–45.

_____. "The Work of the Landmark Club of

Southern California." *American Institute of Architects Journal* 2 (September 1914): 469–81.

Beronius, George. "Those Astonishing Murals of East Los Angeles." *Home Magazine, Los Angeles Times* (11 April 1976): 12–17, 22–23.

_____. "Paradise for Porkers." *Home Magazine, Los Angeles Times.* (18 April 1976): 19–21.

Betsky, Aaron. *Violated Perfection.* New York: 1990.

_____. "Shambles Instead of Shangri-La." *L.A. Architect* (December 1991): 5.

_____. "Remaking L.A.," *Los Angeles Times Magazine,* (15 December 1992): 58–61.

Billiteu, Bill. "Simon Rodia's Incredible Towers." *Art News* 78 (April 1979): 92–96.

Bledsoe, Jane. "Added-on Ornament," *Home Sweet Home, American Domestic Vernacular Architecture.* (edited by Charles W. Moore, et al.), 30–34. New York, 1983.

Bottles, Scott L. *Los Angeles and the Automobile.* Berkeley, Los Angeles, London: 1987.

Boutelle, Sara Holmes. *Julia Morgan Architect.* New York: 1988.

Bowman, Lynn. *L.A.: Epic of a City.* Los Angeles: 1974.

Boyarsky, Nancy and Bill. "The Highway Game." *West Magazine, Los Angeles Times* (28 February 1971): 7–15.

Bradley, Bill. *The Last of the Great Stations.* Glendale: 1979.

_____, comp. *Commercial Los Angeles 1925–1947.* Glendale: 1981.

Brady, Francis. "The Spanish Colonial Revival in California Architecture." Master's thesis, California State University, Long Beach, 1962.

Brantner, Cherri and Gregory Cloud, eds. "The Essential Pico Blvd." *Scan* 1 (November 1978): 2–7.

Braupton, Ernest. *The Garden Beautiful in California.* Los Angeles: 1946.

Breeze, Carla. *L.A. Deco.* New York: 1991.

Bricker, David. "Cliff May and the California Ranch House after 1945." Master's thesis, University of California, Santa Barbara, 1983.

Bricker, Lauren Weiss. "The Residential Architecture of Roland E. Coate." Master's thesis, University of California, Santa Barbara, 1982.

Brino, Giovanni. *La Citta Capitalista Los Angeles.* Florence: 1978.

Brodsly, David. *L. A. Freeway: An Appreciative Essay.* Berkeley: 1981.

Brook, Harry Ellington. *Los Angeles, California: The City and County.* Los Angeles: 1915.

Brown, Robert G. "The California Bungalow in Los Angeles: A Study of Origins and Classification." Master's thesis, University of California, Los Angeles, 1964.

Browne, F. E. *Comfortable Los Angeles Homes and What People Say Who Live in Them.* Los Angeles: 1896.

Bryant, Lynn. "Edward Huntsman-Trout, Landscape Architect," *Review* (Southern California Chapter, Society of Architectural Historians) II, no. 1 (Winter 1983): 1–6.

Buergen, Anne Luise, et al. "Downtown L.A." *L.A. Architect* 5 (February 1979): 3–6.

Burdette, Robert J. *Greater Los Angeles and Southern California.* Chicago: 1906.

Calistro, Paddy and Betty Goodwin. *L.A. Inside and Out.* New York: 1992.

California Institute of Technology (Baxter Art Gallery). *Caltech, 1910–1950.* (Exhibition catalog with essays by Alice Stone, et al.) Pasadena, 1983.

Cameron, Robert. *Above Los Angeles.* Los Angeles: 1976.

Campbell, Regula. "Notes on Landscape Design in Southern California." *L.A. Architect* (October 1981): 4–5.

Cardwell, Kenneth H. *Bernard Maybeck Artisan, Architect, Artist.* Salt Lake City: 1977.

Case, Walter. *History of Long Beach and Vicinity.* New York: 1927; 1974.

Caughey, John W. and La Ree. *Los Angeles: Biography of a City.* Berkeley: 1976.

Chalk, Warren. "Up the Down-ramp." *Architectural Design* 38 (September 1968): 404–7.

Chapman, John L. *Incredible Los Angeles.* New York: 1967.

Chase, John. "Map Guide to Recent Architecture in L.A." *L.A. Architect* 7 (October 1981): 2, 7.

_____. *Exterior Decoration: Hollywood's Inside-out Houses.* Los Angeles: 1982.

_____. "Typecasting Style: New Condominiums in Santa Monica, California." *Arts & Architecture* 1 (1982): 51–58.

_____. "The Garret, the Boardroom, and the Amusement Park." *Journal Los Angeles Institute of Contemporary Art* 4 (1983): 21–27.

Chase, John and John Beach. "The Stucco Box," *Home Sweet Home, American Domestic Vernacular Architecture* (1983): 118–129.

Cheney, Charles H. "Palos Verdes: Eight Years of Development," *Architect and Engineer* 100 (January 1930): 35–83.

Clark, Alson. "The California Architecture of Gordon Kaufmann," *Review* (Southern California Chapter, Society of Architectural Historians) I, no. 3 (Summer 1982): 1–7.

_____. "The Architecture of Los Angeles: An Introduction," *Review* (Southern California Chapter, Society of Architectural Historians) II, no. 1 (Winter 1983): 6–7.

Clark, David. *L.A. on Foot.* Los Angeles and San Francisco: 1972.

_____. *Los Angeles: A City Apart.* Woodland Hills: 1981.

Clark, Robert Judson and Thomas S. Hines. *Los Angeles Transfer: Architecture in Southern California, 1880–1980.* (William Andrews Clark Memorial Library, UCLA). Los Angeles: 1983.

Cohen, Gloria. "Allyn E. Morris, Architect." *L.A. Architect* (May 1982): 2–3.

Coombs, Robert. "The New Victorians," *Westways* 75 (May 1983): 31–33, 69.

Crocker, Donald W. *Within the Vale of Annandale.* Pasadena: 1968.

Crofutt, George A. *Crofutt's New Overland Tourist and Pacific Coast Guide.* Chicago: 1878–79.

Croly, Herbert D. "The California Country House." *Architect and Engineer* 7 (December 1906): 24–39.

Crouch, Dora P., Daniel J. Garr, & Axel I. Mundigo, *Spanish City Planning in North America.* Cambridge: 1982.

Crump, Spencer. *Ride the Big Red Cars.* Los Angeles: 1962.

Culbertson, Judy, and Tom Randell. *Permanent Californians.* Clelsa, Vermont: 1989.

Current, William R. and Karen. *Greene and Greene, Architects in the Residential Style.* Fort Worth: 1974.

Cutts, Anson B., Jr. "The Hillside Home of Ramon Navarro, A Unique Setting Created by Lloyd Wright." *California Arts and Architecture* 44 (July 1933): 11–13, 31.

Dash, Norman. *Yesterday's Los Angeles.* Miami: 1976.

David, Arthur C. "An Architect of Bungalows in California." *Architectural Record* 20 (October 1906): 306–15.

Davis, Genevieve. *Beverly Hills: An Illustrated History.* Chatsworth: 1988.

Davis, Mike. *City of Quartz.* New York: 1990.

Del Zoppo, Annette and Jeffrey Stanton. *Venice, California 1904–1930.* Venice: 1978.

Dickinson, R. B. *Los Angeles Today— Architecturally.* Los Angeles: 1896.

Dietz, Lawrence. "There Was Once a Woman Who Lived in a Shoe." *West Magazine, Los Angeles Times* (30 November 1969): 12–15.

_____. "Raymond Chandler's L.A." *Western Architect* 32 (August 1969): 87–90.

Direccicon General De Arquitectura y Vivienda. MOPU 1984. *R. M. Schindler Arquitectura* (with articles by Esther McCoy, et al.) Madrid.

Diskin, Steve, et al. *Los Angeles at 25 MMPH.* New York: 1993.

Duell, Prentice. "The New Era of California Architecture." *Western Architect* 32 (August 1923): 87–90.

Dumke, Glen S. *The Boom of the Eighties in Southern California.* San Marino: 1970.

Dunitz, Robin J. *Street Gallery: Guide to 1000 Los Angeles Murals.* Los Angeles: 1993.

Faulstick, Paul. *A Guide to Claremont Architecture.* Claremont: 1977.

Feldman, Eddy S. *The Art of Street Lighting in Los Angeles.* Los Angeles: 1972.

Fink, Augusta. *Time and the Terraced Land.* Berkeley: 1966.

Flanagan, Barbara. "Terminal Oasis: The Uncanny Survival of Union Station." *L.A. Architect* 6 (February 1980): 2–3.

Flood, Francis B. "A Study of the Architecture of the Period 1868–1900 Existing in Los Angeles in 1940." Master's thesis, University of Southern California, Los Angeles, 1941.

Fogelson, Robert M. *The Fragmented Metropolis Los Angeles, 1850–1930.* Cambridge: 1967.

Foster, Mark S. "The Model-T, The Hard Sell, and Los Angeles during the 1920s," *Pacific Historical Review* 44 (1975): 459–98.

Frierman, Jay D., Roberta S. Greenwood. *Historical Archaeology of Nineteenth-Century California.* Los Angeles: 1992.

Gallion, Arthur B. "Architecture of the Los Angeles Region." *Architectural Record* 119 (May 1956): 159–66.

Garr, Daniel. "Hispanic Colonial Settlements in California: Planning and Urban Development on the Frontier, 1769–1850." Ph.D. thesis, Cornell University, Ithica, 1971.

Gaut, Helen Lukens. A frequent contributor to *The Craftsman* (1901–16) and other journals, she was a Pasadenan who had strong ties to the Arts and Crafts movement. See, as examples:

_____. "An Example of Progressive Architecture from the West Coast," *The Craftsman* 18 (June 1910): 380–83.

_____. "How the California Bungalow Illustrates the Right Use of Building Materials," *The Craftsman* 19 (November 1910): 200–201.

Gebhard, David. "The Case Study Houses," *Art Forum* 2 (October 1963): 24–25.

_____. "Architecture in Los Angeles." *Art Forum* 2 (Summer 1964): 10–11.

_____. *George Washington Smith.* Santa Barbara: 1964.

_____. "The Spanish Colonial Revival in Southern California." *Journal of the Society of Architectural Historians* 26 (May 1967): 131–47.

_____. "L.A., The Stucco Box." *Art in America* 58 (May–June 1970): 130–33.

_____. *Schindler.* London and New York, 1972. Reprint, Salt Lake City, 1980.

_____. "Getty's Museum." *Architecture Plus* 2 (September–October 1974): 56–61.

_____. "Charles Moore and the West Coast." *Architecture and Urbanism* 5 (1978): 45–48.

_____. "Los Angeles: An Architectural Tour." *Portfolio* 2 (September–October 1980): 106–9.

_____. "Architectural Imagery: The Missions and California." *Harvard Architectural Review* 1 (Spring 1980): 136–45.

_____. "The Monterey Tradition: History Re-ordered." *New Mexico Studies in the Fine Arts* 7 (1982): 14–19.

_____. "Tile, Stucco Walls, and Arches; The Spanish Tradition in the Popular American House." *Home Sweet Home, American Domestic Vernacular Architecture* (edited by Charles W. Moore): 104–11. New York, 1983.

_____. "Preserving the Common Place." *Journal L.A.I.C.A.* 4 (Spring 1983): 50–57.

_____. "The Reign of Spain," *Arts & Architecture* 4 (July 1985): 71–76.

_____. "Civic Presence in California Cities," *Architectural Design* 57 (October 1987): 74–80.

_____. "Some Observations on California's Monterey Tradition," *Journal of the Society of Architectural Historians* 46 (June 1987): 157–170.

_____. *Romanza: The California Architecture of Frank Lloyd Wright.* (with photographs by Scott Zimmerman), San Francisco: 1988.

_____. "California Modernist: Design Stardom at Last," *Metropolitan Home* (October 1989): 93–98.

_____. *Lutah Maria Riggs: A Woman in Architecture, 1921–1980.* Santa Barbara: 1992.

_____. *Robert Stacy-Judd: Maya Architecture, The Creation of a New Style.* Santa Barbara: 1993.

_____. *The Architectural Drawings of R. M. Schindler.* New York: 1993.

Gebhard, David and Susan King. *A View of California Architecture, 1960–1976.* San Francisco: 1976.

Gebhard, David and Harriette Von Breton. *1868–1968: Architecture in California.* Santa Barbara: 1968.

_____. *Kem Weber: The Moderne in Southern California, 1920–1941.* Santa Barbara: 1969.

_____. *Lloyd Wright, Architect.* Santa Barbara: 1971.

_____. *L.A. in the Thirties.* Los Angeles: 1989.

Gebhard, David, Harriette Von Breton, Lauren Weiss. *The Architecture of Gregory Ain: The Play Between the Rational and High Art.* Santa Barbara: 1980.

Gebhard, David, Harriette Von Breton, Robert Winter. *Samuel and Joseph Cather Newsom: Victorian Architectural Imagery in California, 1878–1908.* Santa Barbara: 1979.

Gebhard, David, Lauren Weiss Bricker, David Bricker. *Fort MacArthur, San Pedro—A Public Report.* Washington, D.C.: 1982.

Gebhard, David and Robert Winter. *A Guide to Architecture in Southern California.* Los Angeles: 1965.

_____. *A Guide to Architecture in Los Angeles and Southern California.* Salt Lake City: 1977.

_____. *Architecture in Los Angeles: A Compleat Guide.* Salt Lake City: 1985.

Germany, Lisa. *Harwell Hamilton Harris.* Austin, Texas: 1991.

Gill, Brendan. *The Dream Come True: The Great Houses of Los Angeles.* New York: 1982.

Gill, Irving J. "The Home of the Future: The New Architecture of the West." *The Craftsman* 30 (May 1916): 140–41; 220.

Giovannini, Joseph. As architectural critic for the Los Angeles Herald Examiner from 1978 to 1983, Giovannini contributed greatly to our understanding of the local architectural and planning scene.

_____. "The Environment of Movement." *California History* 60 (Spring 1981): 82–83.

_____. *Real Estate As Art: New Architecture in Venice.* Venice: 1984.

_____. "A Chronicler of California Architecture." *The New York Times* (21 June 1984): 21.

Gleen, Constance W. *Egypt in L.A..* Long Beach: 1977.

Gleye, Paul. *The Architecture of Los Angeles.* Los Angeles: 1981.

Goodhue, Bertram G. and Carleton M. Winslow. *The Architecture and the Gardens of the San Diego Exposition.* San Francisco: 1916.

Greene, Charles S. "Bungalows." *The Western Architect* 12 (July 1908): 3.

_____. "Impressions of Some Bungalows and Gardens." *The Architect* 10 (December 1915): 251–52, 278.

Grenier, Judson. *A Guide to Historic Places in Los Angeles County.* Dubuque, Iowa: 1978.

Grenier, Judson A., Doyce B. Nunis, Jr., Jean Bruce Poole. *A Guide to Historic Places in Los Angeles County.* Los Angeles: 1978.

Grey, Elmer. "Architecture in Southern California." *Architectural Record* 17 (January 1905): 1–17.

_____. "Architecture in Southern California," *Arts and Decoration* 30 (January 1926): 40–41, 78.

_____. "Some Country House Architecture in the Far West." *Architectural Record* 51 (January 1922): 308–15.

Griffin, Helen S. "Some Two-Story Adobe Houses of Old California." *Historical Society of Southern California Quarterly* 20 (March 1938): 5–21.

Gudde, Erwin G. *California Place Names: Origin and Etymology of Current Geographic Names.* Berkeley: 1968.

Guinn, J. M. "Los Angeles in the Adobe Age." *Historical Society of Southern California Quarterly* 4 (1897): 49–55.

Haley, A. L. *Modern Apartments.* Los Angeles: ca. 1910.

Halprin, John. *Los Angeles: Improbable City.* New York: 1979.

Hamlin, Talbot F. "What Makes it American: Architecture in the Southwest and West." *Pencil Points* 20 (December 1939): 762–76.

_____. "California Whys and Wherefores." *Pencil Points* 22 (May 1941): 339–44.

Hampton, Edgar Lloyd. "Architecture of California," *House and Garden* 51 (February 1927): 104–5, 154, 156.

Hancock, Ralph. *Fabulous Boulevard (Wilshire).* New York: 1949.

_____. *The Forest Lawn Story.* Los Angeles: 1955.

Hannaford, Donald R. and Revel Edwards. 1931. *Spanish Colonial or Adobe Architecture in California, 1800–1850.* New York. (republished, 1990, Stamford; "Preface," David Gebhard).

Hanson, A. E. *Rolling Hills: The Early Years.* Rolling Hills: 1978.

_____. 1984. *An Arcadian Landscape: The California Gardens of A. E. Hanson.* (edited and Introduction David Gebhard). Los Angeles.

Hanson, Earl and Paul Beckett. *Los Angeles: Its People and Its Homes.* Los Angeles: 1944.

Harlow, Neal. *Maps and Survey of the Pueblo Lands of Los Angeles.* Los Angeles: 1976.

Harrel, Mary Ann Beach. "The Vernacular Castle." *Home Sweet Home, American Domestic Vernacular Architecture.* (edited by Charles W. Moore). 72–75. New York: 1983.

Harris, Allen. "Southern California Architects: Walker and Eisen." *Building Review* 22 (October 1922): 43–52.

Harris, Frank and Weston Bonenberger. *A Guide to Contemporary Architecture in Southern California.* Los Angeles: 1951.

Harris, Harwell Hamilton. *Harwell Hamilton Harris—A Collection of His Writings.* Raleigh, N.C.: 1965.

Hastings, Miles. "The Continuous House." *Sunset* 32 (January 1914): 110–16.

Hatheway, Roger. "El Pueblo: Myth and Realities," *Review* (Southern California Chapter, Society of Architectural Historians) I:1 (Fall 1981): 1–5.

Hays, William C. "One Story and Open-Air Schoolhouses in California." *Architectural Forum* 27 (September 1917): 57–65.

Heiman, Jim and Rip George. (Introduction by David Gebhard.) *California Crazy.* San Francisco: 1980.

Heisley, George D. "Seeing America: Los Angeles." *Outwest* 30 (March 1909): 193–224.

_____. "Seeing America: Some More About Los Angeles." *Outwest* 30 (May 1909): 509–18.

Henstell, Bruce. *Los Angeles: An Illustrated History.* New York: 1980.

_____. *Sunshine and Wealth: Los Angeles in the Twenties and Thirties.* San Francisco: 1984.

Hess, Alan. "Golden Architecture." *Journal Los Angeles Institute of Contemporary Art* (Spring 1983): 28–30.

_____. "California Coffee Shops," *Arts & Architecture* 2 (1983): 42–50.

_____. *Googie: Fifties Coffee Shop Architecture.* San Francisco: 1985.

Hill, Laurence L. *La Reina: Los Angeles in Three Centuries.* Los Angeles: 1929.

Hines, Thomas S. "Housing, Baseball, and Creeping Socialism: The Battle of Chavez Ravine, Los Angeles, 1949–1959." *Journal of Urban History* 8 (February 1982): 123–45.

_____. *Richard Neutra and the Search for Modern Architecture.* New York: 1982.

Hitchcock, Henry-Russell. "An Eastern Critic Looks at Western Architecture." *California Arts and Architecture* 57 (December 1940): 21–23, 40.

Hoffmann, Donald. *Frank Lloyd Wright's Hollyhock House.* New York: 1992.

Holder, Charles. *Southern California—A Guide Book.* Los Angeles: 1888.

Honnold, Douglas. *Southern California Architecture: 1769–1956.* New York: 1956.

Hopkins, Una Nixon. "The Development of Domestic Architecture on the West Coast." *The Craftsman* 13 (January 1908): 450–57.

Hudson, Karen E. *Paul R. Williams, Architect: Legacy of Style.* New York: 1993.

Hume, H., comp. *Los Angeles, Architecturally.* Los Angeles: 1902.

Humes, Edward. "Downtown is a Bust," *Buzz* 4 (April 1993): 62–67, 101–3.

Hunt, Myron. "The Work of Messrs. Allison and Allison." *Architect and Engineer* 42 (1912): 39–75.

_____. "Personal Sources of Pacific Coast Architectural Development," *American Architect* 129 (5 January 1926): 51–54.

Hunter, Paul and Walter L. Reichardt, eds. *Residential Architecture in Southern California.* Los Angeles: 1939.

Hylen, Arnold. *Bunker Hill: A Los Angeles Landmark.* Los Angeles: 1976.

_____. *Los Angeles Before the Freeways.* Los Angeles: 1981.

Inaya, Beata, et al. *The Three Worlds of Los Angeles.* Los Angeles: 1974.

Jackson, Helen Hunt. *Ramona.* Boston: 1884.

_____. *Glimpses of California and the Missions.* Boston: 1904.

James, George Wharton. *California Romantic and Beautiful.* Boston: 1914.

_____. *In and Out of the Old Missions.* Boston: 1927.

Jaeger, Roland. "Von Altona nach Los Angeles: Jukob Petlef Peters (1889–1934)." *Architektor in Hamburg: Jahrbuch 1993.* Hamburg: 1993.

Jencks, Charles. "The Los Angeles Silvers." *Urbanism* (October 1976): 13–14.

_____. *Daydream Houses of Los Angeles.* New York: 1978.

_____. *Architecture Today.* London and New York: 1982.

Jenney, William L. E. "The Old California Missions and Their Influence on Design." *Architect and Engineer* 6 (September 1906): 25–33.

Johnson, Cheryle, et al. *75th Anniversary of the Los Feliz Improvement Association, 1916–1991.* Los Angeles: 1991.

Johnson, Paul, ed. *Los Angeles: Portrait of An Extraordinary City.* Menlo Park: 1968.

Johnson, Reginald D. "Development of Architectural Styles in California." *Architect and Engineer* 87 (October 1926): 108–9.

Jones, A. Quincy and Frederick E. Emmons. *Builder's Homes for Better Living.* New York: 1957.

Jordy, William H. *Progressive and Academic Ideals at the Turn of the Century.* New York: 1972.

Kamerling, Bruce. *Irving Gill: The Artist as Architect.* San Diego: 1979.

_____. *Irving J. Gill, Architect.* San Diego: 1993.

Kammerman, Roy. *L. A. Superlatives.* New York: 1987.

Kaplan, Sam Hall. *L.A. Lost and Found.* New York: 1987.

_____. *Follies: Design and Other Diversions in a Fractured Metropolis.* Santa Monica: 1989.

Kapp, Glenn and Geoff Miller. "Our Backyard Riviera." *Los Angeles* 2 (April 1961): 18–21.

Karasick, Norman M., and Dorothy K. Karasick. *The Oilman's Daughter: A Biography of Aline Barnsdall.* Encino: 1993.

Kennelley, Joe, and Roy Hankey. *Sunset Boulevard: America's Dream Street.* Burbank: 1981.

Kirker, Harold. *California's Architectural Frontier.* San Marino: 1960. (Reprint 1973, Salt Lake City).

_____. "California's Architecture and its Relations to Contemporary Trends in Europe and America." *California Historical Society Quarterly* 51 (Winter 1972): 289–305.

Knight, Arthur and Eliot Elisofon. *The Hollywood Style.* New York: 1969.

Kuehn, Gernot. *Views of Los Angeles.* Los Angeles: 1978.

Lacy, Bill, and Susan deMenli, eds. *Angeles and Franciscans: Innovative Architecture from Los Angeles and San Francisco.* New York: 1992.

Lancaster, Clay. "The American Bungalow." *Art Bulletin.* 15 (September 1958): 239–53.

_____. *The Japanese Influence in America.* New York: 1963.

Laporte, Paul. *Simon Rodia's Towers in Watts.* Los Angeles: 1962.

Lautner, John. "You've Got to Fight for Great Design." *Home Magazine, Los Angeles Times.* (14 February 1971): 16–18, 21.

Lazlo, Paul. *Paul Lazlo—Designed in the U.S.A. 1937–1947.* Beverly Hills: 1947.

Le Barthon, J. L. *Our Architecture Morgan and Walls, John Parkinson, Hunt and Eager.* Los Angeles: 1904.

Levick, Melba, and Helaine Kaplan Prentice. *The Gardens of Southern California.* San Francisco: 1991.

Leviseur, Elsa. "California Ecology," *Architectural Review* (April 1991): 52–55.

Lewin, Susan Grant and Stanley Tigerman. *The California Condition: A Pregnant Architecture.* La Jolla: 1982.

Lewis, Oscar. *Here Lived the Californians.* New York: 1957.

Lindley, Walter, and J. P. Widney. *California of the South.* New York: 1896.

Lingenbrink, William. *Modernistic Architecture.* Los Angeles: undated (ca. 1933).

Littlejohn, David. *Architecture: The Life and Work of Charles W. Moore.* New York: 1984.

Litter, Charles. "A Dream Come True." *California A.I.A.* (June 1939): 28–29.

Long Beach Museum of Art. *Arts in California: I: Architecture.* (Introduction Jerome Allen Donson). Long Beach: 1957.

Los Angeles Architectural Club. *Yearbook.* Los Angeles: 1910, 1912, and 1913.

Los Angeles Chamber of Commerce. *Los Angeles and Vicinity.* Los Angeles: 1904.

Los Angeles Conservancy (The Conservancy has printed a number of tours of Los Angeles.) Among them (undated) are:
Alvarado Terrace House Tour.
Buildings Reborn in Los Angeles.
Cruisin' L.A.
Old Monrovia House Tour.
Would You Believe Hollywood Boulevard?
Would You Believe Los Angeles?

The Los Angeles Conservancy's *News,* also contains helpful information about architecture and planning in Los Angeles.

Los Angeles Regional Planning Commission. *Annual Reports.* Los Angeles. 1940, 1941, and 1942.

_____. *A Comprehensive Report on the Master Plan for Highways for Los Angeles County.* Los Angeles: 1941.

_____. *Master Plan for Land Use—Inventory and Classification.* Los Angeles: 1941.

Los Angeles Department of Planning. *City Planning in Los Angeles: A History.* Los Angeles: 1964.

Luitjens, Helen. *The Elegant Era.* Palm Desert: 1968.

Luitjens, Helen and Katherine La Hue. *A Sketch Book of Pacific Palisades, California.* Santa Monica: 1975.

Lummis, Charles F. "The Making of Los Angeles." *Outwest* 30 (April 1909): 227–57. (See also his many other articles for this journal and its predecessor, *The Land of Sunshine*).

Mackey, Margaret G. *Los Angeles Proper and Improper.* Los Angeles: 1938.

Makinson, Randell L. "Greene and Greene," in *Five California Architects,* by Esther McCoy. 102–147. New York: 1960.

_____. *A Guide to the Work of Greene and Greene.* Salt Lake City: 1974.

_____. *Greene and Greene: Architecture as a Fine Art*. Salt Lake City: 1977.

_____. *Greene and Greene: Furniture and Related Designs*. Salt Lake City: 1979.

Margolies, John. "Roadside Mecca." *Progressive Architecture* 54 (November 1973): 123–28.

_____. *The End of the Road*. New York: 1980.

_____. *Signs of Our Time*. New York: 1993.

Marsh, Norman F. "Venice of America." *Architect and Engineer* 3 (January 1906): 19–25.

Marquez, Ernest. *Port of Los Angeles*. San Marino: 1976.

May, Cliff. *Sunset Western Ranch House*. Menlo Park: 1952.

Mays, Morrow. *Los Angeles*. New York: 1933.

McClurg, Verner B. *A Catalogue of Small Homes of California*. Hollywood: 1945.

McCoy, Esther. *Roots of California Contemporary Architecture*. Los Angeles: 1956.

_____. *Irving Gill, 1870–1936*. Los Angeles: 1958.

_____. *Five California Architects*. New York; Salt Lake City: 1960, 1975.

_____. *Richard Neutra*. New York: 1960.

_____. "Wilshire Boulevard," (with Marvin Rand) *Western Architect and Engineer* 222: 3 (September 1961): 25–51.

_____. *Modern California Houses: Case Study Houses, 1945–1962*. New York: 1962.

_____. "R. M. Schindler," *Lotus* 5 (1968): 92–105.

_____. *Craig Ellwood, Architect*. New York: 1968.

_____. *Vienna to Los Angeles: Two Journeys*. Santa Monica: 1979.

_____. "The Greenhouse: Energy Efficient Home in Venice, California." *Arts & Architecture* 1: 3 (1982): 45–59.

_____. "Charles Greene's Presence," *Review* (Southern California Chapter, Society of Architectural Historians) 1: 2: (Spring 1982): 1–2.

_____. *The Second Generation*. Salt Lake City: 1984.

McCoy, Esther and Evelyn Hitchcock. "The Ranch House," *Home Sweet Home, American Domestic Vernacular Architecture*. (edited by Charles W. Moore): 84–89. New York: 1983.

McGroarty, John Steven. *Los Angeles from the Mountains to the Sea*. Chicago: 1921.

McMillan, Elizabeth. *1929–1979: A Legend Still: Bullocks Wilshire*. Los Angeles: 1979.

_____. "Five Basic Classifications of Building Production." *Journal, Los Angeles Institute of Contemporary Art* 4 (Spring 1983): 43–49.

McMillan, Elizabeth and Leslie Heumann. "Old Venice-New Venice." *Newsletter* (Southern California Chapter, Society of Architectural Historians) 5 (April 1981): 1–6.

McPherson, William. *Homes of Los Angeles City and County*. Los Angeles: 1873.

McWilliams, Carey. *Southern California: An Island on the Land*. (Reprinted 1973 with new introduction). Salt Lake City: 1946.

Melnick, Robert and Mimi. *Manhole Covers of Los Angeles*. Los Angeles: 1974.

Mikosell, Stephen. *Historic Bridges of California*. Sacramento: 1990.

Millon, Wendy, et al. *The Best of Los Angeles: A Discriminating Guide*. Los Angeles: 1980.

Moore, Charles W. "You Have to Pay for the Public Life." *Perspecta* 9/10 (1966): 57–97.

_____. "Plug It in Rameses and See if It Lights Up." *Perspecta* 11 (1967): 33–43.

Moore, Charles W. and Gerald Allen. *Dimensions: Face, Shapes, and Scale in Architecture*. New York: 1976.

Moore, Charles W., Kathryn Smith, and Peter Becker, eds. *Home Sweet Home, American Domestic Vernacular Architecture*. New York: 1983.

Moore, Charles W., Peter Becker, and Regula Campbell. *Los Angeles: The City Observed—A Guide to its Architecture and Landscapes*. New York: 1984.

Moran, Thomas. "L.A. Pop Architecture." *Los Angeles Free Press* 13 (7–8 April 1976): 6–7.

Moran, Thomas and Tom Sewell. *Fantasy by the Sea: A Visual History of the American Venice*. Venice: 1978.

Morrow, Irving F. "The Work of Allison and Allison," *Pacific Coast Architect* 23 (February 1923): 15–21.

_____. "Recent Architecture of Allison and Allison," *Architect and Engineer* 133 (May 1938): 2–34.

Murmann, Eugene O. *California Gardens*. Los Angeles: 1915.

Murphy, Paul Edgar. *American Mercury* 13 (April 1928): 450–53.

Muschamp, Herbert. "The L.A. Museum of Contemporary Art: What's in a Name." *Architectural Record* 187 (May 1987): 83–85, 89.

Nadeau, Remi. *Los Angeles, from Mission to Modern City*. New York: 1960.

_____. *City Makers: The Story of Southern California's First Boom*. Los Angeles: 1965.

Nairn, Janet. "Frank Gehry: The Search for 'No Rules' Architecture." *Architectural Record* 159 (June 1976): 95–102.

Neff, Wallace. *Architecture in Southern California*. Chicago: 1964.

Neff, Wallace, Jr., (text by Alson Clark). *Wallace Neff: Architect of California's Golden Age*. Santa Barbara: 1986.

Neuerburg, Norman. *Herculaneum to Malibu*. Malibu: 1975.

Neutra, Richard J. "Architecture Conditioned by Engineering and Industry." *Architectural Record* 66 (September 1929): 272–74.

_____. *Life and Shape*. New York: 1962.

Newcomb, Rexford. *The Spanish House for America*. Philadelphia: 1927.

_____. *Mediterranean Domestic Architecture in the United States*. Cleveland: 1928.

_____. *The Old Mission and Historic Houses of California*. Philadelphia: 1925.

_____. *Spanish Colonial Architecture in the United States*. New York: 1937.

Newhall, Ruth W. *A California Legend: The Newhall Land and Farming Company*. Valencia: 1992.

Newman, David J., ed. *Postmodernism and Beyond: Architecture as the Critical Art of Contemporary Culture*. Irvine: 1989.

Newsom, Joseph Cather. *Artistic Buildings and Homes of Los Angeles*. San Francisco: 1888. (Reprinted 1981 with an introduction by Jenne C. Bennett, and a foreword by R. L. Samsell, Los Angeles.)

_____. *Picturesque and Artistic Homes and Buildings of California*. San Francisco: 1890.

_____. *Modern Homes of California*. San Francisco: ca. 1893.

Newsom, Samuel and Joseph Cather Newsom. *Picturesque California Homes*. (No. 1); *Picturesque California Homes*. (No. 2). San Francisco: 1884. (Reprinted in 1978 with an introduction by David Gebhard. Los Angeles.)

Nordhoff, Charles. *California for Pleasure and Residence*. New York: 1878.

Nunis, Doyce B., ed. *Los Angeles and its Environs in the Twentieth Century: A Bibliography of a Metropolis*. Los Angeles: 1973.

Nystrom, Richard Kent. *UCLA, An Interpretation Considering Architecture and Site*. Los Angeles: unpublished, 1968.

Oberhind, Robert. *The Chili Bowls of Los Angeles*. Los Angeles: 1977.

O'Conner, Ben H. "Planning the Supermarket." *Architect and Engineer* 146 (September 1941): 14–19.

O'Flaherty, Joseph. *An End and a Beginning: The South Coast and Los Angeles, 1850–1887*. Hicksville, N.Y.: 1977.

_____. *Those Powerful Years: The South Coast and Los Angeles, 1887–1917*. Hicksville, N.Y.: 1978.

O'Sullivan, Judy. *The Pasadena Playhouse*. Pasadena: 1992.

Ostroff, Roberta. "Up Against the Wall." *West Magazine, Los Angeles Times*. (31 January 1971): 22–27.

Ouellet, Philip J. *City Planning in Los Angeles: A History*. Los Angeles: 1964.

Owen, J. Thomas. "The Church by the Plaza: A History of the Pueblo Church of Los Angeles." *Historical Society of Southern California Quarterly* 42 (June 1960): 186–204.

Padilla, Victoria. *Southern California Gardens*. Berkeley: 1961.

Papademitriou, Peter. "Images from a Silver Screen." *Progressive Architecture* 57 (October 1976): 70–73.

Parker, Robert Miles. *L.A.* San Diego: 1984.

_____. "Evaluation; Utility and Fantasy in Los Angeles's 'Blue Whale'." *American Institute of Architects Journal* 67 (May 1974): 38–45.

_____. "Downtown Los Angeles: Guide Map." *Arts & Architecture* 1 (Fall 1981): 49–53.

_____. "MOCA Builds." *Arts & Architecture* 2 (1983): 31–35.

Peand, Frank F. (publisher) *Land of Heart's Desire—Southern California: Her People, Homes and Pleasures, Art and Architecture*. Los Angeles: 1911.

Pearce, Phyllis M.; Claire G. Redford; Mary Ann Rummel. *Founders and Friends*. Whittier: 1977.

Pelli, Cesar. "Tour Days in May." *Architecture and Urbanism* 45 (September 1974): 19.

Peterson, Kirk. "Eclectic Stucco," *Home Sweet Home, American Domestic Vernacular*

Architecture. (edited by Charles M. Moore); 112–21. New York: 1983.

Peters, William Fredrick. "Lockwood de Forest, Landscape Architect: Santa Barbara, California, 1896–1949." Master's thesis, University of California, Berkeley, 1980.

Phillips California Guide. Los Angeles: Phillips and Co., 1889.

Pildas, Ave. *Art Deco Los Angeles.* New York: 1979.

Pinney, Joyce. *A Pasadena Chronology, 1769–1977: Remembering—When—Where.* Pasadena: 1978.

Plagens, Peter. "Los Angeles: The Ecology of Evil." *Artforum* 11 (December 1972): 67–76.

———. "The L.A. Connections," *Architectural Design* 43 (August 1973): 571–74.

Polyzoides, Stefanos, Roger Sherwood, and James Tice, with photographs by Julius Shulman. *Courtyard Housing in Los Angeles.* Berkeley: 1982.

Powell, Lawrence Clark. *Land of Fiction.* Los Angeles: 1952.

Price, C. Matlock. "Panama-California Exposition: Bertram G. Goodhue and the Renaissance of Spanish Colonial Architecture." *Architectural Record* 37 (March 1915): 229–51.

Rand, Christopher. *Los Angeles, the Ultimate City.* New York: 1967.

Rand-McNally Guide to Los Angeles and Environs. New York: ca. 1925.

Rawls, James J. "The Californian Mission as Symbol and Myth." *California History* 71 (Fall 1992): 342–61.

Reavill, Gil. *Los Angeles.* Oakland: 1992.

Regan, Michael. *Mansions of Los Angeles.* Los Angeles: 1965.

———. *Mansions of Beverly Hills.* Los Angeles: 1966.

Rey, Felix. "A Tribute to the Mission Style." *Architect and Engineer* 76 (October 1924): 77–78.

Richards, Susan, and Sally R. Simms. "The California Post Offices of Allison and Allison," *Prologgue* 20 (Summer 1988): 100–117.

Richey, Elinor. *Remain to Be Seen: Historic Houses Open to the Public.* Berkeley: 1973.

Rickard, J. A. "Los Angeles—The Wonder City of America." *Engineering News Record* 91 (4 October 1923): 554–58.

Rider, Freemont. *Rider's California: A Guide Book for Travelers.* New York: 1925.

Robbins, George W. and Deming L. Tilton, eds. *Los Angeles: Preface to a Master Plan.* Los Angeles: 1941.

Robinson, Charles Mulford. "Los Angeles Parks," *House and Garden* 10 (September 1906): 114–15.

———. *The City Beautiful—Suggestions for Los Angeles.* Los Angeles: 1909.

Robinson, Paul, and Walter Reichardt. *Residential Architecture in Southern California.* Los Angeles: 1939.

Robinson, W. W. *What They Say About Los Angeles.* Pasadena: 1942.

———. *Panorama: A Picture-History of Southern California.* Los Angeles: 1953.

———. *Los Angeles: A Profile.* Norman, Okla: 1968.

———. *Los Angeles from the Days of the Pueblo: A Brief History and Guide to the Plaza Area.* Los Angeles: 1981.

Rolle, Andrew F. *California, A History.* New York: 1963.

Rubin, Barbara. "A Chronology of Architecture in Los Angeles," *Annals of the Association of American Geographers* 67 (1977): 4: 521–37.

Rubin, Barbara, Robert Carlton, and Arnold Rubin. *L.A. In Installments. Forest Lawn.* Santa Monica: 1979.

Ruscha, Edward. *Some Los Angeles Apartments.* Los Angeles: 1965.

———. *Every Building on the Sunset Strip.* Los Angeles: 1966.

———. *Thirty-four Parking Lots.* Los Angeles: 1967.

Sanford, Trent E. *The Architecture of the Southwest.* New York: 1950.

Saylor, Henry H. *Bungalows.* New York: 1917.

Scheid, Ann. *Pasadena: Crown of the Valley.* Northridge: 1986.

Schindler, Pauline, ed. "Special Issue Devoted to Modern Architecture in Southern California." *California Arts and Architecture* 47 (January 1935).

Schmidt-Brummer, Horst. *Venice, California: An Urban Fantasy.* New York: 1973.

Schuyler, Montgomery. "Round About Los Angeles." *Architectural Record* 24 (December 1908): 430–40.

Scott, Mcl. *Cities are for People.* Los Angeles: 1942.

_____. *Metropolitan Los Angeles: One Community*. Los Angeles: 1949.

Sears, Urmy. "A Community Approaches Its Ideal." *California Arts and Architecture* 38 (June 1930): 19–21, 70, 72.

Seidenbaum, Art. "Los Angeles: The New Neighborhood." *Home Magazine, Los Angeles Times* (31 December 1972): 6–12.

_____. *This Is California: Please Keep Out*. New York: 1975.

Seidenbaum, Art and John Malmin. Foreword by Will Durant. *Los Angeles 200: A Bicentennial Celebration*. New York: 1980.

Seims, Charles. *Trolly Days in Pasadena*. San Marino: 1982.

Sewell, Elaine K., Ken Tantanaka, and Katherine W. Rinne. "A. Quincy Jones: The Oneness of Architecture," *Process: Architecture* 41 (1983).

Sexton, Randolph W. *Spanish Influence on American Architecture and Decoration*. New York: 1927.

_____. "A New Yorker's Impression of California Architecture." *California Arts and Architecture* 39 (October 1930): 23–25, 64.

Sheine, Judith. "Los Angeles Builds on Transportation." *Architecture* 82 (August 1993): 93–99.

Shinn, Charles. *Pacific Coast Rural Handbook*. San Francisco: 1878.

Shulman, Julius. "The Architect's Perspective." *Architectural Digest* (May–June 1962): 72–79.

_____. *Cultural-Historic Monuments*. Los Angeles: 1968.

_____. "A Photographer's Perspective on Neutra." *American Institute of Architects Journal* 66 (March 1977): 54–61.

Sillo, Terry and John Manson. *Around Pasadena: An Architectural Study of San Marino, Sierra Madre, and Arcadia*. Pasadena: 1976.

Smith Elizabeth, ed. *Blueprints for Modern Living: History and Legacy of the Case Study Houses*. Los Angeles, Cambridge: 1989.

Smith, Jack. *The Big Orange*. Los Angeles: 1976.

_____. *Jack Smith's L.A.* New York: 1980.

Smith, Kathryn. "Frank Lloyd Wright, Hollyhock House and Olive Hill, 1914–1924." *Journal of the Society of Architectural Historians* 38 (March 1979): 15–33.

_____. *Hollyhock House and Olive Hill*. New York: 1992.

Smith, Sarah Bixby. *Adobe Days*. Fresno: 1925, revised 1974.

Solomon, Barbara Stauffacher. *Good Mourning California*. New York: 1992.

Spalding, William A., comp. *History and Reminiscences: Los Angeles, City and County, California*. Los Angeles: 1931.

Stacy-Judd, Robert B. "Some Local Examples of Mayan Adaptions." *Architect and Engineer* 116 (February 1934): 21–30.

Starr, Kevin. *Americans and the California Dream*. New York. 1973, Reprint 1980, Salt Lake City.

_____. *Inventing the Dream: California Through the Progressive Era*. New York: 1985.

_____. *Material Dreams: Southern California Through the 1920s*. New York: 1990.

Steele, James. *Barnsdale House: Frank Lloyd Wright*. London: 1992.

_____. *Los Angeles Architecture: The Contemporary Condition*. London and San Francisco: 1993.

Stein, Achva Benzinberg, and Jacqueline Claire Moxley. "In Defense of Nonnative: The Case of the Eucalyptus," *Landscape Journal* 11 (Spring 1992): 35–50.

Stephens, James C. "The Development of County Planning in California." Los Angeles: Master's thesis, University of California, 1937.

Strand, Janann. *A Greene and Greene Guide*. Pasadena: 1974.

Streatfield, David. "The Evolution of the Southern California Landscape: 1. Settling into Arcadia," *Landscape Architecture* 66 (January 1976): 39–78.

_____. "The Evolution of the California Landscape: 2. Arcadia Compromised," *Landscape Architecture* 66 (March 1976): 117–27.

_____. "The Evolution of the California Landscape: 3. The Great Promotions," *Landscape Architecture*. 66 (May 1977): 229–39.

_____. "The Evolution of the California Landscape: 4. Suburbia at the Zenith," *Landscape Architecture* 67 (September 1977): 417–24.

_____. *California Gardens: Creating a New Eden*. New York: 1993.

Suisman, Douglas R. *Los Angeles Boulevard: Eight X-Rays of the Body Public*. Los Angeles: 1989.

Sutro, Dirk. *West Coast Waves*. New York: 1993.

Sweeney, Robert L. *Wright in Hollywood*. New York: 1992.

Thompson and West, (publisher). *History of Los Angeles County*. (Reprint, 1959), Berkeley: 1880.

Tomlinson, Russell P. "Mobile Home Parks as a Settlement Type in Los Angeles, Orange, and Riverside Counties." Master's thesis, California State University, Los Angeles, 1968.

Torrance, Bruce. *Hollywood: The First 100 Years*. Hollywood: 1979.

Tracy, Robert Howard. *John Parkinson and the Beaux-Arts City Beautiful Movement in Downtown Los Angeles 1894–1935*. Ph.D. thesis, University of California, Los Angeles, 1982.

Trillin, Calvin. "Simon Rodia: Watts Towers," in *Naives and Visionaries*. Walker Art Center, Minneapolis: 1974: 21–31.

Truman, Ben. C. *Semi-Tropical California*. San Francisco: 1874.

_____. *Homes and Happiness in the Golden State of California*. San Francisco: 1885.

Van Dyke, Theodore S. *Southern California*. New York: 1886.

Van Petten, O. W. "Westwood: The Case of the Bartered Bride," *West Magazine, Los Angeles Times* (26 October 1969): 23–33.

Voelkel, Richard. *Architecture: A Window on the Past*. Santa Ana: 1988.

Walker, Derek, ed. *Los Angeles: Architectural Design Profile—AD/USC Look at L.A.* London: 1981.

Warner, Charles Dudley. *Our Italy*. New York: 1891.

Warren, Violet Lockhart. "The Eucalyptus Crusade," *Historical Society of Southern California Quarterly* 51 (March 1961): 31–41.

Weaver, John D. *El Pueblo Grande*. Los Angeles: 1973.

Weber, Msgr. Francis J. *Saint Vibiana's Cathedral*. Los Angeles: 1976.

Weitzc, Karen. *California's Mission Revival*. Los Angeles: 1983.

Welch, Ileana. *Historic-Cultural Monuments as Designated by the Cultural Heritage Board, Los Angeles*. Los Angeles: 1980.

West, Nathanael. *The Day of the Locust*. New York: 1950.

Whitnall, Gordon. "Tracing the Development of Planning in Los Angeles." *Annual Report of the Los Angeles Planning Commission*. Los Angeles: 1930.

Whittlesey, Charles F. "Concrete Construction." *Architect and Engineer*. (December 1905): 43–47.

_____. "Reinforced Concrete Construction— Why I Believe in It." *Architect and Engineer* 12 (March 1908): 35–57.

Wiley, Stephen. "Los Angeles: 200 Years, 200 Buildings." *L.A. Architect* 6 (September 1976).

Williams, Paul R. *The Small Home of Tomorrow*. Hollywood: 1945.

_____. *New Homes of Today*. Hollywood: 1946.

Wilson, William. "The Colossus of the Roads (The Billboard as Pop Art)." *West Magazine, Los Angeles Times*. (31 December 1970): 14–21.

_____. "Where Has All the Neon Gone?" *West Magazine, Los Angeles Times*. (19 April 1970): 8–11.

_____. "The L.A. Fine Arts Squad: Venice in the Snow and Other Visions." *Art News* 72 (Summer 1973): 28–29.

Winter, Robert W. "The Arroyo Culture." *California Design 1910*. Pasadena. 1974, Reprint 1980, Salt Lake City.

_____. *The California Bungalow*. Los Angeles: 1980.

_____. "The Architecture of the City Eclectic." *California History* 60 (Spring 1981): 72–75.

_____. "The Common American Bungalow," *Home Sweet Home, American Domestic Vernacular Architecture*. (edited by Charles W. Moore): 98–101. New York: 1983.

Withey, Henry F. and Elsie R. *Biographical Dictionary of American Architects*. (Reprint 1970), Los Angeles: 1956.

Wolfe, Tom. "I Drove Around Los Angeles and It's Crazy: The World is Upside Down." *West Magazine, Los Angeles Times*. (1 December 1968): 18–22, 24, 27.

Wood, Ruth K. *The Tourist's California*. Los Angeles: 1915.

Woodbridge, Sally. *California Architecture: Historic American Building Survey*. San Francisco: 1988.

_____. *Bernard Maybeck Visionary Architect*. New York: 1992.

Woollett, William L. "Los Angeles Landmarks." *Historic Preservation* 18 (July–August 1966): 160–63.

Works Progress Administration (WPA). *California: A Guide to the Golden State.* New York: 1939.

_____. *A Guide to the City of Los Angeles.* New York: 1941.

Wurman, Richard Saul. *L.A./Access.* Los Angeles: 1982.

Yoch, James J. *Landscaping the American Dream.* New York: 1989.

Yost, Lloyd Morgan. "Greene and Greene of Pasadena." *American Institute of Architects Journal.* (September 1950): 115–25.

Young, Betty Lou and Randy Young. *Rustic Canyon and the Story of the Uplifters.* Santa Monica: 1975.

_____. *Pacific Palisades, Where the Mountains Meet the Sea.* Pacific Palisades: 1985.

_____. *Street Names of Pacific Palisades.* Pacific Palisades: 1990.

Young, Robert B. *Architecture of Robert B. Young.* Los Angeles: 1905.

Zarakov, Barry Neil. *California Planned Communities of the 1920s.* Master's thesis, University of California, Santa Barbara, 1977.

Zierer, Clifford M., ed. "San Fernando, A Type of Southern California Town." *Annuals of the Association of American Geographers* 24 (1934): 1–28.

A Design Group (David Cooper, Michael W. Folonis, George Blain, and Richard Clemenson), 34
Condominium Town Houses, 1979, (#17)34
Condominium Town Houses, 1980, (#26)35
Condominium Town Houses, 1981, (#18)34 (see also **Janotta-Breska Associates**)
Aaron Brothers Building, c. 1928, (#69)158
Abbey Building, 217
Abell, Thornton M., 4, 13, 17, 23, 46, 57, 96, 98, 99, 102, 107, 111
Abell House, 1937, (#8)13
Abell Office Building, 1954, (#4)96
Beck House, 1955, (#11)102
Haines House, 1943, (#9)13
Haines House, 1951, (#24)17
LeBrun House, 1963, (#6)4
Leslie House, 1950, (#12)96
Maslon House, 1970, (#8)111
Miller House, 1948, (#1)57
Newfield House, 1961, (#39)99
Pray House, 1969, (#4)57
Rich House, 1968, (#26)98
Shonerd House, 1935, 46
Siskin Companies Office Building, 1972, (#11)107
Siskin House, 1966, (#38)99
Ullman House, 1955, (#15)23
Adams, Charles Gibbs (landscape architect), xx, 77, 123, 345
Robinson House and Garden, 1911, 1924, (#13)123
Workman House ("Shadow Ranch"), 1869-72, (#3)345
Adams, George, 321
St. Robert Bellarmine Church, 1939, (#7)321
Adams, George G.; Walter S. Davis; Ralph C. Flewelling; Eugene Weston, Jr.; Lewis E. Weston; Lloyd Wright, 258; 298
Aliso Village, 1941-53, (#1a)258
Ramona Gardens Public Housing, 1940-41, (#5)298
Adams, William, 37
Adaori, Kazumi and Dike Naggana, 250
Fort Moore Pioneer Memorial, 1949-57, (#1)250
Adelman, Abraham A., S. Tildern Norton, and David C. Allison, 203
Wilshire Boulevard Temple, 1922-29, (#35)203
Adlai E. Stevenson House, 1895, (#17)269

Administration Building, Los Angeles County Hospital, c. 1912, (#2)298
Adobe Los Cerritos, 1844, (#4)79
Adobe San Rafael, 1865, (31)320
Aeroscopic Building, c. 1935, (#38)320
Ahmanson Center, 245
Ain, Gregory, xxi, xxii, xxiii, 82, 86, 122, 123, 136, 139, 140, 148, 169, 178, 179, 182, 188, 292, 328, 334, 335, 361
Ain House, 1941, (#22)139
Beckman House, 1938, (#10)188
Brownfield Medical Building, 1938, (#10)82
Byler House, 1937, (#7)292
Daniels House, 1939, (#9)178
Dunsmuir Apartment Building, 1937, (#12)87
Edwards House, 1936, (#9)169
Elterman House, 1961, (#14)335
Ernest House, 1937, (#8)169
Feldman House, 1953, (#41)182
Hay House, 1939, (#3)328
Lewin House, 1962, (#4)361
Mesner House, 1951, (#8)334
Tierman House, 1938-39, (#14)179
Vorkapich Garden House, 1938, (#7)123
Ain, Johnson and Day, 44, 83, 96, 125, 174, 180, 334, 367
Avenel Housing, 1948, (#25)180
Cole House, 1948, (#31)174
Mar Vista Houses, 1946-48, (#48)44
Miller House, 1948, (#25)125
One-Hundred Fifty-Third Street School Building, 1957, (#15)83
Orans House, 1941, (#15)179
Ralphs House, 1950, (#2)367
Shairer House, 1949, (#5)96
Ainsworth, Robert H., 373, 382, 394, 417
Apartment Building, 1926, (#63)382
Grover Cleveland Elementary School, 1934, (#40)373
House, 1948, (#17)417
Pasadena Humane Society Building, 1932, (#8)394
"Alamo, The" c. 1929, (#4)422
Alexander, Robert E., 89, 90, 218, 246, 274, 348
Baldwin Hills Shopping Center, 1954, (#25)89
Bunker Hill Towers, 1968, (#1)218
University Elementary School, 1948; 1950, (#27)90
Alhambra, 300-303
Alhambra Fire Station and City Administration Building, c. 1938, (#8)303

Alhambra Women's Club, c. 1915, (#2)302
Aliso Apartments, 258
Allen, F. S., 432
Allen, William, and W. George Lutzi, (#18)283, 322
Burbank City Hall, 1940-41, (#8)322
Allied Architects, 246, 256
Patriotic Hall, 1926, (#6)256
Allied Architects of Long Beach (Hugh Gibbs and Donald Gibbs; Frank Holmelka and Associates; Killingsworth, Brady and Associates; Kenneth S. Wing, Sr., and Kenneth S. Wing, Jr.), 71
Long Beach City Hall and Public Library, 1973-76, (#2)71
Allied Architects of Los Angeles, 148, 242, 246, 298
Hall of Justice Building, 1925, (#8)246
Los Angeles County/USC Medical Center, 1928-33 and later, (#1)298
Allison and Rible, 445
Claremont-McKenna, 1948 and later, (#19)445
Allison, David C., 242
Allison, John and David C. Allison, 51, 55, 106, 115, 116, 117, 118, 129, 156, 171, 195, 202, 215, 222, 228, 236
Administration Building, UCLA, 1937, (#13)118
Beverly Hills Post Office Building, 1932-33, (#21)129
"Dome, The" (#3)106
First Congregational Church, 1930-32, (#37)215
First Unitarian Church, 1930, (#26)202
Friday Morning Club Building, 1923-24, (#21)222
Kerckoff Hall (UCLA), 1930, (#6)117
Malaga Cove School, 1926, (#12)55
Physics-Biology Building (UCLA), 1928-29, (#4)117
Redondo Beach High School, 1931 and later, (#12)51
Royce Hall, 1928-29, (#1)116
Southern California Edison Building, 1930-31, (#39)228
Thirteenth Church of Christ, Scientist, 1930, (#23)171
U.S. Post Office, Hollywood Branch, 1937, (#60), 156
Wilshire United Methodist Church, 1924, (#50)195
Women's Athletic Club, 1924, (#87)236
Women's Gymnasium, 1932, (#11)117
Alpaugh, Norman W., 215
Town House, The, 1928, (#36)215

Altadena, 409-411
Alvarado Terrace Houses, (#5)208
Ambassador College, 366
Ambassador Foundation Campus,
(#55)381
Andersen, Tim, 379, 381, 383, 386, 396
Anderson, Andy, 341
Anderson House, Andy, 1937-38,
(#7)341
Anderson, Edward O., 112
*The Los Angeles Temple of The Church
of Jesus Christ of Latter-day Saints,
(Mormon), 1955*, (#17)112
Anderson House, 1922, 17
Andre, Steve, (see **Urban Forms**)
Andres Pico Adobe, 352
Angelino Heights, 183-85
Angels Flight, 1900, (#57)233
Anshen and Allen, 116
Biochemistry Building (UCLA), 116
Anthony and Langford, 310
Library, 1976, (#3)310
Arcadia, 427-429
Architects Collaborative (John Hayes),
227
801 Tower, 1991, (#32)227
Archsystems, 218
Sheraton Grande Hotel, 1978-83,
(#3)218
Armet, Louis, and Eldon Davis, 88, 158,
180
Carolina Motel Building, 1959, (#66)158
Conrad's Drive-In, 1958, (#26)180
Pann's Restaurant, 1958, (#22)88
**Armstrong and Sharfman (landscape
architects),** 5
Pepperdine University, 1971-73, (#12)5
Arroyo Guild of Fellow Craftsmen, 285
Atchinson, John, 416
House, 1929, (#6)416
August Furst Castle, 357
Austin Company, 405
Austin Automobile Showroom, c. 1927,
(#10)405
Austin, Field, and Fry, 153, 245, 246
*Hall of Administration Building, 1956-
61,* (#6)246
Hollywood Masonic Temple, 1922,
(#28)153
Los Angeles County Courthouse, 1958,
(#4)245
Austin, John C., xix, 118, 242, 259, 270,
405
*Grace Methodist Episcopal Church,
1906,* (#10)259
*Holliston Avenue United Methodist
Church, 1899,* (#11)405
House, 1904-5, (#19)270
**Austin, John C. and A. M. Edelman, G.
Albert Lansburgh,** 270
*Shrine Civic Auditorium (Al Malaikah
Temple), 1920-26,* (#24)270
Austin, John C. and F. M. Ashley, 171,
195, 290, 429
Arroyo Seco Bank Building, 1926,
(#28)290

*Business Administration and Economics
Building (UCLA), 1948,* (#15)118
*Griffith Park Observatory and
Planetarium, 1935,* (#22)171
Memorial Library, 1930, (#37)195
Monrovia High School, 1928, (#1)429
**Austin, John C., John and Donald
Parkinson, and Albert C. Martin,** 246
Los Angeles City Hall, 1926-28,
(#10)246
**Austin, John C., Sumner Spaulding,
Earl Heitschmidt, and Henry C.
Newton,** 258
Pico Gardens Public Housing, 1941-42,
(#1d)258
Austin, Mary, 285
Austin, W. Horace, 69, 70, 72, 79 (see
also **MacDowell, J. Harold**)
City Beautiful City Hall, 1921, 1934, 69,
70
*Farmers and Merchants Bank Building,
1922,* (#9)72
Long Beach Airport Terminal, 1940-41,
(#5)79
Automobile Service Garage, c. 1925,
(#47)44
Avila Adobe, c. 1818, (#3)251
Ayers, Dr. Samuel, 427
Aztec Hotel, 429
Azusa, 432

B.H.A. Associates, 217
BPO Elks Monument, c. 1910, 34
Babcock, Everett Phipps, 400
Casa Torre Garden Court, 1927,
(#49)400
Singer Building, 1926, (#43)400
Baca, Judy, 327
"The Great Wall" (murals), 1974-83,
(#9)327
*Bailey House (The Old Ranch House),
1887,* (#7)306
**Bailey, Van E. and William Gray
Purcell,** 387
Prospect Houses, 1948, (#17)387
**Bakewell, John, Jr. and Arthur Brown,
Jr.,** 366, 396
Pasadena City Hall, 1925-27, (#29)396
Balch and Stanberry, 261, 440
Boulevard Theater, c. 1937, (#28)261
Fox Theater, 1931, (#16)440
Balch, W. Cliff, 192
El Rey Theater, c. 1928, (#32)192
Baldwin, E. J. "Lucky," 427, 428
Baldwin Hills, Culver City, 84-93
Baldwin Motel, c. 1934, (#46)44
Ballin, Hugo, xxxiv, 171
*Griffith Park Observatory and
Planetarium, 1935,* (#22)171
Banning Homes, 1942, 62
Banning House, 1864, (#6)65
Banning, Phineas, 61, 153
Barber, Thomas B., 150, 400
First United Methodist Church, 1926,
(#42)400
First United Methodist Church, 1929,
(#16)150

Barcume and King, 164
House, 1937-39, (#9)164
Barker and Ott, 74, 321
Jefferson-Bellarmine High School, 1945,
(#7)321
*Saint Anthony's Roman Catholic
Church, 1952,* (#30)74
Barker, M. L. and G. Lawrence, 48, 97
*Mount St. Mary's College, 1939-40 and
later,* (#18)97
Sacred Heart Chapel, 1953, 48
Barlow, Fred Jr. (landscape architect),
(see also **Bashford, Katherine and
Frederick Barlow, Jr.)** 82
**Barlow, Fred and Fred Edmunson
(landscape architects),** (#26)89
Barlow-Saxton Emplacements, 1916, 63
Barmore House, c. 1902, (#5a)208
**Barnes, Edward Larabee; John M. Y.
Lee and Partners with Gruen
Associates,** 107
*Armand Hammer Museum of Art and
Culture, 1989-90,* (#8)107
Barnett, Robert, (#23)
Sunset Car Wash, 1972, (#23)140
Barnsdall Park, 171
**Barton, Arthur G. (landscape archi-
tect),** 345
**Bashford, Katherine (landscape archi-
tect),** xx, 378, 391
**Bashford, Katherine and Frederick
Barlow, Jr. (landscape architects),** 83,
258, 280, 298, 417
Aliso Village, 1941-53, (#1a)258
Avalon Gardens, 1941-42, (#2)280
Bourne House, 1937, (#18)417
Pepperdine College (old campus), 1937,
(#12)83
*Ramona Gardens Public Housing, 1940-
41,* (#5)298
Batchelder, Ernest A., 378
Batchelder House, 1909, 1913, (#27)378
Bates, Richard M., Jr., 214
Westlake Theater, 1926, (#30)214
Batey-Mack, 381
Condominium, 1982, (#59)381
Bath Building, 217
Baume, Edward James, 28
Packard Show Rooms, 1928, (#53)28
Beachey, Catharine S., 340
Beck, Marvin and Santini Bouchard,
128
Gallery Building, 1972-73, 128
Becket, Ellerbe (Graeme Morland), 274,
327
DWP, Distribution Headquarters, 1992,
(#8)327
*Helen Topping Architecture and Fine
Arts Library Addition, 1989,* 274
Becket, Ellerbe (Mehrdad Yazdani), 256
*Central Distribution Center, Department
of Water and Power, 1988-89,* (#10)256
Becket, Welton and Associates, 29, 32,
46, 47, 115, 117, 118, 134, 144, 155, 242,
244, 248, 280, 345, 348, 440
Ackerman Union Building, 1959-60,
(#7)117

Beverly Center, 1982, (#47)144
Bullock's Northridge, 1972, 348
Bullock's Woodland Hills, 1972-73,
(#5)345
*Capitol Records Tower Building, 1954-
56,* (#48)155
Colorado Place, 1981-84, (#59)29
High-rise Dormitories, 1959-64, 115
Los Angeles Music Center, 1964-69,
(#3)244
Northrop Complex, 1982-83, (#10)134
Parker Center, 1955, (#13)248
Pomona Central Library, 1965,
(#20)440
*Pomona City Hall and Council
Chambers, 1969,* (#19)440
Santa Monica Civic Auditorium, 1959,
(#4)32
Schoenberg Hall, 1955, (#17)118
**Becket, Welton Associates (Robert
Taylor),** xxiv, 227
*O'Melveny and Myers Office Building,
1982,* (#34)227
Becket, William S., 97, 142
Shoor House, 1952, (#20)97
William S. Beckett Office Building, 1950,
(#33)142
Beelman, Claude, 93, 106, 156, 188, 213,
233, 236
*A. J. Heinsbergen Decorating Company,
1925,* (#5)188
Bankers Building, 1930, (#61)233
Eastern Columbia Building, 1929,
(#85)236
Garfield Building, 1928-30, (#64)233
*MGM Studios (Goldwyn Studios)
Building, 1938-39,* (#43)93
Ninth and Broadway Building, 1929,
(#84)236
*U.S. Post Office, Hollywood Branch,
1937,* (#60), 156
Woodbury College Building, 1937,
(#22)213
Bel Air, 9, 101-4
Bell, Alphonzo Sr., 9, 94, 101
Bellflower, 313
Bemis, Kenneth, 234
White Log Coffee Shop, 1932, (#67)234
Bender, Rebecca L., xxvi, 43, 100, 116,
117, 335
Ackerman Union Addition, 116
Armacost Duplex, 1989-90, (#50)100
Bernstein House, 1985, (#12)335
Brenta Apartments, 1990, (#38)43
Gardner House, 1992, (#39)43
South Venice Apartments, 1991, 43
Benedict, Edson A., 122
Benker, G. E. (engineer), 107
*Distribution Station #28, Department of
Water and Power, 1945-46,* (#12)107
Bennett, Arthur A., 428
Bennett, Cyril, 396
Pasadena Winter Garden, 1940,
(#17)396
Bennett and Haskell, 366, 394, 395, 399,
401
California State Armory, 1932, 395

First Trust Building, 1928 (#51)401
Kinney-Kendall Building, 1925, (#12)395
Masonic Temple, 1926, (#37)399
Parish House and rectory, 1930,
(#38)399
*Pennsylvania Oil and Tire Warehouse,
1930,* (#2)394
United California Bank, 1929, (#11)394
Bennett, Parsons, and Frost, 59, 366
Wrigley Monument, 1924, (#3)59
Benton, Arthur B., xvii, xxvii, 214, 260,
264, 299, 358, 361, 242, 428, 435
Anoakia, 1910, 428
Butts House, 1894, (#10)431
Church of the Advent, 1925, (#1)264
Epiphany Chapel Sanctuary, 1913,
(#9)299
Holy Trinity Episcopal Church, 1910,
435
Ivy Chapel, 1903, 260
*Mary Andrews Clark Memorial Home
(YWCA), 1912-13,* (#27)214
McGroarty House, 1923, (#1)358
San Gabriel Civic Auditorium, 1923-27,
(#9)424
Wallace House, 1911, (#3)361
Bergstrom, Edwin, 366, 398
Pasadena Civic Auditorium, 1932,
(#34)398
Berkus, Barry, 354
Bertoia, Harry, xxiv
Betsford House, c. 1890, (#1)183
Bevash, Jack, 342
Beverly Hills Hotel, 1912, 122
Beverly Hills, North, 121-26
Beverly Hills, South 126-132
B.H.A. Associates, 217
Bird, Mr., 9
House, c. 1935, (#2)9
Bishop, H. W., 134
Bixby, B. D., 153
Rexall Drug Company Building, 1935,
(#36)153
Black, Milton J., 17, 111, 145, 153, 174,
191, 202
Apartment Building, 1936, (#27)202
Apartment Building, 1938, (#23)191
El Cadiz Apartment Building, 1936,
(#30)153
Cernitz House, 1938, (#29)17
House, 1936, (#53)145
Ulm House, 1937, (#30)174
*Westwood-Ambassador Apartments,
1940,* (#9)111
Blain, George (see **A Design Group**)
*B'Nai David Synagogue and School
Building, c. 1929,* (#9)87
**Blake + Au (Perry Austin Blake and
Alan Kong Au),** 37
Blanton, John, 51, 55
Davidheiser/Kroll House, 1988, (#4)51
Garmire/Russell House, 1989, (#9)51
Marsh House, 1974, (#1)51
McNulty House, 1975, 51
Provost House, 1975, (#2)51
Roy Condominiums, 1991, (#5)51
Shelton Apartments, 1974, 51

Shelton Apartments #5, 1988, (#3)51
Stannard House, 1974, (#17)55
"Blarney Castle," c. 1925, (#4)359
Blick, Joseph J., 380, 390, 401
Lunkenheimer House, 1906, (#20)390
Post House #2, 1903, (#44)380
Scottish Rite Cathedral, 1924, (#58)401
Blick, J. J.; The Postle Company, 360
Newcomb House "El Roble," 1910,
1922, (#14)360
Bliss, G. S. (contractor), 388
Flintoft House, c. 1910, (#3)388
Blood House, 1911, (#13)390
**Blume, Louis and Merrill Butler (engi-
neers),** 240
6th Street Viaduct Bridge, 1932,
(#118)240
Bobrow, Thomas and Associates, 146,
404
*Senior Citizens Housing Project, 1978-
80,* (#62)146
Borghlum, Gutzon, 316
Borgmeyer, Edward J., 200
Forum Theater Building, 1921-24,
(#15)200
Bosworth, B. H., 335
Zimbalist Apartment Building, 1973,
(#22)335
Boyd, Visscher, 179
Tierman House, 1938-39, (#14)179
Boyle Heights, 257-62
Bradbeer and Ferris, 270, 382
Blankenhorn-Lamphear House, 1893,
(#65)382
House, 1890, (#21)270
House, 1891, (#22)270
Bradbeer, James H., 285, 396
McClure House 1889, (#2)285
Stoutenburgh House, c. 1887, (#23)396
Bradbury, 432
Brent, Goldman, Robbins, and Brown,
102
Mirman School, 1972-73, (#6)102
Brentwood, 94-100
Breur, Marcel, 351
*Torrington Manufacturing Company,
1953,* (#11)351
Brockway, L. C., 376
House, 1927, (#11)376
Brown, Carroll H., 267
Stimson House, 1891, (#1)267
Browne, Clyde, 285, 286
Abbey San Encino, 1909-25, (#7)286
Brown's Burger Bar, c. 1940, 348
Brugen, Coosje van, 38
Bruner, E. L., 91
Helms Bakery Building, 1930, (#33)91
Brunnier, H. H., 281
Owens-Illinois Pacific Building, 1937,
(#5)281
Bryant, Leland A., 137, 141
Romanesque Villa Apartments, 1928,
(#26d)141
*Sunset Tower Apartment Building, 1929-
31,* (#10)137
Buchanan and Brockway, 400
First Congregational Church, 1904,

1916, (#39)400
Buchanan, C. W., 395
Entrance to Old Pasadena Public
Library, 1887, (#14)395
Buff and Hensman, 296, 369, 378, 380
House, 1983, (#24)378
Paxson House, 1971, (#8)296
Vista Grande Townhouses, 1981,
(#50)380
Buff, Straub, and Hensman, 410, 416
Case Study House #20, 1958, (#9)410
Thompson House, 1958, (#3)416
Bulfinch, Charles, xvi
Burbank, 321-24
Burke, Kober, Nicolais, and Archuleta,
194
AVCO Savings Building, 1973, (#45)194
Burnham, Daniel H. and Company, xix,
362
Mount Wilson Observatory, 1913
(#10)362
Burnham, F. P., 400, 445
Carnegie Building, 445
First Church of Christ Scientist, 1909,
(#44)400
Burns, Silas R. 287, 290
Ebell Club, 1912, (#15)287
Southwest Museum, 1910-14, and later,
(#25)290
Burr House, 1893, (#11)431
Burrell and Company (builders), 396
Don Carlos Court, 1927, (#22)396
Burroughs, Edgar Rice, 338
Burton, Harold W., 200
Wilshire Ward Chapel, Church of Jesus
Christ of Latter-day Saints (Mormon),
1928, (#14)200
Burton, J. Lee, 95
Chapel, 1900, 94
Street-car Station, c. 1900, 95
Bushnell, David S., 306, 307
Wardman Theater, 1932, (#11)307
Whittier Theater, 1928, 306
Butler, Merrill (engineer), 240
4th Street Viaduct Bridge, 1930-31,
(#117)240
Byers, John, xix, 11, 12, 20, 22, 23, 24,
26, 28, 99, 361
Armstrong-Cobb House, 1926, (#16)23
Boswell House, 1925, 24
Bradbury House, 1992, (#1)12
Bundy House, 1925, (#6)22
Byers House, 1917, (#24)23
Byers House, 1924, (#4)22
Carrillo House, 1925, (#14)23
Flint Houses, 1928, (#57)28
Fuller House, 1920-22, (#12)23
Gorham-Holliday House, 1923-24,
(#21)23
Laidlow House, 1924, (#13)23
MacBennel House, 1921-22, (#17)23
Miles Memorial Playhouse, 1929,
(#42)26
Netcher House, 1926, 28
Thompson House, 1924-25, (#3)22
Tinglof House, 1925-26, (#7)22
Zimmer House, 1924, (#5)22

Byers, John, and Edla Muir, xxii, 10, 11,
18, 98, 100
Barclay House, c. 1927, (#38)18
Boland House, c. 1925, (#41)100
Hamilton House, 1931-33, (#42)100
House, c. 1925, (#34)18
House, c. 1935, (#9)10
Kenaston House, 1936-37, (#31)18
Kerr House, 1930, (#45)100
Murray House, c. 1935, (#46)100
Stedman House, 1935-36, (#43)100
Temple House, 1935-36, (#28)98
Byles, H. Douglas and Eugene Weston
III, 373
Byles and Weston House, 1950,
(#41)373

Calabasas, 340-41
Calabasas Park, 340
California Institute of Technology, 1908-
present, 403-4
California State Polytechnic University,
Pomona, (#21)440
California State University at Long Beach,
1949 and later, (#12)77
California Veteran's Building, 71
Callister, Warren, 399
Cameron, William, 123
Menzies House, 1926, (#4)123
Campbell and Campbell (landscape
architects), xx, 11, 13, 32, 60, 93, 130,
224, 398, 427
Beverly Hills Civic Center, 1981-92,
(#23)130
Cabrillo Mole Terminal Complex, 1993-
94, (#7)60
Carousel Park, 1982-86, (#1b)32
Pasadena Police Department Building,
1989-90, (#30)398
Sony Pictures Entertainment, Child Care
Center, 1993-94, (#41)93
Sony Pictures Entertainment, Digital
Production Building, 1993-94, (#41)93
St. Matthew's Episcopal Church, 1982-
83, (#12)11
Cannon, Georgius Y., 319
Glendale Second Ward, Church of Jesus
Christ of Latter-day Saints (Mormon),
1937, (28)319
Canoga Park, 344-46
Canyon Elementary School, 1894, (#4)13
Capital Mill, 1884, (#17)253
Carde/Killefer, 34
Conference Room, 1982, (#21)34
Carleton Hotel, 1924, 240
Carnation Research Building, 1952-53,
(#7)350
Carney's Express Restaurant, c. 1978, 332
Carney's Restaurant Building, (#9)137
Carol, Claudia (see also **Chase, John**),
26
Jacobs Studio, 1984, (#37)26
Carr, John, 376
John Carr Real Estate Company
Building, 1950, (#5)376
Carrol Avenue, 183-85

Carter, Nathaniel C., 424
Carter, Robert Herrick (landscape
architect), 80, 133, 134
Century Plaza Hotel, 1966, (#3)133
Century Plaza Towers, 1969-75, (#5)134
Fox Plaza, 1985-87, (#2)133
Inglewood Civic Center, 1973, (#5)80
Carthay Circle, 134
Casa de Jose Perez, "Adobe Flores,"
1839, 1849-50, (#25)388
Casa San Pedro, 1823, 63
Case House, 1887, (#18)431
Castle Miniature Golf Course, (#23)336
Castle Park Recreation Center, 1978,
(#24)69
Cathedral of SS Pietro e Paolo, 116
Caudill, Rowlett, and Scott, 444
Four College Science Center, 1970,
(#10)444
Caughey, James H., 10
Caughey, Milton H., 96, 164
Garred House, 1949, (#5)164
Goss House, 1950, (#8)96
Centinela Park, 80
Centinela Ranch House (Ygnacio
Marchado Adobe), 1844, (#2)80
Central Hollywood, 147-162
Central Office of Architecture (Ron
Golan, Eric Kahn, Russell Thomsen), 43
Brig Restaurant, 1990-91, (#41)43
Century City, 133-34
Chambers and Hubbard, 294
Chambers, H. C., 294
Chambers House, 1923, (#5)296
Chandler, Dorothy Pavilion, 245
Chapel of the Pines, 1903, 206
Chapman Building, 204
Charles E. Chapman Building, c. 1923,
(#83)236
Charles House, 1893, (#12)308
Charlotte Perkins Gilman House, c. 1900,
(#39)373
Charlton, James, Wayne R. Williams
and Associates, and Garrett Eckbo
(landscape architects), 97
Mutual Housing Association
Community, 1947-50, (#21)97
Charnock Block, 1888, (#103)238
Chase, Clyde, 143
Chase, John (see also **Carol, Claudia**),
xxiv, 26, 126, 135, 148
Jacobs Studio, 1984, (#37)26
Chateau Marmont, 141
Chatsworth, 347
Chemical and Physical Testing
Laboratories, City of Long Beach, c. 1915,
(#13)72
Cheney, Charles H., 53, 54
Cheney, Charles H. and C. E. Howard,
55
Cheney House, 1924, (#18)55
Chester Place, 1895, 268
Chickering, Allen (landscape architect),
77
Child's House, 264
Children's Museum, 242
Christie, J. H., H. L. Gilman, R. J.
Wirth, 252

Union Passenger Terminal, 1934-39, (#11)252
Church of Il Santissimo Crocifisso, 116
Church of the Incarnation Roman Catholic Church, 1951, (#26)319
Church of the Nazarene, 1890, (#14)427
Church of Our Savior (Episcopal), 1872-later, (#11)424
Church of St. Ambrosio, 116
Church of St. Sepolcro, 116
Church, Thomas D. (landscape architect), 405
  Stuart Pharmaceutical Company, (#13)405
Citizen Publishing and Printing Company Building, 1929, (#39)92
City Beautiful Civic Center, 241
City Hall East, 248
City of Los Angeles Building Department, 290
  Northeast Police Station, 1925, (#26)290
Clapp House, 1874, (#40)379
Claremont, 441
Clark, Alson, 376
  Clark House, 1968, (#6)376
Clark, George A., 378
  Clark House, c. 1910, (#28)378
Clarke, Marie Rankin, 310
Claudio Grau Building, 1990, (#72)159
Clearman's Village, 429
Cleland, Robert Glass, 432
Clemenson, Richard, (see **A Design Group**)
Clements and Clements/Benito A. Sinclair and Associates, 248
  Los Angeles Department of Water and Power Central District Headquarters, Phase II, 1988-92, (#14)248
Clements, Stiles, xix, 6, 80, 82, 87, 89, 132, 242, 253, 284, 312
  Hollywood Turf Club, 1937, 80, (#7)82
  Supermarket Building, c. 1940, (#11)87
  Swimming Pool Building, Beverly Hills High School, c. 1937, (#31)132
  Thomas Jefferson High School, 1936, (#23)284
  U.S. Naval and Marine Corps Armory, 1939-40, (#18)253
  Vons Super Market, 1947-48, 89
Clifton's Cafeteria, 217
Cline, Edgar, 56
  Schoolcraft House, 1926, (#22)56
Close, J. M., xx, 160, 213
  Ahmed Apartment Building, 1925, (#83)161
  Apartment Building, 1926, (#78)160
  Karnak Apartment Building, 1925, (#82)160
  Osiris Apartment Building, 1926, (#26)213
Coast Savings Office Building, 1987, (#15)128
Coate, Roland E., xix, xxii, 103, 123, 125, 169, 267, 378, 385, 386, 390, 414, 416, 417, 418, 421
  All Saints Episcopal Church, 1925, (#33)125
  Automobile Club of Southern California

1921-23, (#3)267
Baer House, 1930, (#22)415
Barber House, 1925, (#23)378
Campbell House, 1924, (#22)390
Davis House, 1936-37, (#7)385
Fitzgerald House, 1919, (#22)418
Forrest House, 1930-31, (#11)123
Heath House, 1930, (#16d)417
House, 1926, (#21)415
House, 1932, (#4)416
Le Fens House, 1933, (#16b)417
Mays House, 1927, (#9)417
Milligan House, 1928, (#16a)417
Norcross House, 1927, (#15)103
Pitcairn House, 1906, (#9d)386
Pitner House, 1928, (#16c)417
Rupple House, 1934, (#36)421
Vinmont House, 1926, (#10)169
Coate, Roland E., Jr., 111, 366, 399, 400, 440
  Mudd House, 1969, (#7)111
  Pasadena Town Club, 1931, (#48)400
Coate, Roland E. Jr. and Stanley Kamebins, 52
  United California Bank Building, 1970 (#15)52
Cobb, Henry, 118
Cohn-Goldwater Building, 1909, (#3)255
Cohn House, c. 1887, (#2m)184
Collins, Russell, 106
  Ralph's Grocery Store Building, 1929, (#2)106
Colorado Street Bridge, 1912-13, 366
Community United Methodist Church, 1929, (#13)11
Conrad, Albert (landscape architect), 59
  Mount Ada, 1921, (#1)59
Conway, James N., 111
  Monterey Garden Apartment Building, c. 1930, (#12)111
Cook and Hall (landscape architects), 242
Cook and Hill (landscape architects), 134, 304, 430
  Park, 1923, (#5)430
Cook, Hill, and Cornell (landscape architects), 84, 302
  Cascades Park, c. 1928, (#7)302
  Monte Mar Vista, 1924, 84
Cook, Wilbur David (landscape architect), xx, 122, 270, 419
Cooper, David, (see **A Design Group**)
Cooper, John M., 234
  Roxie Theater, 1932, (#70)234
Cooper, Thomas, 83
  Pepperdine College, (old campus) 1937, (#12)83
  Coral Gables Bungalow Court, c. 1932, (#28)141
Corbett, Cooper B., 264
  Louise Denkin House, 1912, (#4)264
Cornell, Bridgers and Troller (landscape architects), 243, 244
  Los Angeles Music Center, 1964-69, (#3)244
Cornell, Bridges, Troller, and Hazlett, 115, 119, 248
  Los Angeles Mall, 1973-74, (#11)248

  Murphy Sculpture Court, 1969, (#28)119
Cornell, Ralph D. (landscape architect), xx, 79, 115, 118, 243, 265, 278, 445
  Harwood Garden, 1921, 445
  Pomona College, 1887 and later, (#18)445
  Pueblo del Rio Public Housing, 1941-42, (#1)278
  William Andrews Clark Memorial Library (UCLA), 1924-26, (#11)265
Cortelyon, H. P. (engineer), 240
  1st Street Viaduct Bridge, 1928, (#116)240
Council, Lucile (landscape architect), xx
  "Courthouse, The" 1978-79, (#23)69
  Covina, West Covina, El Monte, Irwindale, Glendora, 435-36
Coxhead, Ernest A., 78, 259, 298, 299, 300, 376, 424
  Bixby House, c. 1885-later (#2)78
  Church of the Angels, 1889, (#8)376
  Church of the Ascension, 1888, (#3)424
  Epiphany Chapel, 1888-89, 298, (#9)299
  Sturgis House, 1889-90, (#14)300
  Craig Adobe, "The Hermitage," c. 1880, (#13)408
Cram and Ferguson, 275, 276
  Alan Hancock Foundation and Memorial Museum, 1940, (#13)276
  Edward L. Doheny, Jr. Memorial Library, 1932, (#11)275
Cram, Goodhue, and Ferguson (Carleton M. Winslow, Sr.), 413
  St. James Episcopal Church, 1907, (#13)413
Crane, C. Howard, 236
  Texaco/United Artists Building, 1927, (#86)236
Crawford, Roland H., 32
  Sears, Roebuck and Company Store, 1946-47, (#2)32
  "Crawford's Corner" Shopping Center, c. 1965, (#5)302
  Crenshaw Shopping Plaza, 1947-48, (#24)89
Criley and McDowell, 444, 445
  Pitzer College, 1964 and later, (#14)445
Cross, Harold and A. F. Wicker, 200
  Arlington Avenue Christian Church, 1926, (#13)200
Crowhurst, F. Scott, 176
  Walt Disney House, 1932, (#47)176
  Culver Theater, c. 1950, (#36)92
Curlett, Aleck, 155
  Hollywood Equitable Building, 1929 (#46c)155
Curlett and Beelman, 72, 74, 214
  Elks Building, 1923-24, (#34)214
  Farmers and Merchants Bank Building, 1922, (#9)72
  Pacific Coast Club, 1925-26, (#33)74
  Security Trust and Savings Building, 1923-25, (#7)72
Curlett, William and Son, 238
  Merchants National Bank Building, 1915, (#95)238
Cutter, Kirkland, 53, 54, 55, 56
  Buchanan House, 1927, 53, 54, (#21)56

Cameron House, 1926, 54
Gard House, 1927, (#6), 55
Gilmore House, 1927, 54
Paull House, 1926, 54
Sisson House, 1927, 54
Stein House, 1928, (#5)54

Daggs House, c. 1910, (#11)444
Dailey, Gardner, 104
Dana, Richard Henry, (1840), 61
Daniel, Mann, Johnson, and
Mendenhall, xxv, 26, 37, 48, 49, 126,
133, 134, 145, 203, 348, 381, 388, 434
Auditorium (Ambassador Foundation
Campus), 1974, (#55f)381
Busway Terminal (El Monte), 1973, 434
Century Bank Building, 1972, (#55)145
Century City Medical Plaza, 1969,
(#1)133
Federal Aviation Agency Building, 1973,
(#14)49
Grieger Building, 1972, (#28)388
Hertz Vehicle Maintenance Turnaround
Facility, 1982, (#3)48
Lawrence Welk Plaza, 1973; General
Telephone Building; Wilshire West
Apartments, (Cesar Pelli, P. J. Jacobson,
and Dwight Williams) (#39)26
Manufacturers Bank Building, 1973,
(#3)126
One Park Plaza, 1971-72, (#40)203
San Diego Savings and Loan
Association Building, 1972, (#9)134
Santa Monica City College: Business
Education and Vocational Building,
1981, (#23)34
Worldwide Postal Center, 1967, (Cesar
Pelli and Anthony Lumsden) (#2)48
Daniels, Mark, 9, 52, 97, 101
Administration Building, c. 1928, 101
Mount St. Mary's College, 1930-31,
(#18)97
Reid House, 1928, (#17)52
Times Demonstration House, 1927-28,
(#4)9
Davidson, J. R., xxii, xxiii, 18, 22, 95,
100, 102, 108, 175, 362
Buki House, 1941, (#14)108
Drucker Apartments, 1940, (#48)100
Four Apartment Units, 1966, (#3)95
House, 1945-48, (#11)362
Kingsley Houses, 1946, (#33)18
Mann House, 1941, (#37)18
Rabinowitz House, 1960, (#9)102
Sabsay House, 1940, (#30)181
Schapiro House, 1949, (#38)175
Stothart-Phillips House, 1937-38, (#9)22
Davies, Hugh R., 70, 73, 281
Huntington Park Civic Center, 1945-51,
(#9)281
Long Beach Polytechnic High School,
1932-36 and later, (#23)73
Davis, Ferdinand, 440
Ebell Club, c. 1910, (#13)440
Masonic Hall, c. 1900, (#18)440
Seventh-Day Adventist Church, c. 1895,
(#15)440

Davis, Hugh R. (Long Beach
Architectural Club), 73
Post Office and Federal Building, 1931-
32, (#16)73
Davis, J. H. (engineer), 72
Buffman's Autoport, 1941, (#5)72
Davis, Mildred (landscape architect), xx
Davis, Pierpont, 54, 55
Garden Apartments, 1937, (#3)54
La Venta Inn, 1923, (#19)56
Davis, Pierpont and Walter S., 141, 144,
149, 181, 188, 267
Churchill House, 1928, (#11)188
El Greco Apartment Building, 1929,
(#43)144
St. John's Episcopal Church, 1922-23,
(#4)267
The Roman Gardens, 1926, (#12)149
Villa d'Este, 1928, (#26f)141
Davis, Sam, 37
Commercial Building, 1987, (#1)37
de Armond, Bea, (with Jason and
Michelle Walker), 313
Bear Tree, 1982-83, 313
de Armond, Jay and Bea, 313
Doll and Toy Museum, 1979, 313
de Bretteville, Peter, 139
de Bretteville-Simon Houses, 1976,
(#21)139
South Pasadena Civic Center, 1985-88,
(#11)413
de Bretteville, Peter and Stefanos
Polyzoides, 144, 274, 373, 391, 404, 413,
424
De Forest, Lockwood (landscape archi-
tect), xx
Decanso Court, c. 1915, (#1)302
Dedijer-Michich, Milica, 39
Michich-Small House, 1981, (#10)39
Dedrick and Bobbe, 70
Municipal Utilities Building, 1932, 70
Delapp, Tony, 28
Wave, The, 1989, (#56)28
Dennis and Farwell, 151, 154, 212, 268
Dennis House, 1910, (#17)212
Janes House, 1903, (#42)154
Lane House, 1909, (#20)151
Wilson House, 1916, 268
Denton, D. M., 360
Park House ("The Rock of Ages
House"), c. 1925, (#13)360
Dentzel, Carl S., xxviii, 348
Derrah, Robert V., 154, 157, 227, 255
Coca-Cola Bottling Company Plant,
1936-37, (#4)255
Crossroads of the World, 1936,
(#63)157
Southern Counties Gas Company
Building, 1939-40, (#33)227
Descanso Gardens, 1937, 1941-later,
(#9)362
Diamond Bar, 441
Diamond, Katherine, xxvi
Diamond, Siegel, 47
Airport Traffic Control Tower and
Administrative Base Building, 1993-95,
47

Dillon, Kenneth, 146
Orlando/Waring Condominiums, 1974,
(#61)146
Disney Studio Buildings, (#11)323
Dixon, Maynard, 288, 346, 428
Doctor's House, c. 1887, (#34)320
Dodd and Richards, 230
Clifton's Silver Spoon Cafeteria, 1922,
(#39)230
Dodd, William J., 14
Uplifters Club, 1923, (#14)14
Dodge, Walter, 135
Dodson House, c. 1887, (#15)63
Dolena, J. E., 111
Garden Apartment and Retail Shop, 111
Dominguez Ranch House, 1826, (#20)283
Don the Beachcomber Restaurant, c.
1937, (#32)153
Donlay, Roy W., (with David S. Allison),
316
Cathedral/Auditorium, 1950, (#2)316
Dora Apartments, 1906, (#3)208
Dorman, Richard L. and Associates, 354
Nature Center, 1973, 354
Dorman/Munselle Associates, 340
Dorn, Fred R., 288
Mount Washington Cable Car Station,
1909, (#22)288
Downey, 311
Downtown, 216-240
Downtown, Civic Center, 241-248
Downtown, Plaza and Northeast, 249-253
Downtown, South, 254-256
Drake, Gordon, 1, 181
Berns House, 1951, (#3)1
Presley House, 1946, (#35)181
Dreiser, Theodore, 135
Dreyfuss, Henry, 242, 386
Drum Barracks, 1859, (#5)65
Dryden, Nathaniel, 123, 320
Brand House ("El Miradero"), 1902-04,
(#34)320
Robinson House and Garden, 1911,
1924, (#13)123
Duarte, 432
Dumas, 359
Weatherwolde Castle, 1928, (#6)359
Dumond House, c. 1925, (#8)430
Durfee, Eugene, 27, 28
Central Tower Building, 1929, (#46)27
Store and Office Building, 1927, (#50)28
Dutch Village Shopping Center, c. 1960,
313
Dworsky, Daniel and Associates, xxxiii,
47, 69, 73, 83, 116, 119, 120, 231, 232
Angelus Plaza, 1981, (#55)232
Bill Hopkins Lincoln-Mercury Agency
Building, 1966, (#21)69
Great Western Savings Association
Building, 1968, (#17)73
Jerry Lewis Neuromuscular Research
Center, 1976-79, (#33)119
Los Angeles Branch, Federal Reserve
Bank of San Francisco, 1985-87,
(#52)231
Northrop Electronics Division
Headquarters, 1982, (#16)83

Track and Field Stadium, 1969,
(#29)119
UCLA Hospital Parking Structure,
1979-80, 116, (#35)120
Dyment House, 1923, (#17)411

EDC, Inc. Architects (Walter Abronson
and Ko Kiyohara), 182
Silverview Condominiums, 1983,
(#38)182
EKONA, 398
Pasadena Police Department Building,
1989-90, (#30)398
Eager and Eager, 377
Jevne House, 1913, (#17)377
Eager, Frank O., 431
Mellenthin House, c. 1912, (#20)431
Eager, Wesley, 175
Apartment Building for Dr. F. Haight,
1937, (#42)175
Eagle Rock, 293-296
Eagles Building, 1949, (#14)52
Eames, Charles, 17, 125, 143 (see also
Eero Saarinen)
Entenza House, 1949, (#27)17
Herman Miller Showroom Building,
1949, (#35)143
Eames, Charles and Ray, 17, xxiii, xxiv,
38
Eames House and Studio, 1947-49,
(#26)17
East Hollywood, 167-176
East Pasadena, 403-5
Eastlake-Gothic Methodist Church, 1904,
347
Easton, Louis B., 365, 379, 381, 390,
396, 408, 425
Coldwell House, c. 1907, (#7)425
House, c. 1906, (#1)408
House, 1910, (#35)379
Ioannes House, 1911, (#11)390
Mead House, 1910, (#56)381
Two Houses, 1905, (#21)396
Volney-Craig House, 1908, (#32)379
Echo Park, 183-85
Eckbo, Dean, and Associates (landscape
architects), 394, 414
Eckbo, Garrett (landscape architect), xx
Edwards, H. Arden, 356
Antelope Valley Indian Museum, 1928,
356
Edwards, W. B., 383
Egasse and Brauch, 296
Brauch House, 1923, (#11)296
Eggers, Henry, 368
House, 1946, (#4)368
Egyptian Gardens, c. 1935, 361
Eggers, Henry and Walter W.
Wilkman, 386, 391
Gladys Peterson Building, 1962,
(#9f)386
Hamish House, 1951, (#27)391
Library, 1962, (#9f)386
Ranney House Classrooms, 1962,
(#9f)386
Ehrenkrantz and Eckstut, xxxii
Ehrlich, Steven, xxvi, 3, 40, 41

Douroux Canal House, 1991, 41
Ed Moses Studio, 1987, 40
House, 1990, (#23)40
Okulick Studio, 1989, 41
Ripple House, 1989, 41
Ehrlich, Steven and Associates, 40, 45,
93, 205
Ace Market, 1989, (#20)40
Hampstead House, 1993, (#45)44
Race Through the Clouds, 1987, (#20)40
Shatto Recreation Center, 1991,
(#46)205
Sony Pictures Entertainment, Child Care
Center, 1993-94, (#41)93
Sony Pictures Entertainment, Digital
Production Building, 1993-94, (#41)93
Windward Circle, (#20)40
Windward Circle Art Building, 1988,
(#20)40
Eichler, Alfred W., 134
Eichler, Joseph, 349
Eisen, Theodore, 196, 268, 270, 287, 288
"Casa de Adobe," 1917, (#21)287
The Doheny, 1898-1900, 268
Donova House ("Sunshine Hill"), c.
1910, (#56)196
Kiefer House, 1894, (#18)270
Eisener, Simon and Lyle Stewart, 323
The Golden Mall, 1967, (#9)323
Eisenstadt, Sidney, 102, 126, 146
Steven S. Wise Temple, Chapel and
School Facilities, 1975, (#7)102
Temple Emmanuel and School, 1954,
(#60)146
Wells Fargo Bank, 1973, (#1)126
El Molino Viejo, 1816, (#26)391
El Segundo Elementary School, 1936,
(#15)49
Eliot Construction Company, 396
Byran's Cleaners, 1938, (#18)396
Elisen, T. A., A. R. Walker, Norman R.
Marsh, David D. Smith, Herbert J.
Powell, and Armand Monaco, 258
William Mead Homes, 1941-42,
(#1c)258
Elliot, Daniel A., 321, 434
Public Service Department Building,
1945, (#2)321
Water Filtration and Softening Plant,
1940, 434
Ellwood, Craig, xxiii, 1, 5, 15, 98, 100,
103, 104, 144, 351
Anderson House, 1950, (#19)15
Broughton House, 1950, (#24)104
Carson-Roberts Building, 1958-60,
(#50)144
Case Study House #16, 1951, (#21)103
Elton House, 1951, (#20)15
Epstein House, 1949, (#24)98
Hunt House, 1955-57, (#10)5
Pierson House, 1961-64, (#2)1
Zimmerman House, 1950, (#45)100
Ellwood, Craig and Associates, 49, 87,
99, 123, 128, 144, 156, 168, 170, 320,
369, 373, 438
Art Center College of Design, 1977,
(#45)373

Brown House, 1949, (#9)123
Courtyard Apartments, 1952, (#56)156
Ellwood Office Building, 1965-66,
(#10)87
Gerwin-Ostrow Office Building, 1960,
(#45)144
Hale House, 1949, (#8)123
Joy Company, 1972-73, (#37)320
Kubly House, 1964, (#11)369
Moore House, 1964, (#15)170
Rosen House, 1962, (#33)99
Scientific Data System Building, 1966-
68, (#13)49
Security Pacific Bank Building, 1972-73,
(#4)168
Security Pacific Place, 1969, (#8)128
State Savings Bank, 1972-73, 128
Xerox Corporation Manufacturing
Facility, 1967, (#1)438
Elysian Park, 183-85
Emma and Lewis Grigsby Mausoleum,
206
Emmons, Frederick E. (see also **Noyes,**
Eliot)
Encino, 337
Engine Company No. 1 Fire Station, 1940,
(#10)299
Ennis, Lyman, 375
Kempton House, 1961, (#2)375
Erickson, Arthur Architects, xxxiii, 130,
231, 231
California Plaza and *Two California*
Plaza, 1983-, (#53)231
Erikson, Peters, Thomas, and
Associates, 400
Ernst, Gerd (for **Daniel, Mann,**
Johnson, and Mendenhall), 381
Student Center (Ambassador Foundation
Campus), 1966, (#55e)381
Esplanade Del Rey Townhouse, 1982,
(#11)49
Essick House, c. 1905, (#16)427
Estep, J. M., (see **Parkinson, Donald B.**
and J. M. Estep)
Evergreen Cemetery, 1877, (#22)260
Evison, Leland, 368, 385
House, 1950, (#2)385
Schonbach House, 1946, (#3)368
Exposition Park, (#25)270
Exposition Park, East, 267-72
Exposition Park, West; Leimert Park, 263-
66

Farmdale School Building, 1889,
(#16)300
Farmer John's (Cloughtan Packing
Company), 1953 and later, 278, (#4)280
Farmer's Market, 1934-37, (#2)187
Farquhar, Robert, 23, 226, 265, 370
The California Club, 1929-30, (#29)226,
370
Clark Library, 370
Fenyes House, 1906, (#28)370
Gorham House, 1910, (#22)23
William Andrews Clark Memorial
Library (UCLA), 1924-26, (#11)265
Farrand, Beatrix, 404

Farrell and Miller, 68
  Torrance High School, 1923, 1929, and c. 1935, (#14)68
Farver, Rick Associates, 206
  Mount Vernon Office, Pacific Savings Building, 1960, (#3)206
Feil and Paradice, (#41)294
Field and Silverman, 120
  UCLA Guest House, 1982-83, (#40)120
  Film Exchange, Inc. Building, c. 1928, (#79)160
Fine, Jud, 224
Fiore d'Italia Restaurant Building, c. 1965, (#11)335
First Christian Church, 1923, (#5)306
First Hebrew Christian Church, 1905, (#11)259
First Methodist Episcopal Church, 1875-76, (#9)33
First National Bank Building, 1925, 312
First Presbyterian Church, c. 1900, (#6)436
Fisher, Frederick, xxxii
Fisher, Frederick and Thane Roberts, 39
  Caplin House, 1979, (#12)39
Fisher, Sergio, 237
  Los Angeles Theater, 237
Fitzhugh, Thornton, 238
  Pacific Electric Building, 1903-5, (#105)238
Fleischman, Maurice, 239
  Gerry Building, 1947, (#109)239
Flewelling and Moody, 88
  Robert Lee Frost Auditorium, Culver City High School and Middle School, 1964, (#17)88
Flewelling, Ralph C., 125, 129, 242, 275, 276
  Beverly Hills Post Office Building, 1932-33, (#21)129
  Colonel Seeley Wintersmith Mudd Memorial Hall of Philosophy, 1928-29, (#9)275
  Harris Hall of Architecture and Fine Arts (USC), 1939, (#12)276
  Hawthorne School, 1929, (#31)125
Flores, Miguel Angelo and Associates, 26, 40, 43, 141
  Snipper House, "La Rotonda," 1988, (#22)40
  Stayden Duplex, 1986, (#43)43
  "Villa de Malaga" Apartments, 1988, (#27)141
  Villa de Malaga Townhouse, 1982-83, (#34)26
Flour Tower, 274
Folonis, Michael W. (see **A Design Group**)
Folonis, Michael W. and Associates, 34, 42, 125
  411 Venice House, 1991, (#34)42
  Beverly House, 1990, (#19)34
  Chambers/Folonis House, 1988, (#20)34
  Sierra Mar House, 1991, (#29)125
Fong and Associates (landscape architects), 218, 256
  Central Distribution Center, Department

of Water and Power, 1988-89, (#10)256
  Promenade Towers, 1985, (#2)218
Fong, Miller, 417
  Font House, 1976, (#12)417
Ford ("Beaudry Street") House, c. 1885, (#24e)289
Forker, Donald M., 312
  Post Office Building, 1970-71, 312
Fort MacArthur, 1914 and later, 62, (#11)63
The Forthman House, 274
Fosayke, George, 170
  Barcelona and Coruna Apartments, 1932, (#20)170
Foster, William E., 26
  Shangri-la Apartments, 1939-40, (#40)26
Fowler, Edward W., 369
  Andalusian House, 369
  Basque House, 369
  Fowler House, 1927, (#9)369
  Majorcan House, 369
  Foy House, 1873, (#2g)184
Francisco Grazide Adobe, c. 1875, (#2)436
Frank, Ron, 14 (see **Urban Innovations Group**)
Fraser, Robert Gordon (landscape architect), 380, 383, 386
  Old Mill of Banbury Cross, c. 1907, (#13)387
  Pergola House, c. 1910, (#73)383
Freese, Ernest Irving, 414
  Spears House, 1925, (#17)414
French Care, Marcel and Jeanne, c. 1930, (#2)304
Fulton, J. E., 310

Gable and Wyant, 22, 47
  Crenshaw House, 1925-26, (#2)22
  Hangar No. 1, 1929, 47
Gage, Merrill, 413
Gage, William J. 130
  Beverly Hills City Hall, 1932, (#22)130
Gallion, Arthur B., 377
  Gallion House, 1956, (#18)377
Ganapathi, S. M., 341
  Sree Venkateswara Temple, 1982-88, (#2)341
Gano, Dr., 59
  Gano House, 1889, (#4)59
Gardena, 84
Gardner, Albert B., 89
  Broadway-Crenshaw Department Store, 1948, 89
Garner, Archibald, 171
  Griffith Park Observatory and Planetarium, 1935, (#22)171
Garnier Block, 1890, (#8)252
Garnsey, Julian, 224
Garrett, Stephen, xxvi, 7
  J. Paul Getty Museum, 1972-73, (#21)7
Gartz Court, 1910, (#37)373
Gasoline Service Station, c. 1925, (#24)73
Gate House ("Doll's House"), c. 1925, (#5)123
Gault, Charles, 192
  Cochran Avenue Court, c. 1928, (#34)192

Gazzeri, E., 316
Geddes, Norman Bel, 49
Gehry, Frank O., xxvi, 37, 139, 243, 342, 398
Gehry, Frank O. and Associates, 4, 24, 28, 32, 38, 39, 40, 63, 100, 116, 120, 130, 132, 144, 148, 154, 159, 210, 239, 244, 271, 327, 341, 342
  Arnoldi Triplex, 1981, (#6)38
  Benson House, 1981-84, (#8)341
  Bubar's Jewelers, 1981, 28
  Cabrillo Maritime Museum, 1981, (#12)63
  California Aerospace Museum, 1982-84, 271
  Chiat/Day/Mojo Advertising Agency Building, 1985-91 (#2)38
  Danziger Studio, 1965, (#73)159
  Davis House, 1972, (#9)4
  Disney Concert Hall, 1988-94, (#2)244
  Edgemar Development, 1984-88, (#7)32
  Francis Howard Regional Branch Library, 1985, (#45)154
  Frank O. Gehry Offices, 1988, (#54)28
  Gehry House, 1978, (#29)24
  Gemini Studio Building, 1976, (#44)144
  Loyola University Law School Building, 1981-84, (#12)210
  Norton House, 1982-84, (#21)40
  Rebecca's Restaurant, 1982-85, (#16)39
  Santa Monica Place, 1979-81, (#49)28, 398
  Schnabel House, 1986-89, (#47)100
  Sirmai-Peterson House, 1983-88, 343
  Spiller House, 1980, (#14)39
  Student Placement and Career Planning Center (UCLA), 1976-77, 116, (#34)120
  "The Temporary Contemporary" Museum, Los Angeles Museum of Contemporary Art, 1982-83, (#115)239
  World Savings Building, 1982, (327
  Wosk House, 1981-84, (#30)132
Gensler and Associates, xxxiii, 26, 47
  Wilshire Professional Building, 1979-80, (#39)26
Gentry, Francis H. (see **Wright, Parker O. and Francis H. Gentry**)
George, Julian (landscape architect), 340
Georgi, Boyd, 376, 408
  Altadena Public Library, 1967, (#3)408
  Puelicher House, 1960, (#10)376
Gerhardt, Herbert J., 431
  Wood House, c. 1925, (#23)431
Geronimo Lopez Adobe, 1878, 352
Gervigian, Raymond, 437
Getschell, Eugene, 406
  "Mansion Adena" (Lewis House), 1886, (#3)406
Getty Museum, 9
Gibbons, Cedric, 13 (see also **Honnold, Douglas**)
  Delores del Rio House, 1929, (#6)13
Gibbs and Gibbs, 324
  Warner/Elektra/Atlantic Corporation Building, 1981, (#14)324
Gilbert House, c. 1902, (#5c)208

Gill and Pearson, (Irving J. Gill), 310
Marie and Chauncey Clarke House,
1919-22, (#6)310
Gill, Irving J., xvii, xviii, xxi, 32, 66, 67,
68, 75, 100, 134, 135, 149, 161, 265, 270,
296, 310, 381, 408, 414, 424
Brighton Hotel, 1912, (#6)67
Clarke House, 310
Colonial Hotel and United Cigar
Building, 1912, (#5)67
Fuller Shoe Manufacturing Company
Building (Casa Del Amo), 1912, (#8)67
Gartz Duplex, 1921, (#12)408
Horatio West Court, 1919-21, (#6)32
Miltimore House, 1911, (#20)414
Morgan House, 1917, (#88)161
Murray Hotel, 1912, (#4)67
Pacific Electric Railroad Bridge, 1912,
(#1)67
Pacific Electric Railroad Station, 1912,
(#2)67
Raymond House, 1918, (#1)75
Roi Tan Hotel, 1912, (#3)67
Rubbercraft Corporation of California
Building, 1913, 67
Salem Manufacturing Company
Building, 1913, (#9)67
Sierra Madre Garden Apartment Houses
(Lewis Courts), 1910, (#2)424
Worker's Single-Family Housing, 1912,
(#17)68
Gilman, H. L., 394
Santa Fe (AMTRAK) Railroad
Passenger Station, 1935, (#9)394
Glendale, 315-20
Glendale Chamber of Commerce Building,
c. 1925, (#3)316
Glendale Federal Savings Building, 1959,
(#4)317
Glendora, 433
Goff, Bruce, 193, 339
Price Museum of Oriental Art, 193
Struckus House, 1982-84, 339
Gogerty and Weyl, 154, 155
Baine Building, 1926, (#41)154
Yucca-Vine Tower Building, 1928,
(#47)155
Gogerty, Henry. L., 46, 320
Grand Central Air Terminal, 1928,
(#35)320
Goldman/Brandt (Ron Goldman), 332
Riverside Law Building, 1972, (#23)332
Goldman/Firth/Associates, 5
Office Building, 1987, (#11)5
Goldman, Herb, 74
Oil Drilling Islands, 1967-68, (337)74
Goodell, James and Associates, xxxii
Goodhue, Bertram G. xx, 276, 298, 365,
380, 385, 403, 404
Bridge Physics Laboratory (California
Institute of Technology), 1922, (#8b)404
Jeffries House, 1922, (#3)385
Memorial Flagpole, 1927, (#52)380
West Court Buildings, 1928-30, (#8c)404
Goodhue, Bertram and Elmer Grey, 404
Gates Chemistry Laboratory, 1917,
(#8a)404

Goodhue, Bertram G. and Carleton M.
Winslow, 223
Los Angeles Public Library, 1922-26,
(#25)223
Gougeon, John, 424, 425
Saint Rita's Church, 1969, (#4)425
Gougeon-Woodman, 401
Pasadena Presbyterian Church, 1976,
(#52)401
Gould, Raymond, 376
Gould House ("Villa Evarno"), 1911-
later, (#9)376
Grable and Austin (contractors/design-
ers), 379
Austin House, 1909, (#30)379
House, 1905, (#38)379
Williams House, 1911, (#33)379
Graham, Robert (sculptor), 41, 225, 272
Doumani House, 1982, (#24)41
Granada Hills, Mission Hills, 349
Grand Central Market Building, 234
Grand Central Square, 234
Graves, Michael, 142, 323
Disney Studio Office Building, 1992,
(#11b)323
Sunar Showroom, 1981, 142
Gray, David L., 37
Gray, Paul (Warner and Gray), 419-21
Virginia Steele Scott Gallery of
American Art, 1983-84, 419
Great Scot Restaurant, c. 1967, 429
Great Western Savings Bank, c. 1970,
(#6)350
Green, Burton E., 122
Green Dog and Cat Hospital, c. 1936,
(#21)283
Greenberg, Tony, 37
Greene, Charles and Henry, xviii, 14,
23, 24, 74, 79, 104, 123, 124, 200, 365,
367, 369, 370, 372, 379, 380, 381, 383,
384, 386, 387, 390, 392, 394, 395, 400,
401, 402, 409, 410, 424, 426, 431, 445
Anthony House, 1909, (#14)123
Bentz House, 1906, (#35)372
Blacker House, E. J., 1912, (#12)390
Blacker House, R. R., 1907, (#19)390
Bolton House, 1906, (#57)381
Bowen House, 1905, (#7)409
Brandt-Serrurier House, 1905, (#13)410
Camp House, Edgar, 1904, (#8)426
Charles Sumner Greene House, 1901,
1906, 1912, 1914, (#22)370
Cole House, 1906, (#30)370
Crow-Crocker House, 1909, (#15)390
Culbertson House, Cordelia, 1911,
(#34)392, 410
Culbertson House, James A., 1902,
1914, 23, (#21)370
Darling House, 1903, (#16)445
De Forest House, 1906, (#37)379
Duncan-Irwin House, 1900, 1906,
(#20)370
Earl Apartment House, 1912, (#54)401,
410
Freeman Ford House, 1907, (#47)380
Gamble House, xviii, 367, 370, (#31)372
Garfield House, 1904, (#19)387

Halsted House, 1905, (#13)369
Hawks House, 1906, (#25)370
Hollister House, 1899, (#67)383
Kinney-Kendall Building, 1897,
(#12)395
Longley House, 1897, 1910, (#20)387
Mervin House, 1904, (#10)386
Oaklawn Bridge and Waiting Station,
1906, (#23)387
Oaklawn Gates, 1905, (#22)387
Phillips House, 1906, (#69)383
Pitcairn House, 1906, (#9d)386
Ranney House, 1907, (#27)370
Reeves House, 1904, (#3)79
Robinson House, 1905, (#48)380
Rolland House, 1903, (#11)386
Sanborn House, 1903, (#3)402
Smith House, E. W., 1910, (#36)400
Spinks House, 1909, (#29)392
Stahlhuth House, 1907 (#4)394
Tichenor House, 1904, (#34)74
Van Rossem House, 1904, (#18)369
Van Rossem-Neill House, 1903, 1906,
(#24)370
Ware House, 1913, (#68)383
Wheeler House, 1905, (#8)200
White Sisters House, 1903, (#23)370
Willet House, 1905, (#26)370
Williams House, 1915, (#15)410
Witbeck House, 1917, (#26)24
Greene, Henry, 406, 408
Savage House, 1924, (#1)406
Thum House, 1925, 408
Greene, Henry George, 133
ABC Entertainment Center, 1972,
(#4)133
Greene, Isabelle (landscape architect), 5
Office Building, 1987, (#11)5
Greg, John W. (landscape architect),
115
Grey, Elmer, (see also **Myron Hunt**) 23,
60, 72, 123, 152, 190, 210, 401, 401
Beverly Hills Hotel, 1911-12, (#12)123
Bowen House, 1925, (#18)190
Bungalow Court, 1910, (#56)401
First Church of Christ, Scientist, 1912,
(#6)210
Gillis House, 1906, 23
Murdock House, 1929, (#6)60
Pasadena Playhouse, 1924-25, (#50)400
Second Church of Christ, Scientist,
1916-25, (#12)72
Grey, Elmer Associates, 101, 389, 401
Grey House, 1911, (#7)389
Grey, Harry, (#6)286
Grey, Melinda, 4, 6, 51
Downey House, 1991, (#4)4
Guerra House, 1992, (#3)12
Tate House, 1989, (#7)51
Walker House, 1992, (#20)6
Griffith, Col. Griffith J., 167
Griffith House, 1923, (#5)409
Griffith Park, 167-176, 168
Griffith Park Equestrian Center, 176
Grinstein/Daniels, 205
Kentucky Fried Chicken, 1990, (#48)205
Grist Mill Restaurant, c. 1950, (#10)323

Grossman, Greta Magnusson, 124
  Grossman House, 1949, (#23)124
Gruen Associates, xxv, 71, 88, (#8)107, 256
  Downtown Plaza Building, 1981-82, (#3)71
  Fox Hills Shopping Mall, 1973-76, (#18)88
  Los Angeles Convention Center, (#9)256
  Parking Structure, 1981-82, (#4)71
Gruen and Associates (Cesar Pelli), 68, 107
  Ohrbach's Del Amo Fashion Square, 1971, (#20)68
Gruen and Krummeck, 48
Gruen, Victor Associates, 37, 51, 102, 142, 203, 354, 436
  Leo Baeck Temple, 1962, (#4)102
  Millron's Department Store Building, 1949 (#4)48
  Puente Hills Mall, 1974, (#1)436
  Redondo Beach Civic Center, 1962, (#11)51
  Pacific Design Center ("Blue Whale"), 1975; 1985-88, (#32)142
  Tishman Building, 1956, (#39)203
Grundfor, Jack, 170
  Los Feliz Manor Apartment Building, 1929, (#19)170

Haas, Solon I., 431
  House, c. 1887, (#14)431
Haenke, J. Martyn, 195, 254
  Fremont Place Entrance Gates, 1911, (#51)195
Hale, George Ellory, 404
  Hale House, c. 1910, (#16)408
Haley, A. L., 208, 362
  Lanterman House ("El Retiro"), 1915, (#7)362
  Powers House, 1903, (#5d)208
Halprin, Lawrence, 224, 225, 227, 398
  Bunker Hill Steps, 1989-90, (#26)225
  Doubletree Inn, 1989-90, (#31)398
  Grand Hope Park, 1989-93, (#36)227
Hamburger Mausoleum, 1931, 261
Hamlin, Ralph, 15
Hancock Foundation Building, 273
Hancock, Henry, 121
Hancock Park, 186-197
Hansen, Albert E., 317
  Glendale City Hall, 1940-42, (#10)317
Hansen, Frederick A. (landscape architect), 316
  Forest Lawn Memorial Park, 1917-present, (#2)316
Hanson, A. E. (landscape architect), xx, 54, 103, 264, 342, 377
  Young House, 1927, (#14)377
Harbor Hills, 1939-41, 62
Hardy, Holzman and Pfeiffer, 193, 224
  Los Angeles County Museum of Art, 1982-83, (#38a)193
Harper, Franklin, 215
  Granada Building, 1927, (#35)215
Harrington, Edward H., xxxii
Harrington, M. R., 351, 352

Harris, George, 359
  Bolton House, 1913, (#3)359
  Harris House, c. 1910, (#2)359
Harris Hall/Fisher Gallery Building, 273
Harris, Harwell H., xxi, xxii, xxiii, 12, 13, 104, 111, 122, 124, 148, 164, 179, 180, 181, 182, 185, 215, 291, 319, 327, 334, 375, 376, 410, 419, 424
  Alexander House, 1941, (#13)179
  Bauer House, 1938, (#23)319
  Birtcher-Share House, 1942, (#2)291
  Charles Croze Studio, 1948, (#40)215
  Dean McHenry House, 1940, (#6)111
  Elliott House, 1951, 327
  English House, 1950, (#18)124
  Entenza House, 1937, (#7)13
  Granstedt House, 1938, (#11)164
  Hansen House, 1951, (#23)180
  Harris House, 1939, (#4)376
  Hawk House, 1939, (#27)181
  Hopmans House, 1951, (#18)180
  Johnson House, 1949, (#28)104
  Laing House, 1935, (#1)375
  Lowe House, 1934, (#8)410
  Meier House, 1942, (#16,)185
  Mulvihill House, 1949, (#1)424
  Pumphrey House, 1939, (#5)13
  Schwenck House, 1940, (#5)334
  Sobieski House, 1946, (#26)419
  Walther House, 1937, (#40)182
Harrison, Beckhart, and Mill, 380
Harrison, Wallace K., 242
Harrison, William H., 306, 307, 308
  El Rancho High School, 1954-55, (#1)306
  Lincoln School, c. 1935, (#4)306
  Lou Henry Hoover School, 1938, (#8)306
  National Trust and Savings Building, c. 1935, (#10)307
  Whittier Civic Center, 1955-59, (#14)308
Hartranft, M. V., 358
Harvey, Arthur E., 196, 205, 207
  American Storage Company Building, 1928-29, (#6)207
  Selig Retail Store Building, 1931, (#50)205
  Wilshire Professional Building, 1929, (#59)196
Harvey, C. W. House, 1888, (#6)306
Haskin House, c. 1888, (#2j)184
Haynes, Paul, 377, 378
  Messler House, c. 1950, (#20)378
  Tabor House, 1950, (#12)377
Haywood, Jack and Vincent J. Proby, 272
  Museum of Afro-American History, 1983-84, 272
Hazlett, Jere H. (landscape architect), 115
Hearst, William Randolph, 255
Heath and Gore, 170
  Greek Theater, 1913, 1929-30, (#21)170
Heather Hill, 1922-23, 14
Heaton, Culver, 361
  Lutheran Church in the Foothills, 1965, (#5)361

Heim House, 1887-88, (#2c)183
Heineman, Alfred, 14, 151, 172, 365, 379
  House, 1924, (#25)172
  Marco Hellman Cabin, 1923-24, (#15)14
  Norton House, 1905, (#36)379
Heineman, Arthur S., (Alfred Heineman, Associate) 14, 151, 196, 206, 365, 372, 379, 389, 390, 392, 403, 406, 411
  Bowen Court, 1913, (#5)406
  Bungalows, c. 1910-25, (#1)206
  Freeman House, 1913, (#30)392
  Fuller House, 1924, (#23)151
  Gless House, 1916, (#54)196
  Hindry House, 1909, (#34)372
  House, c. 1911, (#14)390
  House, c. 1913, (#21)390
  House, c. 1915, (#6)403
  O'Brien House, 1912, (#23)390
  Parsons Bungalow, 1910, (#19)411
  Ross House, 1911, (#19)389
Heitschmidt and Thompson, 444
Heitschmidt, Earl C., 242
Heitschmidt, Earl T., 117, 123
Hellmuth, Obata and Kassebaum, 317
  550 North Brand Building, 1987, (#7)317
Herbergon, Arthur S., Jr., 331
  Rodgers House, 1937, (#14)331
Heritage Park, 1987, (#7)311
Heritage Square, (#24)289
Hershberger, Gilbert S., 381, 382
  Fitzpatrick House, 1980, (#62)382
  Jacobs House, 1992, (#60)381
Hershey, J. Wilmer, 365, 410
  "Little Normandy," 1925, (#11)410
Hertrich, William (landscape architect), 77
Hewitt, Harwood, 201
  Alice Lynch House, 1922-23, (#16)201
High Tower, The, c. 1920, (#7)149
Highland Park, 285-290
Highway 101 West, 341-43
Hillside Memorial Park, (#19)88
Hoag, Paul Sterling, 11, 15, 102, 125, 176, 334
  Dyer House, 1980, (#6)334
  Harrison House, 1950, (#18)11 & (#22)15
  Parker House, 1951, (#30)125
  Rajagopal House, 1983, (#48)176
  Zeigler House, 1952, (#3)102
Hobart, Lewis P., 386
  Cravens House, c. 1929, (#12)386
Hobby City, 313
Hodges, Thomas, 6
  Hodges Castle, 1977-79, (#14)6
Hodgetts + Fung Design Associates, 116, 117, 146, 166, 325
  Click Agency Building, 1991-92, (#66)146
  Panasonic Building, 1991, 325
  Temporary Undergraduate Library (UCLA), 1992-93, (#12)117
  UCLA Gateway, 116
  Viso House, 1989, (#15)166

Hodson, Garvin, 385
Perrin House, 1926, (#8)385
Hoffman, Joseph, 120
Holdredge, William D., 421
Stanwyck House, 1940, (#39)421
Hollenbeck Presbyterian Church, 1884,
(#12)259
Hollywood Bowl, 1924 to present, (#2)148
Hollywood Hills, 163-66
**Holstock, Peter (for O. K. Earl
Corporation),** 381
*Information and Administration Center,
1969,* (#55d)381
Holt, Hinshaw, Pfau, and Jones, 116
*Chiller Plant and Co-Generation
Facility,* 116
*Holy Virgin Mary Russian Orthodox
Cathedral, 1928,* (#1)178
Home of Peace Cemetery, 1931, (#26)261
Homer Laughlin Building, 234
Honnold and Rex, 103, 246, 445
Anderson House, 1951, (#13)103
Hall of Records Building, 1961-62,
(#7)246
Memorial Bell Tower, 1960, 445
Honnold, Douglas, 13, 102, 157 (see also
Cedric Gibbons)
Delores del Rio House, 1929, (#6)13
*Tiny Naylor's Drive-in Restaurant,
1950,* (#65)157
Honnold, Reibsamen, and Rex, 156, 161,
219, 338
Barclays Bank Building, 1971, 338
*Hollywood-Wilshire Health Center,
1968,* (#87)161
Linder Plaza, 1973-74, (#8)219
Sunset-Vine Tower, 1964, (#59)156
Horns, J. R., 188
Commercial Building, 1930, (#7)188
Hot Cha Restaurant, 1936, (#27)74
Hotel Cordova, 217
Houghton, E. W., 406
Rust-Smiley House, 1887, (#4)406
Houseman, Elwood, 141
Villa Sevilla, 1931, (26e)141
Howard, Coy, 62
McCafferty Studio House, 1979, (#5)62
**Howard, Ed and Paul J. (landscape
architects),** 77
Howard, George A., Jr., 250, 287
Hall of Letters, 1904-5, (#16)287
Howard, John Galen, 114, 117
Berkeley's Student Union, 1923, 117
Hromadka House, 1937, (#11)22
Hubbard, Elbert, 396
Hudson and Munsell, 208, 239, 264, 270
Cohan House, c. 1902, (#5b)208
Fire Station No. 29, 1910, (#107)239
*Gusti Villa (Busby Berkeley Estate),
1910,* (#6)264
*Los Angeles County Historical and Art
Museum, 1910,* (#25)270
Mary L. Briggs House, 1912, (#5)264
Murphy House, c. 1906, 264
Hudson, Frank, 395
Renaissance Revival Block, 1894, 395
Hugo Reid Adobe, 428
Hunt and Burns, xx, 196, 267, 290

*Automobile Club of Southern California,
1921-23,* (#3)267
Ebell Club, 1924, (#52)196
Mayan Entrance, 1919, 290
Hunt and Chambers, 366
Hunt and Eager, 210
Evanardy-Kinney House, 1902, (#5f)210
Raphael House, c. 1902, (#5e)210
Hunt and Eggers, 33
Trask House, 1903, 33
Hunt, Eager, and Burns, 287
Bent House, c. 1909, (#20)287
Hunt, George, 396
Hunt Offices and Display Rooms, 1925,
(#19)396
Hunt, Louis L., 240
4th Street Viaduct Bridge, 1930-31,
(#117)240
Hunt, Myron, xix, 23, 53, 122, 294 (see
Elmer Grey), 242, 294, 366, 367, 369,
370, 378, 391, 403, 404, 409, 445
Bridges Hall of Music, 1915, 445
Gillis House, 1906, 23
Hong House, 1917, (#4)409
La Casita del Arroyo, 1934, (#22)378
Myron Hunt House, 1905, (#16)369
Occidental College, 1911-13, (#4)294
Polytechnic School, 1907, (#7)403
Speirs House, 1904, (#19)370
Swan, Johnson, and Fowler halls, 1914,
(#4a)294
Wentworth Hotel, 1913, (#25)391
Hunt, Myron and Elmer Grey, 151, 419
Henry E. Huntington Art Gallery, 1910,
(#31)419
Wattles House and Gardens, 1905,
(#25)151
Hunt, Myron and H. C. Chambers, 53,
54, 55, 128, 294, 295, 336, 363, 380, 381,
396
Bird Hillside Theater, 1925, (#4m)295
Booth Music-Speech Center, 1929,
(#4f)295
Clapp Library, 1924, (#4b)294
Comptroller's House, 1932, (#4k)295
Dean of the Faculty House, 1932,
(#4l)295
Elks Club Building, 1911, (#54)381
Erdman Hall, 1927, (#4h)295
F. L. Olmsted Jr.'s House, 1924-25, 53
Faculty Club, 1922, (#4i)295
Flintridge Biltmore, 1927, (#18)363
Flintridge Country Club, 1921, (#14)363
Freeman Union, 1928, (#4d)294
House, 1928, (#16)363
*I. Magnin and Company Store Building,
1939,* (#7)128
Olmsted House, 1924-25, (#13)55
Orr Hall, 1925, (#4g)295
Palos Verdes Public Library, 1926-30,
(#2)54
Pasadena Public Library, 1927,
(#28)396
Thorne Hall (Auditorium), 1938,
(#4e)295
Throop Hall (Pasadena Hall), 1910, 404
Welbourne House, 336
Hunt, Sumner P., xvii, xxvii, 268, 269,

270, 290, 444
Balch Administration Building, 1929,
444
Casa de Rosas (Froebel Institute), 1894,
(#11)269
The Doheny, 1898, 268
Ebell Club, 1912, (#15)287
Kiefer House, 1895, (#18)270
Southwest Museum, 1910-14, and later,
(#25)290
**Hunt, Sumner; Theodore Eisen;
Charles Lummis,** 288
*Lummis House, ("El Alisal"), 1895-
1910,* (#23)288
Hunter, Paul Robinson, 115, 118
**Hunter, Paul, Walter Benedict, Herbert
Kahn, Edward Tarrell,** 171
Dickson Art Building, 1952, 115,
(#16)118
Junior Arts Center, 1967, (#24)171
Huntington, Henry E., xxxii, 415
**Huntsman-Trout, Edward (landscape
architect),** xx, 82, 99, 444
Hollywood Turf Club, 1937, (#7)82
Johnson House, 1919, (#37)99
Rex House, #1, 1949, (#30)99
Scripps College, 1927-later, (#13)444
Hupp, Tita, 309
Hutchinson and Hutchinson, 118
Faculty Center (UCLA), 1959, (#21)118
Huxley, Aldous, 15, 135

Iglesia Presbiteriana, c. 1900, 432
Industry, La Puente, 437
Inglewood, Hawthorne, 80-83
Inglewood Memorial Park, 1905-later,
(#8)82
Innes House, 1887-88, (#2i), 184
Inwood, Reginald R., 76
Belmont Theater Building, 1929, (#5)76
Irving, Peridian, 262
Irwin and Associates, 78
Bay City Center, 1979-80, (#16)78
Irwin, Robert, 398
Isosaki, Arata, 39, 231
House, 1986, (#9)39
Museum of Contemporary Art, 1983-87,
(#54)231
Israel and Moss, xxvi
Israel, Franklin D., xxvi
Israel, Franklin D. Design Associates,
38, 39, 91, 122, 132, 148, 159, 162
"Art Pavilion," 1991, (#1)122
Bright and Associates Building, 1990,
(#3)38
Goldberg/Bean House, 1991, (#3)148
Lamy/Newton House, 1988, (#93)162
Limelight Productions, 1991, (#76)159
Propaganda Films Building, 1988,
(#75)159
Speedway Cafe, 1991, (#18)40
Tisch/Avnet Building, 1991, (#32)91
Virgin Records, 1991, (#27)132

Jackson, Foster Rhodes, 443, 444
House, c. 1965, 444
James, George Wharton, xvii
Janotta-Breska Associates, 33, 34

Condominium Town Houses, 1981, (#15)33
Condominium Town Houses, 1981, (#16)34
Condominium Town Houses, 1981, (#18)34
Janss Investment Company, 105, 114
Janus Gallery, c. 1928, (#49)144
Japan American Theater, 239
Japanese American Cultural and Community Center, 239
Jeffers, Robinson, 287
Jefferson Junior High School Building, 1936, (#8)76
Jeffrey, Van Trees, and Millar, 365, 378, 379
    Cheesewright House #1, 1909-10, (#34)379
    Cheesewright House #2, 1912, (#25)378
Jeffries, Jim, 292
    Jeffries House, c. 1905, (#10)292
Jencks, Charles, 15
Jerde Partnership, 325
    City Walk, 1992, 325
Johnson, C. Raimond, 275, 276
    Alan Hancock Foundation and Memorial Museum, 1940, (#13)276
    Methodist Episcopal University Church, 1931, (#10)275
Johnson, Harry (assisted by John Byers), 99
    Johnson House, 1919, (#37)99
Johnson House, 1963, (#1)164
Johnson, Kaufman, and Coate, 392, 399, 404
    All Saints Episcopal Church, 1925,(#38)399
    Griffith House, 1924, (#33)392
    Hale Solar Laboratory, 1924, (#9)404
Johnson, Reginald D., xix, 117, 242, 303, 332, 366, 377, 380, 385
    Church of St. Simon and Jude (Episcopal Home for the Aged), 1926, (#9)303
    Francis House, 1929, (#41)380
    Saint Savior's Chapel, Harvard School, 1914, (#20)332
    Tanner-Behr House, 1917, (#4)385
    Tod Ford House, 1919, (#46)380
    University Residence (Chancellor's House), 1930, (#8)117
Johnson, Reginald D., Wilson and Merrill, Robert E. Alexander, 89
    Baldwin Hills Village, 1940-41, (#26)89
Johnson, William Templeton, 445
    Bridges Auditorium (Pomona College), 1931, 445
Jones, A. Quincy, xxii, xxiii, 92, 102, 113, 139 (see also Noyes, Eliot)
    The Barn, 1965, (#20)113
    Jones House and Studio, 1938, (#18)139
    Murphy Buick Showroom and Garage, c. 1949, (#38)92
    Nordlinger House, 1948, (#1)102
    Winans Apartments, 1948, (#2)102
Jones, A. Quincy and Associates, 277,324
    Cinema-Television Center, 1983, (#23)277

Warner Brothers Records Buildings, 1975, (#12)324
Jones and Emmons, 9, 11, 15, 24, 119, 276, 318, 319, 332, 349
    Campbell Hall School, 1951, (#17)332
    Emmons House, 1954, (#18)15
    Faculty Center (USC), 1960, (#14)276
    Fuller House, 1948-49, (#20)319
    House, 1952, (#6)9
    House, 1952, (#7)9
    Leavitt House, 1948, (#14)318
    Shorecliff Tower Apartments, 1963, (#25)24
    University Research Library (UCLA), 1964, and 1967, (#23)119
Jones, H., 119
    UCLA Extension Building, 1976, (#32)119
    Jones House, 1894, (#10)33
    Jones House, 1907, (#18)23
    Jones House, c. 1913, 24
Jones, Robert Trent, 340
    Juan Matias Sanchez Adobe, 1945, (#4)304
Juarez, Fernando, (#27)261
    David Wark Griffith Junior High School, 1978, (#27)261
Judson Studios, 1901, (#4)285
Judson, William Lees, 285, 286
    Judson House, c. 1895, (#5)286
Justice Building (Huntington Park Civic Center), 1951, 282

Kahn, Kappe, and Lotery, 41, 126
    Barclay Bank and Shops Building, 1973, (#2)126
    Stone Condominium, 1973, (#26)41
Kahn, Louis, 348
Kahrs, George, 70
    Veteran's Memorial Building 1936-37, 70
Kajima Associates (George Shinno), 239
    Japan American Theater, (#113)239
    Weller Court, 1982, (#114)239
Kaku Associates, xxxiii
Kalionzes, Gus, Charles A. Klingerman, and Albert R. Walker, 200
    St. Sophia's Greek Orthodox Cathedral, 1948, (#10)200
Kamebins, Stanley, (see Coate, Roland E. Jr.)
Kamnitzer and Cotton, 218, 231, 295 (see also Gruen Associates,)
    California Plaza and Two California Plaza, 1983-, (#53)231
    Keck Theater, 1987-88, (#4o)295
    Promenade Towers, 1985, (#2)218
Kamnitzer and Marks, 37
    Mariner's Village Apartments, 1980, 37
Kamnitzer, Marks, and Vreeland, 335
    Esplanade Apartment Building, 1967, (#10)335
Kanner Architects, (Stephen Kanner) 25, 107, 202
    Harvard Apartments, 1992-93, (#28)202
    Montana Collection, 1992, (#33)25
    Weyburn/Gayley Building, 1990-91, (#7)107

Kapin, George, 294
    Kapin House, 1935, (#2)294
Kaplin, McLaughlin and Diaz, 128
    Two Rodeo Drive, 1989-90, (#14)128
Kappe, Finn, 17
Kappe, Lotery, and Boccato, 28, 49, 80
    Santa Monica Bus (Transportation) Center, 1982-84, (#51)28
    Stanford M. Anderson Water Treatment Plant, 1977, (#4)80
    University Gymnasium, Athletic and Recreational Complex (Loyola University), 1978-80, 49
Kappe, Raymond L., 14, 15, 51, 56, 86, 97, 330, 335
    Barsha House, 1959, (#15)335
    Bernheim House, 1961, (#17)97
    Elliott House, 1951, 327
    Fredonia Apartment Building, 1964, (#7)330
    Gates-Dorman House, 1961, 15
    Gertler House, 1970, (#13)14
    Gould House, 1969, (#19)97
    Handman House, 1963, (#16)335
    House, 1987, (#6)51
    Kappe House, 1968, (#21)15
    National Boulevard Apartment Building, 1954, (#3)86
    Pregerson House, 1966, 15
    Ravenspur Condominiums, 1966, (#25)56
Kassler, Charles M., 224
Katkov, Richard, (see Mulder, Miriam and Richard Katkov)
Kaufmann, Gordon B., xix, 63, 102, 103, 106, 122, 125, 237, 242, 278, 281, 366, 369, 377, 394, 404, 427, 444
    Aluminum Company of America Building, 1938, (#6)281
    Athenaeum, 1930, (#8d)404
    Dennison Library, 1930, 444
    Doheny House ("Greystone"), 1925-28, (#26)125
    Dormitories (California Institute of Technology), 1931, (#8e)404
    Gordon B. Kaufmann House, c. 1929, (#22)103
    Helms House, 1933, (#2)122
    Lohman House, 1925, 103
    Royal Laundry Building, 1927, (#7)394
    San Pedro High School, 1935-37, (#14)63
    Scripps College, 1927-later, (#13)444
    Security Trust and Savings Bank Building, 1907, (#93)237
    Times-Mirror Building, 1931-35, (#88)237
    Wilbur House, 1928, (#8)369
Kawana, Koichi, 337
    Donald C. Tillman Japanese Gardens, 1983, 337
Kay, Carl, 144, 149, 169
    Apartment Building, c. 1925, (#41)144
    Apartment Building, c. 1938, (#13)169
Keating, Richard, 129
Keim, T. Beverly, 389
    Rochester House, c. 1910, (#6)389

Kelham, George W., 114, 116, 117, 228
Haines Hall (UCLA), 1928, (#3)117
Men's Gymnasium (UCLA), 1932,
(#10)117
Moore Hall of Education (UCLA), 1930,
(#5)117
Powell Undergraduate Library (UCLA),
1927-29, (#2)116
Standard Oil Company Office Building,
1923-24, (#37)228
Kellen, David, 37
Keller Block, c. 1890, (#47)27
Kelley, H. Roy, xxii, 55, 102, 385, 418,
421, 429
Baird House, 1938, (#37)421
Chappellett House, c. 1925, (#10)102
Day House, 1932, (#24)418
Goodrich House, 1928, (#10)55
Koebig House, 1927, (#5)385
Phillips House, 1934, (#36)421
Kelley, H. Roy, Edgar F. Bissantz, and
H. G. Spielman, 333
"Model House," 1935, (#1)333
Kelly, Arthur, 1925, 354, 431
Badger House, c. 1912, (#22)
Everest House, c. 1912, (#21)431
Daniels House, 431
Kennedy, Frederick, 400, 402
Throop Memorial Unitarian-
Universalist Church, 1923, (#45)400
Trinity Lutheran Church, 1927, (#2)402
Kerckhoff House, 1900, (#15)269
Kesling, William P., 144, 172, 182
Duplex, 1936, (#42)144
Johnstone House, 1935, (#29)172
Three Houses, 1935-38, (#43)182
Keyes Bungalow, 1911, (#20)411
Khauakani, Kamran, 126
House, 1983-84, (#38)126
Killingsworth, Brady, and Associates,
76, 77, 78, 277, 445
Cambridge Investment Inc. Building,
1966, (#1)78
Duffield Lincoln-Mercury Agency
Building, 1963, (#9)76
Frank House, 1957, (#14)78
McConnell Center, 1967, 445
Ray and Nadine Watt Hall of
Architecture and Fine Arts (USC), 1973,
(#20)277
Sculpture Walk, 1966, 77
Killingsworth, Edward, 77
King, Richard D. 74
Villa Riviera Apartment Building, 1928,
(#32)74
King, Richard Frederick, 328
Dick Powell House, 1934-35, (#2)328
King's Castle Restaurant, c. 1986, (#1)327
Kings Tropical Inn Restaurant Building,
1925, (#31)90
Kingsford, Paul, 321
Jefferson-Bellarmine Elementary
School, 1971, (#7)321
Kinney, Abbot, 36, 42
Kipp, Lyman, 350
U.S. General Services Administration,
1974, (#3)350
Kley House, 1923, 14

Knauer, J., 175
Apartment House, 1939, (#44)175
Knusu Joint Venture Architects, 239
Kober Associates, 366, 398
Plaza Pasadena, 1980, (#33)398
Koenig, Pierre, xxiii, 9, 99, 136, 139, 148
Beagles House, 1963, (#3)9
Case Study House #21, 1958, (#20)139
Case Study House #22, 1959, 139
Seidel House, 1960, (#36)99
Kohn Peterson Fox, 220
1000 Wilshire Building, 1984-87,
(#14)220
Koning/Eizenberg Architecture, xxxiii,
22, 27, 33, 35, 42, 149, 239
31st Street House, 1992-93, (#30)35
Hollywood Duplex, 1990, (#6)149
Ken Edwards Center for Community
Services, 1986-89, (#48)27
Koning-Eizenberg House, 1988-89,
(#10)22
OP12 Dispersed Affordable Housing,
1986-88, (#13)33
Simone Hotel, 1989, (#111)239
St. John's Hospital Housing, 1986-86
and 1987-88, 33
St. Mary's Housing, 1986-88, 33
Twenty-two Twenty-six Town Houses,
1990-92, 33
Venice (Electric) Art Block, 1989-91,
(#33)42
Kozloff, Joyce, 398
Kramer, George W., 289
Lincoln Avenue Methodist Church,
1898-99, (#24f)289
Kucera, Joseph, 377
Martindale House, 1924, (#15)377
Kupper, Eugene, 103
Nilsson House, 1977, (#18)103
Kuromiya, Yosh, 386
Kyson, Charles H., 270, 316
Administration Building (Forest Lawn
Memorial Park), 1918, (#2)316
Kysor, Ezra F., 238, 274, 289, 436
Merced Theater, 1870, (#6)251
Perry House ("Mount Pleasant"), 1876,
(#24b)289
Pico House, 1869-70, (#7)251
St. Vibiana's Cathedral, 1871-76,
(#101)238
Widney (Alumni House) Hall (USC),
1880, (#1)274

LA Group (landscape architects), 5
Office Building, 1987, (#11)5
La Caña Restaurant Building, c. 1935,
(#40)326
La Canada-Flintridge, 361,-63
La Canada Group, xxxii
La Casa de Rancho Los Alamitos, 1806-
later, (#13)77
La Casa de Rocha, 1865, (#34)92
La Casa Pelanconi, 1855, (#4)251
La Casa Primera Adobe (Ygnacio
Palomares Adobe), c. 1837-later, (#5)438
La Crescenta, 360
La Crescenta Valley, 356-57
Ladd and Kelsey, 124, 151, 164, 277,

294, 355, 369, 380, 401, 445
California Institute of the Arts, 1969-70,
354-55
Claremont Hall (Claremont-McKenna
College), 1966, 445
Crippled Children's Society Regional
Office Building, 1969, (#22)151
Fawcett Hall, 1966, 445
First City Bank, 1961, (#59)401
Herrick Chapel, 1964, (#4c)294
Kelsey House, 1961, (#7)369
Pasadena Museum of Art, 1969,
(#53)380
Quen House, 1959, (#16)124
Registration Building (USC), 1964,
(#16)277
Wolff House, 1960, (#2)164
Ladd, Kelton, 368
Ladd House, 1956, (#6)369
Ladd Studio, 1950, (#5)368
Lafayette Park, 198
La Iglesia de Neustra Señora la Reina de
Los Angeles (The Church of Our Lady the
Queen of the Angels), 1818-22, (#2)250
La Mesa Drive, (#1)22
Lammers, Reed, and Reece (engineers),
35
Santa Monica Freeway, interchange with
the San Diego Freeway, 1961-66,
(#29)35
Lancaster, Clay, 379
Landau Partnership, 31, 71, 229
Biltmore Place, 1985-87, (#44)229
Downtown Plaza, 1983, 71
Sea Colony, 1980, 31
Landberg, Kurt Associates, 399
Landsburgh, G. Albert, 236
Orpheum Theater and Office Building,
1911, (#79)236
Langdon and Wilson, xxvi, 7, 127, 215,
229
CNA Building, 1972, (#38)215
Creative Artist Agency Building, 1989,
(associate architects) (#6)127
J. Paul Getty Museum, 1972-73, (#21)7
Pershing Square, (#45)229
Langdon Wilson Mumper, 221 (see also
Pelli, Cesar and Associates)
Citicorp Plaza 777 Tower, 1988-90,
(#18)221
Lane, Howard, 336
Travelers Insurance Building, 1966, 336
Lankershim, Isaac, 314
Lansburgh, G. A. and Anthony B.
Heinsbergen, 202
Warner Brothers Western Theater,
1930-31, (#31)202
Lansburgh, G. Albert, 154
Warner Theater Building, 1926-27,
(#43)154
Lasuen, Padre Fermin, 351
Laszlo, Paul, xxii, 102, 255
Illing of California, 1946-47, (#5)255
Lautner, John, xxiii, xxiv, 1, 44, 108,
120, 124, 136, 137, 164, 166, 179, 292,
335, 346
Bell House, 1940, (#7)164
Carling House, 1950, (#4)164

Crippled Children Society ("Rancho del Valle"), Main Building, 1979, (#7)346
Familian House, 1971, (#15)124
Foster House, 1950, (#13)335
Krause House, 1983, 1
Lautner House, 1939, (#10)179
Malin, Leonard J. House
("Chemosphere"), 1960, (#14)166
Marina Fine Arts Gallery, 1991, (#44)44
Mauer House, 1949, (#4)292
Sagheb House, 1990, (#1)1
Segel House, 1983, 1
Sheets (L'Horizon) Apartments, 1949, (#18)108
"Silvertop" House and Garden, 1957, (#11)179
Stevens House, 1968, 1
Wolff House, 1963, (#6)137
La Verne, 434
La Verne University, 434
Lawrence, G. (see Barker, M. L. and G. Lawrence)
Lawrence Reed Miline Associates (landscape architects), 47
Lawrie, Lee, 224, 404
Layman, T. W., 346
Platt Office Building, 1981, (#8)346
Le Sopha Group/Environmetrics, Inc. (Olivier Vidal), 128
Rodeo Collection, 1980-82, (#12)128
Leason/Pomeroy Associates, 317
First American Title Company of Los Angeles Building, 1987, (#8)317
Lederer, Francis, 344
Canoga Mission Gallery Building, 1934-36, (#1)344
Ledyard House, "Idyllwild," 1909, (#24)390
Lee, Charles and Elizabeth, 119
UCLA Childcare Center, 1987, (#26)119
Lee, S. Charles, 82, 107, 145, 153, 168, 235, 236, 299, 326, 335
Academy Theater, 1939, (#9)82
Bruin Theater, 1930s, (#5)107
DWP Building, 1939, (#4)326
Department of Water and Power Building, c. 1937, (#11)299
Fox Wilshire Theater, 1929, (#56)145
La Reina Theater, 1939, (#9)335
Los Angeles Theater, 1931, (#77)235
MPA Office Building, 1928, (#1)168
Max Factor Building, 1931 (remodeling), (#35)153
Tower Theater, 1925-26, (#80)236
Lees Market Building, c. 1929, (#8)281
Leicht, A. F., 185
Angelus Temple, 1925, (#11)185
Leimert Park, 266
Leonis Adobe, c. 1850, 340
Leonis, Miguel, 340
Lescaze, William, and E. T. Heitschmidt, 156
Columbia Broadcasting System Building, 1937-38, (#58), 156
Leventhal, Michael, 14
Kaplan House, 1973, (#10)14
Levin and Associates, xxxiii

Levin, Brenda, 117
Levin, Brenda and Associates, 224, 295
Lewis, P. O., 107
Fox Westwood Village Theater, 1931, (#6)107
Lewis, P. P., 110
St. Alban's Episcopal Church, 1940-later, (#2)110
Light, Herman Charles and James Friend, 246
Hall of Records Building, 1961-62, (#7)246
Limolti, Lawrence, 146
House Remodeling, 1961, (#64)146
Lincoln Heights, 297-300
Lincoln Park, 1874, 297, 298
Lind, Edward Richard, xxiii, 80, 161
House, 1939, (#85)161
Three Speculative Houses, 1940, (#3)80
Lindeblade Tower, 1987-89, (#29)90
Lindley, Arthur G. and Charles R. Selkirk, 317
Alexa Theater, 1924-25, (#5)317
Lindsey, George M., 175, 317
Glendale Post Office, 1933-34, (#9)317
John Marshall High School, 1930-31, (#40)175
Lingenbrink, William, 340
Lingenbrink Shops, Studio City, 340
Park Moderne, 1929, 340
Locke, Seymour, and Jasper Newton Preston, 380
Bolt House ("Cobbleoak"), 1893, (#42)380
Loma Court, c. 1925, (#25)213
Lomax-Mills Associates, 97, 137
House, 1973-74, (#15)97
Lomax House, 1970-71, (#4)137
Long Beach City Hall, 1933-34, 71
Long Beach Convention Center, 1974-78, 71
Long Beach, Downtown and West, 69-74
Long Beach, East; Naples, and Seal Beach, 75-78
Long Beach Municipal Auditorium, 1930-32, 71
Long Beach Municipal Utilities Building, 1932, 71
Long Beach, North, 78-79
Long Beach Plaza, 72
Long Beach Veteran's Memorial Building, 1936-37, 71
Longfellow-Hastings (Octagonal House), 1893, (#24g)290
Lopez de Lowther Adobe, 1792-1806, (#10)424
Los Angeles County Fairgrounds, (#4)438
Los Angeles Department of Social Service Building, c. 1925, (#1)64
Los Angeles International Airport, 45-49
Los Angeles International Airport, 1925-present, (#1)46
Los Angeles Pacific Railroad Company, Ivy Park Substation, 1907, (#40)175
Los Angeles Railroad, Inglewood Station, 1928, (#6)80
Los Angeles World Zoo, 176

Los Feliz, 167-176
Lotery, Rex, 97, 99, 124, 126
Kritzer House, 1966, (#34)126
Lassoff House, 1989, (#32)99
Lotery House, 1962, (#22)97
Model House for the Trousdale Development Company, 1965, (#20)124
Schacker House, 1956, (#35)126
Loveless, J. E., 73
Saint Mary's Hospital, 1935, 1937, (#20)73
Lovell, Edward (landscape architect), 77
Earl Burns Miller Japanese Garden, 77
Lowe, David Ming-Li, 4, 41, 100
"Gerb in California" Houses, 1990, (#49)100
House, 1962, (#5)4
Ming-Li Lowe Office Building, 1981, (#28)41
Lower Arroyo Seco, North, 374-83
Lower Arroyo Seco, South, 384-87
Loyola University, 1865-present, (#8)48
Luckman, Charles, 97
Luckman, Charles Associates, xxiv, 80, 107, 196, 226, 227, 256, 295
Broadway Plaza, 1972-73, (#31)226
INA-PEG Building, 1960, (#62)196
Inglewood Civic Center, 1973, (#5)80
Los Angeles Convention Center, 1972, (#9)256
United California Bank Building, 1973, (#35)227
U.S. Federal Office Building, 1970, (#10)107
Wilshire West Plaza, 1971, (#9)107
Luckman Partnership, 71, 324
Arco Center Towers, 1979-82, 71
Warner Brothers Office Building, 1979, (#15)324
Lucy Banning House, c. 1900, (#7)65
Ludwig, Emil, 15
Lummis, Charles Fletcher, xvii, xxvii, 285, 288
Lumsden, Anthony, xxv, 37, 337
Sepulveda Flood Control Basin Reclamation Building, 1984, 337
Lunch Pail Restaurant Building, c. 1930, (#17)300
Lunden, Hayward and O'Conner, 248
Health Administration Building, 1953-54, (#12)248
Lunden, Samuel E., 238, 275, 276
Alan Hancock Foundation and Memorial Museum, 1940, (#13)276
Edward L. Doheny, Jr. Memorial Library (USC), 1932, (#11)275
Pacific Coast Stock Exchange, 1929-30, (#96)238
Lustig, Alvin, 86, 128, 137
Beverly-Landau Apartment Building, 1949, (#7)86
Frank Perls Gallery Building, c. 1948, (#10)128
Wayne House, 1950, (#5)137
Lyman, Frederick, 6
Lyman House, c. 1963, (#19)6

Lyndon, Maynard, 4, 118
Bunche Hall, 1964, (#22)118
Lyndon House, 1950, (#7)4
Lynne, Paxton, Paxton, and Cole, 351
*Ninety-fourth Aero Squadron
Headquarters Restaurant, 1973,*
(#10)351
Lyons Building, 234

MacArthur Park, 198
MacArthur Park, East, 208-215
MacArthur Park, North, 206-207
MacArthur Park, West, 198-206
MacDonald and Couchot, 235, 316
Broadway Arcade Building, 1922-23,
(#73)235
*Southern Pacific Railroad Station, c.
1922,* (#1)316
MacDonald, Kenneth, 9, 321
Memorial Rotunda, 1927, (#1)321
Villa de Leon, 1927, (#1)9
**MacDowell, J. Harold and W. Horace
Austin,**
Civic Auditorium, 1930-32, 69
MacFadden House, 1948, (327
MacGowan House, 1912, 264
Mackintosh, Charles Rennie, 281
Maclay, Charles, 314
Macy Street Viaduct, 1926, (#13)253
Maginnis, Walsh, and Sullivan, 200
*St. Thomas the Apostle Roman Catholic
Church, 1905,* (#11)200
Maguire Partners, 217
Maher, George W., 401
Blinn House, 1905-06, (#55)401
Maki, Fumihiko, 94
Mako, Bartolo, 434
Malibu, 1-7
Malibu Canyon Area, 341
Malon, Edward C., 354
Mannheim, Jean, 378
Mannheim House, 1913, (#26)378
Mansfield House, 1916, (#16)411
Marder, Linda, 138
Marina Del Rey, 37
Marlinex Apartment Building, c. 1930,
(#14)211
Marsh and Graham, 40
Hotel Saint Mark, 40
Marsh and Russel, 36, 39, 42
Apartment Building, c. 1905, (#11)39
University of Arts, 1904-5, (#32)42
Marsh, Norman A., 439
First Baptist Church, 1911, (#11)439
Marsh, Norman F. and Company, 33,
36, 256, 412, 415
Parkhurst Building, 1927, (#11)33
*Second Baptist Church (First A.M.E.
Church), 1924,* (#11)256
*South Pasadena Women's Improvement
Association Clubhouse, 1913,* (#25)415
*Watering Trough and Wayside Station,
1905,* (#8)412
Marsh, Smith, and Powell, 24, 51, 157,
273, 413, 418, 426, 434
Carver Elementary School, 1947,
(#25)418

El Monte High School, 1938-39, 434
*Hollywood High School Science
Building, 1934-35,* (#64)157
Pier Avenue School, 1939, (#10)51
Roosevelt School, 1935, (#27)24
Sierra Madre School, c. 1930, (#11)426
South Pasadena High School, 1937,
(#14)413
Marshall, Abbott Partners, 277
Zohrab A. Kaprielian Hall (USC), 1989,
(#24)277
**Marson and Varner (Marion J.
Varner),** 310
Fire Station, 1959, (#1)310
Marston and Maybury, 302, 303, 366,
377, 398, 400, 410
C. F. Braun and Company, c. 1929-37,
(#11)303
Eliot Junior High School, 1944,
(#12)410
Mark Keppel High School, 1939,
(#6)302
Old Pasadena Post Office, 1938 addition,
(#32)398
Warner Building, 1927, (#41)400
Marston and Van Pelt, 380, 390, 396
American Legion Post, 1925, (#27)396
Garford House, 1919, (#18)390
Staats House, 1924, (#45)380
Turner and Stevens Mortuary, 1922,
(#25)396
Marston, Sylvanus, 26, 383, 390
Buckingham House, 1918-19, (#74)383
Gates to Palisades Park, c. 1912,
(#38)26
House, 1910, (#10)390
Thomas House, 1911, (#70)383
Marston, Van Pelt, and Maybury, xix,
65, 380, 386, 400, 407
*Administration Building (Westridge
School), 1923,* (#9a)386
Grace Nicholson Building, 1924,
(#40)400
Shakespeare Club, c. 1925, (#49)380
Westminster Presbyterian Church, 1928,
(#7)407
*Wilmington Branch Public Library, c.
1926,* (#3)65
Martin, Albert C., xix, 26, 234, 261, 267,
299
Abraham Lincoln High School, 1937-38,
(#15)300
Million Dollar Theater, 1918, (#69)234
*St. Monica's Roman Catholic Church,
1925,* (#41)26
*St. Vincent de Paul Roman Catholic
Church, 1923-25,* (#2)267
Martin, Albert C. and Associates, xxiv,
xxv, 89, 117, 134, 200, 203, 213, 218,
219, 220, 221, 222, 226, 244, 274, 303,
318, 334, 335, 338, 342
865 South Figueroa Tower, 1985-87,
(#16)221
Atlantic Richfield Plaza, 1972, (#27)226
Boulevard Theater, 1925, (#6)200
*Glendale Municipal Services Building,
1965,* (#11)318

*Home Savings of America Tower, 1988-
89,* (#20)221
Law Center Addition, 1987, 274
*Los Angeles Department of Water and
Power Building, 1963-64,* (#1)244
Manulife Plaza, 1981-82, (#6)219
Prudential Building, 1978-80, 342
*Sanwa Bank Plaza (Mitsui Fudosan
Building), 1986-89,* (#13)220
Sears Complex, 1971, (#12)303
Security Pacific Plaza, 1973-74,
(#22)222
Sherman Oaks Galleria, 1980, (#21)335
*St. Basi's Roman Catholic Church,
1974,* (#36)203
Sunkist Headquarters Building, 1969,
(#3)334
Union Bank Building, 1968, (#4)218
*Wells Fargo Building (444 Plaza
Building), 1979,* (#23)222
Wilbur Medical Plaza, 1986, (#2)338
Wilshire Financial Building, 1985-86,
(#20)13
Martin, Albert C. and S. A. Marx, 194
*May Company Department Store
Building, 1940,* (#39)194
1900 Avenue of the Stars Building, 1969,
(#7)134
*May Company Crenshaw Department
Store, 1946-47,* 89
Martin and Dovretzky, 338
Fleetwood Center, 1987, (#1)338
Martin, David C. 49
Library, 1977 (Loyola University), 49
Martin, Donald, 296
Martin House, 1966, (#6)296
Martin, Richard Nagy, (#15)78
Martinez, Alfredo Ramos, 444
Mason House, 1916, (#9)296
Masonic Hall, c. 1900, (#3)435
Masonic Temple, 1858, (#5)251
Maston, Carl L., 84, 86, 97, 136, 138,
148, 180, 205, 387, 412, 440
Chiat House, 1967, (#5)412
Dunham House, 1956, (#14)387
Garden Apartment Building, 1955,
(#2)86
Goldwater Apartment Buildings, 1964,
84
Herman House, 1948, (#16)97
*Kenngott-Brossmer Design Studio
Building, 1968,* (#24)180
*Maston Architectural Office Building,
1967,* (#1)148
Maston House, 1948, (#12)138
*The School of Environmental Design,
1971,* 440
Virgil Apartment Building, 1950,
(#45)205
Matcham, Charles O., 117, 123, 242
Mathews, W. J., 238
St. Vibiana's Cathedral, 1871-76,
(#101)238
**Matthews, Mortimer (Pulliam,
Matthews, and Associates),** 367
Matthews House, 1966, (#1)367

Matlin and Dvoretzky, 68
 South Bay Industrial Park, 1974, (#19)68
Maudlin, Lynn V., 415
 House, 1960, (#2)415
May, Cliff, xxii, 98
 "Mandalay" Cliff May House, 1951-80,
 (#29)98
Maybeck, Bernard, 124, 167, 174
 Anthony House, 1927, (#36)174
Mayberry and Parker, 78
Mayers, George (developer/builder), 39
 Duplex, 1978-81, (#8)39
McAlister, G. C., 23
McAllister, Wayne, 324
 Bob's Big Boy Restaurant, 1949,
 (#16)324
McCarthy, J. Harvey, 134
McCarty Memorial Christian Church,
1931, (#2)264
McClean House, 1929, (#18)411
McClellan, Cruz, Gaylord and
Associates, 391
 Wentworth Hotel, 1991, (#25)391
McCoy, Esther, xxiii, 17, 342
McCoy, Ron, 37
McDonough, Michael, 26
 Bernini House, 1991, (#35)26
McKim, Mead, and White, xix, 154, 383
McKinney, 427
 McKinney House ("The Pyramid
 House"), 1972-74, (#18)427
McLarand, Vasquez and Partners,
xxxiii
McLellan, Douglas and Allen McGill,
150
 First Baptist Church, 1935, 150
McLelland, Douglas, 117
 Mira Hershey Residence Hall, 1930,
 (#9)117
McMurray, Donald, 382, 383, 385
 House, c. 1925, (#6)385
 House, 1938, (#1)385
 McCarthy House, 1937, (#66)382
 Swift House, 1927, (#72)383
McNally, A. N., 408
Mead and Requa, 149, 155
 Krotona Court, 1912-13, (#50)155
 Shrader House, c. 1915, (#14)149
Meier, Richard, 1, 94
 J. Paul Getty Center for the Fine Arts,
 1992-94, 94
Melick, Neal A., 356
Melick, Neal A. and Robert A. Murray,
27
 Santa Monica Post Office, 1937, (#44)27
Meltzmann, Max, 25
 Claremont Apartments, 1929-30,
 (#31)25
Memorial Chapel, Calvary Presbyterian
Church, 1870, (#8)65
Meridian Iron Works, c. 1890, (#7)412
Merithew and Ferris, 383
Methodist Church, 1949, (#5)326
Metropolitan Detention Center, 248
Meyer and Allen Associates, xxxiii, 441
 South Coast Air Quality Management
 District Headquarters, 1990-91, 441

Meyer and Holler, 152, 153, 154, 191,
287 (see also **Milwaukee Building**
Company)
 Egyptian Theater, 1922, (#37)154
 Grauman's Chinese Theater, 1927,
 (#27)152
 Los Angeles First National Bank
 Building, 1927, (#33)153
 Professor's Row, 1911-12, (#18)287
 Wilson Building, 1929, (#26)191
Meyer, Frederick, (#8)39
 Duplex, 1978-81, (#8)39
Meyer, Kurt and Associates, 87, 345,
440
 Great Western Savings and Loan
 Association, 1965, (#14)440
 Great Western Savings Building, 1966,
 (#4)345
 Liberty Building, 1966, (#8)87
 Milbank House, 1910-11, (#20)23
 Milk Bottle (Knudson's Dairy), c. 1935,
 (#11)82
Millard, E. 55
 Sias House, 1927, (#9)55
Miller, Bill, 422
 Miller Water Garden, 1925-later,
 (#2)422
Miller, Leroy B., 160
 EVCO Film Library Building, 1968,
 (#77)160
Miller, Marcus, 150, 192
 Chandler's Shoe Store, c. 1938,
 (#30)192
 Dark Room, The, 1938, (#28)192
 Montecito Apartment Building, 1931,
 (#17)150
Millikan, Robert, 404
Mills House, "Mills View," 1887,
(#17)431
Milner Apartment Building, c. 1925,
(#5h)210
Milwaukee Building Company, 23 (later
Meyer and Holler)
 Weaver House, 1910-11, (#19)23
Miralles and Associates, xxxii
Mission San Fernando Rey De España,
351-52
Mission San Gabriel Archangel, 1791-
1806, (#7)423
Mitchell/Giurgola Architect with
DMJM and Edgardo Cantini, 106
 Center West, 1989-90, (#1)106
Moffat, J. Barry, 330
 Wasman House, 1964, (#12)330
Mohr, William H., 431, 446
 Santa Fe Railroad Passenger Station, c.
 1925, (#24)431, (#22)446
Monaco, Armand, 55
 Haggerty House, 1928, (#15)55
Monroe House, 1887, (#15)431
Monroe, William N., 429
Monrovia, 429-431
Montebello, 304-305
Montebello Park, 304
Montgomery, Ross, 260, 272, 395
 Grace Chapel, c. 1900, 261
 Mausoleum of the Golden West, 260

New Calvary Cemetery and Mausoleum,
1927, (#25)260
St. Andrew's Roman Catholic Church,
1927, (#15)395
St. Cecilia's Roman Catholic Church,
1927, (#29)272
Moore and Turnbull, 14
Moore, Charles W., xxv, xxvi, 11, 14, 15,
35, 130 (see **Urban Innovations Group**)
 Beverly Hills Civic Center, 1981-92,
 (#23)130
 Burns House, 1974, (#23)15
 St. Matthew's Episcopal Church, 1982-
 83, (#12)11
Moore, Charles W. and Richard
Chylinski, 112
 Moore/Rogger/Hofflander Condominium
 Building, 1969-75, (#16)112
Moore, Charles W. and William
Turnbull, 113
 Psychoanalytic Building, 1968-69,
 (#18)113
Moore, Lester S., xvii
Moore, Ruble, Yudell, 24, 32, 98, 102,
116, 117, 320, 398
 Bel Air Presbyterian Church, 1991,
 (#5)102
 Carousel Park, 1982-86, (#1b)32
 Doubletree Inn, 1989-90, (#31)398
 First Church of Christ, Scientist, 1989,
 (#32)320
 Microbiology Research Facility, Unit
 III, 116
 The Peter Boxenbaum Arts Education
 Center/Crossroads School, 1984-89
 (#30)24
 Rodes House, 1978-79, (#23)98
Mooser, William and Company, 96
 Eastern Star Home, 1931-33, (#7)96
Mora, J. J., 429
Morgan and Walls, 231, 235, 236, 238
 I. N. Van Nuys Building, 1910-11,
 (#99)238
 Los Angeles Pacific Telephone Company
 Building, 1911, (#50)231
 Globe Theater, 1921, (#82)236
 Kerkhoff Building, 1907 & 1911,
 (#104)238
 Pantages Theater, 1911, (#72)235
 Van Nuys Hotel, 1896, (102)238
Morgan, Julia, 62, 72, 160, 254, 366, 396
 Hollywood Studio Club Building, 1925-
 26, (#80)160
 Los Angeles Herald-Examiner Building,
 1912, (#1)254
 YWCA Building, 1918, (#2)62
 YWCA Building, 1920-22, (#26)396
 YWCA Building, 1925, (#11)72
Morgan, Walls, and Clements, xix, xx,
xxii, 6, 138, 153, 154, 156, 158, 160, 191,
192, 202, 203, 204, 207, 214, 216, 234,
235, 239, 253, 258, 262, 266, 269, 377
 Adamson House, 1928, (#15)6
 Automobile Showroom, c. 1927,
 (#24)191
 Bank of America Building, 1935
 (remodeling), (#34)153

Belasco Theater, 1926, (#66)234
Carl's Supermarket Building, 1933,
(#32)214
Chapman Building, 1928, (#43)295
Chapman Park Market, 1928-29,
(#43)204
The Citadel Outlet Center, 1990-91, 262
Dominguez-Wilshire Building, 1930,
(#29)192
El Capitan Theater Building, 1926,
(#29)153
Fuller Paint Company Warehouse,
1924-25, (#16)253
Gray Company Building, 1928,
(#108)239
Hite Building, 1923-24, (#31)214
Hollenbeck Home for the Aged, 1896;
1908; 1923, (#8)259
Hollywood Cemetery, 1900, (#81a)160
Hollywood Chamber of Commerce
Building, 1925, (#62)156
KFL (KEHE) Radio Station Building,
1936, (#4)207
Leimert Theater, 1931-32, (#14)266
Mayan Theater, 1926-27, (#65)234
McKinley Building, 1923, (#33)203
Odd Fellows Temple Building, 1924,
(#9)269
Owl Drug Company Building, 1934,
(#44)154
Ralph's Supermarket Building, 1927-28,
(#36)192
Richfield Building, 1928, 216
Samson Tyre and Rubber Company
Building (The Citadel), 1929-30,
(#30)262
Security First National Bank of Los
Angeles, 1929, (#27)192
Store and Office Building, c. 1925,
(#13)138
Story Building and Garage, 1916 and
1934, (#76)235
Toberman Storage Warehouse, 1925,
(#67)158
Warner Brothers Western Theater;
Pellissier Building, 1930-31, (#31)202
Morphosis (Thom Mayne and Michael
Rotundi), xxvi, 42, 51, 129, 144
2-4-6-8 House, 1979, (#37)42
House, 1983, (#8)51
House, 1986-87, 42
Kate Mantilini Restaurant, 1985,
(#16)129
Los Angeles Free Clinic (Selick Ostrow
Building), 1989-90, (#48)144
Sedlak House, 1980, (#36)42
Morris, Allyn E. 137, 178, 181, 182, 290
Aldama Apartments, 1961, (#29)290
Duplexes, 1958-62, (#29)181
Landa Apartment Building, 1966,
(#3)178
Muller House, 1990, (#3)137
Murakakami House, 1962, (#29)181
Silverwood Duplex, 1965, (#42)182
Morris, William, xviii, xxvii, 286, 423
Mosher, Drew, Watson Associates, 440
The Student Health Center (School of

Environmental Design), 1976, 440
"Mosque, The" 1980 (#34)421
Moss and Stafford, 255, 399
Condominiums, 1981, (#36)399
Morgenstern Warehouse, 1978, (#2)255
Moss, Eric Owen, xxvi, 10, 37, 86, 90
708 House, 1979-82, (#10)10
8522 National Building, 1986-90,
(#28)90
Gary Group Office Building, 1988-90,
(#29)90
Petal House, 1982, (#1)86
Moss, Eric Owen and James Stafford,
49
Duplex, 1977, (#12)49
Motels R Us, 1983, (#3)294
Mounce, Wendell and Associates, 230
Mount Baldy Inn, 1927, (#5)304
Mount Carmel High School Building,
1934, (#13)83, (#32)272
Mount Pleasant Bakery Building, c. 1885,
(#2)258
*Mount Washington, 290-92
Mr. Blanding's Dream House, 1947-48,
(#17)6
Mr. King, 294
Sparkletts Drinking Water Corporation,
1925-29, (#1)294
Muir, Edla, 20, 99, 113 (see also **Byers,**
John and Edla Muir)
"Grove, The" Bungalow Court, 1932,
(#19)113
Rex House #1, 1949 (#30)99
Mulder, Miriam and Richard Katkov,
37
Mulgreen, L., 188
Commercial Building, 1929, (#8)188
Mulholland, William, 241
Municipal Ferry Building (City
Hall/Harbor Department Building), 1939-
41, (#3)62
Murmann, Eugene O., xviii
Murphy, Brian, 39
Hopper House, 1989, (#7)39
Murphy/Jahn Associates, 106
10940 Wilshire Tower, 1988, (#1)106
Murray, Robert Dennis, (see **Newton,**
Henry C. and Robert Dennis Murray)
Murray, Robert A. (see **Melick, Neal A.**
and Robert A. Murray)
Murrey, Aleck, 327
Masonic Temple (North Hollywood
Temple Association), 1946-51, (#6)327
Mutlow-Domster Partnership, 113
Kelton-Missouri Townhouses, 1980,
(#22)113
Mutlow, John, 208
Pico Union Villa Building, 1980,
(#4)208
Myers, Barton, 272
Multi-cultural Center, 1983-84, 272
Myer, Kurt and Associates, 142
Center for Early Education Building,
1968, (#34)142
Myer, William E., 282
Lane-Wells Company Building, 1938-39,
(#10)282

Myers, Barton Associates, xxxiii, 48, 68,
149, 325
Child/Family Development Center,
1993, (#18)68
Ivan Reitman Productions Building,
1993, 325
Myers House, 1928, 1985, (#5)149
Wang Tower, Howard Hughes Center,
1986, (#6)48
Myers, Barton Associates; Antoine
Predock Architects; Esherick, Homsey,
Dodge and Davis; Gensler Associates,
119
Northwest Campus Housing and
Commons, 1992, (#25)119

Naples, 77
Needham, Paul Arnold, 138
House, c. 1910, (#17)138
Neff, Wallace, xix, xxii, 55, 102, 103,
104, 109, 126, 341, 363, 366, 388, 392,
405, 407, 416, 417, 419, 424, 427, 429
Barlow House, 1923-24, (#17)427
Bertololli House, c. 1928, (#29)419
Bourne House, 1927, (#18)417
"Bubble House," Experimental Dome
House, 1946, (#1)388
Collins House, 1927, (#11)417
Elliott House, 1925, (#32)392
Doane House, Schuyler, 1924, (#5)416
Galli Curci House, 1938, (#21)109
Gartz House, 1930, (#11)55
Haigh House, 1948, (#27)419
Imerman House, 1936, (#37)126
King G. Gillette Ranch (presently Soka
University), 1929, (#1)341
Miller House, 1932, (#17)103
Neff House, Wallace, 1929, (#30)419
O'Bryan House, 1939, 429
Singleton House, 1973, (#30)104
St. Elizabeth's Roman Catholic Church,
1924, (#8)407
Ten Spec Homes, c. 1927, (#14)405
Up de Graff House, c. 1927, (#15)417
Neff, Wallace and Ernest Torrance, 396
Architect's Offices, 1929, (#20)396
Neher, Otto and C. F. Skilling, 299
Federal Bank Building, 1910, (#8)299
Neptune and Thomas, 5, 294, 295, 433
Citrus Junior College, 433
Odell McConnell Law Center, 1979, 5
Neuerberg, Norman, xxvi, xxviii, 7, 423
J. Paul Getty Museum, 1972-73, (#21)7
Neutra and Alexander, 52, 56, 118
Corinne A. Seeds University Elementary
School, 1950, 1957-58, (#18)118
Palos Verdes High School, 1961,
(#24)56
Riviera Methodist Church, 1957-58
(#16)52
University Nursery-Kindergarten
School, 1957-59, (#19)118
Neutra, Dion, 4, 102, 296, 335
Brown House, 1955, (#12)102
Holiday House Motel, 1950, (#8)4
Kester Avenue Elementary School
Building (addition 1957), (#18)335

Neutra, Richard J., xxi, xxii, xxiii, 4, 12, 15, 17, 28, 56, 62, 89, 99, 102, 108, 110, 111, 112, 120, 122, 124, 136, 140, 144, 148, 155, 161, 164, 172, 178, 182, 213, 246, 278, 280, 282, 292, 296, 328, 335, 348, 375, 411, 444
Akai House, 1961, (#37i)182
Bailey House, 1946-48, (#28)17
Beard House, 1934, (#22)411
Beckstrand House, 1940, (#23)56
Bell Avenue School (Corona School), 1935, (#15)283
Branch House, 1942, (#8)164
Brown House, 1955, (#12)102
California Military Academy, 1934-36, (#23)89
Channel Heights Housing Project, 1941-43, 62
Crescent Professional Building, 1959, (#51)144
Elkay Apartments, 1948, (#16)108
Fine Arts Building, 1959, 348
Flavin House, 1958, (#37g)182
Greenberg House, 1949, (#5)111
Hall of Records Building, 1961-62, (with **Robert Alexander**) (#7)246
Hansch House, 1955, 444
Hinds House, 1947, (#3)292
Holiday House Motel, 1950, (#8)4
Icandomi House, 1960, (#37c)182
Jardinette Apartment Building, 1927, (#84)161
Kambara House, 1960, (#37b)182
Kaufmann House, 1937, (#1)110
Kelton Apartments, 1942, (#15)108
Kester Avenue Elementary School Building, 1951, (#18)335
Koblick House, 1937, (#39)182
Kun Houses, 1938 and 1950, (#24)140
Laemmle Building, 1933, 155
Landfair Apartments, 1937, (#19)108
Lewin House, 1938, 28
Lovell House, 1929, (#27)172
McIntosh House, 1939, (#2)178
Mosk House, 1933, (#54)155
Nesbitt House, 1942, 17, (#40)99
Neutra House, 1964, (#36)182
Ohara House, 1961, (#37h)182
Perkins House, 1955, (#3)375
Plywood Model Experimental House, 1936, (#13)108
Ralph Waldo Emerson Junior High School Building, 1937, (#15)112
Reunion House, 1949, (#37f)182
Rourke House, 1949, (#21)124
Ruben House, 1936, (#17)15
Scholts Advertising Company Building, 1937, (#24)213
Singleton House, 1959, (#8)102
Sokol House, 1948, (#37d)182
Sten-Frenke House, 1934, (#2)12
Strathmore Apartments, 1937, (#17)108
Treweek House, 1948, (#37e)182
Van Cleff House, 1942, (#4)111
Von Sternberg House, 1935, 348
Ward House, 1939, (#2)328
Yew House, 1957, (#37a)182

Neutra, Richard J. and Associates, 296
Eagle Rock Playground Clubhouse, 1953, (#12)296
New Robinson Hotel, 1933, 1934, (#14)72
Newberry Company, 154
J. J. Newberry Company Building, 1928, (#40)154
Newcomb House, 1910, 1922, (#15)369
Newhall; Saugus; Valencia, 354-55
Newsom, Joseph Cather, xvi, 202, 212, 214, 265, 268, 299, 316, 333, 349, 376, 424, 426, 431, 433
Double House, c. 1900, (#22)202
Fitzgerald House, 1903, (#9)265
Flint House, 188, (#15b)212
Greenshaw House, 1907, (#7)376
House, c. 1890, (#13)300
House, c. 1900, (#25)202
House, c. 1902, (#16)212
Lewis House, 1889, (#28)214
Pile House, "Idlewild," 1887-88, (#19)431
Pinney House, 1886, (#12)426
Severance House, 1904, (#6)268

Newsom, Samuel, xvi, 376
Newton, Henry C. and Robert Dennis Murray, 64, 112, 215, 363
Church of the Precious Blood, c. 1932, (#39)215
Church of St. Paul the Apostle, 1930-31, (#14)112
La Canada Thursday Club, c. 1930, (#15)363
Saint Peter and Saint Paul Roman Catholic Church, 1930, (#2)64
Newton Rummond House, 1932, (#6)76
Noble House, c. 1910, (#39)379
Noguchi, Isamu, 239
Nomland, Kemper, and Kemper Nomland, Jr., 377
Case Study House #10, (#13)377
Noonan, Frederick, 237
Stowell Hotel Building, 1913, (#91)237
Normandy Towers, 1924, (#92)162
North Hollywood, 326-327
North Pasadena, 406-408
Northridge, 348
Northwood Inn, 429
Norton, Oakley, 296
Four Houses, 1962-68, (#7)296
Norton, S. Tilden, 205, 233
Temple Sinai East, 1926, (#44)205
William Fox Building, c. 1929, (#61)233
Norton, S. Tilden and F. H. Wallis, 154, 170
Greek Theater, 1913, (#21)170
Shane Building, 1930, (#38)154
Norton Simon Museum, 366
Norton, W. F., 289, 412
Graham House, "Wynyate," 1887, (#6)412
Hale ("C. M.") House, c. 1885, (#24c)289
Norwalk, 312
Norwalk Park, 312
Norwalk Shopping Center, 312
Notre Dame High School Building, c.

1938, (#2)333
Nourse, Clinton, 11
Santa Monica Land and Water Company, 1924, (#15)11
Noyes, Eliot; A. Quincy Jones and Frederick E. Emmons, 49
IBM Aerospace Headquarters, 1963 (#9)49
Nybert and Bissner, 388
Royal Building, 1968, (#27)388

Oakland Cemetery, 347
Oaklawn Avenue, 387
Oakley, Charles Warner, 116
Occidental College, 285, 293
Offenhauser, B. R., 415, 417
House, 1970, (#1)415
Marlow House, 1981, (#10)417
Offenhauser, Francis, 146
House, 1970, (#1)415
Ogilvie, David A., 369
Smith House, 1929, (#10)369
Old Pasadena, (#13)395
Old Plaza Firehouse, 1884, (#9)252
Old Saint Peter's Episcopal Church, 1884, (#10)63
Old Vienna Gardens, 1928-37, 357
Oldenburg, Claes, 38, 143
Oldenburg, Claes and Coosje van Bruggen (sculptors), 143
Margo Leavin Gallery Building, 1989, (#36)143
Olmsted and Olmsted (landscape architects), xx, xxi, 11, 12, 53, 54, 55, 56, 66, 122, 263, 386
Haggerty House, 1928, (#15)55
La Venta Inn, 1923, (#19)56
Malaga Cove School, 1926, (#12)55
Palos Verdes Public Library, 1926-30, (#2)54
Olmsted and Olmsted; Charles H. Cheney, 55
Palos Verdes Golf Course, 1922 and later, (#7)55
Olmsted and Olmsted; Charles H. Cheney; Webber, Staunton, and Spaulding, 54
Malaga Cove Plaza, 1922 and later, (#1)54
Oliver, Henry, 122
Spadena House, 1921, (#3)122
Orozco, Jose, xxxiv
Orr, Robert H., 168, 204, 205, 432, 439, 443
Commercial Garage, 1927, (#42)204
Hollywood Christian Church, 1922, (#2)168
Ninth Church of Christ, Scientist, 1924-27, (#47)205
Pilgrim Congregational Church, 1911, (#7)439
Pitzer House, 1910, (#2)443
Wells Fargo Bank, 1918, 432
Wilshire Boulevard Christian Church, 1922-23, (#37)203
Orr, Strange, and Inslee, 434
Church of the Brethren, 1930, 434

Ortega-Vigare Adobe, 1792-1805, (#6)422
Osgood-Farley, Leary-Merrian
Emplacements, 1916, 63
Oud, J. J. P., 49
Our Lady of Guadalupe Church, 1917,
436
Owl Drug Store Building, c. 1930,
(#65)146

Pacific Mutual Building, 1912 etc.,
(#46)230
Pacific Palisades, North, 8-11
Pacific Palisades, South, 12-19
*Pacific Telephone Company Building, c.
1926*, (#7)200
Pacoima, 333
Padua Hills, (#9)444
**Page, Raymond E. (landscape archi-
tect),** 122
Paietta House, 1928, (#13)318
Palisades Elementary School, 1930,
(#14)11
Palmdale; Lancaster, 356
Palmer, Neil Stanton, 69, 240
*Palmetto Construction Headquarters,
Department of Water and Power, 1991-
92*, (#119)240
*Tomunjun Professional Building, 1979-
80*, (#22)69
Palms Railroad Station, c. 1886,
(#24a)289
Palomares Adobe, c. 1850-54, (#2)438
Palos Verdes, North, 53-56
Palos Verdes, South, 57
Paramount Laundry Building, 1987-89,
(#29)90
Paramount Studio Lot, (#81b)160
Parcher, Ellet, 153
Bank of America Building, 1914,
(#34)153
Park House, 1904, (#14)369
Park Place, c. 1920, (#9)439
Parkes, A. B., 365
Parkes, T. W., 387
*Waiting Station and Cobblestone Wall,
c. 1902*, (#24)387
Parkin Architects, 120
John Wooden Center, 1983, (#38)120
Parkinson and Bergstrom, 412
Bilike House, 1905-06, (#3)412
Parkinson and Parkinson, xix, xxii
Parkinson, Donald B. and J. M. Estep,
32
Santa Monica City Hall, 1938-39,
(#3)32
Parkinson, John, 219, 237, 266, 273
Alexandria Hotel, 1906, (#94)237
Brady Block, 1904, (#90)237
Engine Company #28 Building, 1912,
(#10)219
Fire Engine House No. 18, 1904,
(#15)266
Security National Bank Building, 1916,
(#93)237
Parkinson, John and Donald B., 106,
128, 204, 231, 233, 238, 252, 271, 272,
274, 275

Banks-Huntly Building, 1929-31,
(#97)238
Bridge Hall, 1928, (#7)275
*Bullocks-Wilshire Department Store
Building, 1928*, (#41)204
*George Finley Bovard Administration
Building, 1920-21*, (#2)274
*Gwynn Wilson Student Union Building,
1927-28*, (#5)275
Holmby Hall, 1929, (#4)106
Law School Building (USC), 1926,
(#4)275
*Los Angeles Branch, Federal Reserve
Bank of San Francisco, 1930*, (#51)231
Manual Arts High School, 1934-35,
(#28)272
Memorial Coliseum, 1921-23, 271
Pacific Coast Stock Exchange, 1929-30,
(#96)238
*Physical Education Building (USC),
1928*, (#6)275
*Saks Fifth Avenue Store Building, c.
1936-37*, (#9)128
Science Building (USC), 1928, (#8)275
*Title Guarantee Building (Guarantee
Trust), 1929-30*, (#59)233
Union Passenger Terminal, 1934-39,
(#11)252
Parkinson, John and Edwin Bergstrom,
230, 237, 238
Los Angeles Athletic Club, 1911-12,
(#48)230
*Security Trust and Savings Bank
Building, 1907*, (#93)237
Parlee, A. C. (builder), 394
Palmetto Court, 1915, (#6)394
Parr, George, 33
Merle Norman Building, 1935-36,
(#8)33
Union Oil Building, c. 1911, (#98)238
Parson, Arthur, 77
Parsons, A. W., 224
**Parsons, Brinkerhoff, Quade and
Douglas,** xxxii
Parsons Tower, 366
Pasadena, 364
*Pasadena Jewish Temple and Center,
1957*, (#14)408
Patterson, H. M., 72
First Congregational Church, 1914,
(#10)72
Peacock Cafe, 427
Pechey, Archibald Dixon, 287
Hiner House and Sousa Nook, 1922,
(#19)287
Pei, Cobb, Freed & Partners, 118, 127,
256
Creative Artist Agency Building, 1989,
(#6)127
*John E. Anderson Graduate School of
Management, 1994*, 118
Los Angeles Convention Center, (#9)256
Pei, I. M. and Partners, 222, 274
First Interstate World Center, 1988-90,
(#24)222
Pelli, Cesar, xxv, 348
Teledyne Systems Company, 1968, 348

Pelli, Cesar and Associates, 221
Citicorp Plaza 777 Tower, 1988-90,
(#18)221
Pepperdine Center Building, 83
Percy Bitton Limited (developer), 422
San Gabriel Village, c. 1938, (#5)422
Pereira and Luckman, 187, 213, 242,
402, 443
CBS Television City, 1952, (#1)187
Robinson's Pasadena, 402
Signal Oil Company Office Tower, 1958,
(#21)213
*Southern California School of Theology,
1960-61*, (#7)443
Pereira, William and Associates, xxiv, 5,
46, 47, 119, 133, 145, 193, 196, 226, 242,
274, 276, 294, 295, 310, 393
*Ahmanson Center for Biological
Research, 1964*, (#15)276
City Hall, 1967, (#2)310
Coons Administrative Center, 1968, 294
Dickson Art Center, 1965, (#27)119
Fox Plaza, 1985-87, (#2)133
*Great Western Savings Center Building,
1972*, (#58) 145
*Los Angeles County Museum of Art,
1964*, (#38a)193
Lytton Building, 1968, (#55)196
Norris Residence Hall, 1966, (#4n)295
*Parsons Company Office Tower, Ralph
M., 1974*, (#1)393
Pepperdine University, 1971–73,
(#12)5
Security Pacific Building, 1973,
(#30)226
Town Center Hall, 1971, (#4)310
Peridian Group (landscape architects),
391
Peters, Harry, 360
Peters, Jock, 149, 204, 340, 341, 421
*Bullocks-Wilshire Department Store
Building, 1928*, (#41)204
Community Building, 1931, (#2)340
Fountain, 1930, (#3)340
House, 1931, (#1)340
Lingenbrink House, 1930, (#11)149
Sheppard House, 1934, (#32)421
Well-house, 1931, (#6)341
Phelps, Barton and Associates, 103, 104,
116, 118, 124, 248, 265, 326
*East Building; Corinne A. Seeds
University Elementary School, 1990-93*,
(#20)118
Epstein House, 1988-89, (#17)124
Kranz House, 1989-91, (#19)103
*Los Angeles Department of Water and
Power Central District Headquarters,
Phase II, 1988-92*, (#14)248
*North Hollywood Pump Station,
Department of Water and Power, 1989-
92*, (#1)326
North Range, 1989-90, 265
Phelps-Simonson House, 1981-85,
(#27)104
*Tiverton House (Patient Family Guest
House)*, 116
Philharmonic Auditorium Building, 217

Phillip, Clark, 74
Ebell Club Building, 1924, (#29)74
Phillips House, 1875, (#22)440
Phillips House, 1887, (#2a)183
Pico Garden Apartments, 258
Pico, Governor Pio Adobe, 1842, 1882, (#17)309
Pico Rivera, 304-305
Pie, Cobb, Freed and Associates, 116
Anderson School of Management, 116
Eltinge House, 1921, (#34)181
Pierce, Harry L., 431
United Presbyterian Church, c. 1926, (#12)431
Pierce, Harry W., 319
North Glendale Methodist Church, 1941, (#27)319
Pilgrim Congregational Church, c. 1905, (#30)272
Pinney House, 1887, (#21)184
Placerita Canyon State Park and Nature Study Center, 354
Plaza Pasadena, 366, 392
Plummer and Feil, 235
The Dutch Chocolate Shop, 1914, (#75)235
Plummer, Charles F., 213, 235
Schauber's Cafeteria, 1927, (#78)235
Young's Market Building, 1924, (#19)213
Point Fermin Lighthouse, 1874, (#13)63
Police and Fire Station of Venice, c. 1930, (#35)42
Polyzoides, Stefanos, et al., 140
Pomona, 438-40
Ponce de Leon Apartment Building, c. 1905, (#1)208
Pope, John Russell, xxvi, 419
Huntington Mausoleum, 1933, 419
Porter House, 1875, (#16)387
Portman, John and Associates, 218
Bonaventure Hotel, 1974-76, (#5)218
Postle Co., D. E. (designers), 411
Gunther House, 1923, (#23)411
Powers, G. W., 202
Val d'Amour Apartment Building, 1928, (#29)202
Predock, Antoine, 41, 342
Douroux House, 1989-90, (#25)41
Thousand Oaks Art and Civic Center, 1994, 342
Presbyterian Conference Grounds, 1922-later, (#11)10
Price, Roy Selden, 102, 164, 191
Courtyard Retail and Office Building, c. 1926, (#25)191
Margaret Shelby Fillmore House (Edward A. Bailey), 1929, (#13)166
Prisbey, Tressa, 342
Grandma Prisbey's Bottle Village, 1959-74, (#2)342
Priteca, B. Marcus, 62, 129, 155, 233, 282
Fox-Warner Brothers Theater, 1931, (#1)62
Pacific Theater, 1931, (#18)129
Pantages Theater Building, 1929,

(#49)155, (#63)233
Warner Brothers Downtown Building, 1920, (#63)233
Warner Brothers Theater, 1930, (#13)282
Producers Film Center, c. 1928, (#70)158
"Promenade, The," 71
Pulliam, Matthews, and Associates, 123, 332, 367, 377, 401, 403, 405, 434, 440
Apartment Building, 1963, (#5)403
Cunningham House, 1980, (#19)377
Heidemann House, 1972, (#6)123
Kinsey Office Building, 1978, (#25)332
Pasadena Public Library, Lamanda Park Branch, 1966, (#12)405
Retail Shops, 1961, (#60)401
Security Savings Bank, 1976, 434
Student Union, 1976, 440
Pulliam, Zimmerman, and Matthews (Bernard Zimmerman) 332
Dorman/Winthrop Clothiers Building, 1966, (#22)332
Pullman and Matthews, 62
Purdy, Benjamin Morton (landscape architect), 98
Temple House 1935-36, (#28)98
Putnam Place Town House, 1983, (#25)34

Queen Mary, The, 1934, (#36)74
Queen Surf Condominiums, 1974-75, 71

Radio Building, The, c. 1941, (#15)88
Radon, Meyer, 24
Sovereign Hotel and Apartments, 1928-29, (#28)24
Rainer and Adams, 419
House, 1933, (#28)419
Ralph Parsons Company (engineering), 143
Rapid Transit District Bus Maintenance Facility, 1982, (#37)143
Ramirez Design Associates (Lionel Ramirez), 92
Ramona Gardens Public Housing, 1940-41, (#5)298
Rancho de los Encinos, 336
Rancho San Pedro, 1942, 62
Randy's Donuts, 1954, (#1)80
Rankin, J. S., 241
Raymond, J., 132
Cañon Court, 1930, (#29)132
Reavis House, 1923, (#7)359
Reddon, John and John G. Raben, 87
Sears, Roebuck, and Company Store Building, 1939, (#14)87
Reed Jewelers, c. 1929, (#71)235
Reed, John, 6
Reed House, 1960, (#18)6
Reed Neurological Research Center (UCLA), 119
Reid, Hiram, 384
Renton, D. M., 59
Mount Ada, 1921, (#1)59
Rex, John, 57, 99
Ekdale House, 1948, (#3)57
Rex House #2, 1955, (#31)99
Ridgeway, Harry, 365, 395, 401, 408,

410
Lukens House, 1886-88, (#57)401
Venetian Revival Building, 1887, 395
Williams House, "Hillmon," 1887, (#11)408
Woodbury House, 1882, (#10)410
Ridgeway, Henry, 382
MacPherson House, 1894, (#64)382
Rietveld, Gerrit, 33
Riggs, Lutah Maria, 54, 264
Risley, W. L., 55
Palos Verdes Estates Project House #2, 1925, (#14)55
Robbins and Brown, Inc., 106
Ashton Towers, 1989, (#1)106
Robbins House, 1931, 362
Robert Louis Stevenson School, c. 1936, (#26)73
Roberts, Thane, (see **Fisher, Frederick and Thane Roberts)**
Roberts, Tom, 124, 328
Condominiums, 1975, (#1)328
Three Houses, 1976, (#19)124
Rochlin and Baran and Associates, 338, 348
Medical Center of Tarzana, 1973, 338
Northridge Hospital, 1968-later, 348
Rodia, Simon, 283, 342
Watts Towers, 1921-45, 278, (#19)283, 342
Roehrig, Frederick L., 11, 196, 269, 365, 372, 381, 383, 386, 394, 401, 406, 408, 410
Department of Water and Power Building, 1935, (#16)11
Hotel Green, 1898, 1903, (#10)394
House, 1891, (#2)406
Marshall-Eagle House, 1917, (#71)383
McMurran House, 1911, (#33)372
McNally House, 1888, (#2)408
Performing Arts Building, 1909, (#9b)386
Rindge House, 1900, (#14)269
Scofield House, 1909, (#55a)381
Van Nuys House, 1898, (#57)196
Woodbury House, 1882, (#10)410
Roman's Food Mart, c. 1935, (#31)192
Root Beer Barrel Restaurant, c. 1932, (#24)284
Rose Bowl, 366
Rose Gardens, 271
Rose House, 1862, (#1)422
Rosedale Cemetery, (#51)206
Rosenheim, Alfred F., 74, 237, 269
Clunes Broadway Theater, 1910, (#74)235
Hellman Building, 1903, (#89)237
Second Church of Christ, Scientist, 1905-10, (#12)269
Rosenthal, Alfred B., 239
California Theater, 1918, (#106)239
Rosier, Grillias Pirc, 274
Pertusati Bookstore, 1987, 274
Ross, A. Patterson, 316
Church of the Flowers, 1918, (#2)316
Rossiter-Banfield Company, 389
House, 1915, (#5)389

Roth, Ralph, 59
Rotundi, Michael, 178, 219, 253
CDLT 1, 2 House, 1987-92, (#5)178
Carlson Studio-House, 1992, (#15)253
Nicola Restaurant, 1992-93, (#9)219
Route 66—San Gabriel Valley, 364
Rowan Building (Bradley Building), 1930, (#8)72
Rowlett, Caudill, 119
James E. West Alumni Development Center, 1974-76, (#31)119
Ruble, Michael, 436
Ruble House, "The Rock Castle," 1985, (#8)436
Ruck, W. F., and Claude Beelman, 258
Rosehill Courts Public Housing, 1942, (#1b)258
Rucker, Douglas W., 6
Rucker House, 1971, (#13)6
Russell, George Vernon, 102, 149, 386
Gertrude Hall Building and Classrooms, 1955, (#9g)386
Pike House, 1952, (#10)149
Russell House, 1887-88, (#2b)183
Russian Village, 1928-later, 446

Saarinen, Eero, xxiv, 17 (see also
Charles Eames)
Entenza House, 1949, (#27)17
Saarinen, Eliel, 115, 118, 242, 308
Sabin, Palmer, 102, 242, 373
Franks House, 1932, (#38)373
Sachs, Herman (color consultant), 252
Union Passenger Terminal, 1934-39, (#11)252
Sacred Heart Roman Catholic Church, c. 1900 (#7)299
Saemundsson, Nina, 214
Prometheus, 1935, (#33)214
Safdie, Moshe and Associates, 130
Saint John's Episcopal Church, 1883, (#4)65
Saint Paul's Cathedral, 217
**Sakurai, Nagao, with Dudley Fridgett;
Kazuo Nakamura,** 103
Japanese Garden, 1961, (#16)103
**Salisbury, Bradshaw, and Taylor
(Arthur Taylor),** 145
Beverly Hills Water Department Building, 1927, (#59)145
Samuel Wacht Associates, 120
Le Conte-Levering Faculty Housing, 1982-83, (#39)120
San Dimas, 433
San Fernando, 352-53
San Fernando Valley, 314
San Fernando Valley State College, 348
San Gabriel Union Church and School, 1936, (#3)422
San Gabriel Valley, 422-24
San Marino, 415-21
San Pedro, 61-63
Sanders House, 1887, (#2k)184
Santa Catalina Island, 58-60
Santa Fe Passenger Station, c. 1880, (#6)305
Santa Fe Railroad Passenger Station

(Whittier), c. 1889, (#3)306
Santa Fe Railroad Station, c. 1885, 438
Santa Fe Springs, 310-311
**Santa Monica Architectural Group
(Tom Oswald),** 123
O'Neill House and Pavilion, 1978-84, (#10)123
Santa Monica Museum of Art, 32
Santa Monica, North, 20-30
Santa Monica Pier, 1909-21, (#1a)31
Santa Monica, South, 31-35
Saunders, W. J., 158, 381
Community Laundry Building, 1927, (#68)158
Rhodes House, 1906, (#58)381
Savoy, Vincent, 443
Criley-Patterson House, c. 1965, (#5)443
House, c. 1965, (#4)443
Sawtelle Veterans Hospital, (#1)94
Saxsmith, Harold, 421
Townley House, 1936, (#38)421
Schabarum, Peter K., 350
Valley Municipal Building, 1932, (#2)350
Scherer, L. G., 403
Thatcher Medical Center, 1948-49, (#4)403
Scherer, Lester, 188, 260
Meade House ("La Casa de las Campanas"), c. 1927, (#12)188
Our Lady of Lourdes Roman Catholic Church, 1930, (#24)260
Schilling and Schilling, 73
Hancock Motors, 1929, (#21)73
Lafayette Hotel Building, 1929, (#15)73
Pacific Auto Works, 1928-29, (#25)73
Schindler, R. M. xxi, xxii, xxv, 6, 18, 42, 46, 51, 52, 60, 87, 100, 109, 122, 124, 135, 136, 137, 139, 140, 141, 143, 148, 150, 151, 155, 163, 164, 170, 171, 174, 175, 177, 178, 179, 181, 185, 194, 284, 294, 318, 330, 331, 332, 338, 340, 384, 414, 418, 424
Bethlehem Baptist Church, 1944, (#22)284
Braxton House, 51
Bubeshko Apartment Building, 1938 & 1941, (#4)178
Buck House, 1934, (#40)194
Droste House, 1940, (#21)180
Druckman House, 1941, (#3)164
Duplex for De Keysor, 1935, (#15)150
Duplexes, 1922, (#38)143
Elliot House, 1930, (#45)175
Elliott House, 1951, 327
Erlik House, 1952, (#24)151
Falk Apartments, 1939, (#6)178
Fitzpatrick House, 1936, (#12)164
Gold House, 1945, (#10)330
Goodwin House, 1940, (#9)330
Grokowsky House, 1928, (#15)414
House, 1929, (#5)340
Howe House, 1925, (#28)181
Janson House, 1949, (#19)139
Kallis House, 1947, (#6)330
Lacey Duplex, 1922, (#10)185

Laurelwood Apartment Building, 1948, (#8)330
Lechner House, 1948, (#11)339
Lingenbrink Shops, 1939-42, (#19)332
Lowe House #1, 1923, 294
Lowe House #2, 1937, 294
Mackey Apartment Building, 1939, (#13)87
Manola Court (Sachs) Apartment Building, 1926-40,(#7)178
McAlmon House, 1935-36, (#37)174
Medical Arts Building, 1945, (#18)332
Modern Creators Store Building, 1937, (#29)141
Olive House, 1933, (#12)179
Packard House, 1924, (#23)418
Presburger House, 1945, (#16)332
Reis House, 1950, (#7)137
Rodakiewicz House, 1937, (#22)124
Rodriguez House, 1941, (#12)318
Roth House, 1945, (#13)331
Sardi's Restaurant, 1932-34, 155
Schindler Studio House, 1921-22, (#40)143
Schindler Studio Residence A, 1920, (#24)171
Schlesinger House, 1952, (#43)175
Skolnik House, 1952, (#16)170
Sorg House, 1926, (#12)424
Southhall House, 1938, (#13)185
Tischler House, 1949, (#20)109
Tucker House, 1950, (#25)140
Van Dekker House, 1940, 338
Van Patten House, 1934-35, (#16)179
Von Koerber House, 1931-32, (#18)52
Walker House, 1936, (#22)180
Westby House, 1938, (#8)178
Wilson House, 1938, (#17)80
Wolfe House, 1928, (#5)60
Zaczek Beach House, 1936-38, 46
Schuchardt, William, 242
**Schulitz, Helmut (Urban Innovations
Group),** 125
Schulitz House, 1977, (#24)125
Scully, Vincent, Jr., xvii
Schultze and Weaver, 219, 229, 232, 238
Biltmore Hotel, 1922-23, (#43)229
Hellman Commercial Trust and Savings Bank Building, 1924, (#100)238
Jonathan Club, 1924, (#7)219
Subway Terminal Building, 1924-26, (#56)232
Schultze, Leonard and Associates, 123, 187
**Schultze, Leonard and Son and E. T.
Heitschmidt,** 187
Park La Brea Housing (Metropolitan Life Housing Development), 1941-42, (#3)187
Schwartz, Martha (landscape architect), 262
Selkirk, Charles: Honnold and Russel, 136
Sunset Plaza, 1934-36, (#2)136
Senator Madison Jones House, 1902, (#33)320
Serra, Father Junipero, 147, 351

Sessions House, 1888, (#2h)184
Sessions, Kate (landscape architect), xx
Shatto, G., 58
Shattuck, Charles E., 290
  Morrell House, 1906, (#27)290
Shaver Partnership, 434
  *Student Center and Drama Laboratory
  (La Verne University), 1973,* 434
Shaw, Howard, 53
  *Shaw ("Valley Knudson Memorial")
  House, c. 1877,* (#24d)289
Sheets, Millard, xxiv, xxxiv, 28, 331,
  413, 443, 444
  Garrison Theater, 1963, 1970, (#12)444
Shellhorn, Ruth (landscape architect),
  (#37)183, 401
Shepard, Otis, 59
Sherwood Country Club, 1991-92, 342
Sherwood, Roger, 140
**Shipley, Phil and Associates (landscape
architects),** 130, 132
  *Music Corporation of America Building,
  1940, 1968-72,* (#24)130
  Shoreline Square, 1986-87, 71
  Showboat Restaurant, 1968, (#4)328
Shulman, Julius, 140
Sibbert, Edward F., 154
  Kress and Company Building, 1935,
  (#39)154
Siebel, John Associates, 136
  Sunrise Plaza Apartment Building, 1982,
  (#1)136
Siegel Diamond Architects, 83, 113, 120,
207
  Feitler House, 1993-94, (#23)113
  *Multipurpose and Classroom Building,
  Commonwealth Avenue Elementary
  School, 1992-93,* (#5)207
  Richstone Family Center, 1993-94,
  (#17)83
  University of California Parking
  Services and Ridesharing, 1991,
  (#36)120
Siegel, Gwathmey and Associates, 12,
130
Siegel, Skarek and Diamond, 339
  Chateau Office Building, 1985, 339
Sierra Madre, 425-427
Silver Lake, 177-182
Simi Valley, 341
Simon, Louis A., 246, 307, 346, 356
  Canoga Park Post Office, 1938, (#6)346
  *Federal Building and Post Office, 1938-
  40,* (#9)246
  Whittier Post Office, 1935, (#9)307
Sinclair, Bonito A. and Associates, 47
Siple, Allen, 99, 113, 443
  "Grove, The" Bungalow Court, 1932,
  (#19)113
  Siple House, 1949-59, (#35)99
Skidmore, Owings, and Merrill, 84, 129,
  134, 203, 220, 221, 228, 229, 233, 253,
  317, 325, 393
  ABI Tower, 1971, (#8)134
  American Savings Bank Building, 1986,
  (#6)317
  Bank Americard Building (Bank of

America Computer Center), 1979,
(#19)253
Beneficial Plaza, 1967, (#32)203
*Columbia Savings and Loan Building
(I), 1987,* (#19)129
*Columbia Savings and Loan Building
(II), 1987,* (#20)129
Crocker Center, 1982-83, (#38)228
The Gas Company Towers, 1988-91,
(#42)229
Getty Oil Company Building, 1984, 325
*Great Western Savings and Loan
Association, 1952,* 84
International Jewelry Center, 1979-81,
(#60)233
Office Building, 1978-80, (#12)220
Office Buildings, 1979, 1981, (#1)393
One Wilshire Building, 1964, (#41)229
*Seventh Market Place (Bullocks
Department Store), 1985-86,* (#19)221
Smale, Clarence J., 48, 190, 191
  Apartment Building, 1930, (#22)191
  Loyola Theater, 1946, (#5)48
  Smith House, 1929-30, (#17)190
Small, Franklin M.; Walter Webber,
151, 297
  Bernheimer Bungalow, 1913, (#21)151
Smith and Williams, 119, 125, 292, 295,
333, 348, 362, 370, 377, 394, 401, 414,
444
  Blaisdell Medical Building, 1952,
  (#53)401
  Clarke House, 1950, (#28a)125
  Crowell House, 1952, (#16)377
  *Dean of Students' House (Occidental
  College), 1951,* (#4j)295
  1414 Fair Oaks Building, 1959,
  (#16)414
  Friend Paper Company, 1965, (#3)394
  Goldman Medical Building, 1948, 333
  Modern Tract Housing, 1954, 348
  Sale House, 1949, (#28b)125
  *Sunset Canyon Recreation Facility,
  1964,* (#24)119
  Williams House, 1948, (#9)292
Smith, George Washington, xix, 102,
365, 377, 385, 392, 417
  Baldwin House, 1925, (#14)417
  Ostoff House, 1924, (#13)417
  Prindle House, 1926, 1928, (#31)392
  Young House, 1927, (#14)377
Smith, Jones, and Contini, 174
  Griffith Park Girl's Camp, 1949,
  (#33)174
Smith, L. A., 415
  Rialto Theater, 1925, (#24)415
Smith, Powell, and Morgridge, 84
  El Camino College, 1951, 84
Smith, Whitney R., xxii, xxiii, 370, 386,
409, 417, 418, 419
  Coates House, 1938, (#6)409
  *Frank, Laurie and Susan Art Studio,
  1978,* (#9e)386
  *Hoffman Gymnasium-Auditorium
  (Westridge School), 1980,* (#9c)386
  House, c. 1940, (#20)418
  Jordan House, 1941, (#19)417

Mudd, Seeley G. Science Building, 1978,
(#9e)386
Neighborhood Church, 1972, (#29)370
**Smith, Whitney R., A. Quincy Jones,
and Edgardo Contini,** 97
  *Mutual Housing Association
  Community, 1947-50,* (#21)97
Smithley, C. K., 194
  Monterey Apartments, 1925, (#41)194
Solberg and Lowe, 159
  The Burger that Ate L.A., 1989,
  (#71)159
Soriano, Raphael S., xxi, xxii, xxiii, 18,
77, 86, 103, 124, 136, 137, 148, 164, 172,
176, 180, 185, 260, 266, 292, 309, 321
  Adolph's Office Building, 1951-53,
  (#4)321
  C.S.H. House, 1950, (#32)18
  Colby Apartment Building, 1950, (#6)86
  Curtis-Noyes House, 1950, (#20)103
  Gogol House, 1938-39, (#46)176
  House, 1941, (#8)292
  Kimpson-Nixon House, 1939, (#11)77
  Koosis House, 1940, (#18)150
  Krause House, 1950-52, (#15)309
  Lipetz House, 1935, (#19)180
  *Los Angeles Jewish Community Center,
  1937,* (#14)260
  Lukens House, 1940, (#12)266
  Polito House, 1939, (#8)137
  Ross House, 1938, (#15)185
  Schrage-Hallauer House, 1951,
  (#26)172
  Schulman House and Studio, 1950,
  (#10)164
  Strauss-Lewis House, 1940, (#4)86
  Touriel Medical Building, 1950,
  (#13)266
South Beach Area, 50-52
South Carthay, 135
South Pasadena, Central Section, 412-14
*South Pasadena Presbyterian Church,
1906,* (#10)412
*Southern Pacific Railroad Station, c.
1900,* 354
Spanish Colonial Revival Village, c. 1928,
(#29)388
Spanish Kitchen Building, c. 1925,
(#6)188
Spaulding and Rex, 201
  *American National Red Cross Chapter
  Building, 1939,* (#21)201
Spaulding, Sumner, xix, 46, 242
Spaulding, Sumner and John Rex, 48
  Westchester High School, 1952, (#7)48
Sprague, A. A., 381
  Sprague House, 1903, (#55b)381
Sproul, Gilbert House, c. 1889, 312
St. Athanasius Episcopal Church, c. 1890,
(#9)185
*St. Ferdinand's Roman Catholic Church,
1949,* 352
St. Luke's Hospital, 1934, (#15)408
St. Robert Bellarmine Complex, 321
*St. Steven's Servian Orthodox Cathedral,
1949-52,* (#13)303
Stacy-Judd, Robert B., xx, 23, 26, 185,

191, 327, 431
  Atwater Bungalows, 1931, (#14)185
  Aztec Hotel, 1925, (#16)431
  Masonic Temple (North Hollywood
  Temple Association), 1946-51, (#6)327
  Sisson House, 1926, (#19)191
  Worrel House, 1926, (#23)23
Stafford/Bender, 32
  Condominium Town Houses, 1981-82,
  (#5)32
Stafford, James, (see **Moss, Eric Owen**
and James Stafford)
Standard Service Station, 1962, 47
Stanford, Leland, 314
Stanley, George (sculptor), 148
Stanton, J. E., 445
  Honnold Library, 1952, (#15)445
Stanton, J. E., W. F. Stockwell, Paul R.
Williams, Adrian Wilson, 245, 246, 398
  Hall of Administration Building, 1056-
  61, (#6)246
  Los Angeles County Courthouse, 1958,
  (#4)245
  Paseo de los Pobladores, 1961-, (#5)246
Stanton, Reed, and Hibbard, 110, 221
  Doheny Memorial Dormitory for Girls,
  1931, (#3)110
  Hotel Figueroa, 1925, (#17)221
Stanton and Stockwell, 248, 274
  Honnold Library, 1956 addition,
  (#15)445
  Los Angeles Mall, 1973-74, (#11)248
Starkman, Maxwell and Associates, 71,
95, 112, 134, 354
  Crocker Plaza, 1980-82, 71
  First Los Angeles Bank Building, 1975,
  (#6)134
  Ten-Five-Sixty Wilshire Boulevard,
  1980-82, (#13)112
  World Savings Center Building, 1982,
  (#2)95
Staunton, W. F., 390
  McDonald House, c. 1927, (#16)390
Stein, Bill, 43
  Stein Building, 1984, (#40)43
Stein, Clarence S., (#26)89
Stern, Martin Jr., 92
  Ship's Culver City Restaurant, 1957,
  (#37)92
Stern, Robert A. M. (Stern Ehrenkrantz
Ramager), 398
  Pasadena Police Department Building,
  1898-90, (#30)398
Steven Ehrlich Architects, 18, 29, 30
  Ehrlich House, 1988, (#35)18
  Gold-Friedman House, 1991, (#36)18
  Israel House, 1990, (#58)29
  Sony Music Campus, 1992, (#60)30
Stevens, Lawrence Tenney, 438
Stewart, Albert (art advisor), 250
  Fort Moore Pioneer Memorial, 1949-57,
  (#1)250
Stewart House, c. 1887, (#13)431
Stickley, Gustav, xviii, 286, 287, 365
Stimson, G. Lawrence, 197, 365, 380,
382
  House, 1910, (#43)380

House, c. 1910, (#65)197
Wrigley House, 1911, (#61)382
Stirling, James, 39, 94
Stone, Edward D., 49, 126, 277, 395,
405, 443, 444
  Bankamericard Center Building, 1975,
  (#16)395
  Charlotte S. and Davre Davidson
  Conference Center, 1975, (#21)277
  Harvey Mudd College, 1957-later,
  (#8)444
  Stuart Pharmaceutical Company, 1957-
  58, (#13)405
Stone, Edward D. and Associates, xxiv,
203, 277, 443
  Ahmanson Center Building, 1970,
  (#34)203
  Kresge Memorial Chapel, 1961, 443
  Social Science Building (USC), 1968,
  (#18)277
  Von Kleinsmid Center of International
  and Public Affairs, 1966, (#17)277
  Waite Phillips Hall of Education (USC),
  1968 (#19)277
Stonerod, Earl D., 197
  Apartment Building, 1936, (#66)197
  Loyola University Theater, 1963, 49
  Perpetual Savings Bank Building, 1962,
  (#4)126
Stony Point, 347
Street, Arthur Edmund, 376
  Church of the Angels, 1889, (#8)376
Street, George, 376
Studio City, 329-332
Studio Works (Hodgetts and
Mangurian with Frank Lupe and
Audrey Mitlock)
  Gagosian Art Gallery and Apartments,
  1980-81, (#15)39
Styka, Jan, 316
Sullivan, Louis H., 39, 401
Sumner Hall (Pomona College), 445
Sumner House, 1886, (#21)446
Sussman/Prejza Inc., 262
Sutton, Thomas L., Jr., 354, 355
  Magic Mountain Amusement Park, 1970,
  355
Swasey, McNeal, 46
Swinerton and Walberg Company, 325
  Victoria Station, 1980, 325
Symonds/Deenihan, 403
  Burlington Arcade, 1982, (#62)402

Tail-O-the-Pup, 1946, (#46)144
Tamale, The, 1928, (#1)304
Tanaka, Ted Tokio, 42
  Multi-Family Residence, 1989, (#31)42
Taos West Apartments, 1972, (#5)350
Taper, Mark Forum, 245
Tarzana, Woodland Hills, 338-39
Taylor, Edward Cray and Ellis Wing
Taylor, 239
  Wolfer Printing Company Building,
  1929, (#110)239
Taylor, Wood, 394
  House, 1892, (#5)394
Teapot, The, c. 1931, (#14)83

Tedesco Architects, 96, 188
  Churchill House, 1982, (#11)188
  Wyle Guest House, 1983, (#13)96
Temple City, El Monte, 434
Temple, Don Juan, 79
Temple, Walter P., 437
Telesound Studio, c. 1945, (#74)159
Terminal Annex Post Office, 1937-38,
(#12)252
Test, Lawrence (Woodbridge
Dickinson, associate), 365, 373
  Dickinson House, 1941, (#32)372
  Hernly House, 1949, (#44)373
Texas Instruments Computer Discovery
Center, 1982, 355
Thiene, Paul (landscape architect), xx,
xxi, 125
  Doheny House ("Greystone"), 1925-28,
  (#26)125
Thomas and Dorothy Leavey Library
(USC), 276
Thomas, Bobrow, and Associates, 351
  Valley Presbyterian Hospital, 1983-84,
  (#8)351
Thomas Ince Studio Building, 1915,
(#35)92
Thomas, Louis A., 319
  St. Mark's Episcopal Church, 1948,
  (#25)319
Thomas, S. Seymour, 360
  St. Luke's of the Mountains, 1924, 360
Thompson, Tommy, 427
Thompson, W. F., 381
  Merritt House, 1905-6, (#55c)381
Thornton and Fagan Associates, 193,
390, 400
  Discovery of La Brea Museum, 1976,
  (#38b)193
  Pages Victorian Court, 1981, (#47)400
  "Tara West," 1978, (#17)390
Thoryk, Paul, 14
  House, 1976, (#11)14
Tice, James, 140
Tifal Brothers (builders), 430
  Four Bungalows, c. 1910, (#7)430
Tilton, Leon Deming, 105
Tindall, John, Ed McCreany, and Jesse
Hood, 437
  Donut Hole, The, 1968, (#4)437
Tipping, Richard L., 37
Toluca Lake, 327-328
Tom Roberts, 338
  Apartment House, 1976, (#5)338
Tom Roberts Associates, 142
  Office and Showroom Building, 1982,
  (#31)142
Tomson, Tommy, 187, 248
  Health Administration Building, 1953-
  54, (#12)248
Torrance, 66-69
Torrance, Jared Sidney, 66
Tossman, Alan (see Urban Forms)
Tossman/Day, 35
  Condominium Town Houses, 1981,
  (#27)35
Train and Williams, 72, 273, 285, 369,
435

First National Bank Building, 1900, 1905-6, 1907, (#6)72
First National Bank, c. 1918, (#2)435
Robert Williams House, c. 1905, (#1)285
Two Houses, c. 1924, (#12)369
Train, Robert F., 283
Bell High School, 1935, (#16)283
Trona Corporation Building, 1917-18, 63
Trousdale Estates, 125
Trudeau, J. Earl, 88, 93, 326
Saint Anselm Church, 1956-57, (#21)88
St. Augustine Roman Catholic Church, 1956-57, (#44)93
St. Charles Boromeo Roman Catholic Church, 1959, (#2)326
Tujunga, 358-60
Tujunga American Legion Hall, c. 1928, (#9)360
Turner, Burnett C., 118, 242
University Guesthouse (UCLA), 1952, (#14)118
Twitchell, Kent, xxxiv, (#15)229
Tyler, Frank M., 192, 198
Commercial Building, 1927, (#33)192
Scott House, c. 1906, (#2)198

UCLA, 114-20
Ulmar, Terry, 341
Ulmar House, 1939-later, (#1)341
Underwood, Gilbert Stanley, 192, 246, 281
Desmonds Department Store Building, 1928-29, (#35)192
East Los Angeles Union Pacific Railroad Passenger Station, 1928, (#7)281
Federal Building and Post Office, 1938-40, (#9)246
United Auto Workers Union Building, 1961, (#7)305
United Church of Christ, Scientist, 1945, (#1)198
United Methodist Church, 1911, (#3)430
United Methodist Church, c. 1916, (#16)68
Universal City, 325
University of Southern California, 273-77
University of Southern California School of Medicine, Administration Building, c. 1920, (#3)298
Upper Arroyo Seco, 367-73
Urban Forms, 26
Condominiums, 1980, (#36)26
Sun-Tech Town Houses, 1981, (#24)34
Urban Innovations Group (Charles Moore, Ron Frank, and Robert Yudell), xxxiii, 14, 88, 130, 146, 240, 335
Abel House, 1978, (#16)14
Florence Hotel, 1986, (#120)240
Ladera Center, 1983 (#20)88
Senior Citizens Housing Project, 1978-80, (#62)146
Willheim House, 1978-79, (with Elias Torres and John Rubel) (#20)335
U.S. Post Office, Osbourne Station, c. 1928, (#31)153

V.A. Outpatient Clinic, 248
VIP Palace Restaurant Building, c. 1973, (#19)201
Valencia, 354
Van de Kamp Building, c. 1930, (#26)272
Van Keppel, Hendrick, xxiv
Van Meter, Daniel, 335
Tower of Wooden Pallets, 1951, (#19)335
Van Nuys, I. N., 314
Van Nuys, Panorama City, Sepulveda, 349-51
Van Pelt, Garrett, 366, 381, 389
Van Pelt House, 1926, (#8)389
Van Tilburg, Johannes and Partners, 28, 38, 329
Centrum Office Building, 1982, (#5)329
Renaissance Building, 1989, (#4)38
Van Tilburg Office Building, 1979, (#52)28
Vawter House, 1900, (#14)33
Vedanta Temple, 1933 (#53)155
Venice Canals, 1904-5, (#19)40
Venice Center, 1904-5, (#17)40
Venice City Hall, 42
Venturi, Robert, xxvi
Venturi, Scott Brown and Associates (with Payette Associates), 116, 120
Gordon & Virginia MacDonald Medical Research Laboratories, 1991-92, 116, (#37)120
Verbeck Mansion, c. 1897, (#53)196
Vermeulen, Aurele (landscape architect), 267
Automobile Club of Southern California, 1921-23, (#3)267
Vicente Lugo Adobe (El Viejo Lugo Adobe), 1844, (#17)283
Victoria Station Restaurant, 339
Videriksen, Ebbe, 332
Office Building, 1983, (#24)332
Villa Rotunda, c. 1955, 356
Villa Sonora, c. 1922, (#15)68
Vincent Thomas Bridge, 1961-63, 62, (#16)63
Viole, Laurence, 326
Parish Hall, 1938, (#2)326
Viollet-Le-Duc, Eugene, xxvii, xxviii, 423
Vivian Webb Chapel, 1944, 443
Volkswagen Showroom Building, c. 1937, (#28)132
Voss Apartments, 1937-47, (#32)25
Voysey, Charles F. A., 103

W. W. Henry Company, 282
W. W. Orcutt House, ("Rancho Sombra del Roble"), c. 1930, (#2)344
Wachsmann, Konrad and Walter Gropius, 145, 164
General Panel House, 1950, (#6)164
Marshall House, 1948, (#54)145
Wachtel, Elmer, 291
Elmer and Marion Cavanaugh Wachtel House and Studio, 1906, (#1)291
Waddell and Harrington, 378
Colorado Street Bridge, 1912-13, (#21)378

Wadsworth House, 1925, (#42)373
Waid, A. J., 168
Grafield Court Apartments, 1927, (#3)168
Walker and Eisen, xix, 27, 46, 68, 128, 155, 203, 217, 219, 228, 230, 233, 236, 237, 423, 436
Bay City Guaranty Building and Loan Association Building, 1929-30, (#45)27
Beverly-Wilshire Hotel, 1926, (#13)128
Edwards and Wildey Building (California Pacific National Bank Building), 1925, (#40)228
Fine Arts Building, 1925, (#11)219
National Bank of Commerce, 1929-30, (#58)233
Office Building, 1936, (#38)203
Oviatt Building, 1927-28, (#47)230
San Gabriel City Hall and Municipal Buildings, 1923, (#8)423
Sunkist Building, 1935, 217
Taft Building, 1923 (#46a)155
Temple Hall, 1919-23, 436
Texaco/United Artists Building, 1927, (#86)236
Title Insurance and Trust Company Building, 1928, (#92)236
Torrance City Hall and Municipal Auditorium, 1936-37, (#11)68
Torrance Public Library, 1936, (#12)68
Walker and Vawter, 215
Hill House, c. 1911, (#41)215
Walker, J. W., 433
Walker, Rodney A., 17, 104, 332, 335
Bernatti House, 1947, (#25)104
Lohrie House, 1940, (#26)104
Smith House, 1948, (#17)335
Sommer House, 1941, (#29)104
Stevens House, 1941, (#21)332
West House, 1948, (#25)17
Wall, Robert and Lilian, 338
Wall Street Plaza, c. 1988, (#4)338
Walsh, Timothy, 379, 424, 426
House, c. 1910, (#31)379
Passionate Fathers Monastery and Retreat House, 1928-31, (#9)426
Wright House, c. 1909, (#29)379
Ward, R. E (engineer), 194
Firestone Garage, 1937, (#43)194
Wardrobe Cleaners Building, c. 1950, (#13)52
Warnecke, John Carl and Associates, 116, 126, 398, 444
Nieman-Marcus Store Building, 1981, (#5)126
Pasadena Convention Center, 1975, (#35)398
Warner and Grey, xxvi
Warner Brothers West Coast Studios, 1922 (#57), 156
Warshaw, Howard, xxxiv, 119
Untitled Mural, 1970, (#30)119
Washeteria, c. 1955, (#16)88
Watt Bungalow, (#9)431
Webb School, 1922-later, (#1)443
Webb Tower, 274
Webber and Spaulding, 59, 445

Casino, 1928, (#2)59
Frary Hall (Pomona College), 1929, 445
Webber, Staunton, and Spaulding, 54
Weber, Kem, xxii, 323
Studio Buildings, 1939-40, (#11a), 323
Weeks and Day, 236
State Theater, 1921, (#81)236
Weese, Harry and Associates, xxxiii
Wehmueller and Stephens, 171
Municipal Art Gallery, 1971, (#24)171
Weil, Martin Eli, 138
Weismuller, Johnnie, 15
Weitzman, Arnold, 138
Chateau Marmont, 1928
Weller House, 1887, (#8)185
Wells Fargo Bank, 1972, (#17)440
Wemple, Emmett L. and Associates
(landscape architects), xx, 7, 84,
(#36)203, 215, 355
CNA Building, 1972, (#38)215
Goldwater Apartment Buildings, 1964,
84
J. Paul Getty Museum, 1972-73, (#21)7
Wenderoth, Oscar, 398
Old Pasadena Post Office, 1913,
(#32)398
West Hollywood, 135-46
Westlake Village, 342
Weston and Weston, 149, 327, 417
American Legion Headquarters
Building, 1929, (#13)149
Los Angeles County Regional Branch
Library, c. 1929, (#7)327
Weston, Joseph, 435
Subsistence Homestead Project, 1934-
35, (#5)435
Westridge School, 1906-08, (#9)386
Westside Village, 1939-41
Romboz House, 1947, (#7)417
Westwood Hills Congregational Church,
1928, (#21)113
Westwood, South and East, 110-13
Westwood Village, 106
Westwood, West, 105-9
Wetmore, David J., and Loyal Watson,
261
Wyvern Wood Housing Project, 1938-
39, (#29)261
Wetmore, James A., 73, 317
Glendale Post Office, 1933-34, (#9)317
Post Office and Federal Building, 1931-
32, (#16)73
White, Willard, (#5)188
Whittier, 306-309
Whittier College, 1896-1920s, (#13)308
Whittier Public Library, 1959, (#14)309
Whittlesey, Austin (interiors), 246, 316
Administration Building (Forest Lawn
Memorial Park), 1918, (#2)316
Los Angeles City Hall, 1926,28,
(#10)246
Whittlesey, Charles F., 217, 226, 264,
265, 391
Lindsay House, 1908, (#7)264
Mayflower Hotel (Checkers Hotel),
1927, (#28)226
Walker House, 1905-6, (#8)265

Wentworth Hotel, 1906, (#25)391
Whitworth, James, 122
Whizin, Arthur, 35
Chili Bowls, 1931, (#28)35
Widom-Wein and Associates, 132
Burton-Hill Town Houses, 1974,
(#26)132
Widom, Wein and Cohen, 176
The Gene Autry Western Heritage
Museum, 1987-89, (#49)176
Wiemeyer, George, 380
Vista del Arroyo Hotel, 1920, (#51)380
Wilcox, Mr. and Mrs. Horace, 147
William S. Hart Park, 354
Williams, Barney, 365
Williams, John and Associates, 47
Williams, Paul R., xxii, 27, 46, 47, 54,
88, 102, 128, 130, 162, 190, 256, 278,
362, 363, 377
Al Jolson Memorial, 1951, 88
Banning House #1, 1929, (#95)162
Banning House #2 & 3, 1929, (#96)162
Collins House, 1932, (#14)190
Degnan House, 1927, (#8)362
Drive-in Market, 1928, (#43)27
Gabriel Duque House, 1932, (#94)162
Leistikow House, 1923, (#13)190
Mitchell House, 1924, (#17)363
Music Corporation of America Building,
1940, 1968-72, (#24)130
Pueblo del Rio Public Housing, 1941-
42, xxii, xxiii, (#1)278
(with **Adrian Wilson, Gordon B.**
Kaufmann, Wurdeman and Becket,
Richard J. Neutra)
Rothman House, 1926, (#15)190
Saks Fifth Avenue Store Building, c.
1936-37, (#9)128
Second Baptist Church (First A.M.E.
Church), 1924, (#11)256
Williams, Paul R. and Associates, 123,
132, 195, 280
Hacienda Village, 1941-42, (#3)280
Parking Structure for Litton Industries,
1968-72, (#25)132
Paul R. Williams House, 1951, (#48)195
Will Rogers Ranch, 1921-later, (#39)19
Williamson and Norris, 282
Willit, Edwin W., 210
Bungalow Court, 1925, (#10)210
Willmore, W. E., 69
Wilmington, 64-65
Wilshire Boulevard District, 186-197
Wilson, Adrian and Associates, 277,
278, 280
Arnold Schoenberg Institute (USC),
1978, (#22)277
Wilson, Benjamin, 121, 300
Wilson, Henry L., 200
Bungalow, c. 1910, (#9)200
Wilson, Merrill, and Alexander, 282
Wing, Kenneth S., Sr., and Kenneth S.
Wing, Jr., 71, 79
California Veteran's Memorial State
Office Building, 1981-82, (#1)71
Long Beach Airport Terminal, 1940-41,
(#5)79

Winslow, Carleton M., 280, 319, 388,
425, 430, 435
Avalon Gardens, 1941-42, (#2)280
Group of Adobes, 1925-27, (#26)388
St. Luke's Episcopal Church, 1926,
(#6)430
St. Mark's Episcopal Church, 1948,
(#25)319
Winslow, Carleton M., Jr., 435
St. Martha's Episcopal Church, 1956-
62, (#4)435
Winslow, Carleton M., Jr.; Warren
Waltz; Andrew Joncich and William
Lusby, 62, 168
Kleihauer Memorial Chapel, 1967,
(#2)168
Seaman's Center Building, 1954 and
1962, (#6)62
Winslow, Carleton M., Sr. and
Frederick Kennedy, 396
First Baptist Church, 1926, (#24)396
Witmer, David J., 169
House, c. 1925, (#14)169
Wong, Gin and Associates, 187, 213
Arco Center Building, 1988-89,
(#23)213
CBS Television City, 1852, (#1)187
Woodlawn Cemetery Mausoleum, 1924,
(#22)34
Woolf, John, 126, 146, 195
Pendleton House, 1942, (#36)126
Reynolds House, 1958, (#46)195
Woolf Studio Building, 1946-47,
(#63)146
Woollett, William L., xxviii, 234, 242,
275
Elizabeth Von Kleinsmid Hall, 1925,
(#3)275
Million Dollar Theater, 1918, (#69)234
Workman Adobe ("Rancho La Puente"),
1842, (#3)436
Workman House ("Shadow Ranch"),
1869-72, (remodeling 1935-36, Lawrence
Test), (#3)345
Workman, William, 121
World Trade Center Complex, 1986-87,
71
Worthen, Kenneth, Sr., 327
Streamline Moderne House, 1935, 327
Wren, Helen, 443, 445
Lincoln House, c. 1927, (#6)443
Sugg House, c. 1930, (#17)445
Wright and Gentry, 73
York Rite Masonic Temple Building,
1927, (#22)73
Wright, Eric, 9, 138
Soffer House, 1973 (#8)9
Wright, Frank Lloyd, xv, xx, xxi, 6, 9,
14, 39, 97, 122, 124, 128, 138, 146,
148, 150, 152, 170, 171, 367, 372, 381,
401, 432, 443
Anderton Court Building, 1953-54,
(#11)128
Arch Oboler House, 1940, 1941, 194
1946, (#16)6
Barnsdall "Hollyhock" House, 1'
(#24)171

Ennis House, 1924, 152, 170
Freeman House, 1924, (#19)150, 152
Millard House ("La Miniatura")1923, 367, (#36)372
Pauson House, 1940, 6
Pearce House, 1950, 432
Storer House, 1923, (#15)138, 152
Sturges House, 1939, 6, (#14)97
Wright, J. C. for City Engineer's Office, 175
    Franklin Avenue "Shakespeare" Bridge, 1926, (#41)175
Wright, Lloyd, 9, xx, xxi, xxii, 22, 55, 56, 57, 66, 86, 96, 98, 102, 103, 125, 135, 138, 141, 148, 149, 152, 168, 169, 174, 197, 242, 318, 339, 351, #62, 411
    Avery House, 1934-37, (#27)98
    Bowler House, 1963, (#8)55
    Calori House, 1926, (#19)318
    Carr House, 1925, (#35)174
    Colbert House, 1935, (#23)103
    Derby House, 1926, (#18)318
    Dorland House, 1949, (#21)411
    Evans House, 1936, (#10)96
    Farrell House, 1926, (#34)174
    Gainsburg House, 1946, (#12)362
    Greer House, 1940, (#9)351
    Griffith Ranch House, 1936, 339
    Healy House, 1949-52, (#14)103
    Henry Bollman House, 1922, (#26)152
    Hill and Dale Nursery and

Kindergarten, 1949, 1965, (#5)9
Howland House, 1933-34, (#32)125
Karaski House, 1960, (#5)86
Lewis House, 1926, (#21)319
Lombardi House, 1965, (#20)56
Mace House, 1958, (#14)138
Moore House, 1965, (#16)55
Nables House, 1949, (#8)22
Otto Bollman House, 1922, (#8)149
Samuel House, 1934, (#11)96
Samuels-Navarro House, 1926-28, (#7)169
Sowden House, 1926, (#12)169
Storer House, 1923, (#15)138
Taggart House, 1922-24, (#6)168
Wayfarer's Chapel, 1949 and later, (#2)57
Weber House, 1921, (#63)197
Wright House, 1928, (#30)141
Wright-Mooers House, 1894, (#15a)211
Wright, Parker O. and Francis H. Gentry, 73
    Scottish Rite Cathedral, 1926, (#19)73
Wurdeman and Becket, 115, 188, 193, 278, 280, 401
    Bullock's Pasadena, 1947, (#61)401
    Pan-Pacific Auditorium, 1935-38, (#4)188
    Prudential Building, 1948, (#37)193
Wurster, Bernardi, and Emmons, 99
Wurster, William W., 104, 242
    Sperry House, 1953, (#34)99

Wyman, George H., 234
    Bradbury Building, 1893, (#68)234

Yamasaki, Minoru, 133, 134
    Century Plaza Hotel, 1966, (#3)133
    Century Plaza Towers, 1969-75, (#5)134
Yoakum House, c. 1900, (#10)287
Yoch, Florence (landscape architect), xx, 103, 190 (#18)
    Gordon B. Kaufmann House, c. 1929, (#22)103
Yoch, Florence and Lucille Council (landscape architects), 77, 109
    Galli Curci House, 1938, (#21)109
Yudell, Buzz, 15
Yudell, Robert, 14 (see **Urban Innovations Group**)

Zetterberg House, 1906, 445
Zimmer Gunsul Frasca Partnership, 272
    California Museum of Science and Industry, 272
Zwebell, Arthur B. and Nina W., 140, 153, 169
    Andalusia, The, 1927, (#26c)140
    Casa Laguna, The, 1928, (#11)169
    El Cabrillo, 1928, 153
    Patio del Moro, 1925, (#26a)140
    Ronda, The, 1927, (#26b)140